Distributed Database Systems

Principles, Algorithms and Systems

Distributed Database Systems

Principles, Algorithms and Systems

Ikvinderpal Singh
Sukhwant Singh

KHANNA BOOK PUBLISHING CO. (P) LTD.

::: *Publisher of Engineering and Computer Books* :::

Head Office : 4C/4344, Ansari Road, Darya Ganj, New Delhi-110002
Phone : 011-23244447/48 Fax : 011-23244447
Regd. Office : 1694-95, Nai Sarak, Delhi-110006
Phone : 011-23283211 Fax : 011-23256658
E-Mail : contact@khannabooks.com
Website : www.khannabooks.com, www.khannapublishers.com

Distributed Database Systems

Ikvinderpal Singh
Sukhwant Singh

ISBN: 978-93-81068-16-8
Reprint 2015

Published by:
Khanna Book Publishing Co. (P) Ltd.
4C/4344, Ansari Road, Darya Ganj, New Delhi-110 002
Phone: 011-23244448 Telefax: 011-23244447
E-mail: contact@khannabooks.com
Website: www.khannabooks.com

Printed in India by: **S.P.S. Printers & Binders,** Delhi

ACKNOWLEDGEMENT

First we would like to thanks almighty for giving us courage to bring up this book. We duly acknowledge the contribution of our colleagues Prof. Rachhpal Singh, Prof. Harbhajan Singh, Prof. Sukhwinder Kaur, Prof. Kawaljit Kaur, Prof. Mani Arora, Mr. Sukhwant Singh, Mr. Avtar Singh Sandhu, Mr. Rupinder Singh, Mr. Baljinder Singh, Mr. Opinder Singh, Mr. Jagbir Singh, Mr. Nirmaljit Singh, Mr. Lovedeep Singh, Mr. Kanwarpal Singh, Mr. Navjeet Singh, Mr. Manpreet Singh, Mr. Rakesh Kumar, Mrs. Mandeep Kaur, Mrs. Jyoti Maini, Ms. Sapandeep kaur, Ms. Kanwaljit Kaur, Ms. Simranjeet Kaur, Mrs. Sehajpreet Kaur, Mrs. Anureet kaur, Ms. Manpreet Kaur, Ms. Indu bala, Ms. Sukhbir kaur and Kawaljit Singh for their valuable co-operation and guidance. We are grateful to Mr. Puneet Khanna **M/s KHANNA PUBLICATIONS** for his encouragement and motivation during this project.

Special Thanks

Our special thanks go to **Prof. Kawaljit Kaur** for their valuable guidance and timely support during the compilation of this book.

PREFACE

This Book is meant for a wide range of readers who wish to learn the basic concepts of Distributed database systems. It can also be helpful for programmers, researchers and management experts who use distributed database techniques. Distributed database design has been clearly dealt with suitable examples. Query processing and optimization have been discussed in lucid manner, so that a beginner can understand the concepts with minimal effort.

During the 1970s computers were extensively used for building powerful integrated database systems. The technology of database systems has built its theoretical foundations and has been experienced in a large number of applications. At the same time, computer networks have been extensively developed, allowing the connection of different computers and the exchange of data and other resources between them. In recent years the availability of databases and of computer networks has given rise to a new field: distributed database system. A distributed database system is, in brief an integrated database which is built on top of a computer network rather than on a single computer. The data which constitute the database are stored at the different sites of the computer network, and the application programs which are run by the computers access data at different sites. Completely new problems are faced for building and implementing a distributed database system, and a great amount of research work has been done in order to solve them. This research work constitutes a new discipline having its own principles. In order to understand distributed database systems we must know more than the principles of traditional databases and computer networks: we must also integrate this knowledge with the study of the peculiar aspects of the new technology.

This book presents the principles of this new technology. It is intended for those who are professionally interested in having an up-to-date view of the distributed data processing.

This book contains the following chapters:

Chapter 1 is an overview of the characteristics and problems of distributed database systems. It also explains advantages and disadvantages of Distributed database systems. It also covers comparison between centralized and distributed system.

Chapter 2 is on distributed database design. It deals with the issues of fragmentation, allocation, transparency and replication of data at the different sites of the computer network. It also includes various types of distributed database designs.

Chapter 3 discusses the architecture of distributed database systems from the viewpoint of the application programmer. It also includes the architecture of client-server, peer to peer and multidatabase systems.

Chapter 4 deals with distributed query processing. It includes various phases of distributed query processing: Query decomposition, query fragmentation, global query optimization and local query optimization. It also includes join strategies in fragmented relations.

Chapter 5 discusses the distributed query optimization. It includes issues of query optimization, components of query optimization and joins ordering in fragment queries. It also includes global query optimization algorithms: Distributed INGRES, distributed R* and SDD-1 algorithm.

Chapter 6 describes the distributed transaction management. It deals with the properties and goals of transaction management, classification of transactions. It also includes distributed transactions used in oracle.

Chapter 7 presents the distributed concurrency control. It deals with Distributed serializability, locking-based concurrency control protocols, timestamp based techniques, optimistic concurrency control technique, reliability, resolution of inconsistencies, reliability protocols in distributed database systems.

Chapter 8 is devoted to the distributed deadlock management. It mainly focuses on deadlock handling in a distributed environment. It also includes deadlock detection algorithms and recovery from deadlocks.

Chapter 9 deals with distributed recovery management. It includes local recovery protocols, distributed recovery protocols: 2PC, 3PC and other protocols. It also includes network partition protocols: pessimistic protocols and optimistic protocols.

Chapter 10 summarizes distributed database administration. It deals with database security, view management, authorization and protection, integrity constraints and global system catalog.

This book can be used by a wide reader audience, ranging from beginners to practicing professionals. It is well suited for advanced or beginning college level students as a complete book for an introductory Distributed Database Systems, as a supplementary text, or as an effective independent study guide.

Each and Every chapter contains clear statements of definitions and principles together with illustrative and other descriptive material.

We welcome comments from all readers to improve this textbook as a useful guide for the community of engineers and technologists who will become knowledgeable about the potential of distributed database systems for their use in solving the problems that challenge us each day.

CONTENTS

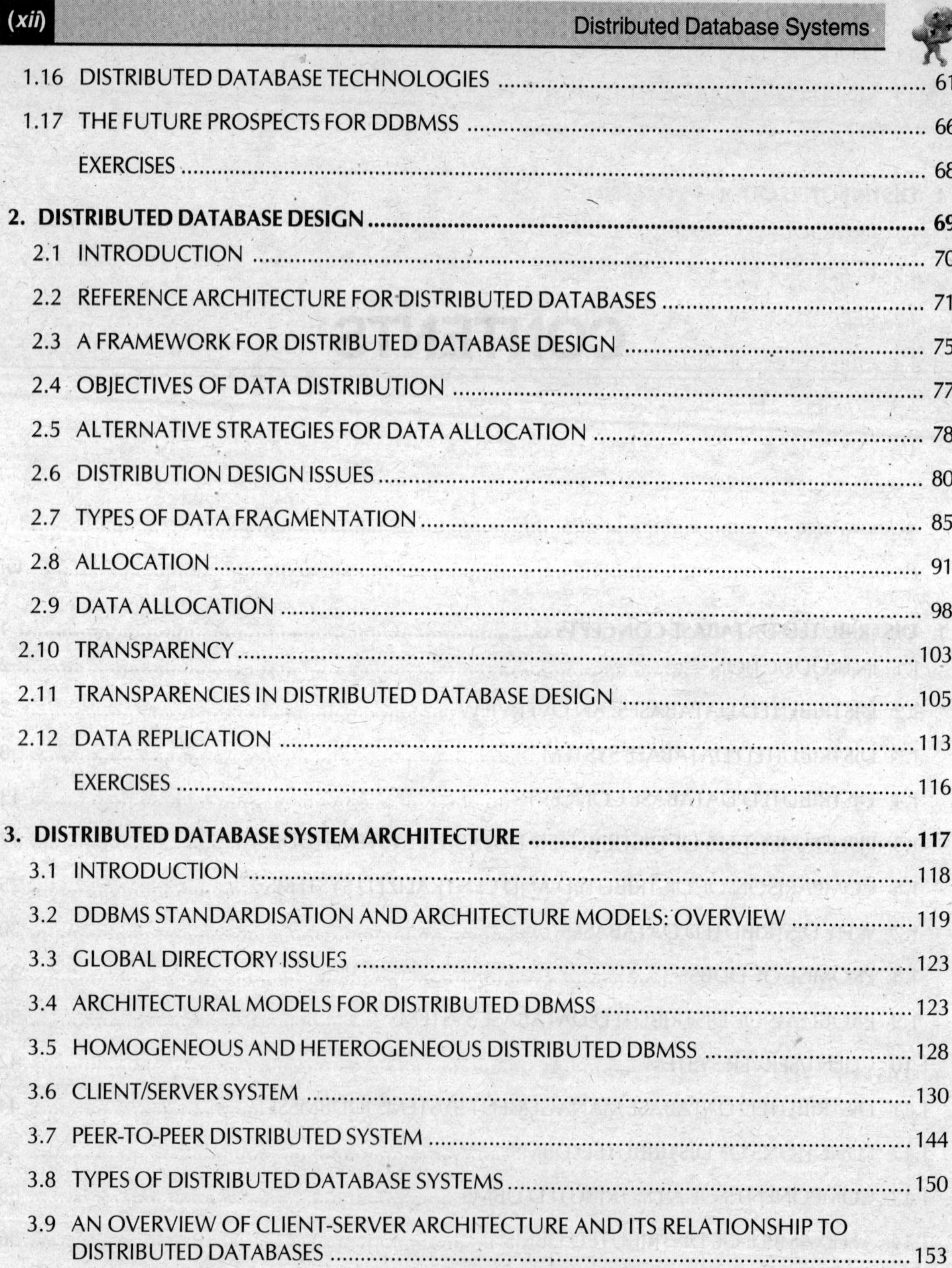

CHAPTER 1

DISTRIBUTED DATABASE CONCEPTS

1.1 INTRODUCTION

In this chapter we turn our attention to distributed databases (DDBs) and distributed database management systems (DDBMSs). The developments in computer networking technology and database systems technology resulted in the development of distributed databases in the mid 1970s. It was felt that many applications would be distributed in the future and therefore the databases had to be distributed also. Although many definitions of a distributed database system have been given, there is no standard definition. A distributed database system includes a distributed database management system (DDBMS), a distributed database and a network for interconnection. The DDBMS manages the distributed database. A distributed database is data that is distributed across multiple databases.

With advances in distributed processing and distributed computing that occurred in the operating systems arena, the database research community did considerable work to address the issues of Distributed database system functions include distributed query management, distributed transaction processing, distributed metadata management and enforcing security, integrity across the multiple nodes and other topics, and developed many research prototypes. However, a full-scale comprehensive DDBMS that implements the functionality and techniques proposed in DDB research never emerged as a commercially viable product. Most major vendors redirected their efforts from developing a "pure" DDBMS product into developing systems based on client-server, or toward developing active heterogeneous DBMSs. Organizations, however, have been very interested in the *decentralization* of processing (at the system level) while achieving an *integration* of the information resources (at the logical level) within their geographically distributed systems of databases, applications, and users. Coupled with the advances in communications, there is now a general endorsement of the client-server approach to application development, which assumes many of the DDB issues.

There are various architectural alternatives for a distributed database system. In one architecture, the control is centralized while the data is distributed. In architecture, the data as well as control are distributed. Then there is the non-multidatabase approach to designing a distributed database system. In this approach, there are no local database management systems (DBMSs).

The DDBMS manages all of the distributed data. Multidatabase architectures are architectures where each local database is managed by a local DBMS and the various DBMSs are connected through a DDBMS. These multidatabase architectures have been studied extensively in the literature. They can be grouped according to whether they are based on tightly coupled or loosely coupled approaches. An orthogonal method is to group the multidatabase systems depending on whether they are based on homogeneous or heterogeneous DBMSs.

The components of a DDBMS include a distributed query processor (DQP) that handles distributed queries, a distributed transaction manager (DTM) for processing distributed transactions, a distributed metadata manager (DTM) for managing distributed metadata, a distributed integrity manager (DIM) for enforcing integrity constraints across the databases and a distributed security manager (DSM) for enforcing security constraints across the databases.

There are two aspects to query processing in a DDBMS: query transformation and query optimization. The query transformation process transforms a global query into equivalent fragment queries. This process is performed according to transformation rules. The query optimization process optimizes the query with respect to the cost of executing the query.

Transaction management in a DDBMS involves the handling of distributed transactions. By a distributed transaction, we mean a transaction which executes at multiple sites. The portion of the transaction, which executes at a particular site is a sub transaction associated with that site. A coordinator controls the execution of the sub transactions. Concurrency control techniques ensure the consistency of the distributed database when transactions execute concurrently. An additional problem of transaction management in a distributed environment is ensuring the consistency of the data in the presence of site and network failures. Various commit protocols have been developed for reliable transaction processing.

Metadata in a distributed environment includes information about the relations, fragmentation of the relations, allocation of the relations and the local schema information. It is usually maintained at two levels. One is the global metadata and the other is the local metadata. Local metadata is the metadata associated with the local DBMS. Integrity issues in a DDBMS include enforcing integrity constraints across multiple DBMSs. Security controls include discretionary security such as enforcing access control rules and multilevel security where the data are assigned different sensitivity levels. We discuss both aspects of security in the sections on multilevel security and discretionary security.

1.2 DISTRIBUTED DATABASES: AN OVERVIEW

In recent years, distributed databases have become an area of information processing, and it is easy to foresee that their importance will rapidly grow. There are both organizational and technological reasons for this trend: distributed databases eliminate many of the shortcomings of centralized da-

tabases and fit more naturally in the decentralized structures of many organizations.

A typical, but rather vague, definition of a distributed database is the following: A distributed database is a collection of data which belong logically to the same system but are spread over the sites of a computer network. This definition emphasizes two equally important aspects of a distributed database:

1. **Distribution**, i.e., the fact that the data are not resident at the same site (processor), so that we can distinguish a distributed database from a single, centralized database.
2. **Logical correlation**, i.e., the fact that the data have some properties which tie them together, so that we can distinguish a distributed database from a set of local databases or files which are resident at different sites of a computer network.

The problem with the above definition is that both properties, distribution and logical correlation, are too vaguely defined to always discriminate between those cases which really belong to distributed databases and those which do not. In order to develop a more specific definition, let us consider a few examples.

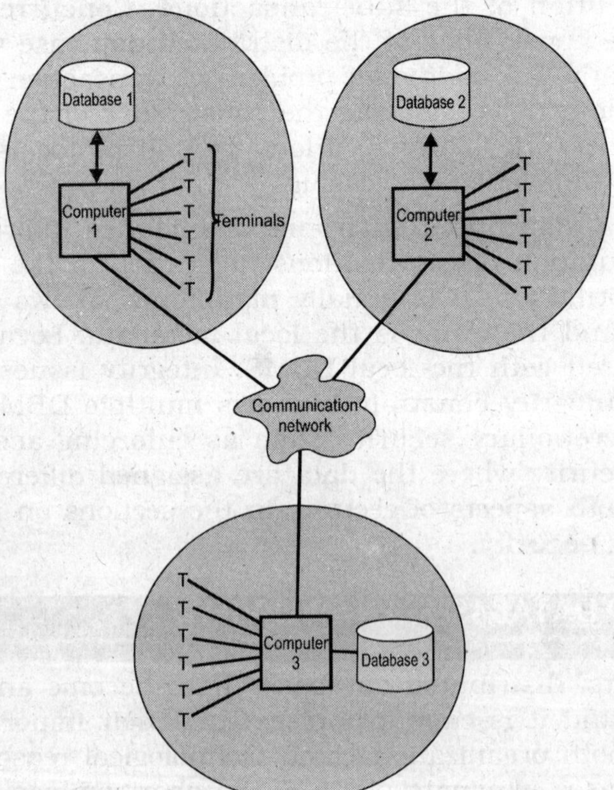

Figure 1.1 A distributed database on a geographically dispersed network.

Example 1.1

Consider a bank that has three branches at different locations. At each branch, a computer controls the teller terminals of the branch and the account database of that branch and the account database of that branch (Figure 1.1). Each computer with its local account database at one branch constitutes one site of the distributed database; computers and connected by a communication network. During normal operations the applications which are requested from the terminals of a branch need only to access the database of that branch. These applications are completely executed by the computer of the branch where they are issued, and will therefore be called local applications. An example of a local application is a debit or a credit application performed on an account stored at the same branch at which the application is requested.

If we try to apply the definition of distributed database to the situation described so far, we find that it is difficult to say whether the logical correlation property holds. Is the fact that the branches contain the information about accounts of the same bank sufficient? Should this be considered an example of a distributed database or of a set of local databases?

In order to answer these questions, let us focus on what makes dealing with a set of local databases different from dealing with the same data considered as a distributed database. From a technological viewpoint, it appears that the really important aspect is the existence of some applications which access data at more than one branch. These applications are called global applications or distributed applications. The existence of global applications will be considered the discriminating characteristic of distributed databases with respect to a set of local databases.

A typical global application is a transfer of funds from an account of one branch to an account of another branch. This application requires updating the databases at two different branches. Note that this application is something more than just performing two local updates at two individual branches (a debit and a credit), because it is also necessary to ensure that either both updates are performed or neither. As we shall see, ensuring this requirement for global applications is a difficult task.

In example 1.1 the computers are at geographically different locations; however, distributed databases can be built also on local networks.

Example 1.2

Consider the same bank of the previous example, with the same applications, however with a system configuration as shown in Figure 1.2. The same processors with their databases have been moved away from the branches to a common building and are now connected with a high-bandwidth local network. The teller terminals of the branches are connected to their respective

computers by telephone lines. Each processor and its database constitute a site of the local computer network.

We see that the physical structure of the connections has changed with respect to Example 1.1; however, the characteristics aspects of the architecture have remained the same. In particular, the same computers execute the same applications accessing the same databases. An application which was local in the previous example is still local, provided that locality is not defined with respect to the geographical distribution of the computers with its own database is involved.

If there are global applications, it is convenient to consider this example a distributed database, because most of the features which characterized the previous example are still valid. However, the fact that the distributed database is implemented on a local network instead of a geographical network, with its mush higher throughput and reliability, will in some cases change the type of solutions which are given to some problems. Let us consider an example of a system which we do not consider a distributed database in this book.

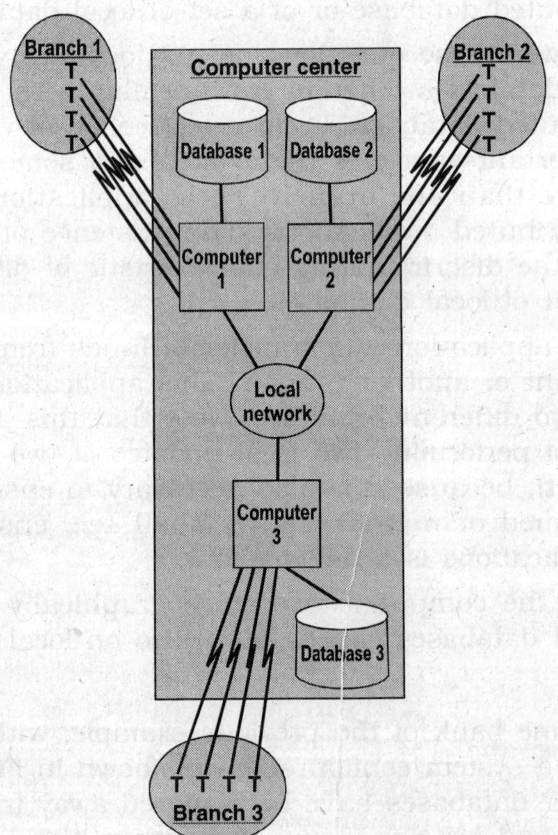

Figure 1.2 A distributed database on a local network.

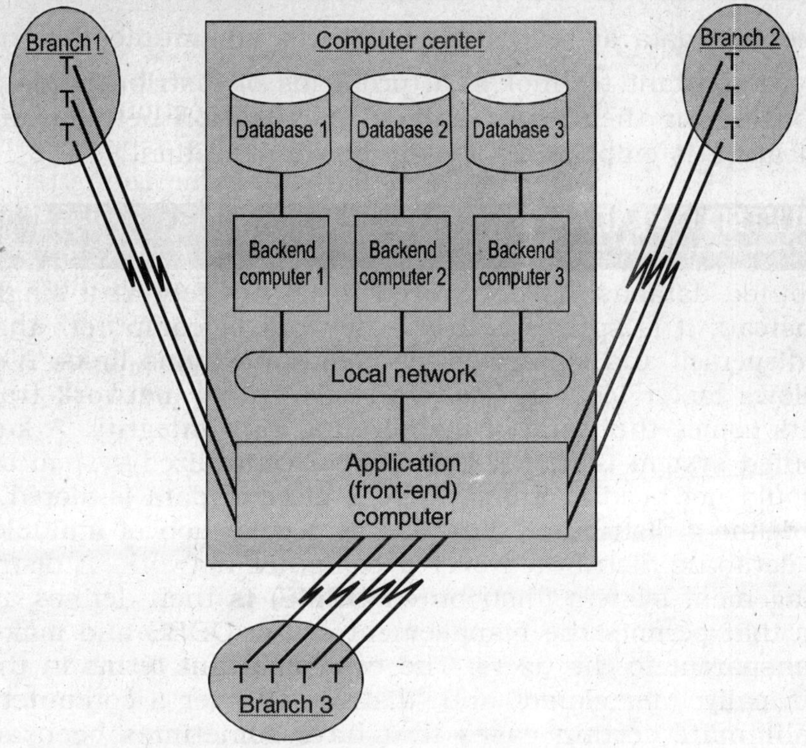

Figure 1.3 A multiprocessor system

Example 1.3

Consider the same bank of the previous example but with the system configuration shown in Figure 1.3. The data of the different branches are distributed on three "backend" computers, which perform the database management functions. The application programs are executed by a different computer, which requests database access services from the backends when necessary.

The reason for not considering this type of system a distributed database is that, although the data is physically distributed over different processors, their distribution is not relevant from the application viewpoint. What we miss here is the existence of local applications in the sence that the integration of the system has reached the point where no one of the computers is capable of executing an application by itself.

We can now summarize the considerations which we have obtained from the above examples in the following working definition:

A distributed database is a collection of data which are distributed over different computers of a computer network. Each site of the network has autonomous processing capability and can perform local applications. Each site also participates in the execution of at least one global application, which

requires accessing data at several sites using a communication subsystem.

The most important technological problems of distributed databases derive from considering them the result of" cooperation between autonomous sites"; this feature is emphasized by the above definition.

1.3 DISTRIBUITED DATABASE SYSTEM

A distributed database is not stored in its entirety at a single physical location. Instead, it is spread across a network of computers that are geographically dispersed and connected via communications links. A distributed database allows faster local queries and can reduce network traffic. With these benefits comes the issue of maintaining data integrity. A key objective for a distributed system is that it looks like a centralized system to the user. The user should not need to know where a piece of data is stored physically.

We can define a distributed database as a collection of multiple. Logically interrelated database distributed over a computer network. A distributed database management system (distributed DBMS) is then defines as the software system that permits the management of the DDBS and makes the distribution transparent to the users. The two important terms in these definitions are "logically interrelated" and "distributed over a computer network." They help eliminate certain cases that have sometimes been accepted to represent a DDBS.

A DDBS is not a "collection of files" that can be individually stored at each node of a computer network. To form a DDBS, filed should not only be logically related, but there should be structure among the files, and access should be via a common interface. We should note that there has been much recent activity in the internet (such as Web pages). In light of this activity, the above requirement may seem unnecessarily strict. However, providing "DBMS-like" access to data is different that a DDBS.

It has sometimes been assumed that the physical distribution of data is not the most significant issue. The proponents of this view would therefore feel comfortable in labelling as a distributed database two (related) database that reside in the same computer system. However, the physical distribution of data is very important. It creates problem that are not encountered when the databases reside in the same computer. Note that physical distribution does not necessarily imply that the computer systems are geographically far apart; they could actually be in the same room. It simply implies that the communication between them is done over a network instead of through shared memory, with the networks as the only shared resource.

This brings us to another point. The definition above also rules out multiprocessor systems as DDBSs. A multiprocessor system is generally considered to be a system where two or more processors share some form of memory, either primary tightly coupled) (Figure 1.4), or secondary memory, when it is called shared disk (also called loosely coupled) (Figure 1.5)[1].

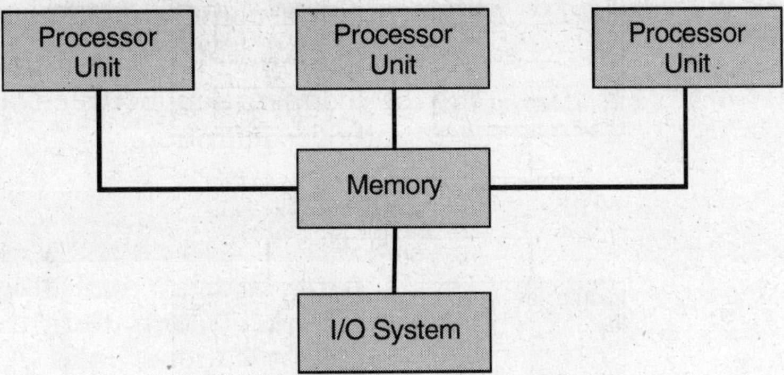

Figure 1.4 Shared memory multiprocessor

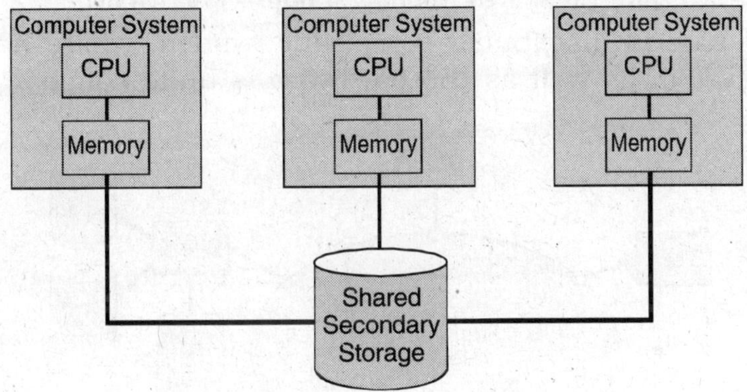

Figure 1.5 Shared Disk Multiprocessor

Another distinction that is commonly made is between shared everything and shared-nothing architectures. The former architectural model permits each processors to access everything (primary and secondary memories, and peripherals) in the system and covers the two models that we described above. Sharing memory enable the processors to communicate without exchanging messages. The shared-nothing architecture (Figure 1.6) is one where each processor has its own primary and secondary memories as well as peripherals, And communicates with other processors over a very high speed interconnect t (e.g., bus or a switch). In this sense the shared-nothing multiprocessors are quite similar to the distributed environment that we consider in this book. However, there are differences between the interactions in multiprocessor architectures and the rather fundamental difference is the mode of operation. A multiprocessor system design is rather symmetrical consisting of a number of identical processor and memory Components, and controlled by one or more copies of the same operating system, which is responsible for a strict control of the task assignment to each processor.

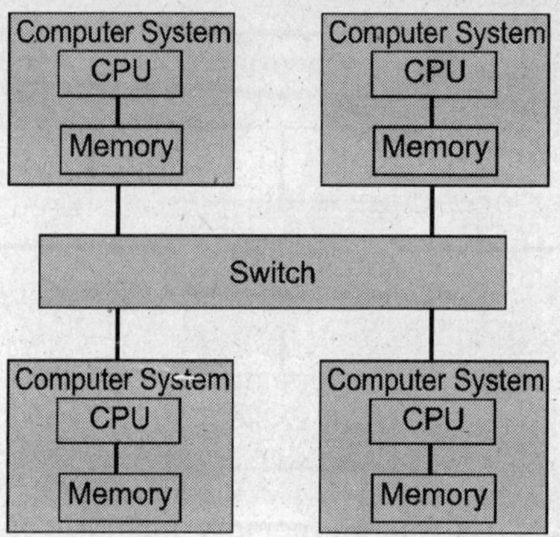

Figure 1.6 Shared Nothing Multiprocessor System

This is not true in distributed computing system, where heterogeneity of the operating system as well as the hardware is quite common.

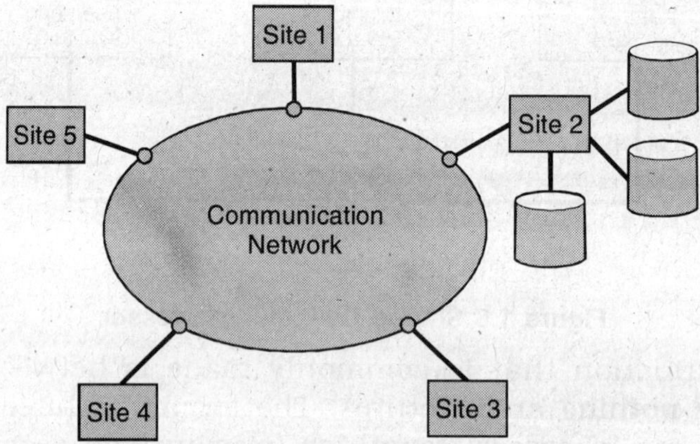

Figure 1.7 Central databases on a network

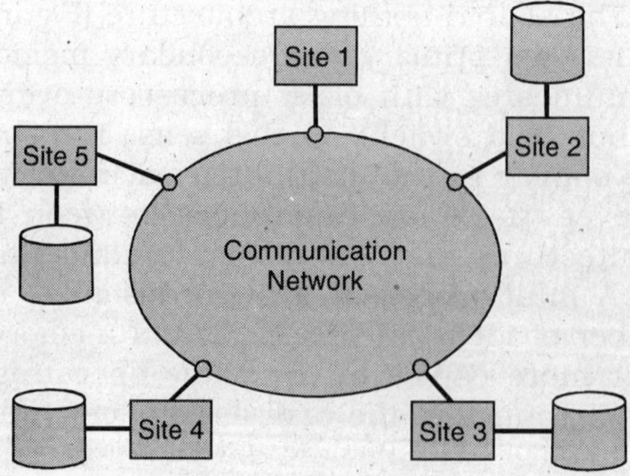

Figure 1.8 Distributed database system environments

In addition, a DDBS is not a system where, despite the existence of a network the database resides at only one node of the network (Figure 1.7.). In this case the problems of database management are no different from the problems encountered in a centralized database environment. The database is centrally managed by one computer system (site 2 in Figure 1.7.) and all requests are routed to that site. The only additional consideration has to do with transmission delays. It is obvious that the existence of a computer network or a collection of "files" is not sufficient to form a distributed database system. What we are interested in is an environment where data is distributed among a number of sites (Figure 1.8.).

1.3.1 FORMS OF DISTRIBUTED DATA

There are five categories of distributed data:

1. Replicated data
2. Horizontally fragmented data
3. Vertically fragmented data
4. Reorganized data
5. Separate-schema data

1. **Replicated Data:** Replicated data means that copies of the same data are maintained in more than one location. Data may be replicated across multiple machines to avoid transmitting data between systems.

   Replicas can be read only or writable. Read only replicas have changes made to the original and then propagated outwards to the replicas. Writable replicas propagate changes back to the original using either a "write through" or a "write back" strategy. Write through implies a synchronous connection and a "real-time" update to the original. The write back strategy allows changes to be propagated when it is most appropriate (i.e., a "store-and-forward" or an asynchronous concept).

   Consider the timeliness of the transactions against the data. How up-to-date or current does the data/replicas have to be? The biggest concern with replicated data is how to handle "collisions." Refer to Issues to Consider When Distributing Data for further information on handling collisions. Replicated data can simplify disaster recovery because data can be restored to the failed site from one of the replicated copies. Replicated data is most effective when data is not updated frequently. This tool suite maintains replicated databases for each installation.

2. **Horizontally Fragmented Data:** Horizontally fragmented data means that data is distributed across different sites based on one or more primary keys. This type of data distribution is typical where, for ex-

ample, branch offices in an organization deal mostly with a set of local customers and the related customer data need not be accessed by other branch offices.

3. **Vertically Fragmented Data:** Vertically fragmented data is data that has been split by columns across multiple systems. The primary key is replicated at each site. For example, a district office may maintain client information such as name and address keyed on client number while head office maintains client account balance and credit information, also keyed on the same client number.
4. **Reorganized Data:** Reorganized data is data that has been derived, summarized, or otherwise manipulated in some way. This type of data organization is common where decision-support processing is performed. There may be some instances where the on-line transaction processing (OLTP) and decision-support database management systems are different. Decision-support typically requires better query optimization and ad hoc SQL support than does OLTP. OLTP usually requires optimization for high-volume transaction processing.
5. **Separate-Schema Data:** Separate-schema data maintains separate databases and application programs for different systems. For example, one system may manage inventory and one may handle customer orders. There may be a certain amount of duplication with separate-schema data.

1.3.2 COMPARISON OF DISTRIBUTED DBMSS AND REPLICATED DATABASES

One of the requirements to maintain data integrity using a distributed database management system (DBMS) is the two-phase commit. A two-phase commit first requires that the data to be updated is locked on all nodes on the network that maintain the data. Only when the originating node receives confirmation from all other nodes that the data is updated can the originating node commit the updates to the database and release the data. A failure on the network at any point during the commit transaction may cause the entire transaction to fail. The two-phase commit approach to updating data becomes less attractive when the network consists of several nodes. The more nodes the more potential for failed transactions.

A better alternative to a distributed DBMS for many applications is data replication. Replication does not require a tightly coupled two-phase commit. Instead, replication allows local copies of the data to be updated and uses behind-the-scenes updating of the same data across the network. Replication technologies rely on asynchronous communications to keep data synchronized. Data updates made at one node are relayed to other nodes at set time intervals. The time interval for the updates depends on the needs of the

user. For example, asynchronous updates may be communicated immediately, every hour, or once a day.

There are many approaches to replication ranging from decision-support replication (DSS-R) technologies that maintain read-only copies of data locally to transaction-processing replication (TP-R) technologies that offer near real time data updates designed to replace distributed DBMS technologies. DSS-R approaches are suited for applications that require historical data such as decision-support applications or backup systems that can be used as standby databases in the event that the main database connection is lost. TP-R approaches are more suited for applications that require current, not historical, data but do not require complete data synchronization, such as a reservation system that allows for overbooking.

The most appropriate approach to data distribution depends on your application. The two-phase commit is still the best approach when the most current data is required, such as for an automated teller machine.

1.4 DISTRIBUTED DATABASE CONCEPTS

Distributed databases bring the advantages of distributed computing to the database management domain. A **distributed computing system** consists of a number of processing elements, not necessarily homogeneous, that are interconnected by a computer network, and that cooperate in performing certain assigned tasks. As a general goal, distributed computing systems partition a big, unmanageable problem into smaller pieces and solve it efficiently in a coordinated manner. The economic viability of this approach stems from two reasons: (1) more computer power is harnessed to solve a complex task, and (2) each autonomous processing element can be managed independently and develop its own applications.

We can define a **distributed database (DDB)** as a collection of multiple logically interrelated databases distributed over a computer network, and a **distributed database management system (DDBMS)** as a software system that manages a distributed database while making the distribution transparent to the user (Note 2). A collection of files stored at different nodes of a network and the maintaining of inter relationships among them via hyperlinks has become a common organization on the Internet, with files of Web pages. The common functions of database management, including uniform query processing and transaction processing, *do not* apply to this scenario yet. The technology is, however, moving in a direction such that distributed World Wide Web (WWW) databases will become a reality in the near future.

1.4.1 PARALLEL VERSUS DISTRIBUTED TECHNOLOGY

Turning our attention to system architectures, there are two main types of multiprocessor system architectures that are commonplace:

- ***Shared memory (tightly coupled) architecture:*** Multiple processors share secondary (disk) storage and also share primary memory.
- ***Shared disk (loosely coupled) architecture:*** Multiple processors share secondary (disk) storage but each has their own primary memory.

These architectures enable processors to communicate without the overhead of exchanging messages over a network (Note 3). Database management systems developed using the above types of architectures are termed **parallel database management systems** rather than DDBMS, since they utilize parallel processor technology. Another type of multiprocessor architecture is called **shared nothing architecture.** In this architecture, every processor has its own primary and secondary (disk) memory, no common memory exists, and the processors communicate over a high-speed interconnection network (bus or switch). Although the shared nothing architecture resembles a distributed database computing environment, major differences exist in the mode of operation. In shared nothing multiprocessor systems, there is symmetry and homogeneity of nodes; this is not true of the distributed database environment where heterogeneity of hardware and operating system at each node is very common. Shared nothing architecture is also considered as an environment for parallel databases.

1.4.2 ADVANTAGES OF DISTRIBUTED DATABASES

Distributed database management has been proposed for various reasons ranging from organizational decentralization and economical processing to greater autonomy. We highlight some of these advantages here.

1. **Management of distributed data with different levels of transparency:** Ideally, a DBMS should be **distribution transparent** in the sense of hiding the details of where each file (table, relation) is physically stored within the system. The following types of transparencies are possible:
   - ***Distribution or network transparency:*** This refers to freedom for the user from the operational details of the network. It may be divided into location transparency and naming transparency. **Location transparency** refers to the fact that the command used to perform a task is independent of the location of data and the location of the system where the command was issued. **Naming transparency** implies that once a name is specified, the named objects can be accessed unambiguously without additional specification.

- ***Replication transparency:*** Copies of data may be stored at multiple sites for better availability, performance, and reliability. Replication transparency makes the user unaware of the existence of copies.
- ***Fragmentation transparency:*** Two types of fragmentation are possible. **Horizontal fragmentation** distributes a relation into sets of tuples (rows). **Vertical fragmentation** distributes a relation into subrelations where each subrelation is defined by a subset of the columns of the original relation. A global query by the user must be transformed into several fragment queries. Fragmentation transparency makes the user unaware of the existence of fragments.

2. **Increased reliability and availability:** These are two of the most common potential advantages cited for distributed databases. **Reliability** is broadly defined as the probability that a system is running (not down) at a certain time point, whereas **availability** is the probability that the system is continuously available during a time interval. When the data and DBMS software are distributed over several sites, one site may fail while other sites continue to operate. Only the data and software that exist at the failed site cannot be accessed. This improves both reliability and availability. Further improvement is achieved by judiciously *replicating* data and software at more than one site. In a centralized system, failure at a single site makes the whole system unavailable to all users. In a distributed database, some of the data may be unreachable, but users may still be able to access other parts of the database.
3. **Improved performance:** A distributed DBMS fragments the database by keeping the data closer to where it is needed most. **Data localization** reduces the contention for CPU and I/O services and simultaneously reduces access delays involved in wide area networks. When a large database is distributed over multiple sites, smaller databases exist at each site. As a result, local queries and transactions accessing data at a single site have better performance because of the smaller local databases. In addition, each site has a smaller number of transactions executing than if all transactions are submitted to a single centralized database. Moreover, interquery and intraquery parallelism can be achieved by executing multiple queries at different sites, or by breaking up a query into a number of subqueries that execute in parallel. This contributes to improved performance.
4. **Easier expansion:** In a distributed environment, expansion of the system in terms of adding more data, increasing database sizes, or adding more processors is much easier.

The transparencies we discussed in (1) above lead to a compromise between ease of use and the overhead cost of providing transparency. Total

transparency provides the global user with a view of the entire DDBS as if it is a single centralized system. Transparency is provided as a complement to **autonomy**, which gives the users tighter control over their own local databases. Transparency features may be implemented as a part of the user language, which may translate the required services into appropriate operations. In addition, transparency impacts the features that must be provided by the operating system and the DBMS.

1.4.3 ADDITIONAL FUNCTIONS OF DISTRIBUTED DATABASES

Distribution leads to increased complexity in the system design and implementation. To achieve the potential advantages listed previously, the DDBMS software must be able to provide the following functions in addition to those of a centralized DBMS:

1. **Keeping track of data:** The ability to keep track of the data distribution, fragmentation, and replication by expanding the DDBMS catalog.
2. **Distributed query processing:** The ability to access remote sites and transmit queries and data among the various sites via a communication network.
3. **Distributed transaction management:** The ability to devise execution strategies for queries and transactions that access data from more than one site and to synchronize the access to distributed data and maintain integrity of the overall database.
4. **Replicated data management:** The ability to decide which copy of a replicated data item to access and to maintain the consistency of copies of a replicated data item.
5. **Distributed database recovery:** The ability to recover from individual site crashes and from new types of failures such as the failure of a communication links.
6. **Security:** Distributed transactions must be executed with the proper management of the security of the data and the authorization/access privileges of users.
7. **Distributed directory (catalog) management:** A directory contains information (metadata) about data in the database. The directory may be global for the entire DDB, or local for each site. The placement and distribution of the directory are design and policy issues.

These functions themselves increase the complexity of a DDBMS over a centralized DBMS. Before we can realize the full potential advantages of distribution, we must find satisfactory solutions to these design issues and problems. Including all this additional functionality is hard to accomplish, and finding optimal solutions is a step beyond that.

At the physical **hardware** level, the following main factors distinguish a DDBMS from a centralized system:

- There are multiple computers, called **sites** or **nodes.**
- These sites must be connected by some type of **communication network** to transmit data and commands among sites.

The sites may all be located in physical proximity—say, within the same building or group of adjacent buildings—and connected via a **local area network,** or they may be geographically distributed over large distances and connected via a **long-haul** or **wide area network.** Local area networks typically use cables, whereas long-haul networks use telephone lines or satellites. It is also possible to use a combination of the two types of networks.

Networks may have different **topologies** that define the direct communication paths among sites. The type and topology of the network used may have a significant effect on performance and hence on the strategies for distributed query processing and distributed database design. For high-level architectural issues, however, it does not matter which type of network is used; it only matters that each site is able to communicate, directly or indirectly, with every other site. For the remainder of this chapter, we assume that some type of communication network exists among sites, regardless of the particular topology. We will not address any network specific issues, although it is important to understand that for an efficient operation of a DDBS, network design and performance issues are very critical.

1.5 FUNDAMENTALS OF DISTRIBUTED DATABASE SYSTEMS (DDBS)

Distributed database systems (DDBS) are systems that have their data distributed and replicated over several locations; unlike the centralized data base system (CDBS), where one copy of the data is stored. Data may be replicated over a network using horizontal and vertical fragmentation similar to projection and selection operations in Structured Query Language (SQL). Both types of database share the same problems of access control and transaction management, such as user concurrent access control and deadlock detection and resolution. On the other hand, however, DDBS must also cope with different problems.

Access control and transaction management in DDBS require different rules to monitor data retrieval and update to distributed and replicated databases. Oracle, as a leading Database Management Systems (DBMS) employs the two-phase commit technique to maintain a consistent state for the databases. The objective of this paper is to explain transaction management in DDBMS and how Oracle implements this technique. To assist in understanding this process, an example is given in the last section. It is hoped that this

understanding will encourage organizations to use and academics to discuss DDBS and to successfully capitalize on this feature of Oracle. The next section presents advantages, disadvantages, and failures in Distributed Database Systems.

Subsequent sections provide discussions on the fundamentals of transaction management, two-phase commit, Oracle's implementation of the two-phase commit, and, finally, an example on how the two-phase commit works.

1.5.1 DISTRIBUTED DATABASE

A distributed database can be defined as consisting of a collection of data with different parts under the control of separate DBMSs running on independent computer systems. All the computers are interconnected and each system has autonomous processing capability serving local applications. Each system participates, as well, in the execution of one or more global applications. Such applications require data from more than one site. The distributed nature of the database is hidden from users and this transparency manifests itself in a number of ways.

Although there are a number of advantages to using a distributed DBMS, there are also a number of problems and implementation issues. Finally, data in a distributed DBMS can be partitioned or replicated or both.

Definition:

A distributed database system consists of a collection of sites, connected together via some kind of communications network, in which:

A. Each site is a full database system site in its own right, but

B. The sites have agreed to work together so that a user at any site can access data anywhere in the network exactly as if the data were all stored at the user's own site.

It is a kind of **virtual database**, whose component parts are physically stored in a number of distinct real databases at a number of distinct sites.

Each site is absolutely independent and can do local work as a complete database system.

The overall distributed system can thus be regarded as a kind of partnership among the individual local DBMSs at the individual local sites.

A new software component at each site provides the necessary partnership functionality, and it is the combination of these new components together with the existing DBMSs that constitutes what is usually called the distributed database management system.

Several sites may even coexist in the same machine (for test) and they can exist in LAN or WAN.

An assumption is each site is **strict homogeneity**.

Data distributedà Database distributed

Distributed database provide the necessary bridges to connect those islands of information together so that to mirror the structure of enterprise. Local data can be kept locally and can be accessed remotely when necessary.

Efficiency of processing (the data is kept close to the point where it is most frequently used)

Increased accessibility (it is possible to access any database from anywhere)

Distributed system is complex from technical view.

Three of the best known are (a) **SDD-1**, which was built in the research division of Computer Corporation of America in the late 1970s and early 1980s; (b) **R***, a distributed version of the System R prototype, built at IBM Research in the early 1980s; and (c) **Distributed Ingres**, a distributed version of the Ingres prototype, also built in the early 1980s at the University of California at Berkeley.

Some modern SQL products offer some distributed database support such as (a) Ingres/Star; the distributed database component of Ingres; (b) the distributed database option of Oracle; and (c) the distributed data facility of DB2.

In fact, there are several reasons why, for a distributed database system to be successful, that system must be relational; relational technology is a prerequisite to (effective) distributed technology.

IMPORTANT NOTE

Care with a distributed database must be taken to ensure the following:

- **The distribution is transparent** — users must be able to interact with the system as if it were one logical system. This applies to the system's performance, and methods of access among other things.
- **Transactions are transparent** — each transaction must maintain database integrity across multiple databases. Transactions must also be divided into subtransactions, each subtransaction affecting one database system.

1.5.2 ADVANTAGES OF DISTRIBUTED DBS

Since organizations tend to be geographically dispersed, a DDBS fits the organizational structure better than traditional centralized DBS. Each location will have its local data as well as the ability to get needed data from other locations via a communication network. Moreover, the failure of one of the servers at one site won't render the distributed database system inacces-

sible. The affected site will be the only one directly involved with that failed server. In addition, if any data is required from a site exhibiting a failure, such data may be retrieved from other locations containing the replicated data. The performance of the system will improve, since several machines take care of distributing the load of the CPU and the I/O. Also, the expansion of the distributed system is relatively easy, since adding a new location doesn't affect the existing ones.

Following are advantages of distributed databases

1. Management of distributed data with different levels of transparency.
2. Increase reliability and availability.
3. Easier expansion.
4. Reflects organizational structure — database fragments are located in the departments they relate to.
5. Local autonomy — a department can control the data about them (as they are the ones familiar with it.)
6. Protection of valuable data — if there were ever a catastrophic event such as a fire, all of the data would not be in one place, but distributed in multiple locations.
7. Improved performance — data is located near the site of greatest demand, and the database systems themselves are parallelized, allowing load on the databases to be balanced among servers. (A high load on one module of the database won't affect other modules of the database in a distributed database.)
8. Economics — it costs less to create a network of smaller computers with the power of a single large computer.
9. Modularity — systems can be modified, added and removed from the distributed database without affecting other modules (systems).
10. Reliable transactions - Due to replication of database.
11. Hardware, Operating System, Network, Fragmentation, DBMS, Replication and Location Independence.
12. Continuous operation...
13. Distributed Query processing.
14. Distributed Transaction management.

Single site failure does not affect performance of system. All transactions follow A.C.I.D. property: a-atomicity, the transaction takes place as whole or not at all; c-consistency, maps one consistent DB state to another; i-isolation, each transaction sees a consistent DB; d-durability, the results of a transaction must survive system failures. The Merge Replication Method used to consolidate the data between databases.

1.5.3 DISADVANTAGES OF DISTRIBUTED DBS

On the other hand, DDBS has several disadvantages. A distributed system usually exhibits more complexity and cost more than a centralized one. This is true because the hardware and software involved need to maintain a reliable and an efficient system. All the replication and data retrieval from all sites should be transparent to the user. The cost of maintaining the system is considerable since technicians and experts are required at every site. Another main disadvantage of distributed database systems is the issue of security. Handling security across several locations is more complicated. In addition, the communication between sites maybe tapped to.

Following are disadvantages of distributed databases

1. **Complexity** — extra work must be done by the DBAs to ensure that the distributed nature of the system is transparent. Extra work must also be done to maintain multiple disparate systems, instead of one big one. Extra database design work must also be done to account for the disconnected nature of the database — for example, joins become prohibitively expensive when performed across multiple systems.
2. **Economics** — increased complexity and a more extensive infrastructure means extra labour costs.
3. **Security** — remote database fragments must be secured, and they are not centralized so the remote sites must be secured as well. The infrastructure must also be secured (e.g., by encrypting the network links between remote sites).
4. **Difficult to maintain integrity** — in a distributed database, enforcing integrity over a network may require too much of the network's resources to be feasible.
5. **Inexperience** — distributed databases are difficult to work with, and as a young field there is not much readily available experience on proper practice.
6. **Lack of standards** — there are no tools or methodologies yet to help users convert a **centralized DBMS into a distributed DBMS.**
7. **Database design more complex** — besides of the normal difficulties, the design of a distributed database has to consider fragmentation of data, allocation of fragments to specific sites and data replication.
8. Additional software is required.
9. Operating System should support distributed environment.
10. Concurrency control: it is a major issue. It is solved by locking and timestamping.

1.5.4 FAILURES IN DISTRIBUTED DBS

Several types of failures may occur in distributed database systems:

1. **Transaction Failures:** When a transaction fails, it aborts. Thereby, the database must be restored to the state it was in before the transaction started. Transactions may fail for several reasons. Some failures may be due to deadlock situations or concurrency control algorithms.
2. **Site Failures:** Site failures are usually due to software or hardware failures. These failures result in the loss of the main memory contents. In distributed database, site failures are of two types:
   - ***Total Failure*** where all the sites of a distributed system fail,
   - ***Partial Failure*** where only some of the sites of a distributed system fail.
3. **Media Failures:** Such failures refer to the failure of secondary storage devices. The failure itself may be due to head crashes, or controller failure. In these cases, the media failures result in the inaccessibility of part or the entire database stored on such secondary storage.
4. **Communication Failures:** Communication failures, as the name implies, are failures in the communication system between two or more sites. This will lead to network partitioning where each site, or several sites grouped together, operates independently. As such, messages from one site won't reach the other sites and will therefore be lost. The reliability protocols then utilize a timeout mechanism in order to detect undelivered messages. A message is undelivered if the sender doesn't receive an acknowledgment. The failure of a communication network to deliver messages is known as performance failure.

1.5.5 FUNDAMENTAL PRINCIPLE OF DISTRIBUTED DATABASE

To the user, a distributed system should look exactly like a non-distributed system. In other words, users in a distributed system should be able to behave exactly as if the system were not distributed. All of the problems of distributed systems are—or should be—internal or implementation-level problems, not external or user-level problems.

Some objectives:

1. Local autonomy
2. No reliance on a central site
3. Continuous operation
4. Location independence
5. Fragmentation independence
6. Replication independence
7. Distributed query processing
8. Distributed transaction management

9. Hardware independence
10. Operating system independence
11. Network independence
12. DBMS independence.

These objectives are not all independent of one another, nor are they necessarily exhaustive, nor are they all equally significant. However, the objectives are useful as a basis for understanding distributed technology in general and as a framework for characterizing the functionality of specific distributed systems.

In a remote data access system, the user might be able to operate on data at a remote site, or even on data at several remote sites simultaneously, but "the seams show"; that is, the user definitely aware, to a greater of lesser extent, that the data is remote and has to behave accordingly. In a true distributed database system, by contrast, the seams are hidden.

1. **Local Autonomy:** The sites in a distributed system should be autonomous. It means all operations at a given site are controlled by that site; no site X should depend on some other site Y.
   Actually, the local autonomy objective is not wholly achievable; so the autonomy objective would thus more accurately be stated: Sites should be autonomous to the maximum extent possible.
2. **No Reliance on a Central Site:** Local autonomy implies that all sites must be treated as equals. So there isn't any central master for some central service such as centralized query processing, centralized transaction management and so on. It seems like a corollary of Local Autonomy, but it is desirable in its own right, even if full local autonomy is not achieved, which is why we spell it out as a separate objective.
   Two reasons are central site might be a bottleneck and more important, the system would be vulnerable –if central site went down.
3. **Continuous Operation:** An advantage of distributed systems in general is that they can provide greater reliability and greater availability:
   Reliability is the probability that the system is up and running at any given moment.
   Availability is the probability that the system is up and running continuously throughout a specified period.
   (Unplanned shutdown)
4. **Location Independence:** The basic idea of location independence also known as location transparency is simple: Users should not have to know where data is physically stored, but rather should be able to behave–at least from a logical standpoint—as if the data were all stored at their own local site. It simplifies application programs and end-user activities and it allows data to migrate from site to site without invalidating any of those programs or activities.

5. **Fragmentation Independence:** A system supports data fragmentation for physical storage purposes, and distinct fragments can be stored at different sites. Data can be stored at the location where it is most frequently used, so that most operations are local and network traffic is reduced. Users should be able to behave, at least from a logical standpoint, as if the data were in fact not fragmented at all. Fragmentation independence implies that users will be presented with a view of the data in which the fragments are logically recombined by means of suitable joins and unions.

6. **Replication independence:** A system supports data replication if a given base relvar—or , more generally, a given fragment of a given base relvar—can be represented in storage by many distinct copies or replicas, stored at many distinct sites.

   Reasons: Better performance (not necessary to access other sites); better availability

   Disadvantage: Update propagation

   Replication should be transparent to the user.

7. **Distributed Query Processing:** It proves why distributed systems must be relational.

8. **Distributed Transaction Management:**

   Recovery: The system must ensure that the set of agents for that transaction either all commit in unison or all roll back in unison.

   Concurrency: concurrency control in most distributed systems is typically based on locking.

   Each **transaction** is said to consist of several agents, where an agent is the process performed on behalf of a given transaction at a given site.

9. **Hardware Independence:** It is desirable to be able to run the same DBMS on different hardware platforms.

10. **Operating System Independence:** It is a corollary of Hardware Independence.

11. **Network Independence:** It is desirable to support a variety of disparate communication networks also.

12. **DBMS Independence:** The strict homogeneity assumption: the DBMS instances at different sites all support the same interface—they do not necessarily all have to be copies of the same DBMS software. It might be possible for the distributed system to be heterogeneous, at least to some degree.

1.6 COMPARISON OF DISTRIBUTED AND CENTRALIZED SYSTEMS

Distributed databases are not simply distributed implementations of centralized databases, because they allow the design of systems which present different features from traditional, centralized systems. It is therefore useful to look at the typical features of traditional databases and to compare them with the corresponding features of distributed database. The features which characterize the traditional database approach are centralized control, data independence, and reduction of redundancy, complex physical structures for efficient access, integrity, recovery, concurrency control, privacy and security.

1. **Centralized control:** This possibility of providing centralized control over the information resources of a whole enterprise or organization was considered as one of the strongest motivations for introducing database; they were developed as the evolution of information systems in which each application had its own private files. The fundamental function of a **database administrator (DBA)** was to guarantee the safety of data; the data itself was recognized to be an important investment of the enterprise which required a centralized responsibility. In distributed databases, the idea of centralized control is much less emphasized. This depends also on the architecture, as can be seen by considering Examples 1.1 and 1.2. Probably, Example 1.2 lends itself more to centralized control than does Example 1.1. In general, in distributed database it is possible to identify a hierarchical control structure based on a global data administrator, administrators, who have the responsibility of their respective local databases. However, it must be emphasized that local database administrators may have a high degree of autonomy, up to the point that a global database administrator is completely missing and the intersite coordination is performed by the local administrators themselves. This characteristic is usually called site autonomy: from complete site autonomy without any centralized database administrator to almost completely centralized control.
2. **Data independence:** Data independence was also considered one of the main motivations for introducing the database approach. Essentially, data independence means that the actual organization of data is transparent to the application programmer. Programs are written having a "conceptual" view of the data, the so called **conceptual schema**. This main advantage of data independence is that programs are unaffected by changes in the physical organization of data. In distributed database, data independence has the same importance as in traditional databases; however, a new aspect is added to the usual notion of data independence, namely, distribution transparency. By distribution

we mean that programs can be written as if the database were not distributed. Thus the correctness of programs is unaffected by the movement of data from one site to another; however, their speed of execution is affected. Data independence was provided in traditional databases through a multilevel architecture having different descriptions of data and mappings between them; the notions of conceptual schema, storage schema, and external schema were developed for this purpose. In a similar way, distribution transparency is obtained in distributed databases by introducing new levels and schemata.

3. **Reduction of redundancy:** In traditional databases, redundancy was reduced as far as possible for two reasons: first, inconsistencies among several copies of the same logical data are automatically avoided by having only one copy, and second, storage space is saved by eliminating redundancy. Reduction of redundancy was obtained by data sharing, i.e., by allowing several applications to access the same files and records.

   In distributed databases, however, there are several reasons for considering data redundancy as a desirable feature: first, the locality of applications can be increased if the data is replicated at all sites where applications need it, and second, the availability of the system can be increased, because a site failure does not stop the execution of applications at other sites if the data is replicated. In general, the same reasons against redundancy which were given for the traditional environment are still valid, and therefore the evaluation of the optimal degree of redundancy requires an evaluation of a rather complex trade-off. As a very general statement, let us say that the convenience of replicating a data item increases with the ratio of retrieval accesses versus update access performed by applications to it. The convenience of data replication increases because if we have several copies of an item, retrieval can be performed on any copy, while updates must be performed consistently on all copies. A more precise discussion of this problem is given in next chapter , when dealing with distributed database design.

4. **Complex physical structures and efficient access:** Complex accessing structures, like secondary indexed, interfile chains, and so on, are a major important part of data base management systems (DBMSs). The reason for providing complex accessing structures is to obtain efficient access to the data. In distributed databases, complex accessing structures are not the right tool for efficient access. Therefore, while efficient access is a main problem in distributed databases, physical structures are not a relevant technological issue. Efficient access to a distributed database cannot be provided by using intersite physical struc-

tures, because it is very difficult to build and maintain such structures and because it is not convenient to "navigate" at a record level is a distributed database. Let us illustrate this point by an example.

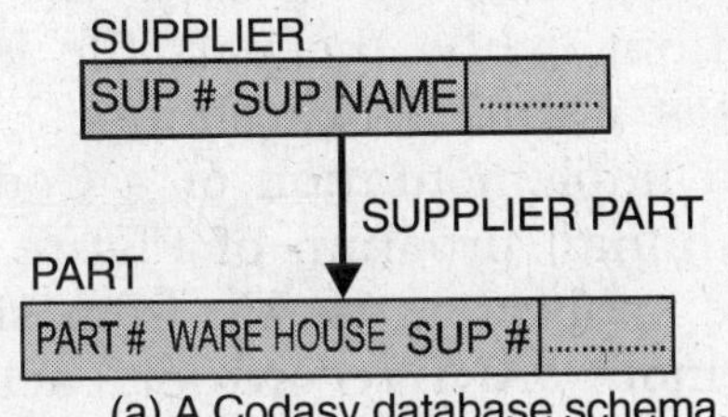

(a) A Codasy database schema.

Find SUPPLIER record with SUP# S1;
Repat until "no more member in set"
Find next PART record in SUPPLIER-PART set:
Output PART record;

(b) A Codasyl-DBMS-like program for finding parts supplied by supplier S1.

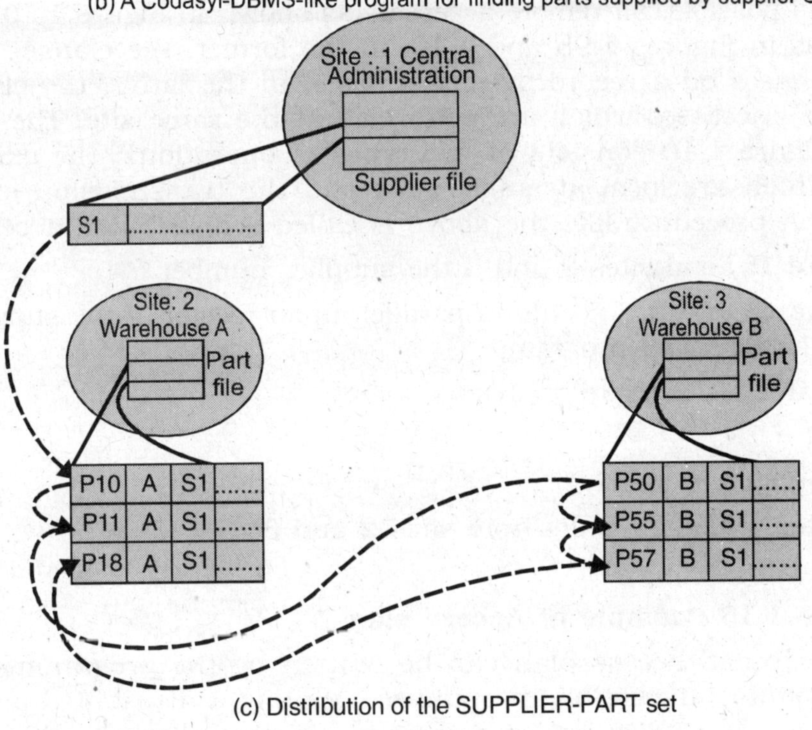

(c) Distribution of the SUPPLIER-PART set

Figure 1.9 A distributed Codasyl-like database

Example 1.4

Consider the schema of the Codasyl-like database shown in Figure 1.9a. There are two record types. SUPPLIER and PART, and one set type, SUPPLIER-PART, which connects supplier records to the parts records supplied by

them. The application "find all PART records supplied by supplier S1" is coded in a Codasyl-like DML as shown in Figure 1.9b.

Let us now assume that the above database is distributed over three sites of a computer network, as shown in Figure 1.9c: the supplier file is located at site 1 (central administration), while the part file is split into two different subfiles located at two sites 2 and 3 (warehouses). Let us further suppose that we have a distributed implementation of a Codasyl system, so that we can run the same (navigational) program of Figure 1.9b on the distributed database. Suppose that the application is run from site 1. Clearly, the system would have to access a remote PART record for each iteration of the "repeat until" loop; therefore, for each access to a record not only the record itself would have to be transmitted, but also several messages would have to be exchanged.

A more efficient implementation of the same application consists of grouping, as far as possible, all remote accesses, as shown in Figure 1.10. Compare the programs in Figures 1.9b and 1.10: in the former, the clause "find next" requires accesses on a record-by-record basis; in the latter, the clause "find all" groups all accesses which are performed at the same site. The procedure shown in Figure 1.10 consists of two types of operations: the execution of programs which are local at single sites and the transmission of files between sites. A procedure like the above is called a distributed access plan.

1. **At site 1:** Send sites 2 and 3 the supplier number SN
2. **At sites 2 and 3:** Execute in parallel, upon receipt of the supplier number, the following program:

   Find all PARTS records having

   SUP # = SN;

   Send result to site 1.
3. **At site 1:** Merge results from sites 2 and 3;

   Output the result.

Figure 1.10 Example of Access plan

A distributed access plan can be written by the programmer or produced automatically by an optimizer. Writing a distributed access plan is similar to navigational programming in centralized databases, in the sense that the programmer specifies how the database must be accessed. However, intersite navigation should be performed at the level of groups of records, while usual one-record-at-a-time navigation can be performed for local processing at each site. Therefore, a navigational language is less appropriate than a nonprocedural, set-oriented language for building access plans.

Several problems are still to be solved in the design of an optimizer which produces automatically an access plan like the one shown in Figure 1.10. It is convenient to divide these problems into two categories: global optimization and local optimization. Global optimization consists of determining which data must be accessed at which sites and which data files must consequently be transmitted between sites. The main optimization parameter for global optimization is communication cost, although the cost of accessing the cost of accessing the local databases should also be taken into account in some cases. The relative importance of these factors depends on the ratio between communication costs and disk access costs, which depends in turn on the type of communication network.

Local optimization consists of deciding how to perform the local database accesses at each site; the problems of local optimization are typical of traditional, nondistributed databases and will not be further considered in this book.

The research on global optimization has produced results which are useful even if access plans are not produced automatically, because it aids in understanding how a distributed database can be efficiently accessed.

5. **Integrity, recovery and concurrency control:** It databases the issues of integrity, recovery, and concurrency control, although they refer to different problems, is strongly interrelated. To a large extent, the solution of these problems consists of providing transactions. A transaction is an atomic unit of execution; i.e., it is a sequence of operations which either are performed in entirety or are not performed at all. The **"funds transfer"** application, given in Example 1.1, is a global application which must be an atomic unit: either both the debit portion and the credit portion are executed or none; it is not acceptable to perform only one of them. Therefore the funds transfer application is also a global transaction. It is clear that in distributed database the problem of transaction atomicity has a particular flavor: how should the system behave if the "debit" site is operational and the **"credit"** site is not operational when the funds transfer is required? Should the transaction be aborted (undoing all operations which have been performed until the moment of site failure), or should a smart system try to execute the funds transfer correctly even if both sites are never simultaneously operational? Of course, the user would be less affected by failures if the latter approach is applied. Clearly, atomic transactions are the means to obtain database integrity, because they assure that either all actions which transform the database from one consistent state into another are performed, or the initial consistent state is left untouched. There

are two dangerous enemies of transaction atomicity: failures and concurrency. Failures may cause the system to stop in the midst of transaction execution, thus violating the atomicity requirement. Concurrent execution of different transactions may permit one transaction to observe an inconsistent, transient state created by another transaction during its execution. **Recovery** deals to a large extent with the problem of preserving transaction atomicity in the presence of failures. In distributed databases this aspect is particularly important, because some of the sites involved in transaction execution might fail, as shown in the previous example. **Concurrency control** deals with ensuring transaction atomicity in he presence of concurrent execution of transactions. This problem can be seen as a typical synchronization problem. In distributed databases, as in all distributed systems, the synchronization problem is harder than in centralized systems.

6. **Privacy and security:** In traditional databases, the database administrator, having centralized control, can ensure that only authorized access to the data is performed. Note, however, that the centralized database approach in itself, without specialized control procedures, is more vulnerable to privacy and security violations than the older approaches based on separate files. In distributed databases, local administrators are faced essentially with the same problem as database administrators in a traditional database. However, two peculiar aspects of distributed databases are worth mentioning: first, in a distributed database with a very high degree of site autonomy, the owners of local data feel more protected because they can enforce their own protections instead of depending on a central database administrator; second, security problems are intrinsic to distributed systems in general, because communication networks can represent a weak point with respect to protection.

1.7 WHY DISTRIBUTED DATABASES?

There are several reasons why distributed databases are developed. The following is a list of the main motivations.

1. **Organizational and economic reasons:** Many organizations are decentralized, and a distributed database approach fits more naturally the structure of the organization. The problems of a distributed organizational structure and of the corresponding information system are the subject of several books and papers. With the recent developments in computer technology, the economy-of-scale motivation for having large, centralized computer centers is becoming questionable. We do not further discuss this subject here; however, the organizational and economic motivations are probably the most important reason for develop-

ing distributed databases.

2. **Interconnection of existing databases:** Distributed databases are the natural solution when several databases already exist in an organization and the necessity of performing global applications arises. In this case, the distribute database is created bottom-up from the preexisting local databases. This process may require a certain degree of local restructuring; however, the effort which is required by this restructuring is much less than that needed for the creation of a completely new centralized database.
3. **Incremental growth:** If an organization grows by adding new, relatively autonomous organizational units (new branches, new warehouses, etc.) then the distributed database approach supports a smooth incremental growth with a minimum degree of impact on the already existing units. With a centralized approach, either the initial dimensions of the system take care of future expansion, which is difficult to foresee and expensive to implement, or the growth has a major impact not only on the new applications but also on the existing ones.
4. **Reduced communication overhead:** In a geographically distributed database like the database of Example 1.1, the fact that many applications are local clearly reduces the communication overhead with respect to a centralized database. Therefore, the maximization of the locality of application is one of the primary objectives in distributed database design.
5. **Performance considerations:** The existence of several autonomous processors results in the increase of performance through a high degree of parallelism. This consideration can be applied to an multiprocessor system, and not only to distributed databases. For instance, the configuration of Example 1.3 also allows parallelism, but it is not considered a distributed database. However, distributed databases have the advantage in that the decomposition of data reflects application dependent criteria which maximize application locality; in this way the mutual interference between different processors, and critical bottlenecks, such as the communication network itself or common services of the whole system, are avoided. This effect is a consequence of the autonomous processing capability requirement for local applications started in the definition of distributed databases.
6. **Reliability and availability:** The distributed database approach, especially with redundant data, can be used also in order to obtain higher reliability and availability. However, obtaining this goal is not straightforward and requires the use of techniques which are still not completely understood. The autonomous processing capability of the different sites does not by itself guarantee a higher overall reliability of the system, but is ensures a graceful degradation property; in other words,

failures in a distributed database can be more frequent than in a centralized one because of the greater number of components, but the effect of each failure is confined to those applications which use the data of the failed site, and complete system crash is rare. The techniques for building reliable distributed databases are presented in Chapter 9.

The above motivations for distributed databases are not new. Why has the development of distributed database systems just begun? There are two main reasons for this: first, the recent development of small computers, providing at a lower cost many of the capabilities which were previously provided by large mainframes, constitutes the necessary hardware support for the development of distributed information system; second the technology of distributed databases is based on two other technologies which have developed a sufficiency solid foundation during the seventies: computer networks technology and database technology. It is a complex task to build a distributed database on top of a computer network and a set of local database management systems at each site; it would be an infeasible effort without these building blocks.

1.8 PROMISE OF DDBSS

Many advantages of DDBSs have been cited in literature, ranging from sociological reasons for decentralization to better economics. All of these can be distilled to four fundamentals which may also be viewed as promises of DDBS technology. In this section we discuss these promises and, in the process, introduce many of the concepts that we will study in subsequent chapters.

1.8.1 TRANSPARENT MANAGEMENT OF DISTRIBUTED AND REPLICATED DATA

Transparency refers to separation of the higher-level semantics of a system from lower-level implementation issues. In other words, a transparent system "hides" the implementation details from users. The advantage of a fully transparent DBMS is the high level of support that it provides for the development of complex applications. It is obvious that we would like to make all DBMSs (centralized or distributed) fully transparent.

Let us start our discussion with an example. Consider can engineering firm that has offices in Boston, Edmonton, Paris and San Francisco. They run projects at each of these sites and would like to maintain a database of their employees, the projects and other related data. Assuming that the database is relational, we can store this information in two relations: EMP (ENO, ENAME, TITLE)[3] and PROJ(PNO, PNAME, BUDGET). We also introduce a third relation to store salary information: PAY (TITLE, SAL) and a fourth relation ASG which indicates which employees have been assigned to which projects for what duration with what responsibility: ASG (ENO, PNO, DUR, RESP). If all of this data was stored in a centralized DBMS, and we wanted to find out the names and employees who worked on a project for more than 12 months, we would specify this using the following SQL query:

```
SELECT     ENAME, SAL
FROM       EMP, ASG, PAY
WHERE      ASG.DOR > 12
AND        EMP.ENO = ASG.ENO
AND        PAY.TITLE = EMP.TITLE
```

However, given the distributed nature of this firm's business, it is preferable, under these circumstances, to localize each data such that data about the employees in Edmonton office are stored in Edmonton, those in the Boston office are stored in Boston, and so forth. The same applies to the project and salary information. Thus, what we are engaged in is a process where we partition each of the relations and store each partition at a different site. This is known as fragmentation and we discuss it further below.

Furthermore, it may be preferable to duplicate some of this data at other sites for performance and reliability reasons. The result is a distributed database which is fragmented and replicated (Figure 1.11). Fully transparent access means that the users can still pose the query as specified above, without paying any attention to the fragmentation, location, or replication of data, and let the system worry about resolving these issues.

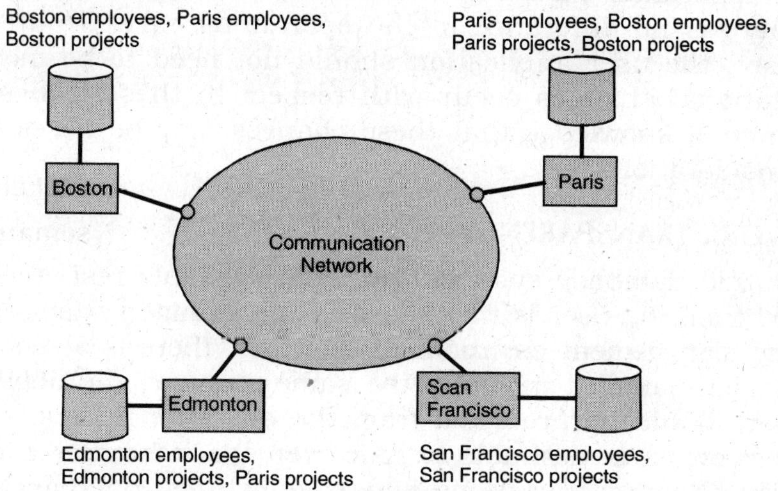

Figure 1.11 A Distributed Application

1.8.1.1 DATA INDEPENDENCE

Data independence is a fundamental form of transparency that we look for within a DBMS. It is also the only type that is important within the context

of a centralized DBMS. It refers to the immunity of user applications to changes in the definition and organization of data, and vice versa.

Data definition can occur at two levels. At one level the logical structure of the data is specified, and at the other level the physical structure of the data is defined. The former is commonly known as the schema definition; whereas the latter is referred to as the physical data description. We can therefore talk about two types of data independence: logical data independence and physical data independence. Logical data independence refers to the immunity of user applications to changes in the logical structure of the database. In general, if a user application operates on a subset of the attributes of a relation, it should not be affected later when new attributes are added to the same relation. For example, let us consider the EMP relation discussed above. If a user application deals with only the address fields of this relation (it might be a simple mailing program), the later additions to the relation of say, skill, would not and should not affect the mailing application.

Physical data independence deals with hiding the details of the storage structure from user applications. When a user application is written, it should not be concerned with the details of physical data organization. The data might be organized on different disk types, parts of it might be organized differently (e.g., random versus indexed-sequential access) or might even be distributed across different storage hierarchies (e.g., disk storage and tape storage). The application should not be involved with these issues since, conceptually; there is no difference in the operations carried out against the data. Therefore, the user application should not need to be modified when data organizational changes occur with respect to these issues. Nevertheless, it is common knowledge that these changes may be necessary for performance considerations.

1.8.1.2 NETWORK TRANSPARENCY

In centralized database systems, the only available resource that needs to be shielded from the user is the data (i.e., the storage system). In a distributed database management environment, however, there is a second resource that needs to be managed in much the same manner: the network. Preferably, the user should be protected from the operational details of the network. Furthermore, it is desirable to hide even the existence of the network, if possible. Then there would be no difference between database applications that would run on a centralized database and those that would run on a distributed database. This type of transparency is referred to as network transparency or distribution transparency.

One can consider network transparency from the viewpoint of either the services provided or the data. From the former perspective, it is desirable to

have uniform means by which services are accessed. From a DBMS perspective, distribution transparency requires that users do not have to specify where data is located.

Some have separated distribution transparency into two: location transparency and naming transparency. Location transparency refers to the fact that the command used to perform a task is independent of both the location of the data and the system on which an operation is carried out. Naming transparency means that a unique name is provided for each object in the database. In the absence of naming transparency, user is required to embed the location name (or an identifier) as part of the object name.

1.8.1.3 REPLICATION TRANSPARENCY

The issue of replicating data within a distributed database is discussed in quite some detail in last chapter. At this point, let us just mention that for performance, reliability, and availability reasons, it is usually desirable to be able to distribute data in a replicated fashion across the machines on a network. Such replication helps performance since diverse and conflicting user requirements can be more easily accommodated. For example, data that is commonly accessed by one user can be placed on that user's local machine as well as on the machine of another user with the same access requirements. This increases the locality of reference. Furthermore, if one of the machines fails, a copy of the data is still available on another machine on the network. Of course, this is a very simple-minded description of the situation. In fact, the decision as to whether to replicate or not, and how many copies of any database object to have, depends to a considerable degree on user applications. Note that replication causes problems in updating databases. Therefore, if the user applications are predominantly update-oriented, it may not be a good idea to have too many copies of the data.

Assuming that data is replicated, the issue related to transparency that needs to be addressed is whether the users should be aware of the existence of copies or whether the system should handle the management of copies and the user should act as if there is a single copy of the data (note that we are not referring to the placement of copies, only their existence). From a user's perspective the answer is obvious. It is preferable not to be involved with handling copies and having to specify the fact that a certain action can and/or should be taken on multiple copies. From a systems point of view, however, the answer is not that simple. Remember that replication transparency refers only to the existence of replicas, not to their actual location. Note also that distributing these replicas across the network in a transparent manner is the domain of network transparency.

1.8.1.4 FRAGMENTATION TRANSPARENCY

The final form of transparency that needs to be addressed within the context of a distributed database system is that of fragmentation transparency. It is commonly desirable to divided each database relation into smaller fragments and treat each fragment as a separate database object (i.e., another relation). This is commonly done for reasons of performance, availability, and reliability. Furthermore, fragmentation can reduce the negative effects of replication. Each replica is not the full relation but only a subset of it; thus less space is required and fewer data items need be managed.

There are two general types of fragmentation alternatives. In one case, called horizontal fragmentation, a relation is partitioned into a set of subrelations each of which have a subset of the tuples (rows) of the original relation. The second alternative is vertical fragmentation where each subrelation is defined on a subset of the attributes (columns) of the original relation.

When database objects are fragmented, we have to deal with the problem of handling user queries that were specified on entire relations but now have to be performed on subrelations. In other words, the issue is one of finding a query processing strategy based on the fragments rather than the relations, even though the queries are specified on the latter. Typically, this requires a translation from what is called a global query to several fragment queries. Since the fundamental issue of dealing with fragmentation transparency is one of query processing.

1.8.1.5 WHO SHOULD PROVIDE TRANSPARENCY?

We discussed various possible forms of transparency within a distributed computing environment. Obviously, to provide easy and efficient access by novice users to the services of the DBMS, one would want to have full transparency, involving all the various types that we discussed. Nevertheless, the level of transparency is inevitably a compromise between ease of use and the difficulty and overhead cost of providing high levels of transparency.

What has not yet been discussed is who is responsible for providing these services. It is possible to identify three distinct layers at which the services of transparency can be provided. It is quite common to treat these as mutually exclusive means of providing the service, although it is more appropriate to view them as complementary.

We could leave the responsibility of providing transparent access to data resources to the access layer. The transparency features can be built into the user language, which then translates the requested services into required operations. In other words, the compiler or the interpreter takes over the task

and no transparent service is provided to the implementer of the compiler or the interpreter.

The second layer at which transparency can be provided is the operating system level. State-of-the-art operating systems provide some level of transparency to system users. For example, the device drivers within the operating system handle the minute details of getting each piece of peripheral equipment to do what is requested. The typical computer user, or even an application programmer, does not normally write device drivers to interact with individual peripheral equipment; that operation is transparent to the user.

Providing transparent access to resources at the operating system level can obviously be extended to the distributed environment, where the management of the network resource is taken over by the distributed operating system. This is a good level at which to provide network transparency if it can be accomplished. The unfortunate aspect is that not all commercially available distributed operating systems provide a reasonable level of transparency in network management.

The third layer at which transparency can be supported is within the DBMS. The transparency and support for database functions provided to the DBMS designers by an underlying operating system is generally minimal and typically limited to very fundamental operations for performing certain tasks. It is the responsibility of the DBMS to make all the necessary translations from the operating system to the higher-level user interface. This mode of operation is the most common method today. There are, however, various problems associated with leaving the task of providing full transparency to the DBMS. These have to do with the interaction of the operating system with the distributed DBMS and are discussed throughout this book.

It is therefore quite important to realize that reasonable levels of transparency depend on different components within the data management environment. Network transparency can easily be handled by the distributed operating system as part of its responsibilities for providing replication and fragmentation transparencies (especially those aspects dealing with transaction management and recovery). The DBMS should be responsible for providing a high level of data independence together with replication and fragmentation transparencies. Finally, the user interface can support a higher level of transparency not only in terms of a uniform access method to the data resources from within a language, but also in terms of structure constructs that permit the user to deal with objects in his or her environment rather than focusing on the details of database description. Specifically, it should be noted that the interface to a distributed DBMS does not need to be a programming language but can be a graphical user interface, a natural language interface, and even a voice system.

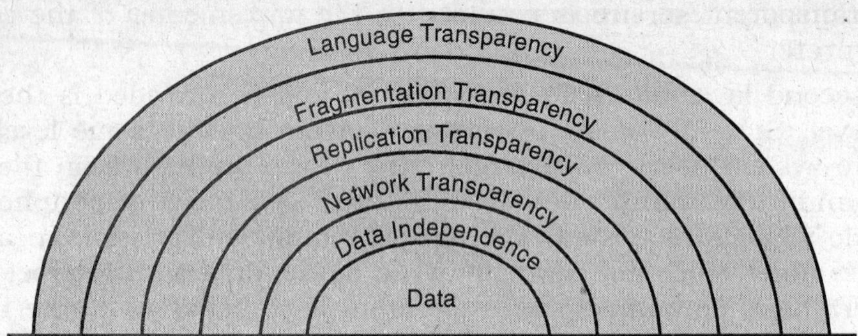

Figure 1.12 Layers of transparency

A hierarchy of these transparencies is shown in Figure 1.12. It is not always easy to delineate clearly the levels of transparency, but such a figure serves an important instructional purpose even if it is not fully correct. To complete the picture we have added a "language transparency" layer, although it is not discussed in this chapter. With this generic layer, users have high-level access to the data (e.g., fourth-generation languages, graphical user interfaces, natural language access).

1.9 PROBLEMS OF DISTRIBUTED DATABASE SYSTEMS

The overriding problem is that communication networks at least, "long-haul" or wide area networks (WANs) are slow. A typically WAN might have an effective data rate of around 5 to 10 thousand bytes per second; the typical disk drive, by contrast, has a data rate of around 5 to 10 million bytes per second. As a consequence, an overriding objective in distributed database is typically, to minimize network utilization i.e. to minimization the number and volume of messages. This objective in turn gives rise to problems in a number of subsidiary areas, the following among them:

1.9.1 QUERY PROCESSING

The objective of minimizing network utilization implies that the query optimization process itself needs to be distributed, as well as the query execution process. In other words, the overall optimization process will typically consist of a global optimization step, followed by local optimization steps at each affected site.

Example: Database

S	{S#, CITY}	10,000 stored tuples at site A
P	{P#, COLOR}	100,000 stored tuples at site B
SP	{S#, P#}	1,000,000 stored tuples at site A

Consider "Get supplier numbers for London suppliers of red parts"

((S JOIN SP JOIN P) WHERE CITY='London' AND
COLOR=COLOR('Red')){S#}

Suppose: Number of red parts=10; Number of shipments by London suppliers=100,000;

Data rate=50,000 bits per second; Access delay=0.1 second

Worst: Join suppliers and shipments at site A, restrict the result to London suppliers, and then, for each of those suppliers in turn, check site B to see whether the corresponding part is red. Each of these checks will involve two messages—a query and a response. The transmission time for these messages will be small compared with the access delay.

T=20000 seconds approx. (5.56h)

Best: Restrict parts at site B to those that are red and move the result to site A. Complete the processing at site A.

T=0.1 seconds

1.9.2 CATALOG MANAGEMENT

In a distributed system, the system catalog will include not only the usual catalog data regarding base relvars, views, integrity constraints, authorizations, and so on, but also all the necessary control information to enable the system to provide the desired location, fragmentation, and replication independence. Where and how should the catalog itself be stored?

1. **Centralized:** The total catalog is stored exactly once, at a single central site.
2. **Fully replicated:** The total catalog is stored in its entirety at every site.
3. **Partitioned:** Each site maintains its own catalog for objects stored at that site. The total catalog is the union of all of those disjoint local catalogs.
4. **Combination of Approaches 1 and 3:** Each site maintains a unified copy of all of those local catalogs, as in Approach 1.

Approach 1 obviously violates the objective of "no reliance on a central site." Approach 2 suffers from a severe loss of autonomy, in that every catalog update has to be propagated to every site. Approach 3 makes nonlocal operations very expensive. Approach 4 is more efficient than Approach3, but violates the objective of "no reliance on a central site" again.

System-wide name

Creator ID (the ID of the user who issued the CREATE operations that created the object in the first place)

Creator site ID (the ID of the site at which the CREATE operation was executed)

Local name (the unqualified name of the object)

Birth site ID (the ID of the site at which the object was initially stored)

MARILYN @ NEWYORK . STATS @ LONDON

USER IDs are unique within site and site IDs are globally unique. Thus, for example, the system-wide name. MARILYN creates the STATS in NEWYORK which is initially stored in LONDON.

1.9.3 UPDATE PROPAGATION

The basic problem with data replication is that an update to any giver logical object must be propagated to all stored copies of that object.

A common scheme for dealing with this problem is the so-called primary copy scheme, which works as follows:

- One copy of each replicated object is designated as the primary copy. The remainder are all secondary copies.
- Primary copies of different objects are at different sites (so this is a distributed scheme once again).
- Update operations are deemed to be logically complete as soon as the primary copy has been updated. The site holding that copy is then responsible for propagating the update to the secondary copies at some subsequent time.

A few further observations

1. The concept of replication in a system with delayed propagation can be thought of as an application of the idea of snapshots.
2. We do not mean to suggest that delayed propagation is a bad idea—it is clearly the right thing to do in appropriate circumstances.
3. One reason why many products implement replication with delayed propagation is that the alternative—that is, updating all replicas prior to COMMIT—requires two-phase commit support, which can be costly in performance.

1.9.4 RECOVERY

Recovery in distributed systems is typically based on two-phase commit, or some variant thereof. Two-phase commit is required in any environment in which a single transaction can interact with several autonomous resource managers; however, it is particularly important in a distributed system, because the resource managers in question—that is, the local DBMS—are operating at distinct sites and are hence very autonomous.

1. The objective of "no reliance on a central site" dictates that the coordinator function must not be assigned to one distinguished site in the network, but instead must be performed by different sites for different transactions. Typically it is handled by the site at which the transaction in question is initiated; thus, each site must be capable of acting as the coordinator site for some transactions and as a participant site for others.
2. The two-phase commit process requires the coordinator to communicate with every participant site—which means more messages and more overhead.
3. If site Y acts as a participant in a two-phase commit process coordinated by site X, then site Y must do what it is told by site X (commit or rollback, whichever applies): a loss of local autonomy, though perhaps a minor one.

Presumed commit, under this scheme, participants are required to acknowledge "rollback" ("undo it") message but not "commit" ("do it") messages, and the coordinator can forget the transaction as soon as it has broadcast its decision, provided that decision is "commit". If an in-doubt participant crashes, then on restart it will (as always) interrogate the coordinator. If the coordinator still remembers the transaction (i.e., the coordinator is still waiting for the participant's acknowledgment), then the decision must have been "rollback"; otherwise, it must have been "commit".

Presumed rollback is the opposite, of course: Participants are required to acknowledge "commit" messages but not "rollback" messages, and the coordinator can forget the transaction as soon as it has broadcast its decision, as long as that decision is "rollback". If an in-doubt participant crashes, then on restart it will interrogate the coordinator. If the coordinator still remembers the transaction (i.e., the coordinator is still waiting for the participant's acknowledgment), then the decision was "commit"; otherwise, it was "rollback".

1.9.5 CONCURRENCY

Concurrency control in most distributed systems is based on locking, just as it is in most nondistributed systems. In a distributed system, however, requests to test, set, and release locks become messages (assuming that the object under consideration is at a remote site), and messages mean overhead.

For example, consider a transaction T that needs to update an object for which there exist replicas at n remote sites. If each site is responsible for locks on objects stored at that site (as it will be under the local autonomy assumption), then a straightforward implementation will require at least 5n messages:

n lock requests, n lock grants, n update messages, n acknowledgments, n unlock requests combine the lock and update, combine the grant and acknowledgment

The usual approach to this problem is to adopt the primary copy strategy already described in the subsection "Update Propagation".

Global deadlock

1. The agent of transaction T2 at site X is waiting for the agent of transaction T1 at site X to release a lock.
2. The agent of transaction T1 at site X is waiting for the agent of transaction T1 at site Y to complete.
3. The agent of transaction T1 at site Y is waiting for the agent of transaction T2 at site Y to release a lock.
4. The agent of transaction T2 at site X is waiting for the agent of transaction T2 at site X to complete: Deadlock!

1.10 CLIENT/SERVER SYSTEM

Client/Server systems can be regarded as a special case of distributed systems in general. More precisely, a client/server system is a distributed system in which (a) some sites are client sites and some are server sites, and (b) all data resides at the server sites, (c) all applications execute at the client sites, and (d) "the seams show" (full location independence is not provided).

Recall that the term client/server refers primarily to an architecture, or logical division of responsibilities; the client is the application (also known as the front end), and the server is the DBMS (also known as the back end). Precisely, because the overall system can be so neatly divided into two parts, however, the possibility arises of overall system can be so neatly divided into two parts, however, the possibility arises of running the two on different machines.

Several clients might be able to share the same server (indeed this is the normal case). A single client might be able to access several servers. This latter possibility divides in turn into two cases:

1. **The client is limited to accessing just one serer at a time—** that is, each individual database request must be directed to just one server; it is not possible, within a single request, to combine data from two or more different servers. Furthermore, the user has to know which particular server stores which pieces of data.
2. **The client can access many server simultaneously—** that is, a single database request can combine data from several servers, which means

that the servers look to the client as if they were really just one server, and the user does not have to know which server store which pieces of data.

1.10.1 CLIENT/SERVER STANDARDS

First of all, certain client/server features are included in the SQL standard.

Next, there is the ISO Remote Data Access standard, RDA. The general intent of RDA is to define formats and protocols for client/server communication.

The third and last standard we mention here is IBM's Distributed Relational Database Architecture standard.

1.10.2 CLIENT/SERVER APPLICATION PROGRAMMING

A client/server system can be thought of as a distributed system in which all requests originate at one site and all processing is performed at another.

1.10.2.1 DBMS INDEPENDENCE

The strict homogeneity assumption is arguably too strong; all that is really needed is that the various DBMSs at different sites all support the same interface. Ingres and Oracle both supported the official SQL standard—no more and no less!

Gateway also mentioned as wrapper, is used to make a DBMS look like another one.

1.10.2.2 DATA ACCESS MIDDLEWARE

Gateways do suffer from a number of obvious limitations. One is that they provide little location independence. Another is that the very same application might need to make use of several distinct gateways, without any support for joins that span sites and so forth.

Any piece of software whose general purpose is to paper over the differences among distinct systems that are supposed to work together somehow might reasonably be regarded as "middleware". However, we focus here on what might be termed data access middleware.

There are clear technical difficulties in trying to provide full DBMS independence, even when all of the participating DBMSs are SQL systems specifically. However, the potential payoff is huge even if the solutions are less than perfect; for this reason, several data access middleware products already exit, and more are likely to appear in the near future.

1.11 DISTRIBUTED DATABASE MANAGEMENT SYSTEMS (DDBMSS)

A **distributed database management system** ('DDBMS') is a software system that permits the management of a distributed database and makes the distribution transparent to the users. A distributed database is a collection of multiple, logically interrelated databases distributed over a computer network. Sometimes "distributed database system" is used to refer jointly to the distributed database and the distributed DBMS.

A centralized distributed database management system (DDBMS) manages the database as if it were all stored on the same computer. The DDBMS synchronizes all the data periodically and, in cases where multiple users must access the same data, ensures that updates and deletes performed on the data at one location will be automatically reflected in the data stored elsewhere.

The users and administrators of a distributed system, should, with proper implementation, interact with the system as if the system was centralized. This transparency allows for the functionality desired in such a structured system without special programming requirements, allowing for any number of local and/or remote tables to be accessed at a given time across the network.

Distributed database management systems are software for managing databases stored on multiple computers in a network. A distributed database is a set of databases stored on multiple computers that typically appears to applications on a single database. Consequently, an application can simultaneously access and modify the data in several databases in a network. DDBMS is specially developed for heterogeneous database platforms, focusing mainly on heterogeneous database management systems (HDBMS).

A distributed database management system supports the creation and maintenance of distributed databases. In analyzing the features of DDBMSs, it is convenient to distinguish between commercially available systems and advanced research prototypes. This distinction is based on present-day state of the art. Clearly, some features which are currently experimental in advanced research prototypes will be incorporated in commercially available systems of the future. In this section, some hints are given on how hard these problems are and in which way the new features will be made commercially systems and most of the research prototypes.

Several commercially, available distributed systems were developed by the vendors of centralized database management systems. They contain an additional component which extends the capabilities of centralized DBMSs by supporting communication and cooperation between several instances of DBMSs which are installed at different sites of a computer network.

The software components which are typically necessary for building a distributed in this case are:

1. The database management component (DB)
2. The data communication component (DC)
3. The data dictionary (DD), which is extended to represent information about the distribution of data in the network
4. The distributed database component (DDB)

These components are connected as shown in Figure 1.13 for a two-site network.

We will use the term "distributed database management system" to refer to the above set of four components, while DDB is only the specialized distributed database component.

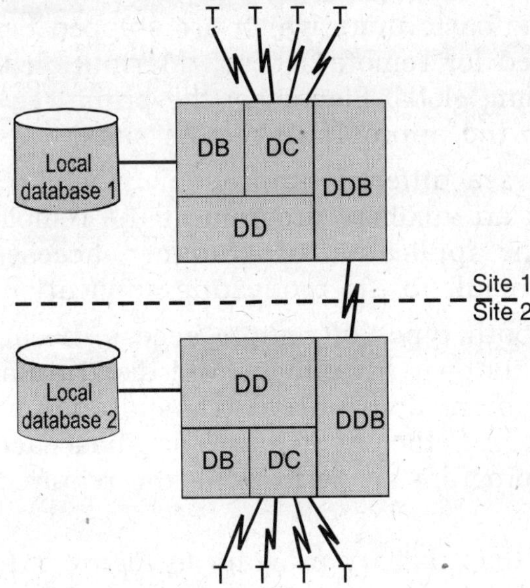

Figure 1.13 Components of a commercial DDBMS.

In a similar way, we will use the term "database management system" to refer to the set of components which serve to manage a nondistributed database, i.e., the DB, DC and DD components.

The services which are supported by the above type of systems are typically:

1. Remote database access by an application program; this feature is the most important one and is provided by all systems which have a distributed database component.

2. Some degree of distribution transparency; this feature is supported to a different extent by different systems, because there is a strong trade-off between distribution transparency and performance.
3. Support for database administration and control; this feature includes tools for monitoring the database, gathering information about database utilization, and providing a global view of data files existing at the various sites.
4. Some support for concurrency control and recovery of distributed transactions.

The access to a remote database by an application can be performed in one of two basic ways, as shown in Figure 1.14a and b. Figure 1.14a shows that the application issues a database access request which refers to remote data. This request is automatically routed by the DDBMS to the site where the data is located; then it is executed at that site, and the result is returned. In this way, the basic units which are shipped between this primitive. If this approach is used for remote access, distribution transparency can be implemented by providing global filenames; the primitives could then be automatically addressed to the appropriate remote sites.

Figure 1.14b shows a different approach, in which the application requires the execution of an auxiliary program at the remote site. This auxiliary program, written by the application programmer, accesses the remote database and returns the result to the requesting application.

DDBMSs provide both types of remote access, because each one of the above approaches has its own advantages and disadvantages. The solution of Figure 1.14a provides more distribution transparency while the solution of Figure 1.14b can be more efficient if many database accesses are required, because the auxiliary program an perform all the required accesses and send only the result back.

If the capability of the auxiliary program in Figure 1.14b is a greater than the capability of the database access primitives of Figure 1.14a, then the second solution can be more efficient. Therefore, having powerful primitives which are capable of manipulating sets of records at a time is a very useful feature of the local DBMS in building a distributed system. However, most commercially available DBMSs are one-record-at-a-time systems, and therefore auxiliary programs are needed.

An important property of DDBMSs is whether they are homogeneous or heterogeneous. Homogeneity and heterogeneity can be considered at different levels in a distributed database: the hardware, the operating system, ant the local DBMSs. However, the important distinction for us is at the level of local DBMSs, because differences at lower levels are managed by the communication software. Therefore, in the following, the term "homogeneous DDBMS" refers to a DDBMS with the same DBMS at each site, even if the computers and/or the operating systems are not the same.

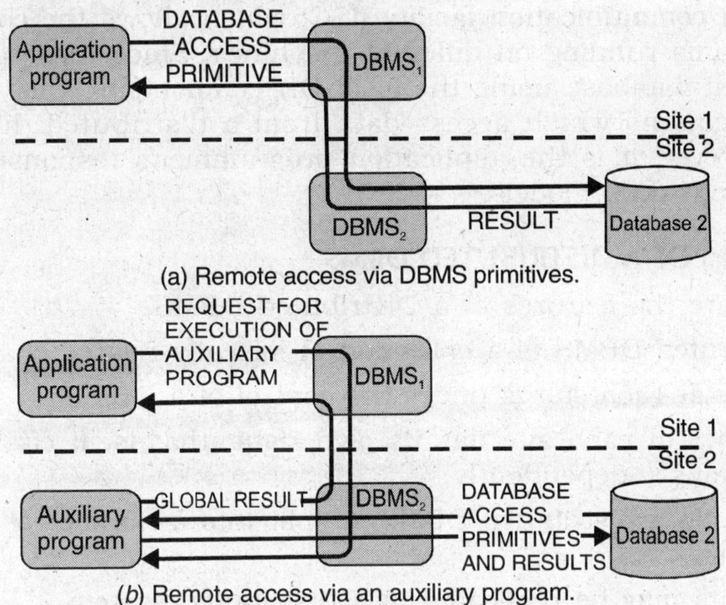

(a) Remote access via DBMS primitives.

(*b*) Remote access via an auxiliary program.

Figure 1.14 Types of accesses to a accesses to a distributed database

Note that this situation is not uncommon, because the same vendor often provides the same DBMS on several computers and because software houses produce DBMSs which run on different computers of different vendors.

A heterogeneous DDBMS used instead at least two different DBMSs. Heterogeneous DDBMSs add the problem of translating between the different data models of the different local DBMSs to the complexity of homogeneous DDBMSs. For this reason, if the development of a distributed database is performed top-down without a preexisting system, it is convenient to develop a homogeneous system. However, as it was stated in the previous section, in some cases the motivation for creating in this case it is required to develop a heterogeneous DDBMS, capable of building a global view of the database.

Although the problems of heterogeneous DDBMSs are very hard, and therefore really heterogeneous DDBMSs exist only as research prototypes, it must be started that commercially available systems provide some degree of support for heterogeneity. While none of these systems performs translation between different data models, which is the really hard problem some of them support the communication between data communication (DC) components. This type of communication was not developed especially for building distributed databases, but was developed for compatibility reasons within a centralized system. Typical examples of this situation are several DBMSs which have

been produced by software houses for running on IBM computers. These DBMSs have an integrated pair of DB/DC components; however, their DC component can be substituted by IBM's standard teleprocessing monitor CICS. CICS has an intersystem communication facility (ISC) which allows the communication between programs running on different machines. Since these programs can access the local database using the local DB components, this allows implementing applications which access data from a distributed, heterogeneous database. However, it is the application programmer's responsibility to deal with the different data models.

1.11.1 FEATURES OF A DISTRIBUTED DBMS

Following are the features of a Distributed DBMS:

(i) A distributed DBMS is a collection of logically related shared data.

(ii) The data at each site is under the control of a DBMS.

(iii) The DBMS at each site has its own right, that is, it can handle local applications independently.

(iv) The data in a distributed DBMS is split into a number of fragments or partitions.

(v) Fragments may be replicated in a distributed system.

(vi) Fragments/replicas are allocated to different sites.

(vii) In a distributed system, the sites are linked by communications network.

(viii) Each DBMS in a distributed system participates in at least one global application.

Every site in a distributed DBMS may have its own local database depending on the topology of the Distributed DBMS.

1.11.2 ADVANTAGES OF DISTRIBUTED DBMS

DDBMS has some advantages. Data is located near the greatest demand site, access is faster, processing is faster due to several sites spreading out the work load, new sites can be added quickly and easily, communication is improved, operating costs are reduced, it is user friendly, there is less danger of a single-point failure, and it has process independence.

Several reasons why businesses and organizations move to distributed databases include organizational and economic reasons, reliable and flexible interconnection of existing database, and the future incremental growth. Companies believe that a decentralized, distributed data database approach will adapt more naturally with the structure of the organizations. Distributed database is more suitable solution when several databases already exist in an organization. In addition, the necessity of performing global application

can be easily performed with distributed database. If an organization grows by adding new relatively independent organizational units, then the distributed database approach support a smooth incremental growth.

Data can physically reside nearest to where it is most often accessed, thus providing users with local control of data that they interact with. This results in local autonomy of the data allowing users to enforce locally the policies regarding access to their data.

One might want to consider a parallel architecture is to improve reliability and availability of the data in a scalable system. In a distributed system, with some careful tact, it is possible to access some, or possibly all of the data in a failure mode if there is sufficient data replication.

A distributed DBMS has several advantages over traditional centralized DBMSs. These are listed in the following:

1. **Sharing of information:** The major advantages in a distributed database system are the provision for sharing information. Users at one site in a distributed system may be able to access data residing at other sites. For example, consider an organization that has a number of branches throughout the country. Each branch stores its own data locally. Similarly, a user in one branch can access data from another branch; thus, information sharing is possible in a distributed system.
2. **Faster data access:** End-users in a distributed system often work with only a subset of the entire data. If such data are locally stored and accessed, data accessing in distributed database system will be much faster than it is in a remotely located centralized system.
3. **Speeding up of query processing:** A distributed database system makes it possible to process data at several sited simultaneously. If a query involves data stored at several sites, it may be possible to split the query into a number of subqueries that can be executed in parallel. Thus, query processing becomes faster in distributed systems.
4. **Capacity and growth:** An advantage of distributed databases is that as the organisation grows, new sites can be added with little or no upheaval to the DBMS. Compare this to the situation in a centralised system, where growth entails upgrading with changes in hardware and software that affect the entire database.
5. **Reliability and availability:** An advantage of distributed databases is that even when a portion of a system (i.e. a local site) is down, the overall system remains available. With replicated data, the failure of one site still allows access to the replicated copy of the data from another site. The remaining sites continue to function. The greater accessibility enhances the reliability of the system.

6. **Increased local autonomy:** In a distributed system, the primary advantage of sharing data by means of data distribution is that each site is able to retain a degree of control over data that are stored locally. In a centralized system, the database administrator is responsible for controlling the entire data in the database system. In a distributed system, there is a global database administrator responsible for the entire system. A part of these responsibilities is delegated to local database administrators residing at each site. Each local administrator may have a different degree of local autonomy or independence depending on the design of the distributed database system. The possibility of local autonomy is often a major advantage of distributed database.
7. **Increased availability:** If one site fails in a distributed system, the remaining sites may be able to continue the transactions of the failed site. In a distributed system, data may be replicated at several sites; therefore, a transaction requiring a particular data item from a failed site may find it at other sites. Thus, the failure of one site does not necessarily imply the shutdown of the system. In distributed systems, some mechanism is required to detect failures and to recover from failures. The system must no longer use the services of the failed site. Finally, when the failed site recovers, it must get integrated and smoothly come back into the system using appropriate mechanisms.
8. **Increased reliability:** Data may be replicated in distributed systems; a single data item may exist at several sites. If one site fails, a transaction requiring a particular data item from that site may access it from other sites. Therefore, the failure of a node or a communication link does not necessarily make the data inaccessible; thus, reliability increases.
9. **Better performance:** The data in a distributed system are dispersed to match business requirements; therefore, data are stored near the site where the demand for them is the greatest. As the data are located near the greatest-demand site and given the inherent parallelism of distributed DBMSs, speed of database access may be better than in a remote centralized database. Moreover, as each site handles only a part of the entire database, there may not be the same level of contention for CPU and I/O services that characterizes a centralized DBMS.
10. **Reduced operating cost:** In the 1970, computing power used to be estimated as being proportional to the square of the cost of equipments; hence, three times the cost would provide nine times the power. This was known as Grosch's Law. It is now generally accepted that the cost will be much lesser to create a system of smaller computers with computing power equivalent to that of a single large computer. Thus, it is

more cost-effective for corporate divisions and departments to obtain separate computers. It is also much more cost-effective to add workstations to a network than to update a mainframe system. The second potential cost savings occurs where databases are geographically remote and the applications require access to distributed data. In such cases, owing to the relative expense of transmitting data across the network as opposed to the cost of local access, it may be much more economic to partition the application and perform the processing locally at each site.

11. **Efficiency and flexibility:** An advantage of distributed databases is that data is physically stored close to the anticipated point of use. Hence if usage patterns change then data can be dynamically moved or replicated to where it is most needed.
12. **Distributed database sharing:** An advantage of distributed databases is that users at a given site are able to access data stored at other sites and at the same time retain control over the data at their own site.
13. **Distributed system reflects organizational structure:** Many organizations are by their nature distributed over several locations. For example, a banking organization can have several branches in different locations throughout the country. In such applications, it is beneficial if data are distributed over these locations and maintained locally. At the same time, the banking organization may wish to make global queries involving the access of data at all or a number of branches. In such organizations, building a distributed system is more beneficial as it reflects the organizational structure.
14. **Integration of existing databases:** When several databases already exist in an organization and the necessity of performing global applications arises, distributed database is the natural solution. In this case, the distributed database is created from the pre-existing local databases using bottom-up approach. Although this process requires a certain degree of local restructuring, the effort required for the creation of a completely new centralized database is much higher than the effort required for local restructuring.
15. **Processor independence:** A distributed system may contain multiple copies of a particular data item. Thus, in a distributed system, users can access any available copy of the data item, and user-requests can be processed by the processor at the data location. Hence, user-requests do not depend on a specific processor.
16. **Modular extensibility:** Modular extension in a distributed system is much easier. New sites can be added to the network without affecting the operations of other sites. Such flexibility allows organizations to

extend their system in a relatively rapid and easier way. Increasing data size can usually be handled by adding processors and storage power to the network.

1.11.3 DISADVANTAGES OF DISTRIBUTED DBMS

DDBMS also has a few disadvantages. Managing and controlling is complex, there is less security because data is at so many different sites.

Distributed databases provide more flexible accesses that increase the chance of security violations since the database can be accessed throughout every site within the network. For many applications, it is important to provide secure. Present distributed database systems do not provide adequate mechanisms to meet these objectives. Hence the solution requires the operation of DDBMS capable of handling multilevel data. Such a system is also called a multi level security distributed database management systems (MLS-DDBMS). MLS-DDBMS provides a verification service for users who wish to share data in the database at different level security. In MLS- DDBMS, every data item in the database has correlated with one of several classifications or sensitivities.

The ability to ensure the integrity of the database in the presence of unpredictable failures of both hardware and software components is also an important features of any distributed database management systems. The integrity of a database is concerned with its consistency, correctness, validity, and accuracy. The integrity controls must be built into the structure of software, databases, and involved personnel.

If there are multiple copies of the same data, then this duplicated data introduces additional complexity in ensuring that all copies are updated for each update. The notion of *concurrency control* and recoverability consume much of the research efforts in the area of distributed database theory. Increasing in reliability and performance is the goal and not the status quo.

1. **Increased complexity:** A distributed DBMS that hides the distributed nature from the users and provides an acceptable level of performance, reliability and availability is inherently more complex. In a distributed system, data may be replicated, which adds additional complexity to the system. All database related tasks such as transaction management, concurrency control, query optimization and recovery management are more complicated than in centralized systems. Management of distributed data is a very complicated task than the management of centralized data.
2. **Increased maintenance and communication cost:** The maintenance costs of a distributed DBMS are much higher than those of a centralized system, as complexity increases. Moreover, a distributed DBMS

requires a network to afford communication among different sites. An additional ongoing communication cost is incurred owing to the use of this network. There are also additional labour costs to mange and maintain the local DBMSs and the underlying network.

3. **Security:** As data in a distributed DBMS are located at multiple sites, the probability of security lapses increases. Further, all communications between different sites in a distributed DBMS are conveyed through the network, so the underlying network has to be made secure to maintain system security.
4. **Increased storage requirements:** Data replication in distributed DBMS requires additional disk storage space. This disadvantage can ignore, because disk storage space is relatively cheap, and it is becoming cheaper. However, disk access and storage management in a widely dispersed data-storage environment are more complex than they would be in a centralized database.
5. **Integrity problem:** Database integrity refers to the validity and consistency of stored data. Database integrity is usually expressed in terms of constraints. A constraint specifies a condition and a proposition that the database is not permitted to violate. Enforcing integrity constraints generally requires access to a large amount of data that define the constraint but are not involved in the actual update operation itself. The communication and processing costs that are required to enforce integrity constraints in a distributed DBMS may be prohibitive.
6. **Database design more complex:** The design of a distributed DBMS involves fragmentation of data, allocation of fragments to specific sites and data replication, besides the normal difficulties of designing a centralized DBMS. Therefore, the database design for a distributed system is much more complex than for a centralized system.
7. **Lack of experience:** Distributed DBMSs have not been widely accepted, although many protocols and problems are well-understood. Consequently, we do not yet have the same level of experience in industry as we have with centralized DBMSs. For a prospective adopter of this technology, this may be a significant restriction.
8. **Lack of standards:** A distributed system can consist of a number of sites that are heterogeneous in terms of processors, communication networks (communication mediums and communication protocols) and DBMSs. This lack of standards significantly limits the potential of distributed DBMSs. There are also no tools or methodologies to help users to convert a centralized DBMS into a distributed DBMS.

1.12 FUNCTIONS OF DISTRIBUTED DBMS

A distributed DBMS manages the storage and processing of logically related data on interconnected computers wherein both data and processing are distributed among several sites.

Following are the various functions of distributed database system:

1. **Applications interfaces:** This feature is most important and is provided by all systems that are distributed in nature. A distributed DBMS provides application interfaces to interact with the end-users or application programs and with remote databases within the distributed system.
2. **Validation and transformation techniques:** A distributed DBMS must contain necessary validation techniques to analyze data requests. It must also contain transformation techniques to determine which data request components are distributed and which ones are local.
3. **Distributed backup and recovery services:** Backup services in distributed DBMSs ensure the availability and reliability of a database in case of failures. Recovery services in distributed DBMSs take account of failures of individual sites and of communication links and preserve the database in the consistent state that prior to the failure.
4. **Distributed concurrency control:** Concurrency control techniques manage simultaneous data access and ensure data consistency across database fragments in the distributed DBMS. They ensure that consistency of replicated data is maintained in spite of concurrent execution of local and global transactions in the distributed DBMS.
5. **Support for global system catalog:** This feature includes tools for monitoring the database, gathering information about database utilization and providing a global view of data files existing at the various sites. A distributed DBMS must contain a global system catalog to store data distribution details for the system.
6. **Support for global database administrator:** Global database administrator in distributed DBMS is responsible for maintaining the overall control of data and programs accessing the data in the distributed system.
7. **Distributed security control:** A distributed DBMS offers security services to provide data privacy at both local and remote databases. This feature is used to maintain appropriate authorization/access privileges to the distributed data.
8. **Distribution transparency:** One major objective of the distributed system is to achieve distribution transparency; that is, users should be

unaware of the distributed nature of the system. This feature is supported to a different extent by different distributed systems, because there is a strong trade-off between distribution transparency and performance.

9. **Mapping and I/O interfaces:** A distributed DBMS must provide mapping techniques to determine the data location of local and remote fragments. It must also provide I/O interfaces to read or write data from or to permanent local storage.
10. **Management of replicated data:** To maintain the consistency of replicated data items, a distributed DBMS must have the ability to decide which copy of a replicated data item is to be selected while executing a data request.
11. **Distributed transaction management:** Transaction management facilities in distributed DBMSs ensure that the local and global transactions move data from one consistent state to another. Consistency of data should not be violated by local and distributed transactions. This consistency maintenance activity includes the synchronization of local and remote transactions as well as transactions across multiple distributed segments.
12. **Extend communication services:** A distributed DBMS supports extended communication services to provide access to remote sites and allows the transfer of queries and data among the sites using a network.
13. **Extend query processing and optimization:** The distributed DBMS supports query processing techniques to retrieve answers of local queries as well as global queries. It also provides query optimization both for local and global queries to find the best access strategy. In the case of global query optimization, the global query optimizer will determine which database fragments are to be accessed in order to execute global queries.

1.13 COMPONENTS OF A DISTRIBUTED DBMS

A Distributed DBMS controls the storage and efficient retrieval of logically interrelated data that are physically distributed among several sites.

Following are the various components used in a distributed DBMS:

1. **Computer workstations:** A distributed DBMS consists of a number of computer workstations that form the network system. The distributed database system must be independent of the computer system hardware.
2. **Networking components:** Each workstation in a distributed system contains a number of network hardware and software components. These

components allow each site to interact and exchange data with each other site. Network system independence is a desirable property of the distributed system.

3. **Communication media:** In a distributed system, any type of communication (data transfer, information exchange) among nodes is carried out through communication media. This is a very important component of a distributed DBMS. It is desirable that a distributed DBMS be communication media independent, that is, it must be able to support several types of communication media.
4. **Transaction processor:** A Transaction processor is a software component that resides in each computer connected with the distributed system and is responsible for receiving and processing both local and remote-applications' data requests. This component is also known as the application processor or the transaction manager.
5. **Data processor:** A Data processor is also a software component that resides in each computer connected with the distributed system and stores and retrieves data located at that site. The Data processor is also known as the data manager. In a distributed DBMS, a Data processor may be a centralized DBMS.

1.14 AN EXAMPLE OF DISTRIBUTED DBMS

Suppose that a Software company has a number of branches in different cities throughout the country. Each branch has its own local system that maintains information regarding all the customers, projects and employees in that particular branch. Each such individual branch is termed a site or a node. All sites in the system are connected via a communication network. Each site maintains three relational schemas: Project for project information, Customer for customer information and Employee for employee information, which is listed below.

Project = (project-id, project-name, project-type, project-leader-id, branch-no, amount)

Customer = (customer-id, customer-name, customer-city, project-id)

Employee = (emp-id, emp-name, designation, salary, emp-branch, project-no)

Here the underlined attributes represent the primary keys for the corresponding relations. There also exists one single site that maintains the information about all branches of the company. The single site containing information about all the customers, projects and employees in all branches of the company maintains an additional relational schema Branch, which is defined as follows:

Branch = (<u>branch-no</u>, branch-name, branch-city, no-of-projects, total-revenue)

Each local branch can access its local data via local applications as well as it can access data from other branches via global applications. During normal operations that are requested from a branch, local applications need only to access the database of that particular branch. These applications are completely executed by the processor of the local branch where they are initiated, and are therefore called local applications. Similarly, there exist many applications that require projects, customers and employees information from other branches also. These applications are called global applications or distributed applications.

1.15 PROBLEM AREAS

We discussed a number of technical problems that need to be resolved to realize the full potential of distributed DBMSs. In this section we discuss them in a more organized fashion as a prelude to our in-depth studies in the rest of the book.

1.15.1 DISTRIBUTED DATABASE DESIGN

The question that is being addressed is how the database and the applications that run against it should be placed across the sites. There are two basic alternatives to placing data: partitioned (or nonreplicated) and replicated. In the partitioned scheme the database is divided into a number of disjoint partitions each of which is placed at a different site. Replicated designs can be either fully replicated (also called fully duplicated) where the entire database is stored at each site, or partially replicated (or partially duplicated) where each partition of the database is stored at more than one site, but not at all the sites. The two fundamental design issues are fragmentation, the separation of the database into partitions called fragments, and distribution, the optimum distribution of fragments.

The research in this area mostly involves mathematical programming in order to minimize the combined cost of storing the database, processing transactions against it, and communication. The general problem is NP-hard. Therefore, the proposed solutions are based on heuristics.

1.15.2 DISTRIBUTED QUERY PROCESSING

Query processing deals with designing algorithms that analyze queries and convert them into a series of data manipulation operations. The problem is how to decide on a strategy for executing each query over the network in the most cost-effective way, however cost is defined. The factors to be considered are the distribution of data, communication costs, and lack of sufficient

locally-available information. The objective is to optimize where the inherent parallelism is used to improve the performance of executing the transaction, subject to the above-mentioned constraints. The problem is NP-hard in nature, and the approaches are usually heuristic.

1.15.3 DISTRIBUTED DIRECTORY MANAGEMENT

A directory contains information (such as descriptions and locations) about data items in the database. Problems related to directory management are similar in nature to the database placement problem discussed in the preceding section. A directory may be global to the entire DDBS or local to each site; it can be centralized at one site or distributed over several sites; there can be a single copy or multiple copies.

1.15.4 DISTRIBUTED CONCURRENCY CONTROL

Concurrency control involves the synchronization of accesses to the distributed database, such that the integrity of the database is maintained. It is, without any doubt, one of the most extensively studies problems in the DDBS field. The concurrency control problem in a distributed context is somewhat different than in a centralized framework. One not only has to worry about the integrity of a single database, but also about the consistency of multiple copies of the database. The condition that requires all the values of multiple copies of every data item to converse to the same value is called mutual consistency.

Let us only mention that the two general classes are pessimistic, synchronizing the execution of user request before the execution starts, and optimistic, executing the request and then checking if the execution compromised the consistency of the database. Two fundamental primitives that can be used with both approaches are locking, which is based on the mutual exclusion of accesses to data items, and timestamping, where the transactions are executed in some order. There are variations of these schemes as well as hybrid algorithms that attempt to combine the two basic mechanisms.

1.15.5 DISTRIBUTED DEADLOCK MANAGEMENT

The deadlock problem in DDBSs is similar in nature to that encountered in operating systems. The competition among users for access to a set of resources (data, in this case) can result in a deadlock if the synchronization mechanism is based on locking. The well-known alternatives of prevention, avoidance and detection/recovery also apply to DDBS.

1.15.6 RELIABILITY OF DISTRIBUTED DBMS

We mentioned earlier that one of the potential advantages of distributed systems is improved reliability and availability. This however, is not a feature that comes automatically. It is important that mechanisms be provided to ensure the consistency of the database as well as to detect failures and recover from them. The implication for DDBBS is that when a failure occurs and various sites become either inoperable or inaccessible, the databases at the operational sites remain consistent and up to date. Furthermore, when the computer system or network recovers from the failure, the DDBSs should be able to recover and bring the databases at the failed sites up-to-date. This may be especially difficult in the case of network partitioning, where the sites are divided into two or more groups with no communication among them.

1.15.7 OPERATING SYSTEM SUPPORT

The current implementation of distributed database systems on top of (or under) the conventional operating systems suffers from the performance bottleneck. The support provided by operating systems for database operations does not correspond properly to the requirements of the database management software. The major operating system-relation problems in single-processor systems are memory management, file system and access methods, crash recovery, and process management. In distributed environments there is the additional problem of having to deal with multiple layers of network software. The work in this area is on finding solutions to the dichotomy of providing adequate and simple support for distributed database operations, as well as providing general operating system support for other applications.

1.15.8 HETEROGENEOUS DATABASES

When there is no homogeneity among the databases at various sites either in terms of the way data is logically structured (data model) or in terms of the mechanisms provided for accessing it (data language), it becomes necessary to provide a translation mechanism between database systems. This translation mechanism usually involves a canonical form of facilitate data translation, as well as program templates for translating data manipulation instructions.

It turns out that heterogeneity is typically introduced if one is constructing a distributed DBMS from a number of autonomous, centralized DBMSs. In this setting the problems are more general than heterogeneity. In fact, such systems, which we call multidatabase systems, should be considered complementary to the distributed DBMSs as defined in this chapter. Thus, all the problems that we have discussed in the preceding sections have complementary specifications for multidatabase systems.

1.15.9 RELATIONSHIP AMONG PROBLEMS

We should mention at this point that these problems are not isolated from one another. The reasons for studying them in isolation are that (1) problems

are difficult enough to study by themselves, and would probably be impossible to present all together, and that (2) it might be possible to characterize the effect of one problem on another one, through the use of parameters and constraints. In fact, each problem is affected by the solutions found for the others, and in turn affects the set feasible solutions for them. In this section we discuss how they are related.

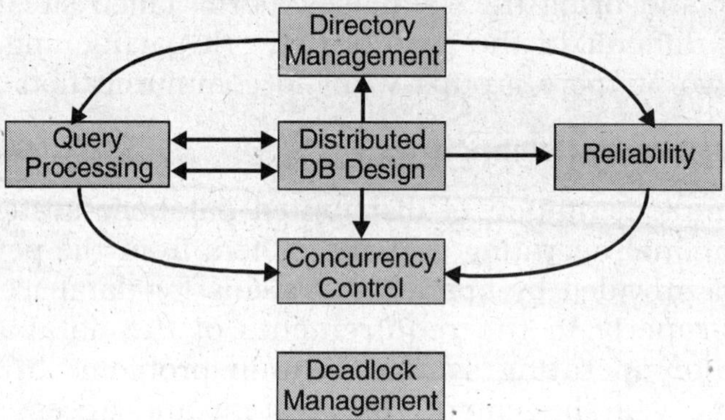

Figure 1.15 Relationship Among Research Issues

The replication of fragments when they are distributed affects the concurrency control strategies that might be employed. Some concurrency control algorithms cannot be easily used with replicated databases. Similarly, usage and access patterns to the database will influence the concurrency control algorithms. If the environment is update intensive, the necessary precautions are quite different from those in a query-only environment.

There is a strong relationship among the concurrency control problem the deadlock management problem and reliability issues. This is to be expected, since together they are usually called the transaction management problem. The concurrency control algorithm that is employed will determine whether or not a separate deadlock management facility is required. If a locking-based algorithm is sued, deadlocks will occur, whereas they will not if timestamping is the chosen alternative.

Reliability mechanisms are implemented on top of a concurrency control algorithm. Therefore, the relationship among them is self-explanatory. It should also be mentioned that the reliability mechanisms being considered have an effect on the choice of the concurrency control algorithm. Techniques to provide reliability also make use of data placement information since the existence of duplicate copies of the data serve as a safeguard to maintain reliable operation.

Two of the problems we discussed in the preceding sections – operating system issues and heterogeneous databases – are not illustrated in Figure 1.15. This is obviously not because they have no bearing on other issues; in fact, exactly the opposite is true. The type of operating system used and the features supported by that operating system greatly influence what solution strategies can be applied in any of the other problem areas. Similarly, the natures of all these problems change considerably when the environment is heterogeneous. The same issues have to be dealt with differently when the machine architecture, the operating systems, and the local database management software vary from site to site.

1.16 DISTRIBUTED DATABASE TECHNOLOGIES

Distributed database systems are based upon several models and their implementations can include a number of different features. This has developed from the many varied situations and requirements organizations are faced with in putting the technology to use. The topics described below are key to understanding the capabilities and limitations of distributed database systems.

1.16.1 FRAGMENTATION

The fragmentation technique for distributed databases involves splitting the centralized database into portions and moving them to different locations. This distribution is accomplished by horizontal and/or vertical partitioning. No data is stored redundantly with the exception of primary keys in the case of vertical fragmentation. Using the relational model, horizontal fragmentation is accomplished by separating rows and vertical fragmentation is accomplished by separating columns. Data is normally fragmented according to the section of the organization which uses or modifies the data most frequently. For example, a firm may use a department code field to determine which department is responsible for each record and where the data should physically reside in a horizontally fragmented system.

Key principles of the fragmented distribution model are that only one copy of the data exists in the database, and that ownership and ability to update the database are shared. This model is similar to the centralized model in that the data is always consistent and current. The only redundancies exist with primary key fields when using vertical fragmentation. Fragmented database systems are more complex than centralized systems, but simpler than replicated systems. The issue of a single point of failure is reduced, but not eliminated. Network usage is generally lower in fragmented systems than in centralized systems.

1.16.2 REPLICATION

Distributed databases can use replication techniques to maintain multiple copies of the same data. Replicated database systems seek to maintain

data consistency while allowing redundancy. There are two basic models for replicated databases: the master/slave model and the update anywhere model. These replication techniques can also be combined with fragmentation for a more complex distribution pattern.

The master/slave model maintains a dedicated master for each individual data element of the database. This master data is used as the source of replication to slave data elements, which are distributed as copies at multiple locations. These distributed replicas are used exclusively for read-only access; all updates must be made directly to the master. All replication is assumed to take place asynchronously to the updating of the master. This means that all of the data replicas are made consistent with the master at some time after an update is made to the master.

The critical component of any master/slave system is the asynchronous replication service. The goal of the replication service is to maintain all replicas in a state of consistency with the master within a timeliness standard required for the replicas to be useful to the application. This is accomplished through complete or incremental refresh of the master to slaves, or through delta propagation of events to slaves. These are also commonly referred to as table-based or transaction-based replication techniques respectively. The choice of which method to use is one the designer makes, taking into account such factors as the data consistency requirements of the system, the network's capabilities, and the anticipated volume of updates to the database. In practice the designer may be constrained, however, since DDBMSs typically employ only one of these two techniques.

Systems using the master/slave model may allow the designation of the master to change from one node to another node containing a copy of the data. This allows the system some flexibility to respond to changing load requirements. For example, the system could move the master designation to a node preparing to perform a large number of batch updates or to an alternate node in the event the master experiences a failure. However, the basic principle of the master/slave model is always in effect. Only one node can be the master at any one time.

The update anywhere model, as its name suggests, allows updates to be performed on any copy of the data in the distributed database - there is no designated master for any data element. Read and update operations may be performed at any location. Updates are propagated to all copies within the database. The update-anywhere model complies with C.J. Date's second rule for distributed databases, "No reliance on a single site".

Replication in the update-anywhere model can be performed either synchronously or asynchronously. Synchronous replication requires the use of the two-phase commit protocol, and ensures all atomicity, consistency, isolation, and durability (ACID) properties of transactions. Asynchronous replication may be used in some cases, with the loss of isolation between transactions operating on identical data at different sites at the same time. The choice between the two methods is one the system designer must make based upon the requirements of the system, the capabilities of the network, and the anticipated volume of updates to the database. The costs of implementing synchronous replication are higher relative to asynchronous replication due to the increased requirements on the network and the database system hardware.

Asynchronous replication under the update-anywhere model can cause a great deal of complexity when data consistency must be maintained. No design using this technique can completely prevent data conflicts from occurring. Conflicts are only detected after they occur, and must be repaired using manual operations or system-generated compensating transactions. Because the original transactions are sometimes undone, this violates the concept of durability of transactions. Undoing transactions can have a ripple effect as undoing one transaction creates referential integrity or other problems for later transactions. Operating update-anywhere databases with asynchronous replication can be compared to running a centralized database with all locking mechanisms off - performance is greatly increased, but transactional integrity is often lost.

1.16.3 CONCURRENCY CONTROL

Concurrency control in replicated databases is implemented only in systems using synchronous replication under the update-anywhere model. Distributed databases which use fragmentation techniques or master/slave replication do not require concurrency control beyond what is required in traditional centralized database systems. Distributed databases using asynchronous replication do not implement distributed concurrency control; instead they rely on conflict detection and compensating transactions.

The two-phase commit protocol is a required component of distributed databases that use synchronous replication. The two-phase commit protocol consists of the coordinating node issuing a transaction to all affected nodes, waiting for each node to acknowledge that it is prepared to commit, and then issuing a commit order to the affected nodes. If not all affected nodes acknowledge that they are prepared to commit after the first phase, then the coordinating node issues a rollback instruction to all nodes. With the two-phase commit protocol, there is a short period of vulnerability between commit times at different nodes during the second phase when data consistency could possibly be lost due to a node or network failure. The probability of this is extremely small, however, and most DDBMSs do not implement any measures to compensate.

1.16.4 FAILURE RECOVERY

One of the advantages of replicated database systems is that they can provide a level of fault-tolerance beyond what can be achieved through more traditional means such as the use of redundant array of inexpensive disks (RAID). By replicating the database so that it is on two separate machines in different physical locations on the network, the probability that failures will cause a loss of service is significantly reduced. Two options for implementing failure recovery through database replication are available: warm standby and hot standby.

Warm standby uses asynchronous replication to maintain the standby server in a state nearly consistent with that of the primary server. Due to the lag between transactions being committed on the primary server and replication to the standby server, a small number of transactions are normally lost during a primary server failure and switchover to the standby server.

Hot standby uses synchronous replication to maintain the standby server in a state always consistent with the primary server. From an availability perspective this is the preferred solution, but the higher costs and potential lower performance of synchronous replication databases cause many organizations to select a warm standby solution. Buretta recommends a combination of local hot standby, normally RAID, and offsite warm standby server.

1.16.5 OLTP/OLAP

In the earliest days of centralized databases, vendors typically used a one-size fits all approach to DBMS software. As database systems grew, increased in importance to the organization, and began operating in diverse applications, it became apparent that DBMSs should be specialized. One of the major shifts occurred when data centers running mainframes with large relational databases optimized for transaction speed began to notice poor performance during times when reports and queries were processed. It was at this point that the different requirements of online transaction processing (OLTP) and online analytical processing (OLAP) became apparent. Some organizations responded to the performance issues by restricting OLAP to late night and other off-peak times. This is less than an ideal solution as it limits the use of OLAP for the competitive advantage it should provide, and may be impossible when an organization operates round the clock or in many time zones.

The solution most commonly implemented now is the establishment of separate data stores for OLTP and OLAP. Each data store is optimized for the type of services it provides. Buretta (1997) outlines the distinctions between the requirements of OLTP and OLAP environments. OLTP environments include relatively short updating transactions; high number of users sharing either the same physical data store or a replica with real-time or near-real-time data consistency with the primary sources; and highly-normalized data structures (usually to third normal form). OLAP environments include complex queries that tend to summarize, consolidate, and apply complex calculations to data; a small number of users sharing data structures with a data latency level that generally does not need to have real time or near-real time consistency with the primary source(s); and denormalized data structures with precalculated values that reduce the number of joins across data structures.

1.16.6 SECURITY

Implementing effective security in a widely distributed database is no small task. Buretta notes that possible security services in a multitier architecture include authentication, authorization, nonrepudiation, confidentiality, and data integrity. Authentication is the process of having each user, host, or application server prove who it says it is. Authorization is the process of ensuring that each authenticated user has the necessary permission level to perform the requested tasks. Nonrepudiation is ensuring that authenticated and authorized users may not deny that they used a designated resource. Confidentiality prevents unauthorized users from accessing sensitive data. Data integrity prevents data from being modified in an unauthorized manner.

Buretta makes some recommendations for implementing security in a replicated database environment. The first is that all stored and/or displayed passwords must be encrypted so that unauthorized persons and processes may not obtain them. Pseudo-user accounts, those established for systems to automatically log on to the network, are common in distributed database environments. Buretta points out that these accounts must comply with the firm's security policies and knowledge of their passwords should be limited. All file systems, raw devices, and/or database structures used to store queued data and/or messages must be secure. This item points out the many avenues in a distributed system available to unauthorized users, which must be protected. Finally, encryption techniques must be integrated within the replication service. This prevents interception of the data transmitted over the network.

Burleson makes the point that distributed database systems may use either application- or data-level security. Application-level security, as its name suggests, is programmed into the application logic. Each application is responsible for governing user access to the data. Data level security is implemented in the database engine. Profiles of acceptable data items and operations are stored and checked by the database engine against the end-user's permission level on each database operation. Burleson recommends that application-level security be removed and replaced with data level security to

make the distributed database more secure. The argument for this is that a skilled end-user with a workstation and commonly available development tools could easily write an application that does not follow the organization's security policy. Such a security hole may be created either unintentionally by a well-meaning employee or intentionally by someone with malicious intent. When data-level security is implemented, such security holes are not possible.

The issues above demonstrate that a good DDBMS must provide security services, and that organizations must know how to properly implement them. As data is distributed and end-users are given more processing power, potential for security problems increases. Organizations with distributed databases must be competent and vigilant in their execution of security.

1.17 THE FUTURE PROSPECTS FOR DDBMSS

DDBMS technology has potential, but its continued growth in popularity is not guaranteed. Just as DDBMSs grew in popularity with client-server, the potential for further growth in their popularity will likely be tied to client-server. The following section examines the potential for future success or failure of DDBMS systems with a focus on client-server trends as indicators of what the future may hold.

1.17.1 GROWTH OF INTERNET COMPUTING

Experience with distributed database client-server architectures has shown that the complexity and expense of these approaches can be overwhelming. As a result, some firms have decided to go back in the direction of centralized databases. A 1998 study by Computer Economics Inc. reported in *Computer Reseller News* found that 37 percent of companies surveyed were using or implementing server-consolidation strategies (Burbank & Roberts, 1998). Vendors have responded to this demand by providing solutions using servers based on mainframe or minicomputer platforms and thin clients, which in most cases run only a web browser. This architecture is sometimes referred to as Internet computing.

Proponents of Internet computing claim that simplifying the distributed components of the architecture and moving data to one professionally-managed location provides higher reliability and lower operating costs. One of the original arguments for client-server was the ability to replace character-based terminals with GUI-based workstations, which are more flexible and easier to use. Internet computing retains the benefits of a central data store and GUI-based workstations. The benefits of Internet computing may generate stiff competition for widely distributed database systems.

1.17.2 IMMATURITY OF CLIENT-SERVER

Although client-server technology has been in widespread use for over a decade, some argue that it is not yet developed to the level to provide sufficient advantages to businesses implementing new systems. A panel of industry experts speaking at the Client-Server Leadership Forum in Toronto in 1996 concluded that the client-server market is still in adolescence (Williamson, 1996). The panel reiterated the popular view that three-tiered client-server systems are far superior to two-tiered systems. Three-tiered architectures require more resources to implement, but are generally more scalable and allow for thinner, easier to maintain clients than two-tiered architectures. The panel saw the client-server industry as immature, due to the low numbers of three-tiered systems implemented - only 4.9 percent of all client-server systems. Many panel members felt that until three-tiered systems become the norm, the benefits of client-server architectures cannot be realized. Some of the members felt that this weakness may lead to client-server being replaced by Internet computing.

1.17.3 LACK OF DDBMS STANDARDS

Of C.J. Date's twelve commandments for a distributed database, four refer to open standards issues required for DDBMSs to reach their full potential. These are hardware independence, operating system independence, network independence, and database independence. Today's DDBMS products are still do not meet these four standards.

Burleson described the causes of lack of open standards in the DDBMS market and the impact this has had on DDBMS growth. Five years later, this is still a fact. DDBMS technology is relatively new, and is still suffering from vendors fighting to develop and hold on to proprietary features. Today the situation is improving, but cross-vendor connectivity is sometimes limited, especially for legacy systems that do not implement newer standards.

EXERCISES

1. What do you mean by distributed databases?
2. Explain in detail concept of distributed database system?
3. Explain various categories of distributed data?
4. Comparison between distributed DBMSs and replicated databases?
5. Difference between parallel versus distributed technology?
6. What are the advantages of distributed databases?
7. Explain additional functions of distributed databases?
8. Explain various fundamentals of distributed database systems (DDBs)?
9. What are the disadvantages of distributed DBs?
10. Explain the failures in distributed DBs?
11. Comparison between distributed and centralized systems?
12. Why distributed databases?
13. Explain the promises of DDBs?
14. Explain the various problems of distributed database systems?
15. What do you mean by client/server system?
16. What do you mean by distributed database management systems (DDBMs)?
17. Explain the various features of a distributed DBMS?
18. What are the advantages of distributed DBMS?
19. What are the disadvantages of distributed DBMS?
20. Explain various functions of distributed DBMS?
21. Explain the various components of a distributed DBMS?
22. Explain an example of distributed DBMS?
23. Explain various problem areas of DDBMS?
24. Explain the various distributed database technologies?
25. Explain the future prospects for DDBMS?

CHAPTER 2

DISTRIBUTED DATABASE DESIGN

2.1 INTRODUCTION

In the 1980s, distributed database systems had evolved to overcome the limitations of centralized database management systems and to cope up with the rapid changes in communication and database technologies. This chapter introduces the fundamentals of distributed database systems. Benefits and limitations of distributed DBMS over centralized DBMS are briefly discussed. The objectives of a distributed system, the components of a distributed system, and the functionality provided by a distributed system are also described in this chapter.

The term **"distributed database design"** has a very broad and unprecise meaning. In this chapter, we concentrate on those aspects which are peculiar to distributed databases, while we do not present design problems which are faced also in the design of centralized databases. The design of a centralized database amounts to:

1. Designing the **"conceptual schema"** which describes the integrated database (i.e., all the data which are used by the database applications).
2. Designing the **"physical database"** i.e., mapping the conceptual schema to storage areas and determining appropriate access methods.

   In a distributed database these two problems become the design of the global schema and the design of the local physical databases at each site; the techniques which can be applied to these problems are the same as in centralized databases.

   The distribution of the database adds to the above problems two new ones:

3. Designing the fragmentation, i.e., determining how global relations are subdivided into horizontal, vertical, or mixed fragments.
4. Designing the allocation of fragments, i.e., determines how fragments are mapped to physical images; in this way, also the replication of fragments is determined.

These two problems fully characterize the design of data distribution. Fragmentation design has been studied only in recent times, since fragmentation has been established as a distinguishing feature of distributed databases; it had, however, been partially analyzed in the context of centralized systems with multiple storage devices. The allocation problem has instead been studied extensively since the development of distributed file systems, and is typically regarded in the literature as the **"file allocation problem."**

The distinction between these two problems is conceptually relevant, since the first one deal with the **"logical criteria"** which motivate the fragmentation of a global relation, while the second one deals with the **"physical"** placement

of data at the various sites. However, this distinction must be introduced with extreme care; in general, it is not possible to determine the optimal fragmentation and allocation by solving the two problems independently, since they are interrelated.

Although the design of application programs is made after the design of schemata, the knowledge of application requirements influences schema design, since schemata must be able to support applications efficiently. Thus, in the design of a distributed database, sufficiently precise knowledge of application requirements is needed; clearly, this knowledge is required only for the more **"important"** applications, i.e., those which will be executed frequently or whose performances are critical. In the application requirements we include:

1. The site from which the application is issued (also called site of origin of the application).
2. The frequency of activation of the application (i.e., the number of activation requests in the unit time); in the general case of applications which can be issued at multiple sites, we need to know the frequency of activation of each application at each site.
3. The number, type, and the statistical distribution of accesses made by each application to each required data **"object."**

Characterizing these features is not trivial; moreover, consider that these data are typically given for global relations and must be properly translated into terms which apply to fragments; since fragmentation is produced as a result of design and is not known a priori, these data must be known for all fragmentation alternatives which are considered during design.

2.2 REFERENCE ARCHITECTURE FOR DISTRIBUTED DATABASES

Figure 2.1 shows reference architecture for a distributed database. This reference architecture is not explicitly implemented in all distributed databases; however, its levels are conceptually relevant in order to understand the organization of any distributed database. We will therefore analyze and understand all the components of this reference architecture.

At the top level of Figure 2.1 is the **global schema**. The global schema defines all the data which are contained in the distributed database as if the database were not distributed at all. For this reason, the global schema can be defined exactly in the same way as in a nondistributed database. However, the data model which is used for the definition of a global schema should be convenient for the definition of the mapping to the other levels of the distributed database. We will use the relational model for this purpose. Using this model, the global schema consists of the definition of a set of global relations.

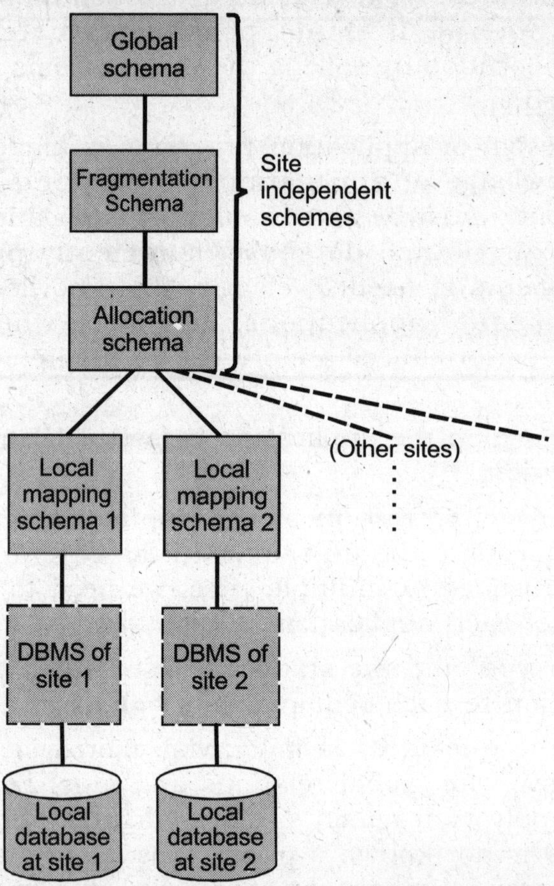

Figure 2.1 A reference architecture for distributed databases

Each global relation can be split into several nonoverlapping portions which are called **fragments**. There are several different ways in which to perform the splitting operation; they are described in the next section. The mapping between global relations and fragments is defined in the fragmentation schema. This mapping is one to many; i.e., several fragments correspond to one to many; i.e., several fragments correspond to one global relation, but only one global relation corresponds to one fragment. Fragments are indicated by a global relation name with an index (fragment index); for example, R_i indicated the ith fragments of global relation R.

Fragments are logical portions of global relations which are physically located at one or several sites of the network. The allocation schema defines at which site(s) a fragment is located. Note that the type of mapping defined in the allocation schema determines whether the distributed database is redundant or nonredundant; in the former case the mapping is one to many, while in the latter case the mapping is one to one. All the fragments which correspond to the same global relation R and are located at the same site j constitute the physical image of global relation R at site j. There is therefore a one to one mapping between a physical image and a pair (global relation site); physical images can be indicated by a global relation name and a site index. To distinguish them from fragments, we will use a superscript; for example, R^j indicates the physical image of the global relation R at site j.

An example of the relationship between the object types defined above is shown in Figure 2.2. A global relation R is split into four fragments R_1, R_2, R_3, and R_4. These four fragments are allocated redundantly at the three sites of a computer network, thus building three physical images R^1, R^2, and R^3.

To complete the terminology, we will refer to a copy of a fragment at a given site, and denote it using the global relation name and two indexes (a fragment index and a site index). For example, in Figure 2.2, the notation R_2^3 indicates the copy of fragment R_2 which is located at site 3. Finally, note that two physical images can be identical. In this case we will say that a physical image is a copy of another physical image. For example, in Figure 2.2, R^1 is a copy of R^2.

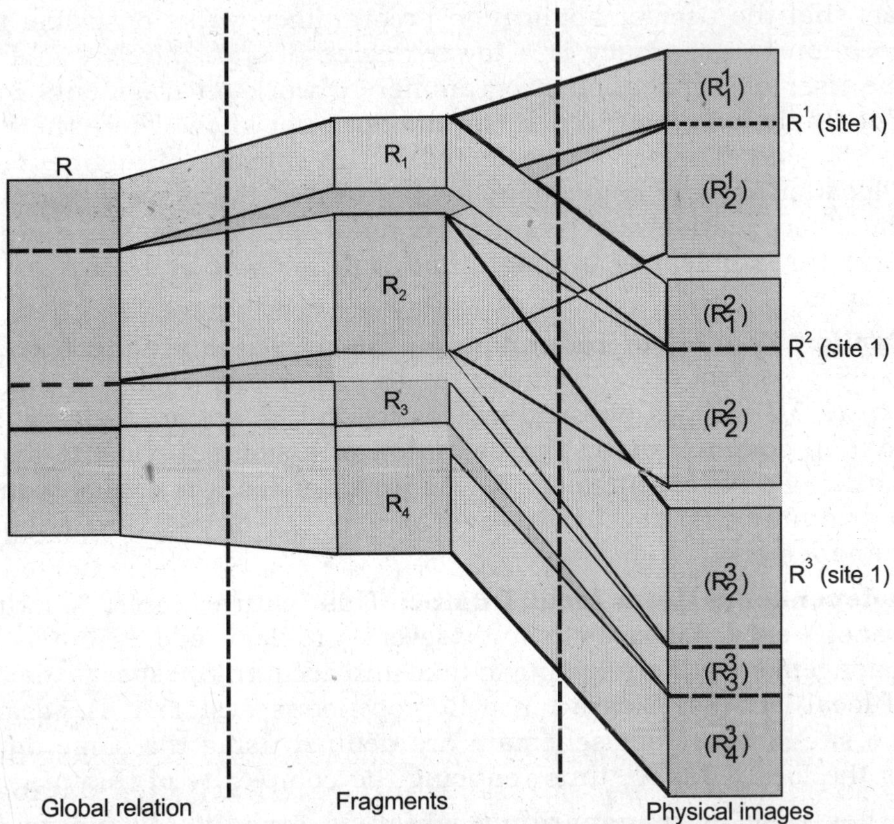

Figure 2.2 Fragments and physical images for a global relation

Let us now go back to the reference architecture of Figure 2.1. We have already described the relationship between the objects at the three top levels of this architecture. These three levels are site independent; therefore, they do not depend on the data model of the local DBMSs. At a lower level, it is necessary to map the physical images to the objects which are manipulated by the local DBMSs. This mapping is called a local mapping schema and depends on the type of local DBMS; therefore in a heterogeneous system we have different types of local mappings at different sites.

This architecture provides a very general conceptual framework for understanding distributed databases. The three most important objectives which motivate the features of this architecture are the separation of data fragmentation and allocation, the control of redundancy, and the independence from local DBMSs.

1. **Separating the concept of data fragmentation from the concept of data allocation:** This separation allows us to distinguish two different levels of distribution transparency, namely fragmentation transparency and location transparency. Fragmentation transparency. Fragmentation transparency is the highest degree of transparency and consists of the fact that the user or application programmer works on global relations. Location transparency is a lower degree of transparency and requires the user or application programmer to work on fragments instead of global relations; however, he or she does not know where the fragments are located. The separation between the concept of fragmentation and allocation is very convenient in distributed database design, because the determination of relevant portions of the data is thus distinguished from the problem of optimal allocation, as will be shown in the next chapter.
2. **Explicit control of redundancy:** The reference architecture provides explicit control of redundancy at the fragment level. For example, in Figure 2.2 the two physical images R^2 and R^3 are overlapping; i.e., they contain common data. The definition of disjoint fragments as building blocks of physical fragment R_2. As we shall see, the explicit control over redundancy is useful in several aspects of distributed database management.
3. **Independence from local DBMSs:** This feature, called local mapping transparency, allows us to study several problems of distributed database management without having to take into account the specific data models of local DBMSs. Clearly, in a homogeneous system it is possible that the site-independent schemata are defined using the same data model as the local DBMSs, thus reducing the complexity of this mapping.

Another type of transparency which is strictly related to location transparency is replication transparency. Replication transparency means that the user is unaware of the replication of fragments: Clearly, replication transparency is implied by location transparency; however, in certain cases it is possible that the user has no location transparency but has replication transparency (thus, he or she uses one particular copy, and the system makes appropriate actions on the other copies). In this book, we do not further distinguish replication transparency from location transparency.

As a final remark on the reference architecture, we can say that it performs the same function as the ANSI/SPARC architecture in traditional DBMSs: it is not necessarily implemented by the existing systems, but it shows which levels and schemata are conceptually relevant.

2.3 A FRAMEWORK FOR DISTRIBUTED DATABASE DESIGN

In a distributed system, data are physically distributed among several sites but it provides a view of single logical database to its users. Each node of a distributed database system may follow the three-tier architecture like the centralized database management system (DBMS). Thus, the design of a distributed database system involves the design of a global conceptual schema, in addition to the local schemas, which conform to the three-tier architecture of the DBMS in each site. The design of computer network across the sites of a distributed system adds extra complexity to the design issue. The crucial design issue involves the distribution of data among the sites of the distributed system. Therefore, the design and implementation of the distributed database system is a very complicated task and it involves three important factors as listed in the following.

- **Fragmentation:** A global relation may be divided into several non-overlapping subrelations called fragments, which are then distributed among sites.
- **Allocation:** Allocation involves the issue of allocating fragments among sites in a distributed system. Each fragment is stored at the site with optimal distribution.
- **Replication:** The distributed database system may maintain several copies of a fragment at different sites.

The definition and allocation of fragments must be based on how the database is to be used. After designing the database schemas, the design of application programs is required to access and manipulate the data into the distributed database system. In the design of a distributed database system, precise knowledge of application requirements is necessary, since database schemas must be able to support applications efficiently. Thus, the database design should be based on both quantitative and qualitative information, which collectively represents application requirements. Quantitative information is used in allocation, while qualitative information is used in fragmentation.

The quantitative information of application requirements may include the following:

- The frequency with which a transaction is run, that is, the number of transaction requests in the unit time. In case of general applications that are issued from multiple sites, it is necessary to know the frequency of activation of each transaction at each site.
- The site from which a transaction is run (also called site of origin of the transaction).
- The performance criteria for transactions.

The qualitative information of application requirements may include the following information about the transactions that are executed:

- The relations, attributes, and tuples accessed by the transactions.
- The type of access (read or write).
- The predicates of read operations.

Characterizing these features is not trivial. Moreover, this information is typically given for global relation and must be properly translated into terms of all fragmentation alternatives that are considered during database design.

2.3.1 ALTERNATIVE APPROACHES FOR DISTRIBUTED DATABASE DESIGN

The distributed database design involves making decisions on the fragmentation and placement of fragmented data across the sites of a computer network. Two alternative design issues have been identified for the distributed database design, namely, top-down and bottom-up design process.

2.3.1.1 TOP-DOWN DESIGN PROCESS

In this process, the database design starts from the global schema design and proceeds by designing the fragmentation of the database, and then by allocating the fragments to the different sites, creating the physical images. The process is completed by performing the physical design of the data at each site, which is allocated to it. The global schema design involved both designing of global conceptual schema and global external schemas (view design). In global conceptual schema designing step, the user needs to specify the data entities and to determine the applications that will run on the database as well as statistical information about these applications. At this stage, the design of local conceptual schemas is considered. The objective of this step is to design local conceptual schemas by distributing the entities over the sites of the distributed system. Rather than distributing relations, it is quite common to partition relations into subrelations, which are then distributed to different sites. Thus, in a top-down approach, the distributed database design involves two phases, namely, fragmentation and allocation.

The fragmentation phase is the process of clustering information in fragments that can be accessed simultaneously by different applications, whereas the allocation phase is the process of distributing the generated fragments among the sites of a distributed database system. In the top-down design process, the last step is the physical database design, which maps the local conceptual schemas into physical storage devices available at corresponding sites. Top-down design process is the best suitable for those distributed systems that are developed from scratch.

2.3.1.2 BOTTOM-UP DESIGN PROCESS

In the bottom-up design process, the issue of integration of several existing local schemas into a global conceptual schema is considered to develop a distributed system. When several existing databases are aggregated to develop a distributed system, the bottom-up design process is followed. This process is based on the integration of several existing schemas into a single global schema. It is also possible to aggregate several existing heterogeneous systems for constructing a distributed database system using the bottom-up approach. Thus, the bottom-up design process requires the following steps:

- The selection of a common model for describing the global schema of the database.
- The translation of each local schema into the common data model.
- The integration of the local schemas into a common global schema.

Any one of the above design strategies is followed to develop a distributed database system.

2.4 OBJECTIVES OF DATA DISTRIBUTION

In a distributed system, data may be fragmented, and each fragment can have a number of replicas to increase data availability and reliability. The following objectives must be considered while designing the fragmentation and allocation of these fragments to different sites in a distributed system (i.e., during the design of data distribution).

(a) Locality of reference: To maximize the locality of references, whenever possible, data should be stored close to where it is used during data distribution. If a fragment is used at several sites, it may be beneficial to store copies of the fragment at different sites.

(b) Improved availability and reliability of distributed data: During data distribution, reliability and availability are improved by replication. A higher degree of availability can be achieved by storing multiple copies of the same information in different sites. Reliability is also achieved by storing multiple copies of the same information, since it is possible

to continue the normal operations of a particular site in case of site failure, by referencing the copy of the same information from other sites.

(c) Workload distribution and improved performance – Bad allocation may result in underutilization of resources, and thereby system performance may degrade. Distributing the workload over the sites is an important feature of distributed database system. Workload distribution should be done to take advantage of system resources at each site and to maximize the degree of parallelism of execution of transactions. Since workload distribution might negatively affect processing locality, it is necessary to consider the trade-off between them during the **design of data distribution.**

(d) Balanced storage capacities and costs: Database distribution must reflect the cost and availability of storage at different sites. The availability and cost of storage at each site must be considered so that cheap mass storage can be used, whenever possible. This must be balanced against locality of reference.

(e) Minimal communication costs: The cost of processing remote requests must be considered during data distribution. Retrieval cost is minimized when locality of reference is maximized or when each site has its own copy of the data. However, when replicated data are updated, the update has to be performed at all sites holding a replica, thereby increasing the communication costs.

2.5 ALTERNATIVE STRATEGIES FOR DATA ALLOCATION

Four alternative strategies have been identified for data allocation. This section describes these different data allocation strategies and also draws a comparison between them.

(i) Centralized: In this strategy, the distributed system consists of a single database and DBMS is stored at one site with users distributed across the communication network. Remote users can access centralized data over the network; thus, this strategy is similar to distributed processing.

In this approach, locality of reference is the lowest at all sites, expect the central site where the data are stored. The communication cost is very high since all users expect the central site have to use the network for all types of data accesses. Reliability and availability are very low, since the failure of the central site results in the loss of entire database system.

(ii) **Fragmented (or Partitioned):** This strategy partitions the entire database into disjoint fragments, where each fragment is assigned to one site. In this strategy, fragments are not replicated.

If fragments are stored at the site where they are used most frequently, locality of reference is high. As there is no replication of data, storage cost is low. Reliability and availability are also low but still higher than centralized data allocation strategies, as the failure of a site results in the loss of local data only. In this case, communication costs are incurred only for global transactions. However, in this approach, performance should be good, and communication costs are low if the data distribution is designed properly.

(iii) **Complete replication:** In this strategy, each site of the system maintains a complete copy of the entire database. Since all the data are available at all sites, locality of reference, availability and reliability, and performance are maximized in this approach.

Storage costs are very high in this case, and hence, no communication costs are incurred due to global transactions. However, communication costs for updating data items are the most expensive. To overcome this problem, snapshots are sometimes used. A snapshot is a copy of the data at a given time. The copies are updated periodically, so they may not be always up-to-date. Snapshots are also sometimes used to implement views in a distributed database, to reduce the time take for performing a database operation on a view.

(iv) **Selective replication:** This strategy is a combination of centralized, fragmented, and complete replication strategies. In this approach, some of the data items are fragmented and allocated to the sites where they are used frequently, to achieve high localization of reference. Some of the data items or fragments of the data items that are used by many sites simultaneously but not frequently updated, are replicated and stored at all these different sites. The data items that are not used frequently are centralized.

The objective of this strategy is to utilize all the advantages of all other strategies but none of the disadvantages. This strategy is used most commonly because of its flexibility.

Table 2.1 Comparison of Strategies for Data Allocation

	Locality of reference	Reliability and availability	Workload distribution and performance	Storage costs	Communication costs
Centralized	Lowest	Lowest	Poor	Lowest	Highest
Fragmented	High	Low for data item, high for system	Satisfactory	Lowest	Low
Complete replication	Highest	Highest	Best for reading	Highest	High for updating low for reading
Selective replication	High	Low for data item, high for system	Satisfactory	Average	Low

2.6 DISTRIBUTION DESIGN ISSUES

In the preceding section we indicated that the relations in a database schema are usually decomposed into smaller fragments, but we did not offer any justification or details for this process. The objective of this section is to fill in these details.

The following set of interrelated questions covers the entire issue. We will therefore seek to answer them in the remainder of this section.

- Why fragmented at all?
- How should we fragment?
- How much should we fragment?
- Is there any way to test the correctness of decomposition?
- How should we allocate?
- What is the necessary information for fragmentation and allocation?

2.6.1 REASONS FOR FRAGMENTATION

From a data distribution viewpoint, there is really no reason to fragment data. After all, in distributed file systems, the distribution is performed on the basis of entire files. In fact, the earlier work dealt specifically with the allocation of files to nodes on a computer network. With respect to fragmentation, the important issue is the appropriate unit of distribution. A relation is not a suitable unit, for a number of reasons. First, application views are usually subsets of relations. Therefore, the locality of accesses of applications is defined not on entire relations but on their subsets. Hence it is only natural to consider subsets of relations as distribution units.

Second, if the applications that have views defined on a given relation reside at different sites, two alternatives can be followed, with the entire relation being the unit of distribution. Either the relation is not replicated and is stored at only one site, or it is replicated at all or some of the sites where the applications reside. The former results in an unnecessarily high volume of remote data accesses. The latter, on the other hand, has unnecessary replication, which causes problems in executing updates (to be discussed later) and may not be desirable if storage is limited.

Finally, the decomposition of a relation into fragments, each being treated as a unit, permits a number of transactions to execute concurrently. In addition, the fragmentation of relations typically results in the parallel execution of a single query by dividing it into a set of subqueries that operate on fragments. Thus fragmentation typically increases the level of concurrency and therefore the system throughput. For the sake of completeness, we should also indicate the disadvantages of fragmentation. If the applications have conflicting requirements which prevent decomposition of the relation into mutually exclusive fragments, those applications whose views are defined on more than one fragment may suffer performance degradation.

It might, for example be necessary to retrieve data from two fragments and then take either their union or their join, which is costly. Avoiding this is a fundamental fragmentation issue.

The second problem is related to semantic data control, specifically to integrity checking. As a result of fragmentation, attributes participating in a dependency may be decomposed into different fragments which might be allocated to different sites. In this case, even the simpler task of checking for dependencies would result in chasing after data in a number of sites.

2.6.2 FRAGMENTATION ALTERNATIVES

Relation instances are essentially tables, so the issue is one of finding alternative ways of dividing a table into smaller ones. There are clearly two alternatives for this: dividing it horizontally or dividing it vertically.

Example 2.1

In this chapter we use a modified version of the relational database scheme. We have added to the PROJ relation a new attribute (LOC) that indicates the place of each project. Figure 2.3 depicts the database schema instance we will use. Figure 2.4 shows the PROJ relation of Figure 2.3 divided horizontally into two relations. Subrelation $PROJ_1$ contains information about projects whose budgets are less than \$200,000, whereas $PROJ_2$ stores information about projects with larger budgets.

EMP

ENO	ENAME	TITLE
E1	J. Doe	Elect. Eng
E2	M. Smith	Syst. Anal.
E3	A. Lee	Mech. Eng.
E4	J. Miller	Programmer
E5	B Casey	Syst. Anal.
E6	L. Chu	Elect. Eng.
E7	R. Davis	Mech. Eng.
E8	J. Jones	Syst. Anal.

ENO	PNO	RESP	DUR
E1	P1	Manager	12
E2	P1	Analyst	24
E2	P2	Analyst	6
E3	P3	Consultant	10
E3	P4	Engineer	48
E4	P2	Programmer	18
E5	P2	Manager	24
E6	P4	Manager	48
E7	P3	Engineer	36
E8	P3	Manager	40

PROJ

ENO	PNAME	BUDGE	LOG
P1	Instrumentation	150000	Montreal
P2	Database Develop	135000	New York
P3	CAD/CAM	250000	New York
P4	Maintenance	310000	Paris

PAY

TITLE	SAL
Elect. Eng.	40000
Syst. Anal.	34000
Mech. Eng.	27000
Programmer	24000

Figure 2.3 Modified Example Database

$PROJ_1$

PNO	PNAME	BUDGET	LOC
P1	Instrumentation	150000	Montreal
P2	Database Develop.	135000	New York

$PROJ_2$

PNO	PNAME	BUDGET	LOC
P3	CAD/CAM	255000	New York
P4	Maintenance	310000	Paris

Figure 2.4 Example of Horizontal Partitioning

Example 2.2

Figure 2.5 shows the PROJ relation of Figure 2.3 partitioned vertically into two subrelations, $PROJ_1$ and $PROJ_2$. $PROJ_1$ contains only the information about project budgets, whereas $PROJ_2$ contains project names and locations. It is important to notice that the primary key to the relation (PNO) is included in both fragments.

$PROJ_1$ $PROJ_2$

PNO	BUDGET
P1	150000
P2	135000
P3	250000
P4	310000

PNO	PNAME	LOC
P1	Instrumentation	Montreal
P2	Database Develop.	New York
P3	CAD.CAM	New York
P4	Maintenance	Paris

Figure 2.5 Example of Vertical Partitioning

The fragmentation may, of course, be nested. If the nesting's are of different types, one gets hybrid fragmentation. Even though we do not treat hybrid fragmentation as a primitive type of fragmentation strategies, it is quite obvious that many real-life partitioning may be hybrid.

2.6.3 DEGREE OF FRAGMENTATION

The extent to which the database should be fragmented is an important decision that affects the performance of query execution. The degree of fragmentation goes from one extreme, that is, not to fragment at all, to the other extreme, to fragment to the level of individual tuples (in the case of horizontal fragmentation) or to the level of individual attributes (in the case of vertical fragmentation).

We have already addressed effects of very large and very small units of fragmentation. What we need, the, is to find a suitable level of fragmentation which is a compromise between the two extremes. Such a level can only be defined with respect to the applications that will run on the database. The issue is, how? In general, the applications need to be characterized with respect to a number of parameters. According to the values of these parameters, individual fragments can be identified.

2.6.4 CORRECTNESS RULES OF FRAGMENTATION

It is important to note the similarity between the fragmentation of data for distribution (specifically, vertical fragmentation) and the normalization of relations. Thus fragmentation rules similar to the normalization principles can be defined.

We will enforce the following three rules during fragmentation, which, together, ensure that the database does not undergo semantic change during fragmentation.

1. **Completeness:** If a relation instance R is decomposed into fragments R_1, R_2, ..., R_n each data item that can be found in R can also be found in one or more of R_i's. This property, which is identical to the lossless decomposition property of normalization, is also important in fragmentation since it ensures that the data in a global relation is mapped into fragments without any loss [Grant, 1984]. Note that in the

case of horizontal fragmentation, the "item" typically refers to a tuple while in the case of vertical fragmentation, it refers to an attribute.

2. **Reconstruction:** If a relation R is decomposed into fragments R_1, R_2, ..., Rn, it should be possible to define a relational operator Ñ such that

$$R = \nabla R_i, \quad R_i \varepsilon F_R$$

The operator ∇ will be different for the different forms of fragmentation; it is important, however, that it can be identified. The reconstruct ability of the relation from its fragments ensures that constraints defined on the data in the form of dependencies are preserved.

3. **Disjointness:** If a relation R is horizontally decomposed into fragments R_1, R_2, ..., R_n and data item d_1 is in R_j, it is not in any other fragment R_k ($k \neq j$). This criterion ensures that the horizontal fragments are disjoint. If relation R is vertically decomposed, its primary key attributed are typically repeated in all its fragments. Therefore, in case of vertical partitioning, disjointness is denned only on the nonprimary key attributes of a relation.

2.6.5 ALLOCATION ALTERNATIVES

Assuming that the database is fragmented properly, one has to decide on the allocation of the fragments to various sites on the network. When data is allocated, it may either be replicated or maintained as a single copy. The reasons for replication are reliability and efficiency of read-only queries. If there are multiple copies of a data item, there is a good change that some copy of the data will be accessible somewhere even when system failures occur. Furthermore, read-only queries that access the same data items can be executed in parallel since copies exist on multiple sites. On the other hand, the execution of update queries cause trouble since the system has to ensure that all the copies of the data are updated properly. Hence the decision regarding replication is a trade-off which depends on the ratio of the read-only queries to the update queries. This decision affects almost all of the distributed DBMS algorithms and control functions.

A nonreplicated database (commonly called a partitioned database) contains fragments that are allocated to sites, and there is only one copy of any fragment on the network. In case of replication, either the database exists in its entirety at each site (fully replicated database), or fragments are distributed to the sites in such a way that copies of a fragment may reside in multiple sites (partially replicated database). In the latter the number of copies of a fragment may be an input to the allocation algorithm or a decision variable whose value is determined by the algorithm. Figure 2.6 compared these three replication alternatives with respect to various distributed DBMS functions.

2.6.6 INFORMATION REQUIREMENTS

One aspect of distribution design is that too many factors contribute to an optimal design. The logical organization of the database, the location of the applications, the access characteristics of the applications to the database, and the properties of the computer systems at each site all have an influence on distribution decisions. This makes it very complicated to formulate a distribution problem.

The information needed for distribution design can be divided into four categories: database information, application information, communication network information, and computer system information. The latter two categories are completely quantitative in nature and are used in allocation models rather than in fragmentation algorithms.

2.7 TYPES OF DATA FRAGMENTATION

The decomposition of global relations into fragments can be performed by applying two different types of fragmentation: horizontal fragmentation and vertical fragmentation. We will first consider these two types of fragmentation separately and then consider the more complex fragmentation which can be obtained by applying a composition of both.

In a distributed system, a global relation may be divided into several non-overlapping subrelations and allocated to different sites, called fragments. This process is called data fragmentation. The objective of data fragmentation design is to determine non-overlapping fragments, which are logical units of allocation. Fragments can be designed by grouping a number of tuples or attributes of relations. Each group of tuples or attributes that constitute a fragment has the same properties.

In all types of fragmentation, a fragment can be defined by an expression in a relational language (we will use relational algebra) which takes global relations as operands and produces the fragment as result. For example, if a global relation contains data about employees, a fragment which contains only data about employees who work at department D_1 can be obviously defined by a selection operation on the global relation.

There are, however, some rules which must be followed when defining fragments:

Completeness condition: All the data of the global relation must be mapped into the fragments; i.e., it must not happen that a data item which belongs to a global relation does not belong to any fragment.

Reconstruction condition: It must always be possible to reconstruct each global relation from its fragments. The necessity of this condition is obvious:

in fact, only fragments are stored in the distributed database, and global relation has to be built through this reconstruction operation if necessary.

Disjointness condition: It is convenient that fragments be disjoint, so that the replication of data can be controlled explicitly at the allocation level. However, this condition is useful mainly with horizontal fragmentation, while for vertical fragmentation we will sometimes allow this condition to be violated. The reason for this exception will be discussed when dealing with vertical fragmentation.

Advantages of Data Fragmentation

Following are the advantages of data fragmentation:

(i) **Better usage –** Our applications work with views, rather than the entire relation. Therefore, it seems to be beneficial to fragment the relations into subrelations and store them into different sites as units of distribution in data distribution.

(ii) **Improved efficiency –** We can store the data to that it can access easily. In addition, data that are not required by local applications are not stored locally, which may result in faster data access, thereby increasing the efficiency.

(iii) **Improved parallelism or concurrency –** We can divide the transaction into several subtransactions that operate on different fragments in parallel. This increases the degree of concurrency or parallelism in the system, thereby allowing transactions to execute in parallel in a safe way.

(iv) **Better security –** Due to security reasons, data that are not required by local applications are not stored locally and, consequently are not available to unauthorized users of the distributed system.

Disadvantages of data fragmentation

Following are the disadvantages of data fragmentation:

(i) **Low Performance –** The performance of global applications that require data from several fragments located at different sites may become slower and, therefore, performance may low. For example, in case of global applications, it may be necessary to retrieve data from more than one fragment located at different sites. In this case, performing either union or join of these fragments becomes slower and costly.

(ii) **Integrity Problem –** Data and functional dependencies may be decomposed into different fragments that might be allocated to different sites across the network of a distributed system. In this situation, checking functional dependencies is very complicated and, consequently, maintaining integrity becomes very difficult.

2.7.1 HORIZONTAL FRAGMENTATION

Horizontal fragmentation consists of partitioning the tuples of a global relation into subsets; this is clearly useful in distributed databases, where each subset can contain data which have common geographical properties. It can be defined by expressing each fragments as a selection operation on the global relation. For example, let a global relation be

SUPPLIER(SNUM, NAME, CITY)

Then the horizontal fragmentation can be defined in the following way:

$SUPPLIER_1 = SL_{CITY = \text{"SF"}}$ SUPPLIER

$SUPPLIER_2 = SL_{CITY = \text{"LA"}}$ SUPPLIER

The above fragmentation satisfies the completeness condition if "SF" and "LA" are the only possible values of the CITY attribute; otherwise we would not know to which fragment the tuples with other CITY values belong.

The reconstruction condition is easily verified, because it is always possible to reconstruct the SUPPLIER global relation through the following operation:

SUPPLIER = $SUPPLIER_1$ UN $SUPPLIR\text{-}_2$

The disjointness condition is clearly verified.

We will call the predicate which is used in the selection operation which defines a fragment its qualification. For instance, in the above example the qualifications are:

q_1: CITY = "SF"

q_2: CITY = "LA"

We can generalize from the above example that in order to satisfy the completeness condition, the set of qualifications of all fragments must be complete, at least with respect to the set of allowed values. The reconstruction condition is always satisfied through the union operation, and the disjointness condition requires that qualifications be mutually exclusive.

2.7.2 DERIVED HORIZONTAL FRAGMENTATION

In some cases, the horizontal fragmentation of a relation cannot be based on a property of its own attributes, but is derived from the horizontal fragmentation of another relation. Consider, for example, a global relation

SUPPLY(SNUM, PNUM, DEPTNUM, QUAN)

where SNUM is a supplier number. It is meaningful to partition this relation so that a fragment contains the tuples for suppliers which are in a given city. However, city is not an attribute of the SUPPLY which corresponds to the suppliers in a given city. The derived fragmentation of SUPPLY can be therefore defined as follows:

$SUPPLY_1 = SUPPLY\ SJ_{SNUM = SNUM}\ SUPPLIER_1$

$SUPPLY_2 = SUPPLY\ SJ_{SNUM = SNUM}\ SUPPLIER_2$

The effect of the semi-join operations is to select from SUPPLY the tuples which satisfy the join condition between $SUPPLIER_1$ or $SUPPLIER_2$ and SUPPLY, thus determining those tuples of SUPPLY which refer to suppliers in San Francisco or Los Angeles, respectively.

The reconstruction of the global relation SUPPLY can be performed through the union operation as was shown for SUPPLIER.

When a global relation R has a derived fragmentation, the qualifications of its fragments cannot be expressed as predicates which use attributes from R; rather, the condition for a tuple t to belong to a given fragment R_{i-} of R is the existence, in some other fragment S_i of S, of a tuple t' such that t and t' satisfy the semi-join specification of the derived fragmentation. Considering the above example, we give a simple representation of this condition (which should in fact include an existential quantifier) as follows:

q_1: SUPPLY.SNUM = SUPPLIER.SNUM AND SUPPLIER.CITY = "SF"

q_2: SUPPLY.SNUM = SUPPLIER.SNUM AND SUPPLIER.CITY = "LA"

The meaning of the above qualifications is to state, for any tuple of $SUPPLY_1$ ($SUPPLY_2$), the existence of a supplier from San Francisco (Los Angeles) with the same supplier number.

The completeness of the above fragmentation requires that there be no supplier numbers in the SUPPLY relation which are not contained also in the SUPPLIER relation. This is a typical, and reasonable, integrity constraint for this database, and usually is called the referential integrity constraint.

The disjointness condition is satisfied if a tuple of the SUPPLY relation does not correspond to two tuples of the SUPPLIER relation which belong to two different fragments. In this case this condition is easily verified, because the supplier numbers are unique keys of the SUPPLIER relation; however, in general it can be difficult to prove that this condition holds.

2.7.3 VERTICAL FRAGMENTATION

The vertical fragmentation of a global relation is the subdivision of its attributes into groups; fragments are obtained by projecting the global relation over each group. This can be useful in distributed databases where each group of attributes can contain data which have common geographical properties. The fragments; moreover, it must be possible to reconstruct the original relation by joining the fragments together. Consider, for example, a global relation

EMP(EMPNUM, NAME, SAL, TAX, MGRNUM, DEPTNUM)

A vertical fragmentation of this relation can be defined as

$EMP_1 = PJ_{EMPNUM,\ NAME,\ MGRNUM,\ DEPTNUM}\ EMP$

$EMP_2 = PJ_{EMPNUM,\ SAL,\ TAX}\ EMP$

This fragmentation could, for instance, reflect an organization in which salaries and taxed are managed separately. The reconstruction of relation EMP can be obtained as

$EMP = EMP_1\ JN_{EMPNUM = EMPNUM}\ EMP_2$

because EMPNUM is a key of EMP. In general, the inclusion of a key of the global relation into each fragment is the most straightforward way to guarantee that the reconstruction through a join operation is possible. An alternative way to provide the reconstruction property is to generate tuple identifiers which are used as system-controlled keys. This can be convenient in order to avoid the replication of large keys; moreover, tuple identifiers cannot be modified by users.

Let us finally consider the problem of fragment disjointness. First, we have seen that at least the key should be replicated in all fragments in order to allow reconstruction. In general, we can say that in vertical fragmentation the main motivation for having disjoint fragments (i.e., to control replication) is not as important as in horizontal fragmentation. In fact, if we include the same attribute in two different vertical fragments, we know exactly that the replicated data is constituted by the column which corresponds to this attribute; if instead we allow two horizontal fragments to overlap, by permitting nonmutually exclusive qualifications, then we cannot refer directly to the overlapping portion.

For example, consider the following vertical fragmentation of relation EMP:

$EMP_1 = PJ_{EMPNUM,NAME,MGRNUM,DEPTNUM}\ EMP$

$EMP_2 = PJ_{EMPNUM,NAME,SAL,TAX}\ EMP$

The attribute NAME is replicated in both fragments. We can explicitly eliminate this attribute when we reconstruct relation EMP through an additional projection operation:

$EMP = EMP_1\ JN_{EMPNUM = EMPNUM}\ PJ_{EMPNUM,SAL,TAX}\ EMP_2$

2.7.4 MIXED FRAGMENTATION

The fragments which are obtained by the above fragmentation operations are relations themselves, so that it is possible to apply the fragmentation operations recursively, provided that the correctness conditions are satisfied each time. The reconstruction can be obtained by applying the reconstruction rules in inverse order. The expressions which define fragments are more complex in this case; consider, for example, the same global relation

EMP(EMPNUM, NAME, SAL, TAX, MGRNUM, DEPTNUM)

The following is a mixed fragmentation which is obtained by applying the vertical fragmentation of the previous example, followed by a horizontal fragmentation on DEPTNUM:

$EMP_1 = SL_{DEPTNUM \leq 10} PJ_{EMPNUM,NAME,MGRNUM,DEPTNUM}\ NUM$

$EMP_2 = SL_{1 < DEPTNUM \leq 20} PJ_{EMPNUM,NAME,MGRNUM,DEPTNUM}\ EMP$

$EMP_3 = SL_{DEPTNUM > 20} PJ_{EMPNUM,NAME,MGRNUM,DEPTNUM}\ EMP$

$EMP_4 = PJ_{EMPNUM,\ NAME,\ SAL,\ TAX}\ EMP$

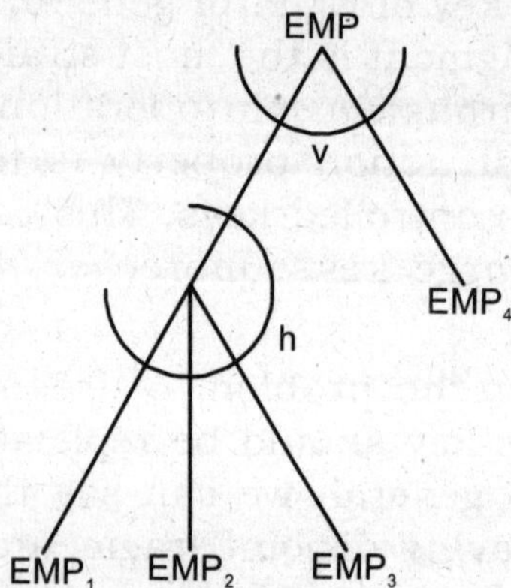

Figure 2.6 The fragmentation tree of relation EMP.

The reconstruction of relation EMP is defined by the following expression:

$EMP = UN\ (EMP_1, EMP_2, EMP_3)\ JN_{EMPNUM} = EMPNUM$

$PJ_{EMPNUM,SAL,TAX}\ EMP_4$

Mixed fragmentation can be conveniently represented by a fragmentation tree. In a fragmentation tree, the root corresponds to a global relation, the leaves correspond to the fragments, and the intermediate nodes correspond to the intermediate results of the fragment-defining expressions. The set of nodes which are sons of a given node represent the decomposition of this node by a fragmentation operation (vertical or horizontal). For example, Figure 2.6 shows the fragmentation tree of relation EMP. The root (relation EMP) is vertically fragmented into two portions: one portion corresponds to a leaf node of the tree (EMP_4); the other portion is horizontally partitioned, thus generating the other three leaves, corresponding to fragments EMP_1, EMP_2, and EMP_3.

2.7.5 NO FRAGMENTATION

A final strategy of the fragmentation is not to fragment a relation. If a relation contains a smaller number of tuples and not updated frequently, this is better not to fragment the relation. It will be more sensible to leave the relation as a whole and simply replicate the relation at each site of the distributed system.

2.8 ALLOCATION

The allocation of resources across the nodes of a computer network is an old problem that has been studied extensively. Most of this work, however, does not address the problem of distributed database design, but rather that of placing individual files on a computer network. We will examine the differences between the two shortly. We first need to define the allocation problem more precisely.

2.8.1 ALLOCATION PROBLEM

Assume that there are a set of fragments F = $\{F_1, F_2, \ldots, F_n\}$ and a network consisting of sites 5 = $\{S_1, S_2, \ldots, S_m\}$ on which a set of applications Q = $\{q_1, q_2, \ldots, q_q)$ is running. The allocation problem involves finding the "optimal" distribution of F to S.

One of the important issues that need to be discussed is the definition of optimality. The optimality can be defined with respect to two measures [Dowdy and Foster, 1982]:

1. **Minimal cost:** The cost function consists of the cost of storing each F_i at a site S_j, the cost of querying F_i at site S_j the cost of updating Ft at all sites where it is stored, and the cost of data communication. The allocation problem, then, attempts to find an allocation scheme that minimizes a combined cost function.
2. **Performance:** The allocation strategy is designed to maintain a performance metric. Two well-known ones are to minimize the response time and to maximize the system throughput at each site.

Most of the models that have been proposed to date make this distinction of optimality. However, if one really examines the problem in depth, it is apparent that the "optimality" measure should include both the performance and the cost factors. In other words, one should be looking for an allocation scheme that, for example, answers user queries in minimal time while keeping the cost of processing minimal. A similar statement can be made for throughput maximization. One can then ask why such models have not been developed. The answer is quite simple: complexity.

Let us consider a very simple formulation of the problem. Let F and S be defined as before. For the time being, we consider only a single fragment, F_k. We make a number of assumptions and definitions that will enable us to model the allocation problem.

1. Assume that Q can be modified so that it is possible to identify the update and the retrieval-only queries, and to define the following for a single fragment F_k:

   $T = \{t_1, t_2, \ldots, t_m\}$

where t_i is the read-only traffic generated at site S_i for F_k and
$U = \{u_1, u_2, ..., u_m\}$
where u_i is the update traffic generated at site S_i for F_k.

2. Assume that the communication cost between any two pair of sites S_i and S_j is fixed for a unit of transmission. Furthermore, assume that it is different for updates and retrievals in order that the following can be defined:

   $C(T) = \{c_{12}, c_{13}, ..., c_{1m}, ..., c_{m-1,m}\}$

   $C'(U) = \{c'_{12}, c'_{13}, ..., c'_{1m}, ..., c'_{m-1,m}\}$

   where C_{ij} is the unit communication cost for retrieval requests between sites S_i and S_j, and c'_{ij} is the unit communication cost for update requests between sites S_i and S_j.
3. Let the cost of storing the fragment at site S_i be d_j. Thus we can define $D = \{d_1, d_2, ..., d_m\}$ for the storage cost of fragment F_k at all the sites.
4. Assume that there axe no capacity constraints for either the sites or the communication links.

Then the allocation problem can be specified as a cost-minimization problem where we are trying to find the set I Í S that specifies where the copies of the fragment will be stored. In the following, x_j, denotes the decision variable for the placement such that

$$x_j = \begin{cases} 1 \text{ if the fragment of } F_k \text{ is assigned to site } S_j \\ 0 \text{ otherwise} \end{cases}$$

The precise specification is as follows:

$$\min \left[\left(\sum_{i=1}^{m} \sum_{j|S_j \varepsilon I} x_j u_j c'_{ij} + t_j \min_{j|S_j \varepsilon I} c_{ij} \right) + \sum_{j|S_j \varepsilon I} x_j d_j \right]$$

subject to

$$x_j = 0 \text{ or } 1$$

The second term of the objective function calculates the total cost of storing all the duplicate copies of the fragment. The first term, on the other hand, corresponds to the cost of transmitting the updates to all the sites that hold the replicas of the fragment, and to the cost of executing the retrieval-only requests at the site, which will result in minimal data transmission cost.

This is a very simplistic formulation that is not suitable for distributed database design. But even if it were, there is another problem. This formulation, which comes from [Casy, 1972], has been proven to be NP-complete [Eswaran, 1974]. Various different formulations of the problem have been proven to be just as hard over the years (e.g., [Sacca and Wiederhold, 1985] and [Lam and Yu, 1980]). The implication is, of course, that for large problems (i.e., large number of fragments and sites), obtaining optimal solutions is probably not computationally feasible. Considerable research has therefore been devoted to finding good heuristics that provide suboptimal solutions.

There are a number of reasons why simplistic formulations such as the one we have discussed are not suitable for distributed database design. These are inherent in all the early file allocation models for computer networks.

1. One cannot treat fragments as individual files that can be allocated one at a time, in isolation. The placement of one fragment usually has an impact on the placement decisions about the other fragments which are accessed together since the access costs to the remaining fragments may change (e.g., due to distributed join). Therefore, the relationship between fragments should be taken into account.
2. The access to data by applications is modelled very simply. A user request is issued at one site and all the data to answer it is transferred to that site. In distributed database systems, access to data is more complicated than this simple "remote file access" model suggests. Therefore, the relationship between the allocation and query processing should be properly modelled.
3. These models do not take into consideration the cost of integrity enforcement; yet locating two fragments involved in the same integrity constraint at two different sites can be costly.
4. Similarly, the cost of enforcing concurrency control mechanisms should be considered [Rothnie and Goodman, 1977].

In summary, let us remember the interrelationship between the distributed database problems. Since the allocation is so central, its relationship with algorithms that are implemented for other problem areas needs to be represented in the allocation model. However, this is exactly what makes it quite difficult to solve these models. To separate the traditional problem of file allocation from the fragment allocation in distributed database design, we refer to the former as the file allocation problem (FAP)and to the latter as the database allocation problem (DAP).

There are no general heuristic models that take as input a set of fragments and produce a near-optimal allocation subject to the types of constraints discussed here. The models developed to date make a number of simplifying assumptions and are applicable to certain specific formulations. Therefore, instead of presenting one or more of these allocation algorithms, we present

a relatively general model and then discuss a number of possible heuristics that might be employed to solve it.

2.8.2 INFORMATION REQUIREMENTS

It is at the allocation stage that we need the quantitative data about the database the applications that run on it, the communication network, the processing capabilities and storage limitations of each site on the network. We will discuss each of these in detail.

2.8.2.1 DATABASE INFORMATION

To perform horizontal fragmentation, we defined the selectivity of midterms. We now need to extend that definition to fragments, and define the selectivity of fragments F_j with respect to query q_r. This is the number of topples of F_j that need to be accessed in order to process q_r. This value will be denoted as seli (F_j).

Another piece of necessary information on the database fragments is their size. The size of the fragment F_j is given by

size (F_j) = card (F_j) * length (F_j) where

length (F_j) is the length (in bytes) of a tuple of fragment F_j.

2.8.2.2 APPLICATION INFORMATION

Most of the application-related information is already compiled during the fragmentation activity, but a few more are required by the allocation model. The two important measures are the number of read accesses that a query (q_i makes to a fragment F_j during its execution (denoted as RR_{ij}), and its counterpart for the update accesses (UR_{ij}). These may, for example, count the number of block accesses required by the query.

We also need to define two matrices UM and RM, with elements u_{ij} and r_{ij}, respectively, which are specified as follows:

$$u_{ij} = \begin{cases} 1 \text{ if query } qi \text{ updates fragment } F_i \\ 0 \text{ otherwise} \end{cases}$$

$$r_{ij} = \begin{cases} 1 \text{ if query } qi \text{ retrives from fragment } F_i \\ 0 \text{ otherwise} \end{cases}$$

A vector O of values o(i) is also defined, where o(i) specifies the originating site of query q_1. Finally, to define the response-time constraint, the maximum allowable response time of each application should be specified.

2.8.2.3 SITE INFORMATION

For each computer site, we need to know about its storage and processing capacity. Obviously, these values can be computed by means of elaborate functions or by simple estimates. The unit cost of storing data at site Sk will be denoted as USC_k. There is also a need to specify a cost measure LPC_k as the cost of processing one unit of work at site Sk. The work unit should be identical to that of the RR and UR measures.

2.8.2.4 NETWORK INFORMATION

In our model we assume the existence of a simple network where the cost of communication is defined in terms of one frame of data. Thus g_{ij} denotes the communication cost per frame between sites S_i and S_j. To enable the calculation of the number of messages, we use f size as the size (in bytes) of one frame. There is no question that there are more elaborate network models which take into consideration the channel capacities, distances between sites, protocol overhead, and so on. However, the derivation of those equations is beyond the scope of this chapter.

2.8.3 ALLOCATION MODEL

We discuss an allocation model that attempts to minimize the total cost of processing and storage while trying to meet certain response time restrictions. The model we use has the following form: min

(Total Cost)

subject to response-time constraint storage constraint processing constraint.

In the remainder of this section we expand the components of this model based on the information requirements. The decision variable is x_{ij}, which is defined as

$$x_{ij} = \begin{cases} 1 \text{ if the fragment } F_i \text{ is stored at site } S_j \\ 0 \text{ otherwise} \end{cases}$$

Total Cost

The total cost function has two components: query processing and storage. Thus it can be expressed as

$$TOC = \sum_{\forall q_i \varepsilon Q} QPC_i + \sum_{\forall s_{ki} \varepsilon S} STC_{jk} \sum_{\forall F_{ji} \varepsilon F} STC_{jk}$$

where QPC_i is the query processing cost of application q_i, and STC_{jk} is the cost of storing fragment F_j at site S_k.

Let us consider the storage cost first. It is simply given by

$$STC_{jk} = USC_k * size(F_j) * x_{jk}$$

and the two summations find the total storage costs at all the sites for all the fragments.

The query processing cost is more difficult to specify. Most models of the file allocation problem (FAP) separate it into two components: the retrieval-only processing cost, and the update processing cost. We choose a different approach in our model of the database allocation problem (DAP) and specify it as consisting of the processing cost (PC) and the transmission cost (TC). Thus the query processing cost (QPC) for application q_i is

$$QPC_i = PC_i + TC_i$$

The processing component, PC, consists of three cost factors, the access cost (AC), the integrity enforcement cost (IE), and the concurrency control cost (CC):

$$PC_i = AC_i + IE_i + CC_i$$

The detailed specification of each of these cost factors depends on the algorithms used to accomplish these tasks. However, to demonstrate the point, we specify AC in some detail.

$$AC = \sum_{\forall S_{ki} \varepsilon S} \sum_{\forall F_{ki} \varepsilon F} (u_{jk} * UR_{ij} + r_{ij} * RR_{jk} * LPC_k$$

The first two terms in the formula above calculate the number of accesses of user query q_i to fragment F_j. Note that (UR_{ij} + RR_{ij}) gives the total number of update and retrieval accesses. We assume that the local costs of processing them are identical. The summation gives the total number of accesses for all the fragments referenced by q_i. Multiplication by LPC_k gives the cost of this access at site S_k. We again use x_{jk} to select only those cost values for the sites where fragments are stored.

A very important issue needs to be pointed out here. The access cost function assumes that processing a query involves decomposing it into a set of subqueries, each of which works on a fragment stored at the site, followed by transmitting the results back to the site where the query has originated. As we discussed earlier, this is a very simplistic view which does not take into consideration the complexities of database processing. For example, the cost function does not take into account the cost of performing joins (if necessary), which may be executed in a number of ways. In a model that is more realistic than the generic model we are considering, these issues should not be omitted.

The integrity enforcement cost factor can be specified much like the processing component, except that the unit local processing cost would probably

change to reflect the true cost of integrity enforcement. Since the integrity checking and concurrency control methods are discussed later in the book, we do not need to study these cost components further here. The transmission cost function can be formulated along the lines of the access cost function. However, the data transmission overhead for update and that for retrieval requests are quite different. In update queries it is necessary to inform all the sites where replicas exist, while in retrieval queries, it is sufficient to access only one of the copies. In addition, at the end of an update request, there is no data transmission back to the originating site other than a confirmation message, whereas the retrieval-only queries may result in significant data transmission.

The update component of the transmission function is

$$TCU_i = \sum_{\forall S_{ki} \varepsilon S} \sum_{\forall F_{ki} \varepsilon F} u_{ij} * x_{jk} * g_{o(i),k} + \sum_{\forall S_{ki} \varepsilon S} \sum_{\forall F_{ki} \varepsilon F} u_{ij} * x_{jk} * g_{k,o(i)}$$

The first term is for sending the update message from the originating site o(i) of q_i to all the fragment replicas that need to be updated. The second term is for the confirmation.

The retrieval cost can be specified as

$$TCR_i = \sum_{\forall F_{ki} \varepsilon F} \min_{S_k \varepsilon S} \left(u_{ij} * x_{jk} * g_{o(i),k} + r_{ij} * x_{jk} \frac{sel_i(F_j) * length(F_j)}{f\ size} * g_{k,o(i)} \right)$$

The first term in TCR represents the cost of transmitting the retrieval request to those sites which have copies of fragments that need to be accessed. The second term accounts for the transmission of the results from these sites to the originating site. The equation states that among all the sites with copies of the same fragment, only the site that yields the minimum total transmission cost should be selected for the execution of the operation.

Now the transmission cost function for query q_i can be specified as

$$TC_i = TCU_i + TCR_i$$

which fully specifies the total cost function.

Constraints

The constraint functions can be specified in similar detail. However, instead of describing these functions in depth, we will simply indicate what they should look like. The response-time constraint should be specified as

execution time of $q_i \leq$ maximum response time of $q_i, \forall S_k \varepsilon S$

whereas the processing constraint is

$\sum_{\forall q_i \varepsilon Q}$ processing load of q_i at site $S_k \leq$ processing capacity of S_k, $\forall S_k \varepsilon S$

This completes our development of the allocation model. Even though we have not developed it entirely, the precision in some of the terms indicates how one goes about formulating such a problem. In addition to this aspect, we have indicated the important issues that need to be addressed in allocation models.

2.8.4 SOLUTION METHODS

In the preceding section we developed a generic allocation model which is considerably more complex than the FAP model. Since the FAP model is NP-complete, one would expect the solution of this formulation of the database allocation problem (DAP) also to be NP-complete. Even though we will not prove this conjecture, it is indeed true. Thus one has to look for heuristic methods that yield suboptimal solutions. The test of "goodness" in this case is, obviously how close the results of the heuristic algorithm are to the optimal allocation.

A number of different heuristics have been applied to the solution of FAP and DAP models. It was observed early on that there is a correspondence between FAP and the plant location problem that has been studied in operations research. In fact, the isomorphism of the simple FAP and the single commodity warehouse location problem has been shown [Rammamoorthy and Wah, 1983]. Thus heuristics developed by operations researchers have commonly have been adopted to solve the FAP and DAP problems. Examples are the knapsack problem solution [Ceri et al., 1982b], branch-and-bound techniques [Fisher and Hochbaum, 1980], and network flow algorithms [Chang and Liu 1982].

There have been other attempts to reduce the complexity of the problem. One strategy has been to assume that all the candidate partitioning have been determined together with their associated costs and benefits in terms of query processing. The problem, then, is modelled so as to choose the optimal partitioning and placement for each relation [Ceri et al., 1983]. Another simplification frequently employed is to ignore replication at first and find an optimal nonreplicated solution. Replication is handled at the second step by applying a greedy algorithm which starts with the nonreplicated solution as the initial feasible solution, and tries to improve upon it ([Ceri et al., 1983] and [Ceri and Pernici, 1985]). For these heuristics, however, there is not enough data to determine how close the results are to the optimal.

2.9 DATA ALLOCATION

The data allocation problem has bee widely analyzed in the context of the "file allocation problem"; references to describe several analytical models which build the optimal allocation of files under very different assumptions and with different objectives. The easiest way to apply this work to the fragment

allocation problem is to consider each fragment as a separate file; however, this approach is not convenient for the following reasons:

1. Fragments are not properly modelled as individual files; since in this way we do not take into account the fact that they have the same structure or behaviour.
2. There are many more fragments than original global relations, and many analytic models cannot compute the solution of problems involving to many variables.
3. Modelling application behaviour in file systems is very simple (typically, applications make a "remote file access"), while in distributed databases application can make a sophisticated use of data.

Some of these problems have not yet been solved satisfactorily; for instance, problem 3 is particularly difficult, since the correct approach would be to evaluate data distribution measuring how "optimized" applications should behave with it. This, however, requires optimizing all the important applications for each possible data allocation; solving query optimization as a subproblem of data allocation is probably too hard, since it requires either an excessive amount of simulation or an excessively complex analytic computation.

We do not present in this section any of the models for file allocation (short descriptions of some of them can be found in the annotated bibliography). There are, however, some general criteria that can be used for allocating fragments; we concentrate on them, and we given empirical, simple measure to evaluate costs and benefits of fragmentation.

2.9.1 GENERAL CRITERIA FOR FRAGMENT ALLOCATION

In determining the allocation of fragments, it is important to distinguish whether we design a final nonredundant or redundant allocation.

Determining a nonredundant final allocation is easier. The simplest method is a "best-fit" approach; a measure is associated with each possible allocation, and the site with the best measure is selected. This approach gives a solution which disregards the "mutual" effect of placing a fragment at a given site if a related fragment is also at that site.

Replication introduces further complexity in the design, because:

1. The degree of replication of each fragment becomes a variable of the problem.
2. Modelling read applications is complicated by the fact that the applications can now select among several alternative sites for accessing fragments.

For determining the redundant allocation of fragments, either of the following two methods can be used:

1. Determine the set of all sites where the benefit of allocating one copy of the fragment is higher that the cost, and allocate a copy of the fragment to each element of this set; this method selects "all beneficial sites."
2. Determine first the solution of the nonreplicated problem, and then progressively introduce replicated copies starting from the most beneficial; the process is terminated when no "additional replication" is beneficial.

Both methods have some disadvantages. In the "all beneficial sites" method, quantifying costs and benefits for each individual fragment allocation is more critical than in the nonredundant case, because it disregards the "mutual" effects of allocating different copies of the same fragment. The "additional replication" method is a typical heuristic approach; with this method, it is possible to take into account that the increase in the degree of redundancy is progressively less beneficial. Both the reliability and availability of the system increase if there are two or three copies of the fragment, but further copies give a less than proportional increase.

2.9.2 MEASURE OF COSTS AND BENEFITS OF FRAGMENT ALLOCATION

Finally, we give very simple formulas for evaluating costs and benefits of the allocation of fragments of a global relation R. Let us first introduce some definitions:

i is the fragment index

j is the site index

k is the application index

f_{kj} is the frequency of application k at site j

r_{ki} is the number of retrieval reference of application k to fragment i

u_{ki} is the number of update references of application k to fragment i

$n_{ki} = r_{ki} + u_{ki}$

2.9.2.1 HORIZONTAL FRAGMENTATION

1. Using the "best-fit" approach for a nonreplicated allocation, we place R_i at the site where the number of references to R_i is maximum. The number of local references of R_i at site j is

$$B_{ij} = \sum_k f_{kj} n_{ki}$$

R_i is allocated at site j* such that B_{ij}, is maximum.

2. Using the "all beneficial sites" method for replicated allocation, we place R_i at all sites j where the cost of retrieval references of applications is larger than the cost of update references to R_i from applications at any other site. $B\text{-}_{ij}$ is evaluated as the difference:

$$B_{ij} = \sum_k f_{kj} n_{ki} - C \times \sum_k \sum_{j' \neq j} f_{kj'} u_{ki}$$

C is a constant which measure the ratio between the cost of an update and a retrieval access; typically, update accesses are more expensive, since they require a larger number of control messages and local operations (thus, $C \geq 1$).

R_i is allocated at all sites j* such that B_{ij^*} is positive; when all B_{ij} are negative a single copy of R_i is placed at the site such that B_{ij^*} is maximum

3. Using the "additional replication" method for replicated allocation, we can measure the benefit of placing a new copy of R_i in terms of increased reliability and availability of the system. As we have stated, this benefit does not grow proportionally to the degree of redundancy of R_i. Let d_i denote the degree of redundancy of R_i, and let F_i denote the benefit of having R_i fully replicated at each site. In reference [4.11] the following function $\beta(d_i)$ we introduced to measure this benefit:

$$\beta(d_i) =)1 - 2^{1-d_i})F_i$$

Note that $\beta(1) = 0$, $\beta(2) = F_i/22$, $\beta(3) = 3F_i/4$, and so on. Then, we evaluate the benefit of introducing a new copy of R_i at site j by modifying the formula of case 2 as follows:

$$B_{ij} = \sum_k f_{kj} n_{ki} - C \, X \sum_k \sum_{j' \neq j} f_{kj'} u_{ki} + b(d_i)$$

This formula takes into account the degree of replication.

2.9.2.2 VERTICAL FRAGMENTATION

Here we measure that benefit of vertically partitioning a fragment R_i, allocated at site r, into two fragments R_S and R_t allocated at sites s and t. By the effect of this partitioning:

1. There are two sets A_S and A_t of applications, issued at sites s or t, which use only attributes of R_S or R_t and become local to sites s and t, respectively; these applications save one remote reference.
2. There is a set A_1 of applications formerly local to r which use only attributes of R_s or R_t; these applications now need to make an additional remote reference.

3. There is a set A_2 of applications formerly local to r which reference attributes of both R_{s-} and R_t; these applications make two additional remote references.
4. There is a set A_3 of applications at sites different than r, s, or t which reference attributes of both R_{s-} and R_t; these applications make one additional remote reference.

We evaluate the benefit of this partitioning as

$$B_{ist} = \sum_{k \varepsilon A_s} f_{kt} n_{ki} + \sum_{k \varepsilon A_1} f_{kr} n_{ki}$$

$$- \sum_{k \varepsilon A_2} 2X f_{kr} n_{ki} - \sum_{k \varepsilon A_3} \sum_{j \notin r,s,t} f_{kj} n_{ki}$$

For simplicity, this formula counts the number of accesses; in order to distinguish between retrieval and update access, taking into account their different costs, it is sufficient to use $(r_{ki} + C X u_{ki})$ instead of n_{ki}.

This formula can be used within an exhaustive "splitting" algorithm to determine whether splitting R_i at site i into R_s at site s and R_t at site t is convenient by trying all possible combinations of sites s and t; some care must be used when r = s or r = t.

2.9.2.3 VERTICAL CLUSTERING

We measure the benefit of the vertical clustering of a fragment R_i, allocated at site r, into two fragments R_s and R_t, allocated at sites s and t, with overlapping attributes I. The clustering requires reconsidering the groups of applications introduced for vertical partitioning:

1. A_s includes applications which are local to site s because they either:
   - Read any attribute of R_s, or
   - Update attributes of R_s which are not in the overlapping part I.

   The same holds for A_t.
2. A_{2-} includes update applications formerly local to r which make an update to attributes of I, since now they need to access both R_s and R_t.
3. A_3 includes the applications at sites different than r, s, or t which update attribute of I, which also need to access both R_{s-} and R_t.

We evaluate the benefit of this clustering using the above expression for B_{ist}.

2.10 TRANSPARENCY

Any change in a computing system, such as new feature or new component, is transparent if the system after change adheres to previous external interface as much as possible while changing its internal behaviour. The purpose is to shield from change all systems (or human users) on the other end of the interface. Confusingly, the term refers to overall invisibility of the component; it does not refer to visibility of component's internals (as in white box or open system). The term transparent is widely used in computing marketing in substitution of the term invisible, since the term invisible has a bad connotation (usually seen as something that the user can't see and has no control over) while the term transparent has a good connotation (usually associated with not hiding anything). The vast majority of the times, the term transparent is used in a misleading way to refer to the actual invisibility of a computing process.

The term is used particularly often with regard to an abstraction layer that is invisible either from its upper or lower neighbouring layer.

Also temporarily used later around 1969 in IBM and Honeywell programming manuals the term referred to a certain programming technique. An application code was transparent when it was clear of the low-level detail (such as device-specific management) and contained only the logic solving a main problem. It was achieved through encapsulation - putting the code into modules that hid internal details, making them invisible for the main application.

For example, the Network File System is transparent, because it introduces the access to files stored remotely on the network in a way uniform with previous local access to a file system, so user might even not notice it while using the folder hierarchy. Earlier File Transfer Protocol (FTP) is considerably less transparent, because it requires each user to learn how to access files through an ftp client.

Similarly, some file systems allow transparent compression and decompression of data, enabling users to store more files on a medium without any special knowledge; some file systems encrypt files transparently. This approach does not require running compression or encryption utility manually.

In software engineering, it is also considered good practice to develop or use abstraction layers for database access, so that the same application will work with different databases; here, the abstraction layer allows other parts of the program to access the database transparently.

In object oriented programming, transparency is facilitated through the use of interfaces that hide actual implementations done with different underlying classes.

2.10.1 TYPES OF TRANSPARENCY IN DISTRIBUTED SYSTEM

Transparency means that any form of distributed system should hide its distributed nature from its users, appearing and functioning as a normal centralized system.

There are many types of transparency:

1. **Access transparency:** Regardless of how resource access and representation has to be performed on each individual computing entity, the users of a distributed system should always access resources in a single, uniform way.
2. **Location transparency:** Users of a distributed system should not have to be aware of where a resource is physically located.
3. **Migration transparency:** Users should not be aware of whether a resource or computing entity possesses the ability to move to a different physical or logical location.
4. **Relocation transparency:** Should a resource move while in use, this should not be noticeable to the end user.
5. **Replication transparency:** If a resource is replicated among several locations, it should appear to the user as a single resource.
6. **Concurrent transparency:** While multiple users may compete for and share a single resource, this should not be apparent to any of them.
7. **Failure transparency:** Always try to hide any failure and recovery of computing entities and resources.
8. **Persistence transparency:** Whether a resource lies in volatile or permanent memory should make no difference to the user.
9. **Security transparency:** Negotiation of cryptographically secure access of resources must require a minimum of user intervention, or users will circumvent the security in preference of productivity.
10. **Scalability transparency:** Means that users and programmers do not know whether a replica or a master provides a service. Scalability transparency depends on replication and migration transparency.
11. **Performance transparency:** Means that users and programmers are unaware how good system performance is maintained. Performance transparency depends on replication and migration transparency. Replication of components provides the basis for a technique called *load balancing*, which achieves performance transparency.

Formal definitions of most of these concepts can be found in RM-ODP, the Open Distributed Processing Reference Model (ISO 10746).

The degree to which these properties can or should be achieved may vary widely. Not every system can or should hide everything from its users. For

instance, due to the existence of a fixed and finite speed of light there will always be more latency on accessing resources distant from the user. If one expects real-time interaction with the distributed system, this may be very noticeable.

2.11 TRANSPARENCIES IN DISTRIBUTED DATABASE DESIGN

Transparency refers to the separation of the higher-level semantics of a system from lower-level implementation issues. In a distributed system, transparency hides the implementation details from users of the system. In other words, the user believes that he or she is working with a centralized database system, and that all the complexities of a distributed database are either hidden or transparent to the user. A distributed DBMS may have various levels of transparency.

In a DDBMS, the following four main categories of transparency have been identified:

1. Distribution transparency
2. Transaction transparency
3. Performance transparency
4. DBMS transparency

2.11.1 DISTRIBUTION TRANSPARENCY

Distribution transparency allows the user to perceive the database as a single, logical entity. In other words, distribution transparency refers to the degree or extends to which details of fragmentation, replication and location transparency are hidden from users. If a user sees all fragmentation, allocation and replication the distributed DBMS is said to have no distribution transparency. The user needs to know that the data are fragmented and the location of fragments for retrieving data, then it is called local mapping transparency. If a system supports higher degree of distribution transparency, the user sees a single integrated schema with no details of fragmentation, allocation or distribution. The distributed DBMS stores all the details in the distribution catalog. All these distribution transparencies are discussed in the following:

(a) Fragmentation transparency – Fragmentation transparency means that objects are accessed without knowledge of any possible fragmentation. Fragmentation transparency hides the fact from users that the data are fragmented. This is the highest level of distribution transparency. If a distributed system has fragmentation transparency, then the user must not be aware regarding the fragmentation of data. As a result, database accesses must be based on global schema and the user need not to specify the particular fragment names or data locations.

Example 2.3

Consider the relation Employee (<u>emp-id</u>, emp-name, designation, salary, emp-branch, project-no) is fragmented and stored in different sites of a distributed DBMS. Further assume the fragmentation of the Employee relation. Therefore, to retrieve the names of all employees of branch number 20 from Employee relation, the user will write the following SQL statement:

Select emp-name from Employee where emp-branch = 20

This SQL statement is same as centralized DBMS.

(b) Location transparency – In other words it is an idea that the resources can be accessed by a user from anywhere on the network without knowing where the resource is located. A file could be on the user's own PC, or thousands of miles away on other servers. Location transparency is the middle level of distribution transparency. To retrieve data from a distributed database with location transparency, the end user or programmer has to specify the database fragment names but need not specify where these fragments are located in the distributed system.

Example 2.4

Suppose that the tuples of the above Employee relation is horizontally partitioned into two fragments EMP1 and EMP2 depending on the selection predicates "emp-id ≤ 100" and "emp-id>100". Hence the user is aware that the Employee relation is horizontally fragmented into two relations EMP1 and EMP2, but they have no idea in which sites these relations are stored. Thus, the user will write the following SQL statement for the above query "retrieve the names of all employees of branch number 20".

Select emp-name from EMP1 where emp-branch = 20
union
Select emp-name from EMP2 where emp-branch = 20.

(c) Replication transparency - A distributed system often employs data replication to ensure a fast response from databases and to enable the system to be resilient to hardware errors. Replication transparency is the term used to describe the fact that the user should be unaware that data is replicated. Replication transparency is closely related to location transparency and it is implied by location transparency. However, it may be possible for a distributed system not to have location transparency but to have replication transparency. In such cases, the user has to mention the location of the fragments of the replication transparency. In such cases, the user has to mention the location of the fragments of a relation for data access. The replication transparency is illustrated in the example 2.4.

Example 2.5

Suppose that the horizontal fragments EMP1 and EMP2 of the Employee relation in example 2.3 are replicated and stored in different sites of the distributed system. Furthermore, assume that the distributed DBMS supports replication transparency. In this case, the user will write the following SQL statement for the query "retrieve the names of all employees of branch number 20 whose salary is greater than Rs. 50,000":

Select emp-name from copy1 EMP1 where emp-branch = 20 and salary > 50,000

union

Select emp-name from EMP2 where emp-branch = 20 and salary > 50,000

Similarly, the above query can be rewritten as follows for a distributed DBMS with replication transparency which does not exhibit location transparency.

Select emp-name from EMP1 at site 1 where emp-branch = 20 and salary > 50,000

union

Select emp-name from EMP2 at site where emp-branch = 20 and salary > 50,000

(d) Local mapping transparency –Local transparency refers that user are aware regarding both the fragment names and the location of fragments, taking into account that any replication of the fragments may exist. If a distributed system has local mapping transparency, then the user has to explicitly mention both the fragment name and the location for data access. It is the lowest level of distribution transparency.

Example 2.6

Let us consider the relation Project (<u>project-id</u>, project-name, project-type, project-leader-id, branch-no, amount) is horizontally partitioned into two fragments P1 and P2 depending on the project-type "inside" and "abroad". Assume that the fragmented relations P1 and P2 are replicated and stored in different sites of the distributed DBMS. With local mapping transparency, the user will write the following SQL statement for the query "retrieve project names and branch numbers of all the projects where the project amount is greater than Rs. 10,000,000":

Select project-name, branch-no from copy1 of P1 at site 1 where amount > 10000000

union

Select project-name, branch-no from copy3 of P2 at site 1 where amount > 10000000

Hence, it is assumed that replicas of fragments p1 and P2 of the Project relation are allocated to different sites of the distributed system such as site1, site3, and site4.

(e) Naming transparency – Naming transparency means that a unique name is provided for each object in the database. If a system supports naming transparency, the user will specify the alias names of database objects for data accessing. In a distributed database system, each database object must have a unique name. The distributed DBMS must ensure that no two sites create a database object with the same name. To ensure this, one solution is to create a central name server, which ensures the uniqueness of names of database objects in the system.

Disadvantages of naming transparency as follows:

- Loss of some local autonomy, because during creation of new database objects, each site has to ensure uniqueness of names of database objects from the central name server.
- Performance may be degraded, if the central site becomes a bottleneck.
- Low availability and reliability because if the central site fails, the remaining sites cannot create any new database object. As availability decreases, reliability also decreases.

A second alternative solution is to prefix a database object with the identifier of the site that created it. This naming method will also be able to identify each fragment along with each of its copies. Therefore, copy2 of fragment 1 of Employee relation created at site 3 can be referred as S3. Employee.F1.C2.The only problem with this approach is that it results in loss of distribution transparency.

One solution that can overcome the disadvantages of the above two approaches is the use of aliases (sometimes called synonyms) for each database object. It is the responsibility of the distributed database system to map an alias to the appropriate database object.

The distributed system R* differentiates between an object's name and its system-wide name (global name). The printname is the name through which the users refer to the database object. The system-wide or global name is a globally unique internal identifier for the database object that is never changed. The system-wide name contains four components as follows:

- **Creator ID** – This represents a unique site identifier for the user who created the database object.
- **Creator site ID** – It indicates a globally unique identifier for the site from which the database object was created.
- **Local name** – It represents an unqualified name for the database object.

- **Birth-site ID** – This represents a globally unique identifier for the site at which the object was initially stored.

For example, the system-wide name, Project-leader@India.localBranch@kolkata, represents and objects with local name local Branch, created by Project Leader in India site and initially stored at the Kolkata site.

Distribution transparency is supported by a distributed data dictionary or a distributed data catalog. The distributed data catalog contains the description of the entire database as seen by the database administrator. The database description is known as distributed global schema.

Example 2.7

In this example, data distribution transparencies for update application have been considered. Assume that the relational schema Employee (emp-id, emp-name, designation, salary, emp-branch, project-no)is fragmented as follows:

EMP1: $s_{\text{emp-branch}\leq 10} (\tilde{O}_{\text{emp-id, emp-name, emp-branch, project-no}} (\text{Employee})$

EMP2: $s_{\text{emp-branch}\leq 10} (\tilde{O}_{\text{emp-id, salary, design}} (\text{Employee})$

EMP3: $s_{\text{emp-branch}>10} (\tilde{O}_{\text{emp-id, emp-name, emp-branch, project-no}} (\text{Employee}))$

EMP44: $s_{\text{emp-branch}>10} (\tilde{O}_{\text{emp-id, salary, design}} (\text{Employee}))$

Consider an update request is generated in the distributed system that the branch of an Employee with emp-id 55 will be modified from emp-branch 20. The user written queries are illustrated in the following for different levels of transparency such as fragmentation transparency, location transparency, and local mapping transparency.

Fragmentation transparency:

Update Employee

set emp-branch = 20

where emp-id = 55.

Local transparency:

Select emp-id = 55

where emp-id = 55

Select salary, design into $slary, $design, from Emp2

where emp-id = 55

Insert into Emp3 (emp-id, emp-name, emp-branch, project-no)

values (55, $emp-name, 20, $project-no)

Insert into Emp4 (emp-id, salary, design)

values (55, $salary, $design)

Delete from Emp1 where emp-id = 55

Delete from Emp2 where emp-id = 55

Local Mapping transparency:

Select emp-name, project-no, into $emp-name, $project-no from Emp1 at site 1

where emp-id = 55

Select salary, design into $salary, $design from Emp2 at site 2

where emp-id = 55

Insert into Emp3 at site 3 (emp-id, emp-name, emp-branch, project-no)

values (55, $emp-name, 20, $project-no)

Insert into Emp3 at site 7 (emp-id, emp-name, emp-branch, project-no)

values (55, $emp-name, 20, $project-no)

Insert into Emp4 at site 4 (emp-id, salary, design)

Values (55, $salary, $design)

Delete from Emp1 at site 1 where emp-id = 55

Delete from Emp1 at site 5 where emp-id = 55

Delete from Emp2 at site 2 where emp-id = 55

Delete from Emp2 at site 6 where emp-id = 55

Hence, it is assumed that the fragment Emp1 has two replicas stored at site 1 and site 5, respectively, the fragment Emp2 has two replicas stored at site 2 and site 6, respectively, the fragment Emp3 as two replicas stored at site 3 and site 7, respectively, and the fragment Emp4 has two replicas stored at site 4 and site 8, respectively.

2.11.2 TRANSACTION TRANSPARENCY

Transaction transparency in a distributed DBMS ensures that all distributed transactions maintain the distributed database integrity and consistency. A distributed transaction can update data stored at many different sites connected by a computer network. Each transaction is divided into several subtransactions (represented by an agent), one for each site that has to be accessed. Transaction transparency ensures that the distributed transaction will be successfully completed only if all subtransactions executing in different sites associated with the transaction are completed successfully. Thus, a distributed DBMS requires complex mechanism to manage the execution of distributed transactions and to ensure the database consistency and integrity. Moreover, transaction transparency becomes more complex due to fragmentation, allocation, and replication schemas in distributed DBMS. Two

further aspects of transaction transparency are concurrency transparency and failure transparency, which are discussed in the following:

(a) Concurrency transparency – While multiple users may compete for and share a single resource, this should not be apparent to any of them. Concurrency transparency in a distributed DBMS ensures that all concurrent transactions (distributed and non-distributed) execute independently in the system and are logically consistent with the results, that are obtained if transactions are executed one at a time in some arbitrary serial order. The distributed DBMS requires complex mechanism to ensure that both local and global transactions do not interfere with each other. Moreover, the distributed DBMS must ensure the consistency of all subtrasactions involved with a global transaction.

Replication adds extra complexity to the issue of concurrency in a distributed DBMS. For example, if a copy of a replicated data item is updated, then the update must be propagated eventually to all copies. One obvious solution to update all copies of a data item is to propagate the changes as part of the original transaction, making it an atomic operation. However, the update process is delayed if one of the sites holding a copy is not reachable during update due to site or communication link failure. If there are many copies of the data item, the probability of succeeding the transaction decreases exponentially.

An alternative solution is to propagate the update to those sites only that are currently available. The remaining sites must be updated when they become available. Therefore, a further strategy is to update the copies of a data item asynchronously, sometimes after the original update.

(b) Failure transparency – In a distributed system, **failure transparency** refers to the extent to which errors and subsequent recoveries of hosts and services within the system are invisible to users and applications. For example, if a server fails, but users are automatically redirected to another server and never notice the failure, the system is said to exhibit *high failure transparency.*

Failure transparency in a distributed DBMS promises that the system will continue its normal execution in the event of failure and it must maintain the atomicity of the global transaction. The atomicity of global transaction ensures that subtransaction of the global transaction are either all committed or all aborted. Thus, the distributed DBMS must synchronize the global transaction to ensure that all subtransactions have completed successfully before recording a final COMMIT for the global transaction. Failure transparency also ensures the durability of both local and global transactions. In addition to all different types of failures in centralized system, the following additional types of failures can occur in a distributed environment:

- The loss of a message
- The failure of a communication link
- The failure of a site
- Network partitioning

Functions that are due to failures will be picked up by another network node and continued.

Failure transparency is one of the most difficult types of transparency to achieve since it is often difficult to determine whether a server has actually failed, or whether it is simply responding very slowly. Additionally, it is generally impossible to achieve full failure transparency in a distributed system since networks are unreliable.

There is also usually a trade-off between achieving a high level of failure transparency and maintaining an adequate level of system performance. For example, if a distributed system attempts to mask a transient server failure by having the client try to contact the failed server multiple times; performance of the system may be negatively affected. In this case, it would have been preferable to have given up earlier and tried another server.

2.11.3 PERFORMANCE TRANSPARENCY

Performance transparency in a distributed DBMS ensures that it performs its tasks as centralized DBMS. Performance transparency in a distributed assures that the system does not suffer from any performance degradation due to the distributed architecture and it will choose the most cost-effective strategy to execute a request. In a distribute environment, the distributed Query processor maps a data request into an ordered sequence of operations on local databases. In this context, the added complexity of fragmentation, allocation and replication schemas is to be considered.

The distributed query processor has to take decision regarding the following issues:

- To perform a data request as to which fragment to access.
- If the fragment is replicated, which copy of the fragment to use.
- Which data location should be used to perform a data request?

The distributed Query processor determines an execution strategy that would be optimized with respect to some cost function.

Typically, the costs associated with a distributed data request include the following:

- The access time (I/O) cost involved in accessing the physical data on disk.

- The CPU time cost incurred when performing operations on data in main memory.
- The communication cost associated with the transmission of data across the network.

Number of query processing and query optimization techniques have been developed for distributed database system: some of them minimize the total cost of query execution time [Sacco and Yao 1982], and some of them attempt to maximize the parallel execution of operations [Epstein etal., 1978] to minimize the response time of queries.

2.11.4 DBMS TRANSPARENCY

DBMS transparency in a distributed environment hides the knowledge that the local DBMSs may be different and is, therefore, only applicable to heterogeneous distributed DBMSs. This is also known as heterogeneity transparency, which allows the integration of several different local DBMSs (relational, network, and hierarchical) under a common global schema. It is the responsibility of distributed DBMS to translate the data requests from the global schema to local DBMS schemas to provide DBMS transparency.

2.12 DATA REPLICATION

Replication is useful in improving the availability of data. The most extreme case is replication of the *whole database* at every site in the distributed system, thus creating a fully replicated distributed database. This can improve availability remarkably because the system can continue to operate as long as at least one site is up. It also improves performance of retrieval for global queries, because the result of such a query can be obtained locally from any one site; hence, a retrieval query can be processed at the local site where it is submitted, if that site includes a server module. The disadvantage of full replication is that it can slow down update operations drastically, since a single logical update must be performed on every copy of the database to keep the copies consistent. This is especially true if many copies of the database exist. Full replication makes the concurrency control and recovery techniques more expensive than they would be if there were no replications.

The other extreme from full replication involves having no replication—that is, each fragment is stored at exactly one site. In this case all fragments *must be* disjoint, except for the repetition of primary keys among vertical (or mixed) fragments. This is also called nonredundant allocation.

Between these two extremes, we have a wide spectrum of partial replication of the data—that is, some fragments of the database may be replicated whereas others may not. The number of copies of each fragment can range from one up

to the total number of sites in the distributed system. A special case of partial replication is occurring heavily in applications where mobile workers—such as sales forces, financial planners, and claims adjustors—carry partially replicated databases with them on laptops and personal digital assistants and synchronize them periodically with the server database (Note 5). A description of the replication of fragments is sometimes called a replication schema.

Replication is the process of sharing information so as to ensure consistency between redundant resources, such as software or hardware components, to improve reliability, fault-tolerance, or accessibility. It could be data replication if the same data is stored on multiple storage devices or computation replication if the same computing task is executed many times. A computational task is typically replicated in space, i.e. executed on separate devices, or it could be replicated in time, if it is executed repeatedly on a single device. The access to a replicated entity is typically uniform with access to a single, non-replicated entity. The replication itself should be transparent to an external user. Also, in a failure scenario, a failover of replicas is hidden as much as possible.

It is common to talk about active and passive replication in systems that replicate data or services. Active replication is performed by processing the same request at every replica. In passive replication, each single request is processed on a single replica and then its state is transferred to the other replicas. If at any time one master replica is designated to process all the requests, then we are talking about the primary-backup scheme (master-slave scheme) predominant in high-availability clusters. On the other side, if any replica processes a request and then distributes a new state, then this is a multi-primary scheme (called multi-master in the database field). In the multi-primary scheme, some form of distributed concurrency control must be used, such as distributed lock manager.

Load balancing is different from task replication, since it distributes a load of different (not the same) computations across machines, and allows a single computation to be dropped in case of failure. Load balancing, however, sometimes uses data replication (esp. multi-master) internally, to distribute its data among machines.

Backup is different from replication, since it saves a copy of data unchanged for a long period of time. Replicas on the other hand are frequently updated and quickly lose any historical state.

2.12.1 REPLICATION IN DISTRIBUTED SYSTEMS

Replication is one of the oldest and most important topics in the overall area of distributed systems. Whether one replicates data or computation, the objective is to have some group of processes that handle incoming events. If we replicate data, these processes are passive and operate only to maintain the stored data, reply to read requests, and apply updates. When we replicate computation, the usual goal is to provide fault-tolerance. For example, a replicated service might be used to control a telephone switch, with the objective of ensuring that even if the primary controller fails, the backup can take over its functions. But the underlying needs are the same in both cases: by ensuring that the replicas see the same events in equivalent orders, they stay in consistent states and hence any replica can respond to queries.

2.12.2 REPLICATION MODELS IN DISTRIBUTED SYSTEMS

A number of widely cited models exist for data replication, each having its own properties and performance:

1. **Transactional replication:** This is the model for replicating transactional data, for example a database or some other form of transactional storage structure. The one-copy serializability model is employed in this case, which defines legal outcomes of a transaction on replicated data in accordance with the overall ACID properties that transactional systems seek to guarantee.
2. **State machine replication:** This model assumes that replicated process is a deterministic finite state machine and that atomic broadcast of every event is possible. It is based on a distributed computing problem called distributed consensus and has a great deal in common with the transactional replication model. This is sometimes mistakenly used as synonym of active replication.
3. **Virtual synchrony:** This computational model is used when a group of processes cooperate to replicate in-memory data or to coordinate actions. The model defines a new distributed entity called a process group. A process can join a group, which is much like opening a file: the process is added to the group, but is also provided with a checkpoint containing the current state of the data replicated by group members. Processes can then send events (multicasts) to the group and will see incoming events in the identical order, even if events are sent concurrently. Membership changes are handled as a special kind of platform-generated event that delivers a new membership view to the processes in the group.

Levels of performance vary widely depending on the model selected. Transactional replication is slowest, at least when one-copy serializability guarantees are desired (better performance can be obtained when a database uses log-based replication, but at the cost of possible inconsistencies if a failure causes part of the log to be lost). Virtual synchrony is the fastest of the three models, but the handling of failures is less rigorous than in the transactional model. State machine replication lies somewhere in between;

the model is faster than transactions, but much slower than virtual synchrony. The virtual synchrony model is popular in part because it allows the developer to use either active or passive replication. In contrast, state machine replication and transactional replication are highly constraining and are often embedded into products at layers where end-users would not be able to access them.

EXERCISES

1. What do you mean by distributed database design?
2. Explain the reference architecture for a distributed database?
3. Explain the framework for distributed database design?
4. Explain the alternative approaches for distributed database design?
5. What are the objectives of data distribution?
6. What are the different alternative strategies for data allocation?
7. Explain various distribution design issues?
8. Explain various types of data fragmentation?
9. What do you mean by allocation?
10. What do you mean by data allocation?
11. Explain the concept of transparency?
12. Explain various types of transparencies in distributed system?
13. Explain the transparencies in distributed database design?
14. What do you mean by data replication?
15. Explain replication models in distributed systems?

CHAPTER 3

DISTRIBUTED DATABASE SYSTEM ARCHITECTURE

3.1 INTRODUCTION

A **distributed database** is a database that is under the control of a central database management system (DBMS) in which storage devices are not all attached to a common CPU. It may be stored in multiple computers located in the same physical location, or may be dispersed over a network of interconnected computers. Collections of data (e.g. in a database) can be distributed across multiple physical locations. A distributed database can reside on network servers on the Internet, on corporate intranets or extranets, or on other company networks. Replication and distribution of databases improve database performance at end-user worksites. To ensure that the distributive databases are up to date and current, there are two processes: replication and duplication. Replication involves using specialized software that looks for changes in the distributive database. Once the changes have been identified, the replication process makes all the databases look the same. The replication process can be very complex and time consuming depending on the size and number of the distributive databases. This process can also require a lot of time and computer resources. Duplication on the other hand is not as complicated. It basically identifies one database as a master and then duplicates that database. The duplication process is normally done at a set time after hours. This is to ensure that each distributed location has the same data. In the duplication process, changes to the master database only are allowed. This is to ensure that local data will not be overwritten. Both of the processes can keep the data current in all distributive locations.

Besides distributed database replication and fragmentation, there are many other distributed database design technologies. For example, local autonomy, synchronous and asynchronous distributed database technologies. These technologies' implementation can and does depend on the needs of the business and the sensitivity/confidentiality of the data to be stored in the database, and hence the price the business is willing to spend on ensuring data security, consistency and integrity. The architecture of a system reflects the structure of the underlying system. It defines the different components of the system, the functions of these components and the overall interactions and relationships between these components. This concept is true for general computer systems as well as for software systems. The software architecture of a program or computing system is the structure or structures of the system, which comprises software elements or modules, the externally visible properties of these elements and the relationships between them. Software architecture can be thought of as the representation of an engineering system and the process(es) and discipline(s) for effectively implementing the design(s) of such a system. A distributed database system can be considered as a large-scale software system; thus, the architecture of a distributed system can be defined in a manner similar to that of software systems. This chapter introduces the different alternative reference architectures of distributed database systems such as client/server, peer-to-peer and MDBSs.

3.2 DDBMS STANDARDISATION AND ARCHITECTURE MODELS: OVERVIEW

Figure 3.1 shows the alternatives in implementing DDBMSs. Basically, there are three dimensions for databases, DDBMSs, and applications:

- distribution, which means that databases, DDBMSs, and applications can be located centrally or distributed in a network,
- autonomy, means that the control of databases, DDBMSs, and applications can be done centrally, or autonomous, or in between, and
- heterogeneity means that databases, DDBMSs, and applications can be of the same type or of different types.

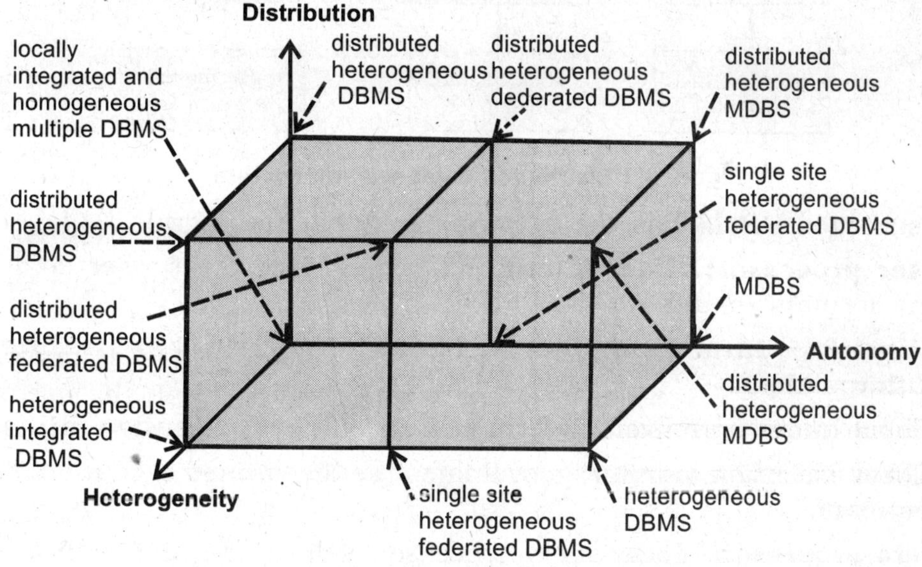

Figure 3.1 DDBMS implementation alternatives

Broadly speaking, we can category all DDBSs into three types of architectures using the ANSI/SPARC DBMS architecture: distributed database architecture, federated database architecture, and multidatabase architecture. Figure 3.2 shows a distributed database architecture where

- **External schema:** supports user applications and user access to the database.

- **Global conceptual schema:** supports the enterprise view of the data and describes the logical structure of the data at all the sites.
- **Local conceptual schema:** supports the logical organisation at each site.
- **Local internal schema:** supports the physical data organisation on each site.
- **Global directory/Dictionary:** supports global mappings.

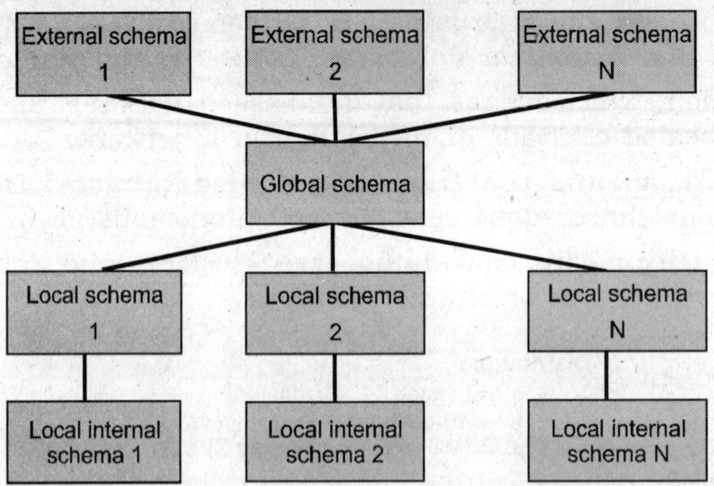

Figure 3.2 Distributed database architecture

A distributed DBMS has the following components (Figure 3.3):

- **User processor:** User interface handler: interprets user commands and formats results
- Semantic data controller: checks integrity constraints and authorisations
- Global query optimizer: determines an efficient execution strategy
- Global execution monitor: coordinates the distributed execution of user requests.
- **Data processor:** Local query processor: selects the best path to access data
- Local recovery manager: manages the local database consistency in case of failures
- Runtime support processor: is the interface to the OS.

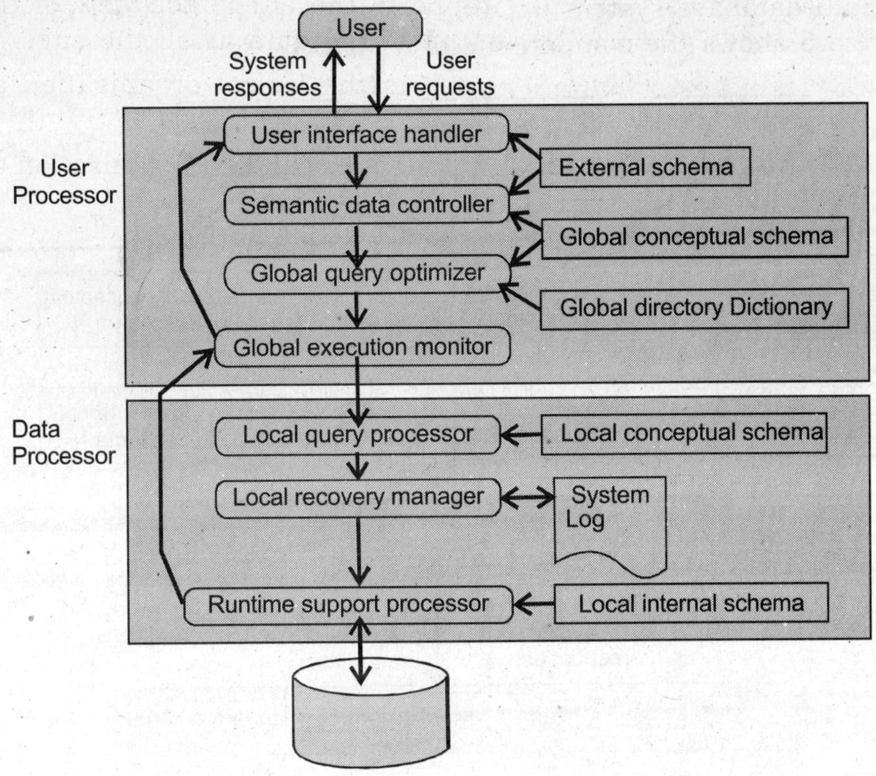

Figure 3.3 Components of a distributed DBMS

Figure 3.4 depicts a federated database system (FDBS) architecture.

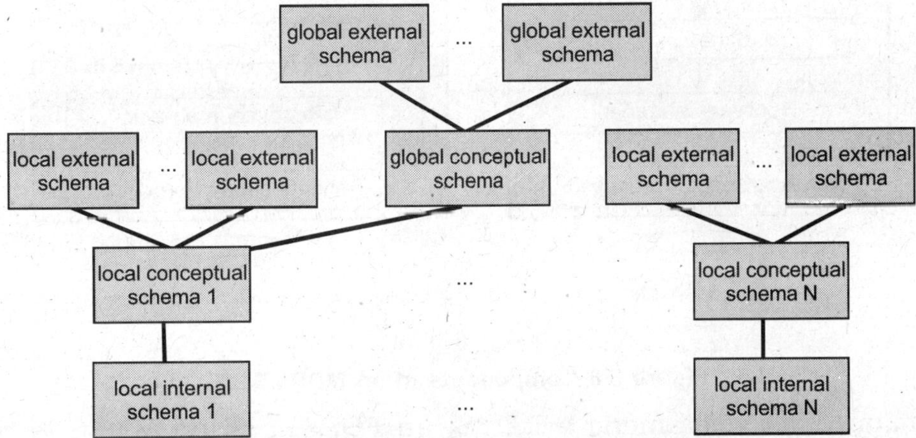

Figure 3.4 Federated database architecture

The multi-database system (MDBS) architecture is depicted in Figure 3.5 and Figure 3.6 shows the components of a MDBS.

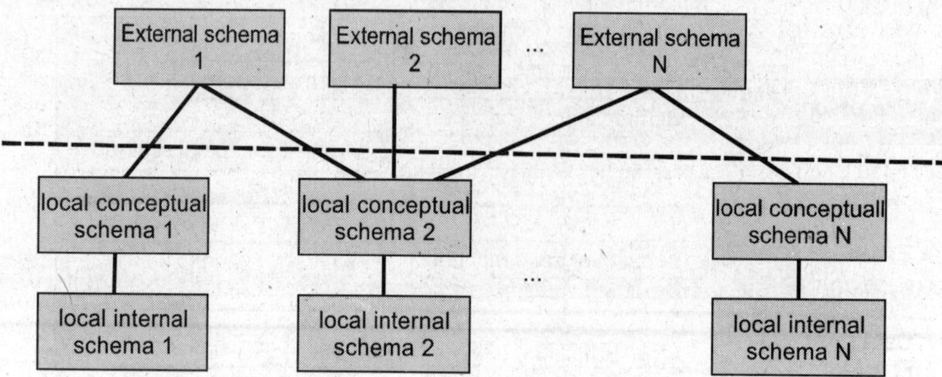

Figure 3.5 Multi-database system architecture

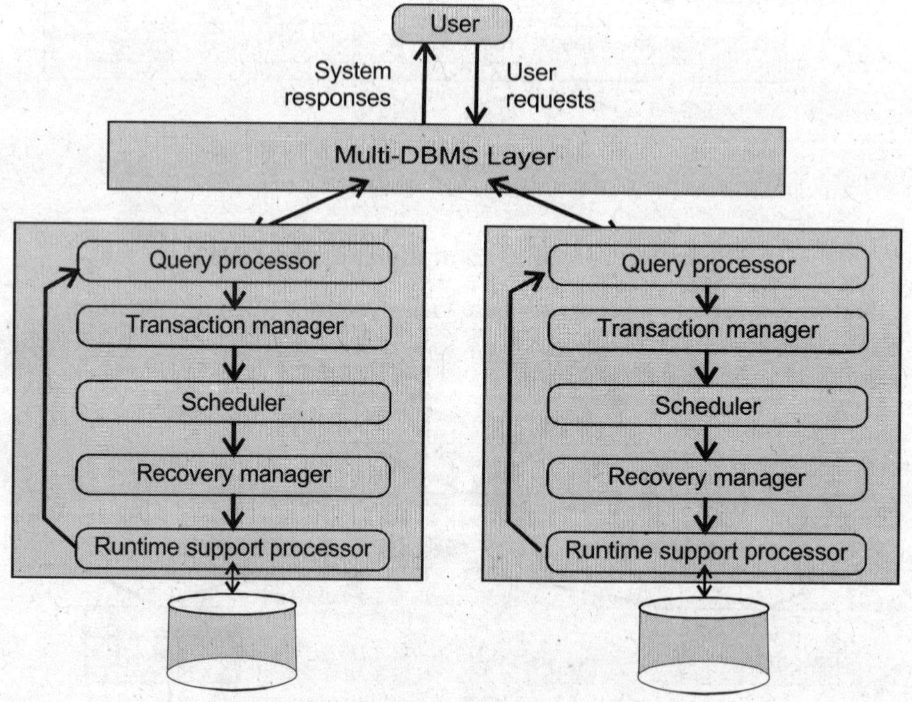

Figure 3.6 Components of an MDBMS

The main difference among a DDBS, an FDBS, and an MDBS is that, a DDBS has a global schema and all accesses to the DDBS have to go through the global schema. While an FDBS also has a global schema, the accesses to the FDBS can go through the global schema, or through individual databases. An MDBS has no global schema, but may have some external schemas that group the views of several databases. The accesses to the MDBS can go through an external schema, or through individual databases. For convenience, however, we use DDBS to include the meanings of DDBS, FDBS and MDBS, unless we explicitly distinguish them.

3.3 GLOBAL DIRECTORY ISSUES

There are three ways to view the management of the global directory of a DDBS.

- **Types:** A global directory to the entire database or many local directories to each site
- **Location:** Maintained centrally at one site or in a distributed fashion by a number of sites
- **Replication:** A single copy of the directory or multiple copies.

Figure 3.7 shows the strategies for managing the global directory in a DDBS:

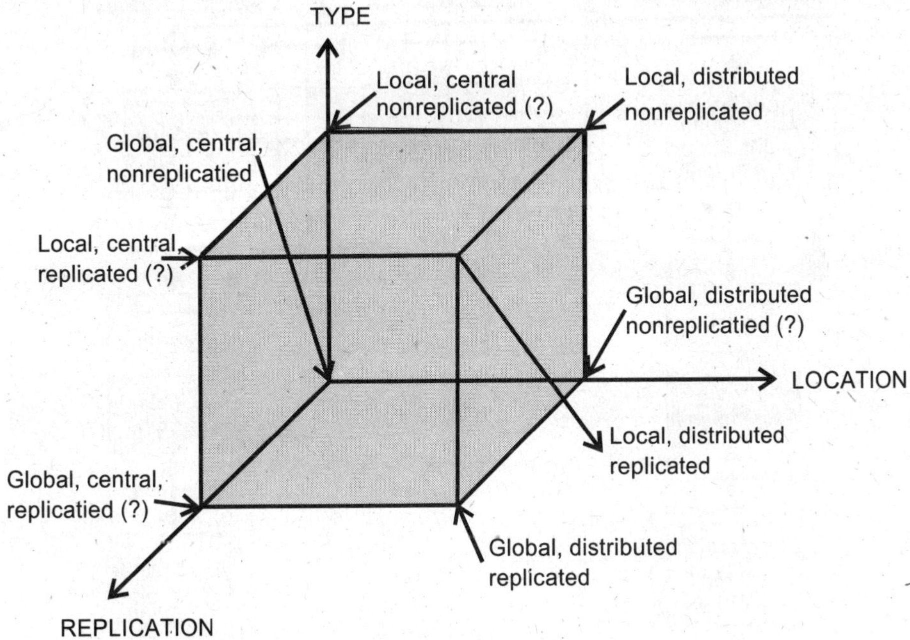

Figure 3.7 Alternative directory management strategies

3.4 ARCHITECTURAL MODELS FOR DISTRIBUTED DBMSS

Let us consider the possible ways in which multiple databases may be put together for sharing by multiple DBMSs. We use a classification (Figure 3.8)

that organizes the systems as characterized with respect to (1) the autonomy of local systems, (2) their distribution, and (3) their heterogeneity.

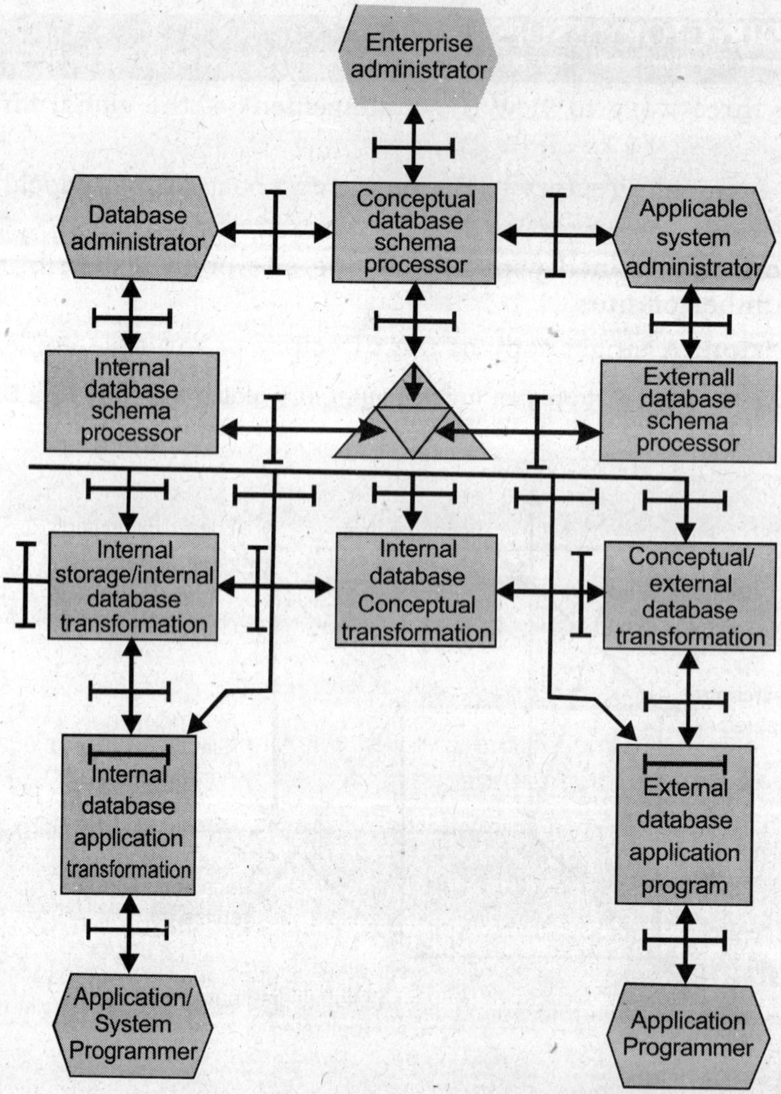

Figure 3.8 Partial Schematic of the ANSI/SPARC Architectural Model.

3.4.1 AUTONOMY

Autonomy refers to the distribution of control, not of data. It indicates the degree to which individual DBMSs can operate independently. Autonomy is a function of a number of factors such as whether the component systems exchange information, whether they can independently execute transactions, and whether one is allowed to modify them. Requirements of an autonomous system have been specified in a variety of ways. For example lists these requirements as follows:

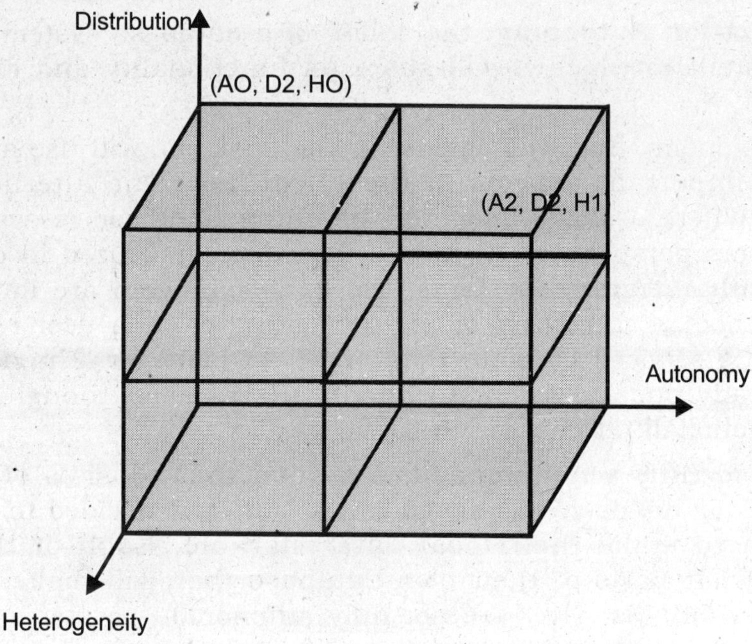

Figure 3.9 DBMS Implementation Alternatives

1. The local operations of the individual DBMSs are not affected by their participation in the multidatabase system.
2. The manner in which the individual DBMSs process queries and optimize them should not be affected by the execution of global queries that access multiple databases.
3. System consistency or operation should not be compromised when individual DBMSs join or leave the multidatabase confederation.

The concept of database autonomy refers to the ability of each local database system to have control over its own data and to perform various operations on its own data. Bukhres et al. define database autonomy as "the ability of each local database system to control access to its data by other database systems, as well as the ability to access and manipulate its own data independently of other systems". Sheth and Larson describe four types of autonomy:

1. **Design Autonomy:** the ability of a database system to choose its own design with respect to data model, query language, semantic interpretation of the data, the operations supported by the system, and the implementation of the system (e.g., concurrency control algorithms).

2. **Communication Autonomy:** the ability of a database system to decide whether and when to communicate with other database systems.
3. **Execution Autonomy:** the ability of a database system to decide how to execute local operations without interference from external operations, and the order in which to execute external operations.
4. **Association Autonomy:** the ability of a database system to determine the extent to which it will share its functionality and resources with others.

In the taxonomy that we consider in the book, we will use a classification that covers important aspects of these features. One alternative is tight integration. Where a single-image of the entire database is available to any user who users perspective the data is logically centralized in one database. In these tightly-integrated systems, the data managers are implemented so that one of them is in control of the processing of each user request even if that request is serviced by more than one data manager. The data managers do not typically operate as independent DBMSs even though they usually have the functionality to do so.

Next we identify semiautonomous system that consists of DBMSs that can (and usually do) operate independently, but have decided to participate in a federation to make their local data sharable. Each of these DBMSs determines what parts of their own database they will make accessible to users of other DBMSs. They are not fully autonomous systems because they need to be modified to enable them to exchange information with one another.

The last alternative that we consider is total isolation, where the individual systems are stand-alone DBMSs, which know neither of the existence of other DBMSs nor how to communicate with them. In such systems, the processing of user transactions that access multiple databases is especially difficult since there is no global control over the execution of individual DBMSs.

It is important to note at this point that the three alternatives that we consider for autonomous systems are not the only possibilities. We simply highlight the three most popular ones.

3.4.2 DISTRIBUTION

Whereas autonomy refers to the distribution of control, the distribution dimension of the taxonomy deals with data. Of course we are considering the physical distribution of data over multiple sites; as we discussed in Chapter 1, the user sees the data as one logical pool. There are a number of ways DBMSs have been distributed. We abstract these alternatives into two classes: Client/server distributed option, the taxonomy identifies there alternative architectures.

The client/server distribution, which has become quite popular in the last number of years, concentrates data management duties at servers while the clients focus on providing the application environment including the user interface. The server DBMSs represent the first attempt at distributing functionally. There are a variety of ways of structuring them each providing a different level of distribution. Which we devote to client/server DBMS architectures. What is important at this point is that the sites on a network are distinguished as "clients" and "servers" and their functionally is different.

In peer-to-peer systems, there is no distinction to client machines versus servers. Each machine has full DBMS functionally and can with other machines execute queries transactions. These systems which are also called fully distributed are our main focus in this book, even though many of the techniques carry over to client/server systems as well.

3.4.3 HETEROGENEITY

Heterogeneity may occur in various forms in distributed systems ranging from hardware heterogeneity and difference in networking protocols to variations in models managers. The important ones from the transaction management protocols. Representing data with different tools create heterogeneity because of the inherent expressive powers and limitations of individual data models. Heterogeneity in paradigms in different data models (set-at-a-time access in relational system versus record-at-a-time access in network and hierarchical system), but also covers differences in languages even what the individual systems use the same data model. Different query languages that use the same data model often select very different methods expressing identical requests (e.g., DB2 uses SQL, while INGRES uses QUEL).

3.4.4 ARCHITECTURAL ALTERNATIVES

Let us consider the architectural alternatives starting at the origin in Figure 3.9 and moving along the autonomy dimension. For identification, we use a notation based on the alternatives along the three dimensions. The dimensions are identified as A (autonomy), D (distribution) and H(heterogencity). The alternatives courses have different meaning along each of the dimensions. Along the autonomy dimension, 0 represents tight integration, 1 represents semiautonomous systems and 2 represents total isolation. Along distribution 0 is for no distribution 1 is for client/server systems and 2is for peer-to-peer distribution. Finally along the heterogeneous systems. In figure 3.9, we have identified two alternative architectures that are focus of this book. (A0, D2, H0) which is a (peer-to-peer) distributed homogeneous DBMS and (A2, D2, H1) which is a (peer-to-peer) architectural alternatives that are identified system. We should note all the architectural that are identified by this design space are meaningful. We will, nevertheless discuss each and indicate the unrealistic architectures where appropriate.

The dimensions are identified as A (autonomy), D (distribution) and H (heterogeneity).

- (A0, D0, H0): *composite system* by logically integrated. The system has no distribution or heterogeneity but a set of multiple DBMSs.
- (A0, D0, H1): one has multiple data managers that are heterogeneous but provide an integrated view to the user such as the access to network, hierarchical, and relational database residing on a single machine.
- (A0, D1, H0): the database is distributed even though an integrated view of the data is provided to users; e.g., client/server distribution.
- (A0, D2, H0): the same type of transparency is provided to the user in a fully distributed environment. No distinction among clients and servers, each site provides identical functionality; e.g., peer-to-peer distribution.
- (A1, D0, H0): *semiautonomous systems*, which are commonly termed federated DBMS.
- (A1, D0, H1): *heterogeneous federated DBMS*, mostly found in everyday; e.g., if we wish to provide an integrated view to the users, then it is necessary to hide the autonomy and heterogeneity of the component systems and establish a common interface.
- (A1, D1, H1): *distributed, heterogeneous federated DBMS*, place component systems on different machines for distribution; herein, autonomy and heterogeneity are more important than distribution.
- (A2, D0, H0): *multi-database system* (MDBS) architectures with full autonomy. There's no concept of cooperation and they do not even know how to talk to each other. A multi-database management system (multi-DBMS) provides for the management of this collection of autonomous databases and transparent access to it.
- (A2, D0, H1): maybe even more realistic than (A1, D0, H1), we want to build applications which access data from multiple storage systems with different characteristics.

  (A2, D1, H1) and (A2, D2, H1): both represent the case where component databases that make up the MDBS are distributed over a number of sites – called *distributed MDBS*, dealing with similar interoperability. In the case of client/server (A2, D1, H1), most of the interoperability concerns are delegated to *middleware systems* resulting in a *three layer architecture*.

3.5 HOMOGENEOUS AND HETEROGENEOUS DISTRIBUTED DBMSS

A distributed DBMS may be classified as homogenous or heterogeneous. In an ideal distributed database system, the sites would share a common global schema (although some relations may be stored only at some local sites), all sites would run the same database management software and the sites are aware of the existence of other sites. In a distributed system, if all sites use the same DBMS product, it is called a homogenous distributed database system. However, in reality, a distributed database has to be constructed by linking multiple already-existing database systems together, each with its own schema and possibly running different database management software. Such systems are called heterogeneous distributed database systems. In a heterogeneous distributed database system, sites may run different DBMS products that need not be based on the same underlying data model, and thus, the system may be composed of relational, network, hierarchical, and object-oriented DBMSs.

Homogeneous distributed DBMS provides several advantages such as simplicity, ease of designing and incremental growth. It is much easier to design and manage a homogeneous distributed DBMS than a heterogeneous one. In a homogeneous distributed DBMS, making the addition of a new site to the distributed system is much easier, thereby providing incremental growth. These systems also improve performance by exploiting the parallel processing capability of multiple sites.

Heterogeneous systems are usually constructed over a number of existing individual sites where each site has its own local databases and local DBMS software, and integration is considered at a later stage. To allow the necessary communications among the different sites in a heterogeneous distributed system, interoperability between different DBMS products is required. If a distributed system provides DBMS transparency, users are unware of the different DBMS products is required. If a distributed system provides DBMS transparency, users are unaware of the different DBMS products in the system, and therefore it allows users to submit their queries in the language of the DBMS at their local sites. Achieving DBMS transparency increases system complexity. Heterogeneity may occur at different levels in a distributed database system as listed in the following.

- different hardware
- different DBMS software
- different hardware and different DBMS software

If the hardware is different but the DBMS software is the same in a distributed system, the translation is straightforward between sites involving the change of codes and word lengths. Moreover, the differences among the sites at lower levels in a distributed system are usually managed by the communication software. Therefore, homogeneous distributed DBMS at each site, even if the processors and/or the operating systems are not the same.

If the DBMS software is different at different sites, the execution of global transactions becomes very complicated, as it involves the mapping of data

model to the equivalent data structures in another data model. For example, relations in the relational data model may be mapped into records and sets in the network data mode. The translation of query languages is also necessary. If both the hardware and DBMS software are different at different sites in a distributed system, the processing of global transactions becomes extremely complex, because translations of both hardware and DBMS software are required. The provision of a common conceptual schema, which is formed by integrating individual local conceptual schemas, adds extra complexity to the distributed processing. The integration of data models in different sites can be very difficult owing to the semantic heterogeneity.

Some relational systems that are part of a heterogeneous distributed DBSM use gateways, which convert the language and data model of each different DBMS into the language and data model of the relational system. Gateways are mechanisms that provide access to other systems. In a gateway, one vendor (e.g., Oracle) provides single direction access through its DBMS to another database managed by a different vendor's DBMS (e.g., IBM DB2). The two DBMSs need not share the same data model. For example, many RDBMS vendors provide gateways to hierarchical and network DBMSs. However, the gateway approach has some serious limitations as listed below.

- The gateway between two systems may be only a query translator, that is, it may not support transaction management even for a pair of systems.
- The gateway approach generally does not address the issue of homogenizing the structural and representational differences between different database schemas; that is, it is only concerned with the problem of translating a query expressed in one language into an equivalent expression in another language.

In this context, one solution is a multi-database system (MDBS) that resides on top of existing databases and file systems and provides a single logical database to its users. An MDBS maintains only the global schema against which users issue queries and updates.

3.6 CLIENT/SERVER SYSTEM

The **client–server model** of computing is a distributed application structure that partitions tasks or workloads between the providers of a resource or service, called servers, and service requesters, called clients. Often clients and servers communicate over a computer network on separate hardware, but both client and server may reside in the same system. A server machine is a host that is running one or more server programs which share their resources with clients. A client does not share any of its resources, but requests a server's content or service function. Clients therefore initiate communication sessions with servers which await incoming requests.

Client-server software architecture is versatile and flexible in today's fast-changing IT landscape. It is modular in structure and relies on messaging services for communication between components. They were designed to improve flexibility, usability, scalability, and interoperability. Software flexibility implies the ability for a program to change easily according to different users and different system requirements.

Usability refers to human-computer interaction and the ability of a software application to accomplish a user's goal. Some defining features are ease-of-use and a clear, logical process of evolution towards a goal. Scalability refers to a product's (be it hardware or software) ability to change in size or volume gracefully to meet user requests. Interoperability is the ability of software or hardware to function with other systems without requiring human intervention and manpower. Client-server software architecture aims to increase productivity through improvements in all of these categories.

Client-server architecture developed as a response to the limitations of file-sharing architectures, which require tons of bandwidth and can often stall or jam a network causing it to crash. They require low shared usage and low volume of data to be transferred. In client-server architecture, the database server replaced the file server. Relational data base management systems (DBMSs) answered user queries directly. Since only specific queries were being answered, only that data was transferred instead of entire files that slow down networks. It also improved consistency in data between users, since all users had access to the same updated information.

The general forces that drive the move to client/server systems are as follows:

- A strong business requirement for decentralized computing horsepower.
- Standard, powerful computers with user-friendly interfaces.
- Mature, shrink-wrapped user applications with widespread acceptance.
- Inexpensive, modular systems designed with enterprise class architecture, such as power and network redundancy and file archiving network protocols, to link them together.
- Growing cost/performance advantages of PC-based platforms.

Client-server architecture can be considered as a network environment that exchanges information between a server machine and a client machine where server has some resources that can be shared by different clients.

The client/server system is a versatile, message-based and modular infrastructure that is intended to improve usability, flexibility, interoperability and scalability as compared to centralized, mainframe, time-sharing computing.

In the simplest sense, the client and the server can be defined as follows:

- A client is an individual user's computer or a user application that does a certain amount of processing on its own and sends and receives requests to and from one or more servers for other processing and/or data.
- A Server consists of one or more computers or an application program the receives and processed requests from one or more client machines. A server is typically designed with some redundancies in power, network, computing, and file storage.

Usually, a client is defined as a requester of services, and a server is defined as the provider of services. A single machine can be both a client and a server depending on the software configuration. Sometimes, the term server or client refers to the software rather than the machines. Generally, server software runs on powerful computers dedicated for exclusive use of business applications. On the other hand, client software runs on common PCs or workstations. **The properties of a server are:**

- Passive (slave)
- Waiting for requests
- On request serves clients and sends reply.

The properties of a client are:

- Active (Master)
- Sending requests
- Waits until reply arrives.

A server can be stateless or stateful. A stateless server does not keep any information between requests. A stateful server can remember information between requests.

3.6.1 ADVANTAGES AND DISADVANTAGES OF CLIENT/SERVER SYSTEM

A client/server system provides a number of advantages over a powerful mainframe centralized system. The major advantage is that it improves usability, flexibility, interoperability and scalability as compared to centralized, time-sharing, mainframe computing.

3.6.1.1 ADVANTAGES OF CLIENT/SERVER ARCHITECTURE

The client/server model is particularly recommended for networks requiring a high degree of reliability, the main advantages being:

- **centralized resources**: given that the server is the centre of the network, it can manage resources that are common to all users, for example: a central database would be used to avoid problems caused by redundant and inconsistent data

- **improved security**: as the number of entry points giving access to data is not so important
- **server level administration**: as clients do not play a major role in this model, they require less administration
- **scalable network**: thanks to this architecture it is possible to remove or add clients without affecting the operation of the network and without the need for major modification
- A client/server system allows the end user to use a microcomputer's graphical user interfaces, thereby improving functionality and simplicity.
- It provides better performance at a reduced cost for hardware and software than alternative mini or mainframe solutions.
- A client–server architecture enables the roles and responsibilities of a computing system to be distributed among several independent computers that are known to each other only through a network. This creates an additional advantage to this architecture: greater ease of maintenance. For example, it is possible to replace, repair, upgrade, or even relocate a server while its clients remain both unaware and unaffected by that change.
- All data is stored on the servers, which generally have far greater security controls than most clients. Servers can better control access and resources, to guarantee that only those clients with the appropriate permissions may access and change data.
- Since data storage is centralized, updates to that data are far easier to administer in comparison to a P2P paradigm. In the latter, data updates may need to be distributed and applied to each peer in the network, which is both time-consuming and error-prone; there can be thousands or even millions of peers.
- Many mature client–server technologies are already available which were designed to ensure security, friendliness of the user interface, and ease of use.
- It functions with multiple different clients of different capabilities.
- A client/server system has the ability to distribute the computing workload between client workstations and shared servers.

3.6.1.2 DISADVANTAGES OF THE CLIENT/SERVER MODEL

Client/Server architecture also has the following drawbacks:

- **increased cost**: due to the technical complexity of the server
- As the number of simultaneous client requests to a given server increases, the server can become overloaded. Contrast that to a P2P

network, where its aggregated bandwidth actually increases as nodes are added, since the P2P network's overall bandwidth can be roughly computed as the sum of the bandwidths of every node in that network.

- The client/server architecture creates a more complex environment in which it is often difficult to manage different platforms (LANs, operating systems, DBMS etc.)
- In a client/server system, the operating system software is distributed over many machines rather than a single system, thereby increasing complexity.
- A client/server system may suffer from security problems as the number of users and processing sites increases.
- **A weak link**: the server is the only weak ling in the client/server network, given that the entire network is built around it! Fortunately, the server is highly fault tolerant (primarily thanks to the RAID system)
- The workstations are geographically distributed in a client/server system, and each of these workstations is administrated and controlled by individual departments, which adds extra complexity. Furthermore, communication cost is incurred with each processing.
- The client–server paradigm lacks the robustness of a good P2P network. Under client–server, should a critical server fail, clients' requests cannot be fulfilled. In P2P networks, resources are usually distributed among many nodes. Even if one or more nodes depart and abandon a downloading file, for example, the remaining nodes should still have the data needed to complete the download.
- The maintenance cost of a client/server system is greater than that of an alternative mini or mainframe solution.

3.6.2 ARCHITECTURE OF CLIENT/SERVER DISTRIBUTED SYSTEMS

Client/server architecture is a prerequisite to the proper development of client/server systems. The Client/server architecture is based on hardware and software components that interact to form a distributed system. In a client/server distributed database system, entire data can be viewed as a single logical database while at the physical level data may be distributed. Form the data organizational view, the architecture of a client/server distributed database system is mainly concentrated on software components of the system, and this system includes three main components: clients, servers and communications middleware.

(i) A **Client** is an individual computer or process or user's application that requests services from the server. A Client is also known as front-end application, as the end user usually interacts with the client process.

The software components required in the client machine are the client operating system, client DBMS and client graphical user interface. Client process is run on an operating system that has at least some multi-tasking capabilities. The end users interact with client side, which is responsible for managing the data that is cached in the client. In some client/server architectures, communication software is embedded into the client machine, as a substitute for communication middleware, to interact efficiently with other machines in the network.

(ii) A **Server** consists of one or more computers or is a computer process or application that provides services to clients. A Server is also known as back-end application, as the server process provides the background services for the client processes. A server provides most of the data management services such as query processing and optimization, transaction management, recovers management, storage management and integrity maintenance services to the clients. In addition, sometimes communication software is embedded into the server machine, instead of communication middleware, to manage communication with clients and other servers in the network.

Communication middleware is any process (es) through which clients and servers communicate with each other. The communication middleware is usually associated with a network that controls data and information transmission between clients and servers. Communication middleware software consists of three main components: application program interface (API), database translator and network translator. The API is public to client applications through which they can communicate with the communication middleware. The middleware API allows the client process to be database server-independent. The database translator translates the SQL requests into the specific database server syntax, thus enabling a DBMS from one vendor to communicate directly with a DBMS from another vendor, without using a gateway. The network translator manages the network communications protocols; thus, it allows clients to be network protocol-independent. To accomplish the connection between the client and the server, the communication middleware software operates at two different levels. The physical level deals with the communications between the client and the server computers (computer to computer) whereas the logical level deals with the communications between the client and the server processed (interprocess). The basic client/server architecture is illustrated in figure 3.10.

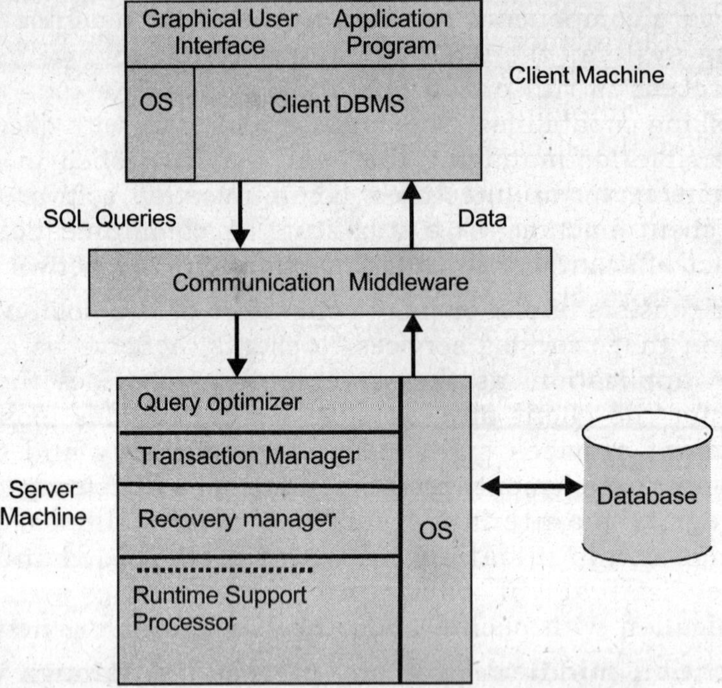

Figure 3.10 Client/Server Reference Architecture

The client/server architecture is intended to provide a scalable architecture, whereby each computer or process on the network is either a client or a server.

3.6.3 ARCHITECTURAL ALTERNATIVES FOR CLIENT/SERVER SYSTEMS

A client/server system can have several architectural alternatives known as two-tier, three-tier and multi-tier or n-tier.

Two-tier architecture – Two tier client-server software architectures improve usability and scalability. Usability is increased though user-friendly, form-based interfaces. Scalability is improved because two tiered systems can hold up to 100 users, whereas file server architectures can only accommodate 12. Two tiered architecture is best suited to homogeneous environments processing non-complex, non-time sensitive information.

A client/server architecture has two types of nodes on the network: clients and servers. As a result, these generic architectures are sometimes referred to as two-tier architectures.

Two tier architectures consist of three components: user system interfaces, processing management, and database management. User system interface (USI) is a component of an organization's decision support system, which includes human decision-makers. It provides a user friendly layer of communication to make requests of the server and offers multiple forms of input and output. USIs include features like display management services, sessions, text input, and dialog. Processing management includes process development, process implementation, process monitoring, and process resources services. Database management includes database and file services.

Two tier client-server designs derive its name from how it distributes work between client and server. Clients access databases through the user system interface. Database management, on the server side, distributes processing between both client and server. Both tiers, the client and the server, are responsible for some of the processing management. Simply put, the client uses the user interface to make requests through database management on the server side. The general two-tier architecture of a Client/Server system is illustrated in figure 3.11.

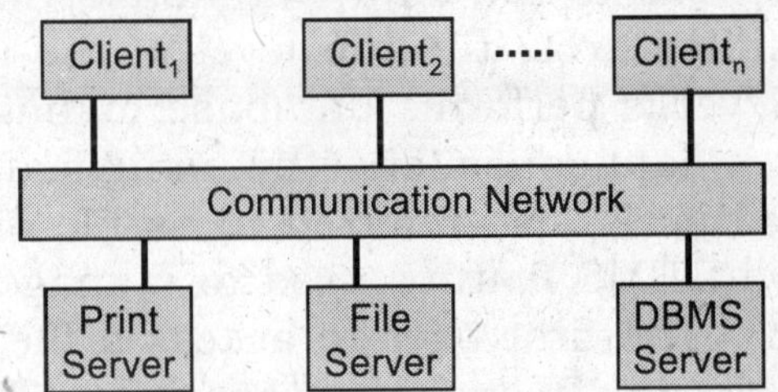

Figure 3.11 Two-tier Client/Server Architecture

In a two-tier client/server system, it may occur that multiple clients are served by a single server, called multiple clients-single server approach. Another alternative is multiple servers providing services to multiple clients, which is called multiple clients-multiple servers approach. In the case of multiple clients-multiple servers approach, two alternative management strategies are possible: either each client manages its own connection to the appropriate server or each client communicates with its home server, which further communicates with other servers as required. The former approach simplifies server code but complicates the client code with additional functionalities, which leads to a heavy (fat) client system. On the other hand, the latter approach loads the server machine with all data management responsibilities and thus leads to a light (thin) client system. Depending on the extent or which the processing is shared between the client and the server, a server can be described as fat or thin. A fat server carries the larger proportion of the processing load, whereas a thin server carries a lesser processing load.

Most of the application processing takes place on the client side, while the database management system (DBMS), on the server side, focuses on processing data through stored procedures. Connectivity between the tiers can be dynamically altered depending on users' requests and the services they are demanding. Two tier client server architectures work well for groups

or businesses of up to 100 users on an LAN (Local Area Network), any more and service would deteriorate. Also, this software architecture offers limited flexibility by requiring the writing of manual code to move program functionality to a different server.

Three-tier Architecture – Three tier client server architecture is also known as multi-tier architecture and signals the introduction of a middle tier to mediate between clients and servers. The middle tier exists between the user interface on the client side and database management system (DBMS) on the server side. This third layer executes process management, which includes implementation of business logic and rules. The three tier models can accommodate hundreds of users. It hides the complexity of process distribution from the user, while being able to complete complex tasks through message queuing, application implementation, and data staging or the storage of data before being uploaded to the data warehouse.

As in two tiered architectures, the top level is the user system interface (client) and the bottom level is performs database management. The database management level ensures data consistency by using features like data locking and replication. Data locking is also referred to as file or record locking. This is a first-come, first-serve DBMS feature used to manage data and updates in a multi-user environment. The first user to access a file or record denies any other user access or "locks it". It opens up again and becomes accessible to other users once the update is complete.

The middle tier is also called the application server. It contains a centralized processing logic, which facilitates management and administration. Localizing system functionality in the middle tier makes it possible for processing changes and updates to be made once and be distributed throughout the network available to both clients and servers. Sometimes the middle tier is divided into two or more units with different functions. This makes it a multi-layer model. The typical three-tier architecture of a client/server system is depicted in figure 3.12.

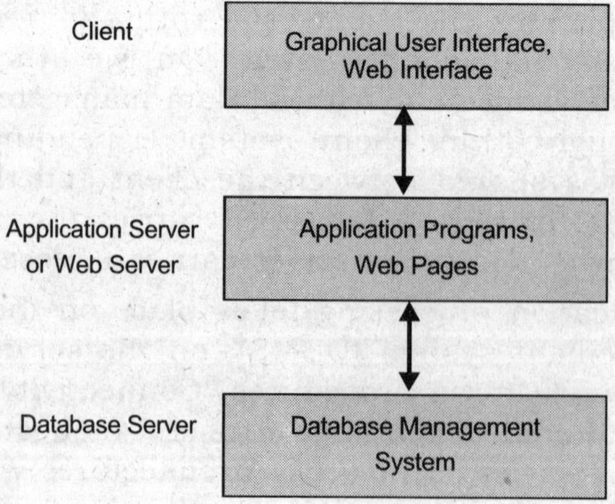

Figure 3.12 Three-tier Client/Server Architecture

On of the most basic ways of configuring the middle layer in three tier architecture is through TP (transaction process) monitoring. Here, the middle layer takes care of processing through a system of prioritizing messages, queuing messages, scheduling transactions. This allows the user to connect to the TP monitor and then work on other things while the TP monitor manages the transaction until it is complete. TP monitoring allows multiple DBMSs to be updated in a single transaction. It also provides connectivity to a variety of data sources and can attach priorities to transactions.

Messaging servers also provide a middle layer in three tier client-server architectures. They also prioritize messages. The messages contain priority information, addresses and identification numbers to locate requested data on relational DBMSs and other data sources. However, in this context, the intelligent information is found in the content of the message and headings. In TP monitors, intelligence is located in the monitor itself.

In three tier application server architecture, most application functions run on a shared host. This makes them more secure and scalable since it lessens the burden of software placed on the client-side. Application servers are also less expensive to install since it is installed on a single server and not on every desktop in the network.

ORB (Object Request Broker) architecture in a three tiered model increases interoperability. Technologies like CORBA (Common Object Request Broker Architecture) and COM/DCOM (Common Object Model/Distributed Common Object Model) support distributed objects and allow requests to be processed across platforms and across programming languages.

Finally, distributed/collaborative enterprise architecture is based on ORB, but advances CORBA. Developed in 1993, it shares and reuses not just objects, but also business models on an enterprise-wide scale. Enterprise, here, refers to as an organization's multiple business systems that must all work together. Distributed/collaborative enterprise architecture increases flexibility and efficiency operationally. The limitations of this model include a lack of commercial object-oriented analysis and design tools to work with applications.

The major advantage of three-tier client/server architecture is that it provides better performance for groups with a large number of users and improves flexibility compared to two-tier approach. In the case of three-tier architecture, as data processing is separated from different servers, it provides more scalability. The disadvantage of three-tier architecture, it is much more difficult to develop and test software than in two-tier architecture, because more devices have to communicate to complete a user's transaction.

In general, a multi-tier (or n-tier) architecture may deploy any number of distinct services, including transitive relations between applications served implementing different functions of business logic, each of which may or may not employee a distinct or shared database system.

For example, in web applications, the client side is usually written in HTML meanwhile the application servers are usually written in C++ or Java. By using a scripting language embedded in HTML, web servers act as translation layers that allow for communication between the client and server layers.

This layer receives requests from clients and generates HTML responses after requesting it from database servers. Popular scripting languages include JavaScript, ASP (Active Server Page), JSP (JavaScript Pages), PHP (Hypertext Preprocessor), Perl (Practical Extraction and Reporting Language), and Python. One of the major benefits of three tier architecture is the ability to partition software and "drag and drop" modules onto different computers in a network.

3.6.4 THE THREE-TIER CLIENT-SERVER MODEL

In the 1990s the client-server model has been used extensively to develop a huge number and variety of applications. The reasons are simple. It is a very clean model which adheres well to the software modularity and usability requirements. This model allows the programmer to develop, test and install applications very quickly. It simplifies maintenance and lowers its costs. It also allows proving correctness of code. Figure 3.13 depicts the basic client-server model.

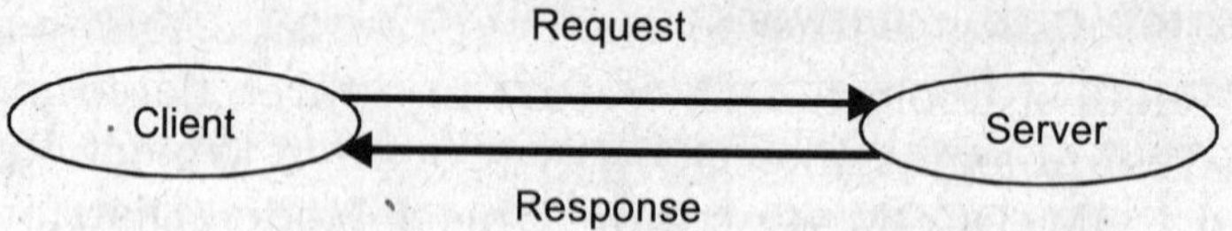

Figure 3.13 Basic client-server model

According to this model there are two processes, the client, which requests a service from another process, the server, which is the service provider. The server performs the requested service and sends back a response. This response could be a processing result, a confirmation of completion of the requested operation or even a notice about a failure of an operation. From the user's point of view a distributed computing system can provide the following services: printing, electronic mail, file service, authentication, naming, database service and computing service. These services are provided by appropriate servers. Because of the restricted number of servers (implied by a restricted number of resources on which these servers were implemented), clients compete for these servers.

Some definitions of the client-server model:

- **Service:** A service is a software entity that runs on one or more machines. It provides an abstraction of a set of well-defined operations.
- **Server:** A server is an instance of a particular service running on a single machine.
- **Client:** A client is a software entity that exploits services provided by servers. A client can but does not have to interface directly with a human user. The physical implementation of the client-server model is shown in Figure 3.14

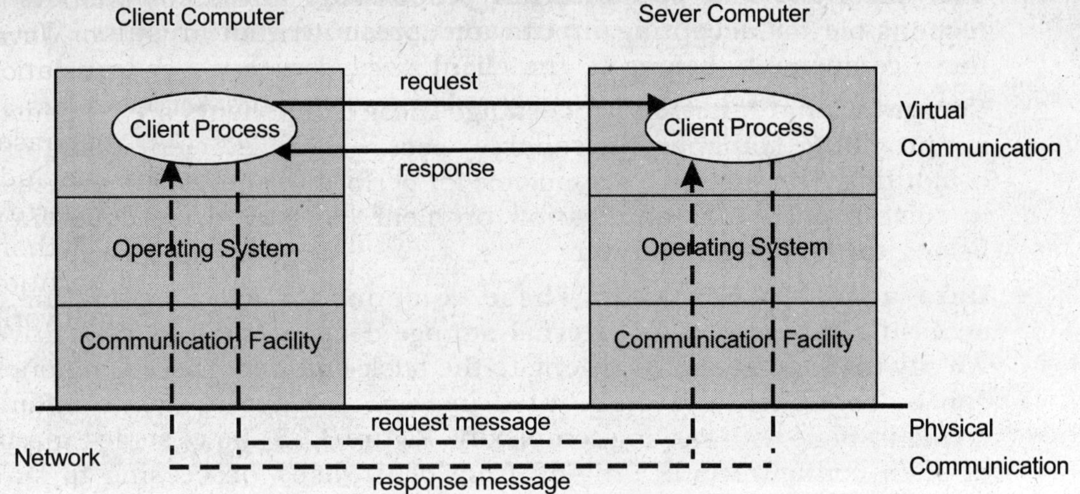

Figure 3.14 Client-server model: the physical implementation

The most important features of the client-server model are simplicity, modularity, extensibility and flexibility. Simplicity manifests itself by closely matching the flow of data with the control flow. Modularity is achieved by organising and integrating a group of computer operations into a separate service. Also any set of data with operations on this data can be organised as a separate service. The whole distributed computing system developed based on the client-server model can be easily extended by adding new services in the form of new servers. The servers which do not satisfy user requirements can be easily modified or even removed. Only the interfaces between the clients and servers must be maintained.

Advantages of the client-server model:

- Simplicity
- Modularity
- Extensibility
- Flexibility

The three major problems of the client-server model:

- A server failure may affect the service
- A server is a potential bottleneck
- The cost/reliability trade-off

The three-tier client-server architecture extends the basic client-server model by adding a middle tier to support the application logic and common services.

In this architecture, a distributed application consists of the following three types of components:

- **User interface and presentation processing:** These components are responsible for accepting inputs and presenting the results. We say these components belong to the client tier;
- **Computational function processing:** These components are responsible for providing transparent, reliable, secure, and efficient distributed computing. They are also responsible for performing necessary processing to solve a particular application problem. We say these components belong to the application tier.
- **Data access processing:** These components are responsible for accessing data stored on external storage devices (such as disk drives). We say these components belong to the back-end tier. These components can be combined and distributed in various ways to create different configurations with varying complexity. Figure 3.15 shows some examples of such configurations ranging from centralised processing to three-tier distribution. In particular, Figure 3.15(a) shows a centralised configuration where all the three types of components are located in a single computer. Figure 3.15(b) shows three two-tier configurations where the three types of components are distributed on two computers. Figure 3.15(c) shows a three-tier configuration where all the three types of components is distributed on different computers.

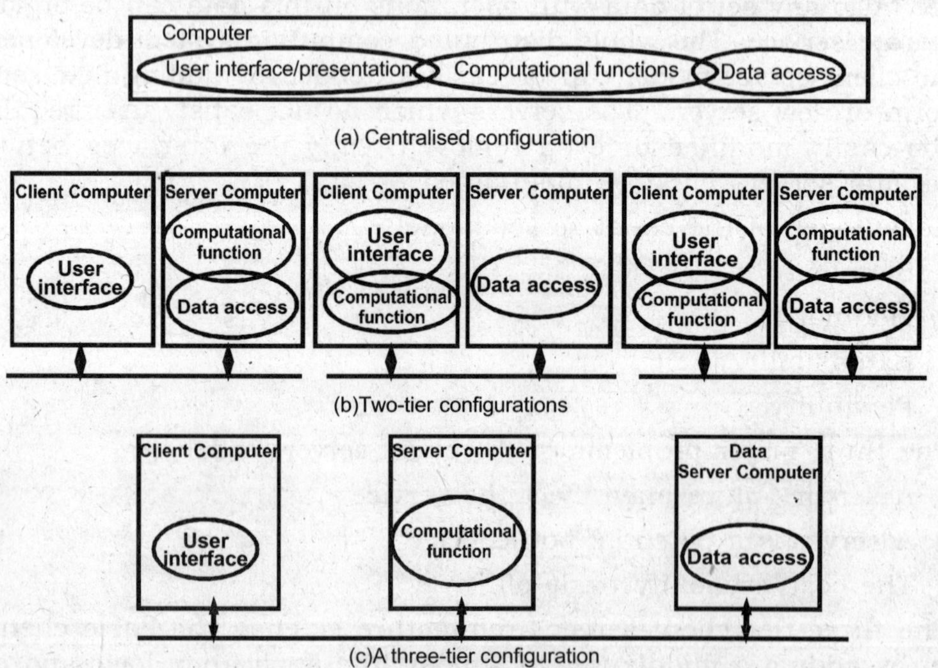

Figure 3.15 Examples of three-tier configurations

When the business logic becomes very complex and involves accessing multiple data servers, the middle tier representing the complex business logic is split into a layered structure to separate the concerns. Thus, the layered middle-tier forms a multi-tier (more than three-tier) architecture. Figure 3.16 illustrates an example implementation of the three-tier architecture. In this example, the upper tier consists of client computers that run user interface processing software. The middle tiers are computers that run computational function processing software. The bottom tier is back-end data servers. In three-tier client-server architecture, application clients usually do not interact directly with the data servers, instead, they interact with the middle tier servers to obtain services. The middle tier servers will then either fulfil the requests themselves, sending the result back to the clients, or more commonly, if additional resources are required, servers in the middle tier will act (as clients themselves) on behalf of the application clients to interact with the data servers in the bottom tier or other servers within the middle tier.

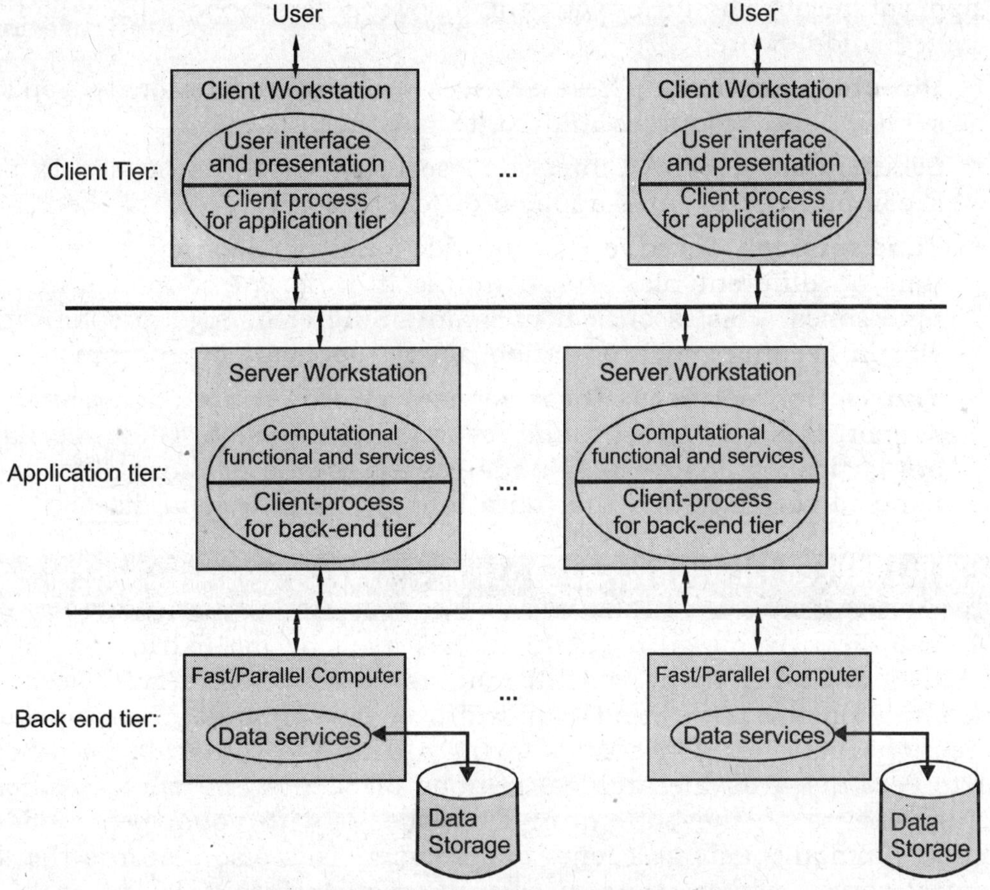

Figure 3.16 Example of a three-tier architecture

Compared with normal two-tier client-server architecture, the three-tier client-server architecture has the following two important advantages:

- **Better transparency:** The servers within the application tier of the three-tier architecture allow an application to detach user interface from back-end resources and therefore provide better location and migration transparency. That is, the location or implementation of back-end resources can be changed without affecting the programs within the client tier;
- **Better scalability:** The centralised and two-tier architectures do not scale well to support large applications. The servers within the application tier of the three-tier architecture, however, inject another dimension of scalability into the client-server environment.

Other benefits that the three-tier client-server architecture may achieve include better concurrency, flexibility, reusability, load balancing, and reliability. In addition to providing services for business logic and applications, the application tier should provide the following key services (they sometimes are called middleware):

- **Directory services:** These services are required to locate application services and resources and route messages there.
- **Security services:** An integrated security service is needed to provide a comprehensive inter-application client-server security mechanism.
- **Time services:** These services provide a universal format for representing time on different platforms running in different countries in various time zones. This is critical in maintaining error logs and timestamps, and in keeping synchronisation among application processes.
- **Transaction services:** These services provide transaction semantics to support commit, rollback, and recovery mechanisms. These mechanisms are critical to ensure that updates across one or more databases are handled correctly and that data integrity is not jeopardised.

3.7 PEER-TO-PEER DISTRIBUTED SYSTEM

Peer-to-Peer Architecture distinguishes itself by its distribution of power and function. Rather than concentrating its power in the server, Peer-to-Peer models rely on the power and bandwidth of participants. They form *ad hoc* connections between nodes for sharing all kinds of information and files. Peer-to-Peer discards hierarchical notions of clients and servers (clients at the top, servers on the bottom) and replaces it with equal peer nodes that function simultaneously as clients and servers. This also discards the idea of a central server, which exists in Client-Server Architecture.

The peer-to-peer architecture is a good way to structure a distributed system so that it consists of many identical software processes or modules, each module running on a different computer or node. The different software modules stored at different sites communicate with each other to complete the processing required for the execution of distributed applications. Peer-to-peer architecture provides both client and server functionalities on each computer. Therefore, each node can access services from other nodes as well as providing services to other nodes. In contrast with the client/server architecture, in a peer-to-peer distributed system each node provides user interaction facilities as well as processing capabilities.

From our point of view, Peer-to-Peer systems include the following features:

1. A Peer-to-Peer system should have a decentralized structure
2. The nodes in a Peer-to-Peer system should be able to share resources among each other (processing power, storage space, etc.)
3. A Peer-to-Peer system has no fixed hierarchy
4. Each node in a Peer-to-Peer system may have the potential of communicating with each other directly, with no control or interference from a centralized point.

There are several classifications of Peer-to-Peer networks. These include pure/hybrid and structured/unstructured Peer-to-Peer networks.

Pure P2P networks merge the role of clients and servers as equals and do not provide a central server for managing the network or a central router that forwards requests to other networks.

Hybrid P2P models, on the other hand, do contain a central server that stores peer information and responds to request for information stored on that server. In this configuration, peers host available resources since there no central server provides this function. Peers also make central servers aware of what resources they want to share and make those resources available to peers that request them. Also, route terminals function as used addresses and are indexed to find an absolute address.

The structure of P2P networks is determined by the nature of the overlay network, which consists of all participating peers as equal nodes. Nodes in an overlay network are connected through virtual or logical links that create a path to the underlying network. Essentially, overlay networks are network built on top of other networks. Peer-to-Peer networks are considered overlay networks because they are usually built on top of the Internet. Structured P2P networks use a global protocol so that searches can be routed TO any peers/nodes BY any peers/nodes on the network. To retrieve rare files, more structured overlay links are required. The most common structured P2P network

is the distributed hash table (DHT). DHTs are decentralized distributed systems that store names and values. Any participating node in the network can lookup and retrieve values. Maintenance of the DHT mapping is distributed among the nodes. The ownership of each file is assigned to a peer, but the addition or deletion of peers or files doesn't cause major disruptions. This makes them very scalable.

Unstructured P2P networks establish links more arbitrarily. To join, a peer only has to copy the links of an existing node and then add its own links as it develops. To find a desired file, however, the request must be flooded throughout the network. This doesn't always necessarily return the desired results if the file being requested is rare. There is no correlation between peer and content. Also, flooding increases network traffic, slowing down responses and file sharing.

The primary advantage of P2P networks is that all clients contribute their resources. These resources include computing power, bandwidth, and storage space. In traditional Client-Server models there are a fixed number of servers, so the addition of clients slows down network processing. In Peer-to-Peer models, as nodes are added, system resources increase (contributed by the added nodes) to accommodate demand.

As a database management system, each node in a peer-to-peer distributed system provides all data management services and it can execute local queries as well as global queries. Thus, in this system there is no distinction between client DBMS and server DBMS. As a single-application program, DBMS at each node accepts user requests and manages execution. Like in client/server system, also in a peer-to-peer distributed database system data is viewed as a single logical database although the data is distributed at the physical level. In this context, the identification of the reference architecture for a distributed database system is necessary.

3.7.1 REFERENCE ARCHITECTURE OF DISTRIBUTED DBMSS

In distributed DBMSs, it is more difficult to represent a common architecture that is generally applicable for all applications. However, it may be useful to represent a possible reference architecture that addressed data distribution. Data in a distributed system are usually fragmented and replicated. Considering this fragmentation and replication issue, the reference architecture of a distributed DBMS consists of the following schemas (as depicted in figure 3.17):

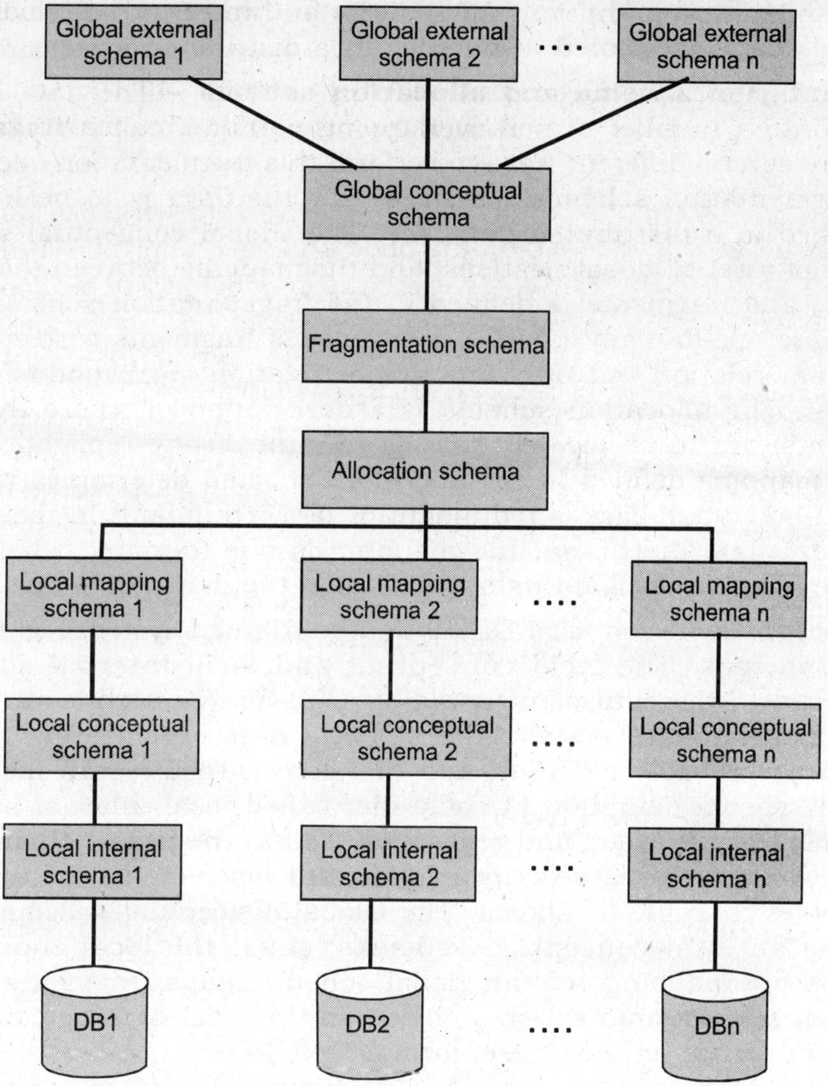

Figure 3.17 reference Architecture of Distributed DBMS

1. **Global external schema** – User application and user accesses to the distributed database are represented by a number of global external schemas. This is the topmost level in the reference architecture of a distributed DBMS. This level describes the part of the distributed database that is relevant to different users.
2. **Global conceptual schema** – The Global conceptual schema represents the logical description of the entire database as if it is not distributed. This level corresponds to the conceptual level of the ANSI-SPARC

architecture of centralized DBMS and contains definitions of all entities, relationships among entities and security and integrity information for the whole database stored at all sites in a distributed system.

3. **Fragmentation schema and allocation schema** – The data can be divided into a number of non-overlapping portions, called **fragments**. There are several different ways to perform this fragmentation operation. The fragmentation schema describes how the data is to be logically partitioned in a distributed database. The Global conceptual schema consists of a set of global relations, and the mapping between the global relations and fragments is defined in the fragmentation schema. This mapping is one-to-many, that is, a number of fragments correspond to one global relation but only one global relation corresponds to one fragment. The allocation schema is a description of where the data (fragments) are to be located, taking account of any replication. The type of mapping defined in the allocation schema determines whether the distributed database is redundant or non-redundant. In the case of redundant data distribute, the mapping is one-to-many, whereas in the case of non-redundant data distribution the mapping is one-to-one.
4. **Local schemas** – Each local DBMS in a distributed system has its own set of schemas. The local conceptual and local internal schemas correspond to the equivalent levels of ANSI-SPARC architecture. In a distributed database system, the physical data organization at each machine is probably different, and therefore it requires an individual internal schema definition at each site, called local internal schema. To handle fragmentation and replication issues, the logical organization of data at each site is described by a third layer in the architecture, called local conceptual schema. The Global conceptual schema is the union of all local conceptual schemas; thus, the local conceptual schemas are mappings of the global schema maps fragments in the allocation schema onto external objects in the local database, and this mapping depends on the type of local DBMS.

Therefore, in a heterogeneous distributed DBMS, there may be different types of local mappings at different nodes. This architecture provides a very general conceptual framework for understanding distributed databases. Furthermore, such databases are typically designed in a top-down manner; therefore, all external-view definitions are made globally.

3.7.2 COMPONENT ARCHITECTURE OF DISTRIBUTED DBMSS

There are four major components of a distributed DBMS that has been identified are as follows:

1. Distributed DBMS (DDBMS) component

2. Data communications (DC) component
3. Global system catalog (GSC)
4. Local DBMS (LDBMS) component

1. **Distributed DBMS (DDBMS) component:** It is used to control the entire system. This component provides the different levels of transparencies such as data distribution transparency, transaction transparency, performance transparency and DBMS transparency (in the case of heterogeneous DDBMS). DDBMS has subdivided into four major components as given below:
   (a) **User interface handler** – It is responsible for interpreting user commands as they come into the system and formatting the result data as it is sent to the user.
   (b) **Semantic data controller** – It is responsible for checking integrity constraints and authorizations that are defined in the Global system catalog, before processing the user requests.
   (c) **Global query optimizer and decomposer** – It determines an execution strategy to minimize a cost function and translates the global queries into local ones using the global and local conceptual schemas as well as the global system catalog. The global query optimizer is responsible for generating the best strategy to execute distributed join operations.
   (d) **Distributed execution monitor** – It coordinates the distributed execution of the user request. This component is also known as distributed transaction manager. During the execution of distributed queries, the execution monitors at various sites may and usually do communicate with one another.
2. **DC component:** The DC component is the software that enables all sites to communicate with each other. The DC component contains all information about the sites and the links.
3. **Global system catalog (GSC):** The Global system catalog provides the same functionality as system catalog of centralized DBMS. In addition to metadata of the entire database, a Global system catalog contains all fragmentation, replication and allocation details considering the distributed nature of a DDBMS. It can itself be managed as a distributed database and thus, it can be fragmented and distributed, fully replicated or centralized like any other relations in the system.
4. **Local DBMS (LDBMS) component:** The LDBMS component is a standard DBMS, stored at each site that has a database and responsible for controlling local data. Each LDBMS component has its own local system catalog that contains the information about the data stored at that

particular site. In a homogeneous DDBMS, the LDBMS component is the same product, replicated at each site, while in a heterogeneous DDBMS, there must be at least two sites with different DBMS products and/or platforms.

The major components of an LDBMS are as follows:

(a) **Local query optimizer** – It is used as the access path selector and responsible for choosing the best access path to access any data item for the execution of a query.

(b) **Local recovery manager** – The local recovery manager ensures the consistency of the local database in spite of failures.

(c) **Run-time support processor** – It physically accesses the database according to the commands in the schedule generated by the query optimizer and is responsible for managing main memory buffers. The run-time support processor is the interface to the operating system and contains the database buffer manager.

3.7.3 DISTRIBUTED DATA INDEPENDENCE

The reference architecture of a DDBMS is an extension of ANSI-SPARC architecture; therefore data independence is supported by this model. Distributed data independence means that upper levels are unaffected by changes to lower levels in the distributed database architecture. Like a centralized DBMS, both distributed logical data independence and distributed physical data independence are supported by this architecture.

In a distributed system, the user queries data irrespective of its location, fragmentation or replication. Furthermore, any changes made to the Global system catalog do not affect the user views in the global external schemas. Thus, distributed logical data independence is provided by global external schemas in distributed database architecture. Similarly, the Global system catalog provides distributed physical data independence in the distributed database environment.

3.8 TYPES OF DISTRIBUTED DATABASE SYSTEMS

The term distributed database management system can describe various systems that differ from one another in many respects. The main thing that all such systems have in common is the fact that data and software are distributed over multiple sites connected by some form of communication network. In this section we discuss a number of types of DDBMSs and the criteria and factors that make some of these systems different.

The first factor we consider is the **degree of homogeneity** of the DDBMS software. If all servers (or individual local DBMSs) use identical software and all users (clients) use identical software, the

DDBMS is called **homogeneous;** otherwise, it is called **heterogeneous.** Another factor related to the degree of homogeneity is the **degree of local autonomy.** If there is no provision for the local site to function as a stand-alone DBMS, then the system has **no local autonomy.** On the other hand, if *direct access* by local transactions to a server is permitted, the system has some degree of local autonomy.

At one extreme of the autonomy spectrum, we have a DDBMS that "looks like" a centralized DBMS to the user. A single conceptual schema exists, and all access to the system is obtained through a site that is part of the DDBMS—which means that no local autonomy exists. At the other extreme we encounter a type of DDBMS called a *federated DDBMS* (or a *multidatabase system*). In such a system, each server is an independent and autonomous centralized DBMS that has its own local users, local transactions, and DBA and hence has a very high degree of *local autonomy.* The term **federated database system (FDBS)** is used when there is some global view or schema of the federation of databases that is shared by the applications. On the other hand, a **multidatabase system** does not have a global schema and interactively constructs one as needed by the application. Both systems are hybrids between distributed and centralized systems and the distinction we made between them is not strictly followed. We will refer to them as FDBSs in a generic sense.

In a heterogeneous FDBS, one server may be a relational DBMS, another network DBMS, and a third an object or hierarchical DBMS; in such a case it is necessary to have a canonical system language and to include language translators to translate subqueries from the canonical language to the language of each server. We briefly discuss the issues affecting the design of FDBSs below.

3.8.1 FEDERATED DATABASE MANAGEMENT SYSTEMS ISSUES

The type of heterogeneity present in FDBSs may arise from several sources. We discuss these sources first and then point out how the different types of autonomies contribute to a semantic heterogeneity that must be resolved in a heterogeneous FDBS.

- ***Differences in data models:*** Databases in an organization come from a variety of data models including the so-called legacy models (network and hierarchical, see Appendix C and Appendix D), the relational data model, the object data model, and even files. The modeling capabilities of the models vary. Hence, to deal with them uniformly via a single global schema or to process them in a single language is challenging. Even if two databases are both from the RDBMS environment, the same information may be represented as an attribute name, as a relation name, or as a value in different databases. This calls for an intelligent

query-processing mechanism that can relate information based on metadata.

- ***Differences in constraints:*** Constraint facilities for specification and implementation vary from system to system. There are comparable features that must be reconciled in the construction of a global schema. For example, the relationships from ER models are represented as referential integrity constraints in the relational model. Triggers may have to be used to implement certain constraints in the relational model. The global schema must also deal with potential conflicts among constraints.
- ***Differences in query languages:*** Even with the same data model, the languages and their versions vary. For example, SQL has multiple versions like SQL-89, SQL-92 (SQL2), and SQL3, and each system has its own set of data types, comparison operators, string manipulation features, and so on.

3.8.2 SEMANTIC HETEROGENEITY

Semantic heterogeneity occurs when there are differences in the meaning, interpretation, and intended use of the same or related data. Semantic heterogeneity among component database systems (DBSs) creates the biggest hurdle in designing global schemas of heterogeneous databases. The **design** which in turn affect the eventual complexity of the FDBS:

- ***The universe of discourse from which the data is drawn:*** For example, two customer accounts databases in the federation may be from United States and Japan with entirely different sets of attributes about customer accounts required by the accounting practices. Currency rate fluctuations would also present a problem. Hence, relations in these two databases which have identical names—CUSTOMER or ACCOUNT may have some common and some entirely distinct information.
- ***Representation and naming:*** The representation and naming of data elements and the structure of the data model may be prespecified for each local database.
- ***The understanding, meaning, and subjective interpretation of data:*** This is a chief contributor to semantic heterogeneity.
- ***Transaction and policy constraints:*** This deal with serializability criteria, compensating transactions, and other transaction policies.
- ***Derivation of summaries:*** Aggregation, summarization, and other data-processing features and operations supported by the system.

Communication autonomy of a component DBS refers to its ability to decide whether to communicate with component DBSs. **Execution autonomy**

refers to the ability of a component DBS to execute local operations without interference from external operations by other component DBSs and its ability to decide the order in which to execute them. The **association autonomy** of a component DBS implies that it has the ability to decide whether and how much to share its functionality (operations it supports) and resources (data it manages) with other component DBSs. The major challenge of designing FDBSs is to let component DBSs interoperate while still providing the above types of autonomies to them.

Typical five-level schema architecture to support global applications in the FDBS environment. In this architecture, the **local schema** is the conceptual schema (full database definition) of a component database, and the **component schema** is derived by translating the local schema into a canonical data model or common data model (CDM) for the FDBS. Schema translation from the local schema to the component schema is accompanied by generation of mappings to transform commands on a component schema into commands on the corresponding local schema. The **export schema** represents the subset of a component schema that is available to the FDBS. The **federated schema** is the global schema or view, which is the result of integrating all the shareable export schemas. The **external schemas** define the schema for a user group or an application, as in the three-level schema architecture (Note 6).

All the problems related to query processing, transaction processing, and directory and metadata management and recovery apply to FDBSs with additional considerations. It is not within our scope to discuss them in detail here.

3.9 AN OVERVIEW OF CLIENT-SERVER ARCHITECTURE AND ITS RELATIONSHIP TO DISTRIBUTED DATABASES

As we pointed out in the chapter introduction, full-scale DDBMSs have not been developed to support all the types of functionalities that we discussed so far. Instead, distributed database applications are being developed in the context of the client-server architecture. The section further discusses client-server in the context of DDBMS.

Exactly how to divide the DBMS functionality between client and server has not yet been established. Different approaches have been proposed. One possibility is to include the functionality of a centralized DBMS at the server level. A number of relational DBMS products have taken this approach, where an **SQL server** is provided to the clients. Each client must then formulate the appropriate SQL queries and provide the user interface and programming language interface functions. Since SQL is a relational standard, various SQL servers, possibly provided by different vendors, can accept SQL commands.

The client may also refer to a data dictionary that includes information on the distribution of data among the various SQL servers, as well as modules for decomposing a global query into a number of local queries that can be executed at the various sites. Interaction between client and server might proceed as follows during the processing of an SQL query:

1. The client parses a user query and decomposes it into a number of independent site queries. Each site query is sent to the appropriate server site.
2. Each server processes the local query and sends the resulting relation to the client site.
3. The client site combines the results of the subqueries to produce the result of the originally submitted query.

In this approach, the SQL server has also been called a **transaction server** (or a **database processor (DP)** or a **back-end machine**), whereas the client has been called an **application processor (AP)** (or a **front-end machine**). The interaction between client and server can be specified by the user at the client level or via a specialized DBMS client module that is part of the DBMS package. For example, the user may know what data is stored in each server, break down a query request into site subqueries manually, and submit individual subqueries to the various sites. The resulting tables may be combined explicitly by a further user query at the client level. The alternative is to have the client module undertake these actions automatically.

In a typical DDBMS, it is customary to divide the software modules into three levels:

1. The **server** software is responsible for local data management at a site, much like centralized DBMS software.
2. The **client** software is responsible for most of the distribution functions; it accesses data distribution information from the DDBMS catalog and processes all requests that require access to more than one site. It also handles all user interfaces.
3. The **communications software** (sometimes in conjunction with a **distributed operating system)** provides the communication primitives that are used by the client to transmit commands and data among the various sites as needed. This is not strictly part of the DDBMS, but it provides essential communication primitives and services.

The client is responsible for generating a distributed execution plan for a multisite query or transaction and for supervising distributed execution by sending commands to servers. These commands include local queries and transactions to be executed, as well as commands to transmit data to other clients or servers. Hence, client software should be included at any site where multisite queries are submitted. Another function controlled by the client (or coordinator) is that of ensuring consistency of replicated copies of a data item by employing distributed (or global) concurrency control techniques. The client must also ensure the atomicity of global transactions by performing global recovery when certain sites fail. One possible function of the client is to *hide* the details of data distribution from the user; that is, it enables the user to write global queries and transactions as though the database were centralized, without having to specify the sites at which the data referenced in the query or transaction resides. This property is called **distribution transparency.** Some DDBMSs do not provide distribution transparency, instead requiring that users be aware of the details of data distribution.

3.10 GLOBAL DIRECTORY ISSUES

The global directory issue is relevant only for a distributed DBMS or a multi-DBMS that uses a GCS.

- The extensions of the directory as described in the ANSI/SPARC report.
- Including the location and makeup of the fragments.
- The database containing meta-data.

The first issue – type, global or local?

- May be either global to the entire database or local to each site.
- May be maintained centrally at one site, or distribute it over a number of sites.

The second issue – location, centralized or distributed directories?

- Keep the directory at one site – increase the load at that site and cause traffic.
- Distribute directories over a number of sites – increase complexity of managing directories.

The third issue – replication, single copy or multiple copies?

- Multiple copies would provide more reliability for higher possibility to reach the directory.
- Multiple copies also cause lower delays in accessing the directory due to less contention and the relative proximity of the directory copies.
- The multiple copy case only works for distributed DBMS; MDBS only maintain single directory.

Alternative Directory Management Strategies

- Refer Figure 3.7 for three dimensions with orthogonal to one another.
- The question mark (?) represents the unrealistic combinations.

- The choice of an appropriate directory management scheme should also depend on the query processing and the transaction management techniques.

3.11 FEDERATED DATABASE SYSTEM

A **federated database system** is a type of meta-database management system (DBMS) which transparently integrates multiple autonomous database systems into a single **federated database**. The constituent databases are interconnected via a computer network, and may be geographically decentralized. Since the constituent database systems remain autonomous, a federated database system is a contrastable alternative to the (sometimes daunting) task of merging together several disparate databases. A federated database, or **virtual database**, is the fully-integrated, logical composite of all constituent databases in a federated database system.

McLeod and Heimbigner were among the first to define a federated database system, as one which "define[s] the architecture and interconnect[s] databases that minimize central authority yet support partial sharing and coordination among database systems".

Through data abstraction, federated database systems can provide a uniform user interface, enabling users and clients to store and retrieve data in multiple noncontiguous databases with a single query — even if the constituent databases are heterogeneous. To this end, a federated database system must be able to decompose the query into subqueries for submission to the relevant constituent DBMS's, after which the system must composite the result sets of the subqueries. Because various database management systems employ different query languages, federated database systems can apply wrappers to the subqueries to translate them into the appropriate query languages.

- **Note:** this description of federated databases does not accurately reflect the McLeod/Heimbigner definition of a federated database. Rather, this description fits what McLeod/Heimbinger called a *composite* database. McLeod/Heimbigner's federated database is a collection of autonomous components that make their data available to other members of the federation through the publication of an export schema and access operations; there is no unified, central schema that encompasses the information available from the members of the federation.

Among other surveys, defines a Federated Database as a collection of cooperating component systems which are autonomous and are possibly heterogeneous. The three important components of an FDBS as pointed out in are autonomy, heterogeneity and distribution. Another dimension which

has also been considered is the Networking Environment Computer Network, e.g., many DBSs over a LAN or many DBSs over a WAN update related functions of participating DBSs (e.g., no updates, nonatomic transitions, atomic updates). Master data management or MDM is a relatively new term for similar practices.

3.11.1 FDBS ARCHITECTURE

A DBMS can be classified as either centralized or distributed. A centralized system manages a single database while distributed manages multiple databases. A component DBS in a DBMS may be centralized or distributed. A multiple DBS (MDBS) can be classified into two types depending on the autonomy of the component DBS as federated and no federated. A non-federated database system is an integration of component DBMS that are not autonomous. A federated database system consists of component DBS that are autonomous yet participate in a federation to allow partial and controlled sharing of their data.

Federated architectures differ based on levels of integration with the component database systems and the extent of services offered by the federation. A FDBS can be categorized as loosely or tightly coupled systems.

- **Loosely Coupled system** requires component databases to construct their own federated schema. A user will typically access other component database systems by using a multi-database language but this removes any levels of location transparency, forcing the user to have direct knowledge of the federated schema. A user imports the data they require from other component databases and integrates it with their own to form a federated schema.
- **Tightly coupled system** consists of component systems that use independent processes to construct and publicize an integrated federated schema.

  Multiple DBS of which FDBS are a specific type can be characterized along three dimensions: Distribution, Heterogeneity and Autonomy. Another characterization could be based on the dimension of networking For e.g. single databases or multiple databases in a LAN or WAN.

3.11.1.1 DISTRIBUTION

Distribution of data in an FDBS is due to the existence of a multiple DBS before an FDBS is built. Data can be distributed among multiple DB which could be stored in a single computer or multiple computers. These computers could be geographically located in different places but interconnected by a network. The benefits of data distribution help in increased availability and reliability as well as improved access times.

3.11.1.2 HETEROGENEOUS DATABASE SYSTEM | HETEROGENEITY

Heterogeneities in databases arise due to several factors. Some of them occur due to differences in structures, semantics of data, the constraints supported or query language. Differences in structure occur when two data models provide different primitives such as object oriented (OO) models that support specialization and inheritance and relational models that do not. Differences due to constraints occur when two models support two different constraints. For example the set type in CODASYL schema may be partially modeled as a referential integrity constraint in a relationship schema. CODASYL supports insertion and retention that are not captured by referential integrity alone. The query language supported by DBMSs can also contribute to heterogeneity between other component DBMSs. For example differences in query languages with same data models or different versions of query languages could contribute heterogeneity.

Semantic heterogeneities arise when there is a disagreement about meaning, interpretation or intended use of data. At the schema and data level, some of the possible classifications of Heterogeneities that occur are

- **Naming Conflicts** e.g. Databases using different names to represent the same concept.
- **Domain Conflicts or Data Representation conflicts** e.g. Databases using different values to represent same concept.
- **Precision Conflicts** e.g. Databases using same data values from domains of different cardinalities for same data.
- **Metadata Conflicts** e.g. same concepts are represented at schema level and instance level.
- **Data Conflicts** e.g. Missing attributes
- **Schema Conflicts** e.g. Table versus table conflict which includes naming conflicts, data conflicts etc.

In creating a federated schema, one has to resolve such heterogeneities before integrating the component DB schemas.

3.11.1.3 SCHEMA MATCHING, SCHEMA MAPPING

Dealing with incompatible data types or query syntax is not the only obstacle to a concrete implementation of an FDBS. In systems that are not planned top-down, a generic problem lies in matching semantically equivalent, but differently named parts from different schemas (=data models) (tables, attributes). A pairwise mapping between n attributes would result in n(n-1)/2 mapping rules (given equivalence mappings) - a number that quickly gets too large for practical purposes. A common way out is to provide a global schema that comprises the relevant parts of all member schemas and provide mappings

in the form of database views. Two principal solutions can be realized, depending on the direction of the mapping:

1. **Global as View (GaV):** the global schema is defined in terms of the underlying schemas
2. **Local as View (LaV):** the local schemas are defined in terms of the global schema

Both are explained in more detail in the article Data integration. Alternate approaches to the schema matching problem and a classification of the same are explained in more detail in the article Schema Matching

3.11.1.4 AUTONOMY

Fundamental to the difference between an MDBS and an FDBS is the concept of autonomy. It is important to understand the aspects of autonomy for component databases and how they can be addressed when a component DBS participates in an FDBS. There are four kinds of autonomies addressed

- **Design Autonomy** which refers to ability to choose its design irrespective of data, query language or conceptualization, functionality of the system implementation.

Heterogeneities in an FDBS are primarily due to design autonomy.

- **Communication autonomy** refers to the general operation of the DBMS to communicate with other DBMS or not.
- **Execution autonomy** allows a component DBMS to control the operations requested by local and external operations.
- **Association autonomy** gives a power to component DBS to disassociate itself from a federation which means FDBS can operate independently of any single DBS.

The ANSI/X3/SPARC Study Group outlined a three level data description architecture, the components of which are the conceptual schema, internal schema and external schema of databases. The three level architecture is however inadequate to describing the architectures of an FDBS. It was therefore extended to support the three dimensions of the FDBS namely Distribution, Autonomy and Heterogeneity. The five level schema architecture is explained below.

3.11.2 CONCURRENCY CONTROL

The *Heterogeneity* and *Autonomy* requirements pose special challenges concerning concurrency control in an FDBS, which is crucial for the correct execution of its concurrent transactions (see also global concurrency control). Achieving global serializability, the major correctness criterion, under these requirements has been characterized as very difficult and unsolved.

Commitment ordering, introduced in 1991, has provided a general solution for this issue (See Global serializability; See Commitment ordering also for the architectural aspects of the solution).

3.11.3 FIVE LEVEL SCHEMA ARCHITECTURE FOR FDBSS

The five level schema architecture includes the following:

- **Local Schema** is the conceptual concept expressed in primary data model of component DBMS.
- **Component Schema** is derived by translating local schema into a model called the canonical data model or common data model. They are useful when semantics missed in local schema are incorporated in the component. They help in integration of data for tightly coupled FDBS.
- **Export Schema** represents a subset of a component schema that is available to the FDBS. It may include access control information regarding its use by specific federation user. The export schema helps in managing flow of control of data.
- **Federated Schema** is an integration of multiple export schemas. It includes information on data distribution that is generated when integrating export schemas.
- **External Schema** defines a schema for a user/applications or a class of users/applications.

While accurately representing the state of the art in data integration, the Five Level Schema Architecture above does suffer from a major drawback, namely IT imposed look and feel. Modern data users demand control over how data is presented; their needs are somewhat in conflict with such bottom-up approaches to data integration.

3.12 MULTI-DATABASE SYSTEM (MDBS)

An MDBS is a software that can be manipulated and accessed through a single manipulation language with a single common data model in a heterogeneous environment without interfering with the normal execution of the individual database systems. The MDBS has developed from a requirement to manage and retrieve data from multiple databases within a single application while providing complete autonomy to individual database systems. To support DBMS transparency, MDBS resides on top of existing databases and file systems and presents a single database to its users. An MDBS maintains a global schema against which users issue queries and updates, and this global schema is constructed by integrating the schemas of local database. To execute a global query, the MDBS first translates it into a number of subqueries, and converts these subqueries into appropriate local queries for running on local

DBMSs. After completion of execution, local results are merged and the final global result for the user query is generated. An MDBS controls multiple gateways and manages local databases through these gateways. MDBSs can be classified into two different categories based on the autonomy of the individual DBMS. These are non-federated MDBSs and federated MDBSs. A federated MDBS is again categorized as loosely coupled federated MDBS and tightly coupled federated MDBS based on who manages the federation and how the components are integrated. Further, a tightly coupled federated MDBS can be classified as single federation tightly coupled federated MDBS and multiple federations tightly coupled federated MDBS. The complete taxonomy of MDBSs [Sheth and Larson, 1990] is depicted in figure 3.18.

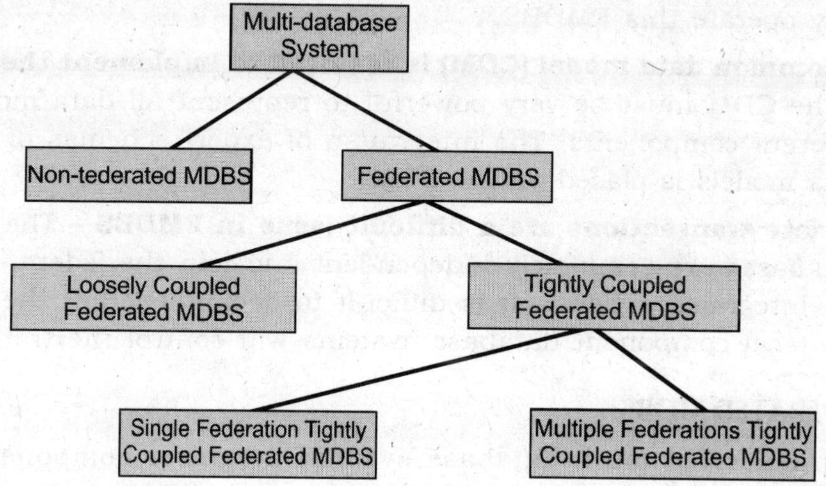

Figure 3.18 Taxonomy of Multi-database Systems

Federated MDBS (FMDBS): It is a collection of cooperating database management systems that are autonomous but participate in a federation to allow partial and controlled sharing of their data. In a federated MDBS, all component DBMSs cooperate to allow different degrees of integration. There is no centralized control in a federated architecture because the component databases control access to their data. To allow controlled sharing of data while preserving the autonomy of component DBMSs and continued execution of existing applications, a federated MDBS supports two types of operations: local or global (or federation). Local operations are directly submitted to a component DBMS, and they involve data only from that component database. Global operations access data from multiple databases managed by multiple component DBMSs via the FMDBS. Thus, an FMDBS is a cross between a DDBMS and a centralized DBMS. It is a distributed system to global users whereas a centralized DBMS to local users. In a simple way, an MDBS is said

to be an FMDBS, if users interface to the MDBS through some integrated views, and there is no connection between any two integrated views.

Following are the features of an FMDBS are given below:

- **Integrated schema exists –** The FMDBS administrator (MDBA) is responsible for the creation of integrated schemas in a heterogeneous environment.
- **Component databases are transparent to users –** Users are not aware of the multiple component DBMSs in an FMDBS; thus, the users only need to understand the integrated schemas to implement the operations on an FMDBS. They cannot change the integrated components when they operate this FMDBS.
- **A common data model (CDM) is required to implement the federation** – The CDM must be very powerful to represent all data models in the different components. The integration of export schemas of component data models is placed on the CDM.
- **Update transactions are a difficult issue in FMDBS –** The component databases are completely independent and join the federation through the integrated schema. It is difficult to decide whether the FMDBS or the local component database systems will control the transactions.

NON-FEDERATED MDBS

A non-federated multi-database system integrates component systems that are not autonomous but still heterogeneous. It has only one level of management, and all operations are performed uniformly. A nonfederated database system does not distinguish local and nonlocal users. Thus, in a non-federated MDBS, all applications are global applications (because there is not local user) and data are accessed through a single global schema. It logically appears to its users like a distributed database.

3.12.1 FIVE-LEVEL SCHEMA ARCHITECTURE OF FEDERATED MDBS

The terms federated database system and federated database architecture was introduced by Heimbigner and McLeod (1985) to facilitate interactions and sharing among independently designed databases. Their main purpose was to build up a loosely coupled federation of different component databases. Sheth and Larson (1990) have identified five-level schema architecture for a federated MDBS to solve the heterogeneity of FMDBSs, which is depicted in figure 3.19.

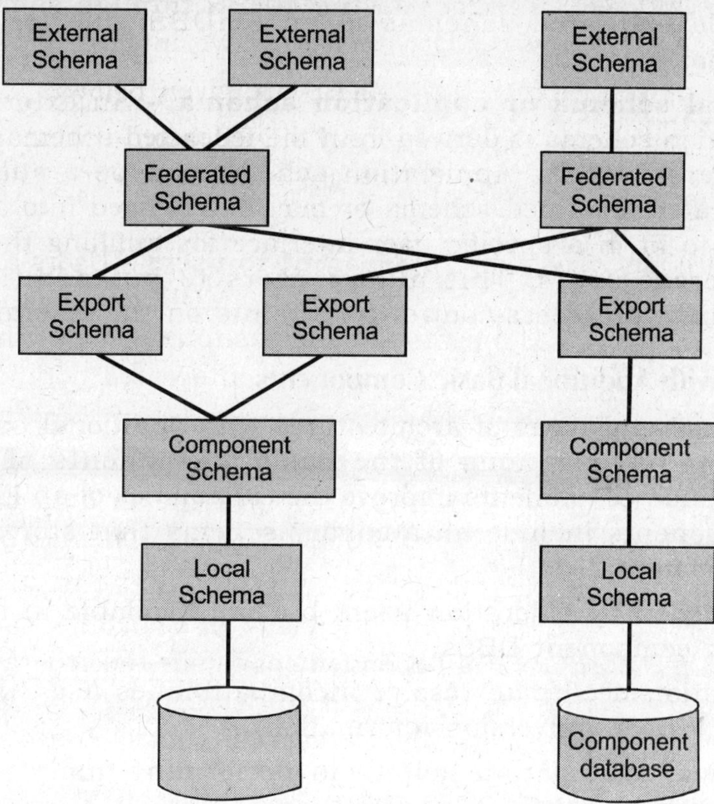

Figure 3.19 Five-level Schema Architecture of Federated MDBS

(i) **Local schema** – A local schema is used to represent each component database of a federated MDBS. A local schema is expressed in the native data model of the component DBMS, and hence different local schemas can be expressed in different data models.

(ii) **Component schema** – A component schema is generated by translating local schemas into a data model called the canonical or CDM of the FMDBS. A component schema is used to facilitate negotiation and integration among divergent local schemas to execute global tasks.

(iii) **Export schema** – An export schema is a subset of a component schema, and it is used to represent only those portions of a local database that are authorized by the local DBMS for accessing of non-local users. The purpose of defining export schemas is to control and manage the autonomy of component databases.

(iv) **Federated schema** – A federated Schema is an integration of multiple export schemas. It is always connected with a data dictionary that stores the information about the data distribution and the definitions

of different schemas in the heterogeneous environment. There may be multiple federated schemas in an FMDBS, one for each class of federation users.

(v) **External schema or application schema** – An external schema or application schema is derived from the federated schema and is suitable for different users. Application schema can be a subset of a large complicated federated schema or may be changed into a different data model, to fit in a specific user interface for fulfilling the requirements of different users. This allows users to put additional integrity constraints or access-control constraints on the federated schema.

Architectures with Additional Basic Components

There are several types of architectures with additional components that are extensions or variations of the basic components of the reference architecture. Such components improve the capabilities of an FDBS. Examples of such components include an auxiliary schema that stores the following types of information:

- data needed by federation users but not available in any of the pre-existing component DBSs.
- information needed to resolve incompatibilities (e.g., unit translation tables, format conversion information).
- statistical information helpful in performing query processing and optimisation.

Extended federated architectures

To allow a federation user to access data from systems other than the component DBSs, the five-level schema architecture can be extended in additional ways, for example, by replacing a component database by a collection of application programs. It is conceptually possible to replace some database tables by application programs. For example, a table containing pairs of equivalent Fahrenheit and Celsius values can be replaced by a procedure whereby calculated values on one scale give values on the other.

3.12.2 REFERENCE ARCHITECTURE OF TIGHTLY COUPLED FEDERATED MDBS

An FDBS is tightly coupled if the federation and its administrator(s) have the responsibility for creating and maintaining the federation and actively control the access to component DBSs. Tightly coupled federations take the form of schema integration and may have one or more federated schemas. A tightly coupled FDBS is said to have single federation if it allows the creation and management of only one federated schema; it is said to have multiple federations if it allows the creation and management of multiple federated schemas. It provides location, replication, and distribution transparency. The

process for the administration of a tightly coupled FDBS is as follows. First, export schemas are created by negotiation between a component DBA and the federation DBA; the component DBA has control over what is included in the export schemas. Then the federation DBA creates and controls the federated schema as s/he is usually allowed to read the component schemas to help determine what data are available and where they are located and then negotiate for their access. Finally, external schemas are created by negotiation between a federation user and the federation DBA who has the authority to decide what is included in each external schema. DDTS can be categorised as tightly coupled FDBSs with single federation. The reference architecture of a tightly coupled FMDBS is depicted in figure 3.20.

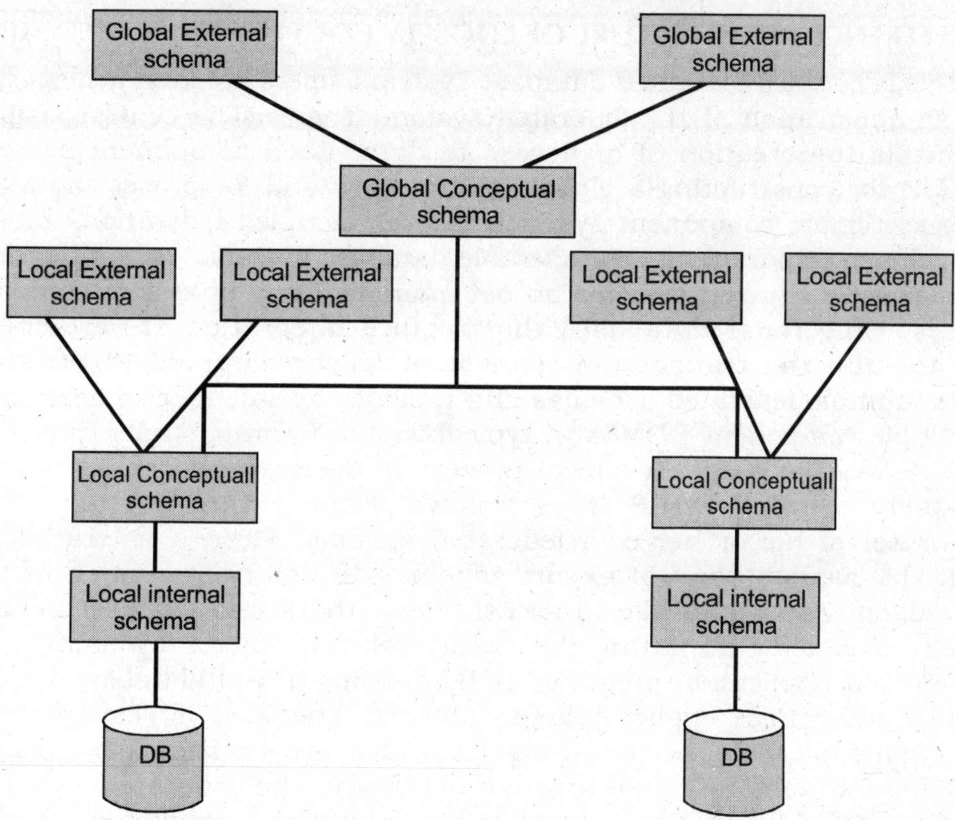

Figure 3.20 Reference Architecture of Tightly Coupled Federated MDBS

The architecture of an FMDBS is primarily determined by which schemas are present, how they are arranged and how they are constructed. The reference architecture is necessary to understand, categorize and compare different architectural options for developing federated database systems. This section describes the reference architecture of a tightly coupled FMDBS.

Usually, and FMDBS is designed in a bottom-up manner to integrate a number of existing heterogeneous databases. In a tightly coupled FMDBS, federated schema takes the form of schema integration. For simplicity, a single (logical) federation is considered for the entire system, and it is represented by a GCS. A number of export schemas are integrated into the GCS, where the export schemas are created through negotiation between the local databases and the GCS. Thus, in an FMDBS, the GCS is a subset of local conceptual schemas and consists of the data that each local DBMS agrees to share. The GCS of a tightly coupled FMBDS involves the integration of either parts of the local conceptual schemas or the local external schemas. Global external schemas are generated through negotiation between global users and the GCS.

3.12.3 REFERENCE ARCHITECTURE OF LOOSELY COUPLED FEDERATED MDBS

In loosely coupled federated database systems, users are largely responsible for the administration of the federated system. There is no central authority that controls the creation of or access to data. Each component system is responsible for constructing a global schema view and for processing queries that access remote component systems. Loosely coupled federations take the form of schema importation, interoperable database systems, or multidatabase systems. Loosely coupled systems do not maintain hard links into component databases. Only those databases that require integration are attached as needed to fulfil the transaction request. A loosely coupled FDBS always supports multiple federated schemas and provides an interface to deal directly with multiple component DBMSs. A typical way to formulate queries is to use a multidatabase language. A typical process of developing federated schemas in a loosely coupled FDBS is as follows. Each federation user is the administrator of his or her own federated schema. First, a federation user looks at the available set of export schemas to determine which of these describe data s/he would like to access. Next, the federation user defines a federated schema by importing the export schema objects by using a user interface or an application program, or by defining a multidatabase language query that references export schema objects. The user is responsible for understanding the semantics of the objects in the export schemas and resolving the DBMS and semantic heterogeneity. Finally, the federated schema is named and stored under the account of the federation user who is its owner.

The loosely coupled approach may be inappropriate for more traditional business or corporate databases, where system control is desirable, where the users are naïve and would find it difficult to perform negotiation and integration themselves, or where location, distribution, and replication transparencies are desirable. The loosely coupled approach provides a greater degree of autonomy for the component systems, because no central authority is imposed. In addition, loose coupling generally tends to scale better to very large systems. On the other hand, maintaining consistency is more difficult in a system that lacks a central authority. The reference architecture of a loosely coupled FMDBS is depicted in figure 3.21.

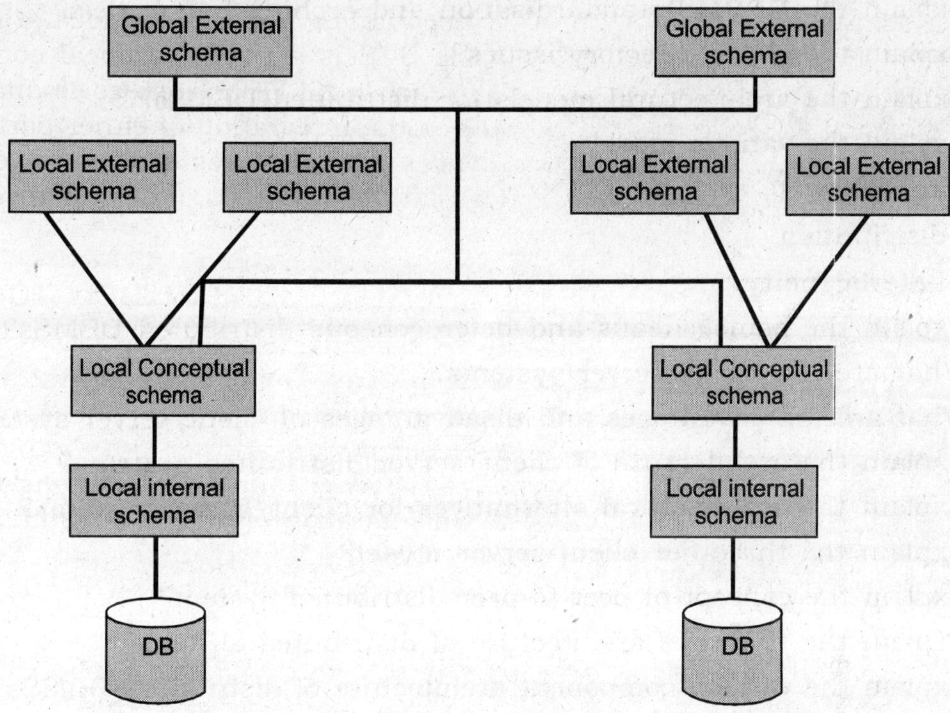

Figure 3.21 Reference Architecture of Loosely Coupled Federated MDBS

Breitbart believes that the Federated approach is more advantageous than the global schema approach; it is popular, and many currently developed systems use this approach for resolving heterogeneity problems between databases. This avoids constructing a global schema and is easier to maintain. To achieve this, a system must maintain knowledge about the contents of each database to know what to include in a query and to help in resolving conflicts between sources, since there is no global schema to provide information about the semantics of the databases. In this case, federated schemas for global users are defined by importing export schemas using a user interface or an application program or by defining a multi-database language query that references export schema objects of local databases. Export schemas are created based on local component databases. Thus, in a loosely coupled FMDBS, a global external schema consists of one or more local conceptual schemas.

EXERCISES

1. What are distributed database systems?
2. Explain the architecture of distributed database systems?
3. Explain the DDBMS standardisation and architecture models?
4. Explain the global directory issues?
5. Explain the architectural models for distributed DBMSs?
6. Explain the various models:
   - autonomy
   - distribution
   - heterogeneity
7. Explain the homogeneous and heterogeneous distributed DBMSs?
8. What are the client/server systems?
9. What are the advantages and disadvantages of client/server system?
10. Explain the architecture of client/server distributed systems?
11. Explain the architectural alternatives for client/server systems?
12. Explain the three-tier client-server model?
13. Explain the concept of peer-to-peer distributed system?
14. Explain the reference architecture of distributed DBMSs?
15. Explain the various component architecture of distributed DBMSs?
16. What do you by distributed data independence?
17. Explain the various types of distributed database systems?
18. Explain the overview of client-server architecture and its relationship to distributed databases?
19. Explain the federated database system?
20. Explain the architecture of federated database system?
21. Explain the concept of multi-database system?
22. Explain the five-level schema architecture of federated MDBS?
23. Explain the reference architecture of tightly coupled federated MDBS?
24. Explain the reference architecture of loosely coupled federated MDBS?

CHAPTER 4

DISTRIBUTED QUERY PROCESSING

4.1 INTRODUCTION

The amount of data handled by a database management system increases continuously, and it is no longer unusual for a DBMS to manage data sizes of several hundred gigabytes to terabytes. In this context, a critical challenge in a database environment is to develop an efficient query processing technique, which involves the retrieval of data from the database. A significant amount of research has been dedicated to develop highly efficient algorithms for processing queries in different databases, but here the attention is restricted on relational databases. There are many ways in which a complex query can be executed, but the main objective of query processing is to determine which one is the most cost-effective. This complicated task is performed by a DBMS module, called query processing. In query processing, the database users generally specify what data is required rather than the procedure to follow to retrieve the required data. Thus, an important aspect of query processing is query optimization. A query typically has many possible execution strategies, and the process of choosing a suitable one for processing a query is known as query optimization.

A query is expressed by using a high-level language such as SQL (Structured Query Language) in a relational data model. The main function of a relational query processor is to transform a high level query into are equivalent lower-level query (relational algebra), and the transformation must achieve both correctness and efficiency. The lower-level query (relational algebra) and the transformation must achieve both correctness and efficiency. The lower-level query actually implements the execution strategy for the given query. In a centralized DBMS, query processing can be divided into four main steps: query decomposition (consisting of scanning, parsing and validation), query optimization, code generation and query execution. In the query decomposition step, the query parser checks the variety of the query and then translates it into an internal form, usually a relational algebraic expression or something equivalent. The query examines all relational algebraic expressions that are equivalent to the given query and chooses the optimum one that is estimated to be the cheapest. The code generator generates the code for the access plan selected by the query optimizer and the query processor actually executes the query. The steps of query processing in centralized DBMS are illustrated in figure 4.1.

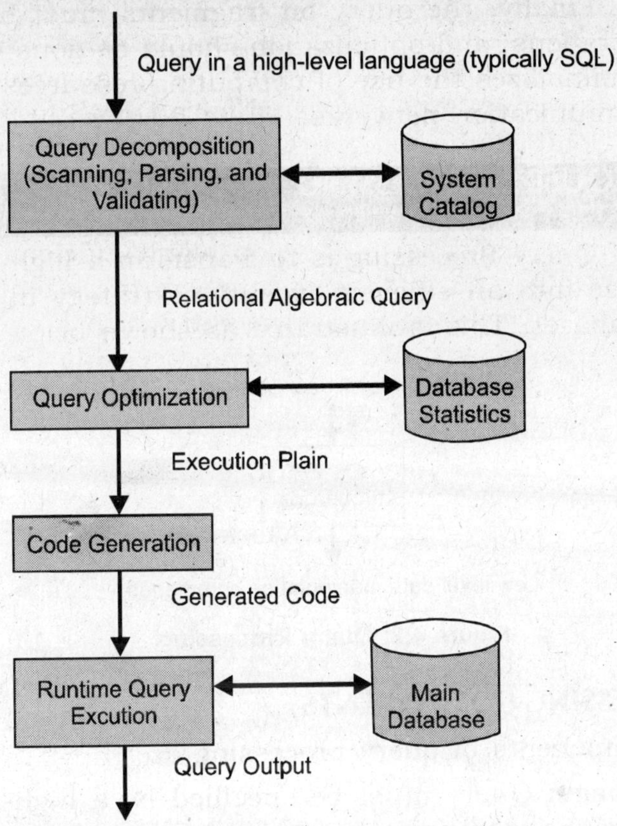

Figure 4.1 Steps for Query Processing in Centralized DBMS

Query optimization is a critical performance issue in a centralized database management system, and the main challenge is to choose one execution strategy that minimizes the consumption of computing resources. Another objective of query optimization is to reduce the total execution time of the query, which is the sum of the execution times of all individual operations that make up the query. There are two main techniques for query optimization in a centralized DBMS, although the two methods are usually combined in practice. The first approach uses heuristic rules that order the operations in a query, whereas the second approach compares different strategies based on their relative costs and selects the one that requires minimum computing resources. In a distributed system, several additional factors further complicate the process of query execution. In general, the relations are fragmented in a distributed database; therefore, the distributed query processor transforms a high-level query on a logically distributed database (entire relation) into a sequence of database operations (relational algebra) on relation fragments. The data accessed by the query in a distributed database must be localized so that the database operations can be performed on local data or

relation fragments. Finally, the query on fragments must be extended with communication operations, and optimization should be done with respect to a cost function that minimizes the use of computing resources such as disk I/Os, CPUs and communication networks.

4.2 CONCEPTS OF QUERY PROCESSING

The objective of Query Processing is to transform a high-level query on a distributed database into an efficient execution strategy in a low-level language on local databases. This is illustrated as shown below:

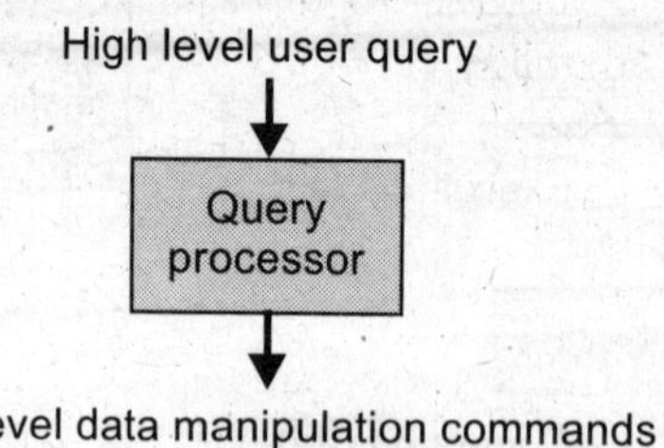

Figure 4.2: Query Processing

4.2.1 QUERY PROCESSING COMPONENTS

Three main components of query processing are:

1. **Query Language:** Query must be specified by a high-level query language. SQL is the most widely used declarative query language.
2. **Query Execution Methodology:** This includes low-level physical steps for executing high-level (declarative) user queries.
3. **Query Optimization:** The process to determine the best execution plan for a query.

4.2.3 STEPS OF QUERY PROCESSING

Following are the steps involved in processing a query:

- Any high-level query (SQL) on a database must be processed, optimized and executed by the DBMS
- The high-level query is scanned, and parsed to check for syntactic correctness
- An internal representation of a query is created, which is either a query tree or a query graph
- The DBMS then devises an execution strategy for retrieving the result of the query. (An execution strategy is a plan for executing the query by accessing the data, and storing the intermediate results)

- The process of choosing one out of the many execution strategies is known as query optimization

4.3 REPRESENTATION OF DATABASE OPERATION IN FORM OF A QUERY

Query Processing means to transform a high-level query (typically, in relational calculus) into an equivalent lower-level query (typically in relational algebra). The low-level query actually implements the execution strategy for the query. The transformation must achieve both correctness and efficiency. It is correct if the low-level query has the same semantics as the original query i.e. if both queries produce the same result. The well-defined mapping from relational calculus to relational algebra results into achieving correctness. So the query processing problem is to produce efficient execution strategy.

Thus Query processing problem includes:

4.3.1 SELECTING ALTERNATIVES

A calculus query may have many equivalent algebra queries. So the problem is to select execution strategy that could minimize execution time, or total resource consumption. It is a computationally intractable problem. Thus problem is to choose a solution close to the optimum. In distributed databases, communication cost for data exchange occurs. So query processing problem reduces to select best sites to process data and possibly the way data should be transferred.

Example 4.1

Consider the following two tables for an Employee (EMP) and Assignment of Project (ASG).

EMP(ENO,ENAME,TITLE)

Where ENO is Employee No., ENAME is Employee Name, TITLE is Title of Employee in the Company.

ASG(ENO,PNO,RESP,DUR)

Where ENO is Employee No., PNO is Project No., RESP is Responsibility of an Employee within a project and DUR is duration of assignment in months.

Now consider the query:

Find the names of employees whose project duration is greater than 37 months.

The expression of query in relational calculus using the SQL syntax is:

SELECT ENAME

FROM EMP, ASG

WHERE EMP.ENO = ASG.ENO

AND DUR > 37

Two equivalent relational algebra queries to above query are:

$$\Pi_{ENAME}(\sigma_{DUR>37 \wedge EMP.ENO=ASG.ENO}(EMP \times ASG))$$

$$\Pi_{ENAME}(EMP \infty_{ENO}(\sigma_{DUR>37}(ASG)))$$

The second query avoids Cartesian product and thus consumes much less computing resource than the first and thus is better and should be retained.

4.3.2 IMPORTANCE OF SITE SELECTION

In Centralized query processing, execution strategies can be well expressed in an extension of relational algebra and the aim is to choose, for a given query, the best relational algebra query among all equivalent ones. On the other hand, in distributed query processing, relational algebra is not enough to express execution strategies. It must be supplemented with operations for exchanging data between sites. So additionally, distributed query processing includes the selection of best sites to process data and possibly the way data should be transformed thus making query processing significantly more difficult.

Following example illustrates the importance of site selection:

Consider the query

$$\Pi_{ENAME}(EMP \infty_{ENO}(\sigma_{RESP="manager"}(ASG)))$$

Assumptions: Assume that:

Site 1: $ASG_1 = \sigma_{ENO \le}"E3"(ASG)$

Site 2: $AGSG_2 = \sigma_{ENO>"E3"}(ASG)$

Site 3: $EMP_1 = \sigma_{ENO \le "E3"}(EMP)$

Site 4: $EMP_2 = \sigma_{ENO>"E3"}(EMP)$

Site 5: result

Two Equivalent distributed execution strategies for the above query are shown in Figure 4.2 and Figure 4.3 respectively. An arrow from site i to site j labeled with R indicates that relation R is transferred from site i to site j. StrategyA exploits the fact that relations EMP and ASG are fragmented the same way in order to perform the select and join operation in parallel. StrategyB centralizes all the operand data at the result site before processing the query.

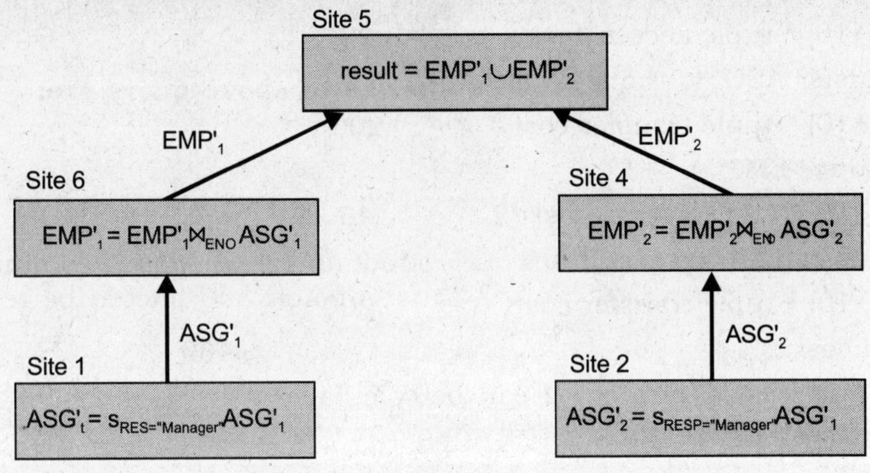

(a) Strategy A

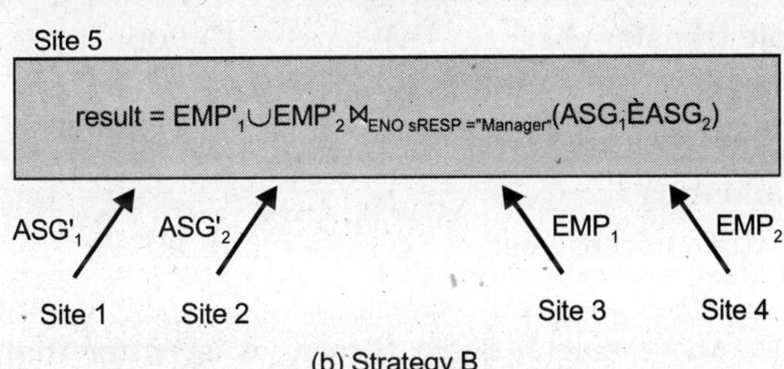

(b) Strategy B

Figure 4.3: Importance of Site Selection

In order to evaluate the resource consumption of these two strategies, we use a simple cost model. **Also consider the following assumptions:**

- size of EMP relation is 400 tuples,
- size of ASG relation is 1000 tuples
- tuple_access_cost is 1 unit
- tuple_transfer_cost is 10 units
- There are 20 managers in ASG
- Data is uniformally distributed among sites.
- Relations ASG and EMP are locally clustered on attributes RESP and ENO respectively.

Therefore, there is direct access to tuples of ASG (respectively, EMP) based on the value of attribute RESP (respectively, ENO).

The total cost of strategy1 can be calculated as:

» produce ASG'
· (10+10) * tuple access cost 20
» transfer ASG' to the sites of EMP
· (10+10) * tuple transfer cost 200
» produce EMP'
· (10+10) * tuple access cost *2 40
» transfer EMP' to result site
· (10+10) * tuple transfer cost 200
Total cost 460

The total cost of strategy 2 can be calculated as:

» transfer EMP to site 5
· 400 * tuple transfer cost 4,000
» transfer ASG to site 5
· 1000 * tuple transfer cost 10,000
» produce ASG': no index due to data transfer
· 1000 * tuple access cost 1,000
» join EMP and ASG'
· 400 * 20 * tuple access cost 8,000
Total cost 23,000

As clear from above calculations, StrategyA is better than StrategyB by a factor of 50. It also provides better distribution of work among sites.

Example 4.2

Consider the following two relations which are stored in a centralized DBMS

Employee (empid, ename, salary, designation, deptno)

Department (deptno, dname, location)

and the following query:

"Retrieve the names of all employees whose department location is 'inside' the campus"

where, empid and deptno are the primary keys for the relations Employee and Department respectively and deptno is a foreign key of the relation Employee.

Using SQL, the above query can be expressed as:

Select ename from Employee, Department where Employee.deptno = Depaartment.deptno and location = "inside"

Two equivalent relational algebraic expressions that correspond to the above SQL statement are as follows:

(i) P_{ename} ($s_{(location = \text{“inside”}) \wedge (Employee.deptno = Department.deptno)}$ (Emoloyee x Department))

(ii) P_{ename} ($Employee_{Employee.deptno = Department.deptno}$ ($s_{(location = \text{“inside”}}$ (Department)))

In the first relational algebraic expression the projection and the selection operations have been performed after calculating the Cartesian Product of two relations Employee and Department, whereas in the second expression the Cartesian Product has been performed after performing the selection and the projection operation from individual relations. Obviously, the use of computing resources is lesser in the second expression. Thus, in a centralized DBMS, it is easier to choose the optimum execution strategy based on a number of relational algebraic expressions that are equivalent to the same query. In a distributed context, the query processing is significantly more difficult because the choice of optimum execution strategy depends on some other factors such as data transfer among sites and the selection of the best site for query execution. The problem of distributed query processing is discussed below with the help of an example.

Example 4.3

Consider the same example 4.2 in a distributed database environment where the Employee and Department relations are fragmented and stored at different sites. For simplicity, let us assume that the Employee relation is horizontally fragmented into two partitions EMP_1 and EMP_{2-}, which are stored at site1 and site2 respectively, and the Department relation is horizontally fragmented into two relations $DEPT_1$ and $DEPT_2$, which are stored in site3 and site4 respectively as listed below.

$EMP_1 = s_{deptno<=10}$ (Employee)

EMP_2 $s_{deptno>10}$ (Employee)

$DEPT_1 = s_{deptn=10}$ (Department)

$DEPT_2 - s_{deptno>10}$ (Department)

Further assume that the above query is at Site5 and the result is required at that site. Two different strategies to execute the distributed environment are depicted in figure 4.4.

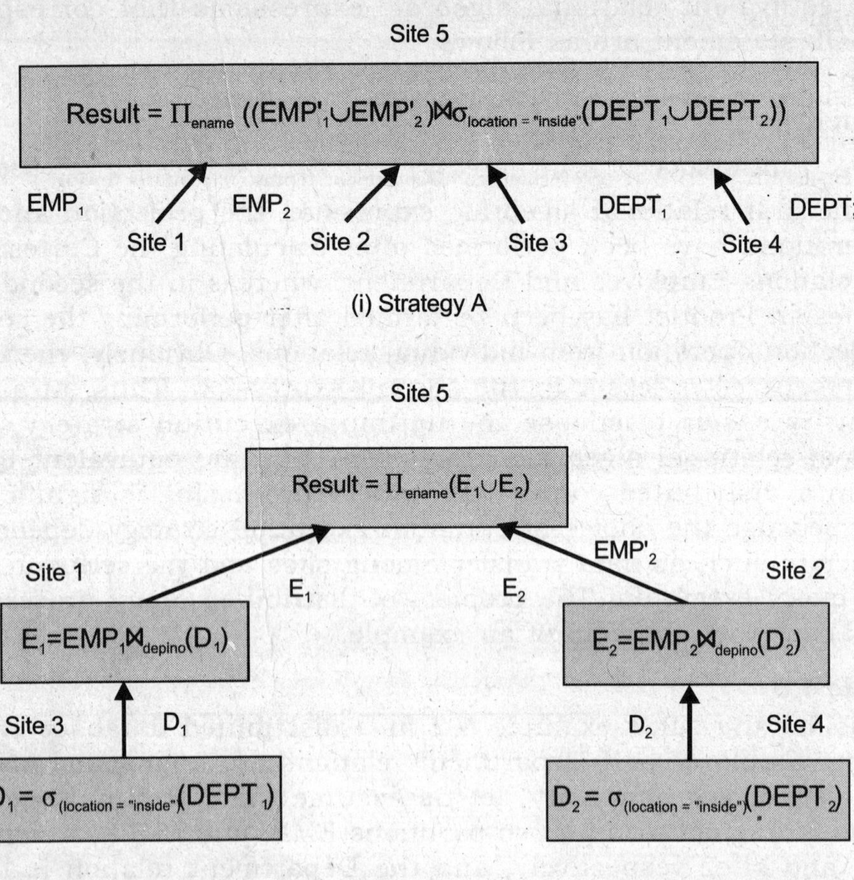

Figure 4.4 Two Equivalent Distributed Query Execution Strategies

In the first strategy, all data are transferred to Site5 before processing the query. In the second strategy, selection operations are performed individually on the fragmented relations $DEPT_1$ and $DEPT_2$ at Site3 and Site4 respectively, and then the resultant data D_1 and D_2 are transferred to Site1 and Site2 respectively. After evaluating the join operations D_1 with EMP_1 at Site1 and D_2 with EMP_2 at Site2, the resultant data are transmitted to Site5 and the final projection operation is performed.

To calculate the costs of the above two different execution strategies, let us assume that the cost of accessing a tuple from any relation is 1 unit, and the cost of transferring a tuple in Employee and Department relation are 1,000 and 20 respectively, among which the location of 8 departments are insite the campus. For the sake of simplicity, assume that the tuples are uniformly distributed among sites, and the relations Employee and Department are locally clustered on attributed "deptno" and "location" respectively.

The total cost for the strategy A is as follows:

(i) The cost of transferring 10 tuples of $DEPT_1$ from Site3 and 10 tuples of $DEPT_2$ from Site4 to Site5 = (10 + 10) * 10 = 200

(ii) The cost of transferring 500 tuples of EMP_1 from Site1 and 500 tuples of EMP_2 from Site 2 to Site5 = (500 + 500) * 10 = 10,000

(iii) The cost of producing selection operations from $DEPT_1$ and $DEPT_2$ = 20 * 1 = 20

(iv) The cost of performing join operation of $EMP_1$and EMP_2 with resultant selected data from Department relation = 1,000 * 8 * 1 = 8,000

(v) The cost of performing projection operation at Site5 to retrieve the employee names = 8 * 1 = 8

In this case, the total cost is = 18,228.

The total cost for the strategy B is listed in the following:

(i) The cost of producing D_1 from $DEPT_1$ and D_2 from $DEPT_2$ (4 + 4) * 1 = 8

(ii) The cost for transferring 4 tuples of D_1 from Site3 to Site1 and 4 tuples of D_2 from Site4 to Site2 = (4 + 4) * 10 = 80

(iii) The cost of producing E_1 at Site1 and E_2 at Site2 = (4 + 4) * 1 * 2 = 16

(iv) The cost for transferring 4 tuples of E_1 from Site1 to Site5 and 4 tuples of E_2 Site2 to Site5 = (4 + 4) * 10 = 80

(v) The cost for evaluating projection operation at Site5 to retrieve the employee names = 8 * 1 = 8.

Hence, the total cost is = 192.

The cost of performing the projection operation and the selection operation on a tuple is same because in both cases it is equal to the cost of accessing a tuple. Obviously, the execution strategy B is much more cost-beneficial than the strategy A. Furthermore, the slower communication between the sites and the higher degree of fragmentation may increase the cost difference between the alternative query processing/execution strategies.

4.4 OBJECTIVES OF DISTRIBUTED QUERY PROCESSING

As stated before, the objective of query processing in a distributed context is to transform a high-level query on a distributed database, which is seen as a single database by the users, into an efficient execution strategy expressed in a low-level language on local databases. We assume that the high-level language is relational calculus while the low-level language is an extension of relational algebra with communication operations. The different layers involved in the query transformation. An important aspect of query processing is query optimization. Because many execution strategies are correct transfor-

mations of the same high-level query, the one that optimizes (minimizes) resource consumption should be retained.

A good measure of resource consumption is the total cols that will be incurred in processing the query [Sacco and Yao, 1982]. Total cost is the sum of all times incurred in processing the operations of the query at various sites and in intersite communication. Another good measure is the response time of the query [Epstein et al., 1978], which is the time elapsed for executing the query. Since operations can be executed in parallel at different sites, the response time of a query may be significantly less than its total cost.

In a distributed database system, the total cost to be minimized includes CPU, I/O, and communication costs. The CPU cost is incurred when performing operations on data in main memory. The I/O cost is the time necessary for disk input/output operations. This cost can be minimized by reducing the number of I/O operations through fast access methods to the data and efficient use of main memory (buffer management). The communication cost is the time needed for exchanging data between sites participating in the execution of the query. This cost is incurred in processing the messages (formatting/deformatting) and in transmitting the data on the communication network.

The first two cost components (I/O and CPU cost) are the only factors considered by centralized DBMSs. The communication cost component is probably the most important factor considered in distributed databases. Most of the early proposal for distributed query optimization assume that the communication cost largely dominates local processing cost (I/O and CPU cost), and thus ignore the latter. This assumption is based on very slow communication networks (e.g., wide area networks with a bandwidth of a few kilobytes per second) rather than on networks with disk bandwidths. Therefore the aim of distributed query optimization reduces to the problem of minimizing communication costs generally at the expense of local processing. The advantage is that local optimization can be done independently using the known methods for centralized systems. However, modern distributed processing environments have much faster communication networks, whose bandwidth is comparable to that of disks. Therefore, more recent research efforts consider significantly to the total cost of evaluating a query[1] [Page and Popek, 1985]. Nevertheless, in distributed environments with high bandwidths, the overhead cost incurred for communication between sites (e.g., software protocols) makes communication cost still an important factor – as important as I/O cost [Valduriez and Gardarin, 1984]. For completeness, let us consider the methods that minimize all cost components.

Distributed query processing involves the retrieving of data from physically distributed database that provide the view of a single logical database to users. It has a number of objectives as listed below.

- The major objective of distributed query processing is to translate a high-level language query on a single logically distributed database (as seen by the users) into low-level language queries on physically distributed local databases.
- There are a number of alternative execution strategies for processing a distributed query. Thus, another important objective of distributed query processing is to select an efficient execution strategy for the execution of a distributed query that minimizes the consumption of computing resources.
- In distributed query processing, the total cost for executing a distributed query should be minimized. If no relation is fragmented in a distributed DBMS, the query execution involves only a local processing cost. On the other hand, if relations are fragmented, a communication cost is incurred in addition to the local processing cost. In this case, the aim of distributed query processing is to minimize the total execution cost of the query, which includes the total processing (sum of all local processing costs incurred at the participating sites) of the query and the communication cost. The local processing cost of a distributed query is evaluated in terms of I/O cost (the number of disk accesses) and CPU cost. The CPU cost is incurred when performing data operations in the main memory of the participating sites. The I/O cost can be minimized by using efficient buffer management techniques. In distributed query execution, the communication cost is incurred for the exchange of data between participating sites. Hence, the communication cost depends on several factors such as the amount of data transfer between participating sites, the selection of best site for query execution, the number of message transfers between the participating sites, and the communication network. In the case of high-speed wide area networks (with a bandwidth of a few kilobytes per.second), the communication cost is the dominant factor, and the optimization of CPU cost and I/O cost can be ignored in such cases. The optimization of local processing cost is greater significance in the case of local networks.
- In distributed query processing, one approach to query optimization is to minimize the total cost of time required to execute a query. Another alternative approach for query optimization is to reduce the response time of a distributed query, which is the time elapsed between the initiation of the query and producing the answer of the query. Therefore, another important objective of distributed query processing is to maximize the parallel execution of operations of a given distributed query so that the response time is significantly less than the total cost time.

4.5 COMPLEXITY OF RELATIONAL ALGEBRA OPERATIONS

The relational algebra is used to express the output of the query. The complexity of relational algebra operations plays a role in defining some of the principles of query optimization. All complexity measures are based on the cardinality of the relation independent of physical implementation details such as fragmentation and storage structures. Following Figure 4.5 shows the complexity of unary and binary operations in the order of increasing complexity and thus of increasing execution time.

Operation	Complexity
Selection Projection (without duplicate elimination)	$O(n)$
Projection (with duplicate elimination) Group	$O(n\log n)$
Join Semi-Join Division Union, Difference	$O(n\log n)$
Cartesian Product	$O(n^2)$

Figure 4.5: Complexity of Relational Algebra Operations

Where n= cardinality of relations

As shown in above table, Complexity is O (n) for unary operations and complexity is O (n* log n) for binary operations if each tuple of one relation must be compared with each tuple of the other on the basis of the equality of selected attributes. Projects with duplicate elimination and group operations require that each tuple of the relation must be compared with each other tuple and thus have O (n*log n) complexity. Finally, Complexity is $O(n^2)$ for the Cartesian product of two relations because each tuple of one relation must be combined with each tuple of the other.

Following conclusions can be drawn from above Complexity table:

- Selections that reduce cardinalities should be performed first.
- Operations should be ordered by increasing complexity.

4.6 QUERY PROCESSOR AND ITS CHARACTERISTICS

A query processor is a module in the DBMS that performs the tasks to process, to optimize and to generate execution strategy for a high-level query .For a DDBMS, the query processor also does data localization for the query based on the fragmentation scheme and generates the execution strategy

that incorporates the communication operations involved in processing the query.

4.6.1 CHARACTERISTICS OF QUERY PROCESSORS

Following are important characteristics of query processors:

4.6.1.1 LANGUAGES

The input language to the query processor can be relational algebra or calculus. If input language is relational calculus, it requires an additional phase to decompose a query expressed in relational calculus into relational algebra. In a distributed context, the output language is relational algebra (annotated with communication primitives). The operations of the output language are directly implemented in the system. The query processor must efficiently map input language to output language.

4.6.1.2 TYPES OF OPTIMIZATION

Query Optimization means to choose the best query execution strategy. Most common method is to predict the cost of each strategy and select the strategy with minimum cost. Although this method is effective in selecting the best strategy, it may incur a significant processing cost for the optimization itself.

The output language specification represents the execution strategy. There can be many such strategies, the best one can be selected through exhaustive search, or by applying heuristic (minimize size of intermediate relations). For distributed databases semi joins can be applied to reduce data transfer.

Following are various types of optimizers or optimization techniques:

(i) Cost-based: This includes an exhaustive search whereby (almost) all possible execution strategies are considered. This technique can be optimal and has combinatorial complexity in the number of relations. This technique however incurs high cost.

(ii) Heuristics: One way of reducing the cost of exhaustive search is the use of heuristics whose effect is to restrict the solution space so that only a few strategies are considered. In both centralized and distributed systems, a common heuristic is to minimize the size of intermediate relations. This method of heuristics may not be optimal.

Following are commonly used heuristics:

- regroup common sub-expressions
- perform unary operations selection, projection first.
- reorder operations to reduce intermediate relation size
- replace a join by a series of semi joins to minimize data communication.

4.6.1.3 OPTIMIZATION TIMING

A query may be optimized at different times relative to the actual time of query execution. Optimization Timing can be:

(i) Static: In this case, optimization is done before executing the query (at compilation time), cost of optimization amortized over multiple executions, mostly based on exhaustive search. Since sizes of intermediate relations of a strategy are not known until run time, they need to be estimated using database statistics. So errors in the estimates can result in sub optimal strategies.

(ii) Dynamic: Here optimization is done at run time i.e. at every time the query is executed. At any point of execution, the choice of the best next operation can be based on accurate knowledge of the results of the operations executed previously. Therefore database statistics are not needed to estimate the size of intermediate results. The main advantage of dynamic optimization over static query optimization is that it makes use of exact sizes of intermediate relations. The disadvantage is that it is expensive since it is based on heuristics and query optimization must be repeated for each execution of the query.

(iii) Hybrid: This approach mixes static and dynamic approaches. In this case, the approach is mainly static but dynamic query optimization may take place when high difference between predicted and actual sizes is detected.

(iv) Statistics: The effectiveness of query optimization relies on statistics on database. Dynamic query optimization requires statistics in order to choose which operations should be done first. Static query optimization requires estimating size of intermediate relations based on statistical information. In a distributed database, statistics for query optimization include:

- fragment cardinality and size
- size and number of distinct values for each attribute.
- detailed histograms of attribute values for better selectivity estimation.

Example of Statistics:

- relation (cardinality, size of a tuple, join selectivity)
- attribute (cardinality of domain, actual number of distinct values)

Common assumptions

- independence between different attribute values.
- uniform distribution of attribute values within their domain.

Statistics need to be periodically updated.

4.6.1.4 DECISION SITES

When static optimization is used, either a single site or several sites may participate in the selection of the strategy to be applied for answering the query. Decision sites are sites that make a decision.

Following are the possible approaches:

(i) **Centralized:** In this approach, a single site determines the best schedule and thus that site is a decision site. This approach is simple but need knowledge about entire distributed database.

(ii) **Distributed:** This approach requires cooperation among sites to determine the schedule and thus multiple sites are decision sites. This approach needs only local information but includes the cost of cooperation.

(iii) **Hybrid:** In this approach, one site makes a major decision and other sites can make local decisions. For example, System R* uses a hybrid approach.

4.6.1.5 EXPLOITATION OF NETWORK TOPOLOGY

The network topology is generally exploited by the distributed query processor. The networks to be considered are:

(i) **Wide area networks (WAN):** In a wide area network, the cost function to be minimized includes mainly communication cost and all other cost factors are ignored. There is a global schedule to minimize communication cost and local schedules are according to centralized query optimization

(ii) **Local area networks (LAN):** In a local area network, communication costs are comparable to I/O costs as well as CPU costs and thus they need to be considered. Therefore it is reasonable for the distributed query processor to increase parallel execution at the expense of communication cost. Also broadcasting capability of some local area networks can be exploited e.g. for joins to optimize the processing.

4.6.1.6 EXPLOITATION OF REPLICATED FRAGMENTS

In a distributed database, relations are fragmented and then these fragments are replicated. Distributed queries expressed on global relations are mapped into queries on replicated physical fragments of relations. Optimization algorithms exploit the existence of replicated fragments at run time in order to minimize communication times.

The optimization algorithm thus includes:

- larger number of possible strategies
- use of Semi joins
- reducing size of data transfer

- increasing number of messages and local processing
- good for fast or slow networks

4.6.1.7 USE OF SEMIJOINS

The semijoin operation has the important property of reducing the size of the operand relation. When the main cost component considered by the query processor is communication, a semijoin is particularly useful for improving the processing of distributed join operations as it is good for reducing the size of data transfer between the sites. However using semijoins may result in an increase in the number of messages and in the local processing time.

Some examples of distributed DBMSs using semijoins include:

- The early SDD-1 makes an extensive use of semijoins and was designed for slow WAN
- The early System R* do not employ semijoins and System R* assumes faster networks

4.6.1.8 QUERY OPTIMIZER

Queries expressed in SQL can have multiple equivalent relational algebra query expressions. The distributed query optimizer must select the ordering of relational algebra operations; sites to process data, and possibly the way data should be transferred in order to optimize the queries. This makes distributed query processing significantly more difficult.

4.7 PHASES IN DISTRIBUTED QUERY PROCESSING

In a distributed database system, data distribution details are hidden from the users; thus, it provides data distribution transparency. The distributed query processor is responsible for transforming a query on global relations into a number of subqueries on fragmented relations at local databases. Therefore, distributed query processing is more complicated than query processing on centralized DBMS, and it requires some extra steps in addition to all the steps of a distributed system, it follows a sequence of phases to retrieve the answer of the query. These are query decomposition, query fragmentation, global query optimization and local query optimization as illustrated in figure 4.7. The first three phases in distributed query processing are controlled by the site where the query is generated. The local query optimization is done at the participating local sites, and all these optimized local queries are executed on local databases. Finally, the results of local queries are sent back to the site of the distributed system where the query is generated. The details of all these phases are described in the next section.

Phases of distributed query processing are based on flow of data in distributed query processing. This flow is as shown below in figure 4.6:

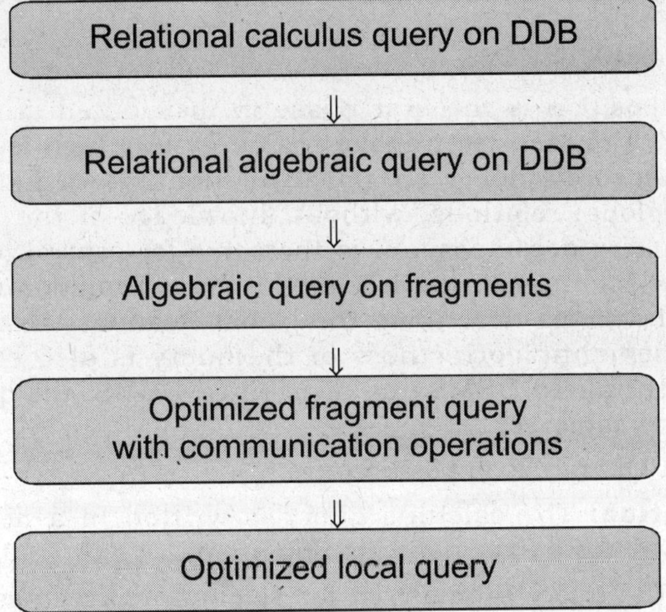

Figure 4.6 Phases in Distributed Query Processing

The steps which are performed to perform distributed query processing are called phases of distributed query processing. These phases are depicted in the following figure:

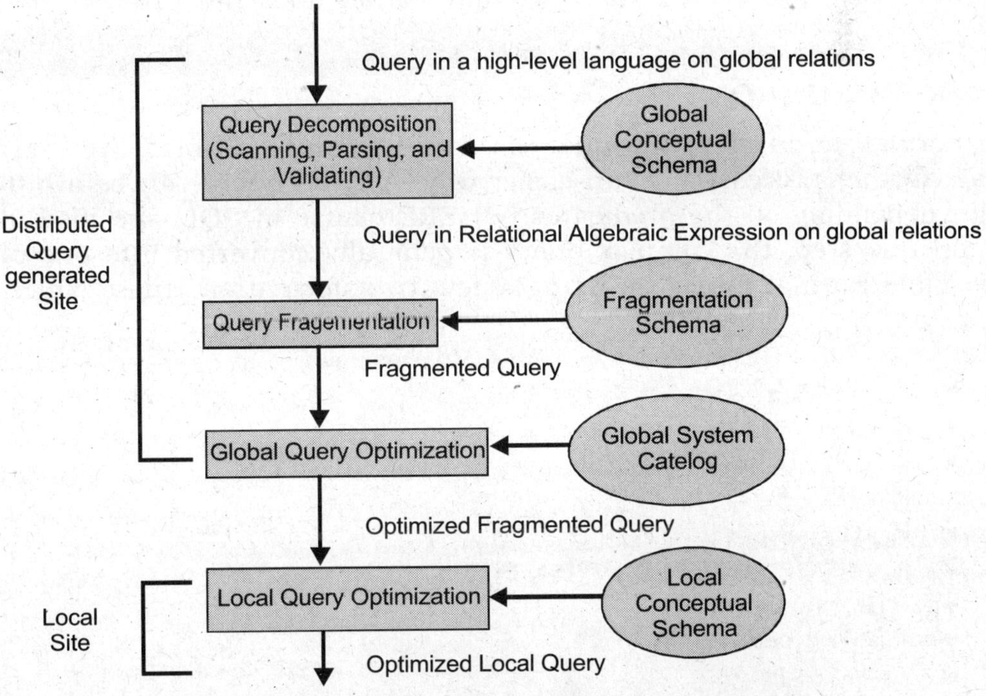

Figure 4.7 Phases in Distributed Query Processing

Following is the description of above layers:

4.7.1 QUERY DECOMPOSITION

Query decomposition is the first phase in distributed query processing. The objective of this phase is to transform a query in a high-level language on global relations algebraic query on global relations. Both input and output queries refer to global relations, without knowledge of the distribution of data. Therefore, query decomposition is the same for centralized and distributed systems. The information needed for this transformation is found in the global conceptual schema describing the global relations. In this phase, the syntactical and semantic correctness of the query is also checked. In the context of both centralized DBMS and distributed DBMS, the query decomposition phase is the same.

Four Steps of Query decomposition are:

- **Normalization:** The calculus query is written in a normalized form (CNF or DNF) for subsequent manipulation
- **Analysis:** The query is analyzed for semantic correctness
- **Elimination of Redundancy (Simplification):** Redundant predicates are eliminated to obtain simplified queries
- **Rewriting or Restructuring:** The calculus query is translated to optimal algebraic query representation

However the process of query decomposition does not produce optimal query.

4.7.1.1 NORMALIZATION

In normalization step, the query is converted into a normalized form to facilitate further processing in an easier way. A given query can be arbitrarily complex depending on the predicates (WHERE clause in SQL) specified in the query. In this step, the complex query is generally converted into one of the two possible normal forms by using a few transformation rules, which are listed below.

- $P_1 \wedge P_2 \Leftrightarrow P_2 \wedge P_1$
- $P_1 \vee P_2 \Leftrightarrow P_2 \wedge P_1$
- $P_1 \wedge (P_2 \wedge P_3) \Leftrightarrow (P_1 \wedge P_2) \wedge P_3$
- $P_1 \vee (P_2 \vee P_3) \Leftrightarrow (P_1 \vee P_2) \vee P_3$
- $P_1 \wedge (P_2 \vee P_3) \Leftrightarrow (P_1 \wedge P_2) \vee (P_1 \wedge P_3)$
- $P_1 \vee (P_2 \wedge P_3) \Leftrightarrow (P_1 \vee P_2) \vee (P_1 \vee P_3)$
- $\neg (P_1 \wedge P_2) \Leftrightarrow \neg P_1 \vee P_2$
- $\neg (P_1 \vee P_2) \Leftrightarrow \neg P_1 \wedge P_2$
- $\neg(\neg p_1) \Leftrightarrow P_1$

where P_i represents a simple predicate specified in the query.

The two possible normal forms are conjunctive normal form and disjunctive normal form.

(i) Conjunctive Normal Form: In conjunctive normal form, preference is given to the AND (^ predicate) operator, and it is a sequence of conjunctions that are connected by the ^ (AND) operator. Each conjunction contains one or more terms connected by the Ú (OR) operator. For instance,

$(P_1 \vee P_2 \vee P_3) \wedge (P_4 \vee P_5 \vee P_6) \wedge \ldots \wedge (P_{n-2} \vee P_{n-1} \vee P_n)$,

where P_i represents a simple predicate, is in conjunctive normal form.

(ii) Disjunctive Normal Form: In disjunctive is in conjunctive normal form, preference is given to the **OR (∨ predicate) operator**, and it is a sequence of disjunctions that are connected with the ∨ (OR) operator. Each disjunction contains one or more terms connected by the ∧ **(AND) operator**. For example,

$(P_1 \wedge P_2 \wedge P_3) \vee (P_4 \wedge P_5 \wedge P_6) \vee \ldots \vee (P_{n-2} \wedge P_{n-1} \wedge P_n)$,

where P_i represents a simple predicate, is in disjunctive normal form. In this normal form, a query can be processed as independent conjunctive subqueries connected by union operations.

Example 4.4

Let us consider the following two relations stored in a distributed database.

Employee (empid, ename, salary, designation, deptno)

Department (deptno, dname, location)

and the following query:

"Retrieve the names of all employees whose designation is 'Manager' and department name is 'Production' or 'Printing'".

In SQL, the above query can be represented as

Select ename from Employee, Department where designation = "Manager" and Employee.

deptno = Department.deptno and dname = "Production" or dname = "Printing"

The conjunctive normal form of this query is as follows"

designation = "Manager" ^ Employee.deptno = Department.deptno ^ (dname = "Production" ∧ dname = "Printing")

The disjunctive normal form of the same query is

(designation = "Manager" ^ Employee.deptno = Department.deptno ^ dname = "Production")

∨ (designation = "Manager" ^ Employee.deptno = Department.deptno ^ dname = "Printing")

Here, in the above disjunctive normal form, each disjunctive normal form, each disjunctive connected by ∨ (OR) operator can be processed as independent conjunctive subqueries.

Example 4.5:

Consider the query: Find the names of employees who have been working on project P1 for 12 or 24 months. Considering the tables EMP and ASG already defined. The above query can be expressed in SQL as:

SELECT ENAME

FROM EMP, ASG

WHERE EMP.ENO = ASG.ENO

AND ASG.PNO = "P1"

AND (DUR ≥ 12 OR DUR = 24)

The conjunctive normal form of above query is:

EMP.ENO = ASG. ENO ∨ ASG. PNO =" P1" ∨ (DUR = 12 ∨ DUR = 24)

While the qualification in disjunctive normal form is

(EMP.ENO = ASG. ENO ^ ASG. PNO =" P1" ^ DUR = 12) ^

(EMP.ENO = ASG. ENO ^ ASG. PNO =" P1" ^ DUR = 24)

4.7.1.2 ANALYSIS

The objective of the analysis step is to reject normalized queries that are incorrectly formulated or contradictory. The query is lexically and syntactically analyzed in this step by using the compiler of the high-level query language in which the query is expressed. In addition, this step verifies whether the relations and attributes specified in the query are defined in the global conceptual schema or not. It is also checked in the analysis step whether the operations on database objects specified in the given query are correct for the object type. When incorrectness is detected in any of the above aspects, the query is returned to the user with an explanation; otherwise, the high-level query is transformed into an internal form for further processing. The incorrectness in the query is detected based on the corresponding query graph or relation connection graph, which can be constructed as follows:

- A node is created in the query graph for the result and for each base relation specifies in the query.
- An edge between two nodes is drawn in the query graph for each join operation and for each project operation in the query. An edge between two nodes that are not result nodes represents a join operation, whereas

an edge whose destination node is the result node represents a project operation.

- A node in the query graph that is not the result node is labelled by a select operation or a self-join operation specifies in the query.

The relation connection graph is used to check the semantic correctness of the subset of queries that do not contain disjunction or negation. Such a query is semantically incorrect, if its relation connection graph is not connected. A join graph is a subgraph of the relation connection graph which represents only join operations specified in the query, and it can be derived from the corresponding query graph. The join graph is useful in the query optimization phase. A query is contradictory if its normalized attribute connection graph [Rosenkrantz & Hunt, 1980] contains a cycle for which the valuation sum is negative. The construction of normalized attribute connection graph for a query is described in the following:

- A node is created for each attribute referenced in the query and an additional node is created for a constant 0.
- A directed edge between two attribute nodes is drawn to represent each join operation in the query. Similarly, a directed edge between an attribute node and a constant 0 node is drawn for each select operation specified in the query.
- A weight is assigned to each edge depending on the inequality condition mentioned in the query. A weight v is assigned to the directed edge $a1 \rightarrow a2$, if there is an inequality condition in the query that satisfies $a1 \leq a2 + v$. Similarly, a weight $-v$ is assigned to the directed edge $0 \rightarrow a1$, if there is an inequality condition in the query that satisfies $a1 \geq n$.

Example 4.6

Let us consider the following two relations:

Student (<u>s-id</u>, sname, address, course-id, year) and

Course (<u>coursc-id</u>, course-name, duration, course-fee, intake-no, coordinator)

and the query:

"Retrieve the names, addresses and course names of all those students whose year of admission is 2008 and course duration is 4 years".

Using SQL, the above query can be represented as:

Select sname, address, course-name from Student, Course where year = 2008 and duration = 4 and Student.course-id = Course.course-id.

Here, course-id is a foreign key of the relation Student. The above SQL query can be syntactically and semantically incorrect for several reasons. For

instance, the attributes sname, address, course-name, year and duration may not be declared in the corresponding schema or the relations Student, Course may not be declared in the corresponding schema. Furthermore, if the operations "= 2008" and "= 4" are incompatible with data types of the attributes year and duration respectively, then the above SQL query is incorrect.

The query graph and the join graph for the above SQL query are depicted in figures 4.8(a) and 4.8(b) respectively.

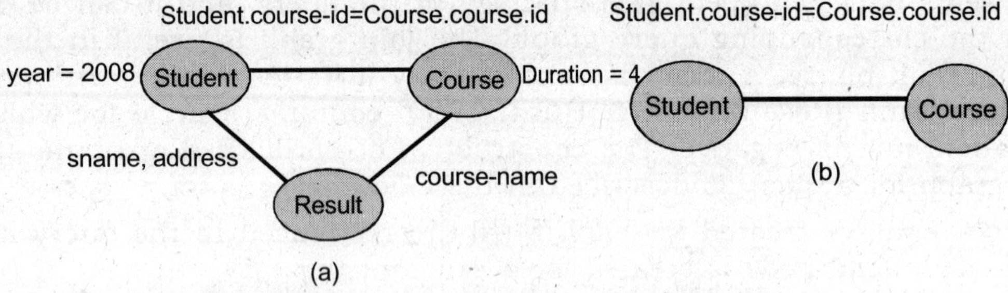

Figure 4.8 (a) Query Graph; (b) Join Graph

In the above SQL query, if the join condition between two relations (that is, Student.course-id = Course.course-id) is missing, then there would be no line between the nodes representing the relations Student and Course in the corresponding query graph [figure 4.8(a)]. Therefore, the SQL query is deemed semantically incorrect as the relation connection graph is disconnected. In this case, either the query is rejected or an implicit Cartesian produce between the relations is assumed.

Example 4.7:

Consider already defined tables EMP and ASG and a new table Project defined as

PROJ (PNO, PNAME, BUDGET)

Where PNO is Project Name, PNAME is Project Name and BUDGET is Project Budget.

Now consider the query in SQL:

SELECT ENAME, RESP

FROM EMP, ASG, PROJ

WHERE EMP.ENO = ASG.GNO

AND ASG.PNO = PROJ.PNO

AND PNAME =" CAD/CAM"

AND DUR $\geq$ 36

AND TITLE = "Programmer"

Thus query graph and join graph for above query is:

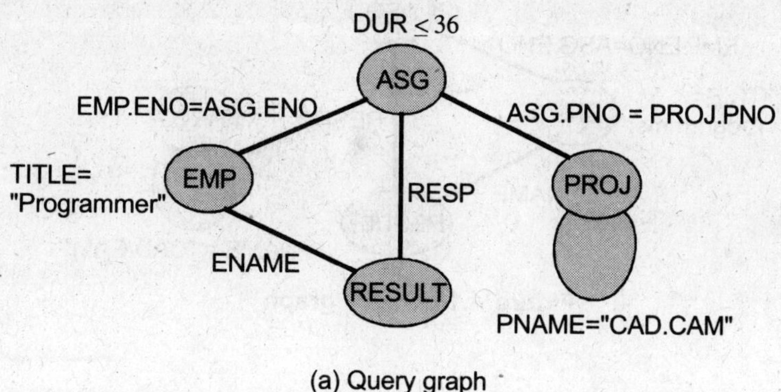

(a) Query graph

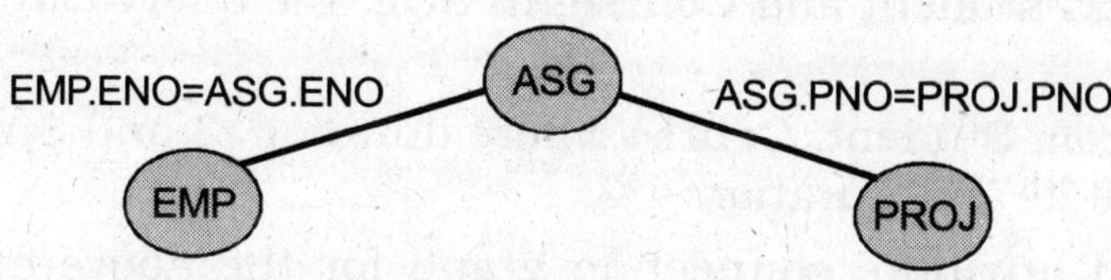

(b) Corresponding join graph

Figure 4.9 Query Graph

A conjunctive query without negation is semantically incorrect if its query graph is NOT connected! E.g.

Example 4.8

Let us consider the following SQL query:

SELECT ENAME, RESP

FROM EMP, ASG, PROJ

WHERE EMP.ENO = ASG.GNO

AND ASG.PNO = PROJ.PNO

AND PNAME = "CAD/CAM"

AND DUR > 36

AND TITLE = "Programmer"

Query graph

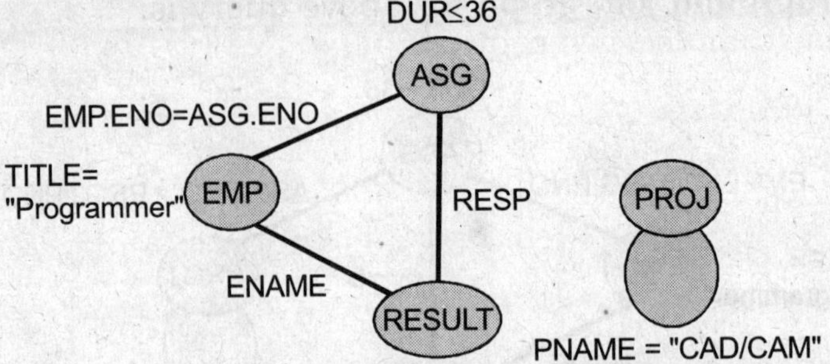

Figure 4.10 Query graph

Example 4.9

Let us consider the query "Retrieve all those student names who are admitted into curses where the course duration is greater than 3 years", that involves the relations student and Course. In SQL, the query can be expressed as:

Select sname from Student, Course where duration>3 and Student.course-id = Course. course-id and duration $\leq$ 2.

The normalized attribute connection graph for the above query is illustrated in figure 4.11.

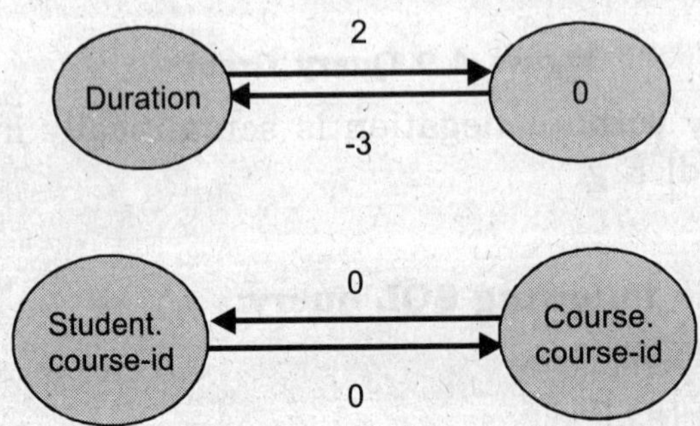

Figure 4.11 Normalized attribute connection graph

In the above normalized attribute connection graph, there is a cycle between the nodes duration and 0 with a negative valuation sum, which indicated that the query is contradictory.

4.7.1.3 SIMPLIFICATION OR ELIMINATION OF REDUNDANCY

In this step, all redundant predicate in the query are detected and the common subexpressions are eliminated to transform the query into a simpler and efficiently computable form. This transformation must achieve the semantic correctness. Typically, view definitions, access restrictions and integrity constraints are considered in this step, some of which may introduce redundancy in the query.

The well-known idempotency rules of Boolean algebra are used to eliminate redundancies from the given query, which are listed below.

- $P \wedge P \Leftrightarrow P$
- $P \vee P \Leftrightarrow P$
- $P \wedge \text{true} \Leftrightarrow P$
- $P \wedge \text{false} \Leftrightarrow \text{false}$
- $P \vee \text{true} \Leftrightarrow \text{true}$
- $P \vee \text{false} \Leftrightarrow P$
- $P \wedge (\sim P) \Leftrightarrow \text{false}$
- $P \vee (\sim P) \Leftrightarrow \text{true}$
- $P \wedge (P \vee Q) \Leftrightarrow P$
- $P \vee (P \wedge Q) \Leftrightarrow P$

Example 4.10

Let us consider the following view definition and a query on the view that involves the relation Employee (<u>empid,</u> ename, salary, designation, deptno).

Create view V1 as select empid, ename, salary from Employee where deptno = 10;

Select * from V1 where deptno = 10 and salary > 10000;

During query resolution, the query will be:

Select empid, ename, salary from Employee where (deptno = 10 and salary > 10000) and deptno = 10;

Here, the predicates are redundant and the WHERE condition reduces to "deptno = 10 and salary > 10,000";

Example 4.11

Query:

```
SELECT TITLE
FROM EMP
WHERE ENAME = "J.Doe"
SELECT TITLE
FROM EMP
WHERE (NOT (TITLE= "Programmer")
AND (TITLE = "Programmer"
OR TITLE = "Electrical Eng.")
AND NOT (TITLE = "Electrical Eng."))
AND ENAME = "J.Doe"
```

Is equivalent to

SELECT TITLE

FROM EMP

WHERE ENAME = "J.Doe"

4.7.1.4 QUERY RESTRUCTURING

In this step, the query in the high-level language is rewritten into an equivalent relational algebraic form. This step involves two substeps. Initially, the query is converted into an equivalent relational algebraic form and then the relational query is restructured to improve performance. The relational algebraic query is represented by a query tree or operator tree which can be constructed as follows:

- A leaf node is created for each relation specifies in the query.
- A non-leaf node is created for each intermediate relation in the query that can be produces by a relational algebraic operation.
- The root of the query tree represents the result of the query and the sequence of operations is directed from the leaves to the root.

In relational data model, the conversion from SQL query to relational algebraic form can be done in an easier way. The leaf nodes in the query tree are created from the FROM clause of the SQL query. The root node is created as a project operation involving the result attributes from the SELECT clause specifies in SQL query. The sequence of relational algebraic operations, which depends on the WHERE clause of SQL query, is directed from the leaves to the root of the query tree. After generating the equivalent relational algebraic form from the SQL query, the relational algebraic query is restructured by using transformation rules from relational algebra, which are listed below. In listing these rules, three different relations R, S and T are considered, where the relation R is defined over the attributes A = $\{A_1, A_2, ..., A_n\}$ and the relation S is defined over the attributes B = $\{B_1, B_2, ..., B_n\}$

(i) Commutativity of binary operators – Binary operators of relational algebra such as Cartesian product, join, union and intersection are commutative:

$$R X S \Leftrightarrow S X R \text{ and } R \infty S \Leftrightarrow S \infty R$$

Similarly, $R \cup S \Leftrightarrow S \cup S \cup R$ and $R \cap S \Leftrightarrow S \cap R$

This rule is not applicable to set difference and semijoin operations of relational algebra.

(ii) Associativity of binary operators – Cartesian product and natural join operation are always associative:

$(R X S) X T \Leftrightarrow R X (S X T)$ and

$(R \infty S) \infty T \Leftrightarrow R \infty (S \infty T)$

(iii) Idempotence of unary operators – Several successive unary operations such as selection and projection on the same relation may be grouped together. Conversely, a single unary operation on several attributes can be separated into several attributes can be separated into several successive unary operations as shown below:

$\sigma_{p(A1)}\ \sigma_{p(A2)}\ (R)) = \sigma_{p(A1)\ \wedge q(A2)}\ (R)$, where p and q denote predicates.

Similarly, $\Pi_{A'}\ (\Pi_{A'}\ (R)) \Leftrightarrow \Pi_{A'}\ (R)$,

Where, A, A' and A" are sets of attributes defined on relation R and A' and A" are subsets of A, and A" is a subset of A'.

(iv) Commutativity of selection and projection – Selection and projection operations on the same relation can be commuted:

$\Pi_{A1,\ldots,\ An}\ (\sigma_{p(Ap)}\ (R)) \Leftrightarrow \Pi_{A1,\ldots,\ An}\ (\sigma_{p(Ap)}\ (\Pi_{A1,\ \ldots,\ An,\ Ap}\ (R)))$,

where Ap is not a member of {A1, ..., An}.

(v) Commutativity of selection with binary operators- Binary operations of relational algebra such as Cartesian product and join operations can be commuted with selection operation as follows:

$\sigma_{p(Ai)}(R \times S) \Leftrightarrow (\sigma_{p(Ai)}(R)) \times S$

$\sigma_{p(Ai)}(\ (R \rhd\lhd_{p(Ai,\ Bj)}\ S) \Leftrightarrow \sigma_{p(Ai)}(R)\ _{p(Ai,\ Bj)}\ S$

$\sigma_{p(Ai)(}R \cup S) \Leftrightarrow \sigma_{p(Ai)}(R) \cup \sigma_{p(Ai)}(S)$

(vi) Commutativity of projection with binary operators- Binary operations of relational algebra such as Cartesian product and join operations can be commuted with projection operation as follows:

$\Pi_C(R \times S) \Leftrightarrow \Pi_{A'}(R) \times \Pi_{B'}(S)$

$\Pi_C(R \rhd\lhd_{p(Ai,\ Bj)}\ S) \Leftrightarrow \Pi_{A'}(R)\ _{p(Ai,\ Bj)}\ \Pi_{B'}(S)$

$\Pi_C\ (R \cup S) \Leftrightarrow \Pi_C(R) \cup \Pi_C(S)$

Proofs of the above transformation rules are available in[aha et.al.,1979]. B applying these rules, a large number of equivalent query trees can be constructed for a given query among which the most cost-effective one is chosen at the optimization phase. However, in this approach, generation of extensively large number of operator trees for the same query is not realistic. Therefore, the above transformation rules are used in methodical way to construct the query tree for a given query. The transformation rules are used in the following sequence.

- Unary operations in the query are separated first two simplify the query.
- Unary operations on the same relation are grouped so that common expressions are computed only once.
- Unary operations are commuted with binary operations.

- Binary operations are ordered.

Example 4.12

Let us consider the following SQL query which involves the relations **Student (s-id, sname, address, course-id, year) and Course (course-id, duration, course-fee, intake-no, coordinator):**

Select sname, course-name from Student, Course where s–id > 0 and year = 2007 and Student. course-id = Course.course–id and duration = 4 and intake-no = 60.

The query tree for the above SQL query is depicted in the figure 4.12.

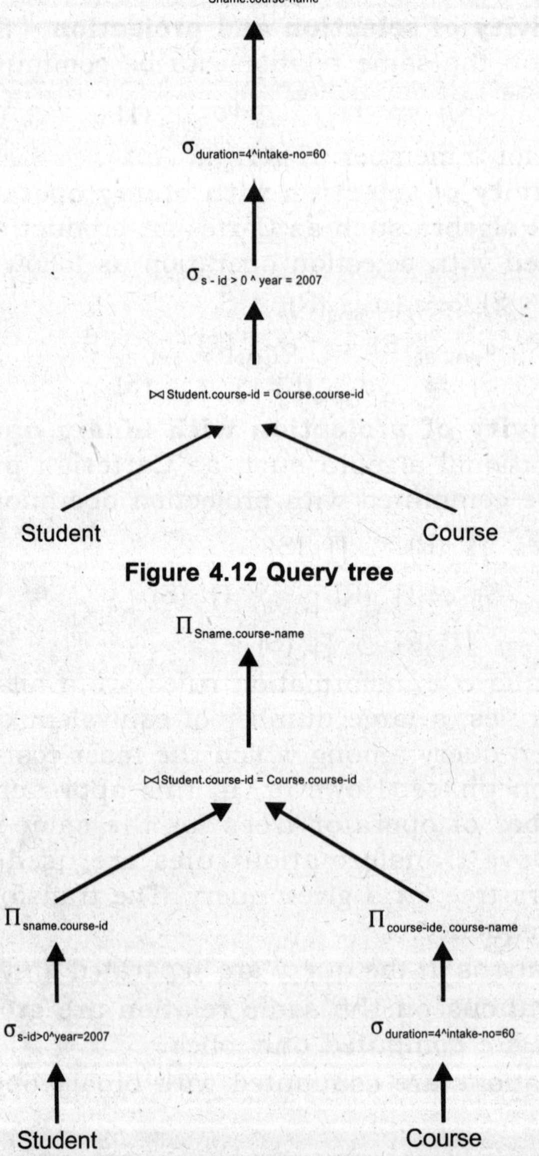

Figure 4.12 Query tree

Figure 4.13 Equivalent Query Tree of Figure 4.12

An equivalent query tree is constructed by applying the above transformation rules as shown in figure 4.13.

Here, unary operations specified in the query are separated first, and all unary operations on the same relation are grouped together to reconstruct the query tree. However, the query tree in the figure 4.13 need not necessarily represent the optimal tree.

The last step of query decomposition rewrites the query in relational algebra.

Rewriting means:

- Rewriting calculus query in relational algebra;
- Straightforward transformation from relational calculus to relational algebra, and
- Restructuring relational algebra expression to improve performance

Relational algebra tree: It is a tree defined by:

- a root node representing the query res
- leaves representing database relations
- non-leaf nodes representing relations produced by operations, and
- edges from leaves to root representing the sequences of operations

How to translate an SQL query into an algebra tree

- Create a leaf for every relation in the FROM clause
- Create the root as a project operation involving attributes in the SELECT clause
- Create the operation sequence by the predicates and operators in the WHERE clause

Example 4.13

Find the names of employees other than J. Doe who worked on the CAD/CAM project for either one or two years.

```
SELECT ENAME
FROM PROJ, EMP, ASG
WHERE ASG.ENO = EMP.ENO
AND ASG.JNO = PROJ.JNO
AND ENAME" J.Doe"
AND PNAME =" CAD/CAM"
AND (DUR = 12 OR DUR = 24)
```

Query tree:

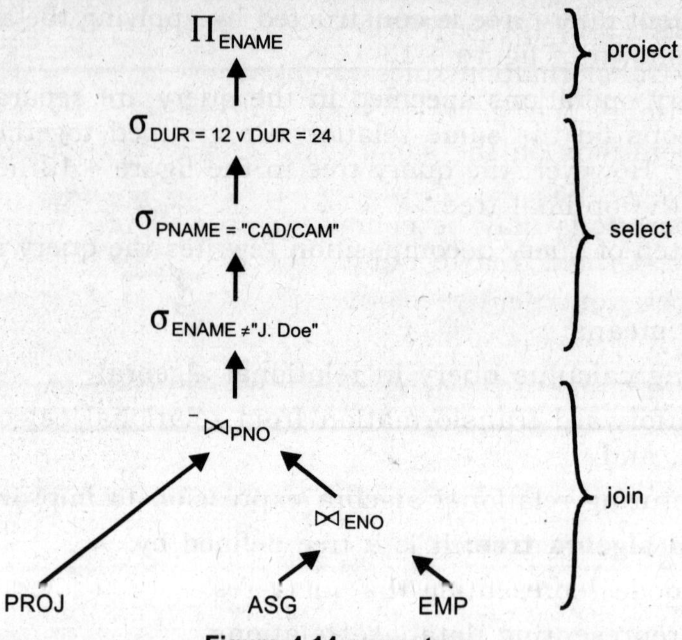

Figure 4.14 query tree

Rewriting — Transformation Rules (I)

1. **Commutativity of binary operations:**

   $R \times S \Leftrightarrow S \times R$

   $R \cup S \Leftrightarrow S \cup R$

2. **Associativity of binary operations:**

   $(R \times S) \times T \Leftrightarrow R \times (S \times T)$

3. **Idempotence of unary operations:** grouping of projections and selections

   2. $\Pi A' (\Pi A'' (R)) \Leftrightarrow \Pi A' (R)$ for $A' \subseteq A'' \subseteq A$

   3. $\sigma\, p1(A1)\, (\sigma\, p2(A2)\, (R)) \Leftrightarrow \sigma\, p1(A1)$ Ùp2(A2) (R)

Rewriting — Transformation Rules (II)

4. **Commuting selection with projection**

   $\Pi_{A1, \ldots, An}(\sigma_{p(Ap)}(R)) \Leftrightarrow \Pi_{A1, \ldots, An}(\sigma_{p(Ap)}(\Pi_{A1, \ldots, An, Ap}(R)))$

5. **Commuting selection with binary operations**

   $\sigma_{p(Ai)}(R \times S) \Leftrightarrow (\sigma_{p(Ai)}(R)) \times S$

   $\sigma_{p(Ai)}((R \bowtie_{p(Ai, Bj)} S) \Leftrightarrow \sigma_{p(Ai)}(R)\ _{p(Ai, Bj)}\ S$

   $\sigma_{p(Ai)(}R \cup T) \Leftrightarrow \sigma_{p(Ai)}(R) \cup \sigma_{p(Ai)}(T)$

6. **Commuting projection with binary operations**

   $\Pi_C(R \times S) \Leftrightarrow \Pi_{A'}(R) \times \Pi_{B'}(S)$

   $\Pi_C(R \bowtie_{p(Ai, Bj)} S) \Leftrightarrow \Pi_{A'}(R)\ _{p(Ai, Bj)}\ \Pi_{B'}(S)$

$$\Pi_C (R \cup S) \Leftrightarrow \Pi_C(R) \cup \Pi_C(S)$$

How to use transformation rules to optimize

- separate unary operations to simplify the query expression
- unary operations on the same relation may be grouped to access the same relation once
- unary operations may be commuted with binary operations, so that may be performed first to reduce the size of intermediate relations
- binary operations may be reordered

Example 4.14

For the optimization of previous query tree, Its Equivalent Query is

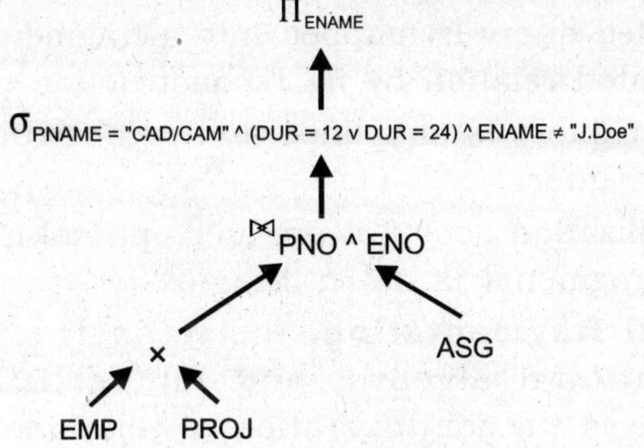

Figure 4.15 query tree

Rewriting or Restructuring of above tree is

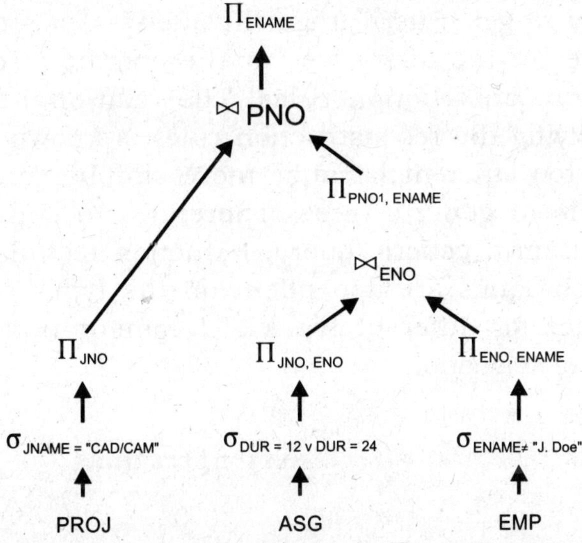

Figure 4.16 Rewriting or Restructuring of above tree

4.7.2 DATA LOCALIZATION OR QUERY FRAGMENTATION

Localization of distributed data means to translate a query on global relation into algebra queries on physical fragment, and optimize the query by reduction. The main role of this phase is to localize the query's data using data distribution information. This phase transforms the distributed query into a fragment query. Fragmentation is defined through fragmentation rules which can be expressed as relational operations. A distributed relation can be reconstructed by applying the fragmentation rules and then deriving a program called a localization program, of relational algebra operations which then acts on fragments.

The process of data localization is carried out in two steps:

1. The distributed query is mapped into a fragment query by substituting each distributed relation by its reconstruction program.
2. The fragment query is simplified and reconstructed to produce to produce a better query.

Again data localization does not produce optimal query because the information regarding fragments is not utilized.

For horizontal fragmentation, the reconstruction rule is the union operation of relational algebra, and for vertical fragmentation the reconstruction rule is the join operation of relational algebra. Thus, query fragmentation is defined through fragmentation rules, and it uses the information stored in the fragment schema of the distributed database. For the sake of simplicity, the replication issue is not considered here.

An easier way to generate a fragment query is to replace the global relations at the leaves of the query tree or the operator tree of the distributed query with their reconstruction rules. The relational algebraic query tree generated by applying the reconstruction rules is known as generic tree. This approach is not too efficient because more simplifications and reconstructions are possible in generic trees. Therefore, to generate a simpler and optimized query from a generic query, reduction techniques are used where the reduction techniques are dependent on the types of fragmentation. Reduction techniques for different types of fragmentation are illustrated with examples in the next section.

Example 4.15:

Assume

- EMP is fragmented into EMP_1, EMP_2, EMP_3 as follows:
- $EMP_1 = \sigma_{\text{"E3"} < ENO < \text{"E3"}}(EMPE)$
- $EMP_2 = \sigma_{\text{"E3"} < ENO \leq \text{"E6"}}(EMP)$
- $EMP_3 = \sigma_{\leq \text{"E6"}}(EMP)$

⇒ ASG fragmented into ASG_1 and ASG_2 as follows:

- $ASG_1 = \sigma_{ENO \geq \text{"E1"}}$
- $ASG_2 = \sigma_{ENO > \text{"E"}}$

Replace EMP by $(EMP_1 \cup EMP_2 \cup EMP_a)$ and ASG by $(ASG_1 \cup ASG_2)$ in any query

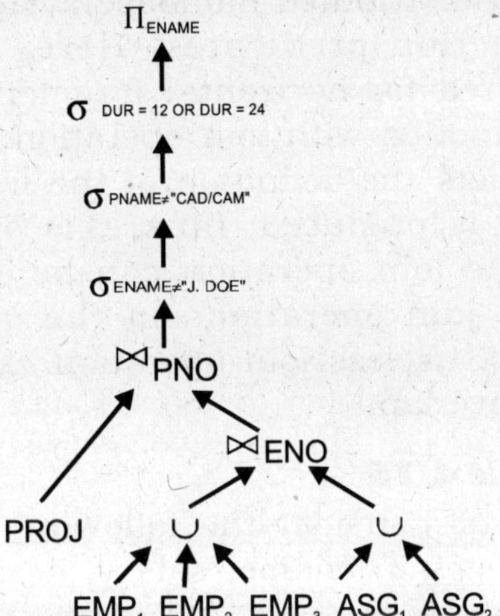

Providing Parallelism

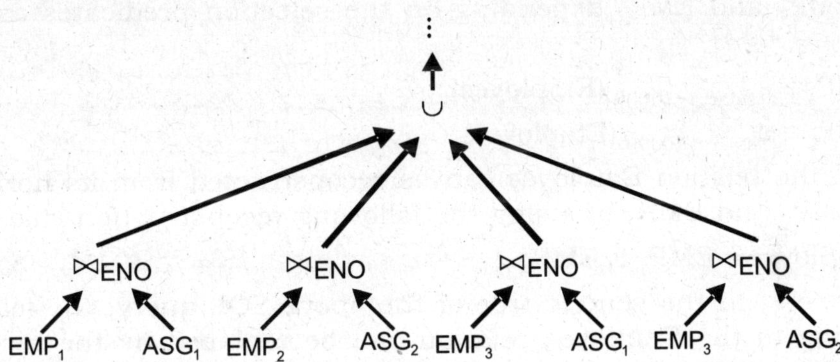

Eliminating unnecessary work

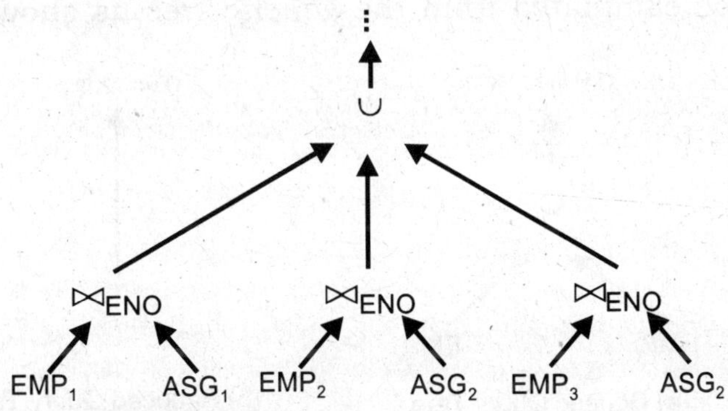

Various reduction techniques are:

4.7.2.1 REDUCTION FOR HORIZONTAL FRAGMENTATION

In a distributed database system, horizontal fragmentation is done based on selection predicates. Here, two different reduction techniques are considered for horizontal fragmentation: reduction with selection operation and reduction with join operation. In the first case, if the selection predicate contradicts the definition of the fragment, then an empty intermediate result relation is produced; thus, this operation can be eliminated. In the second case, the join operation can be commuted with union operation to detect useless join operations in the query, which can be eliminated from the result. A useless join operation exists in a query, if the fragment predicates do not overlap.

Example 4.16

Let us consider the following SQL query that involves the relation Employee (empid, ename, salary, designation, deptno):

Select * from Employee where salary > 10000.

Assume that the Employee relation is partitioned into two horizontal fragments EMP_1 and EMP_2 depending on the selection predicates as mentioned below:

$EMP_1 = s_{salary<=10000}$ (Employee)

$EMP_2 = s_{salary>10000}$ (Employee)

Now, the relation Employee can be reconstructed from its horizontal fragments EMP_1 and EMP_2 by using the following reconstruction rule.

Employee = EMP_1 È EMP_2

Therefore, in the generic tree of the above SQL query, the leaf node corresponding to the Employee relation can be replaced by the reconstruction rule $EMP_1 \cup EMP_2$. Here, the selection predicate contradicts the definition of horizontal fragment EMP_1, thereby producing an empty relation. This operation can be eliminated from the generic tree as shown in figure 4.17.

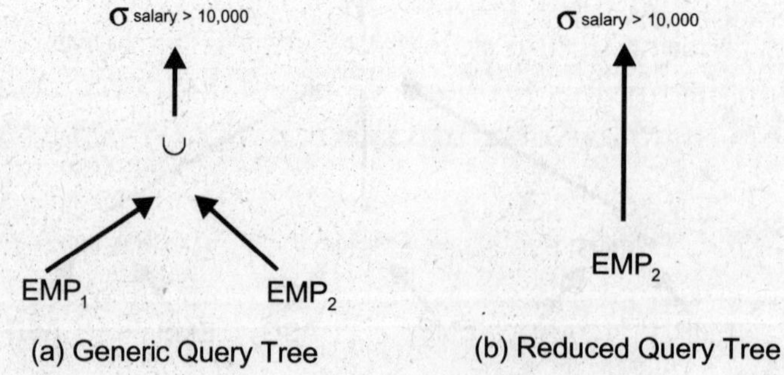

Figure 4.17 Reduction for Horizontal Fragmentation with Selection

Example 4.17

Let us assume that the relation Employee (<u>empid</u>, ename, salary designation, deptno) is horizontally fragmented into two partitions EMP_1 and EMP_2 and the relation Department (<u>deptno,</u> dname, location) is horizontally fragmented into two relations $DEPT_1$ and $DEPT_2$ respectively. These horizontally fragmented relations are defined in the following:

$$EMP_1 = s_{deptno \leq 10}(Employee)$$

$$EMP_2 = s_{deptno > 10}(Employee)$$

$$DEPT_1 = s_{deptno \leq 10}(Department)$$

$$DEPT_2 = s_{deptno > 10}(Department)$$

The reconstruction rules for the above horizontal fragments are as follows:

$$Employee = EMP_1 \text{ È } EMP_2$$

$$Department = DEPT_1 \text{ È } DEPT_2$$

Let us consider the following SQL query in a distributed environment, which involves the relations Employee and Department.

Select * from Employee, Department where Employee.deptno = Department.deptno.

The generic query tree and the reduced query tree for the above query are depicted in figure 4.18. Thus, the commutativity of join operation with union operation is very important in distributed DBMSs, because it allows a join operation of two relations to be implemented as a union operation of partial join operations, where each part of the union operation can be executed in parallel.

4.7.2.2 REDUCTION FOR VERTICAL FRAGMENTATION

The vertical fragmentation partitions a relation based on projection operation; thus, the reconstruction rule for vertical fragmentation is join operation. The reduction technique for vertical fragmentation involves the removal of vertical fragments that have no attributes in common except the key attribute.

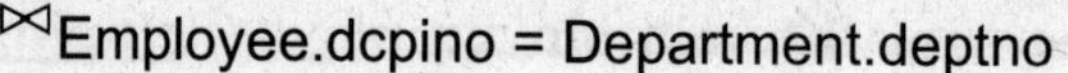

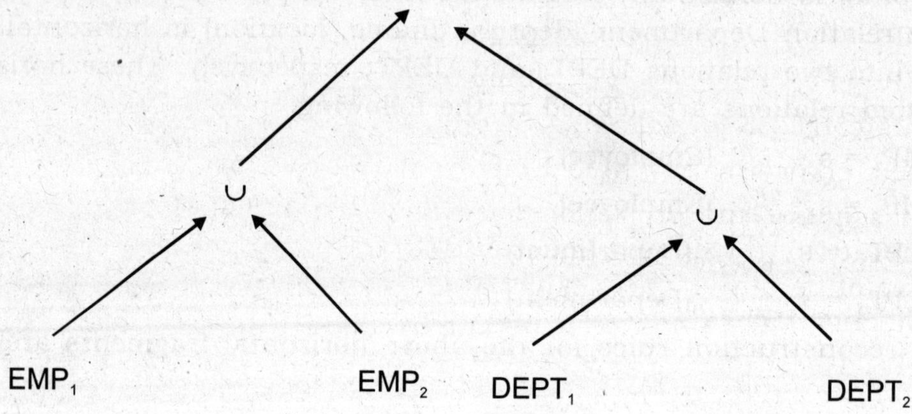

(a) Generic Query Tree

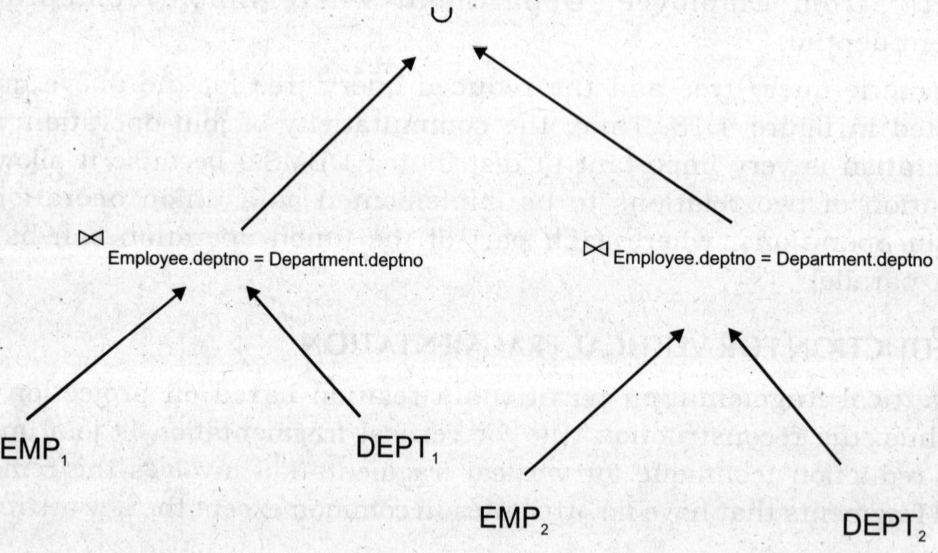

(b) Reduced Query Tree

Figure 4.18 Reduction for Horizontal Fragmentation with Join

Example 4.18

Let us assume that the Employee relation is vertically fragmented into two relations EMP_1 and EMP_2 as defined below:

$EMP_1 = P_{empid,\ ename,\ salary}$ (Employee)

$EMP_2 = P_{empid,\ designation,\ deptno}$ (Employee)

Let us consider the following SQL query.

Select ename, salary from Employee.

In this query, the projection operation on relation EMP_2 is redundant, since the attributes ename and salary are not part of EMP_2. The generic query tree of the above query is illustrated in figure 4.19(a). By commutating the projection operation with join operation and removing the vertical fragment EMP_2 the reduced query tree is produced as shown in figure 4.19(b).

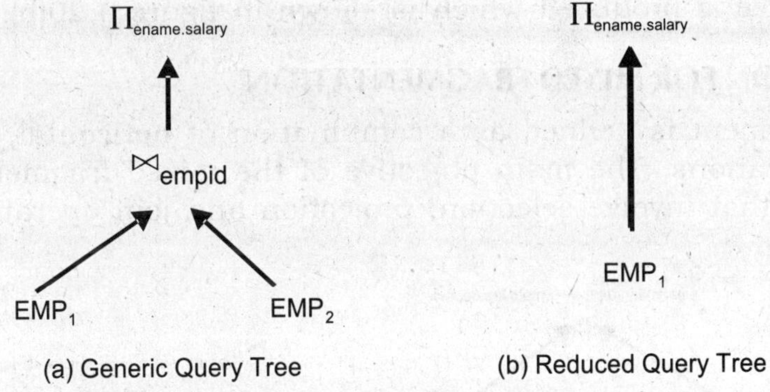

Figure 4.19 Reduction for Vertical Fragmentation

4.7.2.3 REDUCTION FOR DERIVED FRAGMENTATION

The derived fragmentation partitions a child relation horizontally based on the same selection predicate of its parent relation. Derived fragmentation is used to facilitate the join between fragments. The reconstruction rule for derived fragmentation is join operation over union operation. The reduction technique for derived fragmentation involves the commutativity of join operation with union operation and removal of useless join operations and selection operations.

Example 4.19

Let us assume that the relation Department (<u>deptno</u>, dname, location) is horizontally fragmented into two relation $DEPT_1$ and $DEPT_2$ respectively. These horizontally fragmented relations are defined in the following:

$DEPT_1 = s_{deptno \leq 10}$ (Department)

$DEPT_2 = s_{deptno > 10}$ (Department)

Further assume that the fragmentation of Employee relation is derived from Department relation. Thus, EMP_i = Employee $>_{deptno}$ $DEPT_i$ i = 1,2

Let us consider the following SQL query in a distributed environment, which involves the relations Employee and Department.

Select * from Employee, Department where deptno > 10 and Employee.deptno = Department.deptno.

The generic query tree for the derived fragmentation is depicted in figure 4.20(a).

In the above generic query tree, the selection operation on fragment $DEPT_1$ is redundant and can be eliminated. Similarly, as the relation $DEPT_2$ is defined depending on the selection predicate "deptno > 10", the entire selection operation can be eliminated from the above generic tree. By eliminating selection operation and commutating join operation with union operation, the reduced query tree is produced which is shown in figure 4.20(b).

4.7.2.4 REDUCTION FOR MIXED FRAGMENTATION

A mixed fragment is defined as a combination of horizontal, vertical and derived fragmentations. The main objective of the mixed fragmentation is to support queries that involve selection, projection and join operations.

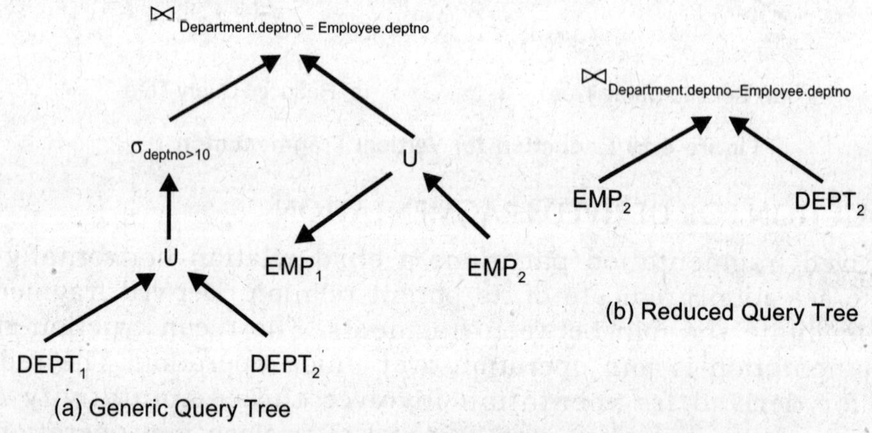

Figure 4.20 Reduction for Derived Fragmentation

The reconstruction rules for mixed fragmentation uses union operations and join operations of fragments. All reduction techniques that are used for horizontal, vertical and derived fragmentation can be used for mixed fragmentation. These reduction techniques are summarized below:

- Removal of empty relations that can be produced by contradicting selection predicates on horizontal fragments.
- Removal of useless relations that can be produced by applying projection operations on vertical fragments.

- Removal of useless join operations that can be produced by distributing join operations over union operations on derived fragments.

4.7.2.5 REDUCTION FOR HYBRID FRAGMENTATION

The combination of horizontal and vertical fragmentation is called hybrid fragmentation. Hybrid fragmentation is obtained by combining the fragmentation functions discussed above. The goal of hybrid fragmentation is to support, efficiently, queries involving projection, selection, and join. Note that the optimization of an operation or of a combination of operations is always done at the expense of other operations. For example, hybrid fragmentation based on selection-projection will make selection only, or projection only, less efficient than with horizontal fragmentation (or vertical fragmentation). The localization program for a hybrid fragmented relation uses unions and joins of fragments.

Example 4.20

EMP is vertically fragmented first, and then horizontally next.

$E_1 = \sigma_{ENO \leq "E_4"}(\pi_{ENO.ENAME}(EMP))$

$E_2 = \sigma_{ENO > "E_4"}(\pi_{ENO.ENAME}(EMP))$

$E_3 = \pi_{ENO.TITLE}(EMP)$

$E = (E_1 \cup E_2) \bowtie_{ENO} E_2$

Combine all discussed three rules to reduce hybrid fragmentation.

Example 4.21

A query on EMP fragmented as above is:

SELECT ENAME

FROM EMP

WHERE ENO =" E5"

Generic qucry tree is

$$\pi_{ENAME}$$
$$\uparrow$$
$$\sigma_{ENO="E5"}$$
$$\uparrow$$
$$\bowtie_{ENO}$$

($\bowtie_{ENO}$ has children $\cup$ and E_3; $\cup$ has children E_1 and E_2)

By rule 3, E3 is eliminated, and by rule 1, E1 is eliminated. The reduced query is

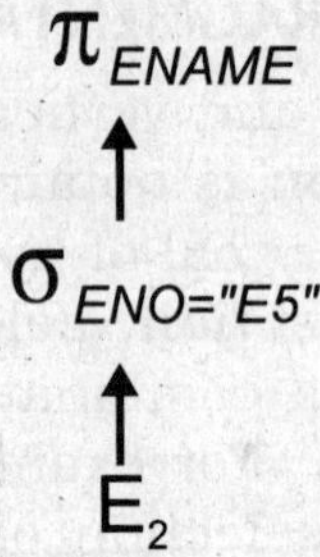

4.7.3 GLOBAL QUERY OPTIMIZATION

The input to the third layer is a fragment query, that is, an algebraic query that is, an algebraic query on fragments. The goal of query optimization is to find an execution strategy for the query which is close to optimal. Remember that finding the optical solution is computationally intractable. An execution strategy for a distribute query can be described with relational algebra operations and communication primitives (send/receive operations) for transferring data between sites. The previous layers have already optimized the query, for example, by eliminating redundant expressions. However, this optimization is independent of fragment characteristics such as cardinalities. In addition, communication operations are not yet specified. By permuting the ordering of operations within one fragment query, many equivalent queries may be found.

Query optimization consists of finding the "best" ordering of operations in the fragment query, including communication operations which minimize a cost function. The cost function, often defined in terms of time units, refers to computing resources such as disk space, disk I/Os, buffer space, CPU cost, communication cost, and so on. Generally, it is a weighted combination of I/O CPU, and communication costs. Nevertheless, a typical simplification made by distributed DBMSs, as we mentioned before, is to consider communication cost as the most significant factor. This is valid for wide area networks, where the limited bandwidth makes communication much more costly than local processing. To select the ordering of operations it is necessary to predict execution costs of alternative candidate orderings. Determining execution costs before query execution (i.e., static optimization) is based on fragment statistics and the formulas for estimating the cardinalities of relational operations. Thus the optimization decisions depend on the available statistics on fragments.

An important aspect of query optimization is join ordering, since permutations of the joins within the query may lead to improvements of orders of magnitude.

One basic technique for optimizing a sequence of distributed join operations is through the semijoin operator. The main value of the semijoin in a distributed system is to reduce the size of the join operands and then the communication cost. However, more recent techniques, which consider local processing costs as well as communication costs, do not use semijoins because they might increase local processing costs. The output of the query optimization layer is an optimized algebraic query with communication operations included on fragments.

This layer optimizes fragment query (e.g., join ordering) with communication operations

- Find an execution strategy close to optimal.
- Find the best ordering of operations in the fragment query, including communication operations.
- Cost function defined in time is required.

Query optimization is the activity of the choosing an efficient execution strategy among several alternatives for processing a query. This is the same both in the contexts of both centralized DBMSs and distributed DBMSs. The selected query execution strategy must minimize the cost of query processing. In a distributed DBMS, the query execution cost is expressed as the total of local processing cost (I/O cost and CPU cost) and communication cost. To simplify the global query optimization, often the local processing cost is ignored, because the communication cost is ignored, because the communication cost is dominant in this case. The optimal query execution strategy is selected by a software module, known as query optimizer, and it can be represented by three components: search space, cost model and optimization strategy. The search space is obtained by applying the transformation rules of relational algebra under the subheading Query restructuring. The cost model determines the cost of a query execution plan. The optimization strategy explores the search space, and it is used to determine the optimal plan using the cost model.

4.7.3.1 SEARCH SPACE

The search space is defined as the set of equivalent query trees for a given query that can be generated by using transformation rules. In query optimization, join trees are particularly important, because they determine the join order of relations involved in a given query, which affects the performance of query processing. If a given query involves many operators and many relations, then the search space is very large, because it contains a large number of equivalent query trees for the given query. Hence, the query optimization process becomes more expensive than the actual execution, and therefore query optimizers typically impose some restrictions on the size of

the search space to be considered. Most query optimizers use heuristics rules that order the relational algebraic operations (selection, projection and Cartesian product) in the query. Another restriction is one that is imposed on the shape of the join tree. There are two different kinds of join trees, known as linear join trees and brushy join trees. In a linear join tree, at least one operand of each operator node is a base relation. On the other hand, a bushy join tree is more general and may have operators with no base relations as operands. Linear join trees reduce the size of search space, whereas bushy join trees facilitate parallelism. The examples of a linear join tree and a bushy join tree are illustrated in figures 4.21(a) and 4.21(b) respectively.

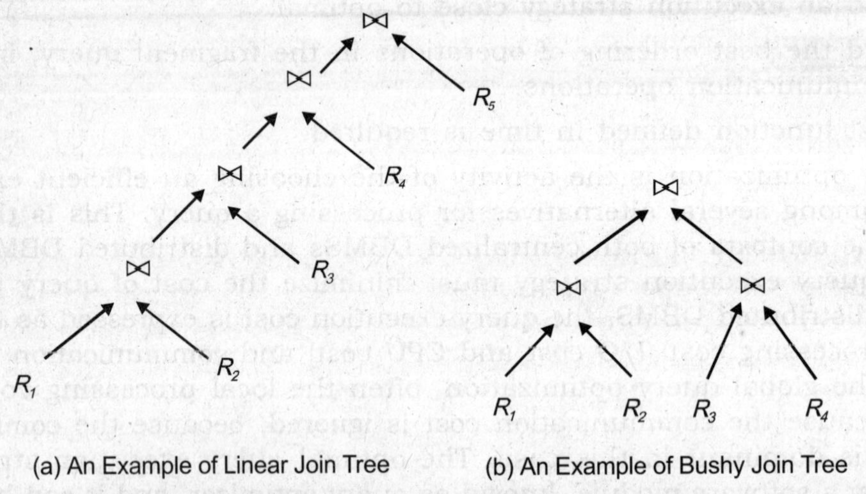

(a) An Example of Linear Join Tree (b) An Example of Bushy Join Tree

Figure 4.21 Two Different Types of Join Trees

4.7.3.2 OPTIMIZATION STRATEGY

There are three different kinds of optimization strategies, known as static optimization strategy, dynamic optimization strategy and randomized optimization strategy, which are described in the following.

(a) Static optimization strategy – In static optimization strategy the given query is parsed, validated and optimized once. This strategy is similar to the approach adopted by a compiler for a programming language. The advantages of static optimization strategy are that the run-time overhead is removed, and there may be more time available for evaluating a large number of execution strategies, which increases the chances of finding a more optimum strategy. The disadvantage with the static optimization strategy is that the optimal execution strategy that is selected at compile-time may no larger be optimal at run-time.

(b) Dynamic optimization strategy – The most popular optimization strategy is dynamic optimization strategy, which is deterministic. In dy-

namic optimization strategy, the execution plan starts from base relations and proceeds by joining one more relation at each step until the complete plan is obtained. The advantage of dynamic optimization strategy is that it is almost comprehensive and ensures the best plan. One disadvantage is that the performance of the query is affected, because the query has to be parsed, validated and optimized each time before execution. Moreover, it is necessary to reduce the number of execution strategies to be analysed to achieve an acceptable overhead, which may have the effect of selecting a less-than-optimum strategy. This strategy is suitable when the number of relations involved in the given query is small.

(c) Randomized optimization strategy – A recent optimization strategy is randomized optimization strategy, which reduces the optimization complexity, but does not guarantee the best execution plan. The randomized optimization strategy allows the query optimization to trade optimization tune for execution time [Lanzeotte et al., 1993]. In this strategy, one or more start plans are built by a greedy strategy, and then it tries to improve the start plan by visiting its neighbours. A neighbour is identified by applying a random transformation to a plan. One typical example of random transformation is exchanging two randomly chosen operand relations of the plan. The randomized optimization strategy provided better performance than other optimization strategies when the number of relations involved in the query increases.

4.7.3.3 DISTRIBUTED COST MODEL

The distributed cost model includes cost functions to predict the cost of operators, database statistics, base data and formulas to calculate the sized of intermediate results.

1. **Cost functions:** In a distributed system, the cost of processing a query can be expressed in terms of the total cost measures or the response time measures [Yu and Chang, 1984]. The total cost measure is the sum of all cost components. If no relation is fragmented in the distributed system and the given query includes selection and projection operations, then the total cost measure involves the local processing cost only. However, when join and semijoin operation s are executed communication costs between different sites may be incurred in addition to the local processing cost. Local processing costs are usually evaluated in terms of the number of disk accesses and the CPU processing time, whereas communication costs are expressed in terms of the total amount of data transmitted. For geographically dispersed computer networks, communication cost is normally the dominant consideration but local processing cost is of greater significance for local networks.

Thus, most early distributed DBMSs designed for wide area networks have ignored the local processing cost and concentrated on minimizing the communication cost. Therefore, the total cost measure can be represented by using the following formula.

$$\text{Total cost measure} = T_{CPU} * \text{insts} + T_{I/O} * \text{ops} + C_0 + C_1 * X$$

where T_{CPU} is the CPU processing cost per instruction, insts represents the total number of CPU instructions, $T_{I/O}$ is the I/O processing cost per I/O ops represents the total number of I/O operations, C_0– is the start-up cost of initiating transmission, C_1 is a proportionality constant, and X is the amount of data to be transmitted. For wide area networks, the above formula is simplified as follows.

$$\text{Total cost measure} = C_0 + C_1 * C.$$

The response time measure is the time from the initiation of the query to the time when the answer is produced. The response time measure must consider the parallel local processing costs and the parallel communication costs. A general formula for response time can be expressed as follows.

Response time measure = T_{CPU} * Seq_insts + $T_{I/O}$ * seq_ops + C_0 + C_1- * seq_X where seq_insts represents the maximum number of CPU instructions that can be performed sequentially, seq_ops represents the maximum number of I/O operations that can be performed sequentially, and seq_X indicates the amount of data that can be transmitted sequentially. If the local processing cost is ignored, then the above formula is simplified into

Response time measure = $C_0 + C_1$ seq_X.

In this case, any processing or communication that is done in parallel is ignored. The following example illustrates the difference between total cost measure and response time measure.

Example 4.22

Let us consider that the amount of data to be transmitted from site1 to site2 is P, and the amount of data to be transmitted from site3 to site2 is Q for the execution of a query as shown in the figure 4.22.

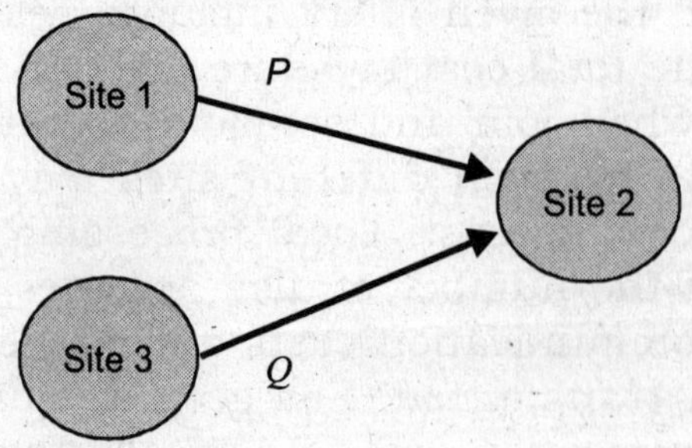

Figure 4.22 Data Transmission for a Query

Here, the total cost measure = $C_0 + C_1 * P + C_0 + C_1 * Q = 2C_0 + C_1 (P + Q)$.

Similarly, the response time measure = max $\{C_0 + C_1 * P, C_0 + C_1 * Q\}$ because the data transmission is done in parallel. In this case, the local processing cost is ignored. The response time measure can be minimized by increasing the degree of parallel execution, whereas the total cost measure can be minimized by improving the utilization of resources.

2. **Database statistics:** The cost of an execution strategy depends on the size of the intermediate result relations that are produced during the execution of a query. In distributed query optimization, it is very important to estimate the size of the intermediate results of relational algebraic operations to minimize the data transmission cost, because the intermediate result relations are transmitted over the network. This estimation is done based on the database stastics of base relations stored in the system catalog and the formulas used to predict the cardinalities of the results of the relational operations. Typically, it is expected that a distributed DBMS will hold the following information in its system catalog to predict the size of intermediate result relations.
   - The length of each attributes Ai in terms of number of bytes denoted by length (Ai).
   - The numbers of distinct values of each attribute Ai in each fragment Rj with the cardinality of the projection of fragment Rj on Ai, denoted y card (Π_{Ai} (Rj)).
   - The maximum and minimum possible values in the domain of each attribute Ai, denoted by Max (Ai) and Min (Ai).
   - The cardinality of the domain of each attribute Ai, denoted by card (dom[Ai]), which represents the number of unique values in the dom[Ai].
   - The number of tuples in the each fragment Rj, denoted by card (Rj).

In addition to the above information, sometimes the system catalog also holds the join selectivity factor for some pairs of relations. The join selectivity factors of two relations R and S is a real value between 0 and 1, and can be defined as follows.

$$SFj\ (R, S)s = card\ (R \infty S)\ / card(R) * card(S).$$

3. **Cardinalities of intermediate results:** To simplify the evaluation of the cardinalities of intermediate results, two assumptions have been made here: first, the distribution of attribute values in a base relation is uniform and second, all attributes are independent, that is, the value of one attribute does not affect the values of others. The formulas to evaluate the cardinalities of the results of basic relational algebraic operations are listed in the following.

(i) *Selection Operation:* The cardinality of selection operation for the relation R is

card (s_F (R)) SF_S (F) * card(R)

where SF_{S-} (F) is dependent on the selection formula. The SF_S (F)s can be calculated as follows.

SF_S (A = value) = 1/card($\tilde{O}_A$ (R))

SF_S (A > value) = max(A) – value/max(A) – min(A)

SF_S (A < value) = value – min(A)/max(A) – min(A)

SF_S (p(Ai) ^p(Aj)) = SF_S(p(Ai) * SF_S (p(Aj)))

SF_S (p(Ai) ^ p(Aj)) = $SF\text{-}_S$ (p(Ai)) + SF_S (p(Aj)) – (SF_S (p(Ai)) * SF_{S-} (p(Aj)))

SF_S (A e {values}) = SF_S (A + value) * card({values})

In this case, Ai and Aj are two different attributes, and p(Ai) and p(Aj) denotes the selection predicates.

(ii) *Projection Operation:* It is very difficult to evaluate the cardinality of an arbitrary projection operation. However, it is trivial in some cases. If the projection of relation R is done based on a single attribute, the cardinality is the number of tuples when the projection is performed. If one of the projected attributes is a key of the relation R, then

card (Π_A (R)) = card (R).

(iii) *Cartesian Product Operation:* The cardinality of the Cartesian product of two relations R and S is denoted as

card (R x S) = card(R) * card(S).

(iv) *Join Operation:* There is no general way to the evaluate the cardinality of the join operation without additional information about the join operation. Typically, the upper bound of the cardinality of the join operation is the cardinality of the Cartesian product. However, there is a common case in which the evaluation is simple. If the relation R with its attribute A is joined with the relation S with its attribute B via an equijoin operation where A is a key of the relation R, and B is a foreign key of relation S, then the cardinality of the join operation can be evaluated as follows.

card (R $\infty_{A=B}$ S) card (S).

In the above evaluation it is assumed that the each tuple of relation R participates in the joini operation; therefore, the above estimation is an upper bound. In other cases, it can be calculated as

SF_{SJ} (R_A S) = card (Π_A S))/card(dom[A])

(v) *Semijoin Operation:* The selectivity factor of the semijoin operation of the relation R by relation S selects the subset of tuples of R that join with tuples of S. An approximation for the semijoin selectivity factor is represented as follows [Henner and Yao, 1979].

$$SF_{SJ}\ (R\ {}_A S) = card\ (\Pi_A\ S))/card(dom[A])$$

The above formula depends on only the attribute A of the relation S. Thus, it is often called the selectivity factor of attribute A of S and is denoted by SF_{SJ} (S.A). Now, the cardinality of the semijoin operation can be expressed by the following formula.

$$card\ (R\ {}_A\ S) = SF_{SJ}\ (S.A) * card(R)$$

This formula is applicable for the common case where the attribute R.A is a foreign key of the relation S. In this case, the semijoin selectivity factor is 1, because $\Pi_A(S)$ = card(dom[A]).

(vi) ***Union Operation:*** It is very difficult to evaluate the cardinality of union operation. The simple formulas for evaluating the upper bound and lower bound cardinalities of union operation are lists in the following.

$$card\ (R \cup S)\ (upper\ bound) = card(R) + card\ (S)$$

$$card\ (R \cup S)\ (lower\ bound) = max\{card(R),\ card(S)\}$$

(vii) ***Set Difference Operation:*** Like union operation, the formulas for evaluating the upper bound and-lower bound cardinalities of set difference operation, denoted by card(R – S0, are card(R) and 0 respectively.

4.7.4 LOCAL QUERY OPTIMIZATION

The last phase is performed by all the sites having fragments involved in the query. Each subquery executing at one site, called a local query, is then optimized using the local schema of the site. At this time, the algorithms to perform the relational operations may be chosen. Local optimization uses the algorithms of centralized systems. This layer optimizes local query. In the context of distributed query processing, local query optimization is the utmost important, because the distributed query is fragmented into several subqueries each of which is processed at local site in a centralized way. Moreover, the query optimization techniques for centralized DBMSs are often extended for use in distributed DBMSs. There are several query optimization techniques for centralized DBMSs. One such centralized query optimization technique, used by the popular relational database system INGRES [Stonebraker et al., 1976], is introduced in the following section.

4.7.4.1 INGRES ALGORITHM

INGRES uses a dynamic query optimization strategy that partitions the high-level query into smaller queries recursively. In this approach, a query is first decomposed into a sequence of queries having a unique relation in common. Each of these single relation queries are their processed by a one-

variable query processor (OVQP). The OVQP optimizes the access to a single relation by selecting, based on the selection predicates, the best access method to that relation. For instance, if there is a selection predicate in the query of the form <A = value>, an index available on attribute A will be used. This algorithm first executes the unary operations and tries to minimize the size of the intermediate results before performing binary operations.

To perform decomposition, two basic techniques are used in the INGRES algorithm: detachment and substitution. The query processor uses the detachment technique to partition a given query into several smaller queries based on a common relation. For example, using detachment technique, the SQL query q1 can be decomposed into two smaller queries q11 and q12 as follows.

q1: Select $R_2.A_2$, $R_3.A_3$,.., $R_n.A_n$
from R_1, R_2,..., R_n
where P_1 ($R_1.A_1$) and P_2 ($R_1.A_1$, $R_2.A_2$,..., $R_n.A_n$)

q11: Select $P_1.A_1$ into R_1
from R_1
where $P_1(R_1A_1)$

q12: Select $R_2.A_2$, $R_3.A_3$,..., $R_n.A_n$
from R_1, R_2,..., R_n
where $P_2(V_1.A_1$, $V_2.A_2)$,..., $V_n.A_n)$

where A_i and A_i, represent lists of attributes of relation R_i, P_1 is a selection predicate involving the attribute A_1, from the relation R_1, and P_2 is a selection predicate involving attributes of relations R_1, R_2, ..., R_n, V_1, ..., V_n represent new names fo relation R_1, ..., R_n after decomposition. This step is necessary to reduce the size of relations before performing binary operations. Detachment technique extracts the selection operations, which are usually the most selective ones.

Multi-relation queries that cannot be further detached are called irreducible. A query is said to be irreducible if and only if the corresponding query graph is a chain with two nodes. Irreducible queries are converted into single relation queries by tuple substitution. In tuple substitution, for a given n-relation query, the tuples of one relation are substituted by their values, thereby generating a set of (n – 1)-relation queries. Tuple substitution can be implemented in the following way. Assume that the relation R is chosen for tuple substitution in an n-relation query q1. For each tuple in R, the attributes referred to in q1 are replaced by their actual values in tuples thereby producing a query q1' with n – 1 relations. Therefore, the total number of queries produced by tuple substitution is card(R). An example of the INGRES algorithm is illustrated in the following.

Example 4.23

Consider the following SQL query that involves three different relations Student(sreg-no, sname, street, city, course-id), Course(course-id, cname, duration, fees), and Teacher (T-id), name, designation, salary, course-id).

Select sna,e name from Student, Course, Teacher where Student.course-id = Course. course-id and Course.couse-id = Teacher.course-id and duration = 4.

Using detachment technique, the above query can be replaced by the following queries, q1 and q2, where Course1 is an intermediate relation.

q1: Select Course.course-id into Course1 from Course where duration = 4.

q2: Select sname, name from Student, Course1, Teacher where Student.course-id = Course1. course-id and Course1.course-id = Teacher.course-id.

Similarly, the successive detachment of q2 may generate the queries q21 and q22 as follows.

q21: Select name, Teacher.course-id into Teacher1 from Teacher, Course1 where Teacher. course-id = Course1.course-id.

q22: Select sname from Student, Teacher1 where Student.course-id = Teacher1.course-id.

Assume that in query q22, three tuples are selected where course-id are C01, C03 and C06 respectively. The tuple substitution of Teacher1 relating produces three one-relation subqueries which are listed below.

q221: Select sname from Student where Student.course-id = "C01"

q222: Select sname from Student where Student.course-id = "C03"

q223: Select sname from Student where Student.course-id = "C06"

4.8 JOIN STRATEGIES IN FRAGMENTED RELATIONS

Thc ordering of join operations is very important in the context of both centralized and distributed query optimization. The algorithms represented in this section do not consider explicitly the fragmentation of relations. Thus, the generic term "relation" is used here to denote either fragmented or non-fragmented relations. There are two basic approaches for join strategies in fragmented relations. One is simple join strategy which tries to optimize the ordering of join operations directly. Another alternative approach is semijoin strategy, which replaces join operations by semijoin operations to minimize communication costs.

4.8.1 SIMPLE JOIN STRATEGY

The objective of simple join strategy is to optimize the ordering of join operations of relations to minimize the query processing cost. For the sake of simplicity, only specific join queries are considered here whose operand relations are stored at different sites, and it is assumed that relation transfers among different sites of the distributed system are to be done in a set-at-a-time basis rather than in a tuple-at-a-time basis. Finally, the time for generating the data at a result site is ignored here.

Let us consider a simple query that involves the joining of two relations R and S that are stored at different sites. In performing $R \infty S$, the smaller relation should be transferred to the site of the large relation. Therefore, it is necessary to calculate the size of the relations R and S. If the query involves one more relation T, then the obvious choice is to transfer the intermediate result $R \infty S$ or the relation T, whichever is smaller.

The difficulty with the simple join strategy is that the join operation may reduce or increase the size of the intermediate results. Hence, it is necessary to estimate the size of the results of join operations. One solution is to estimate the communication costs of all alternative strategies and select the best one for which the communication cost is the minimum. However, the number of alternative strategies will increase as the number of relations increases.

4.8.2 SEMIJOIN STRATEGY

The main drawback of simple join strategy is that the entire operand relation has to be transmitted between the sites. The objective of the semijoin strategy is to minimize the communication cost by replacing join operations of a query with semijoin operations. The join operation between two relations R and S over the attribute A, which are stored at different sites of the distributed system, can be replaced by semijoin operations as follows.

$$R \infty S \Leftrightarrow (R\ {}_A S) \infty_A S \Leftrightarrow R\ {}_A S \infty_A (S\ {}_A R) \Leftrightarrow R\ {}_A S \infty_A S\ {}_A R$$

It is necessary to estimate the cost of the above semijoin operations to understand the benefits of semijoin operations over a join operation. The local processing cost are not considered here for simplicity. The join operation $R \infty_A S$ and the semijoin operation $R\ {}_A S$ and semijoin operation $(R\ {}_A S) \infty_A S$ can be implemented in the following way assuming the relations R and S are stored at site1 and site2 respectively, and size(R) < size(S).

$R \infty_A S$:

1. The relation R is to be transferred to site2.
2. The join operation is performed at site2.

$(R \infty_A S) \infty_A S$:

1. The projection operation $\Pi_A(S)$ is performed at site2 and result is sent to site1.

2. The site1 computes R $_{A}$ S, and the result is, say T.
3. The result T is transferred to site2.
4. The join operation $T \infty_{A}$ S is computed at site2.

The communication cost for the above join operation is $C_0 + C_1$ * size(R), whereas the communication cost for the semijoin operation is $2C_0 + C_1$ *(size(Π_A(S)) + size(R $_A$S)). Thus, the second operation is beneficial if size(Π_A(S)) + size (R $_A$ S) is less than size(R), because C_0 is negligible compared to the cost of data transfer.

In general, the semijoin operation is useful to reduce the size of operand relations involved in multiple join queries. The optimal semijoin program is called a full reduce, which reduces a relation more than other [Chiu and Ho, 1980]. The determination of full reducers is a difficult task. One solution is to evaluate the size of reduction for all possible semijoin strategies and select the best one. Full reducers cannot be found in the group of queries that have cycles in their join graph, known as cyclic queries. For other groups of queries, called tree queries, full reducers exist, but the number of alternative semijoin increases as the number of relations an increase, which complicates the above solution.

The semijoin strategy is beneficial if only a few number of tuples participate in the join operation, whereas the simple join strategy is beneficial if most of the tuples participate in the join operation, because semijoin strategy involves an additional data transfer cost.

Example 4.24

Consider the following join operation that involves three different relations Student, Course, and teacher, and over the attribute course-id.

Student $\infty_{\text{course-id-}}$ Course $\infty_{\text{course-id}}$ Teacher

Further assume that the relations Student, Course and Teacher are stored at site 1, site 2, and site 3 respectively. The corresponding join graph is depicted in figure 4.23.

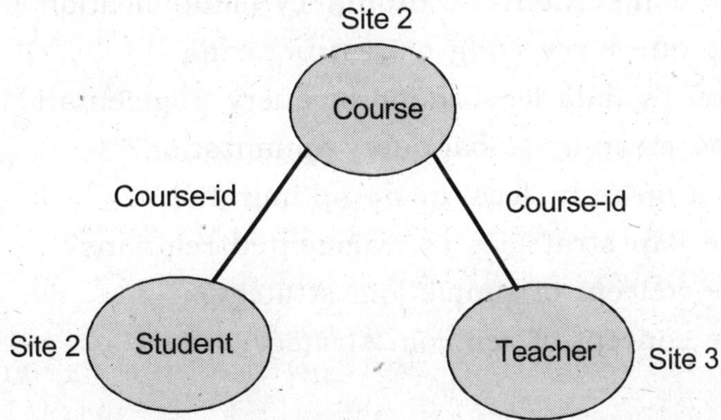

Figure 4.23 Join Graph for a Distributed Query

There are various ways to perform the above join operation, but to select the best one, some more information must be known: size(Student), size(Teacher), size(Course), size(Student ∞ Course) and size (course ∞ Teacher). Moreover, all data transfer can be done in parallel.

If the above join operation is replaced by semijoin operations, then the number of operations will be increased but possibly on smaller operands. In this case, instead of sending the entire Student relation to site2, only the values for the join attribute course-id of Student relation will be sent to site2. If the length of the join attribute is significantly less than the length of the entire tuple, then the semijoin has a good selectivity in this case, and it reduces the communication cost significantly. This is also applicable for performing join operation between the relations Course and Teacher. However, the semijoin operation may increase the local processing time, because one of the two operand relations must be accessed twice.

EXERCISES

1. What are the distributed queries processing?
2. Explain the concepts of query processing?
3. Explain representation of database operation in form of a query?
4. Explain the objectives of distributed query processing?
5. Explain the complexity of relational algebra operations?
6. Explain the query processor and its characteristics?
7. Explain the phases in distributed query processing?
8. Explain the query decomposition?
9. Explain the concept of normalization?
10. Explain the analysis of distributed query processing?
11. Explain the elimination of redundancy (simplification)?
12. Explain the query rewriting or restructuring?
13. What do you by data localization or query fragmentation?
14. What do you mean by global query optimization?
15. What do you mean by local query optimization?
16. Explain the join strategies in fragmented relations?
17. Explain the concept of simple join strategy?
18. Explain the concept of semijoin strategy?

CHAPTER 5

DISTRIBUTED QUERY OPTIMIZATION

5.1 INTRODUCTION

Query optimization is a function of many relational database management systems in which multiple query plans for satisfying a query are examined and a good query plan is identified. This may or not be the absolute best strategy because there are many ways of doing plans. There is a trade-off between the amount of time spent figuring out the best plan and the amount running the plan. Different qualities of database management systems have different ways of balancing these two. Cost based query optimizers evaluate the resource footprint of various query plans and use this as the basis for plan selection.

Typically the resources which are costed are CPU path length, amount of disk buffer space, disk storage service time, and interconnect usage between units of parallelism. The set of query plans examined is formed by examining possible access paths (e.g., primary index access, secondary index access, full file scan) and various relational table join techniques (e.g., merge join, hash join, product join). The search space can become quite large depending on the complexity of the SQL query. There are two types of optimization. These consist of logical optimization which generates a sequence of relational algebra to solve the query. In addition there is physical optimization which is used to determine the means of carrying out each operation.

5.2 QUERY OPTIMIZATION

Query optimization refers to the process of producing an optimal (close to optimal) query execution plan (QEP) which represents an execution strategy for the query. The selected plan minimizes an objective cost function. Selecting the optimal execution strategy for a query is NP-hard in the number of relations. For this research, different operators will be implemented, and we will try to find an optimal strategy (optimizer) and perhaps more important to avoid bad strategy. The main task in query optimization is to consider different orderings of the operations. Query Optimization process is shown in the figure 5.1 below:

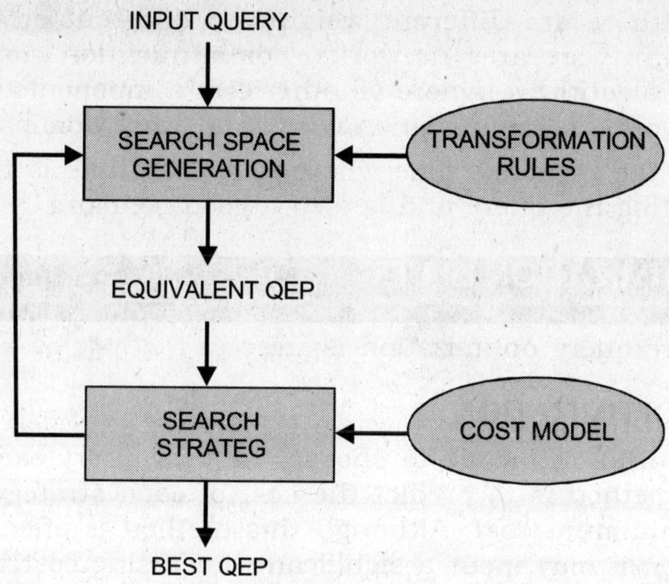

Figure 5.1 Query Optimization Process

Query optimization can be done in centralized databases called centralized query optimization. **The objectives of centralized query optimization are:**

- Find (the best) query execution plan in the space of equivalent query trees
- Minimize an objective cost function
- Gather statistics about relations

Whereas optimization in distributed databases called Distributed query optimization brings additional issues such as:

- Linear query trees are not necessarily a good choice.
- Bushy query trees are not necessarily a bad choice.
- What and where to ship the relations.
- How to ship relations (ship as a whole, ship as needed).
- When to use semi-joins instead of joins.

5.2.1 OBJECTIVES OF QUERY OPTIMIZATION

Following are objectives of query optimization:

1. Minimize the total cost which is sum of all cost (or times) at various sites and in inter-site communication.

   Total Cost = I/O cost + CPU cost + communication cost

However there are different weights in different environments. For Example, in wide area networks, communication cost will dominate and most algorithms ignore all other cost components whereas in local area networks, communication cost is not that dominant

2. Minimize the response time where Response time is the time elapsed for executing the query and is also a good measure.

5.3 QUERY OPTIMIZATION ISSUES

Following are query optimization issues:

5.3.1 TYPES OF OPTIMIZATION

Query Optimization means to choose the best query execution strategy. Most common method is to predict the cost of each strategy and select the strategy with minimum cost. Although this method is effective in selecting the best strategy, it may incur a significant processing cost for the optimization itself.

The output language specification represents the execution strategy. There can be many such strategies, the best one can be selected through exhaustive search, or by applying heuristic (minimize size of intermediate relations). For distributed databases semi-joins can be applied to reduce data transfer.

Following are various types of optimizers or optimization techniques:

(a) Cost-based: This includes an exhaustive search whereby (almost) all possible execution strategies are considered. This technique can be optimal and has combinatorial complexity in the number of relations. This technique however incurs high cost.

(b) Heuristics: One way of reducing the cost of exhaustive search is the use of heuristics whose effect is to restrict the solution space so that only a few strategies are considered. In both centralized and distributed systems, a common heuristic is to minimize the size of intermediate relations. This method of heuristics may not be optimal. Following are commonly used heuristics:

- regroup common sub-expressions
- perform unary operations selection, projection first.
- reorder operations to reduce intermediate relation size
- replace a join by a series of semi joins to minimize data communication.

5.3.2 OPTIMIZATION GRANULARITY

Optimization Granularity means number of queries to be executed at a time.

There are two options:

(a) Single query at a time: This means a single query to be executed at a time. But this method cannot use common intermediate results.

(b) Multiple queries at a time: This means to execute number of queries at a time. This method is efficient if there are many similar queries and decision space is much larger.

5.3.3 OPTIMIZATION TIMING

A query may be optimized at different times relative to the actual time of query execution. **Optimization Timing can be:**

(a) Static: In this case, optimization is done before executing the query (at compilation time), cost of optimization amortized over multiple executions, mostly based on exhaustive search. Since sizes of intermediate relations of a strategy are not known until run time, they need to be estimated using database statistics. So errors in the estimates can result in sub optimal strategies.

(b) Dynamic: Here optimization is done at run time i.e. at every time the query is executed. At any point of execution, the choice of the best next operation can be based on accurate knowledge of the results of the operations executed previously. Therefore database statistics are not needed to estimate the size of intermediate results. The main advantage of dynamic optimization over static query optimization is that it makes use of exact sizes of intermediate relations. The disadvantage is that it is expensive since it is based on heuristics and query optimization must be repeated for each execution of the query.

(c) Hybrid: This approach mixes static and dynamic approaches. In this case, the approach is mainly static but dynamic query optimization may take place when high differences between predicted and actual sizes are detected.

5.3.4 STATISTICS

The effectiveness of query optimization relies on statistics on database. Dynamic query optimization requires statistics in order to choose which operations should be done first. Static query optimization requires estimating size of intermediate relations based on statistical information. In a distributed database, statistics for query optimization include:

- Fragment cardinality and size
- Size and number of distinct values for each attribute.
- Detailed histograms of attribute values for better selectivity estimation.

Example of Statistics:

- relation (cardinality, size of a tuple, join selectivity)
- attribute (cardinality of domain, actual number of distinct values)

Common assumptions

- independence between different attribute values
- uniform distribution of attribute values within their domain
- Statistics need to be periodically updated

5.3.5 DECISION SITES

When static optimization is used, either a single site or several sites may participate in the selection of the strategy to be applied for answering the query. Decision sites are sites that make a decision.

Following are the possible approaches:

(a) ***Centralized:*** In this approach, a single site determines the best schedule and thus that site is a decision site. This approach is simple but need knowledge about entire distributed database.

(b) ***Distributed:*** This approach requires cooperation among sites to determine the schedule and thus multiple sites are decision sites. This approach needs only local information but includes the cost of cooperation.

(c) ***Hybrid:*** In this approach, one site makes a major decision and other sites can make local decisions. For example, System R* uses a hybrid approach.

5.3.6 EXPLOITATION OF NETWORK TOPOLOGY

The network topology is generally exploited by the distributed query processor.

The networks to be considered are:

(a) ***Wide area networks (WAN):*** In a wide area network, the cost function to be minimized includes mainly communication cost and all other cost factors are ignored. There is a global schedule to minimize communication cost and local schedules are according to centralized query optimization.

(b) ***Local area networks (LAN):*** In a local area network, communication costs are comparable to I/O costs as well as CPU costs and thus they need to be considered. Therefore it is reasonable for the distributed query processor to increase parallel execution at the expense of communication cost. Also broadcasting capability of some local area networks can be exploited e.g. for joins to optimize the processing.

5.4 COMPONENTS OF QUERY OPTIMIZER

A query optimizer is a software module that performs query optimization. Following are three components of query optimizer:

1. Search Space
2. Search Strategy
3. Cost Model

The **search space** is the set of execution plans to represent the input query. These plans are equivalent in the sense that they yield the same result but they differ on the execution order of operations and the way these operations are implemented and therefore on performance.

The **search strategy** explores the search space and selects the best plan using the cost model. It defines which plans are examined and in which order.

The **cost model** predicts the cost of a given execution plan. The cost model must have good knowledge about the distributed execution environment.

5.4.1 SEARCH SPACE

Search space is characterized by alternative execution plans. The main issue is to optimize the joins. For *N* relations, there is O (*N*!) equivalent join trees that can be obtained by applying commutativity and associativity rules. For a given query, the search space can thus be defined as the set of equivalent join trees that can be produced using transformation rules.

For Example, Consider the following query:

SELECT ENAME, RESP
FROM EMP, ASG, PROJ
WHERE EMP.ENO=ASG.ENO
AND ASG.PNO=PROJ.PNO

Figure 5.2 show 3 equivalent join trees of the joins in the above query which are obtained by exploiting the associativity of binary operators. Each of these join trees can be assigned a cost based on the estimated cost of each operator. Join tree (c) which starts with a cartesian product may have a much higher cost than the other join trees.

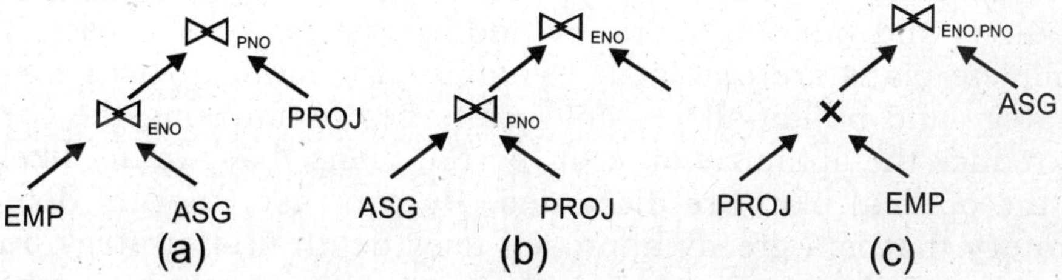

Figure 5.2: Equivalent Join Trees

5.4.1 REDUCTION OF THE SEARCH SPACE

There are two techniques for reduction of the search space:

- **Restrict by means of heuristics:** This means to perform unary operations before binary operations. The most common heuristic is to perform selection and projection when accessing base relations. Another common heuristic is to avoid Cartesian products that are not required by the query.
- **Restrict the shape of the join tree:** There are two kinds of join trees: linear versus bushy trees. A linear tree is a tree such that at least one operand of each operator node is a base relation. A bushy tree is more general and may have operators with no base relations as operands (i.e. both operands are intermediate relations). The restriction regarding the shape of join tree is to consider only linear trees and ignore bushy ones. This reduces the size of the search space to $O(2^N)$. But in case of distributed environment, bushy trees are useful to provide parallelism.

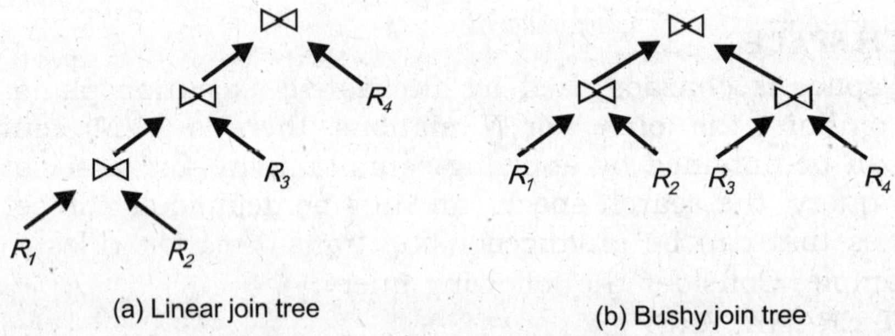

Figure 5.3: The two shapes of join trees.

5.4.2 SEARCH STRATEGY

There are two main strategies to scan the search space:

1. Deterministic
2. Randomized

1. **Deterministic scan of the search space:** Deterministic scan strategy uses dynamic programming approach. It proceeds by starting from base relations and building plans by adding one relation at each step until complete plans are obtained. Dynamic programming uses breadth-first strategy and builds all possible plans before choosing the "best" plan. To reduce the optimization cost, partial plans that are not likely to lead to the optimal plan are discarded. By contrast, another deterministic strategy that is a greedy approach uses depth-first strategy builds only one plan. Following Figure 5.4 illustrates deterministic search strategy.

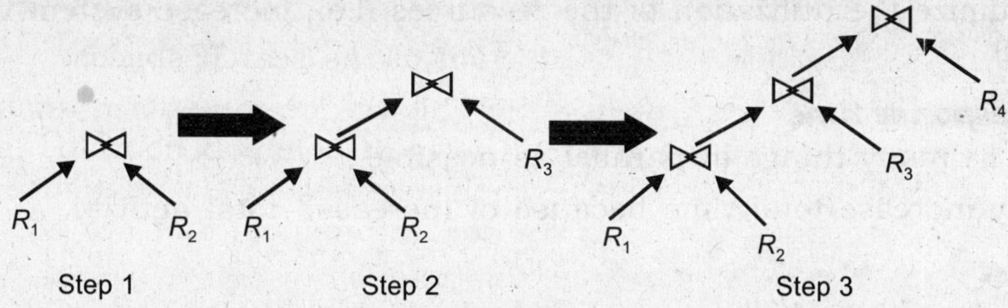

Figure 5.4: Deterministic Search Strategy

Dynamic programming assures searching of best of all plans. In incurs an acceptable optimization cost (in terms of time and space) when the number of relations in the query is small. However this approach becomes too expensive when the number of relations is greater than 5 or 6.

2. **Randomized scan of the search space:** Randomized search strategy concentrates on searching for optimal solutions around a particular starting point. Examples are iterative improvement or simulated annealing techniques. This strategy trades optimization time for execution time. In this strategy First one or more start plans are built by a greedy strategy. Then the start plan is improved by visiting its neighbours. A neighbour is obtained by applying a random transformation to a plan. An example of a typical transformation consists in exchanging two randomly chosen operand relations of the plan. Figure 5.5 illustrates randomized search strategy.

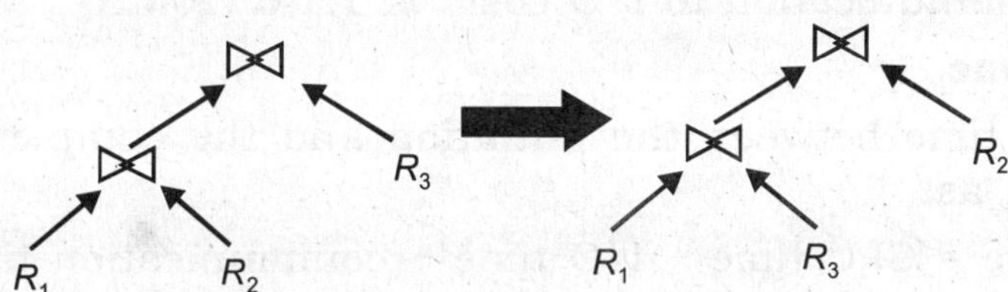

Figure 5.5 Randomized Search Strategy

Randomized search strategy docs not guarantee that the best solution is obtained but avoids the high cost of optimization in terms of memory and time consumption. However this strategy is better when more than 5-6 relations are involved.

5.4.3 DISTRIBUTED COST MODEL

A distributed optimizer cost model includes two different types of cost functions to predict the total cost:

Reduce total time

- Reduce each cost component (in terms of time) individually, i.e. do as little for each cost component as possible

- Optimize the utilization of the resources (i.e., increase system throughput)

Reduce response time

- Do as many things in parallel as possible
- May increase total time because of increased total activity

Total Cost

It is summation of all cost factors and is calculated as:

Total cost = CPU cost + I/O cost + communication cost

CPU cost = unit instruction cost * no. of instructions

I/O cost = unit disk I/O cost * no. of disk I/Os

communication cost = message initiation + transmission

Total Cost Factors

The individual components of the total cost have different weights.

E.g. In wide area network

- Message initiation and transmission costs are high
- Local processing cost is low (fast mainframes or minicomputers)
- Ratio of communication to I/O costs is 20:1

Whereas in local area networks

- Communication and local processing costs are more or less equal
- Ratio of communication to I/O costs is 1:1.6 (10MB/s network)

Response Time

It is elapsed time between the initiation and the completion of a query and is calculated as:

Response time = CPU time + I/O time + communication time

CPU time = unit instruction time * no. of sequential instructions

I/O time = unit I/O time * no. of sequential I/Os

communication time = unit msg initiation time * no. of sequential msg + unit transmission time * no. of sequential bytes

Example 5.1:

Consider the processing of a query at site 3 which requires data from sites 1 and 2.

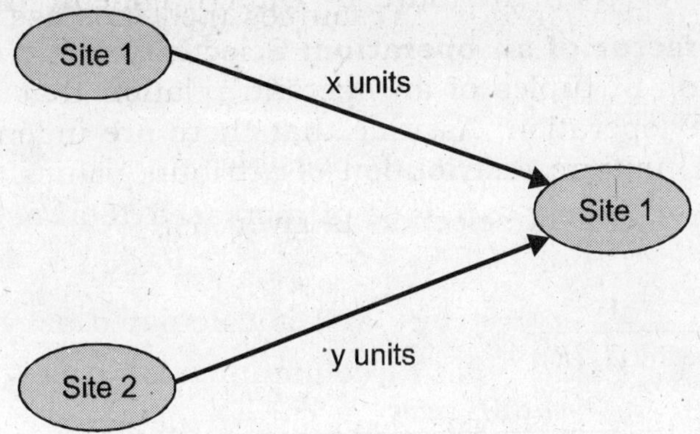

Assume that only the communication cost is considered

Total time = 2 * message initialization time + unit transmission time *$(x+y)$

Response time = max {time to send x from 1 to 3, time to send y from 2 to 3}

Time to send x from 1 to 3 = message initialization time + unit transmission time * x

Time to send y from 2 to 3 = message initialization time + unit transmission time * y

5.5 DATABASE STATISTICS

The primary cost factor is the size of intermediate relations that are produced during the execution and must be transmitted over the network. If a subsequent operation is located on a different site, the intermediate relation must be transmitted over the network. However it is costly to compute the size of the intermediate relations precisely. Instead global statistics of relations and fragments are computed and used to provide approximations

Let $R(A_1, A_2, \ldots, A_k)$ be a relation fragmented into $R_1, R_2, \ldots, R_r$ then database statistics are :

1. **Relation statistics:** Relation statistics consist of following:
   - Minimum and Maximum values of each attribute: min $\{A_i\}$, max$\{A_i\}$.
   - Length of each attribute: length(A_i)
   - Number of distinct values for domain of each attribute in each fragment called its cardinality: card(A_i), (card(dom(A_i)))
2. **Fragment statistics:** Fragment statistics consist of following:
   - cardinality of the fragment i.e. number of tuples in each fragment R_i: card(R_i)

- cardinality of each attribute of each fragment: card $(Ai(R_j))$

3. **Selectivity factor of an operation:** Selectivity factor of an operation is the proportion of tuples of an operand relation that participate in the result of that operation. Assume that there are independent attributes and there is uniform distribution of attribute values.

Thus selectivity factor of selection is given as:

$$SF\sigma(? = value) = \frac{1}{\text{card}(\Pi_A(R))}$$

$$SF_\sigma(A > value) = \frac{max(A) - value}{max(A) - min(A)}$$

$$SF(A < value) = \frac{value - min(A)}{\max(A) - \min(A)}$$

Properties of the selectivity factor of the selection are:

$$SF_\sigma(p(?_2) \wedge p(Aj)) = SF_\sigma(p(A_i))^* SF_\sigma(p(Ai))$$

$$SF_\sigma(p(A_i) \vee p(A_3)) = SF_\sigma(p)(A_i)) + \text{SF}(p)(\text{A}_j)) - (SF_\sigma(p(A_i))^* SF_\sigma(p(A_3))$$

$$SF_\sigma(A\varepsilon\{\text{value}\}) = SF(A = value)^* card(\{values\})$$

5.6 CARDINALITIES OF INTERMEDIATE RESULTS

Database statistics are useful in evaluating the cardinalities of the intermediate results of queries. Two simplifying assumptions are commonly made about the database. The distribution of attribute values in a relation is supposed to be uniform and all attributes are independent meaning that the value of an attribute does not affect the value of any other attribute. These two assumptions are often wrong in practice, but they make the problem tractable. In what follows we give the formulas for estimating the cardinalities of the results of the basic relations algebra operations (selection, projection, Cartesian product, join, semijoin, union, and difference). The operand relations are denoted by R and S. The selectivity factor of an operation, that is, the proportion of tuples of an operand relation that participate in the result of that operation is denoted SF_{OP}, where OP denotes the operation.

1. **Selection:** The cardinality of selection is

$$card(_\sigma p(R)) = SF_\sigma(P)^* card(R)$$

2. **Projection:** Projection can be with or without duplicate elimination. Consider projection with duplicate elimination. Projection is difficult to evaluate because correlations between projected attributes are un-

known. However there are two particularly useful cases where it is trivial. If the projection of relation R is based on a single attribute A, the cardinality is simply the number of tuples when the projection is performed. If one of the projected attributes is a key of R then

$card(\Pi_A(\mathbf{R}) = \mathbf{card(R)}$

3. **Cartesian Product:** The cardinality of Cartesian product of R and S is:

$card(R \times S) = card(R) * card)$

4. **Union:** It is difficult to estimate the cardinality of the union of R and S because the duplicates between R and S are removed by the union. Hence, upper and lower bound are calculated as:

upper bound is :

$card(R \cup S) \leq card(R) + card(S)$

lower bound is :

$card(R \bigcup S) \geq \max\{\text{card(R)}, \text{card(S)}\}$

5. **Set Difference:** Like Union, in case of set difference, upper and lower bounds are calculated as:

upper bound is :

$card(R - S) = card(R)$

And lower bound is 0.

6. **Join:** Selectivity factor for joins is given by:

$$SF\times = \frac{card(R \times S)}{card(R) * card(S)}$$

The upper bound of cardinality of joins is the cardinality of Cartesian product and is given by:

$card(R \times S) \leq card(R) * card(S)$

There are two cases for the cardinality of joins:

(a) General case: If Selectivity factor is given, Cardinality is:

$card(R \times X) = SF \times *(R) * card(S)$

(b) Special case: If R.A is a key of relation R and S.A is a foreign key of relation S then each S-tuple matches with at most one tuple of R and cardinality is given by:

$card(R \times_{R.A.=S.A.} S) = card(S)$

7. **Semijoin:** Selectivity factor for semijoins is the fraction of R-tuples that join with S-tuples. An approximation of the semijoin selectivity factor of A in S is:

$$SF \rhd\!\!< _A S) = SF \rhd\!\!< (S.A) = \frac{card(\Pi_A(S))}{card(dom[A])}$$

Two cases for Cardinality of semijoin

1. **General case:** If Selectivity factor is given, Cardinality of semijoin is:

$$card(R \rhd\!\!< _A S) = SF \rhd\!\!< (S.A.) * card(R)$$

2. **Special case:** If R.A is a foreign key in S (S.A is a primary key) then SF = 1 and the result size corresponds to the size of R.

5.7 JOIN ORDERING IN FRAGMENT QUERIES

Join ordering is an important aspect in centralized DBMS and it is even more important in a distributed DBMS since joins between fragments that are stored at different sites may increase the communication time.

Two approaches exist to order joins in fragment queries:

1. Optimize the ordering of joins directly.
2. Replace joins by combinations of semijoins in order to minimize the communication costs.

5.7.1 JOIN ORDERING

Some algorithms optimize the ordering of joins directly without using semijoins. Distributed INGRES and R* algorithms are representative of algorithms that use joins rather than semijoins. The purpose of this section is to streets the differently that join ordering presents and to motivate the subsequent section, which deals with the use of semijoins to optimize join queries.

A number of assumptions are necessary to concentrate on the main issues. Since the query is localized and expressed on fragments we do not need to distinguish between fragments of the same relation and fragments of different relations. To simplify notation we use the term relation to designate a fragments stores at a particular site. Also, to concentrate to join ordering we ignore local processing time assuming that reducers (selection projection) are executed locally either before or during the join (remember that doing selection first is not always efficient).

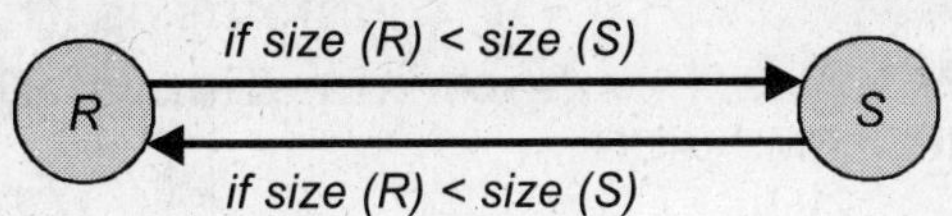

Figure 5.6 transfer of operands in binary Operation

Therefore we consider only join queries whose operand relations are stored at different sites. We assume that relation transfers are set-at-a-time mode rather in a tuple-at-a time mode. Finally we ignore the transfer time for producing the data at a result site.

Let us first concentrate on the simpler problem for operand transfer in a single join. The query is R S, where R and S are relations stored at different sites. The obvious choice relations to transfer is to send site of the larger one, which gives rise two possibility as shown in Figure 5.6. To make this choice we need to evaluate the size of R and S. We now consider join the objective of the join-ordering algorithm is to transmit smaller operands. The difficulty stamps from the fact that the join operations may reduce or increase mandatory but also difficult. A solution is to estimate the communication costs of all alternative strategies and to choose the best one. However, the number of strategies grows rapidly with the number of relations. This approach, used by System R*, makes optimization costly, although this overhead is amortized rapidly if the query is executed frequently.

Thus it moves the smaller relation to the other site

– We have to estimate the size of R and S

- Direct join ordering of queries involving more than two relations is substantially more complex

Example 5.2:

Consider the following query and the respective join graph, where we make also assumptions about the locations of the three relations/fragments

$PROJ \times_{PNO} ASG \times_{ENO} EMP$

Site 2
ENO
PNO
EMP
PROJ
Site 1
Site 3

• Example (Contd.) The query can be evaluated in at least 5 different ways.

- Plan 1: EMP → Site 2
  - Site 2: EMP' = EMP×ASG
  - EMP'→Site
  - Site 3: EMP' ⋈ PROJ
- Plan 2: ASG → Site 1
  - Site 1: EMP' =EMP⋈ASG
  - EMP'→Site 3
  - Site 3: EMP'⋈PROJ
- Plan 3: ASG → Site 3
  - Site 3: ASG' =ASG⋈PROJ
  - ASG'→Site 1
  - Site 1: ASG' ⋈EMP

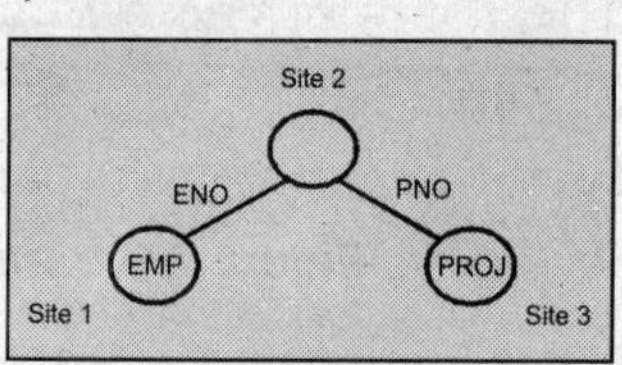

- Plan 4: PROJ→ Site 2
  - Site 2: PROJ'=PROJ×ASG
  - PROJ→'Site 1
  - Site 1: PROJ'⋈EMP
- Plan 5: EMP→ Site 2
  - PROJ→ Site 2
  - Site 2: EMP⋈PROJ⋈ASG

- **Example (contd.):** The query can be evaluated in at least 5 different ways.

To select a plan, a lot of information is needed, including Possibilities of parallel execution if response time is used

5.7.2 SEMIJOIN-BASED ALGORITHMS

In this section we show the semijoin operation can be used to decrease the total time of join queries. The theory of semijoins is defined in [Bernstein and Chiu, 1981]. The main short coming of the join approach described in the preceding section is that entire operand relations must be transferred between sites. The semijoin acts as a size reducer for a relation as a selection does.

The join of two relations R and S over attribute A, stored at sites 1 and 2 respectively, can be computed by replacing one or both by a semojoin with the other relation, using the following rules.

$$R \infty_A S \quad \Leftrightarrow (R, \propto_A S) \infty_A S$$

$$\Leftrightarrow R \propto_A (S \propto_A R)$$

$$\Leftrightarrow R \propto_A S \propto_A (S \propto_A R)$$

The choice between one of the three semojoin strategies requires estimating their respective costs.

The use of the semijoin is beneficial if the cost to produce and send it to the other site is less than a cost of sending the whole operand relation and of doing the actual join. To illustrate the potential benefit of the semijoin, let us compare the costs of the two alternatives: R ∞_A S versus (R $\propto_A$ S) S, assuming the size ® <size (S).

The following program using the notation of 5.7.1, uses the semijoin operation.

1. $\Pi_A \rightarrow$ site 1S
2. Site 1 compute R' = R
3. R' $\rightarrow$ site 2
4. Site 2 computes R' S

For the sake of simplicity let us ignore the constant T_{MSG} in the communication time assuming that the term T_{TR} * size(R) is much larger. We can then compare the two alternatives in terms of the amount of transmitted data. The cost of the join-based algorithm is that of relation R to suite 2. The cost of the semojoin-based algorithm is the 1 and 3 above. Therefore, the semijoin approach is better if

$$\text{size } ((\Pi_A)) + \text{size (RS)} < \text{size(R)}$$

The semijoin approach is better if the semijoin acts as a sufficient reducer, that is, if a few tuples of R participate in the join. The approach id better if almost all tuples of R participate in the join , because the semijoin approach requires an additional transfer of a projection on the join. The cost of the projection step can be minimized by encoding by the result of the projection in bit arrays values. It is important to note that neither approach is systematically the best; they should be considered as complementary. More generally, the semijoin can be useful in reducing the size of the operand relations involved in multiple join queries. However, query optimization becomes more complex in these cases. Consider again the join graph of relations EMP, ADG, and PROJ given in Figure 5.7. We can apply the previous join algorithm using semijoins to each individual join. Thus an example of a program to compute EMP ∞ ASG ∞ PROJ is EMP' ASG' PROJ, where EMP' = EMP ASG and ASG' = ASG PROJ.

However, we may further reduce the size of an operand relation by using morc than one semijoin. For example, EMP' can be replaced in the preceding program by EMP' derived as

EMP" = EMP ∞ (ASG PROJ)

since if size (ASG PROJ) ≤ size (ASG) we have size (EMP") ≤ size(EMP'). In this way, EMP can be reduced by the sequence of semijoins: EMP (ASG PROJ). Such a sequence of semijoins is called a semijoin program for EMP. Similarly, semijoin programs can be found for any relation in a query. For example, PROJ could be reduced by the semijoin program PROJ v (ASG ∞ EMP). However, not all of the relations involved in a query need to be reduced; in particular, we can ignore those relations that are not involved in the final joins.

For a given relation, there exist several potential semijoin programs. The number of possibilities is in fact exponential in the number of relations. But there is one optimal semijoin program; called the full reducer, which for each relation R reduces R more than the others [Chiu and Ho, 1980]. The problem is to find the full reducer. A simple method is to evaluate the size reduction of all possible semijoin programs and to select the best one.

The problems with the enumerative method are twofold:

1. There is a class of queries, called cyclic queries, which have cycles in their join graph and for which full reducers cannot be found.
2. For other queries, called tree queries, full reducers exist, but the number of candidate semijoin programs is exponential in the number of relations, which makes the enumerative approach NP–hard.

In what follows we discuss solutions to these problems.

5.7.3 JOIN VERSUS SEMIJOIN

Compared with the join, the semijoin induces more operations but possibly on smaller operands. Figure 5.8 illustrates these differences with an equivalent pair of join and semijoin strategies for the query whose join graph is given in Figure 5.7. The join of two relations, EMP ∞ ASG in Figure 5.7, is done by sending one relation, ASG, to the site of the other one, EMP, to complete the join locally. When a semijoin is used, however, the transfer of relation ASG is avoided. Instead, it is replaced by the transfer of the join attribute values of relation EMP to the site of relation ASG, followed by the transfer of the matching tuples of relation ASG to the site of relation EMP, where the join is completed. If the join attribute length is smaller than the length of an entire tuple and the semijoin has good selectivity, then the semijoin approach can result in significant savings in communication tune. Using semijoins may well increase the local processing time, since one of the two joined relations must be accessed twice. For example, relation EMP and PROJ are accessed twice in Figure 5.8.

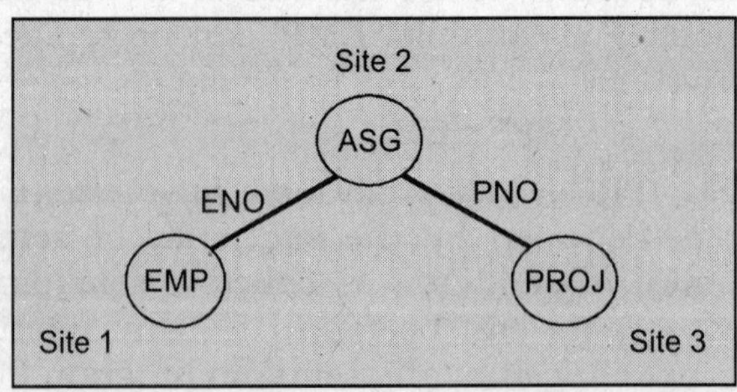

Figure 5.7: join graph for distributed query

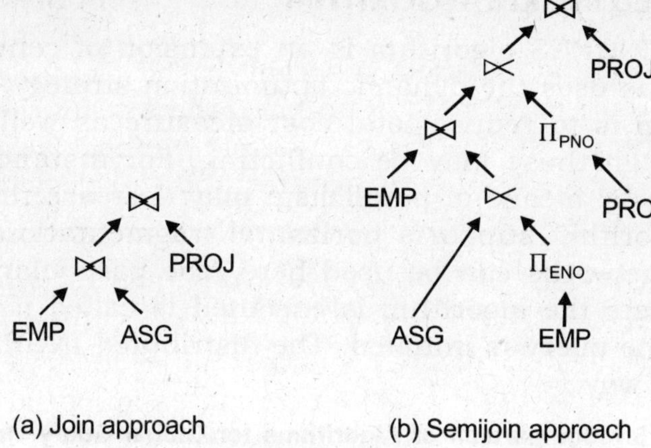

Figure 5.8 Join versus Semijoin Approaches

Furthermore, the join of two intermediate relations produced by semijoins cannot exploit the indices that were available on the base relations. Therefore, using semijoins might not be a good idea if the communication time is not the dominant factor, as is the case with local area networks [Lu and Carey, 1985].

Semijoins can still be beneficial with fast networks if they have very good selectivity and are implemented with bit arrays [Valduriez, 1982]. A bit array BA [1: n] is useful in encoding the join attribute values present in one relation. Let us consider the semijoin R ∞ S. Then BA[i] is set to 1 if there exists a join attribute value A = val in relation S such that h(val) – i, where h is a hash function. Otherwise, BA[i] is set to 0. Such a bit array is much smaller than a list of join attribute values. Therefore, transferring the bit array instead of the join attribute values to the site of relation R saves communication time. The semijoin can be completed as follows. Each tuple of relation R, whose join attribute value is val, belongs to the semijoin if BA [h(val)} = 1.

5.8 GLOBAL QUERY OPTIMIZATION ALGORITHMS

This section introduces three global query optimization algorithms, namely, distributed INGRES algorithm, R* algorithm and SDD-1 algorithm. Al these algorithms are different from one another in a major way depending on several factors such as objective function, optimization strategy and network topology. The comparison between these three algorithms is shown in table 5.1.

5.8.1 DISTRIBUTED INGRES ALGORITHM

Distributed INGRES algorithm is an extension of centralized INGRES algorithm and, thus uses the dynamic optimization strategy. The main objective of this algorithm is to reduce total cost measure as well are response time measure, although these may be conflicting. For instance, increasing communication time by means of parallelism may decrease response time significantly. This algorithm supports horizontal fragmentation, and both general and broadcast networks can be used here. The particular site in the distributes system where the algorithm is executed is called master site, and it is the site where the query is initiated. The distributed INGRES algorithm works in the following way.

Table 5.1 Comparison of Algorithms for Global Query Optimization

Algorithms	Objective function	Optim. Strategy	Comm. Schemes	Optim. Factor	Semijoins	Fragments
Distributed INGRES	Total cost measure or response time measure	Dynamic	General or broadcast	Msg. transfer cost, processing cost	No	Horizontal
SDD-1	Total cost measure	Static	General	Msg. transfer cost	Yes	No
R*	Total cost measure	Static	General or local	Msg. transfer and amount of data transfer cost, I/O cost, CPU cost	No	No

For a given query all monorelation queries (unary operations such as selection and projection) can be detached first and these are processed locally. Then the reduction algorithm [Wong and Youssefi, 1976] is applied to the original query, and it produces two different kinds of subqueries: irreducible subqueries and monorelation subqueries. Reduction is a technique that separates all irreducible subqueries are and monorelation subqueries from the original query by detachment technique. Since monorelation subqueries are already processed locally, no action is taken with respect to then. Assume that the reduction technique produces a sequence of irreducible subqueries q1 → q2 → ... → qn, where at least one relation is common between two consecutive subqueries. It is mentioned in [Wong and Youssefi, 1976] that such a sequence is unique.

Based on the sequence of irreducible subqueries and the size of each fragment, one subquery is chosen from the list, say qi, which has at least tow variables. For processing the subquery qi, initially the best strategy is determined for the subquery. This strategy is expressed by a list of pairs (F, S), where F denotes a fragment that is to be transferred to the processing site S.

After transferring all fragments to the corresponding processing sits, finally the subquery qi is executed. This procedure is repeated for all irreducible subqueries in the sequence q1→ q2→...→ qn, and the algorithm terminates. This algorithm is represented in the following:

Distributed INGRES Algorithm:

Input: Given multi-relation query, q.

Output: Result of the last subquery qn.

Begin

Step 1: Detach all monorelation queries from the given query q and execute by OVQPs (one-variable query processors) at local sites the same way as in centralized INGRES algorithm.

Step 2: Apply reduction technique to q, which will produce a list of monorelation subqueries and a sequence of irreducible subqueries q1→ q2→...→ qn.

Step 3: Ignore all monorelation subqueries (since they are already processed by OVQPs at local sites).

Step 4: for I = 1 to n, repeat Step 5 to Step8 [n is the total number of irreducible subqueries].

Step 5: Choose the irreducible subquery qi involving the smallest fragments.

Step 6: Determine the best strategy, pairs of (F, S) for qi. [F represents a fragment and S represents the processing sites.]

Step 7: For each pair (F, S) transfer the fragment F to the corresponding processing site S.

Step 8: Execute the query qi. Check for the termination o for loop.

Step 9: Output the result.

End.

The query optimization is basically done instep5 and step6 in distributed ingress algorithm in this algorithm subqueries are produced depending on several components and their dependency order since the relation involved in a subquery may be fragmented and stored at different sites the subquery cannot be further subdivided the main difficulty in step6 is to determine how to execute the subquery by selecting the fragments that will be transferred to sites where the processing will take place. For an n-relation subquery, fragments from n – 1 relation must be transferred to the site(s) of fragments of the remaining relation, and then replicated there. Further, the non-transferred relations may be divided into several equal fragments to increase parallelism. This approach is called fragment-and-replicate, which performs a substitution of fragments rather than of tuples as in centralized

INGRES algorithm. The selection of non-transferred relations and the number of processing sites depends on the objective function and the communication scheme. The choice of the number of processing sites is a trade-off between the total time measure and the response time measure. If the number of sites increases, the response time decreases by parallelism, but the total time increases which leads to higher communication cost. The cost of producing the result is ignored here.

The distributed INGRES algorithm is characterized by a limited search of the solution space, an optimization decision taken for each step without considering the consequences of that decision on global optimization. The exhaustive search approach in which all possible strategies are evaluated to determine the best one is an alternative to the limited search approach. However, dynamic optimization strategy is beneficial, because the exact sizes of the intermediate result relations are known.

Example 5.3:

Consider query q1: "Names of employees working on the CAD/CAM project"

```
q1:   SELECT  EMP.ENAME
      FROM    EMP, ASG, PROJ
      WHERE   EMP.ENO = ASG.ENO
      AND     ASG.PNO = PROJ.PNO
      AND     PROJ.PNAME = "CAD/CAM"
```

• Decompose $q1$ into q_{11}'! $q2$:

```
q11:  SELECT  PROJ.PNO INTO JVAR
      FROM    PROJ
      WHERE   PROJ
q':   SELECT  EMP.ENAME
      FROM    EMP, ASG, JVAR
      WHERE   EMP.ENO = ASG.ENO
      AND     ASG.PNO = JVAR.PNO
```

The successive detachments may transform $q2$ into q_{12}'! q_{13}:

```
q':   SELECT  EMP.ENAME
      FROM    EMP,ENO = ASG.ENO
      WHERE   EMP.ENO = ASG.ENO
      AND     ASG.PNO = JVAR.PNO
q12:  SELECT  ASG.ENO INTO GVAR
      FROM    ASG.JVAR
```

```
         WHERE    ASG.PNO = JVAR.PNO
q13:     SELECT   EMP.ENAME
         FROM     EMP,GVAR
         WHERE    EMP.ENO = GVAR.ENO
```

q1 is now decomposed by detachment into q11'! q12 '! q13

q11 is a mono-relation query

q12 and q13 are multi-relation queries, which cannot be further detached and also called irreducible

However tuple substitution allows converting an irreducible query q into mono-relation queries. The steps are:

1. Choose a relation R_1 in q for tuple substitution.
2. For each tuple in R_1, replace the R_1-attributes referred in q by their actual values,

$$q(R_1, R_2, ..., R_n) \text{ is replaced by } \{q'(t_1, R_2, ..., R_n), t_1, \in R_1\}_1$$

thereby generating a set of subqueries q2 with n " 1 relations, i.e.,

Assume that GVAR consists only of the tuples {E1,E2}. Then q13 is rewritten with tuple substitution in the following way

```
q13:   SELECT   EMP.ENAME
       FROM     EMP.GVAR
       WHERE    EMP.ENO = GVAR.ENO

q131:  SELECT   EMP.ENAME            q132:  SELECT   EMP.ENAME
       FROM     EMP                         FROM     EMP
       WHERE    EMP.ENO = "E1"              WHERE    EMP.ENO = "E2"
```

*q*131 and *q*132 are mono-relation queries.

5.8.2 SYSTEM R ALGORITHM

The System R (centralized) query optimization algorithm performs static query optimization based on "exhaustive search" of the solution space and a cost function (IO cost + CPU cost). It takes input a relational algebra tree and produces optimal relational algebra tree as output. In this algorithm Dynamic programming technique is applied to reduce the number of alternative plans.

The optimization algorithm consists of two steps

1. Predict the best access method to each individual relation. (mono-relation query)
   - Consider using index, file scan, etc.
2. For each relation R, estimate the best join ordering

R is first accessed using its best single-relation access method

Efficient access to inner relation is crucial

Considers two different join strategies

- (Indexed-) nested loop join
- Sort-merge join

Example 5.4:

Consider query $q1$: "Names of employees working on the CAD/CAM project"

$PROJ \bowtie_{PNO} ASG \bowtie_{ENO} EMP$

Join graph

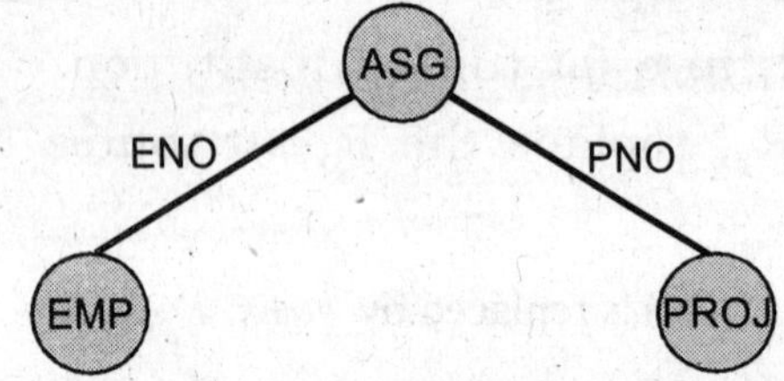

Indexes

- EMP has an index on ENO
- ASG has an indcx on PNO
- PROJ has an index on PNO and an index on PNAME

Step 1 – Select the best single-relation access paths

(a) **EMP:** sequential scan (because there is no selection on EMP)

(b) **ASG:** sequential scan (because there is no selection on ASG)

(c) **PROJ:** index on PNAME (because there is a selection on PROJ based on PNAME)

Step 2 – Select the best join ordering for each relation

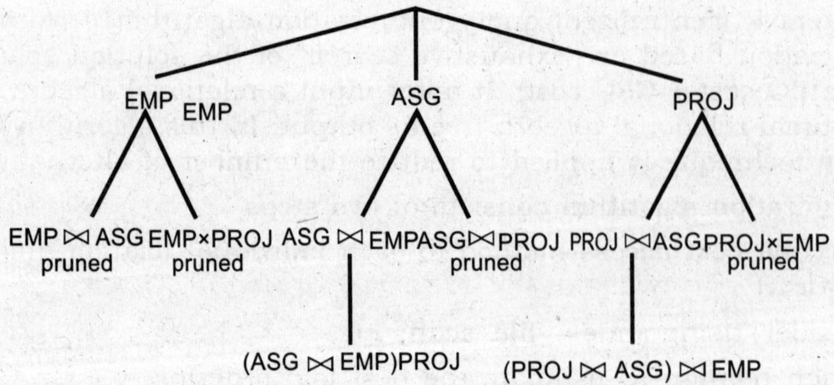

(EMP × PROJ) and (PROJ × EMP) are pruned because they are CPs

(ASG × PROJ) pruned because we assume it has higher cost than (PROJ × ASG);

similar for (PROJ × EMP)

Best total join order ((PROJ ⋊ ASG)⋊EMP), since it uses the indexes best

- Select PROJ using index on PNAME
- Join with ASG using index on PNO
- Join with EMP using index on ENO

ALGORITHM 9.2 R-QOA

```
input: QT: query tree with n relations
output: output: the result of execution
begin
  for each relation Ri ∈ QT do
  begin
  for each access path AP_ij to R_i do
  determine cost(AP_ij)
  end-for
  best AP_i ¬ AP_ij with minimum cost
  end-for
  for each order (R_i1,R_i2, ...R_in) with I = 1, ..., n! do
begin
build strategy (...(( best AP_i1 ∞ R_i2) ∞ R_i3) ∞ ... ∞ R_in)
compute the cost of strategy
end-for
output ¬ strategy with minimum cost
end. { R-QOA}
```

5.8.3 DISTRIBUTED R* ALGORITHM

The objective of distributed R* algorithm [Selinger and Adiba, 1980] is to reduce the total cost measure which includes the local processing costs and communication costs. Distributed R* algorithm uses an exhaustive search approach to select the best strategy. Although exhaustive search incurs an overhead, it can be worthwhile, if the query is executed frequently. The implemented version of distributed R* algorithm does not support fragmentation or replication; thus, it involves relations as its basic units. This algorithm chooses one site as the master site where the query is initiated. The query optimizer

at the master site can take all inter-site decisions, such as the selection of the execution sites, the fragments which will be used, and the method for transferring data. The other participating sites that stores the relations involved in the query, called apprentice sites, can make the remaining glocal decisions and generate local access plans for the query execution. Distributed R* algorithm is implemented in the following way.

Distributed R* Algorithm:

Input: Query tree for the given query

Output: Optimum execution strategy

Begin

Step 1: For each base relation Ri in the query tree, repeat Step2 and Step3.

Step 2: Find each access path of Ri and determine the cost of each access path.

Step 3: Determine the access path with the minimum cost.

Step 4: For I = 1 to n, repeat Step5.

Step 5: For each order (Ri1, Ri2, .., Rin) of the relation Ri, build the best strategy (((APi1, ..., ∞ Ri2) ∞ Ri3) ∞ ....., ∞ Rin) and compute the cost of the strategy.

Step 6: Select the strategy with minimum cost.

Step 7: For J = 1 to M, repeat step8. [M is the total number of sites in the distributed system storing a relation involved in the query]

Step 8: Determine the local optimization strategy at site J and sent.

End

In this algorithm, based on database statistics and formulas used to estimate the size of intermediate results, and access path information, the query optimizer determines the join ordering, the join algorithms and the access path for each fragment. In addition, it also determines the sites of join results and the method of data transfer between sites. For performing the join between two relations, there may be three candidate sites. These are the site of the first relation, the site of the second relation, and the site of the result relation. Two inter-site data transfer techniques are supported by distributed R* algorithm: ship-whole and fetch-as-needed. In ship-whole technique, the join operation. If the join algorithm is merge join, the incoming tuples are processed in a pipeline mode as they arrive at the join site. In this case, the relation need not be stored in the temporary with an external node. In this method, the external relation is sequentially scanned, and for each tuple the join value is sent to the site of the internal relation. The internal tuples that match with the value of the external tuple are selected there, and then the selected tuples are sent to the site of the external relation.

Ship-whole technique requires large data transfer but fewer message transfers than fetch-as-needed technique. Obviously, ship-whole technique is beneficial for smaller relations. On the other hand, the fetch-as-needed technique is beneficial if the relation is large and the join operation has good selectivity. Ir. fetch-as-needed technique, there are four possible join strategies for joining of the external relation with the internal relation over an attribute value. These join strategies and their corresponding costs are calculated in the following, where LC denotes the local processing cost, which involves CPU cost and I/O cost, CC represents the communication cost, and A denotes the average number of tuples of internal relation S that matches with the value of one tuple of external relation R.

Strategy 1: Ship the entire external relation to the site of the internal relation.

In this case, the tuples of external relation R can be joined with the tuples of internal relation S, as they arrive. Therefore,

Total cost measure = LC (retrieving card(R) tuples from R) + CC (size(R)) + LC (retrieving A tuples from internal Relation S) * card(R).

Strategy 2: Ship the entire internal relation to the site of the external relation.

In this case, the tuples of internal relation S cannot be joined with the tuples of external relation R, as they arrive. The entire internal relation S has to be stores in a temporary relation. Hence,

Total cost measure = LC (retrieving card(S) tuples from S) + CC (size(S)) + LC)storing card(S) tuples in T) + LC (retrieving card(R) tuples from R) + LC (retrieving A tuples from T) * card (R).

Strategy 3: Fetch tuples of the internal relation as needed for each tuple of the external relation.

In this case, for each tuple in R, the join attribute value is sent to the site of the internal relation S. The n the A number of tuples from S that matches with this value are retrieved and sent to the site of R to be joined as they arrive. Therefore,

Total cost measure = LC (retrieving card(R) tuples from R) + CC (length(join attribute value)) * card(R) + LC (retrieving A tuples from S) * card(R) + CC (A * length(S)) * card(R).

Strategy 4: Move both relations to a third site and compute the join there.

In this case, the internal relation is first moved to the third site and stored in a temporary relation. Then, the external relation is moved to the third site and the join is performed as the tuples arrive.

Hence,

Total cost measure = LC (retrieving card(S) tuples from S) + CC (size(S)) + LC (storing card(S) tuples in T) + LC (retrieving card(R) tuples from R) + CC (size(R)) + LC (retrieving A tuples from T) * card(R).

The cost of producing the final result is not considered here. In the case of distributed R* algorithm, the complexity increases as the number of relations increases, as it uses the exhaustive search approach based on several factors such as join order, join algorithm, access path, data transfer mode and result site.

5.8.4 HILL-CLIMBING ALGORITHM

In this algorithm, refinements of an initial feasible solution are recursively computed until no more cost improvements can be made. In this semi joins, data replication, and fragmentation are not used. It is devised for wide area point-to-point networks. This first distributed query processing algorithm.

The hill-climbing algorithm proceeds as follows

1. Select initial feasible execution strategy ES0

This means

- a global execution schedule that includes all intersite communication
- Determine the candidate result sites, where a relation referenced in the query exist
- Compute the cost of transferring all the other referenced relations to each candidate site

ES0 = candidate site with minimum cost

2. Split ES0 into two strategies: ES1 followed by ES2
   - ES1: send one of the relations involved in the join to the other relation's site
   - ES2: send the join result to the final result site
3. Replace ES0 with the split schedule which gives

$$\cos t(ES1) + \cos t(local\ join) + \cos t(ES2) < \cos t(ES0)$$

Example 5.5:

What are the salaries of engineers who work on the CAD/CAM project?

$$\Pi_{SAL}(PLAY \bowtie_{TITLE} EMP \times_{ENO} (ASG \bowtie_{PNO} (\sigma_{PNAME="CAD/CAM"}(PROJ)))$$

Schemas: EMP(ENO, ENBAME, TITLE), ASG(ENO, PNO, RESP, DUR), PROJ(PNO, PNAME, BUDGET, LOC), PAY(TITLE, SAL)

Statistics:

Relation	Size	Site
EMP	8	1
PAY	4	2
PROJ	1	3
ASG	10	4

Assumptions:

- Size of relations is defined as their cardinality
- Minimize total cost
- Transmission cost between two sites is 1
- Ignore local processing cost

  *size(EMP ⋈ PAY) = 8, size (PROJ ⋈ ASG ⋈ EMP) = 10

Determine initial feasible execution strategy

- Alternative 1: Resulting site is site 1
  - o Total cost = cost(PAY'!Site1) + cost(ASG'!Site1) + cost(PROJ'!Site1)
  - o = 4 + 10 + 1 = 15
- Alternative 2: Resulting site is site 2
  - o Total cost = 8 + 10 + 1 = 19
- Alternative 3: Resulting site is site 3
  - o Total cost = 8 + 4 + 10 = 22
- Alternative 4: Resulting site is site 4
  - o Total cost = 8 + 4 + 1 = 13

Therefore ES0 = EMP'!Site4; PAY'!Site4; PROJ'!Site4

Candidate split

— Alternative 1: ES1, ES2, ES3

* ES1: EMP → Site2
* ES2: (EMP ⋈ PAY) → Site4
* ES3: PROJ → Site4)

Total_cost = *cost* (EMP → Site2) + *cost* ((EMP ⋈ PAY) → Site4) + *cost* (PROJ → Site4)
= 8 + 8 + 1 = 17

— Alternative 2: ES1, ES2, ES3

* ES1: PAY → Site
* ES2: (PAY ⋈ EMP) → Site4
* ES3: PROJ → Site4

Total_cost = cost(PAYsite → 1) + *cost*((PAY ⋈ EMP) → Site4) + *cost*(PROJ → Site4)
= 4 + 8 + 1 = 13

Both alternatives are not better than ES0, so keep it (or take alternative 2 which has the same cost)

Problems with Hill Climbing Algorithm

- Greedy algorithm determines an initial feasible solution and iteratively improves it
- If there are local minima, it may not find the global minimum
- An optimal schedule with a high initial cost would not be found, since it won't be chosen as the initial feasible solution

Example 5.6:

A better schedule is

$-PROJ \rightarrow Site4$

$-ASG' = (PROJ \ltimes \ ASG) \rightarrow$ Site1

$-ASG' \ltimes EMP) \rightarrow Site\ 2$

$-Total\ cost = 1 + 2 + 2 = 5$

5.8.5 SDD-1 ALGORITHM

The query optimization algorithm of SDD-1 [Bernstein et al., 1981] is derived from an earlier method called the "hill climbing" algorithm, which has the distinction of being the first distributed query processing algorithm. In this algorithm, refinements of an initial feasible solution are recursively computed until no more improvements an initial can be made. The algorithm does not use semijoin nor does it assume data replication and fragmentation. It is devised for wide area point-to-point networks. The cost of transferring the result to the final site is ignored. This algorithm is quite general in that it can minimize an arbitrary objective function, including the total time and response time.

The hill-climbing algorithm proceeds as follows. The input to the algorithm includes the query graph, location of relations, and relation statistics. Following the completion of initial local processing, an initial feasible solution is selected which is a global execution schedule that includes all intersite communication. It is obtained by computing the cost of all the execution strategies that transfer all the required relations to a single candidate result site, and then choosing the least costly strategies ES, followed by ES, where ES, consists of sending one of the relations involved in the join to the resulting relation is transmitted to the chosen result site (specified as schedule ES_2). If the cost of executing strategies ES_1 and ES_2 plus the cost of local join processing is less than that applied recursively to ES_1 and ES_2 until no more benefit can be gained. Notice that if n-way joins are involved. Es_0 will be divided into n subschedules instead of just two.

The hill-climbing algorithm is in the class of greedy algorithms, which start with an initial feasible solution and iteratively it. The main problem is that benefits are ignored. Furthermore, the algorithm may get stuck at a local minimum cost solution and fall to reach the global minimum.

ALGORITHM 9.5 SDD-1-QOA

```
input: QG: query graph with n relationships; statistics for each relation
output: ES: execution strategy
begin
ES ← local operation (QG);
Modify statistics to reflect the effect of local processing
BS ← for each semijoin S J in QG do
if cost (SJ) < benefit(S J) then
BS ← BS ∪ SJ
end-if
end-for
while BS "' do {selection of beneficial semijoins}
begin
SJ ← most_beneficial (BS)   {SJ: semijoin with max (benefit_cost)}
BS ← BS – SJ  {remove SJ from BS}
ES ← ES + SJ {append SJ to execution strategy}
Modify statistics to reflect the effect of incorporating SJ
BS ← BS – nonbeneficial semijoins
BS ← BS  new beneficial semijoins
end-while
{assembly site selection}
AS(ES) ← select the I such that I stores the largest amount of data after
all local operations
ES ← ES ∪ transfers of intermediate relations to AS(ES)
{postoptimization}
for each relation  Ri at AS(ES) do
for each semijoin SJ of Ri by Rj do
if cost (ES) > cost (ES – SJ) then
ES ← ES – SJ
end-if
end-for
end-for
end. {SDD-1-QOA}
```

The initialization phase generosities a set is beneficial semijoins, BS = {SJ_1, SJ_2, ..., SJ_k}, and an execution strategy ES that includes only local processing. The next phase selects the beneficial semijoin from BS by iteratively choosing the most beneficial semijoin, SJ_t, and modifying the database statistics and BS accordingly semijoins in BS that use relation R. The iterative phase terminates when all semijoins in BS have been appended to the execution strategy. The order in which semijoins are appending to ES will be the execution order of the semijoins.

To next phase selects the assembly site of evaluating, for each candidate site the cost of transferring to it all the required data and taking the one with the least strategy if those semijoins that affect only relations stored at the assembly site. This phase is necessary because the assembly site is chosen after all the semijoins have been ordered. The SDD-1 optimize is based on the assumption that relations can be transmitted to another site. This is true for all relations except those stored at the assembly site, which is selected after beneficial semijoins are considered. Therefore, some semijoins may incorrectly be considered beneficial it is the role of postoptimization to remove them from the execution strategy.

EXERCISES

1. What do you distributed query optimization?
2. Explain the concept of query optimization?
3. Explain the issues of query optimization?
4. Explain the components of query optimizer?
5. What do you mean by database statistics?
6. What do you mean by cardinalities of intermediate results?
7. Explain the join ordering in fragment queries?
8. What do you mean by join ordering?
9. Explain the concept of semijoin-based algorithms?
10. Difference between join versus semijoin?
11. Explain the global query optimization algorithms?
12. Explain the distributed INGRES algorithm?
13. Explain the concept of system R algorithm?
14. Explain the concept of distributed R* algorithm?
15. Explain the hill-climbing algorithm in detail?
16. Explain the concept of SDD-1 algorithm?

CHAPTER 6

DISTRIBUTED TRANSACTION MANAGEMENT

6.1 INTRODUCTION

The concept of transaction provides a mechanism for describing logical units of database processing. Transaction processing systems are systems with large databases and hundreds of concurrent users that are executing database transactions. Examples of such systems include systems for reservations, banking, credit card processing, stock markets, supermarket check-out, and other similar systems. They require high availability and fast response time for hundreds of concurrent users. In this chapter we present the concepts that are needed in transaction processing systems. We define the concept of a transaction, which is used to represent a logical unit of database processing that must be completed in its entirety to ensure correctness. We discuss the concurrency control problem, which occurs when multiple transactions submitted by various users interfere with one another in a way that produces incorrect results. We also discuss recovery from transaction failures.

6.2 TRANSACTION MANAGEMENT

Transaction management in a database system deals with the problems of maintaining consistency of data in spite of system failures and concurrent access to data. A transaction consists of a series of operations performed on a database. The important issue in transaction management is that if a database was in a consistent state prior to the initiation of a transaction, then the database should return to a consistent state after the transaction is completed. This should be done irrespective of the fact that transactions were successfully executed simultaneously or there were failures during the execution.

Thus, a transaction is a unit of consistency and reliability. Reliability refers to both the resilience of a system to various types of failures and its capability to recover from them. A resilient system continues its normal execution even when failures occur. A recoverable DBMS always keeps the database in a consistent state either by moving back to a previous consistent state or by moving forward to a new consistent state following various types of failures. The main difference between a query and a transaction is the properties of a transaction: **atomicity** and **durability**. A transaction can ensures the consistency of the database irrespective of the facts that several transactions are executed concurrently and that failures may occur during their execution. A transaction can be considered to be made up of a sequence of

read and write operations on the database, together with some computational steps. In that sense, a transaction may be thought of as a program with embedded database access queries. Each transaction has to terminate. The outcome of the termination depends on the success or failure of the transaction. Once a transaction starts execution, it may terminate in one of the following possible ways:

- Transaction aborts if a failure occurred during its execution
- Transaction commits if it was completed successfully

A transaction may abort due to a variety of reasons:

Rollback: When a transaction is aborted, to maintain the consistency of the data its execution is stopped, and the already executed actions are undone by returning the database to the prior state that existed before then start of the execution.

If a transaction is committed, the result will permanently be stored in the database, and this cannot be undone.

6.3 WHAT IS A TRANSACTION?

A transaction consists of a set of operations that perform a single logical unit of work in a database environment. It may be an entire program, or a part of a program, or a single command (SQL command), and it may involve any number operations on the database. If a transaction is completed successfully, then the database moves from one consistent state of another. This consistency must be ensured irrespective of whether transactions are successfully executed simultaneously or there are failures during execution. Thus, a transaction is a unit of consistency and reliability. The properties of transactions will be discussed later in the properties section.

Each transaction has to terminate. The outcome of the termination depends on the success or failure of the transaction. When a transaction starts executing, it may terminate with one of two possibilities:

1. The transaction **aborts** if a failure occurred during its execution
2. The transaction **commits** if it was completed successfully.

Figure 6.1a shows an example of a transaction that aborts during process 2 (P2). On the other hand, Figure 6.1b shows an example of a transaction that commits, since all of its processes are successfully completed.

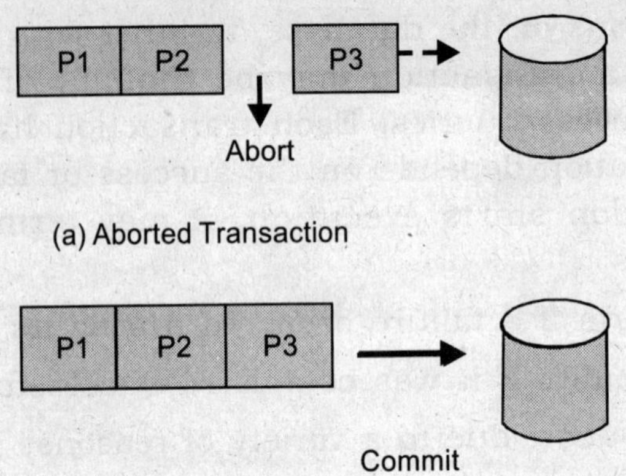

Figure 6.1 Termination types of transaction

Example 6.1

Consider the following Employee relation:

Employee = (emp-id, emp-name, designation, salary, emp-branch, project-no)

and the SQL query

"Update employee salary by 20% for the employee whose emp-id is E0001 in the Employee relation".

The SQL statement for this query is:

```
UPDATE EMPLOYEE
        SET SALARY = SALARY * 2.8
 WHERE EMP-ID = "E0001".
```

This query can be represented as a transaction with the name salary_update using the embedded SQL notation as given below.

```
Begin-transaction salary_update
begin
EXEC SQL
 UPDATE EMPLOYEE SET SALARY = SALARY * 2.8
 WHERE EMP-ID = "E0001"
end
```

The Begin-transaction and end statements represent the beginning and end of a transaction respectively, which is treated as a program that perform a database access.

6.4 DATABASE TRANSACTION

A **database transaction** comprises a unit of work performed within a database management system (or similar system) against a database, and treated in a coherent and reliable way independent of other transactions.

Transactions in a database environment have two main purposes:

1. To provide reliable units of work that allow correct recovery from failures and keep a database consistent even in cases of system failure, when execution stops (completely or partially) and many operations upon a database remain uncompleted, with unclear status.
2. To provide isolation between programs accessing a database concurrently. Without isolation the program's outcomes are possibly erroneous.

A database transaction, by definition, must be atomic, consistent, isolated and durable. Database practitioners often refer to these properties of database transactions using the acronym **ACID**.

Transactions provide an "all-or-nothing" proposition, stating that each work-unit performed in a database must either complete in its entirety or have no effect whatsoever. Further, the system must isolate each transaction from other transactions, results must conform to existing constraints in the database, and transactions that complete successfully must get written to durable storage.

6.4.1 PURPOSE OF DATABASE TRANSACTION

Databases and other data stores which treat the integrity of data as paramount often include the ability to handle transactions to maintain the integrity of data. A single transaction consists of one or more independent units of work, each reading and/or writing information to a database or other data store. When this happens it is often important to ensure that all such processing leaves the database or data store in a consistent state.

Examples from double-entry accounting systems often illustrate the concept of transactions. In double-entry accounting every debit requires the recording of an associated credit. If one writes a check for €100 to buy groceries, a transactional double-entry accounting system must record the following two entries to cover the single transaction:

1. Debit €100 to Groceries Expense Account
2. Credit €100 to Checking Account

A transactional system would make both entries — or both entries would fail. By treating the recording of multiple entries as an atomic transactional unit of work the system maintains the integrity of the data recorded. In other words, nobody ends up with a situation in which a debit is recorded but no associated credit is recorded, or vice versa.

6.4.2 TRANSACTIONAL DATABASES

Most modern[update] relational database management systems fall into the category of databases that support transactions: **transactional databases**.

In a database system a transaction might consist of one or more data-manipulation statements and queries, each reading and/or writing information in the database. Users of database systems consider consistency and integrity of data as highly important. A simple transaction is usually issued to the database system in a language like SQL wrapped in a transaction, using a pattern similar to the following:

1. Begin the transaction
2. Execute several data manipulations and queries
3. If no errors occur then commit the transaction and end it
4. If errors occur then rollback the transaction and end it

If no errors occurred during the execution of the transaction then the system commits the transaction. A transaction commit operation applies all data manipulations within the scope of the transaction and persists the results to the database. If an error occurs during the transaction, or if the user specifies a rollback operation, the data manipulations within the transaction are not persisted to the database. In no case can a partial transaction be committed to the database since that would leave the database in an inconsistent state.

Internally, multi-user databases store and process transactions, often by using a transaction ID or XID.

6.5 FUNDAMENTALS OF TRANSACTION MANAGEMENT

Transaction Management deals with the problems of keeping the database in a consistent state even when concurrent accesses and failures occur.

6.5.1 ATOMICITY

Atomicity requires that database modifications must follow an "all or nothing" rule. Each transaction is said to be atomic. If one part of the transaction fails, the entire transaction fails and the database state is left unchanged. It is critical that the database management system maintain the atomic nature of transactions in spite of any application, DBMS (Database Management System), operating system or hardware failure.

An atomic transaction cannot be subdivided and must be processed in its entirety or not at all. Atomicity means that users do not have to worry about the effect of incomplete transactions.

Transactions can fail for several kinds of reasons:

1. **Hardware failure:** A disk drive fails, preventing some of the transaction's database changes from taking effect.
2. **System failure:** The user loses their connection to the application before providing all necessary information.
3. **Database failure:** E.g., the database runs out of room to hold additional data.
4. **Application failure:** The application attempts to post data that violates a rule that the database itself enforces such as attempting to insert a duplicate value in a column.

6.5.2 CONSISTENCY

It ensures the truthfulness of the database. The consistency property ensures that any transaction the database performs will take it from one consistent state to another. The consistency property does not say how the DBMS should handle an inconsistency other than ensure the database is clean at the end of the transaction. If, for some reason, a transaction is executed that violates the database's consistency rules, the entire transaction could be rolled back to the pre-transactional state - or it would be equally valid for the DBMS to take some patch-up action to get the database in a consistent state. Thus, if the database schema says that a particular field is for holding integer numbers, the DBMS could decide to reject attempts to put fractional values there, or it could round the supplied values to the nearest whole number: both options maintain consistency.

The consistency rule applies only to integrity rules that are within its scope. Thus, if a DBMS allows fields of a record to act as references to another record, then consistency implies the DBMS must enforce referential integrity: by the time any transaction ends, each and every reference in the database must be valid. If a transaction consisted of an attempt to delete a record referenced by another, each of the following mechanisms would maintain consistency:

- abort the transaction, rolling back to the consistent, prior state;
- delete all records that reference the deleted record (this is known as *cascade delete*); or,
- nullify the relevant fields in all records that point to the deleted record.

These are examples of propagation constraints; some database systems allow the database designer to specify which option to choose when setting up the schema for a database. Application developers are responsible for ensuring *application level* consistency, over and above that offered by the DBMS. Thus, if a user withdraws funds from an account and the new balance is lower than the account's minimum balance threshold, as far as the DBMS is concerned, the database is in a consistent state even though this rule (unknown to the DBMS) has been violated.

6.5.3 ISOLATION

Isolation refers to the requirement that other operations cannot access data that has been modified during a transaction that has not yet completed. The question of isolation occurs in case of concurrent transactions (multiple transactions occurring at the same time). Each transaction must remain unaware of other concurrently executing transactions, except that one transaction may be forced to wait for the completion of another transaction that has modified data that the waiting transaction requires. If the isolation system does not exist, then the data could be put into an inconsistent state. This could happen, if one transaction is in the process of modifying data but has not yet completed, and then a second transaction reads and modifies that uncommitted data from the first transaction. If the first transaction fails and the second one succeeds, that violation of transactional isolation will cause data inconsistency. Due to performance and deadlocking concerns with multiple competing transactions, many modern databases allow dirty reads, which is a way to bypass some of the restrictions of the isolation system. A dirty read means that a transaction is allowed to read, but not modify, the uncommitted data from another transaction.

6.5.4 DURABILITY

Durability is the ability of the DBMS to recover the committed transaction updates against any kind of system failure (hardware or software). Durability is the DBMS's guarantee that once the user has been notified of a transaction's success the transaction will not be lost, the transaction's data changes will survive system failure, and that all integrity constraints have been satisfied, so the DBMS won't need to reverse the transaction. Many DBMSs implement durability by writing transactions into a transaction log that can be reprocessed to recreate the system state right before any later failure. A transaction is deemed committed only after it is entered in the log.

Durability does not imply a permanent state of the database. A subsequent transaction may modify data changed by a prior transaction without violating the durability principle.

6.5.5 SERIALIZABILITY

If several transactions are executed concurrently, the result must be the same as if they were executed serially in some order. The activity of guaranteeing transactions' serializability is called concurrency control. If a system provides concurrency control, the programmer can write the transaction as if it were executed alone.

6.5.6 EXAMPLES

The following examples are used to further explain the ACID properties. In these examples, the database has two fields, A and B, in two records. An integrity constraint requires that the value in A and the value in B must sum to 100.

1. **Atomicity failure:** The transaction subtracts 10 from A and adds 10 to B. If it succeeds, it would be valid, because the data continues to satisfy the constraint. However, assume that after removing 10 from A, the transaction is unable to modify B. If the database retains A's new value, atomicity and the constraint would both be violated. Atomicity requires that both parts of this transaction complete or neither.
2. **Consistency failure:** Consistency is a very general term that demands the data meets all validation rules that the overall application expects - but to satisfy the consistency property a database system only needs to enforce those rules that are within its scope. In the previous example, one rule was a requirement that A + B = 100; most database systems would not allow such a rule to be specified, and so would have no responsibility to enforce it - but they would be able to ensure the values were whole numbers. Example of rules that can be enforced by the database system are that the primary key values of a record uniquely identify that record, that the values stored in fields are the right type (the schema might require that both A and B are integers, say) and in the right range, and that foreign keys are all valid.

   Validation rules that cannot be enforced by the database system are the responsibility of the application programs using the database.
3. **Isolation failure:** To demonstrate isolation, we assume two transactions execute at the same time, each attempting to modify the same data. One of the two must wait until the other completes in order to maintain isolation.

Consider two transactions. T_1 transfers 10 from A to B. T_2 transfers 10 from B to A. Combined, there are four actions:

- subtract 10 from A
- add 10 to B.
- subtract 10 from B
- add 10 to A.

If these operations are performed in order, isolation is maintained, although T_2 must wait. Consider what happens, if T_1 fails half-way through. The database eliminates T_1's effects, and T_2 sees only valid data.

By interleaving the transactions, the actual order of actions might be: *A* “ 10, *B* “ 10, *B* + 10, *A* + 10. Again consider what happens, if T_1 fails. T_1 still subtracts 10 from A. Now, T_2 adds 10 to A restoring it to its initial value. Now T_1 fails. What should A's value be? T_2 has already changed it. Also, T_1 never changed B. T_2 subtracts 10 from it. If T_2 is allowed to complete, B's value will be 10 too low, and A's value will be unchanged, leaving an invalid database. This is known as a write-write failure, because two transactions attempted to write to the same data field.

4. **Durability failure:** Assume that a transaction transfers 10 from A to B. It removes 10 from A. It then adds 10 to B. At this point, a "success" message is sent to the user. However, the changes are still queued in the disk buffer waiting to be committed to the disk. Power fails and the changes are lost. The user assumes that the changes have been made, but they are lost.

6.6 GOALS OF TRANSACTION MANAGEMENT

After having considered the characteristics of transactions, let us return to the goals of transaction management: the efficient, reliable, and concurrent execution of transactions. These three goals are strongly interrelated; moreover, there is a trade-off between them, because the effort which is required in order to implement a reliable way the properties of transactions causes an obvious performance penalty.

We considered the main aspects which determine the efficiency of an access plan to a distributed database; the aspects considered in those chapters were completely dependent on the characteristics of the data and of the required application. In this we consider different, and in several cases equally important, efficiency aspects.

1. **CPU and main memory utilization:** This aspect is common to both centralized and distributed databases. Although typical database applications are I/O bound (I.e., they spend much of their time waiting for I/O operations and perform only simple computations), the concurrent execution of many of them (tens or hundreds) in a large system can reveal a bottleneck in main memory or in CPU time. If the operating system has to create a process for each active transaction, most of these processes will be swapped in and out of main memory. Moreover a lot of context switching will be required. In order to reduce this overhead, transaction managers apply specialized techniques which take advantage of the typical characteristics of database applications, and avoid considering them in the same way as the generalized processes which are dealt with by a general-purpose operating system.

2. **Control messages:** In distributed database we have to consider also another aspect of efficiency: the number of control message which are exchanged between sites. A control message is not used to transfer data but is needed in order to control the execution of the application. This aspect is not independent of the previous one, because the cost of a message is constituted not only by its transmission cost, but also by the nontrivial amount of instructions which the CPU has to execute in order to send a message. In many large systems this cost has been estimated to be somewhere between 5,000 and 10,000 instructions. There is agreement on this estimate, although it is not clear why message are so CPU-expensive. This later cost is paid even if the message is exchanged between processes at the same site, without any transmission cost.

   In the minimization of communication costs, only data transfers were considered, not control messages. This approach was correct for two reasons: First, data transfers can be much larger than control messages, especially if no effort is spent in designing a good access plan. Second, data transfer depends only on the required application, while the minimization of control messages is to a large extent dependent on the mechanisms which are provided by the system. This latter reason means that query optimization can be performed to a large extent independent of the problems which are treated in this chapter; however, if two alternative solutions which are obtained with the techniques have comparable costs, then it is worthwhile to compare them also with respect to the efficiency aspects which are related to transaction management.

3. **Response time:** As a third important efficiency aspect, we have to consider the response time of each individual transaction. Clearly, obtaining an acceptable response time can be more critical for distributed applications than for local applications, because of the additional time which is required for communication between different sites.

4. **Availability:** Another aspect which must be considered by the transaction manager of a distributed database is the availability of the whole system. Of course, in a distributed system it is not acceptable for the failure of one site to stop the whole system's operation. Therefore, the algorithms implemented by the transaction manager must not block the execution of those transactions which do not strictly need to access a site which is not operational. As we shall see, the effort of increasing the system's availability in the presence of site failures is a significant characteristic of the algorithms which are used for transaction recovery and concurrency control in distributed databases.

Let us summarize the whole discussion of the last two sections as follows:

The goal transaction management in a distributed database is to control the execution of transactions so that:

1. Transactions have atomicity, durability, serilizability, and isolation properties.
2. Their cost in terms of main memory, CPU, and number of transmitted control messages and their response time are minimized/
3. The availability of the system is maximized.

6.7 IMPLEMENTATION OF TRANSACTION MANAGEMENT

Processing a transaction often requires a sequence of operations that is subject to failure for a number of reasons. For instance, the system may have no room left on its disk drives, or it may have used up its allocated CPU time.

There are two popular families of techniques: write ahead logging and shadow paging. In both cases, locks must be acquired on all information that is updated, and depending on the level of isolation, possibly on all data that is read as well. In write ahead logging, atomicity is guaranteed by copying the original (unchanged) data to a log before changing the database. That allows the database to return to a consistent state in the event of a crash.

In shadowing, updates are applied to a partial copy of the database, and the new copy is activated when the transaction commits.

6.8 LOCKING VS. MULTIVERSIONING

Most databases rely upon locking to provide ACID capabilities. Locking means that the transaction marks the data that it acces6ses so that the DBMS knows not to allow other transactions to modify it until the first transaction succeeds or fails. The lock must always be acquired before processing data, including data that are read but not modified. Non-trivial transactions typically require a large number of locks, resulting in substantial overhead as well as blocking other transactions. For example, if user A is running a transaction that has to read a row of data that user B wants to modify, user B must wait until user A's transaction completes. Two phase locking is often applied to guarantee full isolation.

An alternative to locking is multiversion concurrency control, in which the database provides each reading transaction the prior, unmodified version of data that is being modified by another active transaction. This allows readers to operate without acquiring locks. I.e., writing transactions do not block reading transactions, and readers do not block writers. Going back to the example, when user A's transaction requests data that user B is modifying, the database provides A with the version of that data that existed when user B started his transaction. User A gets a consistent view of the database even if other users are changing data. One implementation relaxes the isolation property, namely snapshot isolation.

6.9 DISTRIBUTED TRANSACTIONS

Database systems implement distributed transactions as transactions against multiple applications or hosts. A distributed transaction enforces the ACID properties over multiple systems or data stores, and might include systems such as databases, file systems, messaging systems, and other applications. In a distributed transaction a coordinating service ensures that all parts of the transaction are applied to all relevant systems. As with database and other transactions, if any part of the transaction fails, the entire transaction is rolled back across all affected systems.

A transaction is always part of an application. When a user types an application code, he or she requests the execution of an application, which does not have the properties of atomicity, durability, serializability, and isolation. At some after its invocation by the user, the application issues a begin_transaction primitive; from this moment, all action which are performed by the application, until a commit or an abort primitive is issued, are to be considered part of the same transaction. In some systems, the beginning of a transaction is implicitly associated with the beginning of the application, until a commit or an abort primitive is issued, are to be considered part of the same transaction. In some systems, the beginning of the application, and commit primitive ends a transaction and automatically begins a new one, so that the explicit begin_transaction primitive is not necessary. However, the model with explicit primitives which is assumed here is more general.

In order to perform functions at different sites, a distributed application has to execute several processes at these sites. We will call these processes the agents of the application. An agent is therefore a local process which performs some actions on behalf of an application.

Note that in the definition of agent we are not interested in knowing whether the agent executes a program written by the application programmer or a primitive function of the system; the programmer can request the execution of a remote primitive or write an auxiliary program, install it at a remote site, and then invoke its execution. We have also discussed the difference between these two approaches from the viewpoint of the application programmer; however, if we consider the execution of the application, there will be some code which is executed at the remote site in order to perform the required function, and it makes little difference for the purpose of this chap-

ter to know how this code is produced. In both cases this code constitutes an agent of the distributed application.

In order to cooperate in the execution of the global operation required by the application, the agents have to communicate. As they are resident at different sites, the communication between agents is performed through messages.

There are different ways in which the agents can be organized to build a structure of cooperating processes. These alternatives will be discussed in a later section. For the purpose of the discussion of atomicity we will assume that:

1. There exists a root agent which starts the whole transaction, so that when the user requests the execution of an application, the root agent is started; the site of the root agent is called the site of origin of the transaction..
2. The root agent has the responsibility of issuing the begin_transaction, commit, and abort primitives.
3. Only the root agent can request the creation of a new agent.

While assumption 1 is intrinsic to the definition of root agent, the other two assumptions are made only for simplifying the presentation of this section and will not apply in later sections. In fact, assumption 2 is adopted by most systems, while only a few systems adopt assumption 3.

6.10 OBJECTIVES OF DISTRIBUTED TRANSACTION MANAGEMENT

This section introduces the objectives of a transaction management subsystem of a distributed DBMS. The responsibilities of the transaction manager in a distributed DBMS is same as those of a corresponding subsystem in a centralized system, but its task is complicated owing to fragmentation, replication and the overall distributed nature of the database. The consistency of the database should not be violated because of transaction executions. Therefore, the primary objective of the transaction manager is not executing transactions in an efficient way in order to preserve the ACID properties of transaction (local as well as global transactions) irrespective of concurrent execution of transactions and system failures. At the same time, the efficiency of transaction executions should be improved to meet the performance criteria. In addition, a good transaction management scheme must consider the following issues.

(i) **CPU and main memory utilization should be improved:** Most of the typical database applications spend much of their time waiting for I/O operations rather then on computations. In a large system, the concurrent execution of these I/O bound applications can turn into a bottle-

neck in main memory or in CPU time utilization. To alleviate this problem, that is to improve CPU and main memory utilization, a transaction manager should adopt specialized techniques to deal with specific database applications. This aspect is common to both centralized and distributed DBMSs.

(ii) Response time should be minimized: To improve the performance of transaction executions the purpose time of each individual transaction must be considered and should be minimized. In case if distributed applications, it is very difficult to achieve an acceptable response time owing to the additional time required to communicate between different sites.

(iii) Available should be maximized: Although the available in a distributed system is between than that in a centralized system, it must maximize for transaction recovery and concurrency control in distributed databases. The algorithms implemented by the distributed transaction manager must not block the execution of those transactions that do not strictly need to access a site that is not operational.

(iv) Communication cost should be minimized: In a distributed system an additional communication cost is incurred for each distributed or global application, because a number of massage transfers are required between sites to control the execution of a global application. These massages arte not only used to transfer data, but are required to control the execution of the application. Preventative measures should be adopted by the transaction manager to minimize the communication cost.

6.11 ACID PROPERTIES OF DISTRIBUTED TRANSACTIONS

A transaction has major four properties that lead to the consistency and reliability of a database management system.

Following are the ACID properties of distributed transactions:

1. Atomicity
2. Consistency
3. Isolation
4. Durability

1. Atomicity: Atomicity refers to the fact that each transaction is a single logical unit of work in a database environment that may consist of a number of operations. All operations of a transaction are to be completed successfully, or none of them are carried out at all. This property is known as all-or-nothing property of a transaction. It is the re-

sponsibility of the DBMS to maintain atomicity even when failures occur in the system. If the execution of a transaction is interrupted by any sort of failures, the DBMS will determine what actions should be performed with that transaction to recover from the failed state.

To maintain atomicity during failures, either the system should complete the remaining operations of the transaction or it should undo all the operations that have already been executed by the transaction before the failure. The execution of a transaction may be interrupted owing to a variety of reasons such as bad input data, deadlock, system crash, processor failure, or media and communication links failures. The recovery after a transaction failure is divided into two different categories based on the different types of failures that can occur in a database environment.

Transaction recovery: The activity of ensuring transaction atomicity in the case of transaction aborts due to failures caused by bad input data, deadlock and other factors.

Crash recovery: The activity of preserving transaction atomicity in the case of system crash or hardware failures.

2. **Consistency:** It refers to the correctness of data. **This property states that:** a transaction must transform the database from one consistency state to another consistency state. It is the responsibility of both the semantic data controller (integrity manager) and the concurrency control mechanisms to maintain consistency of the data. The semantic data controller can ensure consistency by enforcing all the constraints that have been specified in the database schema, such as integrity and enterprise constraints.

Similarly, the responsibility of a concurrency control mechanism is to disallow transactions from reading or updating **"dirty data"**. Dirty data refers to the state of the data at which the data have been updated by a transaction, but the transaction has not yet committed.

A classification of consistency has been defined based on dirty data, which groups databases into four levels of consistency as given below:

Degree 3: A transaction T observes degree 3 consistency if:

1. T does not overwrite dirty data of other transactions.
2. T does not commit any write operation until it completes all its write operations, that is, until the end of the transaction.
3. T does not read dirty data from other transactions.
4. Other transaction in the system does not read any dirty data updated by T before T completes.

Degree 2: A transaction T observes degree 2 consistency if:

1. T does not overwrite dirty data of other transactions.
2. T does not commit any write operation until it completes all its write operations, that is, until the end of the transaction.
3. T does not read dirty data from other transactions.

Degree 1: A transaction T observes degree 1 consistency if:

1. T does not overwrite dirty data of other transactions.
2. T does not commit any write operation until it completes all its write operations, that is, until the end of the transaction.

Degree 0: A transaction T observes degree 0 consistency if:

1. T does not overwrite dirty data of other transactions.

Degree of consistency of higher level covers all the lower levels. These different degrees of consistency provide flexibility to application developers to define transactions that can operate at different levels.

3. **Isolation:** Transactions can execute independently in a database environment; that is, they cannot dependent on each other. In other words, transactions are isolated from one another and the partial effect of incomplete transactions should not be visible to other transactions. This isolation property of transactions is ensured by the concurrency control mechanism of a DBMS. Consequently, no transaction can read or modify data that is being modified by another transaction. If this property is not maintained, one of the following two events as listed below can take place in the database.

   (a) Lost update problem – This problem occurs when an apparently successful completed update operation made one transaction (first) is overridden by another transaction (second). The lost update problem is illustrated in example 6.2.

   (b) Cascading aborts – This problem occurs when one transaction allows other transactions to read its uncommitted data and decides to abort; the transactions that have read or modified its uncommitted data will also abort. Consider the previous example 6.2. If transaction T_1 permits transaction T_2 to read its uncommitted data, then if transaction T_1 aborts, transaction T_2 will also abort consequently.

This type of isolation that is ensured by not allowing uncommitted data to be seen by other transactions is called cursor stability. It is obvious that higher levels of consistency provide more isolation among transactions. If different degrees of consistency are considered from the point of view of the isolation property, then degree 0 prevents lost update problem, degree 2 prevents cascading aborts and degree 3 provides the full isolation by restricting

both the above problems.

A set of isolation levels has been defined by ANSI SQL2 [ANSI, 1992] based on the events dirty read, non-repeatable or fuzzy read and phantom read, when full isolation is not maintained in a database environment. These are read uncommitted, read committed, repeatable read and anomaly serializable. Dirty read refers to the situation when a transaction reads the dirty data of another transaction. Fuzzy read or non-repeatable read occurs when one transaction reads the value of a data item that is modified or deleted by another transaction. If the first transaction attempts to re-read the data item, either that data item may not be found or it may read a different value. Similarly, it is possible that when a transaction is performing a search operation depending on a selection predicate, another transaction may be inserting new tuples into the database satisfying that predicate. This is known as phantom read. The different isolation levels based on these events are listed below.

- **Read uncommitted** – At this isolation level, all the three above events may occur.
- **Read committed** – At this isolation level, non-repeatable read and phantom read are possible, but dirty read cannot occur.
- **Repeatable read** – Only phantom read is possible at this isolation level.
- **Anomaly serializable** – At this isolation level, none of the above events – dirty read, phantom read and fuzzy read – is possible.

4. **Durability:** Durability means that the effects of a successfully completed transaction are permanently recorded in the database and will not be affected by a subsequent failure. This property can ensure that once a transaction commits, the changes are durable and cannot be erased from the database. It is the responsibility of the recovery manager determines how the database is to be durability property of transactions. The recovery manager determines how the database is to be recovered to a consistent state in which all the committed actions are reflected.

Example 6.2

Suppose that there are two concurrent transactions T_1 and T_2 respectively occurring in a database environment. The transaction T_1 is withdrawing Rs.500 from an account with balance B, with an initial value of Rs.2,000, while the transaction T_2 is depositing an amount of Rs.600 into the same account. If these two transactions are executed serially, then the balance B of the account will be Rs.2,100. Consider that both the transactions are started nearly at the same time, and both have read the same value of B, that is,

Rs.2,000. Owing to the concurrent access to the concurrent access to the same data item, when the transaction T_1 is decrementing the value of B to Rs.1,500, the transaction T_2 is incrementing the value of B to Rs.2,600. Thus, update to the item B made by the transaction T_1 will be overridden by the transaction T_2. This is known as lost update problem.

Example 6.3

Suppose that there are concurrent transactions T_1 and T_2 respectively occurring in a database environment. The transaction T_1 is depositing Rs.500 to an account A with an initial value Rs.3,000, while the transaction T_2 is withdrawing an amount Rs.1,000 from the same account A. Further assume that the transaction T_1 is executed first and allows the transaction T_2 to read the uncommitted value Rs.3,500 for A and then aborts. This problem is known as dirty read problem, which is illustrated in the following:

T_1: write(A)
T_2: read(A)
T_1: abort

Thus, the transaction T_2 reads the dirty data of the transaction T_1.

Example 6.4

Consider a situation when one transaction T_1 reads the value of a data item A, while another transaction T_2 updates the same data item. Now, if the transaction T_1 reads the same data item A again, it will read some different value, because the data item is already manipulated by the transaction T_2. This problem is known as non-repeatable or fuzzy read problem, which is illustrated in the following:

T_1: read(A)
T_2: write(A)
T_2: end transaction
T_1: read(A)

In this case, transaction T_1 has read two different values for A.

Example 6.5

The phantom read problem is illustrated below.

T_1: read range [A – B]
T_2: insert A, A<C<B
T_2: end transaction
T_1: read range [A – B]

In this case4, when transaction T_1 performs an operation depending on a criterion, transaction T_2 inserts a new tuple C satisfying that criterion. Now, if the transaction T_1 performs the same operation again, the result will be different. Hence, C is a "phantom" data item.

6.12 AN ABSTRACT MODEL FOR TRANSACTION MANAGEMENT

Here we can represents an abstract model for transaction management in a distributed database environment. In a distributed system, transactions are classified into two different categories:

- **Local transactions:** In this data requirement of a transaction can be fulfilled from the local site or Local transaction access data only from local sites.
- **Global transactions:** In this global transactions access data from remote sited or multiple sites.

It is obvious that the transaction management in a distributed DBMS is more complicated than in a centralized DBMS, as the distributed DBMS must ensure the local sites. This complicated task is performed by four high-level interconnected modules of the DBMS.

1. **Transaction manager:** Transaction manager coordinate's transactions on behalf of application programs by communicating with the scheduler and implements a particular strategy for concurrency control.
2. **Concurrency control manager:** Responsibility of the concurrency control manager is to maximize concurrency, without allowing concurrently executing transactions to interfere with one another, and thereby maintain the consistency of the database as well as the isolation property of the transactions.
3. **Recovery manager:** Recovery manager preserves the database in a consistent state in case of failures.
4. **Buffer manager:** Buffer manager manages the efficient transfer of data between disk storage and main memory.

In a distributed DBMS, all these modules exist in each local DBMS. In addition, a global transaction manager or transaction coordinator is required at each site to control the execution of global transactions as well as of local transactions initiated at that site.

An abstract model of transaction management at each site of a distributed system consists of two different types:

1. **Transaction manager:** Transaction manager at each site manages the execution of the transactions that access data stored at that local site. Each such transaction may be a local transaction or part of a global transaction. The structure of the transaction manager is similar to that of its counterpart in a centralized system, and it is responsible for the following:

   - Maintaining a log for recovery purposes in case of failures.

- Implementing an appropriate concurrency control mechanism to coordinate the concurrent execution of transactions executing at that local site.

2. **Transaction coordinator:** Transaction coordinator at each site in a distributed system coordinates the execution of both local and global transactions initiated at that site. This component or module is not required in centralized DBMSs, as there is only one site in a centralized system. The transaction coordinator at each site performs the following tasks to coordinate the execution of transactions initiated at that local site.
   - It starts the execution of the transactions initiated at that site.
   - It breaks the transactions into a number of subtransactions and distributes these subtransactions to the appropriate sites for execution.
   - It coordinates the termination of the transactions, which may result in the transactions being committed at all sites or aborted at all sites.

The structure of this abstract model is given in figure 6.2.

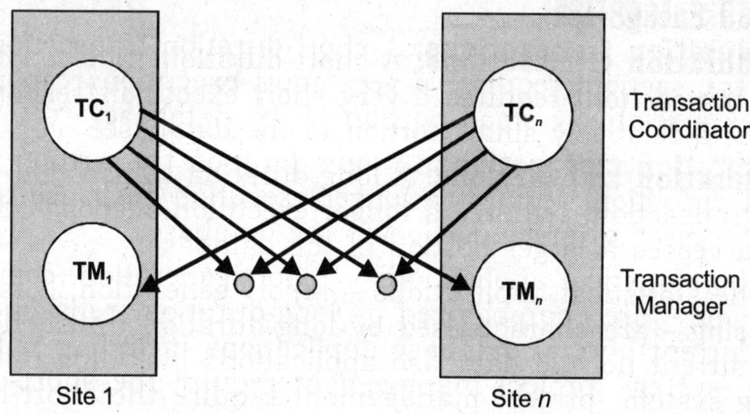

Figure 6.2: A Model for Transaction Management at Each Site in a DDBMS

A transaction is considered as a part of an application. When a user requests for the execution of an application (may be local or global) the application issues a begin_transaction primitive. All actions that are performed by the application after that are to be considered part of the same transaction until a commit or an abort primitive is issued. In some systems, all these primitives are implicitly associated with the application; thus, it is not necessary to define all these primitive explicitly.

To execute a global application generated at site S1, the transaction coordinator of site S1 initiates the transaction and breaks the transaction into a number of subtransactions. It then involves multiple sites by consulting the

global system catalog for parallel execution of these subtransactions at different sites. When these subtransactions are distributed over multiple local sites and perform some tasks on behalf of the application, they are called agents. Agents reside at multiple sites and communicate with each other via message passing. The transaction manager at a local site maintains the log when a local transaction or part of a global transaction is executed at that local site. It also controls the concurrent execution of transactions executing at that site.

The results retrieved from the parallel execution of these subtransaciton sat multiple sites are integrated by the transaction coordinator of site S1, and finally the transaction is terminated.

6.13 CLASSIFICATION OF TRANSACTIONS

These classifications have been defined based on various criteria such as the lifetime of the transaction, organization of read and write operations within the transaction and the structure of the transaction.

Depending on their lifetime or duration, transactions can be classified into two broad categories:

1. **Short-duration transactions:** A short-duration transaction (also called online transaction) requires a very short execution/response time and accesses a relatively small portion of the database.
2. **Long-duration transactions:** A long-duration transaction (also called a batch transaction) requires a longer execution/response time and generally accesses a larger portion of the database.

Most of the statistical applications – report generation, complex queries, image processing – are characterized by long-duration transactions, whereas most of the current normal database applications including railway reservation, banking system, project management require the short-duration category transactions.

Another way to divide transactions into different classes is based on the organization of the read and the write operations within the transaction.

1. **General transactions:** Some transactions have read and write operations are organized in a mixed manner; they do not appear in any specific order. These are called general transactions.
2. **Two-step transactions:** Some transactions restrict the organization of read and write operations in such a way that all the read operations within the transaction are performed before the execution of any write operation.

3. **Restricted (or read-before-write) transactions:** Some transactions may restrict that a data item has to be read before it can be written (updated) within the transaction operation.

If a transaction is characterized by features of both two-step and restricted transactions, then it is called a restricted two-step transaction.

Example 6.6

Consider the transactions T_1, T_2, T_3 and T_4, where T_1 represents a general transaction, T_2 represents a two-step transaction, T_3 represents a restricted transaction and T_4 represents a two-step restricted transaction.

T_1: {read (a1), read (b1), write (a1), read(b2), write(b2), write (b1), commit}

T_2: {read (a1), read (b1), write (b2), read(a1), write(b2), write (b1), commit}

T_3: {read (a1), read (b1), read(b2), write(a1), read(c1), write(b2), read(c2), write(b1), write(c1), write(c2), commit}

T_4: {read(a1), read(b1), read(b2), read(c1), read(c2), write(a1), write (b2), write(b1), write(c1), write(c2) commit}

Transactions can also be classified into three broad categories based on the structure of transactions, namely, flat transactions, nested transactions and workflow models, which are discussed in the following:

(a) Flat Transaction: A flat transaction has a single start point (begin_transaction) and a single end point or terminate point (end_transaction). Most of the typical transaction management database applications are characterized by flat transactions. Flat transactions are relatively simple and perform well in short activities, but they are not well-suited for longer activities.

(b) Nested Transaction: A nested transaction includes other transactions within its own start point and end point; thus, several transactions, called subtransactions, may be nested into one transaction

A nested transaction divided into two types: open nested transaction and closed nested transaction.

1. **Open nested transaction:** It provides flexibility by allowing the commit of the parent transaction before the commit of subtransactions. An example of an open nested transaction is "Saga" [Garcia-Molina and Salem, 1987], which is a sequence of transactions that can be interleaved with other transactions.
2. **Closed nested transaction:** Its commit occurs in a bottom-up fashion, that is, parent transactions are committed after the commit subtransactions or child transactions that are nested within it, although subtransactions are started after the parent transaction.

In "Saga", only two levels of nesting are permitted and it does not support full atomicity at the outer level. Thus, flexibility is provided with respect to ensuring the ACID properties of transactions. The primary advantage of a nested transaction is that it provides a higher level of concurrency among transaction, as a number of subtransactions may be nested or embedded into one transaction.

The nested transaction is also beneficial for recovery, as it is possible to recover independently each subtransaction from failures, thus, leading to less expensive recovery control mechanisms. In the case of nested transactions it is possible to restart only the operations of a particular subtransaction instead of restarting the entire transaction when failures occur in the system.

Finally, the creation of a new transaction is not cumbersome as this can be done by simply inserting the newly created transaction into an existing transaction as a subtransaciton.

Example 6.7

A nested transaction is given below:

```
Begin_transaction Bank_services
Begin
  Begin_transaction Accnts_maintenance
  .......
  end. {Accnts_maintenance}
  Begin_transaction Loan_maintenance
  ...........
  end. {Loan_maintenance}
  Begin_transaction Fixed_deposit
  .............
  end. {Fixed_deposit}
  ............
end. {Bank_services}
```

(c) Workflow models: A workflow is defined as a collection of tasks organized to carry out some business process. Three different types of workflow are identified, which are listed in the following:

- **Human-oriented workflows:** These provide support for collaboration and coordination among humans, but humans themselves are ultimately responsible for the consistency of the operations.

- **System-oriented workflows:** These provide support for specialized tasks that can be executed by a computer such as concurrency control and recovery, automatic task execution, and notification.
- **Transactional workflows:** It has the characteristics of both human-oriented and system-oriented workflows. These workflows provide supports for coordinating execution of multiple tasks and selective use of transactional properties for individual tasks or entire workflows.

There are two main issues involved in workflows: **specification of workflows** and **execution of workflows.**

The key issues involved in specifying a workflow are as follows:

- **Task specification:** The execution structure of each task is defined by providing a set of externally observable execution states and a set of transitions between these states.
- **Tasks coordination requirements:** These are usually represented as inter-task execution dependencies and data flow dependencies, and the termination conditions of the workflow.
- **Execution requirements:** These restrict the execution of the workflow to fulfill application-specific correctness criteria. These include failure/execution atomicity requirements, workflow concurrency control, and recovery requirements.

Example 6.8

Consider the example of patient's health checkup transaction. The entire health checkup activity consists of the following tasks and involves the following data.

- **Task1 (T_1):** A patient requests for health checkup registration and Patient database is accessed.
- **Task2 (T_2 and T_3):** Some medical tests have been performed, and the patient's health information is stored in the Health database. In this case, several medical tests can be performed simultaneously. For simplicity, herc it is assumed that two medical tests have bee performed.
- **Task3 (T_4):** The doctor's advice is taken and hence Doctor Database is accessed.
- **Task4 (T_5):** A bill is generated and the billing information is recorded into the database.

In this patient's health checkup transaction, there is a serial dependency of T_2, T_3 on T_1, and T_4 on T_2, T_3. Hence, T_2 and T_3 can be performed in parallel and T_5 waits until their completion. The corresponding workflow is illustrated in figure 6.3.

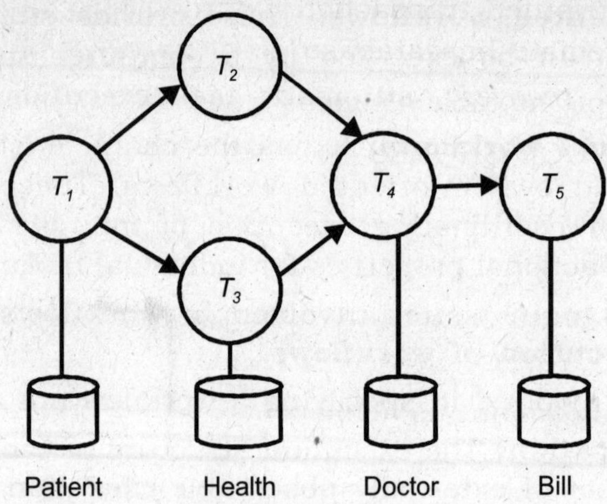

Figure 6.3: An Example of a Workflow

6.14 DISTRIBUTED TRANSACTIONS IN ORACLE

A **distributed transaction** includes one or more statements that, individually or as a group, update data on two or more distinct nodes of a distributed database. For example, assume the database configuration depicted in Figure 6.4:

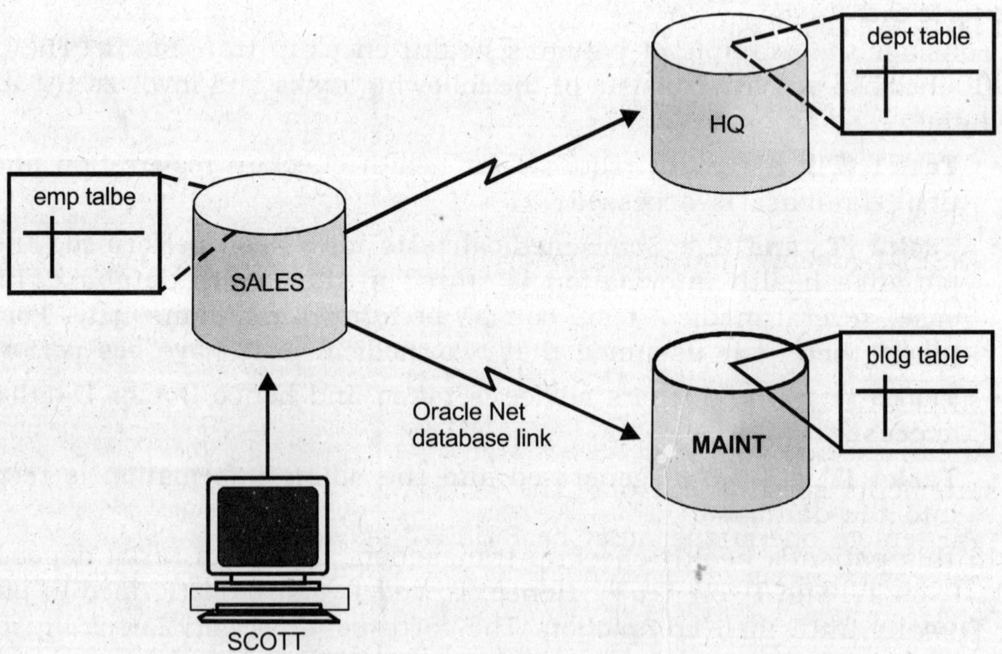

Figure 6.4 Distributed System

The following distributed transaction executed by scott updates the local sales database, the remote hq database, and the remote maint database:

```
UPDATE scott.dept@hq.us.acme.com
  SET loc = 'REDWOOD SHORES'
  WHERE deptno = 10;
UPDATE scott.emp
  SET deptno = 11
  WHERE deptno = 10;
UPDATE scott.bldg@maint.us.acme.com
  SET room = 1225
  WHERE room = 1163;
COMMIT;
```

Note: If all statements of a transaction reference only a single remote node, then the transaction is remote, not distributed.

There are two types of permissible operations in distributed transactions:

- DML and DDL Transactions
- Transaction Control Statements

6.14.1 DML and DDL Transactions

The following are the DML and DDL operations supported in a distributed transaction:

- CREATE TABLE AS SELECT
- DELETE
- INSERT (default and direct load)
- LOCK TABLE
- SELECT
- SELECT FOR UPDATE

You can execute DML and DDL statements in parallel, and INSERT direct load statements serially, but note the following restrictions:

- All remote operations must be SELECT statements.
- These statements must not be clauses in another distributed transaction.

- If the table referenced in the *table_expression_clause* of an INSERT, UPDATE, or DELETE statement is remote, then execution is serial rather than parallel.
- You cannot perform remote operations after issuing parallel DML/DDL or direct load INSERT.
- If the transaction begins using XA or OCI, it executes serially.
- No loopback operations can be performed on the transaction originating the parallel operation. For example, you cannot reference a remote object that is actually a synonym for a local object.
- If you perform a distributed operation other than a SELECT in the transaction, no DML is parallelized.

6.14.2 TRANSACTION CONTROL STATEMENTS

The following are the supported transaction control statements:

- COMMIT
- ROLLBACK
- SAVEPOINT

6.14.3 SESSION TREES FOR DISTRIBUTED TRANSACTIONS

As the statements in a distributed transaction are issued, the database defines a **session tree** of all nodes participating in the transaction. A session tree is a hierarchical model that describes the relationships among sessions and their roles. Figure 6.5 illustrates a session tree:

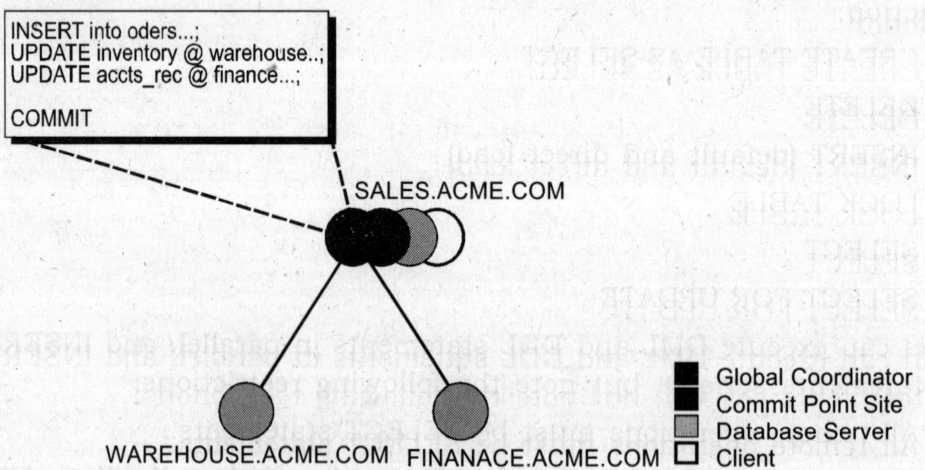

Figure 6.5: Example of a Session Tree

All nodes participating in the session tree of a distributed transaction assume one or more of the following roles:

Role	Description
Client	A node that references information in a database belonging to a different node.
Database server	A node that receives a request for information from another node.
Global coordinator	The node that originates the distributed transaction.
Local coordinator	A node that is forced to reference data on other nodes to complete its part of the transaction.
Commit point site	The node that commits or rolls back the transaction as instructed by the global coordinator.

The role a node plays in a distributed transaction is determined by:

- Whether the transaction is local or remote
- The **commit point strength** of the node ("Commit Point Site ")
- Whether all requested data is available at a node, or whether other nodes need to be referenced to complete the transaction
- Whether the node is read-only

1. **Clients:** A node acts as a client when it references information from a database on another node. The referenced node is a database server. In Figure 6.5, the node sales are a client of the nodes that host the warehouse and finance databases.
2. **Database Servers:** A database server is a node that hosts a database from which a client requests data.

   In Figure 6.5, an application at the sales node initiates a distributed transaction that accesses data from the warehouse and finance nodes. Therefore, sales.acme.com has the role of client node, and warehouse and finance are both database servers. In this cxamplc, sales are a database server *and* a client because the application also modifies data in the sales database.
3. **Local Coordinators:** A node that must reference data on other nodes to complete its part in the distributed transaction is called a local coordinator. In Figure 6.5, sales are a local coordinator because it coordinates the nodes it directly references: warehouse and finance. The node sales also happens to be the global coordinator because it coordinates all the nodes involved in the transaction.

A local coordinator is responsible for coordinating the transaction among the nodes it communicates directly with by:

- Receiving and relaying transaction status information to and from those nodes
- Passing queries to those nodes
- Receiving queries from those nodes and passing them on to other nodes
- Returning the results of queries to the nodes that initiated them

4. **Global Coordinator:** The node where the distributed transaction originates is called the global coordinator. The database application issuing the distributed transaction is directly connected to the node acting as the global coordinator. For example, in Figure 6.5, the transaction issued at the node sales references information from the database servers warehouse and finance. Therefore, sales.acme.com is the global coordinator of this distributed transaction.

   The global coordinator becomes the parent or root of the session tree. The global coordinator performs the following operations during a distributed transaction:

   - Sends all of the distributed transaction SQL statements, remote procedure calls, and so forth to the directly referenced nodes, thus forming the session tree
   - Instructs all directly referenced nodes other than the commit point site to prepare the transaction
   - Instructs the commit point site to initiate the global commit of the transaction if all nodes prepare successfully
   - Instructs all nodes to initiate a global rollback of the transaction if there is an abort response

5. **Commit Point Site:** The job of the commit point site is to initiate a commit or roll back operation as instructed by the global coordinator. The system administrator always designates one node to be the commit point sites in the session tree by assigning all nodes commit point strength. The node selected as commit point site should be the node that stores the most critical data.

Figure 6.6 illustrates an example of distributed system, with sales serving as the commit point site:

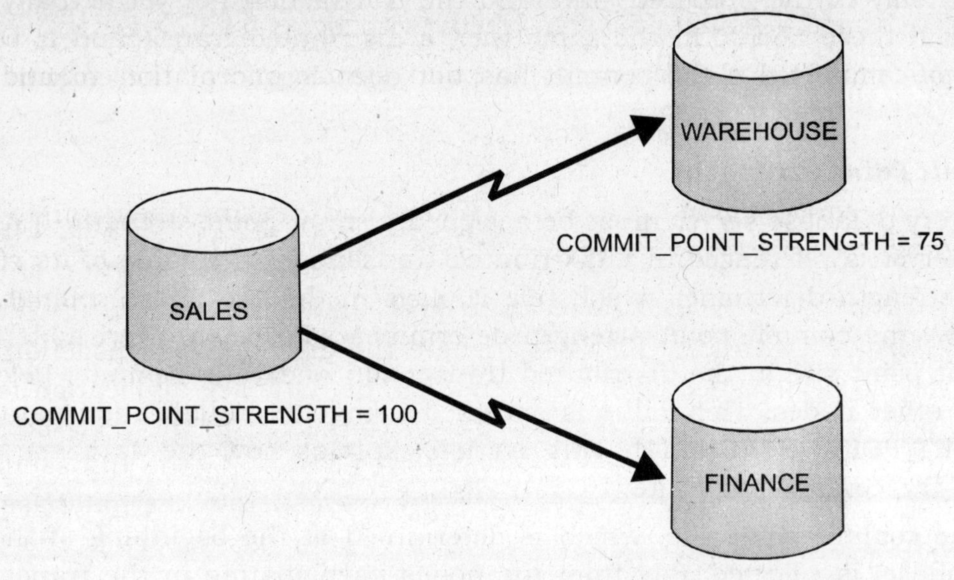

Figure 6.6: Commit Point Site

The commit point site is distinct from all other nodes involved in a distributed transaction in these ways:

- The commit point site never enters the prepared state. Consequently, if the commit point site stores the most critical data, this data never remains in-doubt, even if a failure occurs. In failure situations, failed nodes remain in a prepared state, holding necessary locks on data until in-doubt transactions are resolved.
- The commit point site commits before the other nodes involved in the transaction. In effect, the outcome of a distributed transaction at the commit point site determines whether the transaction at all nodes is committed or rolled back: the other nodes follow the lead of the commit point site. The global coordinator ensures that all nodes complete the transaction in the same manner as the commit point site.

6.14.4 HOW A DISTRIBUTED TRANSACTION COMMITS

A distributed transaction is considered committed after all non-commit-point sites are prepared, and the transaction has been actually committed at the commit point site. The redo log at the commit point site is updated as soon as the distributed transaction is committed at this node.

Because the commit point log contains a record of the commit, the transaction is considered committed even though some participating nodes may

still be only in the prepared state and the transaction not yet actually committed at these nodes. In the same way, a distributed transaction is considered *not* committed if the commit has not been logged at the commit point site.

Commit Point Strength

Every database server must be assigned commit point strength. If a database server is referenced in a distributed transaction, the value of its commit point strength determines which role it plays in the two-phase commit. Specifically, the commit point strength determines whether a given node is the commit point site in the distributed transaction and thus commits before all of the other nodes. This value is specified using the initialization parameter COMMIT_POINT_STRENGTH. This section explains how the database determines the commit point site.

The commit point site, which is determined at the beginning of the prepare phase, is selected only from the nodes participating in the transaction. The following sequence of events occurs:

1. Of the nodes directly referenced by the global coordinator, the database selects the node with the highest commit point strength as the commit point site.
2. The initially-selected node determines if any of the nodes from which it has to obtain information for this transaction has a higher commit point strength.
3. Either the node with the highest commit point strength directly referenced in the transaction or one of its servers with a higher commit point strength becomes the commit point site.
4. After the final commit point site has been determined, the global coordinator sends prepare responses to all nodes participating in the transaction.

Figure 6.7 shows in a sample session tree the commit point strengths of each node (in parentheses) and shows the node chosen as the commit point site:

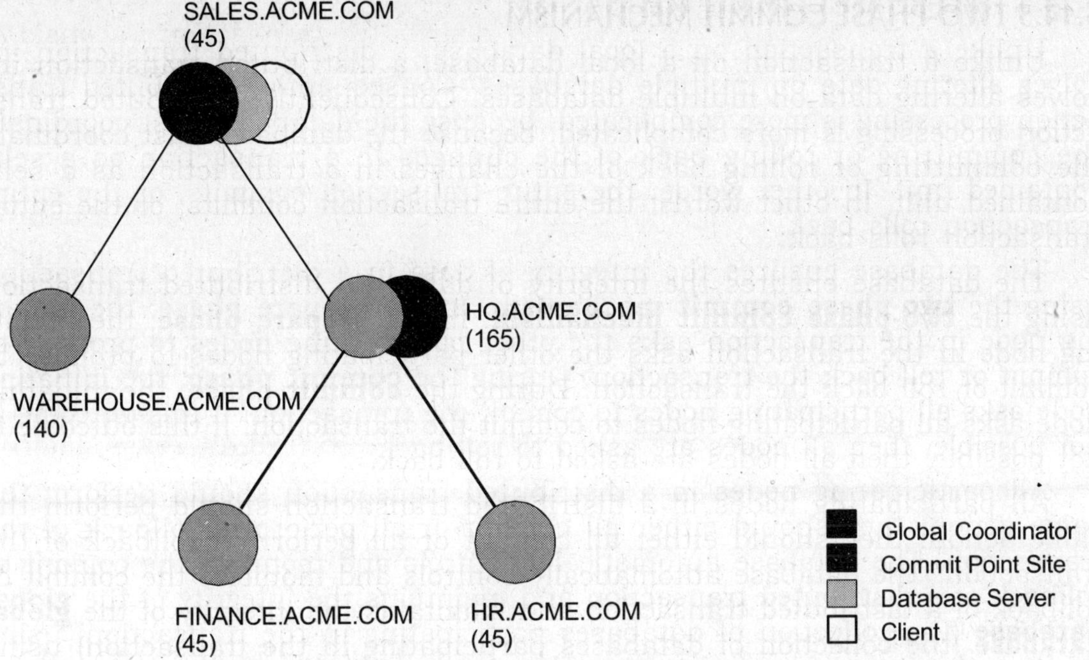

Figure 6.7: Commit Point Strengths and Determination of the Commit Point Site

The following conditions apply when determining the commit point site:

- A read-only node cannot be the commit point site.
- If multiple nodes directly referenced by the global coordinator have the same commit point strength, then the database designates one of these as the commit point site.
- If a distributed transaction ends with a rollback, then the prepare and commit phases are not needed. Consequently, the database never determines a commit point site. Instead, the global coordinator sends a ROLLBACK statement to all nodes and ends the processing of the distributed transaction.

As Figure 6.7 illustrates, the commit point site and the global coordinator can be different nodes of the session tree. The commit point strength of each node is communicated to the coordinators when the initial connections are made. The coordinators retain the commit point strengths of each node they are in direct communication with so that commit point sites can be efficiently selected during two-phase commits. Therefore, it is not necessary for the commit point strength to be exchanged between a coordinator and a node each time a commit occurs.

6.14.5 TWO-PHASE COMMIT MECHANISM

Unlike a transaction on a local database, a distributed transaction involves altering data on multiple databases. Consequently, distributed transaction processing is more complicated, because the database must coordinate the committing or rolling back of the changes in a transaction as a self-contained unit. In other words, the entire transaction commits, or the entire transaction rolls back.

The database ensures the integrity of data in a distributed transaction using the **two-phase commit mechanism**. In the **prepare phase**, the initiating node in the transaction asks the other participating nodes to promise to commit or roll back the transaction. During the **commit phase**, the initiating node asks all participating nodes to commit the transaction. If this outcome is not possible, then all nodes are asked to roll back.

All participating nodes in a distributed transaction should perform the same action: they should either all commit or all perform a rollback of the transaction. The database automatically controls and monitors the commit or rollback of a distributed transaction and maintains the integrity of the **global database** (the collection of databases participating in the transaction) using the two-phase commit mechanism. This mechanism is completely transparent, requiring no programming on the part of the user or application developer.

The commit mechanism has the following distinct phases, which the database performs automatically whenever a user commits a distributed transaction:

Phase	Description
Prepare phase	The initiating node, called the **global coordinator**, asks participating nodes other than the commit point site to promise to commit or roll back the transaction, even if there is a failure. If any node cannot prepare, the transaction is rolled back.
Commit phase	If all participants respond to the coordinator that they are prepared, then the coordinator asks the commit point site to commit. After it commits, the coordinator asks all other nodes to commit the transaction.
Forget phase	The global coordinator forgets about the transaction.

This section contains the following topics:

1. Prepare Phase
2. Commit Phase
3. Forget Phase

1. **Prepare Phase:** The first phase in committing a distributed transaction is the prepare phase. In this phase, the database does not actually commit or roll back the transaction. Instead, all nodes referenced in a distributed transaction (except the commit point site, described in the "Commit Point Site ") are told to prepare to commit. By preparing, a node:
   - Records information in the redo logs so that it can subsequently either commit or roll back the transaction, regardless of intervening failures
   - Places a distributed lock on modified tables, which prevents reads

When a node responds to the global coordinator that it is prepared to commit, the prepared node *promises* to either commit or roll back the transaction later, but does not make a unilateral decision on whether to commit or roll back the transaction. The promise means that if an instance failure occurs at this point, the node can use the redo records in the online log to recover the database back to the prepare phase.

Types of Responses in the Prepare Phase

When a node is told to prepare, it can respond in the following ways:

Response	Meaning
Prepared	Data on the node has been modified by a statement in the distributed transaction, and the node has successfully prepared.
Read-only	No data on the node has been, or can be, modified (only queried), so no preparation is necessary.
Abort	The node cannot successfully prepare.

Prepared Response

When a node has successfully prepared, it issues a **prepared message**. The message indicates that the node has records of the changes in the online log, so it is prepared either to commit or perform a rollback. The message also guarantees that locks held for the transaction can survive a failure.

Read-Only Response

When a node is asked to prepare, and the SQL statements affecting the database do not change any data on the node, the node responds with a **read-only message**. The message indicates that the node will not participate in the commit phase.

There are three cases in which all or part of a distributed transaction is read-only:

Case	Conditions	Consequence
Partially read-only	Any of the following occurs: • Only queries are issued at one or more nodes. • No data is changed. • Changes rolled back due to triggers firing or constraint violations.	The read-only nodes recognize their status when asked to prepare. They give their local coordinators a read-only response. Thus, the commit phase completes faster because the database eliminates read-only nodes from subsequent processing.
Completely read-only with prepare phase	All of following occur: • No data changes. • Transaction is *not* started with `SET TRANSACTION READ ONLY` statement.	All nodes recognize that they are read-only during prepare phase, so no commit phase is required. The global coordinator, not knowing whether all nodes are read-only, must still perform the prepare phase.
Completely read-only without two-phase commit	All of following occur: • No data changes. • Transaction *is* started with `SET TRANSACTION READ ONLY` statement.	Only queries are allowed in the transaction, so global coordinator does not have to perform two-phase commit. Changes by other transactions do not degrade global transaction-level read consistency because of global SCN coordination among nodes. The transaction does not use undo segments.

Note that if a distributed transaction is set to read-only, then it does not use undo segments. If many users connect to the database and their transactions are *not* set to READ ONLY, then they allocate undo space even if they are only performing queries.

Abort Response

When a node cannot successfully prepare, it performs the following actions:

1. Releases resources currently held by the transaction and rolls back the local portion of the transaction.
2. Responds to the node that referenced it in the distributed transaction with an abort message.

These actions then propagate to the other nodes involved in the distributed transaction so that they can roll back the transaction and guarantee the integrity of the data in the global database. This response enforces the primary rule of a distributed transaction: *all nodes involved in the transaction either all commit or all roll back the transaction at the same logical time.*

Steps in the Prepare Phase

To complete the prepare phase, each node excluding the commit point site performs the following steps:

1. The node requests that its descendants, that is, the nodes subsequently referenced, prepare to commit.
2. The node checks to see whether the transaction changes data on itself or its descendants. If there is no change to the data, then the node skips the remaining steps and returns a read-only response (see "Read-Only Response").
3. The node allocates the resources it needs to commit the transaction if data is changed.
4. The node saves redo records corresponding to changes made by the transaction to its redo log.
5. The node guarantees that locks held for the transaction are able to survive a failure.
6. The node responds to the initiating node with a prepared response (see "Prepared Response") or, if its attempt or the attempt of one of its descendents to prepare was unsuccessful, with an abort response (see "Abort Response").

These actions guarantee that the node can subsequently commit or roll back the transaction on the node. The prepared nodes then wait until a COMMIT or ROLLBACK request is received from the global coordinator.

After the nodes are prepared, the distributed transaction is said to be in-doubt (see "In-Doubt Transactions").It retains in-doubt status until all changes are either committed or rolled back.

2. **Commit Phase:** The second phase in committing a distributed transaction is the commit phase. Before this phase occurs, *all* nodes other than the commit point site referenced in the distributed transaction have guaranteed that they are prepared, that is, they have the necessary resources to commit the transaction.

Steps in the Commit Phase

The commit phase consists of the following steps:

1. The global coordinator instructs the commit point site to commit.
2. The commit point site commits.
3. The commit point site informs the global coordinator that it has committed.

4. The global and local coordinators send a message to all nodes instructing them to commit the transaction.
5. At each node, the database commits the local portion of the distributed transaction and releases locks.
6. At each node, the database records an additional redo entry in the local redo log, indicating that the transaction has committed.
7. The participating nodes notify the global coordinator that they have committed.

When the commit phase is complete, the data on all nodes of the distributed system is consistent.

Guaranteeing Global Database Consistency

Each committed transaction has an associated system change number (SCN) to uniquely identify the changes made by the SQL statements within that transaction. The SCN functions as an internal timestamp that uniquely identifies a committed version of the database.

In a distributed system, the SCNs of communicating nodes are coordinated when all of the following actions occur:

- A connection occurs using the path described by one or more database links
- A distributed SQL statement executes
- A distributed transaction commits

Among other benefits, the coordination of SCNs among the nodes of a distributed system ensures global read-consistency at both the statement and transaction level. If necessary, global time-based recovery can also be completed.

During the prepare phase, the database determines the highest SCN at all nodes involved in the transaction. The transaction then commits with the high SCN at the commit point site. The commit SCN is then sent to all prepared nodes with the commit decision.

3. **Forget Phase:** After the participating nodes notify the commit point site that they have committed, the commit point site can forget about the transaction. The following steps occur:
   1. After receiving notice from the global coordinator that all nodes have committed, the commit point site erases status information about this transaction.

2. The commit point site informs the global coordinator that it has erased the status information.
3. The global coordinator erases its own information about the transaction.

6.14.6 IN-DOUBT TRANSACTIONS

The two-phase commit mechanism ensures that all nodes either commit or perform a rollback together. What happens if any of the three phases fails because of a system or network error? The transaction becomes in-doubt.

Distributed transactions can become in-doubt in the following ways:

- A server machine running Oracle Database software crashes
- A network connection between two or more Oracle Databases involved in distributed processing is disconnected
- An unhandled software error occurs

The RECO process automatically resolves in-doubt transactions when the machine, network, or software problem is resolved. Until RECO can resolve the transaction, the data is locked for both reads and writes. The database blocks reads because it cannot determine which version of the data to display for a query.

This section contains the following topics:

- Automatic Resolution of In-Doubt Transactions
- Manual Resolution of In-Doubt Transactions
- Relevance of System Change Numbers for In-Doubt Transactions

1. **Automatic Resolution of In-Doubt Transactions:** In the majority of cases, the database resolves the in-doubt transaction automatically. Assume that there are two nodes, local and remote, in the following scenarios. The local node is the commit point site. User scott connects to local and executes and commits a distributed transaction that updates local and remote.

Failure During the Prepare Phase

Figure 6.8 illustrates the sequence of events when there is a failure during the prepare phase of a distributed transaction:

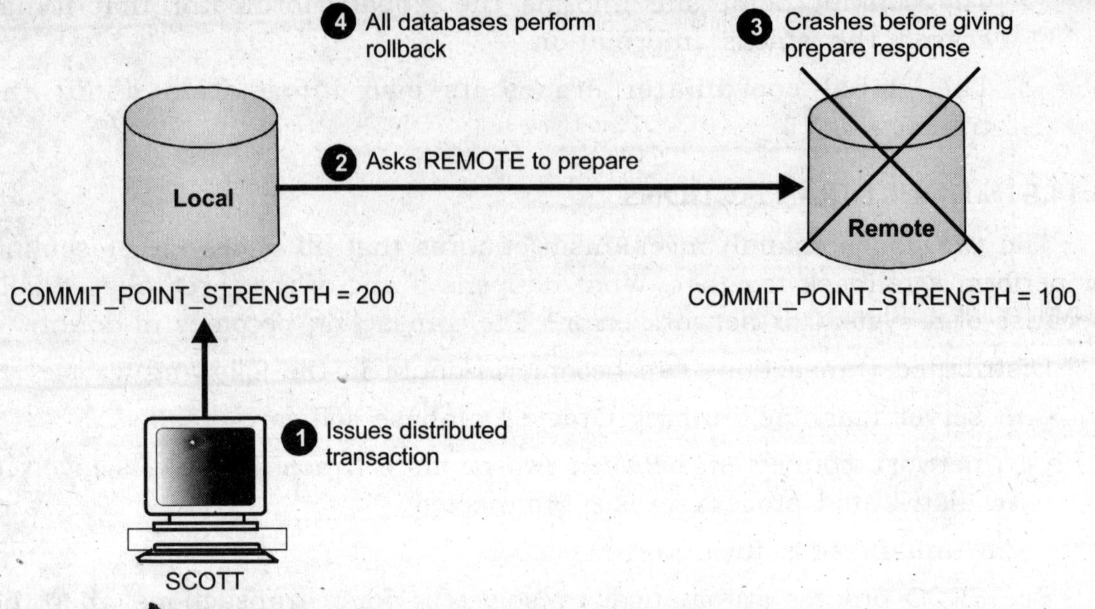

Figure 6.8: Failure During Prepare Phase

The following steps occur:

1. User Scott connects to local and executes a distributed transaction.
2. The global coordinator, which in this example is also the commit point site, requests all databases other than the commit point site to promise to commit or roll back when told to do so.
3. The remote database crashes before issuing the prepare response back to local.
4. The transaction is ultimately rolled back on each database by the RECO process when the remote site is restored.

Failure during the Commit Phase

Figure 6.9 illustrates the sequence of events when there is a failure during the commit phase of a distributed transaction:

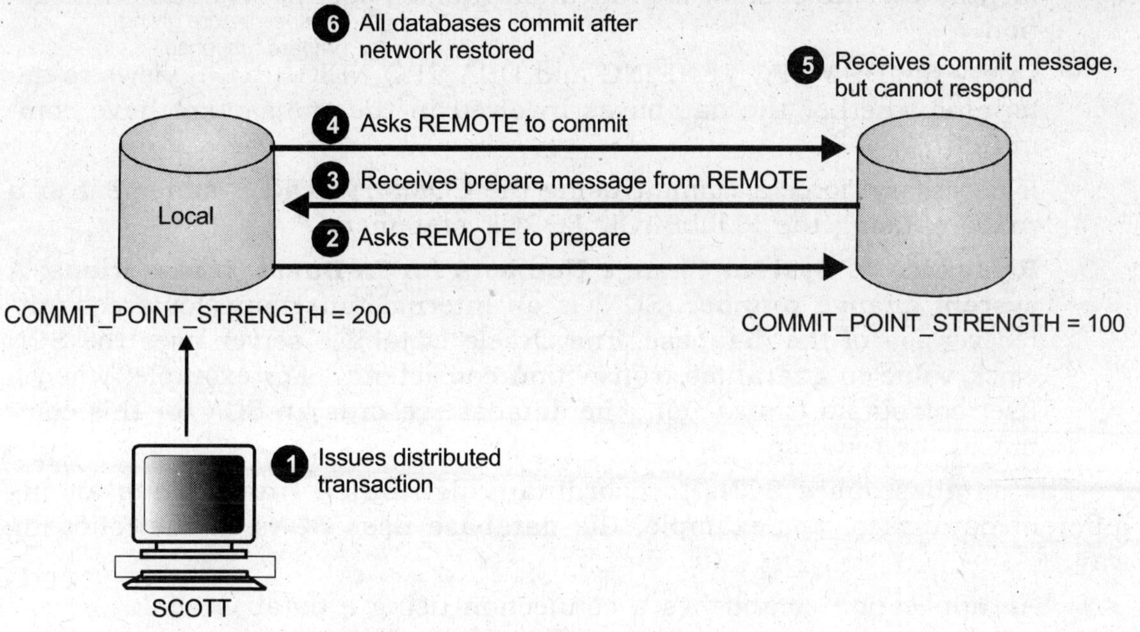

Figure 6.9: Failure During Commit Phase

The following steps occur:

1. User Scott connects to local and executes a distributed transaction.
2. The global coordinator, which in this case is also the commit point site, requests all databases other than the commit point site to promise to commit or roll back when told to do so.
3. The commit point site receives a prepared message from remote saying that it will commit.
4. The commit point site commits the transaction locally, then sends a commit message to remote asking it to commit.
5. The remote database receives the commit message, but cannot respond because of a network failure.
6. The transaction is ultimately committed on the remote database by the RECO process after the network is restored.

2. Manual Resolution of In-Doubt Transactions: You should only need to resolve an in-doubt transaction in the following cases:

- The in-doubt transaction has locks on critical data or undo segments.
- The cause of the machine, network, or software failure cannot be repaired quickly.

Resolution of in-doubt transactions can be complicated. The procedure requires that you do the following:

- Identify the transaction identification number for the in-doubt transaction.
- Query the DBA_2PC_PENDING and DBA_2PC_NEIGHBORS views to determine whether the databases involved in the transaction have committed.
- If necessary, force a commit using the COMMIT FORCE statement or a rollback using the ROLLBACK FORCE statement.

3. **Relevance of System Change Numbers for In-Doubt Transactions:** A **system change number** (SCN) is an internal timestamp for a committed version of the database. The Oracle Database server uses the SCN clock value to guarantee transaction consistency. For example, when a user commits a transaction, the database records an SCN for this commit in the redo log.

The database uses SCNs to coordinate distributed transactions among different databases. For example, the database uses SCNs in the following way:

1. An application establishes a connection using a database link.
2. The distributed transaction commits with the highest global SCN among all the databases involved.
3. The commit global SCN is sent to all databases involved in the transaction.

SCNs are important for distributed transactions because they function as a synchronized commit timestamp of a transaction, even if the transaction fails. If a transaction becomes in-doubt, an administrator can use this SCN to coordinate changes made to the global database. The global SCN for the transaction commit can also be used to identify the transaction later, for example, in distributed recovery.

6.14.7 DISTRIBUTED TRANSACTION PROCESSING: CASE STUDY

In this scenario, a company has separate Oracle Database servers, sales.acme.com and warehouse.acme.com. As users insert sales records into the sales database, associated records are being updated at the warehouse database.

This case study of distributed processing illustrates:

- The definition of a session tree
- How a commit point site is determined
- When prepare messages are sent
- When a transaction actually commits
- What information is stored locally about the transaction

Stage 1: Client Application Issues DML Statements

At the Sales department, a salesperson uses SQL*Plus to enter a sales order and then commit it. The application issues a number of SQL statements to enter the order into the sales database and update the inventory in the warehouse database:

```
CONNECT scott/tiger@sales.acme.com ...;
INSERT INTO orders ...;
UPDATE inventory@warehouse.acme.com ...;
INSERT INTO orders ...;
UPDATE inventory@warehouse.acme.com ...;
COMMIT;
```

These SQL statements are part of a single distributed transaction, guaranteeing that all issued SQL statements succeed or fail as a unit. Treating the statements as a unit prevents the possibility of an order being placed and then inventory not being updated to reflect the order. In effect, the transaction guarantees the consistency of data in the global database.

As each of the SQL statements in the transaction executes, the session tree is defined, as shown in Figure 6.10.

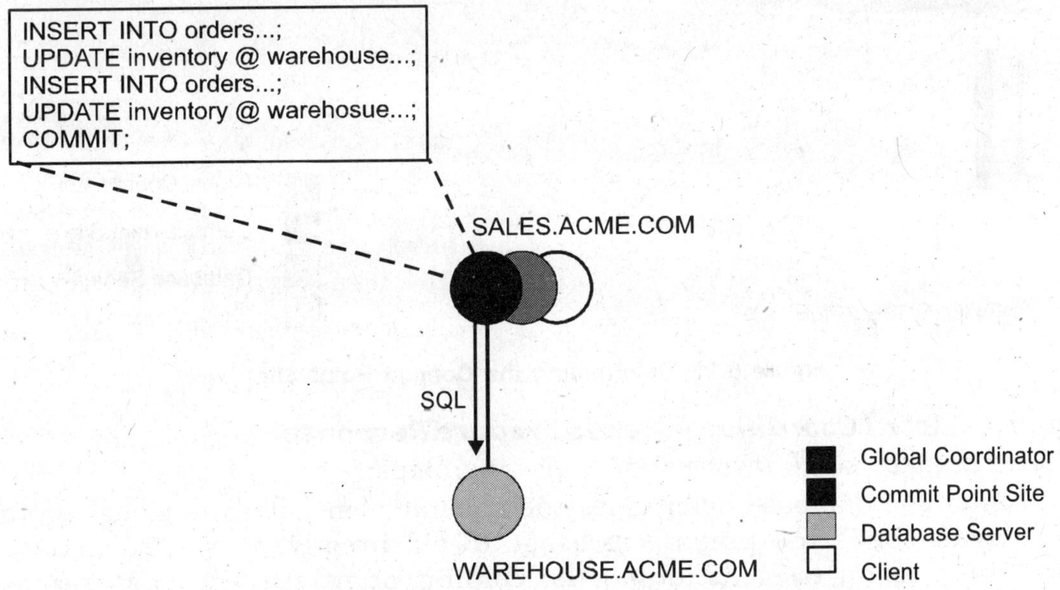

Figure 6.10: Defining the Session Tree

Note the following aspects of the transaction:

- An order entry application running on the sales database initiates the transaction. Therefore, sales.acme.com is the global coordinator for the distributed transaction.

- The order entry application inserts a new sales record into the sales database and updates the inventory at the warehouse. Therefore, the nodes sales.acme.com and warehouse.acme.com are both database servers.
- Because sales.acme.com updates the inventory, it is a client of warehouse.acme.com.

This stage completes the definition of the session tree for this distributed transaction. Each node in the tree has acquired the necessary data locks to execute the SQL statements that reference local data. These locks remain even after the SQL statements have been executed until the two-phase commit is completed.

Stage 2: Oracle Database Determines Commit Point Site

The database determines the commit point site immediately following the COMMIT statement. sales.acme.com, the global coordinator, is determined to be the commit point site, as shown in Figure 6.11.

Figure 6.11: Determining the Commit Point Site

Stage 3: Global Coordinator Sends Prepare Response

The prepare stage involves the following steps:

1. After the database determines the commit point site, the global coordinator sends the prepare message to all directly referenced nodes of the session tree, *excluding* the commit point site. In this example, warehouse.acme.com is the only node asked to prepare.
2. Node warehouse.acme.com tries to prepare. If a node can guarantee that it can commit the locally dependent part of the transaction and can record the commit information in its local redo log, then the node can successfully prepare. In this example, only warehouse.acme.com receives a prepare message because sales.acme.com is the commit point site.

3. Node warehouse.acme.com responds to sales.acme.com with a prepared message.

As each node prepares, it sends a message back to the node that asked it to prepare. Depending on the responses, one of the following can happen:

- If *any* of the nodes asked to prepare responds with an abort message to the global coordinator, then the global coordinator tells all nodes to roll back the transaction, and the operation is completed.
- If *all* nodes asked to prepare respond with a prepared or a read-only message to the global coordinator, that is, they have successfully prepared, then the global coordinator asks the commit point site to commit the transaction.

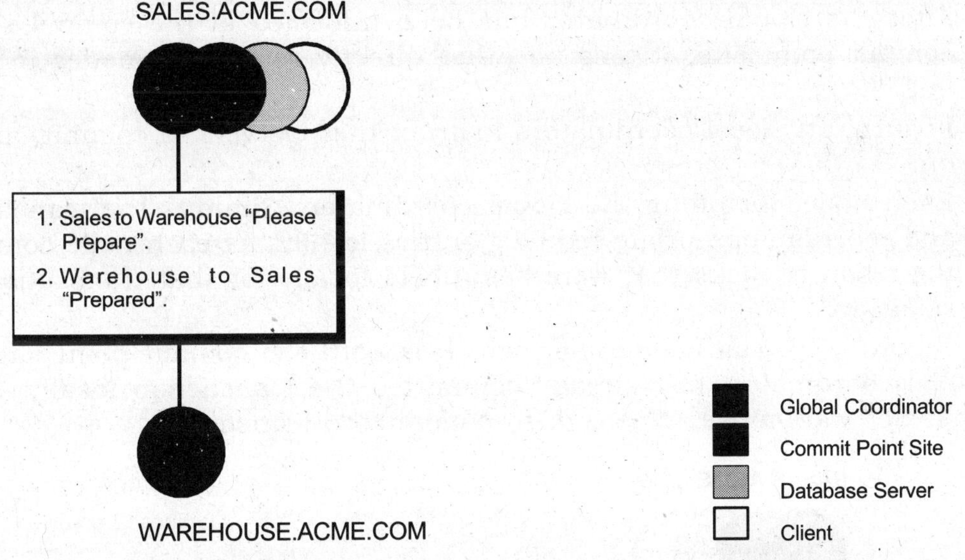

Figure 6.12 Sending and Acknowledging the Prepare Message

Stage 4: Commit Point Site Commits

The committing of the transaction by the commit point site involves the following steps:

1. Node sales.acme.com, receiving acknowledgment that warehouse.acme.com is prepared, instructs the commit point site to commit the transaction.
2. The commit point site now commits the transaction locally and records this fact in its local redo log.

Even if warehouse.acme.com has not yet committed, the outcome of this transaction is predetermined. In other words, the transaction *will* be committed at all nodes even if the ability of a given node to commit is delayed.

Stage 5: Commit Point Site Informs Global Coordinator of Commit

This stage involves the following steps:

1. The commit point site tells the global coordinator that the transaction has committed. Because the commit point site and global coordinator are the same node in this example, no operation is required. The commit point site knows that the transaction is committed because it recorded this fact in its online log.
2. The global coordinator confirms that the transaction has been committed on all other nodes involved in the distributed transaction.

Stage 6: Global and Local Coordinators Tell All Nodes to Commit

The committing of the transaction by all the nodes in the transaction involves the following steps:

1. After the global coordinator has been informed of the commit at the commit point site, it tells all other directly referenced nodes to commit.
2. In turn, any local coordinators instruct their servers to commit, and so on.
3. Each node, including the global coordinator, commits the transaction and records appropriate redo log entries locally. As each node commits, the resource locks that were being held locally for that transaction are released.

In Figure 6.13, sales.acme.com, which is both the commit point site and the global coordinator, has already committed the transaction locally. Sales now instruct warehouse.acme.com to commit the transaction.

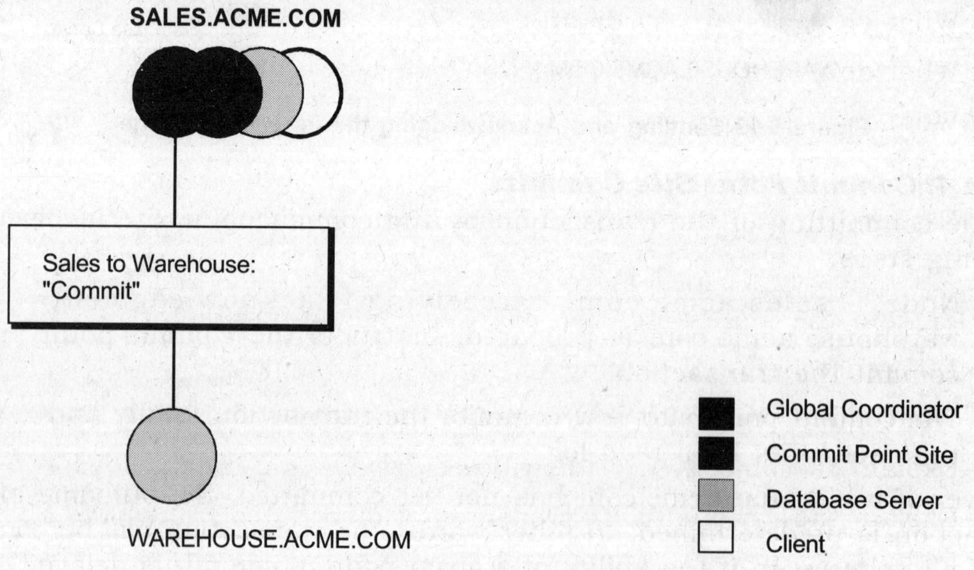

Figure 6.13 Instructing Nodes to Commit

Stage 7: Global Coordinator and Commit Point Site Complete the Commit

The completion of the commit of the transaction occurs in the following steps:

1. After all referenced nodes and the global coordinator have committed the transaction; the global coordinator informs the commit point site of this fact.
2. The commit point site, which has been waiting for this message, erases the status information about this distributed transaction.
3. The commit point site informs the global coordinator that it is finished. In other words, the commit point site forgets about committing the distributed transaction. This action is permissible because all nodes involved in the two-phase commit have committed the transaction successfully, so they will never have to determine its status in the future.
4. The global coordinator finalizes the transaction by forgetting about the transaction itself.

After the completion of the COMMIT phase, the distributed transaction is itself complete. The steps described are accomplished automatically and in a fraction of a second.

EXERCISES

1. What do you mean by distributed transaction management?
2. What do you mean by transaction management?
3. What is a transaction?
4. Explain the concept of database transaction?
5. Explain the fundamentals of transaction management?
6. What are the various goals of transaction management?
7. Explain the implementation of transaction management?
8. Difference between locking vs. multiversioning?
9. What do you mean by distributed transactions?
10. Explain the objectives of distributed transaction management?
11. Explain the various ACID properties of distributed transactions?
12. Explain an abstract model for transaction management?

13. Explain the classification of transactions?
14. Explain the distributed transactions in oracle?
15. How a distributed transaction commits?
16. Explain the concept of two-phase commit mechanism?
17. What are in-doubt transactions?
18. Explain the case study of distributed transaction processing?

CHAPTER 7

DISTRIBUTED CONCURRENCY CONTROL

7.1 INTRODUCTION

In this chapter, we discuss a number of concurrency control techniques that are used to ensure the noninterference or isolation property of concurrently executing transactions. Most of these techniques ensure serializability of schedules, using protocols (that is, sets of rules) that guarantee serializability. One important set of protocols employs the technique of locking data items to prevent multiple transactions from accessing the items concurrently; a number of locking protocols are described. Locking protocols are used in most commercial DBMSs and DDBMSs. Another set of concurrency control protocols use timestamps. A timestamp is a unique identifier for each transaction, generated by the system. Concurrency control protocols that use timestamp ordering to ensure serializability are described. We also discuss multiversion concurrency control protocols that use multiple versions of a data item. In next Section, we present a protocol based on the concept of validation or certification of a transaction after it executes its operations; these are sometimes called optimistic protocols. In the last section, we can explain the concept of reliability and removal of inconsistencies.

7.2 CONCURRENCY CONTROL

Today's Database Management Systems (DBMSs) work in multiuser environment where users access the database concurrently. Therefore the DBMSs control the concurrent execution of user transactions, so that the overall correction of the database is maintained. A transaction is a user program accessing the database. Research in database concurrency control has advanced in a different direction from areas that may appear related such as operating systems concurrency.

Database concurrency control permits users to access a database in a multiprogrammed fashion while preserving the illusion that each user is executing alone on a dedicated system. The main difficulty in achieving this goal is to prevent database updates performed by one user from interfering with database retrievals and updates performed by another.

As an example, consider an on-line airline reservation system. Suppose two customers Customer A and Customer B, simultaneously try to reserve a seat for the same flight. In the absence of concurrency control, these two activities could interfere as illustrated in Figure 7.1. Let Seat No 18 be the first available seat. Both transactions could read the reservation information approximately same time and they reserve the seat No 18 for Customer A and Customer B, and store the result back into the database. The net effect is incorrect: Although two customers reserved a seat, the database reflects only one activity; the other reservation is lost by the system. As it is apparent from the example, it is necessary to establish a correctness criterion for the execution of concurrent user transactions. Serializability is the correctness criterion for the execution of concurrent transactions. The execution of concurrent transactions, which is termed as a history or as a log, is serializable if it produces the same output and has the same effect on the database as some serial execution of the same transactions. A log is serial if, for every pair of transactions, all of the operations of one transaction execute before any of the operations of the other. However, deciding on whether an equivalent serial log exists is an NP_complete problem, that is, there is no known algorithm which will decide in polynomial time on whether any given log is serializable.

Since serializability problem is NP_complete, several subclasses of serializable logs having polynomial time membership test are introduced. The popular subclasses are: the class of serial logs (class S), the class of logs produced by Two_phase locking schedulers (class 2PL), the class of logs produced by Basic Timestamp Ordering schedulers (class BTO) and the class of Conflict Preserving Serializable logs (class CPSR), whose scheduler is based on Serialization Graph Testing (SGT).

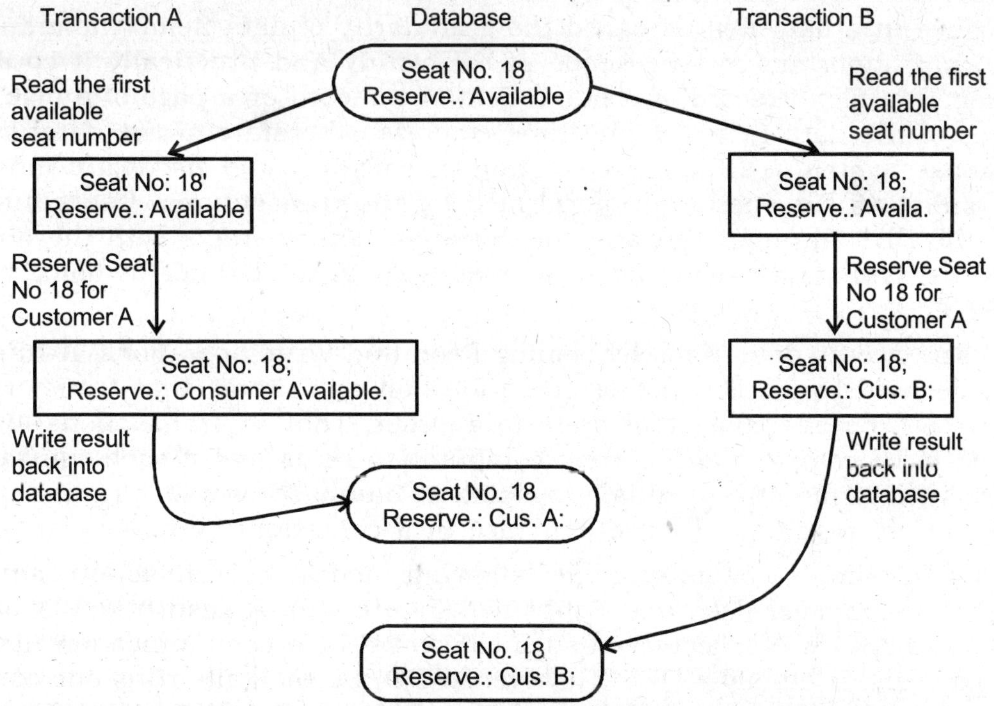

Figure 7.1: Example of an anomaly in database in the absence of concurrency control.

Concurrency control in DBMSs is achieved by a program, called the scheduler, whose goal is to order the operations of transactions in such a way that the resulting log is serializable. Practically, 2PL is the most popular scheduling technique for the centralized DBMSs. However for distributed DBMSs, 2PL induces high communication cost because of the deadlock problem. Therefore, improved algorithms for concurrency control in distributed DBMSs are one of the active research areas in database theory.

Theoretically the class CPSR had been the most attractive log class until 1987, because CPSR was the largest known class of serializable logs in P. However in 1987 a new class of serializable logs in P, called the class WRW is introduced and it is proved that the class WRW is a proper superset of the class CPSR. Almost at the same time the class HD is introduced and it is proved that HD is a proper superset of the class WRW, which makes the HD class the largest known serializable log class in P.

7.3 DATABASE SYSTEM MODEL

A database is a structured collection of data items, denoted {...,x,y,z} that can be accessed concurrently by several transactions. The size of the data contained in a data item is called the granularity of data item. The granularity is not important for the scope of this study and practically it could be chosen as a file, a record of a file, a field of a record or a page of a disk. The values of the data items at any time comprise the state of the database. A Database System (DBS) is a collection of software and hardware modules that supports the operations performed by the transactions. Users interact with the DBS through transactions. A transaction interacts with the outside world by issuing only read and write operations to the DBS or by doing terminal I/O.

Users access data items by issuing Read and Write operations. A transaction, denoted by Ti, is a set of operations on data items that transforms a database from one consistent state to another. That is, transactions are assumed to be complete and correct computation units and if each transaction is executed alone on an initially consistent database, would terminate, produce correct results and leave database in a consistent state.

A DBS simply consists of the following modules: Transaction manager (TM), Data Manager (DM) and Scheduler (Figure 7.2). A Distributed Database System (DDBS) is a collection of sites connected by a communication network and each site is simply a DBS. However in DDBSs each site runs one or more of the following software modules: a TM, a DM or a Scheduler. In DDBSs the schedulers may be distributed, that is there may be a local scheduler at each site. However the local schedulers must cooperate for the consistency of the database. The distributed schedulers must behave as if there is a global

scheduler in the system (Figure 7.3). TM performs the preprocessing of the operations it receives from transactions and DM manages the actual database while the scheduler controls the relative order in which these operations are executed.

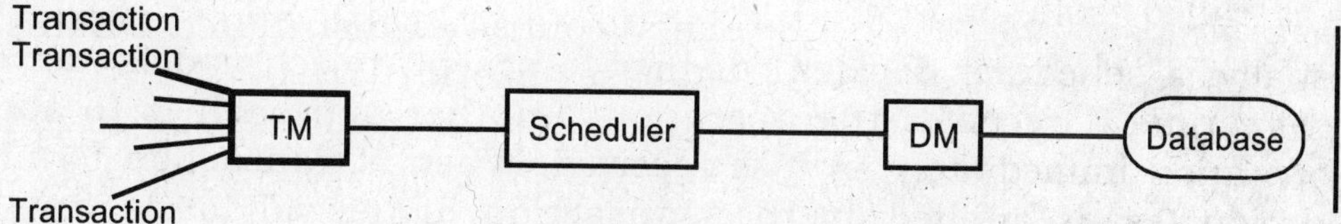

Figure 7.2: Database System Model

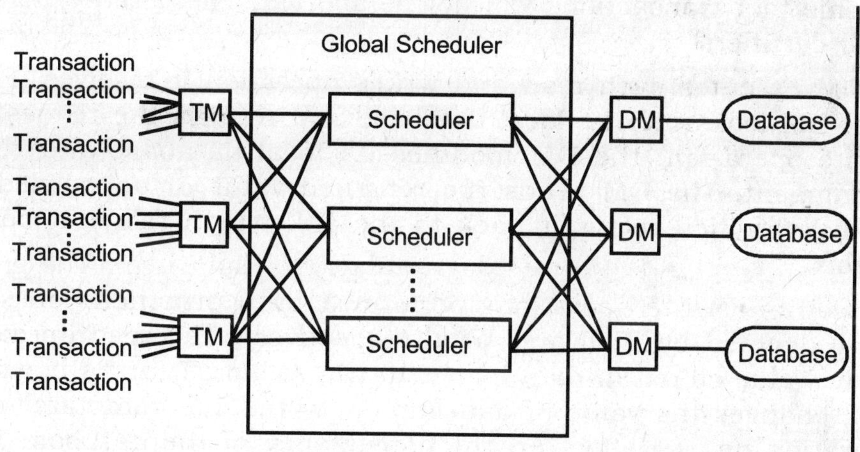

Figure 7.3: Distributed Database System Model

Each transaction issues its operations to a single TM, which receives the operations issued by transactions and forwards them to the scheduler. In DDBSs, the TM is also responsible for determining which scheduler should process the operation submitted by a transaction.

The scheduler is responsible for the consistency of the database. However, a scheduler does not pay attention to the computations performed by the transactions, it makes its decision solely by considering the type of the operations and the data items related to the operations. The scheduler controls the order in which DMs process the read and write operations. When a scheduler receives a read or a write operation, it can either output the operation to the related DM, or delay the operation by holding it for later action, or reject the operation. If an operation of a transaction is rejected, then the transaction should be aborted. Furthermore, every transaction that read a value written by the aborted transaction should also be aborted. This, phenomenon, where an abortion triggers other abortions is called cascading aborts

and it is usually avoided by not allowing a transaction Ti to read another transaction Tj's output until Tj is committed, that is, until the DBS is certain that the transaction Tj will not be aborted. Therefore, an incomplete transaction can not reveal its results to other transactions before its commitment, which is called isolation.

Usually, a scheduler decides whether to accept, reject or delay an operation every time it receives the operation. Another approach is to schedule each operation immediately as it is received. When a transaction terminates, a validation test is applied on the transaction. If the validation test terminates successfully then the transaction is committed, otherwise it is aborted. Such schedulers are called the optimistic schedulers because they optimistically assume that transactions will not be aborted. These schedulers are also called the certifiers.

The DM executes each read and writes operation it receives. For a read operation, DM looks into its local database and returns the requested value. For a write operation, the DM modifies its local database and returns an acknowledgment. The DM sends the returned value or acknowledgment to the scheduler, which relays it back to the TM, which relays it back to the transaction.

The read and write operations performed by transactions on some data item x are denoted by Ri[x] and Wi[x] respectively. The read operation Ri[x] returns the value stored in data item x to transaction Ti and the write operation Wi[x] changes the value of data item x to the one computed by Ti. The read operation has no effect on the consistency of the database. However, since the write operations update the values of the data items, they cause a change in the state of the database. Two operations belonging to different transactions conflict if they operate on the same data item and one of them is a write. The read set, denoted by S(Ri), of a transaction is the set of data items a transaction reads and the write set of a transaction, denoted S(Wi), is the set of data items a transaction writes. The access set or the base set of a transaction is the union of its read and its write sets. When two or more transactions execute concurrently, their operations are executed in an interleaved fashion.

Each transaction starts with a begin operation and ends with a commit or abort operation. Commit indicates that the transaction has completed its execution and the effects of the transaction on the database, that is every write operation processed on behalf of the transaction, should be made permanent. Abort indicates that the transaction has completed abnormally and its effects should be undone by restoring the old values of the data item.

The most common commitment protocol is two phase commitment (2PC). In the fist phase of 2PC, the values of data items in the write set of the

transaction are copied into the secure storage at the related sites without overwriting the old values. If the first phase terminates successfully, the transaction commits and it cannot be aborted from this point on. Then the commit message is sent to the related sites and the effects of the transaction are made permanent by writing the values from the secure storage into the actual database. If a failure occurs during the first phase of 2PC, the transaction is aborted by simply omitting the values copied into the secure storage. If the transactions fail during the second phase of 2PC, there is no need for abortion, however the values copied into the secure storage are written into the actual database when the failed site awakes By the use of 2PC, cascading aborts are also avoided, because the write operations are applied into the database only when the transactions commit.

Let T={T0, T1, ..Tn} be a set of transactions. A Log (or History) is an execution where the operations of the transactions are interleaved such that the orders of the operations within the transactions are preserved.

For example, for T={T1,T2} let

T1= B1 R1[x] R1[y] W1[x] E1

T2= B2 R2[x] W2[x] E2,

Here the operations Bi and Ei i=1,2 are used to denote the beginning and the end of the transactions. Some possible logs over T may be

L1= B1 R1[x] R1[y] B2 R2[x] W1[x] E1 W2[x] E2 or

L2= B2 R2[x] B1 R1[x] R1[y] W1[x] E1 W2[x] E2.

However the execution

B2 R2[x] B1 R1[y] R1[x] W1[x] E1 W2[x] E2

is not a log over T since the order of the operations R11=R1[x] and R12=R1[y] of T1 is not preserved.

Let L be a log over some set T and suppose Wi[x] and Rj[x] are operations in L. We say that Tj reads x from Ti if Wi[x]<Rj[x], (i.e. Wi precedes Rj) and no Wk[x] falls between Wi[x] and Rj[x]. In log

L3 = W0[x] R1[x] W2[x] R3[x] R4[x],

where begin and end operations are not shown for simplicity, T1 reads x from T0 and T3 and T4 reads x from T2.

We call Wi[x], a final write in L if no Wk[x] follows it. In log

L4= W0[x] R2[x] W1[y] W2[y],

W0[x] and W2[y] are final writes.

Two logs over T are equivalent if they represent the same computation, which is in both logs each transaction reads the value written by the same transaction and they have the same final writes.

To consider the initial values of the data items, logs are augmented by an initial transaction Ts, which initially writes all the data items and to consider the effect of final writes, logs are augmented by a final transaction Tf which finally reads all the data items. When the initial and final transactions are augmented log L4 becomes

L4a= Ws[x] Ws[y] W0[x] R2[x] W1[y] W2[y] Rf[x] Rf[y]

Two logs are equivalent if they have the same read from relations when they are augmented by initial and final transactions.

The log L4 is equivalent to log

L5= W0[x] W1[y] R2[x] W2[y],

because they have the same transaction set L4a and L5a have the same read_from relations. However L4 is not equivalent to log

L6= R2[x] W0[x] W2[y] W1[y],

since, T2 reads x from T0 in L4a, but from Ts in L6a and also Tf reads y from T2 in L4a, but from T1 in L6a.

A log is serializable if there exists an equivalent serial log.

The log L4 is serializable because it is equivalent to L5 which is serial. Notice that in L5 the operations of the transactions are not interleaved.

7.4 TWO PHASE LOCKING METHOD

The two phase locking (2PL) schedulers are the most popular type of schedulers in commercial products. In 2PL technique two types of locks, which are the read lock and the write lock, are used on the data items. The read lock is a shared type of lock whereas the write lock is an exclusive type. That is, a transaction can have a read lock on a data item only if there is no write lock on the data item by any other transaction and a transaction can have a write lock on a data item only if there is no read lock or write lock on the data item by any other transaction.

In a database system having 2PL mechanism for the concurrency control, each transaction obeys the following rules:

- a transaction does not request a read or write lock on a data item if it already has that type of lock on that data item;
- a transaction must have a read lock on a data item before reading the data item and it must have a write lock on a data item before writing the data item;
- a transaction does not request any lock after it has released a lock.

Each transaction obeying the third rule has two phases; this is the reason why the technique is called two phase locking. During the first phase,

which is called the growing phase, a transaction obtains its locks without releasing any lock. The point at the end of the growing phase, when a transaction owns all the locks it will ever own, is called the locked point of the transaction. During the second phase, which is called the shrinking phase, the transaction releases the locks it has obtained in the first phase. It should be noted that a transaction can not request a lock in the shrinking phase. When the transaction terminates all the locks obtained by the transaction are released. The locked points of the transactions in a log L determine the serialization order of the transactions.

Two phase locking is sufficient to preserve serializability. However 2PL is not sufficient to preserve isolation. If a transaction Ti releases some of its write locks before its commitment, then some other transaction Tj may read this value. In the case Ti is aborted, Tj and all the other transactions which have read some data item from Ti should also be aborted. In order to guarantee isolation, transactions are required to hold all of their locks until their commitment at the termination.

The log

L7= Ba Ra[x] Bb Rb[y] Wa[x] Ea Wb[x] Wb[y] Eb

is in the class 2PL, all the operations are accepted by the 2PL scheduler without any change on the order. On the other hand, the log

L8= Ba Ra[x] Bb Rb[x] Wa[x] Wa[y] Ea Wb[y] Eb

is not in the class 2PL, since Ta can not obtain the write lock on x before Tb have released it, which is released at Eb operation. 2PL scheduler do not accept Wa[x] request, but blocks it, therefore the output of the 2PL scheduler for L8 will be

L8_2PL= Ba Ra[x] Bb Rb[x] Wb[y] Eb Wa[x] Wa[y] Ea

The deadlock is the most important problem to be handled when a locking scheme is used for concurrency control. A scheduler must be able to discover whether there is a deadlock in the system. In the case of deadlock, one of the transactions in the deadlock state should be chosen as a victim and should be aborted. Deadlocks can be detected by using wait_for graphs or timeouts.

The nodes of the wait_for graph are the transactions and there is an edge from Ti to Tj if and only if the transaction Ti is waiting for a lock, which is held by the transaction Tj. The wait_for graph is cyclic if there is a deadlock in the system, otherwise it is acyclic. In distributed database systems, there may be a system wide deadlock although there is no deadlock when each site in the system is considered separately. Therefore a global deadlock detection mechanism, which requires execution of more complex algorithms, is necessary for the distributed database systems. For global deadlock detection, either each site periodically sends their local wait_for graph to the site having a global

deadlock detector, where a global wait_for graph is constructed by combining the local wait_for graphs, or the information about the paths in the local wait_for graph is sent to the related sited as necessary. Global deadlock detection requires the transmission of many messages among the sites, which is an important portion of communication cost. Furthermore in some situations, although there is no deadlock in the system, the system may decide that there is a deadlock. This phenomenon is called the phantom deadlock and the reason is the delay between the occurrence of the events and the processing time of the messages.

Starvation or livelock is another problem which arises in the case when a transaction is selected as victim repeatedly. Such a transaction may not have the opportunity to finish.

Most of the systems use timeouts for deadlock detection instead of the wait_for graph because of the simplicity of the timeout technique. With the timeout technique, if a transaction waits for a lock to be released longer than a predetermined timeout period, then it is assumed that there is a deadlock in the system and the transaction waiting longer than the timeout period is aborted. In fact, with timeout technique, the existence of a deadlock is only guessed, it is not an actual deadlock detection mechanism. Therefore, the length of the timeout period should be tuned well. If the timeout period is too short, then most of the time, it is decided that there is a deadlock in the system although actually there is not, which results in unnecessary abortions. If the timeout period is chosen too long, transactions stay in deadlock state for a long time until it is decided that there is a deadlock, which results in decrease in the system performance. The starvation problem still remains with the timeout scheme.

Although it is not widely used in distributed systems, deadlock prevention by assigning priorities to the transactions is another solution to the deadlock problem. The priorities of transactions may be decided by considering their submission time to the system. The transaction submitted earlier has greater priority. Assume a transaction Ti waits for a lock which is held by transaction Tj. Wait_die is a strategy which allows Ti to wait only if the priority of Ti is greater than Tj, otherwise Ti is aborted. Another strategy is wound_wait, which allows Ti to wait only if the priority of Ti is less than the priority of Tj, otherwise Tj is aborted. If the priority of an aborted transaction is not updated when it is restarted, the transaction becomes older as time passes, and its priority increases. Therefore the starvation problem is solved by the wait_die and the wound_wait strategies, because these strategies never abort the transactions having higher priorities. As in the time out technique, transactions may be aborted although there is no deadlock.

Deadlock prevention by preordering of the data items is not applicable to 2PL, because in general it is assumed that there is no a priori knowledge about the data items in the read set and write sets of the transactions. The read set and the write set of a transaction are revealed as the transaction is executed. Also the deadlock avoidance techniques are not applicable with the same reasoning.

7.5 TIME STAMP ORDERING METHODS

The time stamp ordering (TO) technique is based on the idea that an operation is allowed to proceed only if all the conflicting operations of older transactions have already been processed. Thus the serializability of the transactions is preserved. This requires knowledge about which transactions are younger than the others.

In the implementation of a distributed timing system, each site in the distributed system contains a local clock or a counter which is used as a clock. The clock is assumed to tick at least once between any two events. Therefore the events within the site are totally ordered. For total ordering of the events at different sites, each site is assigned a unique number and this number is concatenated as least significant bits to the current value of the local clock. Furthermore, each message contains the information about the local time of their site of origin at which the message is sent. Upon receiving a message, the local clock at the receiver site is advanced to be later than the time informed by the message.

In a distributed system having such a clock facility, a timestamp, denoted by TS(A), is assigned to an event A, which is the local time at which the event occurs concatenated with the site identifier. TS(A) uniquely identifies the event itself and for any two events A and B, if event A has happened before the event B, then TS(A) < TS(B).

In timestamp ordering technique, each transaction Ti is assigned a unique timestamp TS(Ti). Each operation issued by the transaction Ti is also assigned the same timestamp TS(Ti) and the conflicting operations are executed in the order of their timestamps. That is the transactions obey the rule known as the TO rule, which states that if pi[x] and qj[x] are conflicting operations belonging to different transactions Ti and Tj, then pi is to be executed before qj iff TS(Ti) < TS(Tj).

Therefore, the transactions are processed such that their execution is equivalent to the execution of a serial log, where the transactions are ordered in the order of their timestamps.

There are several concurrency control methods based on timestamp ordering technique. In the basic timestamp ordering (BTO) method, for each data item x, the largest timestamp of any read operation on data item x and the largest timestamp of any write operation on data item x, which are de-

noted by R_TS(x) and W_TS(x) respectively, are stored along with the data item itself. The BTO scheduler processes a Ri[x] operation if W_TS(x) £ TS(Ti), otherwise Ri[x] is rejected and Ti is aborted. If Ri[x] is not rejected, then it is processed by reading the value of the data item and by setting R_TS(x) to MAX(R_TS(x),TS(Ti)). Similarly BTO scheduler process a Wi[x] operation if R_TS(x) £ TS(Ti) and W_TS(x) £ TS(Ti), otherwise Wi[x] operation is rejected and Ti is aborted. Any Wi[x] operation is processed by updating the value of the data item x and by setting W_TS(x) to MAX(W_TS(x),TS(Ti)). Aborted transactions are restarted by assigning new timestamps.

The log

L9=B1 R1[x] B2 R2[y] W2[y] E2 R1[y] W1[x] E1

is not allowed by the BTO scheduler, since B1<B2 implies that TS1<TS2 and BTO scheduler aborts T1 although the log is serializable. However the log

L10= B1 R1[x] B2 R2[y] R1[y] W2[y] E2 W1[x] E1

can be output of the BTO scheduler without any change on the order of the operations.

It may be assumed that transactions are assigned timestamps when their first operation appears in the execution, that is, the timestamps preserve the order of the first read operations of the transactions, BTO method can further be improved by ignoring the obsolete writes. Let operations Wi[x] and Wm[x] belong to transactions Ti and Tm respectively such that TS(Ti)<TS(Tm). If the scheduler receives the operation Wi[x] after Wm[x] is already processed, then the late operation Wi[x] will be rejected by BTO scheduler, because W_TS(x) would be at least TS(Tm) which is greater than TS(Ti). However in the case R_TS(x) £ TS(Ti), this rejection is unnecessary. If Wi[x] had come before Wm[x], no other transaction by then have read the value written by Wi[x], which is obvious by the fact R_TS(x)TS(Ti), and since Wm[x] then would have overwritten the value written by Wi[x], no other transaction could have the chance to read the value written by Wi[x]. Therefore the operation Wi[x] is obsolete. The result of considering Wi[x] before Wm[x] should be the same as considering Wm[x] only and ignoring Wi[x]. Therefore in such situations Wi[x] may simply be ignored instead of rejecting it, which is known as Thomas' write rule (TWR). Therefore any Wi[x] operation can be scheduled by the use of TWR as follows: If TS(Ti) < R_TS(x) then Wi[x] is rejected, otherwise if W_TS(x)<TS(Ti) then Wi[x] is processed else it is ignored.

In log

L11_BTO = B1 R1[x] B2 R2[y] W2[x] E2 (W1[x]) E1,

the operation W1[x] is ignored by Thomas' Write Rule, and assumed as it is executed before W2[x] operation.

The basic timestamp ordering technique is easy to distribute and the transactions to be aborted are immediately recognized when the operations

are being scheduled. There is no deadlock problem, because the locks are not used and operations are not blocked. However to provide for the reliability, an atomic commitment mechanism is necessary. Extra space is wasted for the read and writes timestamps of the data items. Furthermore many transactions are aborted unnecessarily because of a priori selection of timestamps.

7.6 SERIALIZATION GRAPH TESTING METHOD (SGT OR CPSR)

The serialization graph for a log L, denoted by SG(L), is a directed graph, where the nodes are the transactions in the log. In SG(L) there is an edge from node Ti to Tj if and only if pi[x] and qj[x] are conflicting operations belonging to transactions Ti and Tj respectively and the operation pi[x] precedes qj[x] in the log.

A serialization graph testing (SGT) or conflict preserving serializability (CPSR) scheduler works by explicitly building a serialization graph. When SGT scheduler receives an operation pi[x], it adds the node Ti into the graph if Ti does not already exist in the graph, and then it adds an edge from Tj to Ti for every previously scheduled operation qj[x] that conflict with pi[x]. If the resulting graph is cyclic, then the operation pi[x] is rejected, transaction Ti is aborted and the serialization graph is modified by removing all the edges coming in or out of the node Ti and by removing also node Ti itself.

The log

L12=B1 R1[x] B2 R2[x] W1[x] E1 B3 R3[x] W2[x] E2 W3[y] E3

is not allowed by SGT scheduler, since SG(L12) is cyclic (Figure 7.4.)

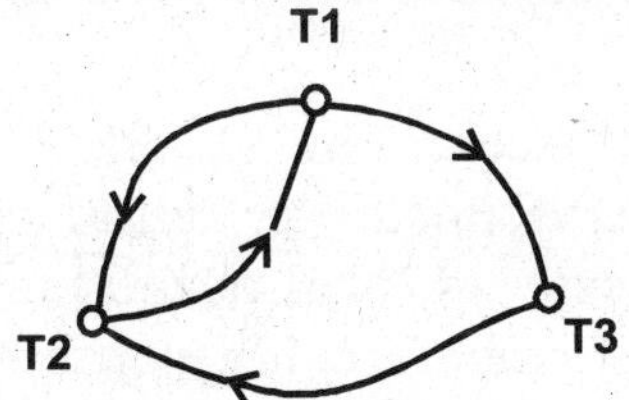

Figure 7.4: SG(H12)

While 2PL and BTO mechanisms totally order the scheduled transactions, the SGT mechanism partially order them. This is the reason why any log which can be handled by 2PL scheduler or BTO scheduler successfully, can also be handled by the SGT scheduler.

Although SGT method provides more concurrency than 2PL and BTO methods, it is not practical to implement the SGT mechanism in the distributed database systems. The problems are similar to the problems in distributed deadlock detection, that is, it is necessary to check the cycles of the serialization graph. If each scheduler maintains a local serialization graph which

reflects only the conflicts on the data items it manages, then local serialization graph may not be cyclic, although the global serialization graph, which reflects all the conflicts in the system, is cyclic. Therefore the local serialization graphs should be combined at a scheduler site to construct the global serialization graph. Such a scheme results in high communication cost and the delay caused by message transmissions are more drastically than in the case of deadlock detection. Furthermore, it is not that easy to handle a crash of the scheduler site.

Another solution for handling global serialization graph is achieved by holding the immediate successors of each transaction at the home site and by distributing the graph by the use of messages containing this information. However if global cycles are likely to occur, again it is quite expensive to search the whole graph in this way.

7.7 OVERVIEW OF CONCURRENCY CONTROL AND RECOVERY IN DISTRIBUTED DATABASES

For concurrency control and recovery purposes, numerous problems arise in distributed DBMS environments that are not encountered in a centralized DBMS environment.

These include the following:

- **Dealing with multiple copies of the data items:** The concurrency control method is responsible for maintaining consistency among these copies. The recovery method is responsible for making a copy consistent with other copies if the site on which the copy is stored fails and recovers later.
- **Failure of individual sites:** The DDBMS should continue to operate with its running sites, if possible, when one or more individual sites fail. When a site recovers, its local database must be brought up to date with the rest of the sites before it rejoins the system.
- **Failure of communication links:** The system must be able to deal with failure of one or more of the communication links that connect the sites. An extreme case of this problem is that **network partitioning** may occur. This breaks up the sites into two or more partitions, where the sites within each partition can communicate only with one another and not with sites in other partitions.
- **Distributed commit:** Problems can arise with committing a transaction that is accessing databases stored on multiple sites if some sites fail during the commit process. The **two-phase commit protocol** is often used to deal with this problem.

- **Distributed deadlock:** Deadlock may occur among several sites, so techniques for dealing with deadlocks must be extended to take this into account.

Distributed concurrency control and recovery techniques must deal with these and other problems. In the following subsections, we review some of the techniques that have been suggested to deal with recovery and concurrency control in DDBMSs.

7.7.1 DISTRIBUTED CONCURRENCY CONTROL BASED ON A DISTINGUISHED COPY OF A DATA ITEM

Primary Site Technique Primary Site with Backup Site Primary Copy Technique Choosing a New Coordinator Site in Case of Failure

To deal with replicated data items in a distributed database, a number of concurrency control methods have been proposed that extend the concurrency control techniques for centralized databases. We discuss these techniques in the context of extending centralized *locking.* Similar extensions apply to other concurrency control techniques. The idea is to designate *a particular copy* of each data item as a **distinguished copy.** The locks for this data item are associated *with the distinguished copy,* and all locking and unlocking requests are sent to the site that contains that copy.

A number of different methods are based on this idea, but they differ in their method of choosing the distinguished copies. In the **primary site technique,** all distinguished copies are kept at the same site. A modification of this approach is the primary site with a **backup site.** Another approach is the **primary copy** method, where the distinguished copies of the various data items can be stored in different sites. A site that includes a distinguished copy of a data item basically acts as the **coordinator site** for concurrency control on that item. We discuss these techniques next.

1. **Primary Site Technique:** In this method a single **primary site** is designated to be the **coordinator site** *for all database items.* Hence, all locks are kept at that site, and all requests for locking or unlocking are sent there. This method is thus an extension of the centralized locking approach. For example, if all transactions follow the two-phase locking protocol, serializability is guaranteed. The advantage of this approach is that it is a simple extension of the centralized approach and hence is not overly complex. However, it has certain inherent disadvantages. One is that all locking requests are sent to a single site, possibly overloading that site and causing a system bottleneck. A second disadvantage is that failure of the primary site paralyzes the system, since all locking information is kept at that site. This can limit system reliability and availability.

Although all locks are accessed at the primary site, the items themselves can be accessed at any site at which they reside. For example, once a transaction obtains a read_lock on a data item from the primary site, it can access any copy of that data item. However, once a transaction obtains a write_lock and updates a data item, the DDBMS is responsible for updating *all copies* of the data item before releasing the lock.

2. **Primary Site with Backup Site:** This approach addresses the second disadvantage of the primary site method by designating a second site to be a **backup site.** All locking information is maintained at both the primary and the backup sites. In case of primary site failure, the backup site takes over as primary site, and a new backup site is chosen. This simplifies the process of recovery from failure of the primary site, since the backup site takes over and processing can resume after a new backup site is chosen and the lock status information is copied to that site. It slows down the process of acquiring locks, however, because all lock requests and granting of locks must be recorded at *both the primary and the backup sites* before a response is sent to the requesting transaction. The problem of the primary and backup sites becoming overloaded with requests and slowing down the system remains undiminished.
3. **Primary Copy Technique:** This method attempts to distribute the load of lock coordination among various sites by having the distinguished copies of different data items *stored at different sites.* Failure of one site affects any transactions that are accessing locks on items whose primary copies reside at that site, but other transactions are not affected. This method can also use backup sites to enhance reliability and availability.
4. **Choosing a New Coordinator Site in Case of Failure:** Whenever a coordinator site fails in any of the preceding techniques, the sites that are still running must choose a new coordinator. In the case of the primary site approach with *no* backup site, all executing transactions must be aborted and restarted in a tedious recovery process. Part of the recovery process involves choosing a new primary site and creating a lock manager process and a record of all lock information at that site. For methods that use backup sites, transaction processing is suspended copies of all the locking information from the new primary site.

If a backup site X is about to become the new primary site, X can choose the new backup site from among the system's running sites. However, if no backup site existed, or if both the primary and the backup sites are down, a process called **election** can be used to choose the new coordinator site. In this process, any site Y that attempts to communicate with the coordinator

site repeatedly and fails to do so can assume that the coordinator is down and can start the election process by sending a message to all running sites proposing that Y become the new coordinator. As soon as Y receives a majority of yes votes, Y can declare that it is the new coordinator. The election algorithm itself is quite complex, but this is the main idea behind the election method. The algorithm also resolves any attempt by two or more sites to become coordinator at the same time. The references in the Selected Bibliography at the end of this chapter discuss the process in detail.

7.7.2 DISTRIBUTED CONCURRENCY CONTROL BASED ON VOTING

The concurrency control methods for replicated items discussed earlier all use the idea of a distinguished copy that maintains the locks for that item. In the **voting method,** there is no distinguished copy; rather, a lock request is sent to all sites that include a copy of the data item. Each copy maintains its own lock and can grant or deny the request for it. If a transaction that requests a lock is granted that lock by *a majority* of the copies, it holds the lock and informs *all copies* that it has been granted the lock. If a transaction does not receive a majority of votes granting it a lock within a certain *time-out period,* it cancels its request and informs all sites of the cancellation.

The voting method is considered a truly distributed concurrency control method, since the responsibility for a decision resides with all the sites involved. Simulation studies have shown that voting has higher message traffic among sites than do the distinguished copy methods. If the algorithm takes into account possible site failures during the voting process, it becomes extremely complex.

7.8 ANOMALIES OF CONCURRENCY CONTROL

The concurrency control is used to prevent interference among users who are simultaneously accessing a database. Here we can introduce the different anomalies that can arise owing to concurrent accesses of data in a multiuser centralized database environment as well as in a distributed database environment. In addition, in a DDBMS an extra problem can arise, namely, multiple-copy consistency problem, as data items may be replicated in distributed databases.

There are mainly five anomalies of concurrency control can be explained below:

1. Lost update anomaly
2. Uncommitted dependency or dirty read anomaly
3. Inconsistent analysis anomaly
4. Non-repeatable or fuzzy read anomaly

5. Phantom read anomaly

1. **Lost update anomaly:** This anomaly can occur when an apparently successful completed update operation made by one transaction is overridden by another transaction. For example, Consider an online electronic funds transfer system accessed via remote automated teller machine (ATMs). Assume that one customer (T_1) is withdrawing Rs.500 from an account with balance B, initially Rs.2,000, while another customer (T_2) is depositing an amount Rs.600 into the same account via ATM from a different place. If these two tasks are executed serially, then the balance B will be Rs.2,100. Further assume that both the tasks are started nearly at the same time and both read the same value Rs.2,000. Due to concurrent access to the same data item, when customer T_1 is decrementing the value of B to Rs.1,500, customer T_2 is incrementing the value of B to Rs.2,100. Thus, update to the data item B made by customer T_1 will be overridden by the customer T_2. Here, the consistency of the data is violated owing to this anomaly, known as lost update anomaly.

2. **Uncommitted dependency or dirty read anomaly:** This anomaly occurs when one transaction allows other transactions to read its data before it has committed and then decided to abort. For example, Suppose two transactions T_1 and T_2 are concurrently accessing an Employee database. The transaction T_1 is updating the salary of an employee by 10 percent whose basic salary is sal_{x1} initially Rs.5,000, while transaction T_2 is calculating tax deduction for the same employee depending on his basic salary sal_x. Transaction T_1 changes the value of sal_x to Rs.5,500, allows transaction T_2 to read this value before transaction T_1 has committed, and then decides to abort. Since transaction T_1 is aborted, sal_x should be restored to its original value Rs.5,000. However transaction T_2 has read the new value of sal_x and calculates the tax deduction depending on this new value Rs.5,500 instead of Rs.5,000. The value of sal_x read by the transaction T_2 is called dirty data, which leads to uncommitted dependency or dirty read anomaly. This problem can be avoided by preventing transaction T_2 from reading the new value of sal_x updated by transaction T_1, until the decision has been made to either commit or abort transaction T_1.

3. **Inconsistent analysis anomaly:** The anomaly of inconsistent analysis occurs when a transaction reads several values from the database but a second transaction updates some of them during the execution of the first. For example, suppose the banking system in which two transactions T_1 and T_2 are accessing the database concurrently. The transaction T_1 is calculating the average balance of all customers of a particu-

lar branch while the transaction T_2 is depositing Rs.1,000 into one customer account with balance bal_x at the same time. Hence, the average balance calculated by the transaction T_1 is incorrect, because the transaction T_2 incremented and updated the balance of one customer during the executing the transaction T_1. This anomaly, known as inconsistent analysis anomaly, can be avoided by preventing the transaction T_2 from reading and updating the value of bal_x until the transaction T_1 completes its execution.

4. **Non-repeatable or fuzzy read anomaly:** Fuzzy read or non-repeatable read anomaly occurs when one transaction reads the value of an item that is subsequently modified or deleted by another transaction. If the first transaction attempts to re-read the data item either that data item may not be found or it may read a different value.

   For example, suppose in the employee database, one transaction T_1 reads the salary of an employee while another transaction T_2 is updating the salary of the same employee (or the same employee record is deleted from the employee database by the transaction T_2) concurrently. Now, if the transactionT_1 attempts to re-read the value of the salary of the same employee, it will read a different value (or that record will be not found) since employee database is updated by the transaction T_2. Thus, two read operations within the same transaction T_1 return different values. This anomaly occurs due to concurrent access of the same data item, known as fuzzy read anomaly.

5. **Phantom read anomaly:** This anomaly occurs when a transaction performing some operation on the database based on a selection predicate another transaction inserts new tuples satisfying that predicate into the same database. For example, suppose that in the employee database, one transaction T_1 retrieves all employees belonging to the R&D department while another transaction T_2 inserts new employees into that department. Hence, if the transaction T_1 re-executes the same operation, then the retrieved data set will contain additional (phantom) tuples that has been inserted by the transaction T_2 in the meantime.

Above anomalies multiple-copy consistency problem can arise in a distributed database system as a results of data distribution. This problem occurs when data item are replicated and stored at different locations in a DDBMS. To maintain the consistency of the global database, when a replicated data item is updated at one site, all other copies of the same data item must be updated. If any copy is not updated the database becomes inconsistent. The updates of the replicated data items are carried out either synchronously to preserve the consistency of the data.

7.9 OBJECTIVES OF DISTRIBUTED CONCURRENCY CONTROL

Concurrency control is the activity of coordinating concurrent accesses to a dataset in a multi-user system. Concurrency control allows users to access a database in a multi-programmed fashion while preserving the consistency of the data.

Main technical difficulty in achieving this goal is the necessity to prevent dataset updates performed by one user from interfering with database retrievals and updated performed by other users.

The concurrency control problem is exacerbated in a distributed DBMS (DDBMS), because in a distributed system users may access data stored at many different sites, and a concurrency control mechanism at one site cannot be aware of transactions at other sites instantaneously. The replication of data items in a distributed database adds extra complexity to the concurrency control mechanism. In this context, it is necessary to discuss the objectives of concurrency control mechanism in a distributed database environment.

Like in centralized DBMSs, the primary goal of the concurrency control mechanism in a DDBMS is to ensure that the consistency of the data items is preserved and each atomic action will be completed in a finite time if the system has not failed.

In addition, a good concurrency control mechanism for a DDBMS has the following objectives:

- Must be resilient to site communication failures.
- Should permit parallel execution to transactions to achieve maximum concurrency, thus satisfying performance requirements.
- Computational methods and storage mechanisms should be modest to minimize overhead.
- Should perform satisfactorily in a network environment taking into consideration that it involves significant communication delay.
- Must impose few constraints on the structure of atomic actions of transactions.

7.10 OVERVIEW OF SERILIZABILITY IN A DISTRIBUTED DATABASE

In distributed database, each transaction performs operations at several sites. The sequence of operations performed by transactions at a site is a local schedule. An execution of n distributed transactions T_1, T_2,...., T_n at m sites is modeled by a set of local schedules S1, S2, ..., S_m.

If we apply at each node a local concurrency control mechanism, we can ensure that all local schedules are serializable. However, the serializability

of local schedules is not sufficient to ensure the correctness of the execution of a set of distributed transactions. Consider, for example, the following two schedules

S1 (site 1): $R_i(x)$ $W_i(x)$ $R_j(x)$ $W_j(x)$

S2 (site 2): $R_j(y)$ $W_j(y)$ $R_i(y)$ $W_i(y)$

Both local schedules are serial; however, there is no global serial sequence of execution of both transactions because $T_i < T_j$ in Serial(S1) and $T_j < T_i$ in Serial(S2). In order to guarantee the serializability of distributed transactions, a stronger condition than the serializability of local schedules is required.

The execution of transactions T_i, ..., T_n is correct if:

1. Each local schedule Sk is serializable
2. There exists a total ordering of T_1, ..., $T\text{-}_n$ such that ,if $T_i < T_j$ in the total ordering, tyhen there is a serial schedule Sk' such that Sk is equivalent to Sk' and $T_i < T_j$ in Serial(Sk'),for each site k where both transactions have executed some action

The above condition can be expressed using the notion of conflicts.

Proposition 8.1

Let T_1,....,T_n be a set transactions, and let E be an execution of these transactions modeled by schedules S1, ...,Sm. E is correct (serializable) if there exists a total ordering of the transactions such that for each pair of conflicting operations O_i and o_j from transactions T_i and T_j, respectively, O_i precedes O_j in any schedule S1,....,Sm if and only if T_i precedes T_j in the total ordering.

We will use proposition 8.1 in order to determine whether an execution of distributed transactions is correct. A distributed concurrency control mechanism is correct if it allows only correct executions of distributed transactions.

7.10.1 DISTRIBUTED SERIALIZABILITY

Transactions can be consist of a sequence of read and write operations together with some computation steps that represents a single logical unit of work in a database environment. All the operations of transaction are units of atomicity; that is, either all the operations should be completed successful or none of them are carried out at all. Ozsu has defined a formal notation for the transaction concept. According to this formalization, a transaction Ti is a partial ordering of its operations and the termination condition. The partial order $P = \{\Sigma, \alpha\}$ defines an ordering among the elements of Σ (called the domain(, where Σ consists of the read and write operations and the termination condition (abort, commit) of the transaction Ti, and a indicates the execution order of these operations within Ti. The execution or execution order-

ing of operations of a transaction is called the schedule. Let E denote an execution sequence of transactions T_1, T_2, ..., T_n,. E is a serial execution or serial schedule if no transactions execute concurrently in E; that is, each transaction is executed to completion before the next one begins. Every serial execution or serial schedule is deemed to be correct, because the properties of transactions imply that a serial execution terminates properly and preserves database consistency. An execution is said to be a non-serial execution or non-serial schedule if the operations from a set of concurrent transactions execute simultaneously. A non-serial schedule (or execution) is serializable if it is computationally equivalent to a serial schedule, which is, if it produces the same result and has the same effect on the database as some serial execution. To prevent data inconsistency, it is essential to guarantee serializability of concurrent transactions. In serializability, the ordering of read and write operations are important. It is necessary to introduce the concept of conflicting transactions. If two transactions perform read or write operations on different data items, then they are not conflicting, and hence the execution order is not important. If two transactions perform read operation on the same data item, then they are non-conflicting. Two transactions are said to be conflicting if they access the same data item concurrently, and at least one transaction performs a write operation. Concurrent read-write operations by two transactions are conflicting. The execution order is important if there is a conflicting operation caused by two transactions. If concurrent accesses of data items are allowed in a database environment, then the schedule may be non-serial, which indicated that the consistency of data may be violated. To allow maximum concurrency and to preserve the consistency of data, it is sometimes possible to generate a schedule from a non-serial schedule that is equivalent to a serial schedule or serial execution order by swapping the order of the non-conflicting operations. If schedule S_1 is derived from a non-serial schedule S_2 by swapping the execution order of non-conflicting operations in S_2, and if S_1 produces the same output as that of a serial schedule S_3 with the same set of transactions, then S_1 is called a serializable schedule. This type of serializability is known as conflict serializability and Schedule S_1 is said to be conflict equivalent to schedule S_2. A conflict serializable schedule orders any conflicting operations in the same way as a serial execution. A directed precedence graph or a serialization graph can be produced to test for conflict serializability. Serializability theory for centralized databases can be extending in a straightforward manner for distributed non-replicated databases. In a distributed system, each local site maintains a schedule or execution order of transactions or subtransactions (part of a global transaction) running at that site, called local schedule. The global schedule or global execution order is the union of all local schedules in a non-replicated distributed database system. Hence, if each local site maintains serializability, then the global schedule also becomes serialization as

the local serialization orders are identical. Replication of data items in a distributed system adds extra complexity in maintaining global serializability or distributed serializability. In this case also, it is possible that local schedules are serializable, but mutual consistency of the replicated data items may not be preserved owing to the conflicting operations on the same data item at multiple sites. Thus, a distributed schedule or global schedule (the union of all local schedules) is said to be distributed serializable if the execution order at each local site is serializable and the local serialization orders are identical. This requires that all subtransactions appear in the same order in the equivalent serial schedule at all sites.

For example, consider a simple transaction T_1 that consists of the following operations:

Transaction T_1: Read(a);
Read(b);
a : = a + b;
write (a);
commit;

The partial ordering of the above transaction T_1 can be formally represented as P = {Σ, α},P = {Σ, α}, Where Σ = (R(a), R(b), W(a), C} and

$$\alpha = \{R(a), W(a)), (R(b), W(a)), W(a), (c)), (R(a), (C)), (R(b), (C))\}$$

Here, the ordering relation specifies the relative ordering of all operations with respect to the termination condition. The partial ordering of a transaction facilitates to derive the corresponding directed acyclic graph (DAG) for the transaction. The DAG of the above transaction T_1 is illustrated in figure 7.5.

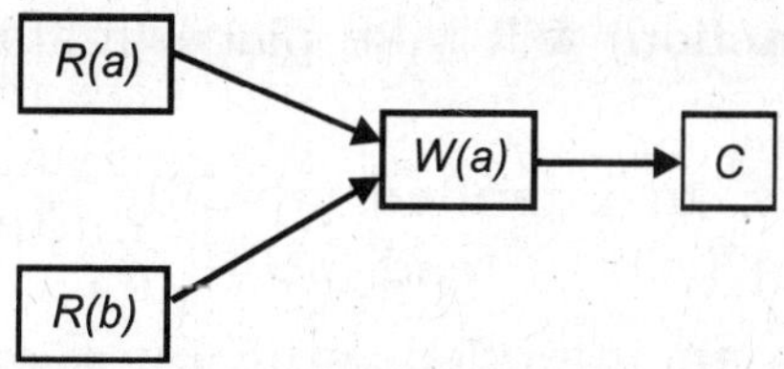

Figure 7.5: Directed Acyclic Graph Representation of transaction Ti

7.11 OVERVIEW OF TWO-PHASE LOCKING IN DISTRIBUTED DATABASES

In databases and transaction processing, two-phase locking, (2PL) is a concurrency control locking protocol, or mechanism, which guarantees serializability. It is also the name of the resulting class (set) of transaction schedules. Using locks that block processes, 2PL may be subject to deadlocks that result from the mutual blocking of two transactions or more.

Note that the two-phase locking protocol shouldn't be confused with the two-phase commit protocol for distributed transactions.

7.11.1 DATA-ACCESS LOCKS

A lock is an object associated with a shared resource such as a row in a database or a page of memory. In a database, a lock on a database object (a data-access lock) may need to be acquired by a transaction before accessing it. Correct use of locks prevents undesired, incorrect or inconsistent operations on shared resources by other concurrent transactions. When a database object with an existing lock acquired by one transaction needs to be accessed by another transaction, the existing lock for the object and the type of the intended access is checked by the system. If the existing lock type does not allow this specific attempted concurrent access type, the transaction attempting access is blocked or even aborted (according to a predefined agreement/locking-scheme).

Two major types of such locks are utilized:

- **Write-lock** (exclusive lock) is associated with a database object by a transaction (the transaction locks it; acquires lock for it) before writing (inserting/modifying/deleting) this object.
- **Read-lock** (shared lock) is associated with a database object by a transaction before reading (retrieving the state of) this object.

The common interaction between these lock types is defined by blocking behavior as follows:

- An existing write-lock on a database object blocks an intended write of the same object by another transaction that has acquired a write-lock for the same object. The second write of the object (requested/issued by the other transaction) will take place (materialize) after the existing lock is released.
- A write-lock blocks an intended (already requested/issued) read by another transaction (with a read-lock).
- A read-lock blocks an intended write by another transaction (with a write-lock).
- A read-lock does not block an intended read by another transaction (with a read-lock). The second read takes place immediately upon being requested by the other transaction.

Several variations and refinements of these major lock types exist, with respective variations of blocking behaviours.

7.11.2 TWO-PHASE LOCKING

According to the two-phase locking protocol, a transaction handles its locks in two distinct, consecutive phases during the transaction's execution:

Phase 1 - Expanding phase: locks are acquired and no locks are released.

Phase 2 - Shrinking phase: locks are released and no locks are acquired.

The serializability property is guaranteed for a schedule with transactions that obey the protocol. The 2PL schedule class is defined as the class of all the schedules comprising transactions with data access orders that could be generated by the 2PL protocol.

7.11.3 STRICT TWO-PHASE LOCKING

The strict two-phase locking (S2PL) class of schedules is the intersection of the 2PL class with the class of schedules possessing the strictness property.

To comply with the S2PL protocol a transaction needs to comply with 2PL, and release its write (exclusive) locks only after it has ended, i.e., being either committed or aborted. On the other hand, read (shared) locks are released regularly during phase 2.

Typically end of phase 1 is safely determined when a transaction has entered its ready state in all its processes (processing has ended, and it is ready to be committed; no additional locking is possible). If several processes (two or more) are involved, then a synchronization point (similar to atomic commitment) among them is needed to determine end of phase 1 for all of them. This is usually too costly, and end of phase 1 is usually postponed to be merged with transaction end (atomic commitment protocol for a multiprocess transaction), which turns S2PL to SS2PL (see below).

S2PL is a special case of 2PL, i.e., the S2PL class is a proper subclass of 2PL.

7.11.4 STRONG STRICT TWO-PHASE LOCKING

To comply with the strong strict two-phase locking (SS2PL) protocol a transaction needs to comply with 2PL, and release both its write (exclusive) and read (shared) locks only after it has ended, i.e., being either committed or aborted. A transaction obeying SS2PL can be viewed as having phase 1 that lasts the transaction's entire execution duration, and no phase 2 (or a degenerate phase 2). Thus, only one phase is actually left, and "two-phase" in the name seems to be still utilized due to the historical development of the concept from 2PL. The SS2PL property of a schedule is also called rigorousness, and an SS2PL schedule is also called a rigorous schedule.

SS2PL is a special case of S2PL, i.e., the SS2PL class of schedules is a proper subclass of S2PL (every SS2PL schedule is also an S2PL schedule, but S2PL schedules exist that are not SS2PL).SS2PL is the concurrency control protocol of choice for most database systems since it provides besides serializability also Strictness, which is instrumental for efficient database recovery, and also commitment ordering (CO) for participating in environments where a CO based global serializability solution is employed. Many variants of SS2PL exist that utilize various lock types with various semantics in different situations, including cases of lock-type change during a transaction. Notable are variants that use multi-granularity locking.

Comment: A more general property than SS2PL exists (a schedule superclass), Strict commitment ordering (Strict CO, or SCO), which as well provides serializability, strictness, and CO, and has similar overhead. SCO does not block upon a read-write conflict (a read-lock does not block acquiring a write-lock; Both SCO and SS2PL have the same behavior for write-read and write-write conflicts), and upon such conflict type has shorter transaction completion time and better performance than SS2PL.

7.12 CONCURRENCY CONTROL TECHNIQUES

Concurrency control in a distributed system involves the activity of controlling the relative order of conflicting operations and thereby ensuring database consistency. There are number of concurrency control techniques are being developed for distributed database systems, and these techniques can be classified into different categories based on different issues such as data distribution and network topology. The most obvious classification is done based on the synchronization approaches that are used in concurrently control techniques to ensure distributed serializability.

Concurrency control techniques are divided into two broad categories based on the synchronization techniques:

1. **Pessimistic concurrency control mechanisms:** Pessimistic algorithms synchronize the concurrent execution of transactions early in their execution life cycle, whereas optimistic algorithms delay the synchronization of transactions until transactions are near to their completion. In pessimistic concurrency control algorithms, the synchronization of transactions is achieved earlier before the starting of transaction executions. The main drawback of pessimistic concurrency control algorithms is that they are neither deadlock-free nor non-blocking algorithms. The pessimistic concurrency control algorithms are further classified into locking-based algorithms, timestamp-based algorithms and hybrid algorithms.
2. **Optimistic concurrency control mechanisms:** Optimistic concurrency control algorithms are based on the assumption that a conflict is rare it

is more efficient to allow transactions to proceed without delays. When a transaction wishes to commit, a check is performed to determine whether a conflict has occurred or not. Therefore, optimistic concurrency control algorithms have the desirable properties of being non-blocking and deadlock-free. The optimistic concurrency control algorithms are also classified into locking-based algorithms and timestamp-based algorithms.

The complete classification of distributed concurrency control techniques is given in figure 7.6.

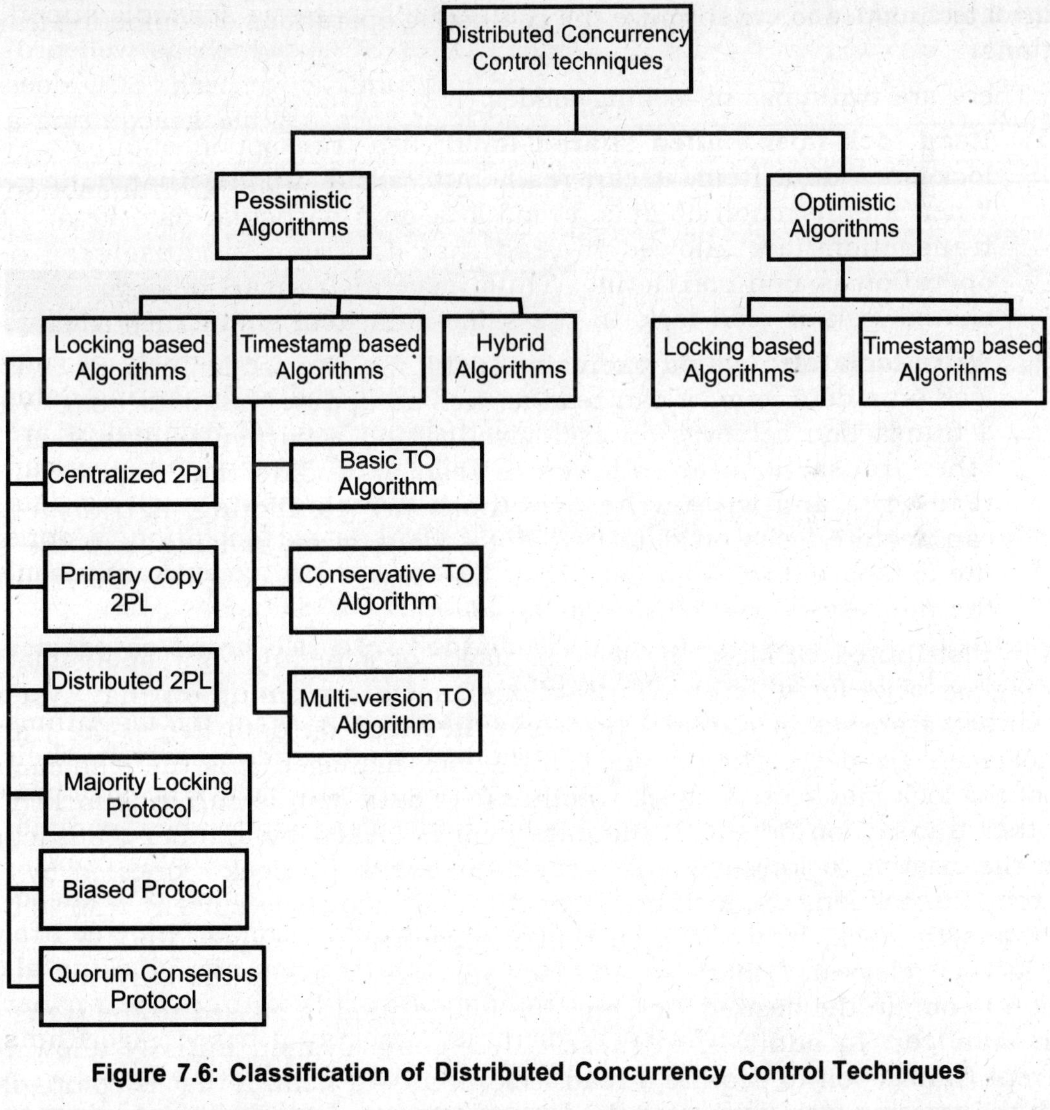

Figure 7.6: Classification of Distributed Concurrency Control Techniques

7.12.1 LOCKING-BASED CONCURRENCY CONTROL PROTOCOLS

In locking-based concurrency control algorithms, the synchronization of transactions is achieved by employing physical or logical locks on some portion of the database or on the entire database. To ensure serializability of concurrent transactions locking methods are the most widely used approach. In this approach, before accessing any data item, a transaction must acquire a lock on that data item. When a transaction acquires a lock on a particular data item, the lock prevents another transaction from modifying that data item. Based on the facts that read-read operation by two different transactions is non-conflicting and the main objective of the locking-based concurrency control techniques to synchronize the conflicting operations of conflicting transactions.

There are two types of locking modes:

1. **Read lock (also called shared lock):** If a transaction obtains a read lock on a data item, it can read, but cannot update that data item. When a transaction obtains a read lock on a particular data item, other transactions are allowed to read that data item because read-read operation is non-conflicting. Thus, several transactions can acquire shared lock or read lock on the same data item simultaneously.
2. **Write lock (also called exclusive lock):** If a transaction obtains a write lock on a data item, it can read as well as update that data item. When a transaction achieves an exclusive lock on a particular data item, no other transactions are allowed to read or update that data item, as read-write and write-write operations are conflicting. A transaction can acquire locks on data items of various sizes, ranging from the entire database down to a data field. The size of the data item determines the fineness or granularity of the lock.

In distributed DBMSs, the lock manager or scheduler is responsible for managing locks for different transactions that are running on that system. When any transaction requires read or writes lock on data items, the transaction manager passes this request to the lock manager. It is the responsibility of the lock manager to check whether that data item is currently locked by another transaction or not. If the data item is locked by another transaction and the existing locking mode is incompatible with the lock requested by the current transaction, the lock manager does not allow the current transaction to obtain the lock; hence, the current transaction is delayed until the existing lock is released. Otherwise, the lock manager permits the current transaction to obtain the desired lock and the information is passed to the transaction manager. In addition to these rules, some system initially allow the current transaction to acquire a read lock on a data item, if that is compatible with the existing lock, and later the lock is converted into a write lock. This is called upgradation of lock. The level of concurrency increases by upgradation of locking. Similarly, to allow maximum concurrency some systems permit the current transaction to acquire a write lock on a data item, and later the lock is converted into a read lock; this is called downgradation of lock. The synchronization of transaction executions in DDBMSs cannot be ensured by implementing locks in transactions only.

Consider the following two transactions Ti and Tj:

```
Ti:  Read(a);            Tj:  Read(a);
     a : = a + 2;                a : = a*10;
     Write(a);                Write(a);
     Read(b);                 Read(b);
     b: b * 2;                b: = b – 5;
     Write(b);                Write(b);
     Commit;                  Commit;
```

In the above transactions, assume that transaction Ti acquires a lock on data item a initially. The transaction Ti release the lock on data item a as soon as the associated operation (read or write) is executed. However, the transaction Ti may acquire a lock on another data item, say b, after releasing the lock on data item a. Although it seems that maximum concurrency is allowed here and it is beneficial for the system, it permits transaction Ti to interfere with other transactions, say Tj, which results in the loss of total isolation and atomicity. Therefore, to guarantee serializability, the locking and releasing operations on data items by transactions need to be synchronized. The most well-known solution is two-phase locking (2PL) protocol.

The 2PL protocol tells that no transaction should acquire a lock after it releases one of its locks. According to this protocol, the lifetime of each transaction is divided into two phases:

1. **Growing phase:** In the growing phase, a transaction can obtain locks on data items and can access data items, but it cannot release any locks.
2. **Shrinking phase:** In the shrinking phase a transaction can release locks but cannot acquire any new locks after that.

Thus, the ending of growing phase of a transaction determines the beginning of the shrinking phase of that transaction. It is not necessary for each transaction to acquire all locks simultaneously and then start processing. Normally, each transaction obtains some locks initially, does some processing, and then requests for additional locks that are required. However, it never releases any lock until it has reached a stage where no more locks are required. If upgradation and downgradation of locks are allowed, then upgradation of locks can take place only in the growing phase, whereas

downgradation of locks can occur in the shrinking phase. When a transaction releases a lock on a data item, the lock manager allows another transaction waiting for that data item to obtain the lock.

However, if the former transaction is aborted and rolled back, then the latter transaction is forced to be aborted and rolled back to maintain the consistency of data. Thus, the rollback of a single transaction leads to a series of rollbacks, called **cascading rollback**. One solution to the cascading rollback problem is to implement 2PL in such a way that a transaction can release locks only when it has reached the end of the transaction or when the transaction is committed. This is called rigorous 2PL protocol. To avoid cascading rollback, another possible variation in 2PL is strict 2PL protocol, in which only write locks are held until the end of the transaction. In a distributed database system, the 2PL protocol is further classified into several categories such as centralized 2PL, primary copy 2PL, distributed 2PL and majority locking depending on how the lock manager activities are managed.

7.12.1.1 CENTRALIZED 2PL

In this method, the lock manager or scheduler is a central component, and hence a single site is responsible for managing all activities of the lock manager for the entire distributed system. Before accessing any data item at any site, appropriate locks must be obtained from the central lock manager. If a global transaction Ti is initiated at site Si of the distributed system, then the centralized 2PL for that global transaction should be implemented in the following say. The transaction manager at the site Si (called coordinator) partitions the global transaction into several subtransactions using the information stored in the global system catalog. Thus, the transaction coordinator is responsible for maintaining consistency of data. If the data items are replicated, then it is also the responsibility of the transaction coordinator to ensure that all replicas of the data item are updated. Therefore, for a write operation, the transaction coordinator requests exclusive locks on all replicas of the data item that are stored at different sites. However, for a read operation, the transaction coordinator can select any one of the replicas of the data item that are available, preferably at its own site. the local transaction mangers of the participating sites request and release locks from/to the centralized lock request, the centralized lock manager checks whether that lock request is compatible with the existing locking status or not. If it is compatible, the lock manager sends a message to the corresponding site that the lock has been granted; otherwise, the lock request is put in a queue until it can be granted. In some systems, a little variable of this method is followed. Here the transaction coordinator sends lock requests to the centralized lock manager on behalf of participating sites. In this case, a global update operation that involves n sites requires a minimum of 2n + 3 messages to implement centralized 2PL method. These are 1 lock request from the transaction coordinator, 1 lock grand message from the centralized lock manager, n update messages from the transaction coordinator, n acknowledgement messages from the n participating sites and 1 unlock request from the transaction coordinator as illustrated in figure7.7

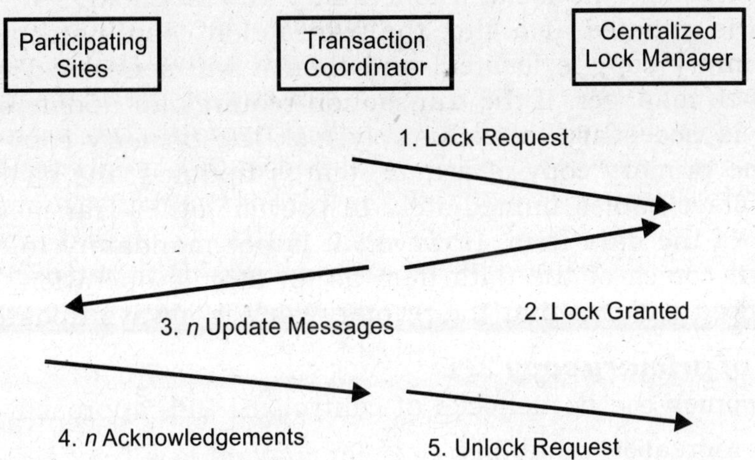

Figure 7.7: Communicating Messages in Centralized 2PL Method

Advantages of centralized 2PL

1. It is a straightforward extension of the 2PL protocol for centralized DBMSs; thus, it is less complicated and implementation is relatively easy.
2. In this case, the deadlock detection can be handled easily, because the centralized lock manager maintains all the locking information. Hence, the communication cost also is relatively low.

Disadvantages of centralized 2PL

1. In the case of DDBMSs, the implementation of centralized 2PL, method is system bottlenecks and lower reliability. For example, as all lock requests go to the centralized lock manager, that central site may become a bottleneck to the system.
2. The failure of the central site causes a major failure of the system; thus, it is less reliable. This method also hampers the local autonomy.

7.12.1.2 PRIMARY COPY 2PL

This method is a straightforward extension of the centralized 2PL method. Here the responsibilities of the centralized lock manager are distributed among a number of sites of the distributed system to overcome the disadvantages of the centralized 2PL method. Thus, in the primary copy 2PL method lock man-

agers are implemented at several sites. Each lock manager is responsible for managing locks for a given set of data items. For replicated data items, one copy is chosen as the primary copy, and the other copies are called slave copies. The choice of the site as the primary site of a data item is flexible. However, it is not necessary that the primary site hold the primary copy of data items to manage the locks [Stonebraker and Neuhold, 1977]. Whenever a transaction is initiated at a site, the transaction coordinator will determine where the primary copy is located, and then it will send lock request to the appropriate lock manager. If the transaction requires an update operation of a data item, it is necessary to exclusively lock the primary copy of that data item. Once the primary copy of a data item is updated, the change is propagated to the slave copies immediately to prevent other transactions reading the old value of the data item. However, it is not mandatory to carry out the updates on all copies of the data item as an atomic operation. The primary copy 2PL method ensures that the primary copy is always updated.

Advantages of primary copy 2PL

1. It overcomes the bottlenecks of centralized 2PL approach.
2. It also increases reliability.
3. This approach incurs lower communication costs because less amount of remote locking is required.

Disadvantages of primary copy 2PL

1. It is only suitable for those systems where the data items are selectively replicated, updates are infrequently and sites do not always require the latest version of the data.
2. Deadlock handling is more complex, as the locking information is distributed among multiple lock managers.
3. In the primary copy 2PL method there is still a degree of centralization in the system, as the primary copy is only handled by one site (primary site). This disadvantage can be partially overcome by nominating backup sites to hold locking information.

7.12.1.3 DISTRIBUTED 2PL

This method implements the lock manager at each site of a distributed system. Thus, the lock manager at each site is responsible for managing locks on data items that are stored locally. If the database is not replicated, then distributed 2PL becomes the same as primary copy 2PL. If the database is replicated, then distributed 2PL implements a read-one-write-all (ROWA) replica control protocol. In ROWA replica control protocol, any copy of a replicated data item can be used for a read operation, but for a write operation, all copies of the replicated data item must be exclusively locked before perform-

ing the update operation. In distributed 2PL, when a global transaction is initiated at a particular site, the transaction coordinator (the transaction manager of that site is called transaction coordinator) sends lock requests to lock managers of all participating sites. In response to the lock requests the lock manager at each participating site can send a lock granted message to the transaction coordinator. However, the transaction coordinator does not wait for the lock granted message in some implementations of the distributed 2PL method. The operations that are to be performed at a participating site are passed by the lock manager of that site to the corresponding transaction manager instead of the transaction coordinator. At the end of the operation the transaction manager at each participating site are passed by the lock manager of that site to the corresponding transaction manager instead of the transaction coordinator.

At the end of the operation the transaction manager at each participating site can send the corresponding message to the transaction coordinator. In an alternative approach, the transaction manager at a participating site can also pass the "end of operation" message to its own lock manager, who can then release the locks and inform the transaction coordinator. The communication between the participating sites and the transaction coordinator when executing a global transaction using distributed 2PL is depicted in figure 7.8.

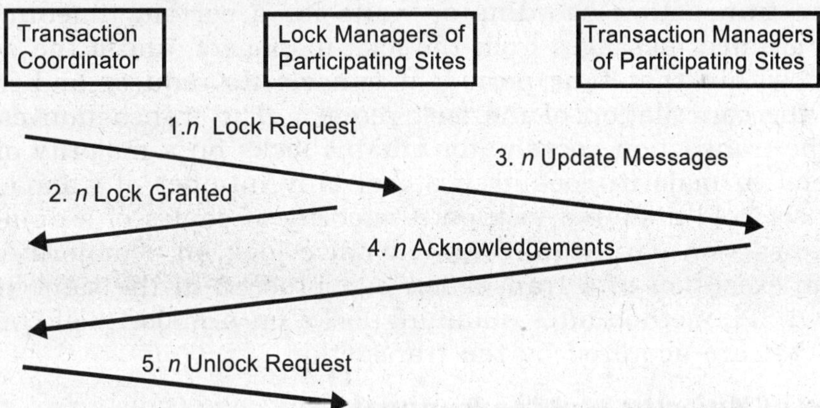

Figure 7.8: Communicating Messages in Distributed 2PL Method

Advantages of Distributed 2PL

1. It overcomes the drawbacks of centralized 2PL method because locks are handled in a decentralized manner.
2. This protocol ensures better reliability than centralized 2PL and primary copy 2PL methods.

Disadvantages of Distributed 2PL

1. Deadlock handling is more complex owing to the presence of multiple lock managers.
2. The communication cost is much higher than in primary copy 2PL, as all data items must be locked before an update operation. In distributed 2PL method, a global update operation that involves n participating sites may require a minimum of 5n messages. These are n lock requests, n lock granted messages, n update messages, n acknowledgement messages and n unlock requests.

7.12.1.4 MAJORITY LOCKING PROTOCOL

This protocol was designed to overcome the disadvantage of distributed 2PL method that all replicas of a data item must be locked before an update operation. In this protocol, a lock manager is implemented at each site to manage locks for all data items stored at that site locally. The majority locking protocol in a DDBMS works in the following way. When a transaction requires to read or write a data item that is replicated at m sites, the transaction coordinator must send a lock request to more than half of the m sites where the data item is stored. Each lock manager determines whether the lock can be granted immediately or not. If the lock request is not compatible with the existing lock status, the response is delayed until the request is granted. The transaction coordinator waits for a certain timeout period to receive lock granted messages from the lock managers, and if the response is not received within that time period, it cancels its request and informs all sites about the cancellation of the lock request. The transaction cannot proceed until the transaction coordinator obtains locks on a majority of copies of the data item. In majority locking protocol, any number of transactions can simultaneously hold a shared lock on a majority of copies of a data item, but only one transaction can acquire an exclusive lock on a majority of copies. However, the execution of a transaction can proceed in the same manner as in distributed 2PL method after obtaining locks on a majority of copies of the data items that are acquired by the transaction.

Advantages of Majority Locking Protocol

1. It avoids the bottlenecks of centralized 2PL method.
2. It is an extension of distributed 2PL.

Disadvantages of Majority Locking Protocol

1. It is more complicated and hence the deadlock handling also is more complex.
2. The communication cost is higher than that of centralized 2PL and primary copy 2PL methods because locking a data item that has m copies requires at least (m + 1)/2 messages for lock requests and (m + 1)/2 messages for unlock requests; thus,

7.12.1.5 BIASED PROTOCOL

This protocol is another replica control approach. This approach assigns more preference to requests for shared locks on data items than to requests for exclusive locks. Like in majority locking protocol, in biased protocol a lock manager is implemented at each site to manage locks for all data items stored at that site. In this protocol, when a transaction requires to read a data item that is replicated at m sites, the transaction coordinator simply sends a lock request to the lock manager of one site that contains a replica of that data item. Similarly, when a transaction needs to lock a data item in exclusive mode, the transaction coordinator sends lock requests to lock managers at all sites that contain a replica of that data item. As before, if the lock request is not compatible with the existing lock status, the response is delayed until the request is granted.

Advantages of Biased Protocol

1. It imposes less overhead on read operations than the majority locking protocol.
2. This scheme is beneficial for common transactions where the frequency of read operations is much higher that the frequency of write operations.

Disadvantages of Biased Protocol

1. It shares the additional overhead on write operations as in distributed 2PL protocol. 2. The deadlock handling is also complicated as in majority locking protocol.

7.12.1.6 QUORUM CONSENSUS PROTOCOL

This protocol is generalization of the majority locking protocol. To implement this protocol, a non-negative weight is assigned to each site of the distributed system. In addition, this approach also assigns integer values to read operations and write operations on each data item, called the read quorum and write quorum of the data item. In quorum consensus protocol, the read quorum and write quorum of a data item P, denoted as P_r- and P_w, are assigned in such a way that satisfy the following conditions:

$P_r + P_w > T$ and $2 * P_w > T$

where T is the total weight of all sites of the distributed system where the data item P resides. To perform a read operation on the data item P, enough number of the data item P stored at different sites must be read, so that their total weight is greater than or equal to P_r. On the other hand, to perform a

write operation on the data item P enough number of copies of the data item P stored at different sites must be written, so that their weight is greater than or equal to P_w. In both cases, the protocol ensures that locks are achieved on a majority of the replicas of the data item P stored at different sites before executing a read or a write operation on P. Hence, the transaction coordinator would send lock requests to different lock managers accordingly.

Advantages of Quorum Consensus Protocol

1. It allows to reduce the cost of read and write operations selectively by appropriately assigning the read and write quorums to data items.

For example, a read operation on a data item with a small read quorum requires reading of fewer replicas of the data item. But the write quorum of that data item may be higher, and hence, to succeed, the write operation needs to obtain locks on more replicas of the data item that are available. Furthermore, if higher weights are assigned to some sites, fewer sites need to be accessed for acquiring locks on a data item. The quorum consensus protocol can simulate the majority locking protocol and the biased protocol if appropriate weights and quorums are assigned.

Disadvantages of Biased Protocol

1. The deadlock handling is also complicated as in majority locking protocol.

Comparison of Lock-based Concurrency Control Strategies

	Implementation Complexity	**Reliability**	**Deadlock Handling**	**Communication Cost**
Centralized 2PL	Very Simple	Lowest reliability	Easy	Lowest
Primary Copy 2PL	Relatively simple	Lower reliability	Relatively complicated	Relatively low
Distributed 2PL	Complicated	Highest reliability	Highly complicated	Highest
Majority Locking Protocol	Complicated	High	Complicated	High
Biased Protocol	Complicated	High	Complicated	High
Quorum Consensus Protocol	Highly complicated	High	Complicated	High

7.13 TIME AND TIMESTAMPS IN A DISTRIBUTED DATABASE

In a distributed system, it is sometimes necessary to know if an event A at some site happened before or after an event B at a different site. Determining the order of events is simple in a centralized system, since it is possible to use the same clock to determine the time at which each event occurs. In a distributed system, instead, it is not realistic to assume that perfectly synchronized clocks are available at all sites.

Several distributed concurrency control and deadlock prevention algorithms need the determination of an ordering of events. The determination of an ordering of events consists in assigning to each event A which occurs in the distributed system a timestamp TS(A) having the following properties:

1. TS(A) uniquely identifies A (i.e., different events have different timestamps)
2. For any two events A and B, if A occurred before B, then TS(A) < TS(B)

The main inconvenience of the above definition is that the meaning of the relationship "occurred before" is not precisely defined if the two events A and B occurred at two different sites, since we do not possess a "global clock" for measuring the exact time of occurrence of al events in the distributed system. Therefore, in this section we first define precisely the meaning of the occur before relationship in a distributed system, and then present an algorithm which produces timestamps having the above two properties.

A precise definition of the occur before relationship in a distributed system is the following. Assume that we know the meaning of the statement "Event A occurred before event B at site i," i.e., that we know the meaning of time ordering at a single site. The relation occurred before, denoted '!, can be generalized to a distributed environment by the following rules:

1. If A and B are two events at the same site and A occurred before B, then A → B.
2. If the event A consists in sending a message and event B consists in receiving the same message, then A → B.
3. If A → B and B → C, then A → C.

The relation → is a partial ordering. We call two events A and B pseudo-simultaneous if neither A → B nor B → A (sometimes the word "concurrent" is used A and B, but we avoid the use of this term because it could be misleading). Consider, for example, Figure 7.9. Events A and D, B and E, B and F, C and E and C and F are pseudo simultaneous. The exact temporal relationship of two pseudo simultaneous events cannot be determined and is not relevant.

The second property of the definition of timestamps can therefore be restarted more precisely as follows:

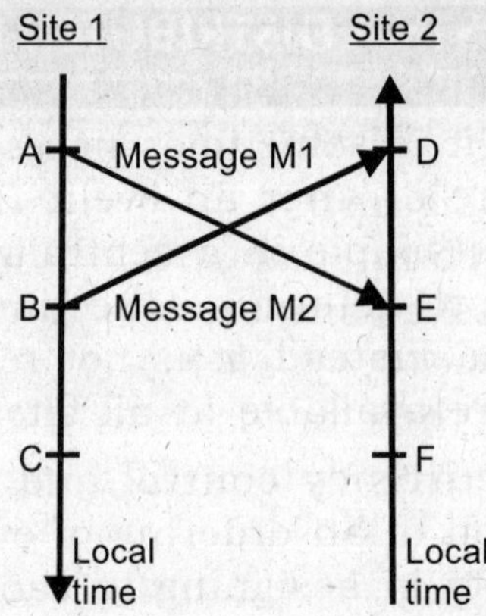

Figure 7.9: The "occurred before" relationship in a two-site system.

2. For any two events A and B, if A → B, then TS(A) < TS(B)

Notice that, if A and B are psedosimltaneous, it is possible that TS(A) < TS(B) or that TS(B) <TS(A). However, after we have assigned timestamps to events, a total ordering is defined between them, even if some are pseudosimultaneous. Therefore, the assignment of timestamps consists of the determination of a total order which is consistent with the partial order defined by the → relation. We say that an event A is younger (older) of an event B if TS(A) > TS(B) (TS(A) < TS(B).

We consider now the generation of timestamps. The first requirement of timestamps, uniqueness can be easily satisfied in a distributed system. It is sufficient that each site add to a locally unique timestamp its site identifier in the least significant position instead of the most significant one avoids the possibility that all timestamps which are generated by one site are greater than all timestamps which are generated by one site are greater than all timestamps which are generated by another site, thus making any attempt to reflect the time ordering in the timestamp ordering impossible.

The second requirement is more complex to satisfy. First, we will use at each site a counter which is steadily incremented, so that the transactions which receive the timestamp at the same site are correctly ordered between themselves. The counter might be simply incremented each time that a new timestamp is generated; however, the synchronization between counters at different sites would be difficult with this approach. It is possible that the counter at a site, say site 1, is used to generate more timestamps than the counter at a different site, say site 2 and hence advances faster.

Fortunately, the counters of the two sites can be kept approximately aligned by simply including in each message the value of the counter of the sending site. If a site receives a message with a timestamp value TS which is greater than its current counter, it increments its counter to be TS + 1. In this way, the counters of cooperating sites are kept approximately synchronized; if two sites are not cooperating, it is not very important if their counters drift away.

Consider the example of Figure 7.9 and assume that the counter at site 1 is initially 0 while the local counter at site 2 is initially 10. Let (x, y) represent the timestamp generated at site y when the local counter has value x. Therefore, initially TS(A) =(0,1) and TS(D) = (10,2). A and D are psedosimulataneous; hence their ordering is arbitrary. When message M2 arrives at site 1, it bears the timestamp of D; hence the local counter at site 1 is bumped and TS(B) = (11,1).When message M1 arrives at site 2,since it bears a smaller timestamp than the current counter of site 2, the counter is simply incremented and TS(E) = (11,2). Note that TS(E) differ from TS(B) only in the site identifier. The two pseudosimultaneous events have obtained "close" timestamps.

Finally, note that we have always used counters, not clocks, in the implementation of timestamps. However, in some applications it may be convenient to use clocks instead of counters. In this way timestamps reflect more closely the real time at which events occur.

7.13.1 TIMESTAMP-BASED CONCURRENCY CONTROL PROTOCOLS

In the case of timestamp-based concurrency control protocols, the synchronization of transactions is achieved by assigning timestamps both to the transactions, and to the data items that are stored in the database. To allow maximum concurrency and to improve efficiency, some locking-based concurrency control algorithms also involve timestamp ordering; these are called hybrid concurrency control algorithms.

The main idea behind the timestamp-based concurrency control techniques is that a unique timestamp is assigned to each transaction to determine the serialization order of transactions in a distributed system. The serialization order is determined depending on the timestamp values of transactions prior to the execution of transactions. A timestamp value is a simple identifier that that is used to identify each transaction uniquely and to permit ordering. In a centralized DBMS, generation of unique timestamp values for transactions can be handled in a simpler way while in a DDBMS timestamp values must be derived from a totally ordered domain. There are two primary methods for generating unique timestamp values in a distributed environment:

1. **Centralized Approach:** In this approach, a single site is responsible for assigning unique timestamp values to all transactions that are generated at different sites of the distributed system. The central site can use a logical counter or its own system clock for assigning timestamp values. The centralized approach is very simple, but the major disad-

vantage of this approach is that it uses a central component for generating timestamp values, which is vulnerable to system failures.

2. **Distributed Approach:** In this approach, each site generates unique local timestamp values by using either a logical counter or its own system clock. To generate unique global timestamp values, unique local timestamp values are concatenated with site identifiers and the pair <local timestamp value, site identifier> represents a unique global position to ensure that the global timestamp value generated in one site is not always greater than those generated in another site. This approach still has a problem: the system clocks at different sites would not be synchronized and one site can generate local timestamp values at a rate faster than that of the possibility of different sites generating the same values on the counter. In this approach, each site generates unique local timestamp values based on its own local logical counter. To maintain uniqueness, each site appends its own identifier to the local counter value, in the least significant position. Thus, the global timestamp value is a two-tuple of the form <local counter value, site identifier>. To ensure the synchronization of all logical counters in the distributed system, each site includes its timestamp value in inter-site messages. After receiving a message, each site compares its timestamp value with the timestamp value in the message and if its timestamp value is smaller, then the site changes its own timestamp to a value that is greater than the message timestamp value. For instance, if site1 sends a message to site2 with its current timestamp value <5, 1> where the current timestamp value of site2 is <7, 2> then site2 would not change its timestamp value. On the other hand, if the current timestamp value of site2 is <8, 2>, then site2 would change its current timestamp value to <11, 2>.

7.13.1.1 BASIC TIMESTAMP ORDERING (TO) ALGORITHM

The basic TO algorithm is a straightforward extension of the TO protocol for centralized DBMSs. Timestamp ordering is a technique by which a serialization order is selected a priori, and transaction execution is forced to obey this order. For two given conflicting operations Oi and Oj belonging to transactions T_1 and T_2 respectively, Oi is executed before Oj if and only if $ts(T_1) < ts(T_2)$, where $ts(T_1)$ and $ts(T_2)$ are the corresponding timestamp values of transactions T_1 and T_2. Here T_1 is the older transaction and T_2 is the younger transactions, and according to the timestamp ordering, operations of transaction T_1 will be executed before those of transaction T_2. In the basic TO algorithm, each transaction is assigned a unique timestamp value by its transaction manager. A timestamp ordering scheduler (which is a software module) is implemented to check the timestamp of each new operation against those of conflicting operations that have already been scheduled. The basic TO implementation distributes the schedulers along with the database. At each site, if the timestamp value of a new operation is found greater than the timestamp values of all conflicting operation that have already been scheduled, then it is accepted; otherwise, the corresponding transaction manager assigns a new timestamp value to the new operation, and the entire transaction is restarted. A timestamp ordering scheduler guarantees that transactions are conflict serializable and that the results are equivalent to a serial schedule in which the transactions are executed chronologically, that is, in the order of the timestamp values.

The comparison between the timestamp values of different transactions can be done only when the timestamp ordering scheduler has received all the operations to be scheduled. In a distributed database environment, it may happen that operations come to the scheduler one at a time, and an operation may reach out of sequence. To overcome this, each data item is assigned two timestamp values: one is a read_timestamp value, which is the timestamp value of the last transaction that had read the data item, and the other is a write_timestamp value, which is the timestamp value of the last transaction that had updated the data item.

Implementation of Basic Timestamp Ordering (TO) Algorithm

The coordinating transaction manager assigns a timestamp value to the transaction T, say ts(T), determines the sites where each data item is stored, and sends the relevant operations to these sites. Let us consider that the transaction T requires to perform a read operation on a data item x located at a remote site. the data item x has a read_timestamp value, which are Rx and Wx respectively. The read operation on the data item x proceeds only if ts(T) > Wx, and a new value ts(T), is assigned to the read_timestamp of data item x; otherwise, the operation is rejected and the corresponding message is sent to the coordinating transaction manager. In other cases, for instance, if ts(T) < Wx, it is indicated that the older transaction T is trying to read a value of the data item x that has been updated by a younger transaction. The older transaction T is too late to read the previous outdated value of the data item x, and the transaction T is aborted here. Similarly, the transaction T can perform a write operation on the data item x, only when the conditions ts(T) > Rx and ts(T) > Wx are satisfied. When an operation (read or write) of a transaction is rejected by the timestamp ordering scheduler, the transaction should be restarted with a new timestamp value, and it is assigned by the corresponding transaction manager.

To maintain the consistency of data, the data processor must execute the accepted operations in the order in which the scheduler passed them. The timestamp ordering scheduler maintains a queue for each data item to en-

force the ordering, and delays the transfer of the next accepted operation on the same data item until an acknowledgement is received from the data processor regarding the completion of the previous operation.

Advantages of Basic Timestamp Ordering (TO) Algorithm

1. Deadlock never occurs. For example, a transaction that is rejected by the timestamp ordering scheduler can restart with a new timestamp value.

Disadvantages of Basic Timestamp Ordering (TO) Algorithm

2. Wastage of time. For example, a transaction may have to restart numerous times to facilitate deadlock freedom.

7.13.1.2 CONSERVATIVE TIMESTAMP ORDERING ALGORITHM

The Conservative TO algorithm is a technique for eliminating transaction restarts during timestamp ordering scheduling and thereby reducing the system overhead. The conservative TO algorithm differs from the basic TO algorithm in the way the operations are executed in each method. In basic TO algorithm, when an operation is accepted by the timestamp ordering scheduler, it passes the operation to the data processor for execution as soon as possible. In the case of conservative TO algorithm, when an operation is received by the timestamp ordering scheduler, the scheduler delays the execution of the operation until it is sure that no future restarts are possible. Thus the execution of operations is delays the execution of the operation until it is sure that no future restarts are possible. Thus, the execution of operations is delayed to ensure that no operation with a smaller timestamp value can arrive at the timestamp ordering scheduler. The scheduler will never reject an operation if the satisfaction of the above condition is assured. Thus, the operations of each transaction are buffered here until an ordering can be established, so that rejections are not possible, and they are executed in that order. The conservative TO algorithm is implemented in the following way.

Implementation of Conservative to Algorithm

In conservative TO algorithm, each scheduler maintains one queue for each transaction manager in the distributed system. Whenever an operation is received by a timestamp ordering scheduler, it buffers the operation according to the increasing order of timestamp values in the appropriate queue for the corresponding transaction manager. For instance, the timestamp ordering scheduler at site p stores all the operations that it has received from the transaction manager of site q in a queue Q_{pq}. The scheduler at each site passes a read or writes operation with the smallest timestamp value from these queues to the data processor for execution. The execution of the operation can proceed after establishing an ordering of the operation can proceed

after establishing an ordering of the buffered operations so that rejections cannot take place.

Above implementation of the conservative TO algorithm suffers from some major problems:

1. First, if some transaction managers never send any operations to a scheduler, the scheduler will get stuck and stop outputting. To overcome this problem, it is necessary that each transaction manager communicate regularly with every scheduler in the system, which is infeasible in large networks.
2. Although conservative TO reduce the number of restarts of the transactions, it is not guaranteed that they will be eliminated completely. For instance, consider that the timestamp scheduler at site S1 has chosen an operation with the smallest timestamp value, say t(x), and passed it to the data processor for execution. It may happen that the site S2 has sent an operation to the scheduler of site S1 with a timestamp value less than t(x) that may still be in transit in the network. When this operation reaches the site S1, it will be rejected, because it violated the TO rule. In this case, the operation wants to access a data item that is already accessed by another operation with a higher timestamp value.

Solutions of above described problems:

First is to ensure that each scheduler chooses an operation for execution and passes it to the data processor only when there is at least one operation in each queue. In the absence of real traffic, when a transaction manager does not have any operations to execute, it will send a null operation to each timestamp scheduler in the system periodically. Thus, the null operations are sent periodically to ensure that the operations that will be sent to schedulers in future will have higher timestamp values than the null operations. This approach is more restrictive and is called extremely conservative TO algorithm.

Another solution for the above problem is transaction classes, which is less restrictive and reduces communications compared to extrcmcly conservative TO algorithm. In this technique, transaction classes are defined based on readset and writeset of transactions, which are known in advance. A transaction T is a member of a class C if readset(T) is a subset of readset(C) and writeset(T) is a subset of writeset(C). However, it is not necessary that transaction classes should be disjoint. The conservative TO algorithm has to maintain one queue for each class instead of maintaining one queue for the transaction manager at each site in the distributed system. With this modification, the timestamp scheduler will choose an operation of a transaction for execution with smallest timestamp value until there is least one operation in each class to which the transaction belongs.

Example 8.6

Consider the following transaction classes and transactions:

Class C_1: readset = {a1}, writeset = {b1, b2}

Class C_2: readset = {a1, b2}, writeset = {b1, b2, c2, c3}

Class C_3: readset = {b2, c3}, writeset = {a1, c2, c3}

Transaction T_1: readset = {a1}, writeset = {b1, b2}

Transaction T_2: readset = {b2}, writeset = {c2, c3}

Transaction T_3: readset{c3}, writeset = {a1}

Hence, T_1 is a member of classes C_1 and C_2, T_2 is a member of classes C_2 and C_3, and T_3 is a member of classes C_3. Now, the conservative TO algorithm has to maintain one queue for each class C_1, C_2, and C_3 instead of maintaining one queue for each transaction manager at each site in the distributed system. The timestamp scheduler will choose an operation of a transaction, with the smallest timestamp value, for execution until there is at least one operation in each class C_1, C_2 or C_3 to which the transaction belongs.

7.13.1.3 MULTI-VERSION TIMESTAMP ORDERING ALGORITHM

Multi-version TO algorithm is another timestamp-based protocol that reduces restart overhead of transactions. In multi-version TO algorithm, the updates of data items do not modify the database, but each write operation creates a new version of a data item while retaining the old version. When a transaction requires reading a data item, they system selects one of the versions that ensure serializability. Multi-version TO algorithm is implemented in the following way. In this method, for each data item P in the system, the database holds a number of versions such as P1, P2, P3, ..., Pn respectively.

Furthermore, for each version of the data item P, the system stores three values: the value of version Pi, read_timestamp(Pi), which is the largest timestamp value of all transactions that have successfully read the version Pi, and write_timestamp(Pi), which is the timestamp value of the transaction that created the version Pi. The existence of versions of data items is transparent to users. The transaction manager assigns a timestamp value to each transaction, which is used to keep track of the timestamp values of each version. When a transaction T with timestamp value ts(T) attempts to perform read or write operation on the data item P, the multi-version TO algorithm uses the following two rules to ensure serializability.

Rule 1: If the transaction T wants to read the data item P, a version Pj is chosen that has the largest write_timestamp value that is less than ts(T), that is, write_timestamp (Pj) < ts (T). In this case, the read operation is sent to the data processor for execution and the value of read_timestamp (Pj) is reset as ts(T).

Rule 2: If the transaction T wishes to perform a write operation on the data item P, it must be ensured that the data item P has not already been read by some other transaction whose timestamp value is greater than ts(T). Thus, the write operation is permitted and sent to the data processor if the version Pj that has the largest write_timestamp of data item P that is less than ts(T) satisfies the condition read_timestamp (Pj) <ts(T). If the operation is permitted, a new version of the data item P, say Pk, is created where write_timestamp(Pk) write_timestamp(Pk) = ts(T). Otherwise, the transaction T is aborted and restarted with a new timestamp value.

Advantages of multi-version TO algorithm

1. The multi-version TO algorithm is a suitable concurrency control mechanism for DBMSs that are designed to support applications that inherently have a notion of versions of database objects such as engineering databases and document databases.

Disadvantages of multi-version TO algorithm

1. It requires more storage space to store the values of different versions of data items with respect to time. To save space, older versions of data items can be deleted if they are no longer required.

7.14 OPTIMISTIC CONCURRENCY CONTROL TECHNIQUE

Optimistic concurrency control techniques is a non-blocking and deadlock free approach for concurrency control. In this technique, it is assumed that the conflicts between transactions are rare, and the transactions are allowed to proceed for execution without imposing delays. When a transaction wants to commit, a validation checking is made to determine whether a conflict has occurred or not. To ensure serializability, the transaction is aborted and restarted if any conflict has occurred. In optimistic concurrency control techniques, the execution of any operation of a transaction follows a sequence of phases depending on whether it is a read operation or an update operation. These are read phase, validate phase and write phase as in figure 7.10.

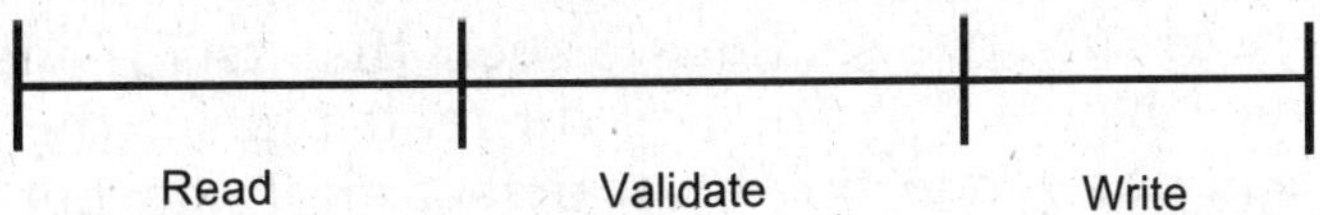

Figure 7.10: Phases of Optimistic Concurrency Control Technique

The read and write operations of each transaction are processed without delay, but no update is made to the actual database. Initially, each transaction makes its updates on local copies of data items and to ensure the consistency of the database, a checking is done on these updates in the validate phase. The changes are made global and written into the actual database if local updates caused no inconsistencies of the database.

Implementation of optimistic concurrency control techniques

The optimistic concurrency control technique for DDBMS based on timestamp ordering [proposed by Ceri and Owicki] is implemented in the following way. Whenever a global transaction is generated at a site, the transaction manager of that site (called the transaction coordinator) divides the transaction into several subtransactions, each of which can execute at many sites. Each local execution can then proceed without delay and follows the sequence of phases of optimistic concurrency control technique until it reaches the validate phase. The transaction manager assigns a timestamp value to each transaction at the beginning of the validate phase that is copied to all its subtransactions. Hence, no timestamp values are assigned to data items and a timestamp value is assigned to each transaction only at the beginning of the validate phase, because its early assignment may cause unnecessary transaction restarts.

Let us consider that a transaction T_p is divided into a number subtransactions, and a subtransaction of T_p that executes at site q is denoted by T_{pq}. To perform the local validation in the validate phase, the following three rules are followed:

Rule 1: For each transaction T_r, if $ts(T_r) < ts(T_{pq})$ (that is, the timestamp value of each transaction T_t- is less than the timestamp value of the subtransaction T_{pq}) and if each transaction T_r has finisthed its write phase before T_{pq} has started it sread phase, the validation succeeds.

Rule 2: If there is any transaction T_r such that $ts(T_r) < ts(T_{pq})$ that completes its write phase while T_{pq} is in its read phase, then the validation succeeds, if none of the data items updated by the transaction T_r are read by the subtransaciton T_{pq} and the transaction T_r completes writing its updates into the database before the subtransaction T_{pq} starts writing. Thus,$WS(T_r) \cap RS(T_{pq}) = \phi$, where $WS(T_r)$ represents the write_timestamp value of the data item S after the transaction T_r completes a write operation on it, and $RS(T_{pq})$ represents the read-_timestamp value of the data items S after the subtransaciton T_{pq} has performed a read operation on S.

Rule 3: If there is any transaction T_r such that $ts(T_r) < ts(T_{pq})$ that completes its read phase before T_{pq} finishes its read phase, then the validation succeeds, if the updates made by the transaction T_r do not affect the read phase or the write phase of the transaction T_{pq}. In this case, $WS(T_r) \cap RS(T_{pq}) = \phi$, and $WS(T_r) \cap WS(T_{pq}) = \phi$.

In this algorithm Rule1 is used to ensure that the transactions are executed serially according to their timestamp ordering. Rule2 indicates that the set of data items written by the older transaction are not read by the younger transaction, and the older transaction completes its write phase before the younger transaction enters its validate phase. Rule3 state that the updates on data items made by the older transaction do not affect the read phase or write phase of the younger transaction, but as in Rule2 it does not require that the older transaction finish writing on data items before the younger transaction starts writing.

Advantages of optimistic concurrency control algorithm

1. It allows higher level of concurrency, since the transactions can proceed without imposed delays.
2. It is very efficient when there are few conflicts, but conflicts can result in the rollback of individual transactions. However, there are no cascading rollbacks, because the rollback involves only a local copy of the data.

Disadvantages of optimistic concurrency control algorithm

1. It incurs higher storage cost. To validate a transaction, the optimistic approach has to store the read and the write sets of several other terminated transactions.
2. Starvation problem. It may happen that a long transaction fails repeatedly in the validate phase during successive trials. This problem can be overcome by allowing the transaction exclusive access to the data items after a specified number of trials, but this reduces the level of concurrency to a single transaction.

7.15 RELIABILITY

Reliability is defined as "a measure of the success with which the system conforms to some authoritative specification of its behavior... when the behavior deviates from that which is specified for it this is called a failure." The reliability of the system is inversely related to the frequency of failures.

7.15.1 RELIABILITY AND CONCURRENCY CONTROL

The problem which we consider in this section is the following: Suppose that there is a failure. How can we maximize the number of transactions which are executed during this failure by the operational part of the system?

Consider a transaction T having read-set RS(T) and write-set WS(T) and suppose that we want to run T alone, so that not concurrency control is needed. I order to run T it is necessary that at least one copy of each data item x belonging to RS(T) be available. If this elementary necessary condition is not satisfied, T cannot be executed, because it lacks input data. The availability of the data items because a list of deferred updates can be produced which will be applied to the database when the failure is repaired. Deferred updates can be implemented using the "spooler" method for solving the remote recovery information problem in the 2-phase-commitment.

The availability of a system which allows only one transaction to be run during failures is not satisfactory; therefore, concurrency control must be taken in account. In fact, the strongest limitation on the execution of transactions in the presence of failures is due to the need for concurrency control.

7.15.1.1 NONREDUDANT DATABASES

If the database is nonredundant, then it is very simple to determine which transactions can be executed. Suppose that 2-phase-locking is used for concurrency control. A transaction tries to lock all data items of its read-and write-sets before commitment. As there is only one copy of each data item, this copy is either available or not. If the unique copy of some data item of the read- or write-set is not available, the transaction cannot commit and must therefore be aborted.

If we assume that only site crashes occur but no partitions, then the availability of the items which belong only to the write-set is not required, and it is possible to spool the up data messages for these items. All transactions which have their read-set available execute completely, including commitment; however, the updates affecting sites which are down are stored at spooler sites. Upon recovery, the restart procedures of the failed sites will receive this list of deferred updates and execute them. In practice, we consider a crashed site as if it were exclusively locked for the transaction; in fact, no other transaction can read the values of data items which are stored there. However, in the case of partitions the deferred update rule will cause inconsistent results to be produced: the failure is catastrophic.

In conclusion if the database is nonredundant, there is not very much to do in order to increase its availability in the presence of failures. Therefore, most reliability techniques consider the case of redundant databases.

7.15.1.2 REDUNDANT DATABASES

The reasons why redundancy is introduced in a distributed database are twofold:

1. To increase the locality of reads, especially in those applications where the number of reads is much larger than the number of writes
2. To increase the availability and reliability of the system

We deal here essentially with the second aspect; however, in designing reliable concurrency control methods for replicated data the first goal also should be kept in mind.

We have already seen that there are three main approaches to concurrency control base on 2-phase-locking in a redundant database: write-locks-all, majority looking, and primary copy locking. Let us review the basic tradeoffs of these approaches with an example.

Write-locks-all: For each transaction and for each type of partition, the group, if any, in which the transaction can be executed. The read-only transaction 10', 11 and 12' are the same as 10, 11, and 12, except that consistency is not required for them; hence, no locks are used. The values of Figure 7.11a confirm the institution: For transactions with a small write-set and especially for read-only transactions, the system is much more available that for transactions with a large write-set. For read-only transactions, the system is much more available than for transactions with a large write-set. For read-only transactions it makes no difference whether consistency is required or not, because the copy which is locked is required anyway for reading. Note that read-only transactions sometimes can run in more than one group, because if the data item has two copies in two different groups, then no update transaction can write on it and read-only transactions can use each copy consistently.

If we make the assumption that no partitions occur, but only site crashes, then the same approach can be used as with a nonredundant database; i.e., the updates of nonavailable copies of data items can be spooled. In this case, the availability of the database for update transactions increases very much. In fact, since only the read-set matters in this case, transactions 1, 4 and 7 have the same availability as transaction 10; transactions 2, 5 and 8 as transaction 11; and transactions 3, 6 and 9 as transaction 12. Obviously, the example must be carefully interpreted. The fact that a transaction can run in a given group means now that it can be run if all other sites are down, instead of building separate groups. The high increase in availability is obtained at the risk of catastrophic partitions.

Let us now consider the locality aspect, which is the other motivation for redundancy. For this purpose we distinguish between the transmission cost of control messages and the transmission cost of data. Requests to lock or unlock a data item and the messages of the 2-phase-commintemnt protocol are required for the control of transactions.

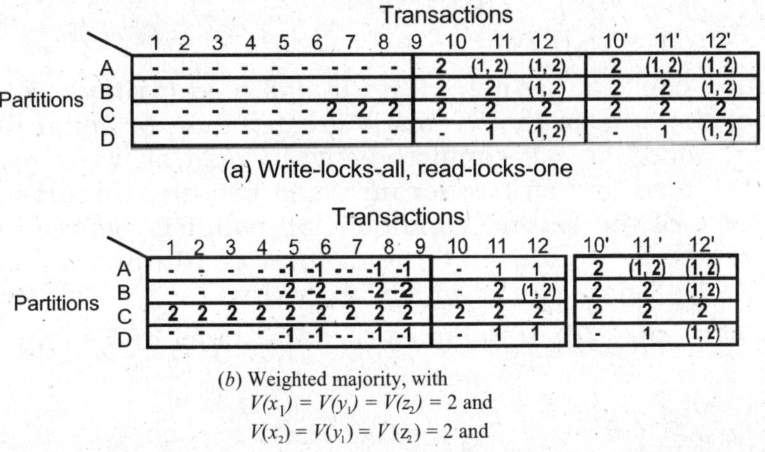

Transactions

Partitions	1	2	3	4	5	6	7	8	9	10	11	12	10'	11'	12'
A	-	-	-	-	-	-	-	-	-	2	(1, 2)	(1, 2)	2	(1, 2)	(1, 2)
B	-	-	-	-	-	-	-	-	-	2	2	(1, 2)	2	2	(1, 2)
C	-	-	-	-	-	-	2	2	2	2	2	2	2	2	2
D	-	-	-	-	-	-	-	-	-	-	1	(1, 2)	-	1	(1, 2)

(a) Write-locks-all, read-locks-one

Transactions

Partitions	1	2	3	4	5	6	7	8	9	10	11	12	10'	11'	12'
A	-	-	-	-	-1	-1	- -	-1	-1	-	1	1	2	(1, 2)	(1, 2)
B	-	-	-	-	-2	-2	- -	-2	-2	-	2	(1, 2)	2	2	(1, 2)
C	2	2	2	2	2	2	2	2	2	2	2	2	2	2	2
D	-	-	-	-	-1	-1	- -	-1	-1	-	1	1	-	1	(1, 2)

(*b*) Weighted majority, with
$V(x_1) = V(y_1) = V(z_2) = 2$ and
$V(x_2) = V(y_1) = V(z_2) = 2$ and

Figure 7.11: Availability of transactions of Example 9.2.

Control messages carry control information and are short. Data messages contain database information and can be long.

When evaluating the opportunity of adding an additional copy of a data item at a site i, the designer have to evaluate the benefit which is obtained by transactions which can read the item locally and the additional cost for updating this copy by all other transactions. With the write-locks-all approach, we have:

1. **Benefit:** For each transaction executed at site i having x in its read-set, one lock message and one data message are saved.
2. **Cost:** For each transaction which is not executed at site i and has x in its write-set, one lock message and one data message are required, plus the messages required by the commitment protocol.

We have made essentially the same assumptions, however without considering the control messages. In fact, it depends on the relative size of the data versus control messages. In fact, it depends on the relative size of the data versus control messages whether control messages are important or not.

Weighted majority locking: The pure majority locking approach is not very suitable for our example, because two copies of each data item exist; hence to lock a majority we must lock both. We will therefore consider a weighted majority approach, or quorum approach, which adopts the same rules which have been used for quorum-based commitment and termination protocols.

These rules, applied to the locking problem, consist of assigning to each data item x a total number of votes V(x), and assigning votes $V(x_i)$ to each copy x, in such a way that V(x) is the sum of all $V(x_i)$. A read quorum $V_r(x)$ and a write quorum $V_w(x)$ are then determined, such that:

$$V_r(x) + V_w(x) > V(x)$$

$$V_w(x) > V(x)/2$$

A transaction can read (write) x if it obtains read (write) locks on so many copies of x that the sum of their votes is greater than or equal to $V_r(x)(V_w(x))$. Due to the first condition, all conflicts between read an write operation on x cannot reach the read and write quorum using two disjoint subsets of copies. Likewise, because of the second condition, all conflicts between write operations are determined. Notice that the second condition can be omitted if transactions read all data items which are written.

Let us assign votes for the copies of data items of Example 9.2 in the following way:

$$V(x) = V(y) = V(z) = 3$$

$$V(x1) = V(y1) = V(z2) = 2$$

$$V(x2) = V(y3) = V(z3) = 1$$

With this assignment we can now consider the availability of the system in the case of partition. We choose the read and write quorums to be 2 for all data items. The availability for the 12 transactions is shown in Figure 7.11b.

The following can be observed:

1. Transaction 1, 2, 3, 4,7, and 20 have all the same availability. They are characterized by the fact that they access all three data items either for reading or for writing or for both. Since the read quorum is equal to the write quorum, it makes no difference whether the data item is read or written from the viewpoint of availability. For the same reason, transactions 5, 6, 8 and 11, which access only data items x and y, have the same availability. Also, transactions 9 and 12 have the same availability of the latter group, because the copy with highest weight for data item x resides at the same site as the copy with highest weight for y.
2. The availability for update transactions is greater with the weighted majority approach than with write-locks-all, while the availability for read-only transactions is smaller.
3. With this method, read-only transactions increase their availability if they can read an inconsistent database, i.e., if they do not need to lock item; in fact, columns 10', 11', and 12' are the same for the majority approach as for the write-locks-all approach.

With the majority approach it is not reasonable to consider the assumption that partitions do not occur. Notice that if we assume the absence of partitions, then the majority approach is dominated by the write-locks-all approach (an approach is dominated by another one if it worse under all circumstances). In fact, we have seen that the majority and quorum ideas have been developed essentially for dealing with partitions.

Consider now the locality aspect. A transaction reads a data item x at its site of origin, if a copy is locally available. Hence, also in this case a data message is saved if a local copy is available. However, read locks must be obtained at a number of copies corresponding to the read quorum. Therefore, the addition of a copy of x can also force transactions which read x to request more read locks at remotes sites. This additional cost depends on the number of copies and on the distribution of votes. The same additional cost is incurred by transactions which have x in their write-set, which must obtain write locks at a number of sites corresponding to the write quorum. Moreover, they have to send a data message to all the sites where there are copies of x.

Primary copy locking: In the primary copy locking approach, all locks for a data items x are requested at the site of the primary copy. We will assume first that also all the real and write operations are performed on this copy; however, writes are then propagated to all other copies. Considering the database of Example 9.2, if we choose x1, y1, and z2 as primary copies, then the

availability of the database for the 12 transactions is the same as in the majority approach (Figure 7.11b), because the assignment of votes which we had applied determined a primary copy situation. This will always happen if we apply weighted voting to items having only two copies. However, this is a particular case; if many copies exist, so that different majorities can be built, then be built, then the two approaches are different. The weighted majority mechanism is more general and can simulate the primary copy approach by a particular assignment of votes.

Several enhancements of the primary exist which make it more attractive. The principal ones are:

1. Allowing consistent reads at different copies than the primary, even if read locks are requested only at the primary; this enhances the locality of reads.
2. Allowing the migration of the primary copy if a site crash makes it unavailable; this enhances availability.
3. Allowing the migration of the primary copy depending on its usage pattern. This also enhances the locality aspect.

The first point deserves a comment. In order to obtain consistent reads at different copies from the primary one, we should use the primary copy method for synchronization, but perform the write and read operations according to the "write all/read one" method. In this approach, the locks are all requested at the primary copy; however, at commitment all copies are updated before releasing the write lock. A read can be performed in this way at any copy, obtaining consistent data.

This method is very similar to write-locks-all, expect that it spends less control messages for write locks but in general more messages for read locks, since a read lock must be requested at the primary copy and not at the local copy. The availability of this method is inferior to the write-locks-all method, since for each data item of the write-set all copies must be available, and for each item of the read-set the primary copy must be available.

7.16 DETECTION AND RESOLUTION OF INCONSISTENCY

When a partition of the network occurs, transactions should be run at most in one group of sites if we want to preserve strictly the consistency of the database. With partitions under this requirement of absolute correctness. However, in some applications it is acceptable to lose consistency in order to achieve more availability. In these cases transactions are allowed to run in all partitions where there is at least one copy of the necessary data. Later, when the failure is repaired, one can try to eliminate the inconsistencies which have been introduced into the database. For this purpose it is necessary first to discover which portions of the data have become inconsis-

tent, and then to assign to these portions a value which is the most reasonable in consideration of what has happened. The first problem is called the detection of inconsistencies; the second is called the resolution of inconsistencies. While exact solutions can be found for the detection problem, the resolution problem has no general solution, because transactions have been executed in the different groups of sites during the partition in a nonglobally serializable way. Therefore the word "reasonable" and not the word "correct" is used for the value which is assigned by the resolution procedure.

7.16.1 DETECTION OF INCONSISTENCIES

Let us assume that, during a partition, transactions have been executed in two or more groups of sites, and that independent updates may have been performed on different copies of the same fragment. Let us first observe that the most naïve solution, consisting of comparing the contents of the copies to check that they are identical, is not only inefficient but also not correct in general. For example, consider an airline reservation system. If, during the partition, we allow taking reservations for the same flight independently on different copies until the maximum number is reached, then all copies might have the same value for the number of reservations; however, the flight would be overbooked in this case.

A correct approach to the detection of inconsistencies can be based on version numbers. Assume that one of the approaches are used for determining, for each data item, the one group of sites which is allowed to operate on it. The copies of the data item which are stored at the sites of this group are called master copies;

During normal operation all copies are master copies and are mutually consistent. For each copy an original version number and a current version number are maintained. Initially the original version number is set to 0, and the current version number is set to 1; only the current version number is incremented each time that an update is performed on the copy. When a partition occurs, the original version number of each isolated copy is set to the value of its current version number of the copies before any "partitioned updates" are performed on it. The original version number is not altered until the partition is repaired. At this time, the comparison of the current and original version numbers of all copies reveals inconsistencies.

Let us consider an example of this method. Assume that copies x1, x2, and x3 of data item x are stored at three different sites. Let V1, V2, and V3 be the version numbers of x1, x2, and x3. Each Vi is in fact a pair with the original and current version number. Initially all three copies are consistently updated. Suppose that one update has been performed, so that the situation is

V1 = (0,2), V2 = (0,2), V3 = (0,2)

Now a partition occurs separating x3 from the other two copies. A majority algorithm, is used which chooses x1 and x2 as master copies. The version numbers become now

V1 = (0,2), V2 = (0,2), V3 = (2,2)

Suppose now that only the master copies are updated during the partition. This version numbers become

V1 = (),3), V2 = (0,3), V3 = (2,2)

and after the repair it is possible to see that x3 has not been modified, since its current and original version numbers are equal. In this case, no inconsistency has occurred, and it is sufficient to perform the updates on x3.

Suppose now that only x3 is updated during the partition. We have

V1 = (0,2), V2 = (0,2), V3 = (2,3)

Since the original version number of x3 is equal to the current version numbers of x1 and x2 the master copies have not been updated. If there are no other copies, then we can simply apply to the master copies the updates of x3, since the situation is exactly symmetrical to the previous one. If there are other isolated copies, for example x4 with V4 = (2,3), we cannot tell whether x4 was updated consistently with x3 even if version numbers are the same; hence we have to assume inconsistency.

Finally, if both the master and the isolated copies have been updated, which also reveals an inconsistency, then the original and the current version number of the isolated copy are different, and the original version number of the isolated copy is also different from the current number of the master copies; for example:

V1 = (0,3), V2 = (0,3), V3 = (2,3)

7.16.2 RESOLUTION OF INCONSISTENCIES

After a partition has been repaired and an inconsistency has been detected, a common value must be assigned to all copies of a same data item. The problem of resolution of inconsistency is the determination of this value.

Since in the different groups transactions have been executed without mutual synchronization, it seems correct to assign as a common value the one which would be produced by some serilizable execution of these same transactions. However, besides the difficulty of obtaining this new value, this is not a satisfactory solution, because the transactions which have been executed have produced effects outside of the system which cannot be undone and cannot be simply ignored.

Note that the transactions requiring the high degree of availability which motivates the acceptance of inconsistencies are exactly those which perform effects outside of the system. For example, take the airline reservation example considered before. The reason for running transactions while the system is partitioned is to tell the customers that flights are available; otherwise, it would be simpler to collect the customers' requests and to apply them to the database after the failure has been repaired.

However, if overbooking has occurred during the partition, then forcing the system to a serializable execution would force the system to perform arbitrary cancellations. From the viewpoint of the application, it might be better to keep the overbookings and let normal user cancellations reduce the number of reservations. A possible way of reducing or eliminating overbooking due to partitions is to assign to each site a number of reservations which is smaller than the total number. This number could be proportional to the size of each group or to some other application-dependent value.

The above example shows that the resolution of inconsistencies is, in general, application-dependent, and hence not within the scope of this book, which deals with generalized mechanism. Reference [9.36] proposes some general principles for designing databases and transactions so that reasonable resolution strategies can be applied.

7.17 RELIABILITY PROTOCOLS IN DISTRIBUTED DATABASE SYSTEMS

Following are the reliability protocols in distributed systems:

7.17.1 RELIABILITY PROTOCOL OVERVIEW

One of the critical functions that database systems have to ensure is correctness and availability. During the course of the database operations, the database system may stop running or some transactions may have to be aborted before the transactions commit. In those situations, atomicity and durability would be compromised if a committed transaction isn't written to the disk or if aborted transaction is written to the disk. It is the role of the transaction manager is to guarantee correctness of database system - all actions in the transaction happen or none happen and if a transaction commits then its effects persist. Furthermore, recovery manager has to be efficient enough so that downtime of the database is minimized and the availability of the database is maximized.

7.17.2 NO STEAL-FORCE METHOD

To ensure correctness, a trivial solution would be to use no steal-force method. In no steal-force method, the effects of transactions are held in the buffer pool until the transaction commits and after the transaction commits the effects are forced (written) to the disk. There are two problems with this

method. In a long transaction, no steal prevents the content of the buffer pool to be replaced until the transaction commits. This will lead to poor throughput in the database system as fewer items get be placed into the buffer manager and disk has to be continuously accessed.. Force writes requires writes to the disk after the transaction but this lead to poor response time. For example, if there is a page that is update frequently, the page has to be forced to the disk at every update. It would be more efficient to have the page in the buffer pool and then write to the disk after most of the updates are finished. However, force is necessary to guarantee durability because what would happen if the database were to crashed before writing the data to the disk? So a desired method is steal-no force method that will also guarantee atomicity and durability.

7.17.3 WRITE AHEAD LOGGING

The solution is to log every action and outcome of every transaction. For example, if the transaction decides to abort, the database system can look at the log and undo all the actions. If the database crashes before committed writes are written to the disk, then once the database comes back up, the recovery manager will read the logs and redo the actions of committed transactions. Lastly, write-ahead logging (WAL) is used to ensure atomicity and durability. In WAL, logs are forced into a stable storage before updates take place or before a transaction commit.

7.17.4 ISSUES IN RECOVERY PROTOCOL IN DISTRIBUTED DATABASE

With distributed databases, guaranteeing atomicity and durability becomes more complicated. Transactions usually span more than one site, so if a transaction commits, and then all the sites that are involved in the transaction have to commit. Also, if the transaction aborts, then all sub-transactions have to abort. The problem is how to do this efficiently. The two-phase commit has been the most popular technique among implemented distributed DBMS and variations have been made to the protocol to make it more efficient in some cases. A more radical variation is called the three-phase commit protocol (3PC) where additional message is sent at the end and in some cases, will lead to better performance.

7.18 TWO-PHASE COMMIT

The two-phase commit (2PC) has been the most popular technique for concurrency control in distributed database as R*, Distributed-INGRES and DDM all use 2PC or variations of it. In the basic form of 2PC, there is a coordinator and subordinates where the coordinator is the site that has initiated the transaction. In the first stage, the coordinator tries to get a uniform decision of either committing or aborting out of the subordinates and in the second stage, the coordinators relay the decision back to them.

The protocol goes as follows:

1. The coordinator will write a "prepare" log on a stable storage and will send "prepare" messages to the subordinates.
2. After the subordinates receives a "prepare" message, they will decide if they can commit or not and sends the response back to the coordinator. If the subordinate decides to commit, a "ready" log will be written to a stable storage on the subordinate's machine.
3. If the coordinator receives an abort reply from any subordinates, the coordinator will send abort message to all subordinates. If all subordinates send "ready" messages, then the coordinator will send another message saying that everyone has signaled commit and write a "global commit" log to the stable storage.
4. If the subordinates get a message saying everyone has decided commit, then the subordinates will commit the data and send back an acknowledgement message back to the coordinator and commit log is written to the local stable storage. If the subordinates get an "abort" message, the subordinates will abort.
5. When the coordinator receives an acknowledgement messages back from all subordinates, the coordinator will record "complete" in the log and the transaction is finished.

If any of the subordinates fails to respond within a set time before the "commit" message have been sent, the coordinator will send abort to all of the subordinates.

7.18.1 RESILIENCE OF TWO-PHASE COMMIT

Two-Phase Commit protocol is able to handle all failures and is able to keep the database systems consistent. The following are possible failures and how 2PC is able to handle them. An important assumption is that each site has its own recovery and concurrency controls to recover from local crashes and failures.

Process	Coordinator Fails	Subordinate Fails
Coordinator sends a "prepare" message	Nothing happens because coordinator hasn't sent any messages yet	Subordinate fails to receive a "prepare" message so after some predetermined time coordinator will abort the transaction and send abort to all subordinates
Subordinates sends either a "ready" or "abort" message	All the subordinates that replied "ready" would wait until the coordinator recover and send a reply back. Until then, the subordinates will continue sending message to the coordinator with request for the reply.	Same as above.
The coordinator sends "commit" or "abort" message.	Same as above.	The coordinator will wait until the subordinate recovers and sends a commit message to the subordinate.
The subordinate will send an acknowledgement.	Same as above	Same as above

7.18.2 TWO-PHASE COMMIT VARIATIONS – PRESUME ABORT

The researchers for the R* System improved the performance of 2PC protocol by assuming abort. In presumed abort, when the coordinator receives an "abort" message from any of the subordinates, the coordinator will send "abort" messages to other subordinates and forget about the entire transaction. If any of the subordinates fail during the process, after the failed subordinate recover, it will ask the coordinator what has happened and from the coordinator's log, it will find that the transaction has been aborted, and the subordinate will abort. The advantage of this variation is reduction of number of control messages between the coordinator and subordinates. However, presume abort becomes less efficient when network is less stable, so it would be better for the subordinates and the coordinator to wait for the network to become reliable again.

7.18.3 TWO-PHASE COMMIT ISSUES AND NON-BLOCKING COMMITMENT PROTOCOL: 3PC

The main issue with traditional 2PC is the blocking factor [2]. Blocking occurs if failure(s) result in other sites having to wait until the failure gets resolved. For example, if there are any network or database failures in any sites after the first phase, then subordinates and/or coordinator have to wait until network communication is restored or until failed site recover from the failure. Since the recovery time can vary from few minutes to few hours or even days, it is very inefficient for sites to wait and hold the locks until a

response is received. The problem is more acute for the case when the coordinator fails since all the subordinates have to wait for the coordinator to recover. In the case that one of the subordinate fail, only the coordinator have to wait for the failed subordinate to recover. This problem led to a non-blocking solution. The goal of a non-blocking solution is to have the transaction keep on going at all operational sites or abort the transaction if the coordinator fails.

The 3PC works as follows:

1. The coordinator will write a "prepare" log on a stable storage and will send "prepare" messages to the subordinates.
2. After the subordinates receives a "prepare" message, they will decide if they can commit or not and sends the response back to the coordinator. If the subordinate decides to commit, a "ready" log will be written to a stable storage on the subordinate's machine.
3. If the coordinator receives an abort reply from any subordinates, the coordinator will send "prepare abort" message to all subordinates. If all subordinates send a ready to commit message, the coordinator will send "prepare commit" message to the subordinates and write a "global commit" log to the stable storage.
4. If the subordinates get a "prepare commit" message, then the subordinates will go into "ready to commit" and send back an "okay" message back to the coordinator and appropriate log is written to the local stable storage. If the subordinates get an "prepare abort" message, the subordinates will do the same.
5. When the coordinator receive "okay" messages back from all subordinates, the coordinator will send "final commit" or "final abort" message to the subordinates and writes appropriate log to a stable storage.

The difference between 3PC and 2PC can be seen when the coordinator fails before sending "prepare commit" message. In 2PC, the subordinates will wait indefinitely until the coordinator comes back again, but in 3PC, a new coordinator is chosen and the new coordinator behaves as follows:

Status of the new coordinator	Actions by the new coordinator	Why the actions are correct
The new coordinator is in "prepare commit" mode	The new coordinator will send "prepare commit" to the subordinates and wait for "Ok" message. Once all "Ok" messages are received, "commit" message is sent to all subordinates.	Nothing has been changed at other sites, so the new coordinator will try to determine the states of other sites and act accordingly.
The new coordinator has committed	"Commit" messages are sent to all subordinates	If the coordinator has committed then other sites should have at least gotten "prepare commit" and sent "Ok" message back to the old coordinator. So other sites should have no problem of committing.
The new coordinator has aborted	"Abort" messages are sent to all subordinates	If the coordinator has aborted then at the worst case, other sites would be at "prepare commit," so there is no inconsistency in aborting at other sites.
The new coordinator is in "prepare" mode	"Abort" messages are sent to all subordinates	Same as above.

7.18.4 THREE PHASE COMMIT ISSUES – QUORUM-BASED PROTOCOLS

Surprisingly, 3PC, in its basic form, do not guarantee consistency. Consider the following case: let and x and y be two groups of operating sites and because of a network failure, communication between two groups are completely gone. Following 3PC, two groups will choose their own coordinators and continue to go through the protocol. So there is a possibility that x and y will act differently. For example, x might choose a coordinator that was in "prepare commit" and later decides to commit. But if y chooses a new coordinator who was in "prepare" mode, then y will uniformly abort.

The solution is to use a quorum of subordinates and the coordinator. If the coordinator fails and a new coordinator is chosen, the coordinator starts collecting information from the subordinates. An addition to the 3PC is the "prepare to abort." Unlike the original 3PC, sites that respond to "prepare to abort" can still commit later on. What "prepare to abort" means is that the site wants to abort but in the same case it doesn't have to and can commit if the situation requires it. This is possible because the quorum is built after all sites have research "prepare" state and in this state, the sites do not care if they commit or abort. Quorum-based protocol also introduced V_A and V_C,

where these are the constants that are defined during the transaction. If V is the total number of sites in a transaction, then $V_A+V_C=V+1$ to ensure that commit or abort in performed. The following the behavior by the new coordinator using quorum-based protocol:

Situation	Actions by the new coordinator	Reason for the actions
At least one of the sites has committed	Send "commit" messages to the subordinates	Since at least one site has committed, other sites should be at "prepare commit" or at "commit." So eventually, all sites should commit.
At least one of the sites has aborted	Send "abort" messages to the subordinates	Since at least one site has aborted, other sites will be at most "prepare." So there is no possibility that other sites will commit.
The number of sites that are in prepared-to-commit state is greater than V_C.	Send "commit" messages to the subordinates	It is more likely that other sites will want to commit so commit is sent.
The number of sites that are in prepared-to-abort state is greater than V_A.	Send "abort" messages to the subordinates.	It is more likely that other sites will want to abort so abort is sent.
The sum of number of sites that are in prepare-to-commit and unknown states is greater than V_C.	"Prepare commit" message is sent to the sites with unknown states and the coordinator waits.	No decision can be made.
The sum of number of sites that are in prepare-to-commit and unknown states is greater than V_A.	"Prepare abort" message is sent to the sites with unknown states and the coordinator waits.	Same as above.
Other cases	The coordinator waits.	Same as above.

7.19 REPLICATION ISSUES AND MISCELLANEOUS ISSUES

Recovery protocols have to account for replication if the distributed database system supports replication. For the copies of the data to be consistent, the copies have to stay the same. This is done through updating every copy and the protocol is same as of 2PC or 3PC. A single copy is used as a coordinator, and the coordinator sends update commands to every copy and tries to commit the copies.

Another issue with 2PC, 3PC or another other protocols are how to resolved commission errors. Commission errors occur when messages are corrupted during transmission or if the coordinator sends wrong commands to the subordinates or if the subordinates do not perform correctly. As possible

solutions to commission error lies in network communication, they will not be discussed in this survey paper.

7.20 FUTURE RESEARCH

There are many possibilities for research in recovery protocols in distributed database systems. While the performance of recovery protocol made be trivial to centralized database system, because of communication costs, recovery protocol has larger role in overall database performance. It would be an important study to research on performance of recovery protocol in different situations. Furthermore, there needs to be research done on how recovery protocol affects the performance of other components of distributed database. For example, how will 3PC affect locking mechanisms of replicated data? Does presume-abort work well in cases where commits are frequent and how fast will locks be acquired and freed? These are some questions that need to be answered for an efficient distributed database system to be implemented.

EXERCISES

1. What do you mean by distributed concurrency control?
2. Explain the concept of concurrency control?
3. Explain the database system model?
4. What do you mean by two phase locking method?
5. Explain the concept of time stamp ordering methods?
6. Explain the concurrency control and recovery in distributed databases?
7. Explain the various anomalies of concurrency control?
8. What are the objectives of distributed concurrency control?
9. Explain the serilizability in a distributed database?
10. What do you mean by distributed serializability?
11. Explain the concept of two-phase locking in distributed databases?
12. Explain the various techniques concurrency control?
13. Explain the locking-based concurrency control protocols?
14. Explain the concept of centralized 2PL?
15. Explain the concept of primary copy 2PL?
16. Explain the concept of distributed 2PL?
17. Explain the concept of majority locking protocol?
18. Explain the concept of biased protocol?

19. Explain the concept of quorum consensus protocol?
20. What do you understand by timestamps in a distributed database?
21. Explain the various timestamp-based concurrency control protocols?
22. What do you mean by basic timestamp ordering (TO) algorithm?
23. What do you mean by conservative timestamp ordering algorithm?
24. What do you mean by multi-version to algorithm?
25. Explain the optimistic concurrency control technique?
26. What do you mean by reliability?
27. Explain the concept of reliability and concurrency control?
28. Explain the detection and resolution of inconsistency?
29. Explain the reliability protocols in distributed database systems?
30. Explain the concept of two-phase commit and three-phase commit protocols?

CHAPTER 8

DISTRIBUTED DEADLOCK MANAGEMENT

8.1 INTRODUCTION

Deadlock occurs when we have a set of processes [not necessarily all the processes in the system], each holding some resources, each requesting some resources, and none of them is able to obtain what it needs, i.e. to make progress. We will usually reason in terms of resources R1, R2, .., Rm and processes P1, P2, .., Pn. A process Pi that is waiting for some currently unavailable resource is said to be blocked.

Resources can be preemptable or non-preemptable. A resource is preemptable if it can be taken away from the process that is holding it [we can think that the original holder waits, frozen, until the resource is returned to it]. Memory is an example of a preemptable resource. Of course, one may choose to deal with intrinsically preemptable resources as if they were non-preemptable. In our discussion we only consider non-preemptable resources.

Resources can be reusable or consumable. They are reusable if they can be used again after a process is done using them. Memory, printers, tape drives are examples of reusable resources. Consumable resources are resources that can be used only once. For example a message or a signal or an event. If two processes are waiting for a message and one receives it, then the other process remains waiting. To reason about deadlocks when dealing with consumable resources is extremely difficult. Thus we will restrict our discussion to reusable resources.

Resources are usually with a multiplicity, i.e. an indication of how many copies of the resource exist. So we may have 3 tape drives, 2 printers, etc. We normally assume that resources have a multiplicity different than 1. If it were always 1 the study of deadlocks could be simplified. In fact, in the case of data bases, or of shared persistent objects, it is usual to have only a single copy of the object (or if there are many copies, as with replicated objects, their access from one user are so different that we can treat the copies as distinct resources with multiplicity one).

8.2 DEADLOCK

A deadlock is a situation when transactions are endlessly waiting for one another. Any lock-based concurrency control algorithm and some timestamp-based concurrency control algorithms may result in a deadlocks, as these algorithms requires transactions to wait for one another. In a lock-based concurrency control algorithms, locks on data items are acquired in a mutually exclusive manner; thus, it may cause a deadlock situation. Whenever a deadlock situation arises in a database environment, outside interference is required to continue with the normal execution of the system. Therefore, the database systems require special procedures to resolve the deadlock situation. Deadlock situations can be characterized by wait-for graphs, directed graphs that indicate which transactions are waiting for which other transactions. In a wait-for graph, nodes of the graph represent transactions and edges of the graph represent the waiting-for relationships among transaction T_i is waiting for a lock on a data item that is currently held by the transaction T_i. Using wait-for graphs, it is very easy to detect whether a deadlock situation has occurred in a database environment or not. There is a deadlock in the system if and only if the corresponding wait-for graph contains a cycle. The resolution of a deadlock situation is much easier in a centralized DBMS than in a distributed DBMS. In a characterized DBMS, only one local wait-for graph (LWFG) is drawn to detect the deadlock situation. The detection of deadlocks in a distributed DBMS is more complicated, because the circular waiting situation, which determines a deadlock, may involve several different sites.

Thus, in a DDBMS it is not sufficient to draw a LWFG for each local DBMS only, but it is also necessary to draw global wait-for graph (GWFG) for the entire system to detect a deadlock situation. In a distributed database, an LWFG is a portion of the GWFG, which consists of only those nodes and edges that are completely contained at a single site.

Three general techniques are available for deadlock resolution in a distributed database system: distributed deadlock prevention, distributed deadlock avoidance and distributed deadlock detection and recovery from deadlock.

Deadlock can only arise in a system where:

- Resources are used in mutual exclusion,
- Resources are acquired piecemeal (i.e. not all the resources that are needed to complete an activity are obtained at the same time in a single indivisible action).
- Resources are not pre-empted (i.e. a process does not take away resources being held by another process). And,
- Resources are not spontaneously given up by a process until it has satisfied all its outstanding requests for resources (i.e. a process, seeing that it cannot obtain some needed resource it does not kindly give up the resources that it is currently holding).

Example 8.1

Suppose that there are two transactions T_1 and T_2 respectively. Further assume that currently the transaction T_1 is holding an exclusive lock on data item Z, and the transaction $T\text{-}_2$ is holding an exclusive lock on data item X. Now, if the transaction T_1 requires a write operation on data item X, the transaction T_1 has to wait until the transaction T_2 releases the lock on the data item X. However, in the meantime if the transaction T_2 requires a read

or a write operation on the data item Z, the transaction T_2 also has to wait for the transaction T_1. In this situation, both the transactions T_1 and T_2 have to wait for each other indefinitely to release their respective locks, and no transaction can proceed for execution; thus a deadlock situation arises.

The formal definition of a deadlock follows.

A deadlock occurs if and only if the following four conditions hold in a system simultaneously:

D1: Mutual Exclusion

At least one of the resources is non-sharable (that is, only a limited number of processes can use it at a time and if it is requested by a process while it is being used by another one, the requesting process has to wait until the resource is released).

D2: Hold and Wait

There must be at least one process that is holding at least one resource and waiting for other resources that are currently being hold by other processes.

D3: No Preemption

No resource can be pre-empted before the holding process completes its task with that resource.

D4: Circular Wait

There exists a set of processes: {P1 , P2 , ...,Pn } such that:

P1 is waiting for a resource held by P2

P2 is waiting for a resource held by P3

.....

Pn-1 is waiting for a resource held by Pn

Pn is waiting for a resource held by P1

Resource Allocation Graphs

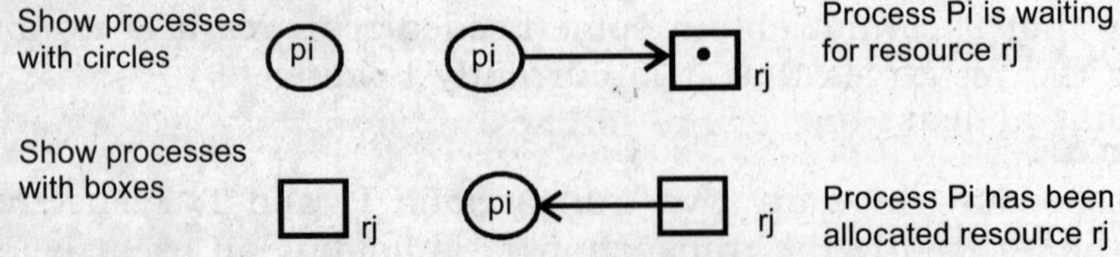

1. If the resource allocation graph contains no cycles then there is no deadlock in the system at that instance.
2. If the resource allocation graph contains a cycle then a deadlock may exist.

3. If there is a cycle and each resource has exactly one instance then a deadlock has occurred.
4. If there is a cycle, and the cycle involves only resources which have a single instance, then a deadlock has occurred.

Example 8.2:

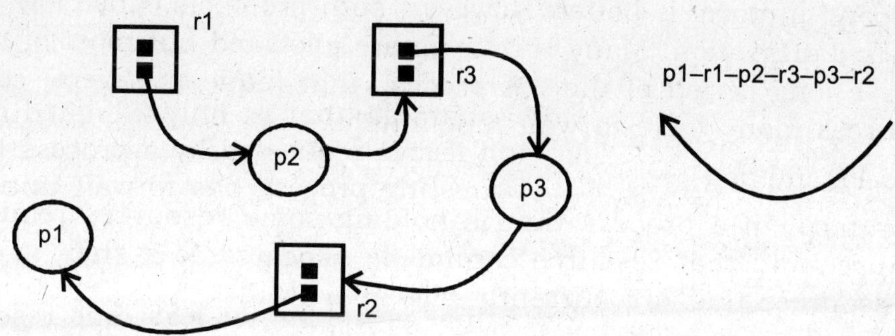

There are cycles, so a deadlock may exist. Actually, p1, p2, and p3 are deadlocked.

Example 8.3:

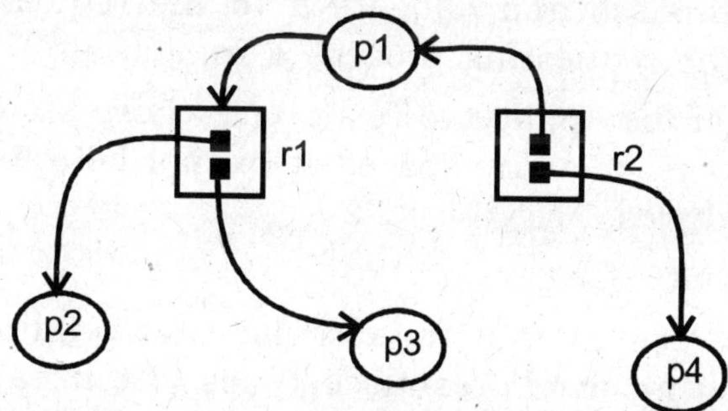

There is a cycle : p1 -> r1 -> p3 -> r2 -> p1

However, there is no deadlock. If p4 releases r2, r2 may be allocated to p3, which breaks the cycle.

8.2.1 DEADLOCK PREVENTION

Ensure that at least one of the four conditions (D1,D2,D3,D4) we discussed cannot hold.

D1: Mutual exclusion

In general we don't have systems with all resources being sharable. Some resources like printers, processing units are non-sharable. So, it is not possible prevent deadlocks by denying mutual exclusion.

D2: Hold-and-wait

One protocol to ensure that hold-and-wait condition never occurs says each process must request and get all of its resources before it begins execution.

Another protocol is: "each process can request resources only when it has no resources allocated."

The second protocol is better. However, both protocols cause low resource utilization and starvation. Many resources are allocated but most of them are unused for a long period of time. A process that requests several commonly used resources many have to wait indefinitely.

D3: No Preemption

One protocol "if a process that is holding some resources requests another resource and that resource cannot be allocated to it then it must release all resources that are currently allocated to it.

Another protocol: "when a process requests some resources, if they are available, allocate them. If a resource it requested is not available, then we check whether it is being used or it is allocated to some other process waiting for other resources. If that resource is not being used, then we preempt it from the waiting process and allocate it to the requesting process. If that resource is used, the requesting process a must wait"

This protocol can be applied to resources whose state can easily be saved and restored (registers, memory space). It cannot be applied to resources like printers and tape drives.

D4: Circular Wait

One protocol to ensure that the circular wait condition never holds : impose a linear ordering of all resource types. Then each process can only request resources in an increasing order of priority.

Example 8.4:

Priority (card reader) = 1

Priority (disk drive) = 2

Priority (tape drive) = 3

Priority (printer) = 4

With these priorities, if process pi wants to use the card reader and the printer, it should first request the card reader, then the printer.

Another protocol: Whenever a process requests a resource rj, it must have released all resources rk with: priority (rk) [3] priority (rj).

With these protocols, the circular wait condition never holds.

8.2.2 RESOURCE ALLOCATION GRAPHS

Resource Allocation Graphs (RAGs) are directed labelled graphs used to represent, from the point of view of deadlocks, the current state of a system.

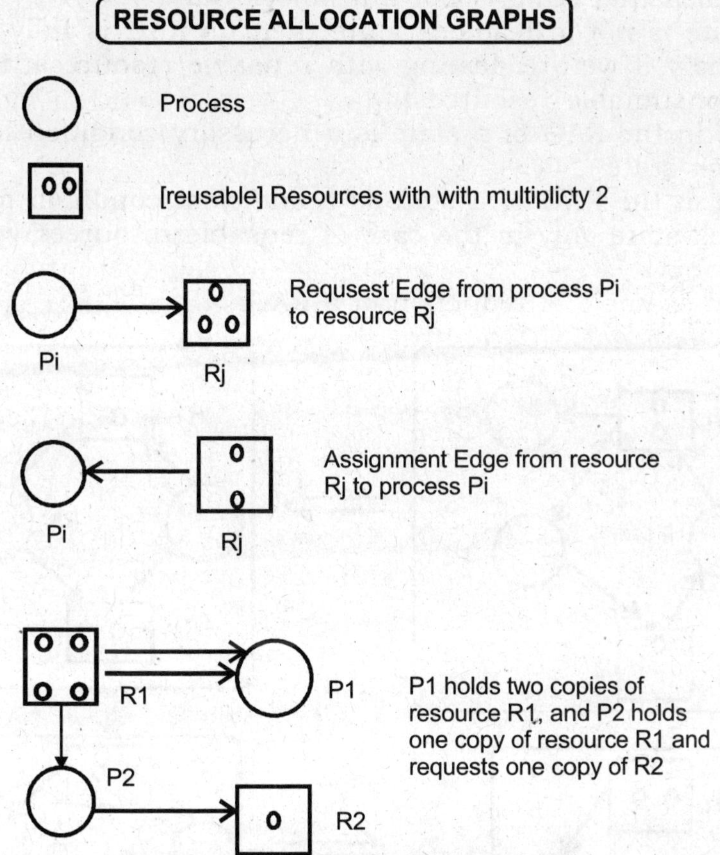

Figure 8.1 Resource allocation graph

State transitions can be represented as transitions between the corresponding resource allocation graphs. Here are the rules for state transitions:

- **REQUEST:** if process Pi has no outstanding request, it can request simultaneously any number (up to multiplicity) of resources R1, R2, ..Rm. The request is represented by adding appropriate requests edges to the RAG of the current state.
- **ACQUISITION:** if process Pi has outstanding requests and they can all be simultaneously satisfied, then the request edges of these requests are replaced by assignment edges in the RAG of the current state
- **RELEASE:** if process Pi has no outstanding request then it can release any of the resources it is holding, and remove the corresponding assignment edges from the RAG of the current state.

Here are some important propositions about deadlocks and resource allocation graphs:

- If the RAG of a state of a system is fully reducible (i.e. it can be reduced to a graph without any edges using ACQUISITION and RELEASE operations) then that state is not a deadlock state.
- If a state is not a deadlock state then its RAG is fully reducible [this holds only if we are dealing with reusable resources; it is false if we have consumable resources]
- A cycle in the RAG of a state is a necessary condition for that being a deadlock state
- A cycle in the RAG of a state is a sufficient condition for that being a deadlock state only in the case of reusable resources with multiplicity one.

Here is an example of reduction of a RAG:

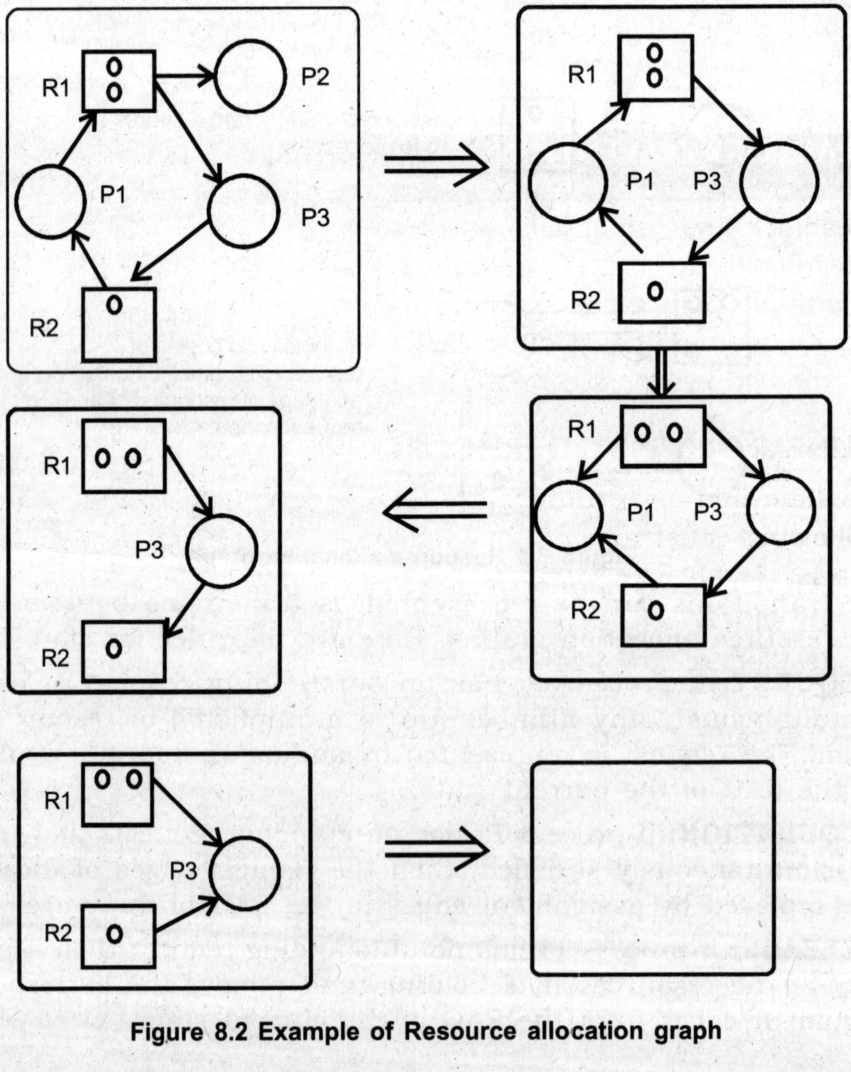

Figure 8.2 Example of Resource allocation graph

And here is a deadlock-free system with a loop.

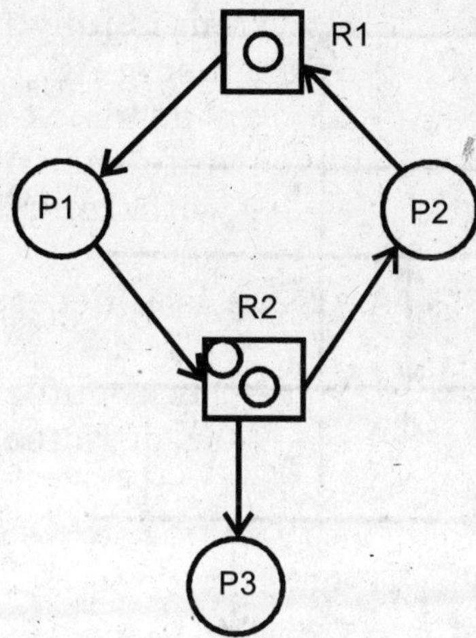

Figure 8.3 Example of Resource allocation graph with loop but no deadlock

8.3 DEADLOCK PREVENTION

Deadlock Prevention is to use resources in such a way that we cannot get into deadlocks. In real life we may decide that left turns are too dangerous, so we only do right turns. It takes longer to get there but it works. In terms of deadlocks, we may constrain our use of resources so that we do not have to worry about deadlocks. Here we explore this idea with two examples.

8.3.1 LINEAR ORDERING OF RESOURCES

Assume that all resources are totally ordered from 1 to r. We may impose the following constraint:

- **LO:** A process cannot request a resource Rk if it is holding a resource Rh with k < h. It is easy to see that with this rule we will not get into deadlocks. [Proof by contradiction.] Here is an example of how we apply this rule. We are given a process that uses resources ordered as A, B, C, D, and E in the following manner:

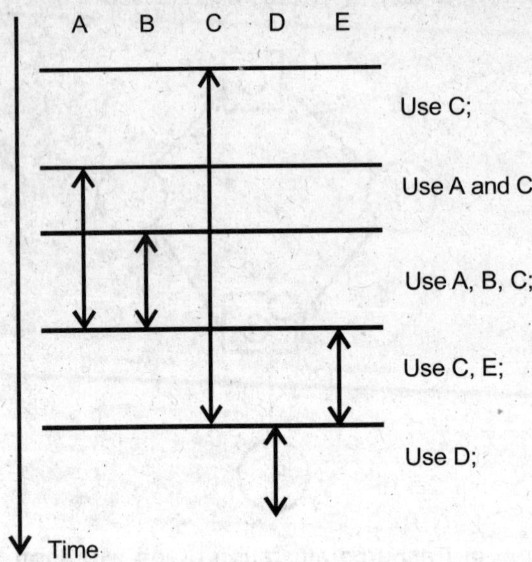

Figure 8.4 linear ordering of resources

Then the process can do the following:

acquire(A); acquire(B); acquire(C);
use C
use A and C
use A, B, C
release(A); release(B); acquire(E);
use C and E
release(C); release(E); acquire(D);
use D
release(D);

A strategy such as this can be used when we have a few resources. It is easy to apply and does not reduce the degree of concurrency too much.

8.3.2 HIERARCHICAL ORDERING OF RESOURCES

Another strategy we may use in the case that resources are hierarchically structured is to lock them in hierarchical order. We assume that the resources are organized in a tree (or a forest) representing containment. We can lock any node or group of nodes in the tree. The resources we are interested in are nodes in the tree, usually leaves. Then the following rule will guarantee avoidance of deadlocks.

- **HO:** The nodes currently locked by a process must lay [simultaneously and at all times until the desired resources are acquired] on all paths from the root to the desired resources.

Here is an example of use of this rule, locking a single resource at a time.

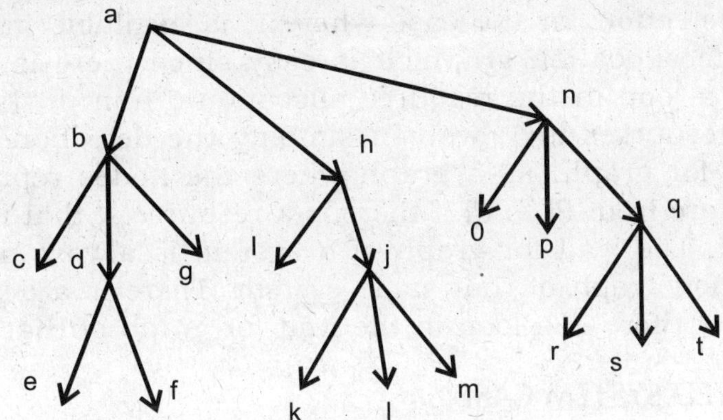

Figure 8.5 Hierarchical Ordering Of Resources

Then if a process wants to use the resources e, f, i, k it uses in sequence the commands:

lock(a); lock(b); lock(h); unlock(a); lock(d); unlock(b); lock(i); lock(j); unlock(h); lock(k); unlock(j); lock(e); lock(f); unlock(d);

Of course by forcing all locking sequences to start at the root of the resource hierarchy we create a bottleneck, since now the root becomes a scarce resource. As always there are trade-offs to be made. An obvious improvement on this prevention policy is to start not by locking the root, but by instead locking the lowest node subsuming all the nodes used by the current activity. For example if we had an activity that accessed only the nodes p, r, and s then we could start by locking n, not a.

8.4 DEADLOCK AVOIDANCE

Deadlock Avoidance, assuming that we are in a safe state (i.e. a state from which there is a sequence of allocations and releases of resources that allows all processes to terminate) and we are requested certain resources, simulates the allocation of those resources and determines if the resultant state is safe. If it is safe the request is satisfied, otherwise it is delayed until it becomes safe.

The Banker's Algorithm is used to determine if a request can be satisfied. It uses requires knowledge of who are the competing transactions and what are their resource needs. Deadlock avoidance is essentially not used in distributed systems.

8.5 DEADLOCK DETECTION

Deadlock Detection, in the case where it is available information about the full resource allocation graph, it is easy since there is deadlock if and only if there is a loop in the resource allocation graph. In the case that the multiplicity of resources is 1, we can simplify the detection of deadlocks by building a wait-for graph, i.e a graph where the nodes represent processes and there is an arc from Pi to Pj if there is a resource R that is held by Pj and requested by Pi. The wait-for graph of a system is always smaller than the resource allocation graph of that same system. There is a deadlock in a system if and only if there is a loop in the wait-for graph of that system.

8.5.1 DISTRIBUTED SYSTEM CASE

It is easy to get into deadlock with transactions that follow two-phase locking and it is easy, if we compute correctly the wait-for graph, to detect a deadlock has occurred. For example, if we have 3 computers 1, 2, and 3, with resources respectively, A, B, and C and D and we have three transactions T1, T2, and T3 that execute as indicate below:

TRANSACTION T1 (Transfer from B to A and D)	TRANSACTION T2 (Transfer from C to B)	TRANSACTION T3 (Transfer from A to C)
Lock(D)		
Deposit to D		
	Lock(B)	
	Deposit to B	
Lock(A)		
Deposit to A		
		Lock(C)
		Deposit to C
Lock(B)		
	Lock(C)	
		Lock(A)
--------------- Deadlock	------------------------------	
Withdraw from B	Withdraw from C	Withdraw from A
Unlock A,B,D	Unlock B,C	Unlock A,C

we have the wait-for diagram

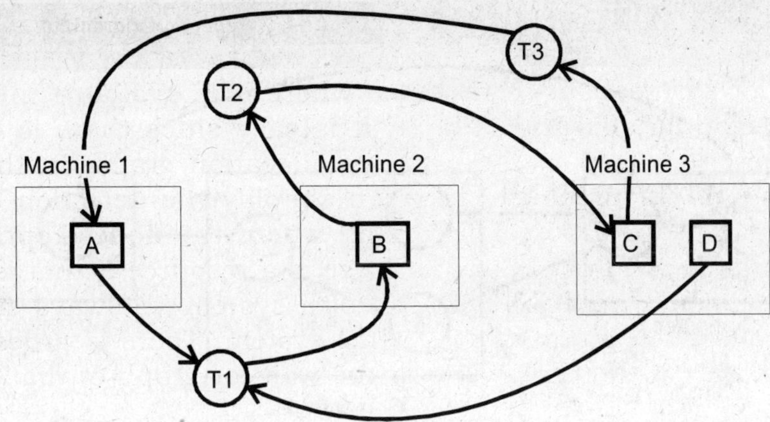

that has a loop, thus we have a deadlock.

As shows, when the wait-for graph is computed at a central location that collects messages from the various systems involved in transactions, it is easy to find also false, or spurious, or phantom deadlocks as in the following picture

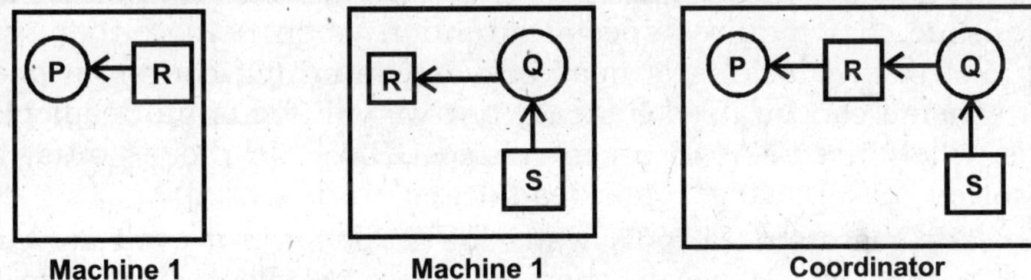

When Q first releases S and then P requests S, but the messages delivered to the coordinator that collects the messages arrive in the wrong order. Then the coordinator believes that a deadlock has arisen and kills unnecessarily P or Q. Of course, if Q was following a 2-phase locking policy, it would not release any lock until it had acquired every lock it needed. Thus phantom deadlocks would not arise if 2-phase locking is followed.

The Chandy-Misra-Haas algorithm detects deadlocks in a distributed system (resources with multiplicity 1) without requiring a coordinator.

When process Pi requests a resource held by process Pj, it sends a message of form

[Requestor of resource, source of message, destination of message]

to Pj, thus in this case Pi sends to Pj the message [i, i, j]. In turn Pj will send to each process Ph such that Pj requests a resource held by process Ph, the message [i, j, h]. The same will be done by Ph, etc. if the original requestor Pi receives a message of form [i, *, i], then it will know that there is a loop, that a deadlock will arise, thus it will delay the request or abort. For example, here is what happens in the following system when process P1 requests a resource held by process P2: indicating that a deadlock arises.

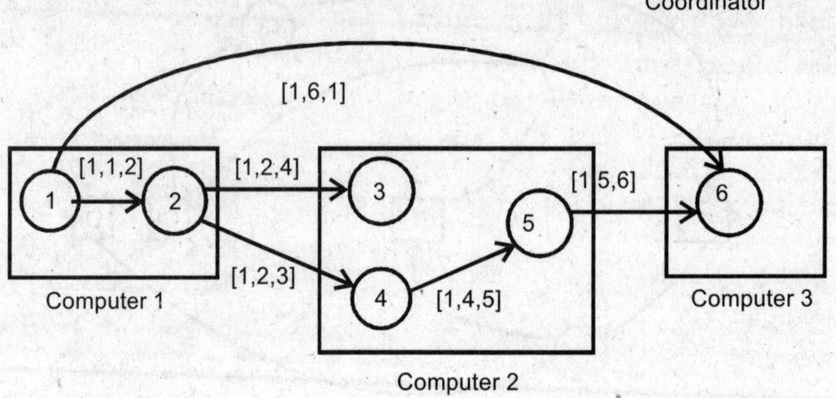

For distributed deadlock prevention can be used timestamps indicating the start of transactions and then ordering priority in case of conflicts on the basis of the time stamp.

8.6 OVERVIEW OF DISTRIBUTED DEADLOCK

One issue that requires special attention when using either primary copy or fully distributed locking is deadlock detection. (Of course, a deadlock prevention scheme can be used instead, but we will focus on deadlock detection, which is widely used.) As in a centralized DBMS, deadlocks must be detected and resolved (by aborting some deadlocked transaction).

Each site maintains a local waits-for graph, and a cycle in a local graph indicates a deadlock. However, there can be a deadlock even if no local graph contains a cycle. For example, suppose that two sites, A and B, both contain copies of objects O1 and O2, and that the read-any write-all technique is used. T1, which wants to read O1 and write O2, obtains an S lock on O1 and an X lock on O2 at Site A, then requests an X lock on O2 at Site B. T2, which wants to read O2 and write O1, meanwhile obtains an S lock on O2 and an X lock on O1 at Site B, then requests an X lock on O1 at Site A. As Figure 8.6 illustrates, T2 is waiting for T1 at Site A and T1 is waiting for T2 at Site B; thus, we have a deadlock, which neither site can detect based solely on its local waits-for graph.

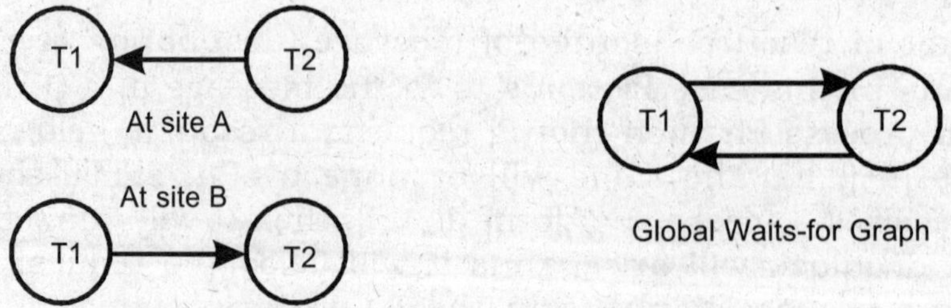

Figure 8.6 Distributed Deadlocks

To detect such deadlocks, a **distributed deadlock detection** algorithm must be used. We describe three such algorithms.

The **first algorithm**, which is centralized, consists of periodically sending all local waits for graphs to some one site that is responsible for global deadlock detection. At this site, the global waits-for graph is generated by combining all the local graphs; the set of nodes is the union of nodes in the local graphs, and there is an edge from one node to another if there is such an edge in any of the local graphs.

The **second algorithm**, which is hierarchical, groups sites into a hierarchy. For instance, sites might be grouped by state, then by country, and finally into a single group that contains all sites. Every node in this hierarchy constructs a waits-for graph that reveals deadlocks involving only sites contained in (the subtree rooted at) this node.

Thus, all sites periodically (e.g., every 10 seconds) send their local waits-for graph to the site responsible for constructing the waits-for graph for their state. The sites constructing waits-for graphs at the state level periodically (e.g., every minute) send the state waits-for graph to the site constructing the waits-for graph for their country.

The sites constructing waits-for graphs at the country level periodically (e.g., every 10 minutes) send the country waits-for graph to the site constructing the global waits-for graph. This scheme is based on the observation that more deadlocks are likely across closely related sites than across unrelated sites, and it puts more effort into detecting deadlocks across related sites. All deadlocks will eventually be detected, but a deadlock involving two different countries may take a while to detect.

The **third algorithm** is simple: If a transaction waits longer than some chosen timeout interval, it is aborted. Although this algorithm may cause many unnecessary restarts, the overhead of deadlock detection is (obviously!) low, and in a heterogeneous distributed database, if the participating sites cannot cooperate to the extent of sharing their waits-for graphs, it may be the only option. A subtle point to note with respect to distributed deadlock detection is that delays in propagating local information might cause the deadlock detection algorithm to identify 'deadlocks' that do not really exist. Such situations are called **phantom deadlocks**, and lead to unnecessary aborts. For concreteness, we discuss the centralized algorithm, although the hierarchical algorithm suffers from the same problem.

Consider a modification of the previous example. As before, the two transactions wait

on each other, generating the local waits-for graphs shown in Figure 8.6, and the local waits-for graphs are sent to the global deadlock-detection site. However, T2 is now aborted for reasons other than deadlock. (For example, T2

may also be executing at a third site, where it reads an unexpected data value and decides to abort.) At this point, the local waits-for graphs have changed so that there is no cycle in the 'true' global waits-for graph. However, the constructed global waits-for graph will contain a cycle, and T1 may well be picked as the victim!

8.7 DISTRIBUTED DEADLOCKS

The detection and resolution of deadlocks constitute important activities of a database management system. The detection of a deadlock corresponds to the determination of a cycle in a wait-for graph. The problem of deadlock detection is more difficult in a distributed database than in a centralized one, because the circular waiting situation which determines a deadlock can involve several sites and not just one.

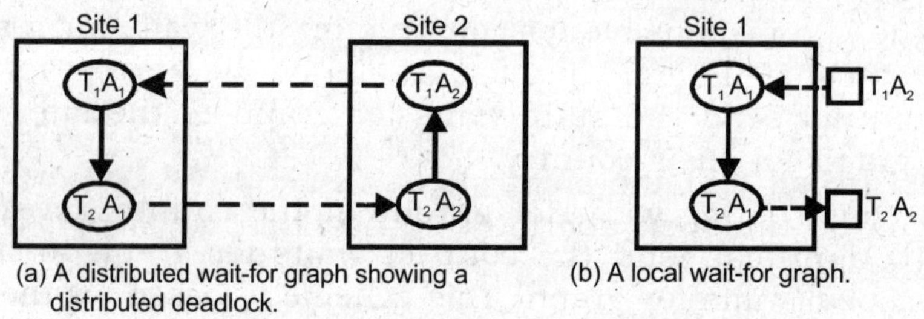

(a) A distributed wait-for graph showing a distributed deadlock.

(b) A local wait-for graph.

Figure 8.7 Distributed and local wait-for graphs.

Figure 8.7a shows a distributed wait-for graph (DWFG) which contains a cycle and thus corresponds to a deadlock situation. The notation T_iA_j refers to agent A_j of transaction T_i. In Figure 8.7a there are two sites and two transactions T_1 and T_2, each consisting of two agents. For simplicity, we assume that each transaction has only one agent at each site where it is executed. A directed edge from an agent T_iA_j to an agent T_rA_s means that T_iA_j is blocked and waiting for T_rA_s. There are two reasons why an agent can be waiting for another one:

1. Agent T_iA_j waits for agent T_iA_j to release a resource which it needs; in this case, T_i is a different transaction from T_r, and the two the two agents are at the same site, because agents request only local resources (recall that agents represent transactions at each site).This type of wait is represented by continuous edges in Figure 8.7a; for instance T_1A_1 is waiting for T_2A_1 to release a resource at site 1.
2. Agent T_iA_j waits for agent T_iA_s to perform some required function; in this case, the two agents belong t the same transaction and agent T_iA_j has requested that agent T_iA_s perform some function at a different site. This type of waiting is represented by the dashed edges in Figure 8.7a.

We call the local wait-for graph (LWFG) the portion of the DWFG consisting only of node and edges which are completely contained at a single site, extended with an indication of the nodes which represent remote agents having an edge connecting them to nodes of the local graph. An example of an LWFG is shown in Figure 8.7b and refers to site 1 of Figure 8.7a. The square nodes are called input ports if they have an edge entering the LWFG and output ports if they receive an edge existing the LWFG.

A deadlock is local if it is caused by a cycle in an LWFG. The determination of local deadlocks is a local task which is not considered here. A deadlock is distributed if it is caused by a cycle in the DWFG which is not contained in any LWFG. The detection of a distributed deadlock is a distributed task, which obviously requires the exchange of information between sites. In the rest of this section we will consider the detection and resolution only of global deadlocks.

Deadlock resolution involves the selection of one or more transactions to be aborted and restarted. When a transaction is aborted, it releases its resources, so that other transactions can proceed. The criteria which are used for the transaction which owns less resources; abort the transaction with smallest abort cost (recall that the abort of a transaction requires that all its previous operations be undone); abort the transaction with the longest expected time to complete.

The redundancy which is often present in a distributed database increases the probability of deadlocks. Consider for example two transactions T_1 and T_2, both of which must lock exclusively the same data item x and nothing else. If x is not replicated, then one transaction will obtain the lock and execute and the other one will wait. No deadlock can arise in this situation. However, if x is replicated, for instance two copies x1 and x2 of x exist at sites 1 and 2 and both transactions use the write-locks-all strategy defined in Chapter 7, then the following sequence of events at sites 1 and 2 determines a deadlock;

At site 1: T_1 locks x1; T_2 waits

At site 2: T_2 locks x2; T_1 waits

At this point the DWFG contains a cycle as in Figure 8.7a.

In the previous chapter we have seen the timeout method for deadlock detection; in the following we will consider several other methods for dealing with deadlocks in a distributed system:

1. Deadlock detection using centralized or hierarchical control
2. Distributed deadlock detection
3. Deadlock prevention

Methods 1 and 2 are based on the idea of transmitting the information of the DWFG between sites to detect deadlocks; method 3 consists in avoiding the occurrence of deadlocks by discovering "dangerous" situations a priori.

8.8 DEADLOCK DETECTION USING CENTRALIZED OR HIERARCHICAL CONTROLLERS

With the centralized controller method, described in reference, a selected site is chosen at which a centralized deadlock detector is run. The centralized deadlock detector has the responsibility of building the DWFG and of discovering cycles in it. Of course, in order to perform this task, the deadlock detector reviews information from all other sites.

At each site there is a local detector. The responsibility of each local deadlock detector is to determine all potential global deadlocks at its site (and to discover also local deadlocks, of course). The idea of a potential global deadlock cycle can be understood by considering again the example of Figure 8.7. Consider the deadlock detector at site 1.The LWFG of site 1 (Figure 8.7b) contains the local edges and edges to remote sites. Since the local deadlock detector cannot know whether at a remote site there is a sequence of edges connecting T_2A_2 to T_1A_2, the sequence of connected nodes constitutes a potential deadlock cycle.

$$T_1A_2 \rightarrow T_1A_1 \rightarrow T_2A_1 \rightarrow T_2A_2$$

In this case the potential deadlock cycle coincides with the whole LWFG; however, this does not occur in general.

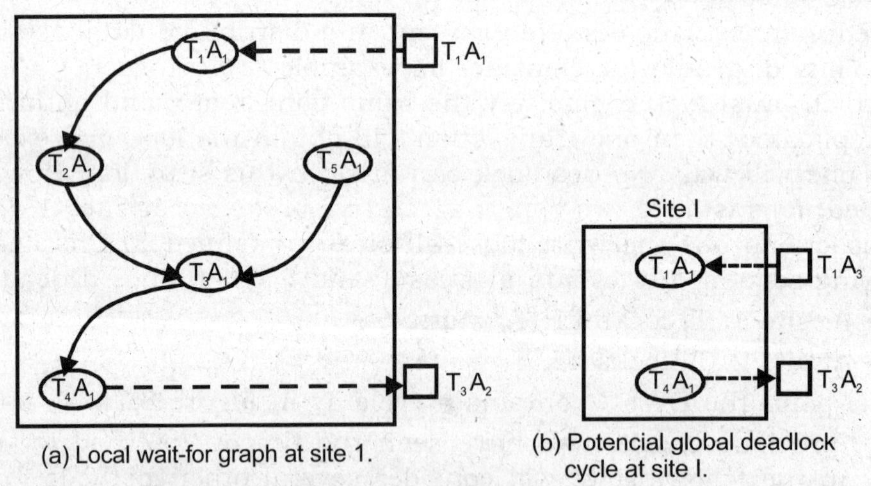

(a) Local wait-for graph at site 1.

(b) Potencial global deadlock cycle at site I.

Figure 8.8 Derivation of a potential global deadlock cycle from a LWFG

Consider now the more complex LWFG shown in Figure 8.8a. In order to determine potential deadlock cycles, the local deadlock detector starts from an input port and searches backward along the local graph until it reaches an output port. This part of the local graph constitutes a potential deadlock cycle. Only the initial and final agents of each potential cycle must be transmitted as it is shown in Figure 8.8b.

The global deadlock detector collects these messages, connects the partial information to build a simplified DWFG, determines cycles, and selects transactions to be aborted. This operation can be performed either periodically or every time there is a change in the situation of the potential deadlock cycles. The actual choice of a period for global deadlock detection is a trade-off between the cost of the detection process and the cost determining deadlocks late.

Centralized deadlock detection is simple, but it has two main drawbacks. First, it is vulnerable to failures of the site where the centralized detector runs. Second, it may require large communications costs, because the centralized detector may be located very far from some other sites of the network. It is possible (and in fact very likely in many applications) that deadlock involves only a few sites which are all close to one another. In this case, they could discover the deadlock without communicating with a distant central site. The hierarchical controller's method aims at exploiting this latter opportunity for reducing communication costs.

With the hierarchical controller's method, described in reference [8, 8] a whole tree of deadlock detectors is built, instead of having a set of local deadlock detectors and a single centralized global deadlock detector. At the leaves of the tree we still have the local deadlock detector. At the leaves of the tree we still have the local deadlock detectors (LDDs), while at nonleaf levels we have nonlocal deadlock detectors (NLDDs). Figure 8.9 shows an example of a hierarchy of deadlock detectors for a network consisting of five sites. Each local deadlock detector (denoted in the figure as LDD1... LDD5) behaves essentially like the local deadlock detectors of the centralized method: it determines local deadlocks and transmits information about potential global cycles to the NLDD at the immediately higher level in the hierarchy. Each nonlocal deadlock detector performs the detection of those deadlocks which involve only the deadlock graph to higher levels in the hierarchy. For example, referring to Figure 8.9, deadlocks involving LDD3, LDD4 and LDD5 are discovered by NLDD2, while a deadlock involving LDD2 and LDD3 is detected only by NLDDO (the highest level detector).

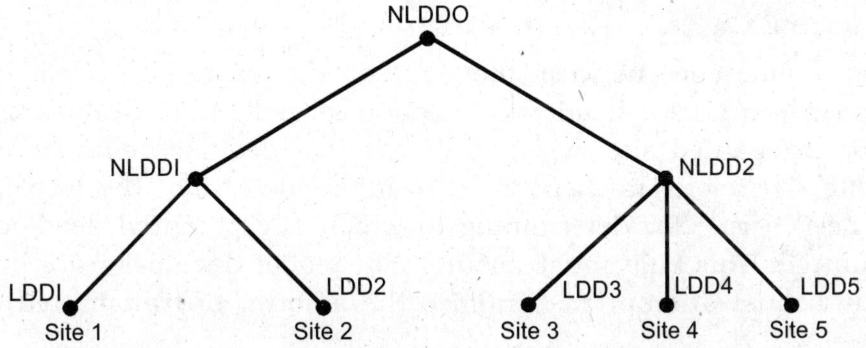

Figure 8.9 A tree of deadlock detectors

The performance of a hierarchical deadlock detection mechanism depends on the choice of the hierarchy. This choice should reflect the network topology and the pattern of access requests to the different sites of the network. For example, assume that a group of sites of the network. For example, assume that a group of sites is determined such that a high percentage of database access requests is within that group and only few requests are to sites outside the group. Such a group is a good candidate for building a subtree under the control of a common nonlocal detector. This problem is similar to the general problem of maximizing the locality of transactions in distributed database design (Chapter 2), with the additional aspect of considering not only locality at one single site but also "group locality," i.e., locality within a group of sites.

8.9 DISTRIBUTED DEADLOCK DETECTION

In a distributed deadlock detection mechanism, there is no distinction between local and nonlocal deadlock detectors. Each site has the same responsibility. Sites exchange information about waiting transactions in order to determine global deadlocks.

Many algorithms have been proposed for distributed deadlock detection in distributed database. We present a simplified version of the algorithm.

This algorithm is based on transmitting the information about potential deadlock cycles, like in the centralized the centralized algorithm. Potential deadlock cycles are detected by each site on their LWFGs. However this algorithm used a slightly different model of an LWFG: all output and input ports are collected into a single node, called external (EX). Moreover, since the indication of agents is irrelevant for the algorithm, only transaction identifiers are used. For example, Figure 8.10a and b represent the same distributed and local wait-for graphs of Figure 8.7a and b. Notice that, with this representation, a potential deadlock cycle is a cycle in the LWFG which contains the node EX.

The main difference between distributed and centralized deadlock detection is that in centralized deadlock detection all potential deadlock cycles are sent to one designated site, while in distributed deadlock detection there is no such site. Therefore, in distributed deadlock detection, the local deadlock detectors need a rule for determining to which site potential deadlock cycles are transmitted. This rule must assure that global deadlocks are eventually detected and must attempt to minimize the amount of transmitted information.

The rule which is used by this distributed deadlock detection algorithm consists in transmitting the potential deadlock information "along" the deadlock cycle itself. For example, consider site 1 of Figure 8.10b. The local deadlock detector has detected a potential deadlock cycle involving T_1, T_2, and EX. Site 1 can choose to send third potential deadlock cycle to the following sites:

1. The site where there is an agent T_1 waiting for T_1 at site 1; this choice corresponds to transmitting potential deadlock information backward along the cycle.
2. The site where there is an agent of T_2 for which T_2 at site 1 is waiting; this choice corresponds to sending the potential deadlock information forward along the cycle.

Clearly, it is not necessary to transmit in both directions. This algorithm transmits only in the forward direction.

If all sites transmit their potential deadlock cycles forward along the cycle, more information is transmitted than necessary. For example, consider the two sites of Figure 8.10b. Since the two situations at sites 1 and 2 are symmetric, both sites would send information about the same global deadlock to each other. This would cause that the same deadlock be discovered twice, which is not necessary. To avoid this unnecessary transmission, the algorithm uses the following rule: the potential deadlock cycle is transmitted only if the transaction identifier of the transaction for which EX waits is greater than the transaction identifier of the transaction waiting for EX. By applying this rule to the situation of Figure 8.10b, we obtain that only site 2 transmits the potential deadlock cycle, because at site 2 EX is waiting for T_2 and T_1 is waiting for EX in the potential cycle. At site 1 we have the opposite situation therefore site 1 does not transmit the potential deadlock cycle. Figure 8.10b shows also how the potential deadlock cycle is transformed into a message to be transmitted: a string is built containing EX followed by the transaction identifiers of the transactions, in the order in which they appear in the cycle.

This algorithm works by successive works by successive iterations. At each iteration each site receives potential deadlock information which was produced by other sites during type previous iteration, then it performs deadlock detection, and communication between local deadlock detectors occurs between different iterations of the algorithm.

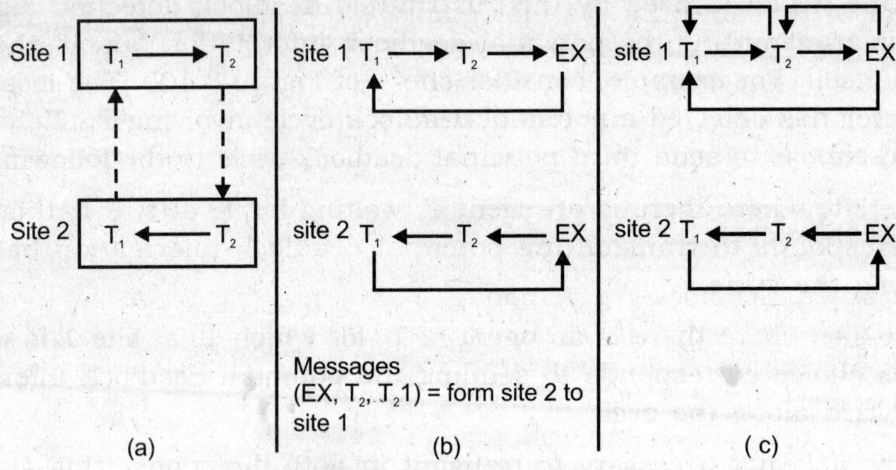

Figure 8.10 Distributed deadlock detection algorithm

At each iteration, the local deadlock detectors at each site perform the following actions:

1. Build the LWFG using local information. The LWFG includes the node EX.
2. For each message which has been received, perform the following modification of the LWFG:
   (a) For each transaction in the message, add it to the LWFG if it does not already exist.
   (b) For each transaction in the message, starting with EX, create an edge to the next transaction in the message. This step has all potential deadlock information received from other sites into the local LWFG. Note that, by effect of action 2b, the modified LWFG contain edges corresponding to wait conditions at emote sites.
3. Find cycles not involving EX in the LWFG. Each such cycle indicates the existence of a deadlock. Deadlock resolution is invoked to eliminate these deadlocks.
4. Find cycles involving EX. These cycles are potential deadlock cycles. The rule described above is used to determine whether a potential deadlock cycle must be transmitted to a different site. If the transmission is required, the message is prepared and transmitted. The transmission of potential deadlock cycles terminates the current iteration of the deadlock detection process.

Example 8.5

Consider the LWFGs of Figure 8.10b. We have seen already that only site 2 sends a message to site 1. The message is shown in the figure.

Figure 8.10c shows the wait-for graph which is obtained by applying the above rules after the message from site 2 has arrived at site 1. The deadlock detector at site 1 searches for cycles not containing EX. Figure 8.10c there is such a cycle between T_2 and $T_{1.}$ A victim is chosen, from Example $T_{1,}$ and an abort message is sent to all sites where the victim was active.

8.10 PREVENTION OF DEADLOCKS

Distributed Deadlock prevention is a cautions scheme in which a transaction is restarted when the system suspects that a deadlock might occur. Deadlock prevention is an alternative method to resolve deadlock situations in which a system is designed in such a way that deadlocks are impossible. In this scheme, the transaction manager checks a transaction when it is first initiated and does not permit to proceed if there is a risk that it may cause a deadlock.

8.10.1 IMPLEMENTATION OF DEADLOCK PREVENTION TECHNIQUE

Consider that a transaction T_i is initiated at a particular site in a distributed database system and that it requires a lock on a data item that is currently owned by another transaction T_j. Here a deadlock prevention test is done to check whether there is any possibility of a deadlock occurring in the system. The transaction T_i is not permitted to enter into a wait state for the transaction T_j, if there is the risk of a deadlock situation. In this case, one of the two transactions is aborted to prevent a deadlock. The deadlock prevention algorithm is called non-preemptive if the transaction T_i is aborted and restarted. On the other hand, if the transaction T_j is aborted and restarted, then the deadlock prevention algorithm is called preemptive. The transaction T_i is permitted to wait for the transaction T_j as usual, if they pass the prevention test. The prevention test must guarantee that if T_i is allowed to wait for T_j, a deadlock can never occur. Here, one simple approach to prevent deadlock situations is to ensure that the transaction T_i never waits for the transaction T_j, but this force a number of restarts. A better approach to implement deadlock prevention test is by assigning priorities to transactions and checking priorities to determine whether one transaction would wait for the other transaction or not. These priorities can be assigned by using a unique identifier for each transaction in a distributed site. For instance, consider that i and j are the priorities of two transactions T_i and T_j respectively. The transaction T_i would wait for the transaction T_j, if T_i has a lower priority than T_j, that is if $i<j$. This approach prevents deadlock, but one problem with this approach is that cyclic restart is possible. Thus, some transactions could be restarted repeatedly without ever finishing.

8.10.2 SOLUTION TO CYCLIC RESTART PROBLEM

We are using the unique timestamp value of each transaction as the priority of that transaction. One way to obtain a global timestamp value for every transaction in a distributed system is assigning a unique local timestamp value to each transaction by its local transaction manager and then appending the site identifier to the low-order bits of this value. Thus, timestamp values are unique throughout the distributed system and do not require that clocks at different sites are synchronized precisely.

There are two different techniques for deadlock prevention:

1. **Wait-die deadlock prevention technique:** Wait-die is a non-preemptive deadlock prevention technique based on timestamp values of transactions and is implemented in the following way. In this technique, when one transaction is about to block and is waiting for a lock on a data item that is already locked by another transaction, timestamp values of both the transactions are checked to give priority to the older transaction. If a younger transaction is holding the lock on the data item then the older transaction is allowed to wait, but if an older transaction is holding the lock, the younger transaction is aborted and restarted with the same timestamp value.. This forces the wait-for graph to be directed from the older to the younger transactions, making cyclic restarts impossible. For example, if the transaction T_i requests a lock on a data item that is already locked by the transaction T_j, then T_i is permitted to wait only if T_i has a lower timestamp value than T_j. On the other hand, if T_i is younger than T_j, then T_i is aborted and restarted with the same timestamp value.
2. **Wound-Wait deadlock prevention technique:** Wound-wait is an alternative pre-emptive deadlock prevention technique by which cyclic restarts can be avoided. In this method, if a younger transaction is allowed to wait until the older transaction releases the corresponding lock. In this case, the wait-for graph flows from the younger to the older transactions, and cyclic restart is again avoided. For instance, if the transaction T_i requests a lock on a data item that is already locked by the transaction T_j, then T_i is permitted to wait only if T_i has a higher timestamp value than T_j, otherwise the transaction T_j is aborted and the lock is granted to the transaction T_i.

8.10.3 COMPARISON OF WAIT- DIE AND WOUND-WAIT TECHNIQUES

Deadlock situation cannot arise and the younger transaction is restarted in both the above methods. The two techniques are different that whether they preempt the active transaction or not. In the wait-die method a transaction can only be restarted when it requires accessing a new data item for the first time. A transaction that has acquired locks on all the required data items will never be aborted. In wound-wait method, it is possible that a transaction that is already holding a lock on a data item is aborted, because another older transaction may request the same data item. Wait-die method gives preference to younger transactions and aborts older transactions, as older transactions wait for younger ones and they tend to wait longer as they get older. On the other hand, wound-wait method prefers older transaction holds the corresponding lock for a long time, while in wound-wait method the older transaction is aborted and restarted only once. The main disadvantage of a deadlock prevention scheme is that it may result in unnecessary waiting the rollback. Furthermore, some deadlock prevention schemes may require more sites in a distributed system to be involved in the execution of a transaction.

8.11 DISTRIBUTED DEADLOCK AVOIDANCE

This technique ensures that deadlock situations will not occur in a distributed system. Preordering of resources is a deadlock avoidance technique in which each data item in the database system is numbered, and each transaction requests locks on these data items in that numeric order. This technique requires that each transaction obtain all its locks before execution. Numbering of data items can be done either globally or locally.

In distributed database systems, it is necessary that all sites are numbered, and transactions that require to access data items from multiple sites must request the corresponding locks by visiting the sites according to the predefined numbers. The priority of a transaction is the highest number among the locks that are already owned by the transaction. In this method, as a transaction can only wait for those transactions that have higher priorities no deadlock situations can occur. Deadlock avoidance methods are more suitable than deadlock prevention schemes for database environments, but they require runtime support for deadlock management, which adds runtime overheads in transaction execution. Furthermore, in addition to requiring predeclaration of locks, a principal disadvantage of this technique is that it forces locks to be obtained sequentially, which tends to increase response time.

8.12 DISTRIBUTED DEADLOCK DETECTION AND RECOVERY

In deadlock detection and recovery method, first it is checked whether any deadlock has occurred in the system. After detection of a deadlock situation in the system, one of the involved transactions is chosen as the victim transaction and is aborted to resolve the deadlock situation. Deadlock situa-

tions are detected by explicitly constructing a wait-for graph and searching it for cycles. A cycle in the wait-for graph indicates that a deadlock has occurred, and one transaction in the cycle is chosen as the victim, which is aborted and restarted. To minimize the cost of restarting, the victim selection is usually based on the number of data items used by each transaction in the cycle. The principal difficulty in implementing deadlock detection in a distributed database environment is constructing the Global Wait For Graph efficiently. In a distributed DBMS, LWFG for each local DBMS can be drawn easily; however, these LWFGs are not sufficient to represent all deadlock situations in the distributed system.

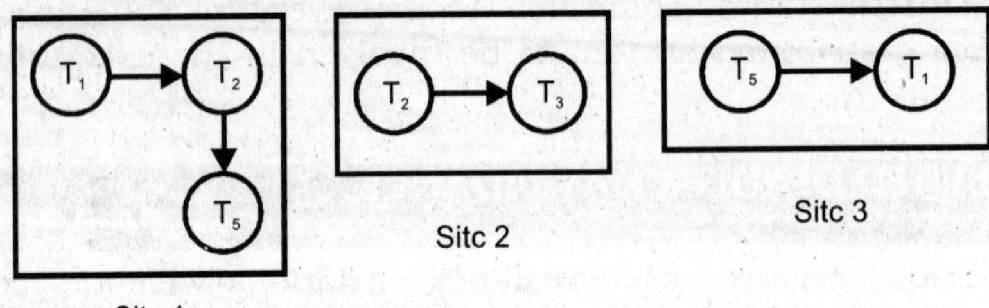

Figure 8.11 Local Wait-for Graphs at Different Sites

Deadlock detection and recovery is the most popular and most suitable technique for deadlock management in a database environment. For example, consider that there are three different sites in a distributed system, and each site has constructed a LWFG as shown in figure 8.11. The LWFG for each site is constructed in the usually manner using local transactions and data items stored at that particular site. A cycle in a LWFG indicates that a deadlock has occurred locally. The LWFGs in figure 8.11 illustrate that no deadlock has occurred locally in the three different sites, as there are no cycles in the LWFGs, but this does not guarantee that no deadlock has occurred globally. To detect a deadlock situation in the distributed system, it is necessary to construct a GWFG from these different LWFGs and to search it for cycles.

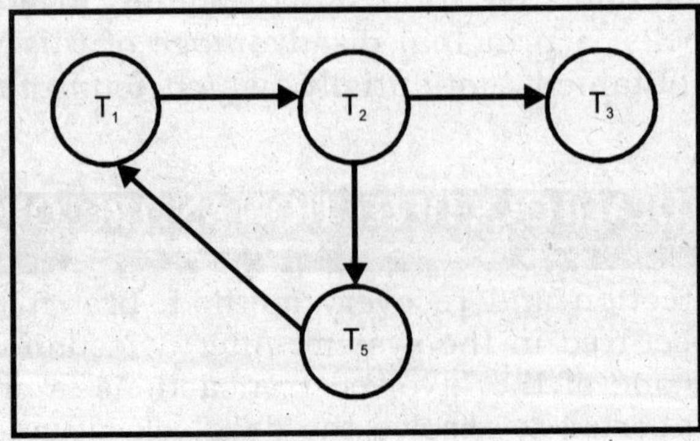

Figure 8.12 Global Wait-for Graph for Figure 8.11

The corresponding GWFG in figure 8.12 illustrate that a deadlock has occurred in the distributed system, although no deadlock has occurred locally.

There are three different techniques for detecting deadlock situations in a distributed system:

1. Centralized deadlock detection
2. Hierarchical deadlock detection
3. Distributed deadlock detection

8.12.1 CENTRALIZED DEADLOCK DETECTION

In Centralized Deadlock Detection method, a single site is chosen as Deadlock Detection Coordinator (DDC) for the entire distributed system. The DDC is responsible for constructing the GWFG for the system. Each lock manager in the distributed database system transmits its LWFG to the DDC periodically. The DDC constructs the GWFG from these LWFGs and checks for cycles in it. The occurrence of a global deadlock situation is detected if there are one or more cycles in the GWFG. The DDC must break each cycle in the GWFG by selecting the transactions to be rolled back and restarted to recover from a deadlock situation. The information regarding the transactions that are to be rolled back and restarted must be transmitted to the corresponding lock managers by the deadlock detection coordinator. To minimize communication cost, the DDC should only send the changes that have to be made in the LWFGs to the lock managers. These changes represent the addition or removal of edges in the LWFGs. The actual length of a period for global deadlock detection is a system design decision, and it is a trade-off between the communication cost of the deadlock detection process and the cost of detecting deadlocks late. The communication cost increases if the length of the period is larger, whereas some deadlocks in the system go undetected if the length of the deadlock detection period is smaller.

Advantages of Centralized Deadlock Detection

1. It is very simple and easy to understand.
2. It is easy to implement.

Disadvantages of Centralized Deadlock Detection

1. This method is less reliable, as the failure of the central site makes the deadlock detection impossible.
2. The communication cost is very high in this case, as other sites in the distributed system send their LWFGs to the central site.
3. False detection of deadlocks can occur, for which the deadlock recovery procedure may be initiated, although no deadlock has occurred. In

this method, unnecessary rollbacks and restarts of transactions may also result owing to phantom deadlocks.

8.12.2 HIERARCHICAL DEADLOCK DETECTION

This method reduces the communication overhead of centralized deadlock detection method. In this approach all sites in a distributed database system are organized into a hierarchy, and a complete tree of deadlock detectors is constructed instead of a single centralized deadlock detector. Each site in the distributed system sends its LWFG to the deadlock detection site above it in the hierarchy. Thus, local deadlock detection is performed in the leaf nodes of the tree, whereas the non-leaf nodes are responsible for detecting any deadlock situation involving all its child nodes. The hierarchical deadlock detection method is explained with an example in figure 8.13. Local deadlock is performed at leaf nodes $site_1$, $site_2$, $site_3$, $site_4$ and $site_5$. The deadlock detector at $site_6$, namely DD_{12}, is responsible for detecting any deadlock situation involving its child nodes $site_1$ and $site_2$. Similarly, $site_3$, $site_4$ and $site_5$ send their LWFGs to $site_7$ and the deadlock detector at $site_7$ searches for any deadlocks involving its adjacent child nodes. A global deadlock detector exists at the root of the tree that would detect the occurrence of global deadlock situations in the entire distributed system. Here, the global deadlock detector resides at $site_8$ and would detect the deadlocks involving $site_6$ and $site_7$. The performance of the hierarchical deadlock detection approach depends on the hierarchical organization of nodes in the system. This organization should reflect the network topology and the pattern of access requests to different sites of the network.

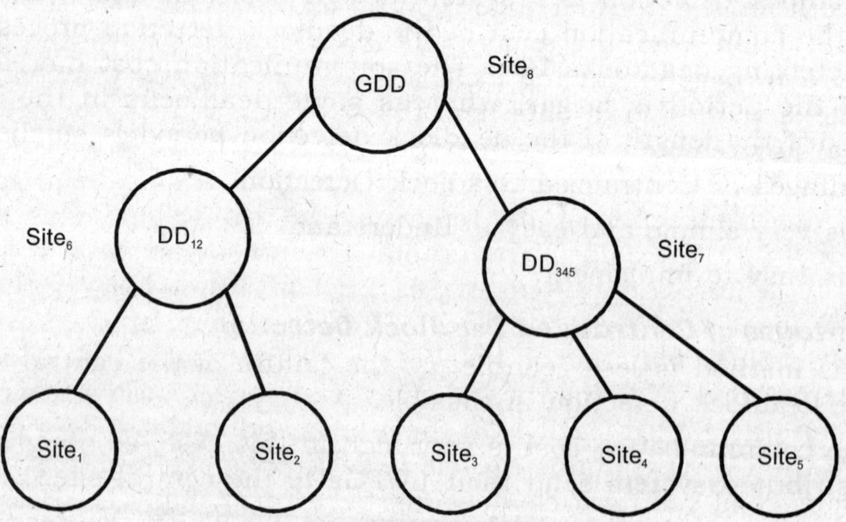

Figure 8.13: Hierarchical Deadlock Detection

Advantages of Hierarchical Deadlock Detection

1. It is very simple and easy to understand.
2. It is easy to implement.
3. It is more reliable than centralized deadlock detection as it reduces the dependence on a central site.
4. It reduces the communication cost.

Disadvantages of Hierarchical Deadlock Detection

1. Its implementation is considerably more complicated, particularly with the possibility of site and communication link failures.
2. Detection of false deadlocks can also occur.

8.12.3 DISTRIBUTED DEADLOCK DETECTION

In distributed deadlock detection method, a deadlock detector exists at each site of the distributed system. In this method, each site has the same amount of responsibility, and there is no such distinction as local or global deadlock detector. A variety of approaches have been proposed for distributed deadlock detection algorithms, but the most well-known and simplified version, which is presented here, was developed by R. Obsermarck in 1982.

Implementation of Distributed Deadlock Detection

In this method, a Local Wait For Graph (LWFG) is constructed for each site by the respective local deadlock detectors. An additional external node is added to the LWFGs, as each site in the distributed system receives the potential deadlock cycles from other sites. In the distributed deadlock detection algorithm, the external node T_{ex} is added to the LWFGs to indicate whether any transaction from any remote site is waiting for a data item that is being held by a transaction at the local site or whether any transaction from the local site is waiting for a data item that is currently being used by any transaction at any remote site. For instance, an edge from the node T_i to T_{ex} exists in the LWFG, if the transaction T_i is waiting for a data item that is already held by any transaction at any remote site. Similarly, an edge from the external node T_{ex} to T_i exists in the graph, if a transaction from a remote site is waiting to acquire a data item that is currently being held by the transaction T_i at the local site. Thus, the local detector checks for two things to determine a deadlock situation. If a LWFG contains a cycle that does not involve the external node T_{ex}, then it indicates that a deadlock has occurred locally and it can be handled locally. On the other hand, a global deadlock potentially exists if the LWFG contains a cycle involving the external node T_{ex}. However, the existence of such a cycle does not necessarily imply that there is a global deadlock, as the external node T_{ex} represents different agents.

The LWFGs are merged so as to determine global deadlock situations. To avoid sites transmitting their LWFGs to each other, a simple strategy is followed here. According to this strategy, one timestamp value is allocated to each transaction and a rule is imposed such shat one site S_i transmits its LWFG to the site S_k, if a transaction say T_k, at site S_k is waiting for a data item that is currently being held by a transaction T_i at site S_i and $ts(T_i) < ts(T_k)$. If $ts(T_i) < ts(T_k)$, the site S_i transmits its LWFG to the site S_k, and the site S_k adds this information to its LWFG and checks for cycles not involving the external node T_{ex} in the extended graph. If there is no cycle in the extended graph, the process continues until a cycle appears and it may happen that the entire GWFG is constructed and no cycle is detected. In this case, it is decided that there is no deadlock in the entire distributed system. On the other hand, if the GWFG contains a cycle not involving the external node T_{ex}, it is concluded that a deadlock has occurred in the system. The distributed deadlock detection method is illustrated in figure 8.14.

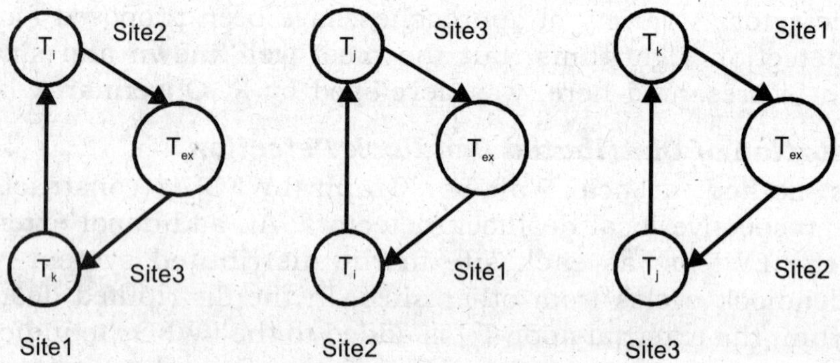

Figure 8.14: Distributed Deadlock Detection

After detecting a deadlock in the system, an appropriate recovery protocol invoked to resolve the deadlock situation. One or more transactions are chosen as victims, and these transactions, together with all their subtransactions, are rolled back and restarted.

Advantages of Distributed Deadlock Detection

1. It is potentially more robust than the centralized or hierarchical methods.
2. It is very simple and easy to understand.
3. It is easy to implement.
4. It is more reliable than centralized deadlock detection as it reduces the dependence on a central site.

Disadvantages of Distributed Deadlock Detection

1. Deadlock detection is more complicated in this method, because no single site contains all the information that is necessary to detect a global deadlock situation in the system.
2. Substantial inter-site communication is required, which increases the communication overhead.
3. It is more vulnerable to the occurrence of false deadlocks than centralized or hierarchical method.

8.13 FALSE DEADLOCKS

The delay which is associated with the transmission of messages which transfer information for deadlock detection can cause the detection of "false" deadlocks. To handle the deadlocks situation in distributed database systems, a number of messages are transmitted among the sites. On the other hand, both in centralized and in hierarchical deadlock detection methods, LWFGs are propagated periodically to one or more deadlock detector sites in the system.

Suppose for example that the deadlock detector receives the information that a transaction Ti is waiting for a transaction Tj, at a given time. Assume that after some time Tj, releases the resource which was requested by Ti , and requests a resource held by Ti . If the deadlock detector receives the information that Tj requests a resource held by Ti before receiving the information that Ti , is not blocked by Tj any more, a false cycle of length 2 is detected.

Another case of false deadlock occurs when a transaction Tj , which blocks a transaction Ti aborts autonomously for some reason which is independent of deadlock detection and at almost the same time Ti requires a resource which was held by Tj . Also in this case it is possible that the message informing the deadlock detector of the latter request arrives earlier than the message informing it of the abort; thus the deadlock detector would determine a false deadlock.

There are two approaches to the problem of false deadlocks: either treating false deadlocks as real ones or validating the detected cycle. The first approach is acceptable if the number of false deadlocks is low. The second approach requires collecting again the information on the presumed cycle: if the deadlock was a real one it will be still present and therefore detected again, otherwise not.

In general, distributed protocols are more vulnerable to the occurrence of false deadlocks than centralized or hierarchical ones.

8.14 LIVELOCK

A **livelock** is similar to a deadlock, except that the states of the processes involved in the livelock constantly change with regard to one another, none progressing. Livelock is a special case of resource starvation; the general definition only states that a specific process is not progressing.

A real-world example of livelock occurs when two people meet in a narrow corridor, and each tries to be polite by moving aside to let the other pass, but they end up swaying from side to side without making any progress because they both repeatedly move the same way at the same time. Livelock is a risk with some algorithms that detect and recover from deadlock. If more than one process takes action, the deadlock detection algorithm can be repeatedly trigger. This can be avoided by ensuring that only one process (chosen randomly or by priority) takes action.

EXERCISES

1. What do you mean by distributed deadlock management?
2. What is deadlock?
3. Explain the concept of deadlock prevention?
4. Explain the concept of resource allocation graphs?
5. Explain various techniques of deadlock prevention?
6. What do you mean by linear ordering of resources?
7. What do you mean by hierarchical ordering of resources?
8. Explain the concept of deadlock avoidance?
9. Explain in detail of distributed deadlock?
10. Explain the deadlock detection using centralized or hierarchical controllers?
11. Explain the various distributed deadlock detection?
12. Explain the distributed deadlock detection and recovery?
13. Explain the concept of centralized deadlock detection?
14. Explain the concept of hierarchical deadlock detection?
15. Explain the concept of distributed deadlock detection?
16. What do you mean by false deadlocks?
17. What do you mean by livelock?

CHAPTER 9

DISTRIBUTED RECOVERY MANAGEMENT

9.1 INTRODUCTION

In a distributed database systems, failures can occur in a owing to a variety of reasons. To maintain the consistency of data, each transaction in a DDBMSs environment must preserve the ACID property. To do this, it is the sole responsibility of a database management system to adopt some appropriate techniques. This complicated task is performed by a DDBMS module, called recovery manager. The major objective of a recovery manager is to deploy an appropriate technique for recovering the system from failures and to preserve the database in the consistent state that existed prior to the failure. In the context of distributed recovery management, two terms are often used: reliability and availability. Hence, it is necessary to differentiate between these two terms. Reliability refers to the probability that the system under consideration does not experience any failures in a given time period.

In general, reliability is applicable for non-recoverable systems. However, the reliability of a system can be measured in several ways that are based on failures. To apply reliability to a distributed database, it is convenient to split the reliability problem into two separate parts, as it is very much associated with the specification of the desired behaviour of the database: application-dependent part and application-independent part. The application-independent specification of reliability consists of requiring that transactions fulfil the system's general specifications, including the consistency constraints. The recovery manager only deals with the application-independent specification of reliability. Availability refers to the probability that the system can continue its normal execution according to the specification at a given point in time in spite of failures. Failures may occur prior to the execution of a transaction and when they have been repaired, the system must be available for continuing its normal operations at that point of time. Thus, availability refers to both the resilience of the DBMS to various types of failures and its capability to recover from them. In contrast with reliability, availability is applicable for repairable systems. In distributed recovery management, reliability and availability are two related aspects. It is accepted that it is easier to develop highly available systems, but it is very difficult to develop highly reliable systems.

9.2 RECOVERY

Recovery is the process of ensuring that a database can achieve a consistent state in the event of failure. The basic unit of recovery in a database system is the transaction. The module of the DBMS tasked with handling recovery must ensure that transactions display the properties of atomicity and durability. This process is complicated by the fact that the management of update activities against a database is not a single-step process. Frequently the writing of changes to a database will involve the steps of reading data from disk into a database buffer, updating data in main memory and writing the database buffer back to disk. The process of transferring data from buffers in main memory to secondary storage is known as flushing. Flushing may occur when triggered by a command such as a commit, may occur automatically when the buffer becomes full or may be set to occur at periodic intervals. The latter approach is known as force-writing the buffer.

Failure can occur either when writing the data to buffers or while flushing the buffers. If a transaction issued a commit but failure occurred before flushing completes, then the changes to the database will not be made permanent. In this case the recovery module will need to redo the transaction updates. If the transaction has not committed when failure occurs, then the recovery module has to undo any changes made to the database to ensure atomicity of transactions.

Most DBMS will provide the following recovery facilities:

- A mechanism which enables backup copies of either the whole or part of a database
- A facility which logs transactions and changes to the database (see above)
- A facility for checkpointing updates to a database
- A facility which permits the system to restore the database to a consistent state after hardware and software failure

The next section considers the issue of checkpointing.

In the case of failure that has caused extensive damage to the database, recovery will involve using the last backup copy of a database in association with the log file to reapply committed transactions. In the case where some failure has left the database in an inconsistent state, we do not need to utilise a backup copy. Instead, we can use the beforc and after images in the log file to restore the database to a consistent state. There are a number of different ways in which recovery can be undertaken in the latter situation. One approach, known as the deferred update protocol, involves updating a database only after transactions have reached their commit point. In the event of failure, uncommitted transactions do not need to be considered because they will not have modified the database. However, committed transactions may need to be redone because their updates may not have modified the database.

9.3 FAILURES IN A DISTRIBUTED DATABASE SYSTEM

There are many types of failures that can affect database processing. Some failures affect the main memory only, while others involve secondary storage.

Following are the types of failure:

1. **Transaction failure –** There are two types of errors that may cause one or more transactions to fail: application software errors and system errors. A transaction can no longer continue owing to logical errors in the application software that is used for database accessing, such as bad input, data not found, overflow or resource limit exceeded. The system enters into an undesirable state (e.g., deadlock) resulting in the failure of one or more transactions, known as system error.
2. **Hardware failure:** Hardware failures may include memory errors, disk crashes, bad disk sectors, disk full errors and so on. Hardware failure can also be attributed to design errors, inadequate (prior) quality control during fabrication, overloading (use of under-capacity components) and wearout of mechanical parts.
3. **Software failure:** Software failure may include failures related to software's such as, operating system, DBMS software, application programs and so on.
4. **System crashes:** System crashes are due to hardware or software errors, resulting in the loss of main memory. There could be a situation that the system has entered an undesirable state, such as deadlock, which prevents the program from continuing with normal processing. This type of failure may or may not result in corruption of data tiles.
5. **Network failures:** Network failures can occur while using a client-server configuration or a distributed database system where multiple database servers are connected by common networks. Network failures such as communication software failures or aborted asynchronous connection will interrupt the normal operation of the database system.
6. **Site failure-** In a distributed DBMS, system failure are typically referred to as site failures, and it can occur owing to a variety reasons as mentioned above. In this context, it is necessary to mention that system failures that result in the loss of the contents of the main memory are only considered here. The system failure may be total or partial failure indicates the failure of some sites in the distributed system while the order sites remain operational. A total failure indicates the simultaneous failure of all sites in a distributed system.
7. **Loss of message-** The loss of messages, or improperly ordered message, is the responsibility of the underlying computer network protocol.

It is assumed that these types of failure are handled by the data communication component of the distributed DBMS, so these are considered here.

8. **Communication link failure-** The performance of a distributed DBMS is highly dependent on the ability of all sites in the network to communicate reliably with one another. Although the communication technology has improved significantly, link failure can still occur in an distributed DBMS.
9. **Media failures:** Such failures are due to head crashes or unreadable media, resulting in the loss of parts of secondary storage. They are the most dangerous failures.
10. **Application software errors:** These are logical errors in the program that is accessing the database, which cause one or more transactions to fail.
11. **Natural physical disasters:** These are failures such as fires, floods, and earthquake or power failures.
12. **Carelessness:** These are failures due to unintentional destruction of data or facilities by operators or users,
13. **Sabotage:** These are failures due to intentional corruption or destruction of data, hardware, or software facilities.

In some cases it is very difficult to distinguish the type of failure that has occurred in the system generally the system identifies that a failure has occurred and initiates the appropriate technique for recovery form the failure.

9.4 STEPS TO BE TAKEN AFTER A FAILURE

The recovery manager must ensure the atomicity of global transactions; that is it must ensure that all subtransactions of a transaction are after committed successfully or none of then are carried out at all. If a DDBMS detected that a site failurc has occurred, then the following steps are to be followed for recovery.

- All transactions that are affected by the failure must be aborted.
- Message must be broadcast about the failure of the site so that no other site will try to access the failed site.
- Checking must be done periodically to see whether the failed site has recovered or not or, alternatively, must wait for the message from the failed site that it has recovered.
- In restart case, the failed site must initiate a recovery procedure to abort all partial transactions that were active at the time of failure.

- After the local recovery, the failed site must update its data to preserve the data consistency.

9.5 LOCAL RECOVERY PROTOCOLS

The local recovery techniques that are used to handle system failure at each site are introduced. The other types of failures are not possible in this case; thus the recovery protocols in a centralized DBMS are used here. The database is permanently stored in secondary storage, which is considered as stable storage in this context. These recovery protocols only deal with the failures that result in the loss of volatile storage. A page is the unit of data storage and access. As the size of the secondary storage is much greater than that of the main memory, pages are transferred from secondary storage to main memory on demand, although some pages are kept in the main memory to enhance access performance. The part of the database that is stored in main memory buffer is called volatile database. Typically, the buffer pages are allocated dynamically. The buffer (main memory space) is efficiently managed by using the page replacement algorithm. The least-recently-used (LRU) algorithm is the most commonly used page replacement algorithm.

The recovery protocols are classified into two different categories based on the method of executing the update operations:

1. In **in-place updating method**, the update operation changes the values of data items in the stable storage, thereby losing the old values of data items. The immediate modification technique is a log-based in-place updating recovery protocol.
2. In **out-place updating method**, the update operation does not change the values of data items in the stable storage, but stores the new values separately. These updated values are integrated into the stable storage periodically. Shadow paging is a non-log-based out-place updating recovery protocol.

9.5.1 IMMEDIATE MODIFICATION TECHNIQUE

In this technique, an update operation changes the value of a data item in the stable storage resulting in the loss of the old value of the data. Now, if a failure occurs before the transaction committed successfully, the database will be in an inconsistent state. To facilitate the recovery of the database to a consistent state, it is necessary to store enough information about the database state changes. This information is stored in a database log. The contents of the database log may differ depending on the implementation, but the typical information that are kept in the database log for each transaction are transaction identifier, type of log record (transaction start, insert, update, delete, abort, commit), identifier of the data item (affected by the database action), updated value of the data item and old value of the data item. Similar to the volatile database, the log information is also maintained in the main memory log buffer and written back to the stable storage.

There are two different ways for writing log buffer into stable storage:

1. **Synchronously:** The addition of a log record forces the database log to move from the volatile storage to the stable storage.
2. **Asynchronously:** The log is moved from the main memory to the stable storage at periodic intervals or when the main memory buffer is full.

The database log is used to protect against system failures in the following ways:

- When a transaction starts, a transaction start record is written in the log.
- When the operation write is performed, a record is written into the log containing the necessary information.
- Once the log record is written, the update is performed in the stable storage.
- When a transaction commits, a transaction commit record is written into the log.

Write-ahead log (WAL) protocol: To facilitate the recovery procedure, it is essential that the log buffers are written into the stable storage before the corresponding write to the permanent database. If updates were made to the database before the log record was written and if a failure occurred, the recovery manager would have no way of undoing the operations.

Under WAL protocol, using immediate modification technique, the recovery manager preserves the consistency of data in the following way, when failures occur.

- Any transaction that has a transaction start record in the log but has no transaction commit record has to be undone. Using the old values of data items, the recovery manager preserves the database in the consistent state that existed before the start of the transaction. The undo operation is performed in the reverse order in which they were written to the log.
- Any transaction that has both a transaction start and transaction commit information in the log must be redone. The redo procedure performs all the writes to the database using the updated values of data items in the log records for the transaction, in the order in which they were written to the log. It is to be noted that the updated values that have already been written into the database have no effect, even though rewriting is unnecessary.

For example, consider a banking transaction T_1 that transfers Rs.1,000 from account A to account B, where the balance of account A is Rs.5,000 and the balance of account B is Rs.2,500 before the transaction starts. Using immediate modification recovery technique, the following information will be written into the database log and into the permanent database to recover from a failure.

Main Memory	Database Log	Permanent Database
read (A, ai)	<T_1, start>	A = 5000, B = 2500
ai = ai – 1000		
write (A, ai)	<T_1, update, A, 5000, 4000>	A = 4000, B = 2500
read(B, bi)		
bi = bi + 1000		
write (B, bi)	<T_1, update, B, 2500, 3500> <T_1, commit>	A = 4000, B = 3500

If the transaction T_1 fails in between the log records <T_1, start> and <T_1, commit>, then it should be undone. On the other hand, if the database log contains both the records <T_1, start> and <T_1, commit> it should be redone.

9.5.2 SHADOW PAGING

Shadow paging is a non-log-based out-place updating recovery protocol in which duplicate stable-storage pages are maintained during the lifetime of a transaction. These are known as current page and shadow page.

- When the transaction starts, the two pages are identical. Whenever an update is made, the old stable-storage page, called the shadow page, is left intact for recovery purpose and a new page with the updated data item values is written into the stable-storage database, called the current page. During the transaction processing, the current page is used to record all updates to the database.
- When the transaction completes, the current page becomes the shadow page. If a system failure occurred before the successful completion of the transaction, the current page is considered as garbage.

Advantages of shadow paging

1. It is significantly faster as there is no need for redo and undo operations.
2. It reduces the overhead of maintaining and searching log records.

Disadvantages of shadow paging

1. Problem of data fragmentation. Further, periodical garbage collection is required to make inaccessible pages accessible for further use.

9.5.3 CHECKPOINTING AND COLD RESTART

Checkpointing is a technique used to limit the amount of searching that needs to be performed against a log file in order to carry out recovery effectively. Checkpointing involves force-writing database buffers to secondary storage at predetermined intervals. Checkpointing technique is used to reduce the searching overhead of log-based recovery protocols. In a log-based recovery protocol, the entire log is searched to find out all the transactions that are need to be redone or undone. The searching overhead is reduced significantly by pointing a location in the database log that indicates that the database is up-to-date and consistent at that point. This process is known as **checkpointing**. In this case, the redo operation has to start from that point and undo operation has to go back to that point only.

Generally, checkpoints are scheduled at predetermined intervals and involve the following operations:

- All log records in the main memory are written into secondary storage.
- All modified pages in the database buffer are written into secondary storage.
- A checkpoint record is written to the log. This record indicates the identifiers of all transactions that are active at the time of checkpoint.

To ensure the atomicity of the checkpointing operations, checkpointing is achieved in three steps [Gray, 1979] as described below:

- A begin_checkpoint record is written into the log.
- The checkpoint data are collected into the stable storage.
- An end_checkpoint record is written into the log.

If a system failure occurs during checkpointing, then the recovery process will not find an end_checkpoint record and will conclude that checkpointing is not completes. When a system failure occurs, the database log is checked and all transactions that have committed since the end_checkpoint are redone, and all transactions that were active at the time of the crash are undone. In this case, the redo operation only needs to start from the end_checkpoint record in the log. Similarly, the undo operation can go in the reverse direction, starting from the end of the log and stopping at the end_checkpoint record. The checkpointing technique described is called transaction-consistent checkpointing. This technique is not the most efficient, as a significant delay is experienced by all transactions. There are many alternative checkpointing mechanisms such as action-consistent checkpointing fuzzy checkpointing and others [Gray, 1979]. Some catastrophic failure may cause the loss of log information on stable storage, or loss of the stable database. In this case it is not possible to reconstruct the current consistent state of the database.

Cold restart technique is required to restore the database to a previous consistent state to maintain the consistency of data in case of loss of information on stable storage. In a distributed database system, the cold restart technique is much more complicated than in a centralized DBMS, because the state of the distributed database as a whole is to be restored to the previous consistent state. The previous consistent state is marked in a database log by a checkpoint. Hence, when the log information on stable storage is lost, it is not possible to restore the database to the previous consistent state using checkpointing. Several techniques have been proposed for performing cold restarts in a distributed database, and most of then produce a high overhead for the system. One solution to handle this situation is to store an archive copy of both the database and the log on a different storage medium. Thus, the DBMS deals with three different levels of memory hierarchy. When loss-of-log failures occur, the database is recovered from the archive copy by redoing and undoing the transactions as stored in the archive log. The overhead of writing the entire database and the log information into a different storage is a significant one. The archiving activity can be performed concurrently with normal processing whenever any changes are made to the database. Each archive version contains only the changes that have occurred since the previous archiving.

Another technique for performing cold restart in a distributed database is to use local logs, local dumps and global checkpoint. A global checkpoint is a set of local checkpoints that are performed at all sites of the network and are synchronized by the following criterion:

- If a subtransaction of a transaction is contained in the local checkpoint at some site, then all other subtransactions of that transaction must be contained in the corresponding local checkpoints at other sites.

The reconstruction is relatively easier if global checkpoints are available. First, at the failed site the latest local checkpoint that can be consider as safe is determined, and this determines which earlier global state has to be reconstructed. Then all other sites are requested to re-establish the local states of the corresponding local checkpoints. The main difficulty with this approach is the recording of global checkpoints.

9.5.4 DISTRIBUTED RECOVERY MANAGEMENT

The recovery process in distributed databases is quite involved. We give only a very brief idea of some of the issues here. In some cases it is quite difficult even to determine whether a site is down without exchanging numerous messages with other sites. For example, suppose that site X sends a message to site Y and expects a response from Y but does not receive it. There are several possible explanations:

- The message was not delivered to Y because of communication failure.
- Site Y is down and could not respond.
- Site Y is running and sent a response, but the response was not delivered.

Without additional information or the sending of additional messages, it is difficult to determine what actually happened.

Another problem with distributed recovery is distributed commit. When a transaction is updating data at several sites, it cannot commit until it is sure that the effect of the transaction on every site cannot be lost. This means that every site must first have recorded the local effects of the transactions permanently in the local site log on disk. The two-phase commit protocol is often used to ensure the correctness of distributed commit.

9.5.4.1 NORMAL EXECUTION AND COMMIT PROTOCOLS

During normal execution, each site maintains a log, and the actions of a subtransaction are logged at the site where it executes. The regular logging activity is carried out and, in addition, a commit protocol is followed to ensure that all subtransactions of a given transaction either commit or abort uniformly. The transaction manager at the site where the transaction originated is called the **coordinator** for the transaction; transaction managers at sites where its subtransactions execute are called **cohorts** (with respect to the coordination of this transaction).

We now describe the **Two-Phase Commit (2PC)** protocol, in terms of the messages exchanged and the log records written. When the user decides to commit a transaction, the commit command is sent to the coordinator for the transaction.

This initiates the 2PC protocol:

1. The coordinator sends a prepare message to each cohort.
2. When a cohort receives a prepare message, it decides whether to abort or commit its subtransaction. It force-writes an abort or **prepare** log record, and then sends a no or yes message to the coordinator. Notice that a prepare log record is not used in a centralized DBMS; it is unique to the distributed commit protocol.
3. If the coordinator receives yes messages from all cohorts, it force-writes a commit log record and then sends a commit message to all cohorts. If it receives even one no message, or does not receive any response from some cohort for a specified time-out interval, it force-writes an abort log record, and then sends an abort message to all cohorts.
4. When a cohort receives an abort message, it force-writes an abort log record, sends an ack message to the coordinator, and aborts the

subtransaction. When a cohort receives a commit message, it force-writes a commit log record, sends an ack message to the coordinator, and commits the subtransaction.

5. After the coordinator has received ack messages from all cohorts, it writes an end log record for the transaction.

The name Two-Phase Commit reflects the fact that two rounds of messages are exchanged:

first a voting phase, then a termination phase, both initiated by the coordinator. The basic principle is that any of the transaction managers involved (including the coordinator) can unilaterally abort a transaction, whereas there must be unanimity to commit a transaction. When a message is sent in 2PC, it signals a decision by the sender. In order to ensure that this decision survives a crash at the sender's site, the log record describing the decision is always forced to stable storage before the message is sent.

A transaction is officially committed at the time the coordinator's commit log record reaches stable storage. Subsequent failures cannot affect the outcome of the transaction; it is irrevocably committed. Log records written to record the commit protocol actions contain the type of the record, the transaction id, and the identity of the coordinator. A coordinator's commit or abort log record also contains the identities of the cohorts.

9.5.4.2 RESTART AFTER A FAILURE

When a site comes back up after a crash, we invoke a recovery process that reads the log and processes all transactions that were executing the commit protocol at the time of the crash. The transaction manager at this site could have been the coordinator for some of these transactions and a cohort for others.

We do the following in the recovery process:

If we have a commit or abort log record for transaction T, its status is clear; we redo or undo T, respectively. If this site is the coordinator, which can be determined from the commit or abort log record, we must periodically resend| because there may be other link or site failures in the system|a commit or abort message to each cohort until we receive an ack. After we have received acks from all cohorts, we write an end log record for T.

If we have a prepare log record for T but no commit or abort log record, this site is a cohort, and the coordinator can be determined from the prepare record. We must repeatedly contact the coordinator site to determine the status of T. Once the coordinator responds with either commit or abort, we write a corresponding log record, redo or undo the transaction, and then write an end log record for T.

If we have no prepare, commit, or abort log record for transaction T, T certainly could not have voted to commit before the crash; so we can unilaterally abort and undo T and write an end log record. In this case we have no way to determine whether the current site is the coordinator or a cohort for T. However, if this site is the coordinator, it might have sent a prepare message prior to the crash, and if so, other sites may have voted yes. If such a cohort site contacts the recovery process at the current site, we now know that the current site is the coordinator for T, and given that there is no commit or abort log record, the response to the cohort should be to abort T.

Observe that if the coordinator site for a transaction T fails, cohorts who have voted yes cannot decide whether to commit or abort T until the coordinator site recovers; we say that T is **blocked**. In principle, the active cohort sites could communicate among themselves, and if at least one of them contains an abort or commit log record for T, its status becomes globally known. In order to communicate among themselves, all cohorts must be told the identity of the other cohorts at the time they are sent the prepare message. However, 2PC is still vulnerable to coordinator failure during recovery because even if all cohorts have voted yes, the coordinator (who also has a vote!) may have decided to abort T, and this decision cannot be determined until the coordinator site recovers.

We have covered how a site recovers from a crash, but what should a site that is involved in the commit protocol do if a site that it is communicating with fails? If the current site is the coordinator, it should simply abort the transaction. If the current site is a cohort, and it has not yet responded to the coordinator's prepare message, it can (and should) abort the transaction. If it is a cohort and has voted yes, then it cannot unilaterally abort the transaction, and it cannot commit either; it is blocked. It must periodically contact the coordinator until it receives a reply. Failures of communication links are seen by active sites as failure of other sites that they are communicating with, and therefore the solutions just outlined apply to this case as well.

9.6 COMMUNICATION FAILURES IN DISTRIBUTED DATABASE

Recovery mechanisms for distributed transactions require understanding also the failures which may occur in the communications between sites. In this section, we classify the main types of communication failures, and state some basic assumptions on the communication network which are relevant in this chapter.

When a message is sent from site X to site Y, we require from a communication network the following behavior:

1. X receives a positive acknowledgment after a delay which is less then some maximum delay DMAX.
2. The message is delivered at Y in proper sequence with respect to other X-Y message.
3. The message is correct.

There is a great variety of possible failures with respect to the above specification; for example, the message might not be correct, the message might be out of order, X might not receive the acknowledgment, with the message being delivered, X might receive the acknowledgment with the message being delivered, and so on.

Most communication networks are capable of eliminating most of these errors, so that we can assume that:

1. If a message from X to Y is delivered at Y, then the message is correct and is in sequence with respect to other X-Y messages.
2. If X receives an acknowledgment, then the message has been delivered.

Note, however, that if, after a delay DMAX, site X has not received an acknowledgment, X cannot know whether the message has been delivered or not. This uncertainly is due to the fact that a lack of acknowledgment can mean two things: either the original message is lost (not delivered), but the acknowledgment message is lost. (not delivered), and hence no acknowledgment message is lost. Although this uncertainty is very inconvenient, there is no way to eliminate it with a finite protocol, i.e., with a protocol which requires a finite number of messages and terminates in a finite time. Therefore, X will typically try to send the message a finite number of times and then assume that the communications network or the site Y has failed.

With modern communication networks, which are capable of routing messages, the following assumption about the network is also reasonable: if site X cannot communicate with size Y but can communicate with site Z, then site Z cannot communicate with site Y either. In this case, when two operating sites X and Y cannot communicate, this means that no communication path is available between them, and the network is partitioned into two or more completely disconnected subnet-works, one including X, and the other one including Y. All the operational sites which belong to the same subnetwork can communicate with each other; however, they cannot communicate with sites which belong to a different subnetwork until the partition is repaired.

We can now summarize the above discussion in the following way. There are two basic types of possible communication errors: lost messages and partitions.

When a site X does not receive an acknowledgment of a message from a site Y within a predefined time interval, X is uncertain about the following things:

1. Did a failure occur at all, or is the system simply slow?
2. If a failure occurred, was it a communication failure, or a crash or site Y?
3. Has the message been delivered at Y or not?

The answer to question 3 does not depend on the answer to question 2, because either the communication failure or the crash can have happened before or after the delivery of the message.

Dealing with network partitions is a harder problem than dealing with site crashes or lost messages. Fortunately, in many computer networks partitions are much less frequent that site crashes. Therefore, several levels of reliability algorithms can be designed, which are capable of dealing with the following failures, in order of increasing difficulty:

Class 1: Site failures only.

Class 2: Site failures and lost messages, but no partitions.

Class 3: Site failures, lost messages, and partitions.

The algorithms of class 1 consider the communication network completely reliable and deal with site failures under this assumption. Hence, if a communication failure occurs, the system, behaves in an erroneous way. We will call catastrophic failures for a reliability mechanism all the failures which cannot be dealt with by it. A network partition is a catastrophic failure for the algorithms of classes 1 and 2.

Multiple failures and K-resiliency: Unfortunately failures do not occur one at a time. A system which can tolerate K failures is called K-resilient. In distributed databases, this concept is applied to site failures and/or partitions. With respect to site failures, an algorithm is said to be K-resilient, if it works properly even if K sites are down. With respect to partitions, K-resiliency refers to the number of subpartitions which have been generated. An extreme case of multiple failures is a total failure, where all sites are down. Many algorithms do not deal with this case, as it is considered extremely rare.

9.7 RECOVERY OF DISTRIBUTED TRANSACTIONS

We can now consider the recovery problem in a distributed database. We assume that at each site a local transaction manager is available, and that it can use the techniques described in Section 9.8 for local recovery.

Each agent can therefore issue begin_transaction, commit and abort primitives to its LTM. After having issued a begin_transaction to its LTM, an agent will possess the properties of a local transaction. We will call an agent which has issued a begin_transaction primitive to its local transaction manager a subtransaction, in order to reflect the fact that it is not an autonomous transaction. Moreover, in order to distinguish the begin_transaction, commit, and abort primitives f the distributed transaction from the local primitives issued by each agent to its LTM, we will call the later local_begin, local_commit, and local_abort.

For the purpose of building a distributed transaction manager (DTM), we require that the LTM has the capabilities of:

1. Ensuring the atomicity of a subtransaction
2. Writing some records on stable storage on behalf of the distributed transaction manager.

We need capability 2 because, in implementing a DTM, some additional information (new types of log records) must also be recorded in such a way that they will survive a failure.

The fact that all agents which participate in performing a distributed transaction are local subtransactions is not sufficient to guarantee the properties of a distributed transaction in other words, the fact that local transaction managers provide atomicity for subtransactions is by itself not sufficient to provide atomicity at the distributed level. The reason for this fact is simple. In order to make sure that either all actions of a distributed transaction are performed or none is performed at all, two conditions are necessary:

1. At each site either all actions are performed or none is performed
2. All sites must take the same decision with respect to the commitment or abort of subtransactions (and must be really capable of performing it)

The existence of local transaction managers, although not sufficient by itself for the implementation of a distributed transaction, is very useful because it allows us to concentrate on the peculiar problem of distributed transaction management, i.e., making sure that all local managers take the same decision, and relieves us from the problem of implementing this decision at each site.

```
FUND_TRANSFER:
Read(terminal, $AMOUNT, $FROM_ACC,$TO_ACC);
Begin-transaction;
Select AMOUNT into $FROM_AMOUNT
from ACCOUNT
where ACCOUNT_NUMBER=$FROM_ACC;
```

```
if $FROM_AMOUNT-$AMOUNT<0 then abort else begin
        Update ACCOUNT
        set AMOUNT=AMOUNT-$AMOUNT
        where ACCOUNT=$TO_ACC;
        Commit,
  end
```

(a) The FUND_TRANSFER transaction at the global level

ROOT-AGENT:

```
Read(termina,$AMOUNT, $FROM-ACC, $TO_ACC);
Begin_transaction;
Select AMOUNT into $FROM_$AMOUNT
from ACCOUNT
where ACCOUNT_NUMBER=$FROM_ACCOUNT;
If $FROM_AMOUNT-$AMOUNT<o then abort else begin
        Update ACCOUNT
        set AMOUNT=AMOUNT-$AMOUNT
        where ACCOUNT=$FROM-ACC);
        Creat AGENT1;
        Send to AGENT1 ($AMOUNT, $TO-ACC);
        Commit
end
```

AGENT$_1$:

```
Receive from ROOT-AGENT($AMOUNT, STO-ACC);
Update ACCOUNT
set AMOUNT=AMOUNT+#AMOUNT
where ACCOUNT=STO_ACC;
```

(b) The FUND_TRANSFER transaction constituted by two agents

Figure 9.1: Fund Transfer

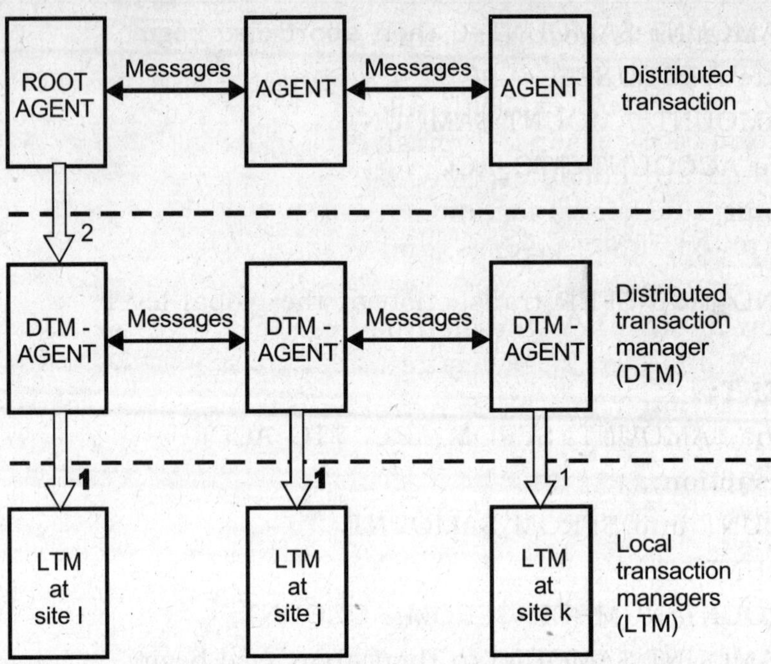

Figure 9.2: A reference model of distributed transaction recovery

The relationship between distributed management and local transaction management is represented in the reference model of a distributed transaction manager shown in Figure 9.2. At the bottom level we have the local transaction managers, which do not need communication between them. The LTMs implement interface (1): local_begin, local_commit, and local_abort. An additional local_create primitive is indicated as part of interface (1), because the creation of a process (agent) is a function of the local systems, although not strictly related to the implementation of the transaction properties.

At the next higher level we have the distributed transaction manager. DTM is by its nature a distributed layer; DTM will be implemented by a set of local DTM-agents which exchange messages between them. DTM as a whole implements interface (2): begin_transactin, commit, abort and (remote) create. The creation of a new agent is a primitive which agents constitute a distributed transaction.

At the next higher level we have the distributed transaction, constituted by the root agent and the other agents. Since we have assumed that only the root agent can issue the begin_transaction, commit, and abort primitives, interface (2) is used only by the root agent.

A word of caution is necessary: this reference model must not be considered as the run-time organization of a distributed transaction; in fact most systems do not implement explicitly all these layers at run time, but reduce them for performance reasons. Typically, some primitives are translated at compile time and are not interpreted at run time. Therefore, the reference model is a conceptual model for understanding how the algorithms work and to which level an operation belongs, and is not necessarily an implementation structure.

We can now analyze how the distributed transaction manager implements the primitives of interface (2) of Figure 9.2.

Begin_transaction When a begin_transaction is issued by the root agent, the DTM will have to issue a local_begin primitive to the LTM at the site of origin and at all the sites at which there are already active agents of the same application, thus transforming all agents into subtransactions; from this time on the activation of a new agent by the same distributed transaction requires that the local_begin be issued to the LTM where the agent is activated, so that the new agent is created as a subtrannsaction.

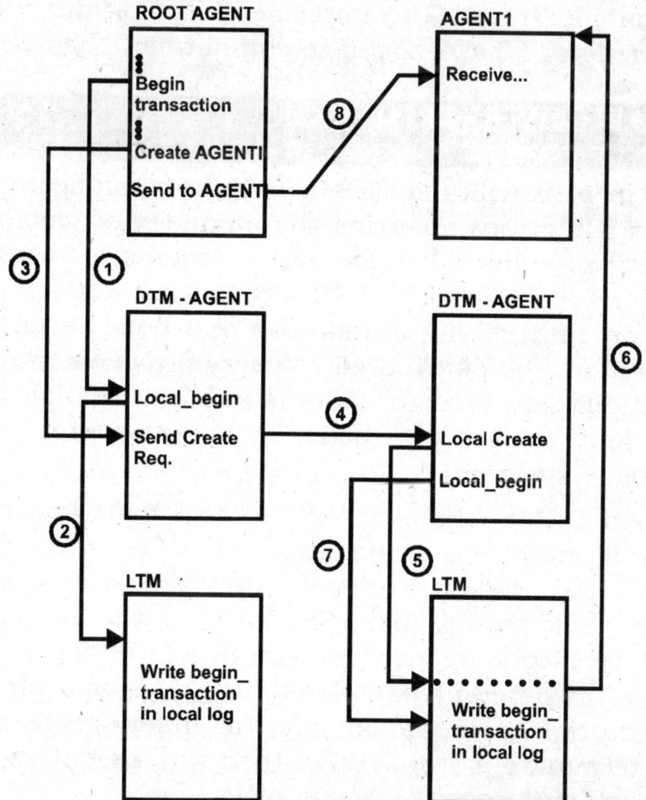

Figure 9.3: Various components of the reference model

As an example, in Figure 9.3 the primitives and messages are shown which are issued by the various components of the reference model for the execution of the distributed FUND_TRANSFER transaction of Figure 9.1 up to point where the parameters are sent from the root agent to $AGENT_1$. The numbers in Figure 9.3 indicate the order in which actions are performed and messages are sent.

Abort: When an abort is issued by the root agent, all existing subtransactions must be aborted. This is performed by issuing local_aborts to the LTMs at all sites where there is an active subtransaction. Clearly, by aborting all subtransactions, the effect of a global abort is obtained, because all actins performed by the agents since the (global) begin_transaction are undone by the LTMs.

Commit: The implementation of the commit primitive is the most difficult and expensive. The main difficulty originates from the fact that the correct commitment of a distributed transaction requires that all its subtransactions commit locally even in the case of failures. It is therefore not acceptable that a subtransaction is locally aborted because of a failure and the other subtransactins commit. In order to implement this primitive for a distributed transaction, the general idea of 2-phase-commitment has been developed.

9.8 DISTRIBUTED RECOVERY PROTOCOLS

The recovery in a distributed DBMS is more complicated than in a centralized DBMS, as it requires ensuring the atomicity of global transactions as well as of local transactions. Therefore, it is necessary to modify the commit and abort processing in a distributed DBMS, so that a global transaction does not commit or abort until all subtransaction of it have successfully committed or aborted. In addition, the distributed recovery protocols must have the capability to deal with different types of failures such as site failures, communication link failures and network partitions. Termination protocols are unique to distributed database systems.

In a distributed DBMS, the execution of a global transaction may involve several sites, and if one of the participating sites fails during the execution of global transaction, termination protocols are used to terminate the transaction at the other participating sites. Similarly, in the case of network partition, termination protocols are used to terminate the active transactions that are being executed at different partitions. One desirable property for distributed recovery protocols in independency. An independent recovery protocol decides hove to terminate a transaction that was execution executing at the time of a failure without consulting any other site.

Moreover, the distributed recovery protocols should cater for different types of failures in a distributed system to ensure that the failure of one site does not affect processing at another site. In other words, operational sites should not be left blocked. Protocols that obey this property are known as non-blocking protocols. It is preferable that the termination protocols are non-blocking. A non-blocking termination protocol allows a transaction to terminate at the operational sites without waiting for recovery of the failed site.

The following section introduces two distributed recovery protocols approaches: Theoretical approach for two-phase commit (2PC) protocol, distributed 2PC, Tree 2PC and three-phase commit (3PC) protocol and Practical approach for two-phase commit (2PC) protocol and three-phase commit (3PC) protocol a non-blocking protocol.

9.9 THEORETICAL APPROACH: DISTRIBUTED RECOVERY PROTOCOLS

Recovery in a distributed DBMS is more complicated than in a centralized DBMS for the following reasons:

- New kinds of failure can arise, namely, failure of communication links and failure of a remote site at which a subtransaction is executing.
- Either all subtransactions of a given transaction must commit, or none must commit, and this property must be guaranteed despite any combination of site and link failures. This guarantee is achieved using a **commit protocol**.

As in a centralized DBMS, certain actions are carried out as part of normal execution in order to provide the necessary information to recover from failures. A log is maintained at each site, and in addition to the kinds of information maintained in a centralized DBMS, actions taken as part of the commit protocol are also logged. The most widely used commit protocols are two-phase commit (2PC) protocol, distributed 2PC, Tree 2PC and three-phase commit (3PC) protocol.

9.9.1 TWO-PHASE COMMIT PROTOCOL

In computer networking and databases, the two-phase commit protocol (2PC, sometimes referred as TPC) is a distributed algorithm that lets all nodes in a distributed system agrees to commit a transaction. The protocol results in either all nodes committing the transaction or aborting, even in the case of network failures or node failures. However, the protocol will not handle more than one random site failure at a time. The two phases of the algorithm are the commit-request phase, in which the coordinator attempts to prepare all the cohorts, and the commit phase, in which the coordinator completes the transactions.

Note that the two-phase commit protocol shouldn't be confused with two-phase locking, a concurrency control locking protocol.

Assumptions

The protocol works in the following manner: one node is designated the coordinator, which is the master site, and the rest of the nodes in the network are designated the cohorts. The protocol assumes that there is stable storage at each node with a write-ahead log that no node crashes forever, that the data in the write-ahead log is never lost or corrupted in a crash, and that any two nodes can communicate with each other. The last assumption is not too restrictive, as network communication can typically be rerouted. The first two assumptions are much stronger; if a node is totally destroyed then data can be lost.

The protocol is initiated by the coordinator after the last step of the transaction has been reached. The cohorts then respond with an agreement message or an abort message depending on whether the transaction has been processed successfully at the cohort.

Basic algorithm

Commit-request phase

1. The coordinator sends a query to commit message to all cohorts and waits until it has received a reply from all cohorts.

2. The cohorts execute the transaction up to the point where they will be asked to commit. They each write an entry to their undo log and an entry to their redo log.

3. Each cohort replies with an agreement message (cohort votes Yes to commit), if the transaction succeeded, or an abort message (cohort votes No, not to commit), if the transaction failed.

Commit phase

Success

If the coordinator received an agreement message from all cohorts during the commit-request phase:

1. The coordinator sends a commit message to all the cohorts.
2. Each cohort completes the operation, and releases all the locks and resources held during the transaction.
3. Each cohort sends an acknowledgment to the coordinator.
4. The coordinator completes the transaction when acknowledgments have been received.

Failure

If any cohort sent an abort message during the commit-request phase:

1. The coordinator sends a rollback message to all the cohorts.
2. Each cohort undoes the transaction using the undo log, and releases the resources and locks held during the transaction.
3. Each cohort sends an acknowledgement to the coordinator.
4. The coordinator undoes the transaction when all acknowledgements have been received.

Disadvantages

The greatest disadvantage of the two-phase commit protocol is the fact that it is a blocking protocol. A node will block while it is waiting for a message. This means that other processes competing for resource locks held by the blocked processes will have to wait for the locks to be released. A single node will continue to wait even if all other sites have failed. If the coordinator fails permanently, some cohorts will never resolve their transactions. This has the effect that resources are tied up forever. The algorithm can block indefinitely in the following way:

If a cohort has sent an agreement message to the coordinator, it will block until a commit or rollback is received. If the coordinator is permanently down, the cohort will block indefinitely, unless it can obtain the global commit/abort decision from some other cohort.

When the coordinator has sent "Query-to-commit" to the cohorts, it will block until all cohorts have sent their local decision. However, if a cohort is permanently down, the coordinator will not block indefinitely: Since the coordinator is the one to decide whether the decision is 'commit' or 'abort' permanent blocking can be avoided by introducing a timeout: If the coordinator has not received all awaited messages when the timeout is over it will decide for 'abort'. This conservative behaviour of the protocol is another disadvantage: It is biased to the abort case rather than the complete case.

A lot of database research has been done on ways to get most of the benefits of the two-phase commit protocol without the costs.

9.9.2 DISTRIBUTED TWO-PHASE COMMIT PROTOCOL

In many cases the 2PC protocol is utilized in distributed environments. The protocol is easily distributed in a network by implementing multiple dedicated 2PC components similar to each other, typically named Transaction Managers (TMs; also referred to as 2PC agents), that carry out the protocol's execution for each transaction. The databases involved with a distributed transaction, the participants, both the coordinator and cohorts, register to

close TMs (typically residing on respective same network nodes as the participants) for terminating that transaction using 2PC. Each distributed transaction has an ad hoc set of TMs, the TMs to which the transaction participants register. A leader, the coordinator TM exists for each transaction to coordinate 2PC for it, typically the TM of the coordinator database. However, the coordinator role can be transferred to another TM for performance or reliability reasons. Rather than exchanging 2PC messages among themselves, the participants exchange the messages with their respective TMs. The relevant TMs communicate among themselves to execute the 2PC protocol schema above, "representing" the respective participants, for terminating that transaction. With this architecture the protocol is fully distributed (does not need any central processing component or data structure), and scales up with number of network nodes (network size) effectively.

This common architecture is also effective for the distribution of other atomic commitment protocols besides 2PC.

9.9.3 TREE TWO-PHASE COMMIT PROTOCOL

A common variant of 2PC in a distributed system, which better utilizes the underlying communication infrastructure, is the Tree 2PC protocol. In this variant the coordinator is the root ("top") of a communication tree (inverted tree), while the cohorts are the other nodes. Messages from the coordinator are propagated "down" the tree, while messages to the coordinator are "collected" by a cohort from all the cohorts below it, before it sends the appropriate message "up" the tree (except an abort message, which is propagated "up" immediately upon receiving it, or if this cohort decided to abort).

The Dynamic two-phase commit (Dynamic two-phase commitment, D2PC) protocol is a variant of Tree 2PC with no predetermined coordinator. Agreement messages start to propagate from all the leaves, each leaf when completing its tasks on behalf of the transaction (becoming ready), and the coordinator is determined dynamically by racing agreement messages, at the place where they collide. They collide either on a transaction tree node, or on an edge. In the latter case one of the two edge's nodes is elected as a coordinator (any node). D2PC is time optimal (among all the instances of a specific transaction tree, and any specific Tree 2PC protocol implementation; all instances have the same tree; each instance has a different node as coordinator): it commits the coordinator and each cohort in minimum possible time, allowing earlier release of locked resources.

9.9.4 THREE-PHASE COMMIT PROTOCOL

In computer networking and databases, the three-phase commit protocol (3PC) is a distributed algorithm which lets all nodes in a distributed system agree to commit a transaction. Unlike the two-phase commit protocol (2PC) however, 3PC is non-blocking. Specifically, 3PC places an upper bound on the amount of time required before a transaction either commits or aborts. This property ensures that if a given transaction is attempting to commit via 3PC and holds some resource locks, it will release the locks after the timeout.

3PC was originally described by Dale Skeen and Michael Stonebraker in their paper, "A Formal Model of Crash Recovery in a Distributed System." In that work, they modeled 2PC as a system of non-deterministic finite state automata and proved that it is not resilient to a random single site failure. The basic observation is that in 2PC, while one site is in the "prepared to commit" state, the other may be in either the "commit" or the "abort" state. From this analysis, they developed 3PC to avoid such states and it is thus resilient to such failures.

Protocol Description

In describing the protocol, we use terminology similar to that used in the two-phase commit protocol. Thus we have a single coordinator site leading the transaction and a set of one or more cohorts being directed by the coordinator.

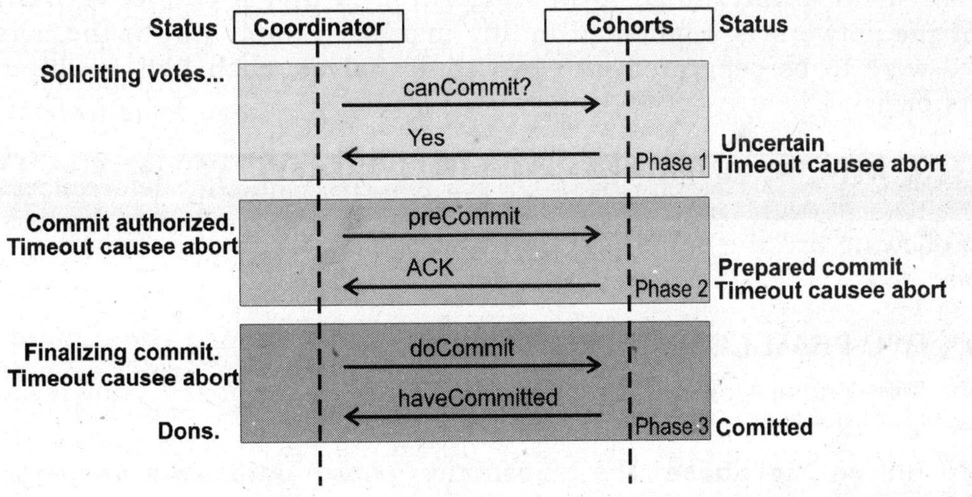

Figure 9.4: Three-Phase Commit Protocol

Coordinator

The coordinator receives a transaction request. If there is a failure at this point, the coordinator aborts the transaction (i.e. upon recovery, it will consider the transaction aborted). Otherwise, the coordinator sends a canCommit? message to the cohorts and moves to the waiting state.

If there is a failure, timeout, or if the coordinator receives a No message in the waiting state, the coordinator aborts the transaction and sends an abort message to all cohorts. Otherwise the coordinator will receive Yes mes-

sages from all cohorts within the time window, so it sends preCommit messages to all cohorts and moves to the prepared state.

If the coordinator fails in the prepared state, it will move to the commit state. However if the coordinator times out while waiting for an acknowledgement from a cohort, it will abort the transaction. In the case where all acknowledgements are received, the coordinator moves to the commit state as well.

Cohort

The cohort receives a canCommit? message from the coordinator. If the cohort agrees it sends a Yes message to the coordinator and moves to the prepared state. Otherwise it sends a No message and aborts. If there is a failure, it moves to the abort state.

In the prepared state, if the cohort receives an abort message from the coordinator, fails, or times out waiting for a commit, it aborts. If the cohort receives a preCommit message, it sends an ACK message back and commits.

Disadvantages

The main disadvantage to this algorithm is that it cannot recover in the event the network is segmented in any manner. Simply put, if the network of nodes were to be separated into two equal halves, each half would continue on its own.

9.10 PRACTICAL APPROACH: DISTRIBUTED RECOVERY PROTOCOLS

Following are the some practical approaches for distributed recovery protocols:

9.10.1 TWO-PHASE COMMIT PROTOCOL

In Two-Phase Commit protocol, there are two phases known as voting phase and decision phase.

In the **voting phase**, the transaction coordinator asks all participants whether they agree to commit the transaction. If one participant votes to abort or fails to vote within a specified time period, the coordinator instructs all participants to abort the transaction. On the other hand, if all participants vote to commit within the time limit, the coordinator instruct all participants to commit the transaction. In this case, any site is free to abort a transaction independently at any time until it votes to commit. This type of abort is called unilateral abort.

In the **decision phase**, a decision is made as to whether the transaction will be aborted or committed. A brief description of the 2PC protocol that does not consider failures as follows:

Phase 1 – The coordinator writes a begin_commit record in its log and sends a "prepare" message to all the participating sites. The coordinator waits for the participants to respond for a certain time interval (timeout period).

Phase 2 – When a participant receives a "prepare" message, it may return an "abort" vote or a "ready_commit" vote to the coordinator. If the participant returns an "Abort" vote, it writes an abort record into the local database log and waits for the coordinator for a specified time period.

On the other hand, if the participant returns a "Ready_commit" vote, it writes a commit record into the corresponding database log and waits for the coordinator for a specified time interval. After receiving votes from participants, the coordinator decides whether the transaction will be committed or aborted. The transaction is aborted, if even one participant votes to abort or fails to vote within the specified time period. In this case, the coordinator writes an "abort" record in its log and sends a "global_abort" message to all participants and then waits for the acknowledgements for a specified time period. Similarly, the transaction is committed if the coordinator receives commit votes from all participants. Here, the coordinator writes a "commit" record in its log and sends a "global_commit" message to all participants. If a participating site fails to send the acknowledgement within that time limit, the coordinator resends the global decision until the acknowledgement is received. Once all acknowledgements have been received by the coordinator, it writes an end_transction record in its log. When a participating site receives a "global_abort" message from the coordinator, it writes an "abort" record it its log and after aborting the transaction sends an acknowledgement to the coordinator. Similarly, when a participating site receives "global_commit" message from the coordinator, it writes a "commit" record it its log and on completion sends an acknowledgement to the coordinator. If a participant fails to receive a vote instruction form the coordinator, it simply times out and aborts. Therefore, a participant can abort a transaction before the voting. In 2PC each participant has to wait for either the global commit" or the "global_abort" message form the coordinator fails to receive the response from a participant, then it is assumed that a site failure has occurred and the termination protocol is invoked. The termination protocol is followed by the operational sites only. The failed sites follow the recovery protocol on restart. The 2PC protocol is illustrated in figure 9.5.

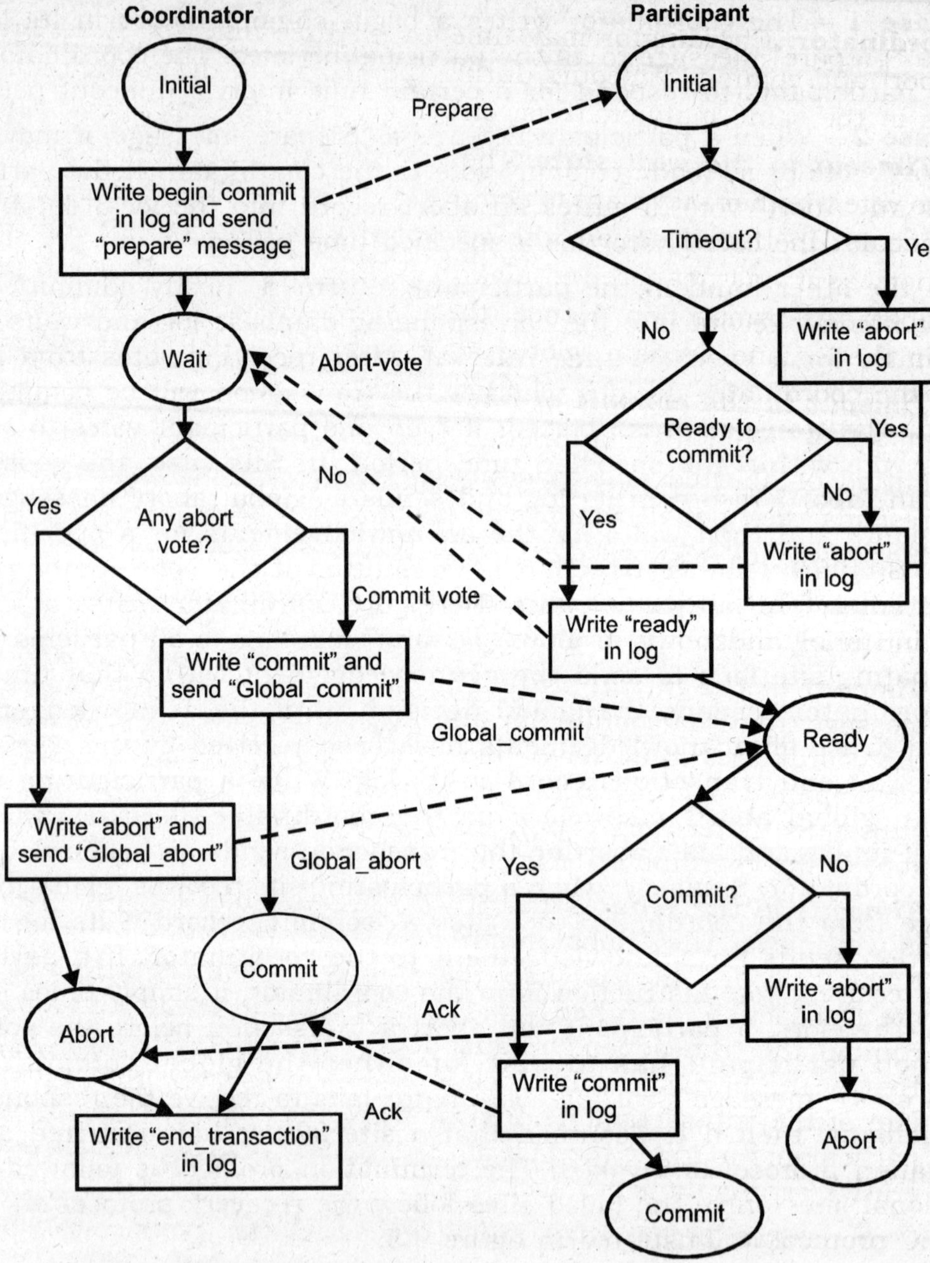

Figure 9.5: Two-phase Commit Protocol

Termination protocols for 2PC

The termination protocol is invoked when the coordinator or a participant fails to receive a message within the time limit. The action that has to be taken in this situation depends on whether the coordinator or the participant has failed and when the timeout has occurred.

Coordinator: Coordinator may timeout in three different states, namely, wait, abort and commit. Timeouts during the abort and the commit states are handles in the same manner; thus, only two cases are explained below:

(i) ***Timeout in the wait state:*** The coordinator is waiting for participants to vote whether they want to commit or abort the transaction and timeout occurs. In this situation, the coordinator cannot commit the transaction, as it has not received all votes. However, it can decide to globally abort the transaction. Hence, the coordinator writes an "abort" record in the log and sends a "global_abort" message to all participants.

(ii) ***Timeout in the commit or abort state:*** The coordinator is waiting for all participants to acknowledge whether they have successfully committed or aborted and timeout occurs. In this case, the coordinator resends the "global_commit" or "global_abort" message to participants that have not acknowledged.

Participant: A participant may timeout in two different states. These are initial and ready as shown in above figure 10.1.

(i) ***Timeout in the initial state:*** The participant is waiting for a "prepare" message from the coordinator and timeout occurs, which indicates that the coordinator must have failed while in the initial state. Hence, the participant can unilaterally abort the transaction. If the participants subsequently receives a "prepare" message, either it can send an "abort" vote to the coordinator or it can simply ignore it.

(ii) ***Timeout in the ready state:*** The participant has voted to commit and is waiting for the "global_commit" decision from the coordinator, and timeout occurs. In this case, the participant cannot unilaterally abort the transaction, as it had voted to commit. The participant also cannot commit the transaction, because it does not know the global decision. Hence, the participant is blocked until it can learn from someone the fate of the transaction. The participant could contact any of the other participants to know the fate of the transaction. This is known as cooperative termination protocol.

The cooperative termination protocol reduces the likelihood of blocking, but still blocking is possible. If the coordinator fails and all participants detect this as a result of executing the termination protocol, then they can elect a new coordinator and thereby resolve the blocking. The state transition diagram for 2PC is depicted in figure 9.6.

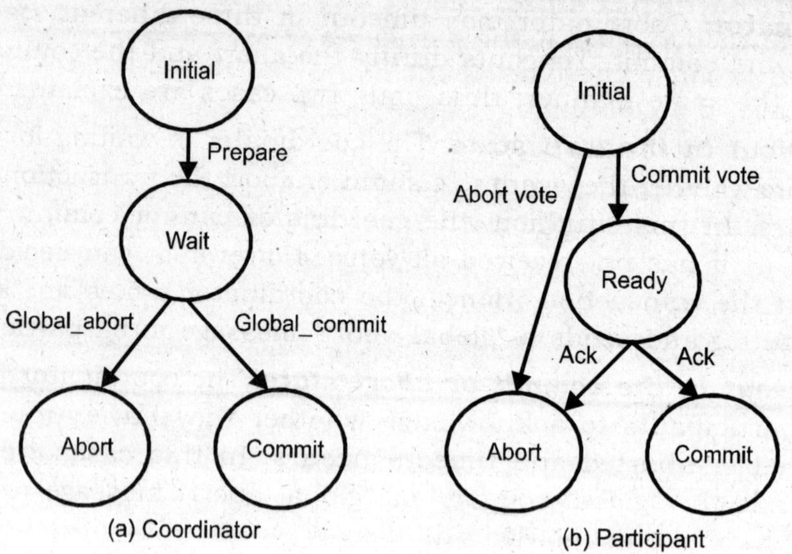

Figure 9.6: State Transition Diagram for 2PC

Recovery protocols for 2PC

Recovery protocols determine the actions to be taken by a failed site on recovery, to maintain the atomicity and the consistency property of transactions. The actions depend on the state of the coordinator or the participant at the time of failure.

Coordinator failure: Here we have given three possible cases of failure of the coordinator.

(i) ***Failure in initial state:*** The coordinator has not yet started the commit procedure. Therefore, it will start the commit procedure on recovery.

(ii) ***Failure in wait state:*** The coordinator has sent the "prepare" message to participants. On recovery, the coordinator will again start the commit procedure from the beginning; thus, it will send the "prepare" message to all participants once more.

(iii) ***Failure in commit or abort state:*** The coordinator has sent the global decision to all participants. On restart, if the coordinator has received all acknowledgements, it can complete successfully. Otherwise, the coordinator will initiate the termination protocol.

Participant failure: The objective of the recovery procedure for a participant is to ensure that it performs the same action as all other participants on restart, and this restart can be performed independently. Here we have given three possible cases of failure of the participant.

(i) ***Failure in initial state:*** The participant has not yet voted to commit the transaction. Hence, the participant can unilaterally abort the transaction, because the participant has failed before sending the vote. In this case, the coordinator cannot make a global commit decision without this participant's vote.

(ii) ***Failure in ready state:*** The participant has sent its vote to the coordinator. On recovery, the participant will invoke the termination protocol.

(iii) ***Failure in commit or abort state:*** The participant has completed the transaction; thus, on restart no further action is necessary.

Communication schemes for 2PC

There are several communication schemes that can be employed for implementing 2PC protocol:

1. **Centralized 2PC:** In the centralized 2PC, communications take place between the coordinator and the participant. The 2PC protocol described above is centralized 2PC. The communication scheme for centralized 2PC is illustrated in figure 9.7.

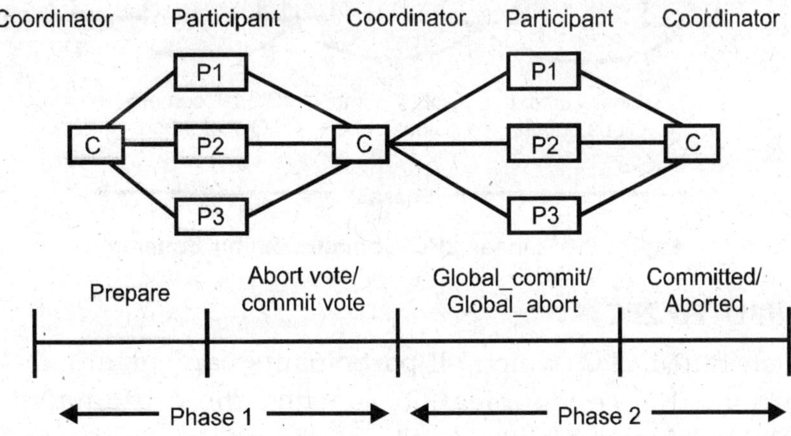

Figure 9.7: Centralized 2PC Communication Scheme

9.10.2 LINEAR 2PC

In the linear 2PC, participants can communicate with one another. In this communication scheme, an ordering is maintained among the sites in the distributed system. Let us consider that the sites are numbered as 1, 2, 3,..., n such that site number 1 is the coordinator and the others are participants. The 2PC is implemented by a forward chain of communication from the coordinator to the participant n in the voting phase and a backward chain of

communication from participant n to the coordinator in the decision phase. In the voting phase, the coordinator passes the voting instruction to site 2, site 2 votes and passes it to site 3, site 3 combines its vote and passes it to site 4 and so on. When the nth participant adds its vote, the global decision is obtained and it is passed backward to the participants, and it is passed backward to the participants, and eventually back to the coordinator. The linear 2PC reduces the number of messages compared to centralized 2PC, but does not provide any parallelism, thus, suffers from low response time performance. It is suitable for networks that do not have broadcasting capability [Bernstein et al., 1987]. The linear 2PC communication scheme is illustrated in figure 9.8.

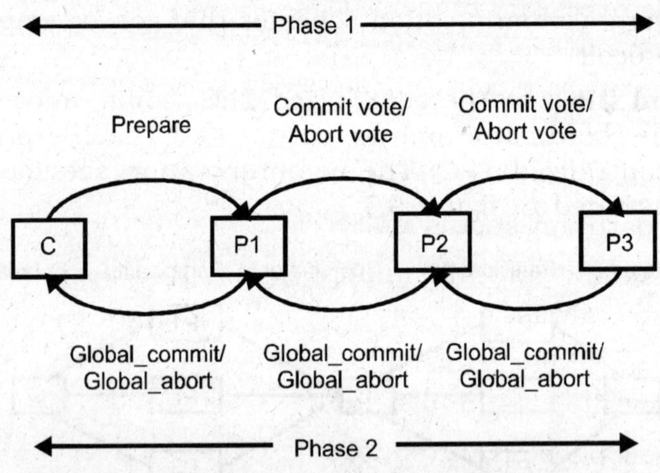

Figure 9.8: Linear 2PC Communication Scheme

9.10.3 DISTRIBUTED 2PC

In the distributed 2PC, which all participants can communicate with each other directly. In this communication scheme, the coordinator sends "prepare" message to all participants in the voting phase. In the decision phase, each participant sends its decision to all other participants and waits for messages from all other participants. As the participants can reach a decision on their own, the distributed-2PC eliminates the requirement for the decision phase of the 2PC protocol. The distributed 2PC communication scheme is illustrated in figure 9.9.

Figure 9.9: Distributed 2PC Communication Scheme

9.10.4 THREE-PHASE COMMIT PROTOCOL

The 3PC protocol [Skeen, 1981] is designed as a non-blocking protocol. In this context, it is necessary to mention that 2PC protocol is not a non-blocking protocol, as in certain circumstances it is possible for sites to become blocked. The coordinator can be blocked in the wait state, whereas the participant can be blocked in the ready state.

The requirements for the 3PC protocol are as follows:

- Network partition should not occur.
- All sites should not fail simultaneously, that is, at least one site must be available always.
- At the most k sites can fail simultaneously, where k is less than total number of sites in the distributed system.

In 3PC, a new phase is introduced known as precommit phase, in between the voting phase and the global decision phase, for eliminating the uncertainty period for participants that have voted commit and are waiting for the global decision from the coordinator. In 3PC, if all participants vote for commit, the coordinator sends a "global precommit" message to all participants. A participant who has received a "precommit" message from the coordinator will definitely commit by itself, if it has not failed. Each participant acknowledges the receipt of "precommit" message to the coordinator and after receiving all acknowledgements the coordinator sends a "global commit" message to all participants. The 3PC protocol is illustrated in the figure 9.10.

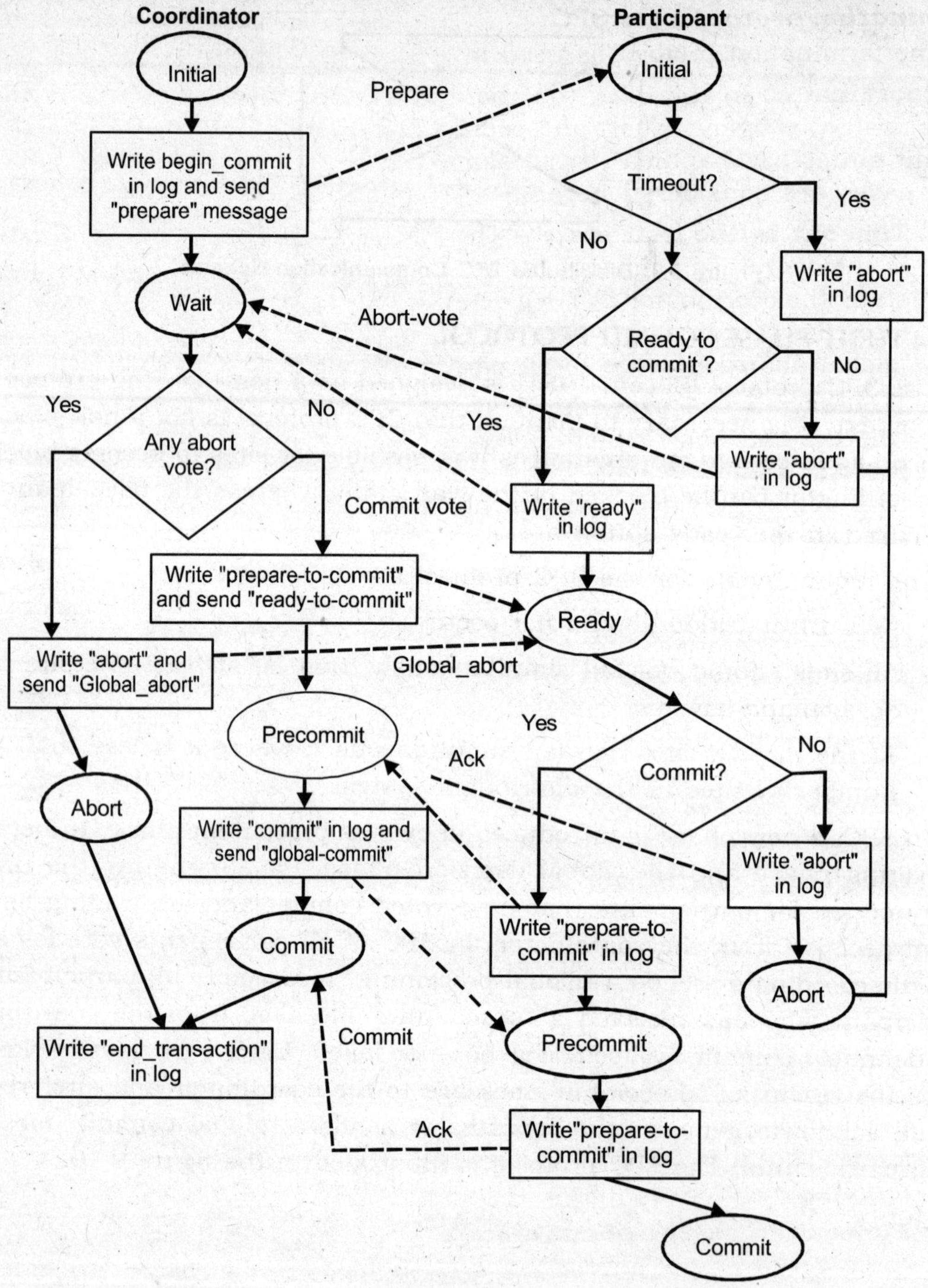

Figure 9.10: Three-phase Commit Protocol

Termination protocols for 3PC

The termination protocol is used in 3PC to handle timeouts.

Coordinator: In the 3PC, the coordinator may timeout in four different states: wait, precommit, abort and commit. Timeouts during the abort and the commit states are handled in the same manner as in 2PC, therefore, only three cases are considered here.

(i) Timeout in the wait state – The action taken here is identical to that in the coordinator timeout in the wait state for the 2PC protocol. In this state, the coordinator can decide to globally abort the transaction. Therefore, the coordinator writes an "abort" record in the log and sends a "global_abort" message to all participants.

(ii) Timeout in the precommit state – The coordinator does not know whether the non-responding participants have already moved to the precommit state or not, but the coordinator can decide to commit the transaction globally as all participants have voted to commit. Hence, the coordinator sends a "prepare-to-commit" message to all participants to move them into the commit state, and then globally commits the transaction by writing a commit record in the log and sending "global_commit" message to all participants.

(iii) Timeout in the commit or abort state – The coordinator is waiting for all participants to acknowledge whether they have successfully committed or aborted and timeout occurs. Hence, the participants are at least in the precommit state and can invoke the termination protocol as listed in case (ii) and case (iii) in the following section. Therefore, the coordinator is not required to take any special action in this case.

Participant: A participant may timeout in three different states: initial, ready and precommit.

(i) Timeout in the initial state – The action taken is identical to that in the termination protocol of 2PC.

(ii) Timeout in the ready state – The participant has voted to commit and is waiting for the global decision from the coordinator. As the communication with the coordinator is lost, the termination protocol continues by electing a new coordinator (the election protocol is discussed later). The new coordinator terminates the transaction by invoking a termination protocol.

(iii) Timeout in the precommit state – The participant has received the "prepare-to-commit" message and is waiting for the final "global_commit" message from the coordinator. This case is handled in the same way as described in case (ii) above.

In the above two cases, the new coordinator terminates the transaction by invoking the termination protocol. The new coordinator does not keep track of participant failures during termination, but it simply guides operational sites for the termination of the transaction. The termination protocol for the new coordinator is described below.

- If the new coordinator is in the wait state, it will globally abort the transaction.
- If the new coordinator is in the precommit state, it will globally commit the transaction and send a "global_commit" message to all participants, as no participant is in the abort state.
- If the new coordinator is in the abort state, it will move all participants to the abort state.

The 3PC protocol is non-blocking protocol, as the operational sites can properly terminate all ongoing transactions. The state transition diagram for 3PC is shown in figure 9.11.

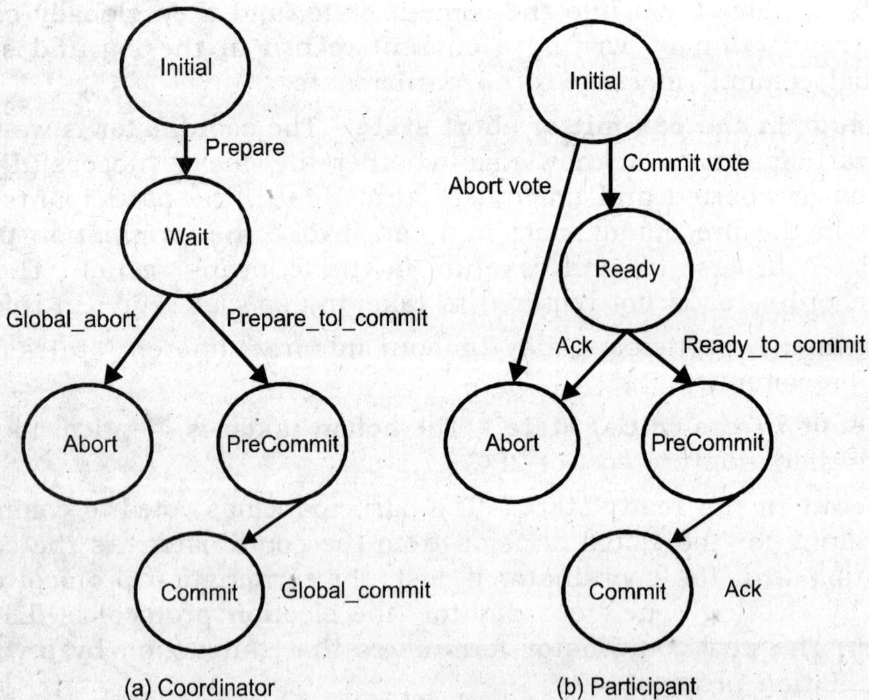

Figure 9.11: State Transition Diagram for 3PC

Recovery protocols for 3PC

There are some differences between the recovery protocol for 3PC and that for 2PC. **Following are the differences:**

(i) Coordinator failure in wait state – The participants have already terminated the transaction during the coordinator failure. On recovery, the coordinator has to learn from other sites regarding the fate of the transaction.

(ii) Coordinator failure in precommit state – The participants has already terminated the transaction. As it is possible to move into the abort state from the precommit state during coordinator failure, on restart, the coordinator has to learn from other sites regarding the fate of the transaction.

(iii) Participant failure in precommit state – The participant has to learn from other participants how they terminated the transaction.

9.10.5 ELECTION PROTOCOL

Whenever the participants detect the failure of the coordinator, the election protocol is invoked to elect a new coordinator. Thus, one of the participating sites is elected as the new coordinator for terminating the ongoing transaction properly.

Implementation of Election Protocol

It is assumed here that each site Si has an order i in the sequence, the lowest being the coordinator, and each site knows the ordering and identification of other sites in the system. For electing a new coordinator, all operational participating sites are asked to send a message to other participants that have higher identification numbers.

The site Si sends message to the sites S_{i+1}, S_{i+2}, S_{i+3} and so on. Whenever a participant receives the message from a lower-numbered participant that participant stops sending messages. Eventually, each participant knows whether there is an operational site with a lower number or not. If not, then it becomes the new coordinator. If the elected new coordinator also times out during this process, then election protocol is again invoked. This protocol is relatively efficient and most participants stop sending messages quite quickly. When a failed site with a lower identification number recovers it forces all higher-numbered sites to elect it as the new coordinator, regardless of whether there is a new coordinator or not.

9.11 NETWORK PARTITION

In communication link failures, network partition can occur in a distributed system. When the network is split into only two partitions, then it is called simple partitioning. On the other hand, when the network is split into more than two partitions, then it is called multiple partitioning. It is very difficult to maintain the consistency of the database in the case of network partition, as messages are lost.

Non-replicated databases: A transaction is allowed to proceed during network partitioning, if it does not require any data from a site outside the partition. Otherwise, the transaction must wait until the sites from which it requires data are available.

Replicated data: This procedure becomes much more complicated. During network partitioning, processing involves a trade-off between availability and consistency [Davidson et al., 1984]. Data consistency is easily provided if no processing is allowed for the replicated data during network partitioning. On the other hand, availability is maximized if there are no restrictions on the processing of replicated data during network partitioning. It is possible to terminate a transaction properly during network partitioning with the help of a non-blocking termination protocol, but unfortunately, there is no such non-blocking termination protocol that can handle network partition.

The recovery technique that is used to handle network partitioning depends on the particular concurrency control strategy being used, as recovery and concurrency control are closely related to each other.

Thus, the recovery techniques that are used to handle network partition can be divided into two categories:

1. Pessimistic protocols
2. Optimistic protocols

9.11.1 PESSIMISTIC PROTOCOLS

Pessimistic protocols emphasize on the consistency of the database, and therefore do not allow the processing of transactions during network partitioning if there is no guarantee that consistency can be mentioned. The termination protocols that deal with network partitioning in the case of non-replicated databases are pessimistic. To minimize blocking, it is convenient to allow the termination of the transaction by at least one group, possibly the largest group, possibly the largest group, during a network partition. However, during network partition, it is impossible for a group to determine whether it is the largest one or not.

The termination protocol can use a pessimistic concurrency control algorithm such as

1. **Primary copy 2PL:** For any transaction, only the partition that contains the primary copies of the data items can execute the transaction. Hence, the recovery of the network involves simply propagating all the updates to every other site. However, this method is vulnerable to the failure of the site that contains the primary copy. In many subnets, a primary site failure is more likely to occur than a partition; thus, this approach can increase blocking, instead of reducing it.

2. **Majority locking:** The above problem can be solved by using majority locking technique. The basic idea of majority locking protocol is that before committing (or aborting) a transaction, a majority of sites must agree to commit (or abort) the transaction. The majority locking protocol cannot be applied with 2PC protocol, as it requires a specialized commit protocol.

   Both of the above approaches are simple, and recovery using these approaches is very much straightforward. However, they require that each site is capable of differentiating network partitioning from site failures.

3. **Quorum-based protocol or weighted majority protocol:** This is straightforward generalization of the majority locking protocol. It can be used as a replica control method for replicated databases as well as a commit method to ensure transaction atomicity in the case of network partitioning. In the case of non-replicated databases the integration of the quorum-based protocols with commit protocol is necessary.

In quorum-based protocol a weight is assigned to each site usually known as a vote. The basic rules for the quorum-based protocol are as follows:

- In the network, each site i is associated a weight or a vote Vi, which is a positive integer. Assume that V is the sum of the votes of all sites in the network.
- A transaction must collect a commit quorum Vc before committing the transaction.
- A transaction must collect an abort quorum Va before aborting the transaction.
- Vc + Va > V.

The last rule ensures that one transaction cannot be aborted and committed at the same time. The rules 2 and 3 ensure that the transaction has to obtain votes before termination.

The integration of 3PC protocol with quorum-based protocols requires a minor modification to the phase 3. To move from precommit state to commit state, it is necessary for the coordinator to obtain a commit quorum from the participants. It is not necessary to implement the rule 3 explicitly, because a transaction that is in the wait or ready state is always willing to abort the transaction; thus, an abort quorum already exists. When network partition occurs, the sites in each partition not possible to know whether a commit quorum or an abort quorum was reached. Therefore, it s necessary for the participants to take an explicit decision before joining either the commit quorum or the abort quorum; the votes cannot be changed afterwards. Since the wait and the ready states do not satisfy these requirements, one new state

"preabort" is added between ready and abort states. The state transition diagram for the modified 3PC is illustrated in figure 10.8.

During network partition, a transaction can be terminated in the following way using quorum 3PC protocol:

- A new coordinator is elected in each partition.
- If at least one participant is in the commit state, the coordinator decides to commit the transaction and sends a "global_commit" message to all participants.
- If at least one participant is in the abort state, the coordinator decides to abort the transaction and sends a "global_commit" message to all participants.
- If a commit quorum is achieved by the votes of the participants in the precommit state, the coordinator decides to commit the transaction and sends a "global_commit" message to all participants.
- If a commit quorum is achieved by the votes of the participants in the precommit state, the coordinator decides to abort the transaction and sends a "global_abort" message to all participants.
- If case 3 is not satisfied but the sum of the votes of the participants in the precommit and ready states are enough to form a commit quorum, the coordinator sends a "prepare-to-commit" message to all participants to move the into precommit state and waits for case 3 to occur.
- If case 3 is not satisfied but the sum of the votes of the participants in the precommit and ready states are enough to form a abort quorum, the coordinator sends a "prepare-to-abort" message to all participants to move the into "preabort" state. The coordinator then waits for case 4 to occur.

The state transition diagram for quorum 3PC protocol is illustrated in figure 9.12. The quorum 3PC protocol is a blocking protocol, but it is capable of handling site failures as well as network partitioning.

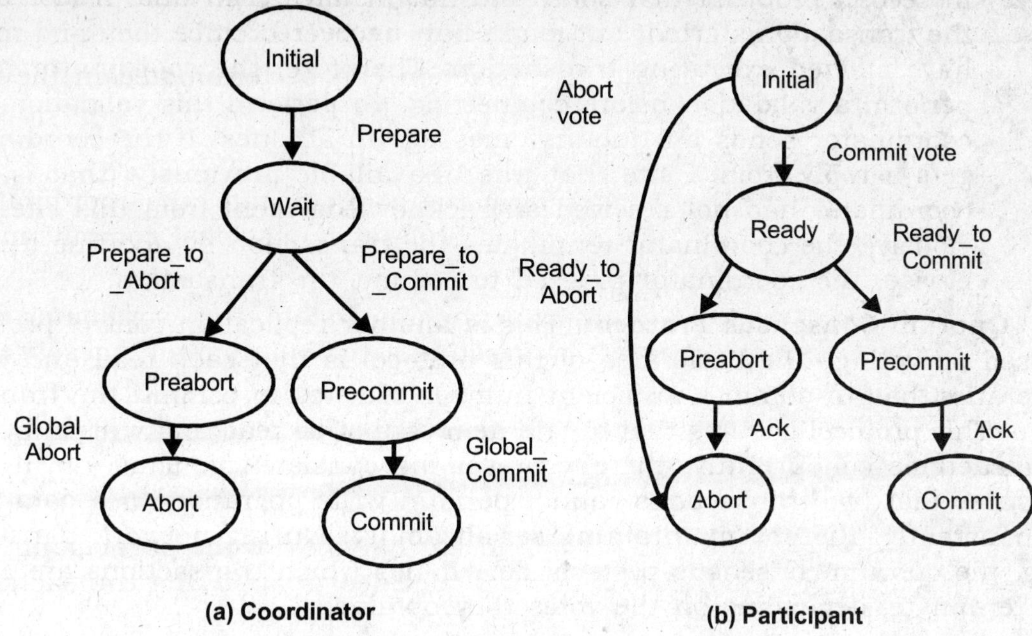

Figure 9.12: State Transition Diagram for Quorum 3PC

9.11.2 OPTIMISTIC PROTOCOLS

Optimistic protocols emphasize on availability and use an optimistic concurrency control approach in which updates are allowed to proceed independently in the various partitions to terminate the transaction. Replication of data items improves availability. In this case, inconsistencies are likely when site recover from network partitioning, but these inconsistencies can be eliminated later. The resolution of inconsistencies depends upon the semantics of the transactions. One protocol for enforcing consistency of replicated data items in ROWA (read-one-write-all) protocol. There are various versions of ROWA protocol. In ROWA-A protocol, update is performed only on all available copies of thc replicated data item, and unavailable copies are updated later. In this approach, the coordinator sends an update message to all sites where replicas of the data item reside and waits for update confirmation. If the coordinator times out before receiving acknowledgements from all sites, it is assumed that the non-responding sites are unavailable and the coordinator continues the update with available sites to terminate the transaction. **There are two problems with this approach:**

1. In first problem, it may so happen that one site containing the replica of a data item has already performed the update and sent the acknowledgement, but as the coordinator has not received it within the specified time interval, the coordinator has considered the site as unavailable.

2. In second problem, that some sites might have been unavailable when the transaction started, but might have recovered since then and might have started executing transaction. Therefore, the coordinator must perform a validation before committing. To perform this validation, the coordinator sends an "inquiry" message to all sites. If the coordinator gets a reply from a site that was unavailable previously (that is, the coordinator had not received any acknowledgement from this site previously), the coordinator terminates the transaction by aborting it; otherwise, the coordinator proceed to commit the transaction.

Quorum-Consensus Protocol: This is another replication control protocol based on voting. The basic idea of this protocol is that each read and write operation has to obtain a sufficient number of votes to commit the transaction. This protocol ensures that a data item cannot be read and written by two transactions concurrently, thereby preserving consistency. Similarly, it also ensures that two transactions cannot perform write operation on a data item concurrently, thereby maintaining serializability. During network partitioning, the quorum-consensus protocol determines which transactions are going to terminate, depending on the votes they obtained.

This protocol also ensures that two different transactions that are initiated at two different partitions and access the same data item cannot terminate simultaneously. The difficulty with the quorum-consensus protocol is that transactions are required to obtain a quorum even to read data. This significantly and unnecessarily slows read access to the database.

9.12 ORACLE DATABASE MANAGEMENT SYSTEM: THE TWO-PHASE COMMIT

The Oracle database is a distributed database management system, which employs the two-phase commit to achieve and maintain data reliability. The following sections explain Oracle's two-phase implementation procedures.

9.12.1 THE SESSION TREE

In each transaction, Oracle constructs a session tree for the participating nodes. The session tree describes the relations between the nodes participating in any given transaction. Each node plays one or more of the following roles:

1. **Client**: A client is a node that references data from another node.
2. **Database Server**: A server is a node that is being referenced by another node because it has needed data. A database server is a server that supports a local database.
3. **Global Coordinator**: The global coordinator is the node that initiated the transaction, and thus, is the root of the session tree. The opera-

tions performed by the global coordinator are as follows In its role as a global coordinator and the root of the session tree, all the SQL statements,

- procedure calls, etc., are sent to the referenced nodes by the global coordinator. Instructs all the nodes, except the COMMIT point site, to PREPARE
- If all sites PREPARE successfully, then the global coordinator instructs the COMMIT point site to initiate the commit phase
- If one or more of the nodes send an abort message, then the global coordinator instructs all nodes to perform a rollback.

4. **Local Coordinator**: A local coordinator is a node that must reference data on another node in order to complete its part. The local coordinator carries out the following functions (Oracle8):

- Receiving and relaying status information among the local nodes
- Passing queries to those nodes
- Receiving queries from those nodes and passing them on to other nodes
- Returning the results of the queries to the nodes that initiated them.

5. **Commit Point Site**: Before a COMMIT point site can be designated, **the COMMIT point strength** of each node must be determined. The COMMIT point strength of each node of the distributed database system is defined when the initial connection is made between the nodes. The COMMIT point site has to be a reliable node because it has to take care of all the messages. When the global coordinator initiates a transaction, it checks the direct references to see which one is going to act as a COMMIT point site. The COMMIT point site cannot be a read-only site. If multiple nodes have the same COMMIT point strength, then the global coordinator selects one of them. In case of a rollback, the PREPARE and COMMIT phases are not needed and thus a COMMIT point site is not selected. A transaction is considered to be committed once the COMMIT point site commits locally.

9.12.2 TWO-PHASE COMMIT AND THE ORACLE IMPLEMENTATION

The transaction manager of the Oracle8 database necessitates that the decision on what to do with a transaction to be unanimous by all nodes. This requires all concerned nodes to make one of two decisions: commit and complete the transaction, or abort and rollback the transaction (Oracle8). The Oracle8 engine automatically takes care of the commit or rollback of all transactions, thus, maintaining the integrity of the database.

The following will describe the two phases of the transaction manager.

1. **PREPARE Phase (PP):** The PP starts when a node, the initiator, asks all participants, except the commit point site, to PREPARE. In the PP, the requested nodes have to record enough information to enable them either to commit or abort the transaction. The node, after replying to the requestor that it has PREPARED, cannot unilaterally perform a COMMIT or abort. Moreover, the data that is tied with the COMMIT or abort is not available for other transactions. Each node may reply with one of three responses to the initiator. These responses are defined below:
   (a) **Prepared:** the data has already been modified and that the node is ready to COMMIT. All resources affected by the transaction are locked.
   (b) **Read-only**: the data on the node has not been modified. With this reply, the node does not PREPARE and does not participate in the second phase.
   (c) **Abort:** the data on the node could not be modified and thus the node frees any locked resources for this transaction and sends an abort message to the node that referenced it.
2. **COMMIT Phase (CP):** Before the CP begins, all the referenced nodes need to have successfully PREPARED. The COMMIT phase begins by the global coordinator sending a message to all the nodes instructing them to COMMIT. Thus, the databases across all nodes are consistent.

9.13 FAILURE OF THE TWO-PHASE COMMIT

A major problem with the two-phase commit occurs when one of the nodes participating in a distributed transaction fails while the transaction is in the PREPARED state. When the failure is for a prolonged period of time, then the data locked on all the other nodes won't be available for other transactions. This will cause a lot of transactions to rollback due to deadlocks. Oracle DBMS, in a new version, introduced an advanced queuing technique to deal with the problem of deadlock. The authors hope to address this technique in another paper in the near future.

9.14 AN EXAMPLE OF A DISTRIBUTED DATABASE SYSTEM

Figure 9.13 illustrates the steps Oracle8 performs in order to PREPARE, Select the COMMIT Point Site, and COMMIT. The example in the figure depicts a company that has several branches located in different cities numbered 1 to 7. Each site has to have access to most of the data in the company in order to check on the status of purchase orders, material acquisition, and several other issues.

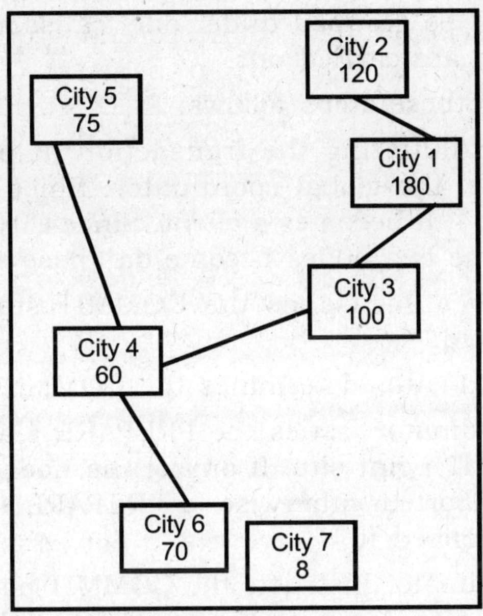

Figure 9.13: An example of distributed databases over several sites

Since new projects are awarded and older projects are completed, project sites tend to change locations. Also, depending on the size and duration of a project, different COMMIT point strength can be assigned and thus, in the same area, different COMMIT point sites can be chosen, for a given location, over a period of time. In this example, City 1 is the head office and thus posses the highest COMMIT point strength. The other sites are assigned the COMMIT point strength based on the Dollar volume of the project. Higher monetary value for a project requires more resource allocation, and as such, will lead to more transactions executed against the data for that project. Since the amount of data involved is large, each site will have the portion of the database pertaining to its operations replicated and stored on a local server. Any transaction will at least affect the database at the head office and one of the sites. If, for example, a material rate, description of an item, accomplished progress, or purchase order is entered, a transaction is initiated that will affect the database at the head office and the database at the concerned site. Other modifications, such as those involving employee transfer or equipment transfer from one site to another, will affect two or more sites. The following discussion explains the steps that entail in processing a distributed transaction:

An employee is to be transferred from City 2 to City 4. The transaction is initiated by City 1 by a personnel employee. The affected sites need to participate in the transaction. The processes that transfer one employee from one site to another should be grouped under one transaction so that either all or none of the processes are carried out.

An explanation of these steps follows:

1. Since City 1 is initiating the transaction, it becomes the root of the session tree, i.e. the global coordinator. Since City 1 updates data in City 2 and City 4, it becomes a client. Since City 1 updates data on City 2 and City 4, the two nodes become database servers.
2. When the application issues the COMMIT statement, the two-phase commit is started.
3. The global coordinator determines the COMMIT point site.
4. The global coordinator issues the PREPARE statement to all nodes except the COMMIT point site. If any of the nodes cannot PREPARE, the transaction is aborted; otherwise, a PREPARED message is sent to the node that referenced it.
5. The global coordinator instructs the COMMIT point site to COMMIT. The COMMIT point site commits the transaction locally and records the transaction in its local redo log.
6. The COMMIT point site informs the global coordinator that it has committed and the global coordinator informs the other nodes by sending the COMMIT message.
7. When all the transactions have committed, the global coordinator informs the COMMIT point site to "forget" about the transaction. The COMMIT point site, after "forgetting" about the transaction, informs the global coordinator, and the global coordinator, in turn, "forgets" about the transaction.

EXERCISES

1. Explain the concept of distributed recovery management?
2. What do you mean by recovery?
3. Explain various failures in a distributed database system?
4. What steps to be taken after a failure?
5. Explain the various local recovery protocols?
6. Explain the immediate modification technique?
7. What do you mean by shadow paging?

8. What do you mean by checkpointing and cold restart?
9. Explain the various communication failures in distributed databases?
10. Explain the recovery of distributed transactions?
11. Explain the various distributed recovery protocols?
12. Explain the theoretical approach: distributed recovery protocols?
13. Explain the practical approach: distributed recovery protocols?
14. Explain the concept of election protocol?
15. Explain the concept of network partition?
16. Explain the concept of pessimistic protocols?
17. Explain the concept of optimistic protocols?
18. Explain the three-phase commit protocol?
19. Explain oracle database management system: the two-phase commit?
20. Explain an example of a distributed database system?

CHAPTER 10

DISTRIBUTED DATABASE ADMINISTRATION

10.1 INTRODUCTION

Database administration refers to a variety of activities for the development, control, maintenance, and testing of the software of the database application. Database administration is not only a technical problem, since it involves the statement of policies under which users can access the database, which is clearly also an organization problem.

In this chapter, we concentrate on the technical aspects of database administration in a distributed environment. Now, we can focus on the following problems:

1. The extension of **protection and authorization** mechanisms to distributed systems; we briefly describe the problems which arise in a distributed environment compared with those which arise in a centralized one.
2. The content and management of the **catalogs**; with this name, we designate the information which is required by the system for accessing the database. In distributed systems, catalogs include the description of fragmentation and allocation of data and the mapping to local names; catalogs themselves become a distributed database, which must be distributed and managed efficiently.

The most important issue in database administration is the degree of **site autonomy** given to each site. There are two extreme solutions, the absence of any local autonomy and complete local autonomy.

10.2 DISTRIBUTED DATABASE SECURITY

As distributed networks become more popular, the need for improvement in distributed database management systems becomes even more important. A distributed system varies from a centralized system in one key respect:

The data and often the control of the data are spread out over two or more geographically separate sites. Distributed database management systems are subject to many security threats additional to those present in a centralized database management system (DBMS). Furthermore, the development of adequate distributed database security has been complicated by the relatively recent introduction of the object-oriented database model. This new model cannot be ignored. It has been created to address the growing complexity of the data stored in present database systems.

Database security is a major concern in the context of both centralized DBMS and distributed DBMS in preserving the consistency of the database. It is an integral part of any database system. Maintaining data security in a distributed DBMS is more complicated than in a centralized DBMS, because the underlying network is to be made secure. Database security is closely related to database integrity.

Data integrity refers to the correctness of data and is represented in terms of integrity constraints. Database security refers to the preventive measures for maintaining data integrity. In a centralized DBMS, database security management typically includes view management, data protection and authorization control, and semantic integrity constraints. All of these can be defined as database rules that the system will automatically enforce. Data that do not satisfy these rules are considered as invalid data, and they are not permitted to be stored in the database. Similarly, any violations of these database rules are automatically detected, and the violating data are rejected by the database system.

For the past several years the most prevalent database model has been relational. While the relational model has been particularly useful, its utility is reduced if the data does not fit into a relational table. Many organizations have data requirements that are more complex than can be handled with these data types. Multimedia data, graphics, and photographs are examples of these complex data types. Relational databases typically treat complex data types as BLOBs (binary large objects). For many users, this is inadequate since BLOBs cannot be queried. In addition, database developers have had to contend with the impedance mismatch between the third generation language (3GL) and structured query language (SQL). The impedance mismatch occurs when the 3GL command set conflicts with SQL.

There are two types of impedance mismatches:

1. **Data type inconsistency:** A data type recognized by the relational database is not recognized by the 3GL. For example, most 3GLs don't have a data type for dates. In order to process date fields, the 3GL must convert the date into a string or a Julian date. This conversion adds extra processing overhead.
2. **Data manipulation inconsistency:** Most procedural languages read only one record at a time, while SQL reads records a set at a time. This problem is typically overcome by embedding SQL commands in the 3GL code. Solutions to both impedance problems add complexity and overhead.

In distributed DBMS context, database security also involves network security, as information is exchanged between different nodes in the system via a computer network. The rules that are used to control data manipulation are a part of the database administration, and generally these are defined by the database administrator (DBA). The cost of enforcing semantic integrity constraints in a centralized DBMS is very high in terms of resource utilization, and it can be prohibitive in a distributed environment. The semantic integrity

constraints are stored in the system catalog. In a distributed DBMS, the global system catalog contains data distribution details in addition to all information that are stored in a centralized system catalog. Maintaining system catalog in a distributed database environment is a very complicated task.

10.2.1 ELEMENTS OF DISTRIBUTED DATABASE MANAGEMENT SYSTEM SECURITY

The distributed database has all of the security concerns of a single-site database plus several additional problem areas. We begin our investigation with a review of the security elements common to all database systems and those issues specific to distributed systems.

A secure database must satisfy the following requirements (subject to the specific priorities of the intended application):

1. It must have physical integrity (protection from data loss caused by power failures or natural disaster),
2. It must have logical integrity (protection of the logical structure of the database),
3. It must be available when needed,
4. The system must have an audit system,
5. It must have elemental integrity (accurate data),
6. Access must be controlled to some degree depending on the sensitivity of the data,
7. A system must be in place to authenticate the users of the system, and
8. Sensitive data must be protected from inference [Pflee89].

The following discussion focuses on requirements 5-8 above, since these security areas are directly affected by the choice of DBMS model. The key goal of these requirements is to ensure that data stored in the DBMS is protected from unauthorized observation or inference, unauthorized modification, and from inaccurate updates. This can be accomplished by using access controls, concurrency controls, updates using the two-phase commit procedure (this avoids integrity problems resulting from physical failure of the database during a transaction), and inference reduction strategies (discussed in the next section).

The level of access restriction depends on the sensitivity of the data and the degree to which the developer adheres to the principal of least privilege (access limited to only those items required to carry out assigned tasks). Typically, a lattice is maintained in the DBMS that stores the access privileges of individual users. When a user logs on, the interface obtains the specific privileges for the user.

According to Pfleeger [Pflee89], access permission may be predicated on the satisfaction of one or more of the following criteria:

1. **Availability of data:** Unavailability of data is commonly caused by the locking of a particular data element by another subject, which forces the requesting subject to wait in a queue.
2. **Acceptability of access:** Only authorized users may view and or modify the data. In a single level system, this is relatively easy to implement. If the user is unauthorized, the operating system does not allow system access. On a multilevel system, access control is considerably more difficult to implement, because the DBMS must enforce the discretionary access privileges of the user.
3. **Assurance of authenticity:** This includes the restriction of access to normal working hours to help ensure that the registered user is genuine. It also includes a usage analysis which is used to determine if the current use is consistent with the needs of the registered user, thereby reducing the probability of a fishing expedition or an inference attack.

   Concurrency controls help to ensure the integrity of the data. These controls regulate the manner in which the data is used when more than one user is using the same data element. These are particularly important in the effective management of a distributed system, because, in many cases, no single DBMS controls data access. If effective concurrency controls are not integrated into the distributed system, several problems can arise.

Bell and Grisom [BellGris92] identify three possible sources of concurrency problems:

1. **Lost update:** A successful update was inadvertently erased by another user.
2. **Unsynchronized transactions** that violate integrity constraints.
3. **Unrepeatable read:** Data retrieved is inaccurate because it was obtained during an update.

Each of these problems can be reduced or eliminated by implementing a suitable locking scheme (only one subject has access to a given entity for the duration of the lock) or a timestamp method (the subject with the earlier timestamp receives priority) [BellGris92].

Special problems exist for a DBMS that has multilevel access. In a multilevel access system, users are restricted from having complete data access. Policies restricting user access to certain data elements may result from secrecy requirements, or they may result from adherence to the principal of least privilege (a user only has access to relevant information). Access policies for multilevel systems are typically referred to as either open or closed.

In an open system, all the data is considered unclassified unless access to a particular data element is expressly forbidden. A closed system is just the opposite. In this case, access to all data is prohibited unless the user has specific access privileges. Classification of data elements is not a simple task. This is due, in part, to conflicting goals. The first goal is to provide the database user with access to all non-sensitive data. The second goal is to protect sensitive data from unauthorized observation or inference. For example, the salaries for all of a given firm's employees may be considered non-sensitive as long as the employee's names are not associated with the salaries. Legitimate use can be made of this data. Summary statistics could be developed such as mean executive salary and mean salary by gender. Yet an inference could be made from this data. For example, it would be fairly easy to identify the salaries of the top executives.

Another problem is data security classification. There is no clear-cut way to classify data. Millen and Lunt [MilLun92] demonstrate the complexity of the problem: They state that when classifying a data element, there are three dimensions:

1. The data may be classified.
2. The existence of the data may be classified.
3. The reason for classifying the data may be classified [MilLun92].

The first dimension is the easiest to handle. Access to a classified data item is simply denied. The other two dimensions require more thought and more creative strategies. For example, if an unauthorized user requests a data item whose existence is classified, how does the system respond? A poorly planned response would allow the user to make inferences about the data that would potentially compromise it. Protection from inference is one of the unsolved problems in secure multilevel database design. Pfleeger [Pflee89] lists several inference protection strategies. These include data suppression, logging every move users make (in order to detect behaviour that suggests an inference attack), and perturbation of data. As we will discuss later, the only practical strategy for the distributed environment that maintains data accuracy is suppression.

10.3 VIEW MANAGEMENT

A view can be defined as a virtual relation or table that is derived from one or more base relations. A view does not necessarily exist in the database as a stored set of data values; only view definitions are stored in the database. When a DBMS encounters a reference to a view, it can be resolved in two different ways. One approach is to look up the definition of the view and translate the definition into an equivalent request against the source tables of the view, and then perform that request. This process is known as view resolution. Another alternative approach stores the view as a temporary table in the database and maintains the changes of the view as the underlying base tables are updated. This process is called view materialization.

In relational data model, a view is derived as the result of a relational query on one or more base relations. It is defined by associating the name of the view with the relational query that specifies it. Views provide several advantages, which are listed in the following:

- **Improved Security** – The major advantage of a view is that it provides data security. It is possible to grant each user the privileges to access the database only through a small set of views that contain the appropriate data for the user, thereby restricting and controlling each user's access to the database.
- **Reduced Complexity** – A view simplifies queries by deriving data from more than one table into a single table and thus converts multi-table queries into single-table queries.
- **Data sharing** – The same underlying base tables can be shared by different users in different ways through views. Therefore, it provides the facility for data sharing and for customizing the appearance of the database.
- **Convenience** – Using views only that portion of the data is presented to the users, in which they are interested. Thus, it reduces the complexity from the user's point of view and provides greater convenience.

In some cases, a view defined by a complex, multi-table query may take a long time to process, because view resolution must join the tables together every time the view is accessed.

10.3.1 VIEW UPDATABILITY

All updates made to a base relation must be reflected in all views that encompass that base relation. Similarly, it is expected that if a view is updated, then the changes will be reflected in the underlying base relations, but all views cannot be manipulated in such a way. Views are classified into two categories, known as updatable views and non-updatable views. The updatability of a view depends on the query expression based on which the view is created. A view is updatable only if the updates to the view can be propagated correctly to the base relations without ambiguity. A view is non-updatable if the corresponding query based on which the view is generated has the following properties.

- The query expression contains DISTINCT, GROUP BY or HAVING clause.
- The query expression includes aggregate functions such as SUM, MAX or MIN.

- The query expression involves more than one base relation or a view which is produced using join, union, intersection or set difference operations.
- If the query contains subqueries.

In addition, no tuple that is added through a view must violate the integrity constraints of the base table.

10.3.2 VIEWS IN DISTRIBUTED DBMS

Views are the same in the context of both distributed DBMS and centralized DBMS, but in distributed DBMS views can be derived from fragmented relations stored at different sites. When a view is created its name and the corresponding definition are stored into the system catalog as base relation descriptions. In a distributed database system, view definitions can be stored centrally at one site or partially or fully replicated depending on the degree of site autonomy offered by the system [William et al., 1982]. In the centralized approach, all view definitions in the distributed system are store in a single central site. In the partially replicated approach, some of the view definitions are replicated and stored at different sites of the distributed system. All view definitions are available at all sites of a distributed system in the fully replicated approach. If a query is generated against a view and the view definition is not available at that site, then remote accessing to the view definition is necessary. The processing of requests is costly against a view that is derived from distributed relations. Moreover, it is likely that several different queries are generated almost at the same time based on the same view. To handle this situation, an approach called view materialization is used. In this approach, the view is stored as a temporary table in the database, called snapshot or materialized view, when the view is first referenced. A snapshot represents a particular state of the database and is therefore states. Snapshots do not reflect updates to base relations and these are only useful for the applications that do not require the most updated version of the database. Snapshots are very useful in many new applications such as data warehousing, replication server, data visualization and mobile systems. The difficulty with view materialization is in maintaining the changes of the view while the base tables are being updated. The process of updating a snapshot in response to changes to the underlying data is called view maintenance. The objective of view maintenance is to apply only those changes that are necessary to keep the view current. However, this can be done when the system is idle.

10.4 AUTHORIZATION AND PROTECTION

In this section, we briefly indicate which problems in authorization and protection are due to distribution, and suggest some solutions for them; a

general treatment of authorization and protection in a centralized environment. Authorization and data protection are two very important aspects of database security, and they are closely related to each other. Protection is required to prevent unauthorized disclosure, alteration or destruction of data. Data protection is generally provided by file systems in both centralized and distributed operating systems. A well-known method for data protection is data encryption. Data encryption is suitable for both storing the information on the disk as well as data exchange through the network. In data encryption method, the data is encoded into ciphertext, and it can be decoded into original data as required by using an algorithm. The algorithms used for encoding and decoding data are called key. There are various standard data encryption techniques such as symmetric key encryption and asymmetric key encryption. The granting of rights or privileges that enable users to have legitimate access to a system or a system's objects is called authorization. Authorization ensures that only the authorized users are accessing the data. An authorization control must have the ability to identify authorized users and thereby to restrict unauthorized accessing of data. Authorization control was being provided by operating systems for a long time, and recently by distributed operating systems as a service of the file system. Generally, a centralized approach is used for authorization control. In this approach, the centralized control creates database objects and provided permission to other users to access these objects. Database objects are identified by their external names. Another aspect of authorization is that different users can have different privileges on the same database objects in a database environment.

In a relational DBMS, the DBA uniformly controls authorizations using high-level constructs. A DBA is usually responsible for allowing users to have access to database objects by creating individual user accounts. In a distributed DBMS, a decentralized authorization control approach is more suitable than a centralized authorization control approach. Authorization control in distributed DBMSs is more complicated because database objects and users may be distributed among different sites.

10.4.1 CENTRALIZED AUTHORIZATION CONTROL

In authorization control, three main entities are involved: users, database objects and operations that can be performed on database objects. Therefore, an authorization can be defined as a triple (user, operation, object), which indicates that the specified user has the right to perform an operation of the specified type on the specified object. Authorization control checks whether a given triple can be permitted to process or not. A user is introduced into the system by the pair (username, password). The username is used to identify each user uniquely in the system, and the password is used to authenticate the user. Both of this information is required to login into the

database environment, thereby preventing unauthorized users from entering into the database system. A database is a collection of database objects. In relational data model, a database object can be defined by its type, which is expressed as (view, relation, tuple, attribute), as well as by its content using selection predicates. A right or privilege represents a relationship between a user and a database object for a particular set of operations. In SQL, an operation is defined by a high-level statement such as INSERT, DELETE, UPDATE, ALTER, SELECT, GRANT, REFERENCES or ALL and privileges are defined using GRANT and REVOKE statements. The keyword public is used to mean all users in the system. In centralized authorization control, the DBA has all privileges on all database objects, and he/she is allowed to grant (or take away) permissions to (from) other users.

In developing a distributed database, one of the first questions to answer is where to grant system access. Bell and Grisom [BellGris92] outline two strategies:

1. Users are granted system access at their home site.
2. Users are granted system access at the remote site.

The **first case** is easier to handle. It is no more difficult to implement than a centralized access strategy. Bell and Grisom point out that the success of this strategy depends on reliable communication between the different sites (the remote site must receive all of the necessary clearance information). Since many different sites can grant access, the probability of unauthorized access increases. Once one site has been compromised, the entire system is compromised. If each site maintains access control for all users, the impact of the compromise of a single site is reduced (provided that the intrusion is not the result of a stolen password).

The **second strategy**, while perhaps more secure, has several disadvantages. Probably the most glaring is the additional processing overhead required, particularly if the given operation requires the participation of several sites. Furthermore, the maintenance of replicated clearance tables is computationally expensive and more prone to error.

Finally, the replication of passwords, even though they're encrypted, increases the risk of theft. A third possibility offered by Woo and Lam [WooLam92] centralizes the granting of access privileges at nodes called policy servers. These servers are arranged in a network. When a policy server receives a request for access, all members of the network determine whether to authorize the access of the user. Woo and Lam believes that separating the approval system from the application interface reduces the probability of compromise.

In decentralized authorization control, the creator of a database object is the owner of that object. The owner has the right to grant permission to other users to perform certain operations on the database object. In this case, the authorization control is distributed among the owners of database objects. If the owner grants the GRANT permission on a database object to some other user, then that specified user can subsequently grant permissions to other users on this specified database object. The revoking process must be recursive, and to perform revoking the system must maintain a hierarchy of grants per database object where the owner of the database object is the root.

The privileges on database objects are stored in the system catalog as authorization rules. There are various ways to store authorization rules in the system catalog; authorization matrix is one of them. In the authorization matrix, each row represents a user (or a subject) each column represents a database object and each cell, which is a pair (user, database object), indicates the authorized operations for a particular user on a particular database object. The authorized operations are specified by their operation type, and in the case of SELECT operation type, sometimes the selection predicates are also mentioned to further restrict the access to database objects. The authorization matrix can be stored in three different ways: by row, by column and by element. When the authorization matrix is stored by row, each user is associated with the list of objects that can be accessed with the corresponding access rights. Similarly, when the authorization matrix is stored by column, each object is associated with the list of users who can access it with the corresponding access rights. In both of the above two approaches, authorizations can be enforced efficiently, but the manipulation of access rights per database object is not efficient as all user profiles must be accessed. This disadvantage can be overcome if the authorization matrix is stored by element, that is, by relation (user, database object, right).

This approach provides faster access in right manipulation per user per database object. A sample authorization matrix is shown in table 10.1.

Table 10.1 A Sample Authorization Matrix

	Employee	**Department**	**Project**
User 1	SELECT	INSERT	ALTER
User 2	INSERT	DELETE	SELECT WHERE project-type="inside"
User 3	SELECT	INSERT	UPDATE
User 4	UPDATE	SELECT	DELETE

Example 10.1

Given SQL statement grants SELECT, UPDATE and DELETE permissions on the database object Employee to all users.

GRANT SELECT, UPDATE, DELETE ON Employee TO PUBLIC.

Similarly, the SQL statement

GRANT ALL PRIVILEGES ON Employee TO user2

grants all permission on the database object Employee to the user user2.

GRANT SELECT ON Employee TO user1 WITH GRANT OPTION.

The above SQL statement allows user1 to grant SELECT permission on Employee database object to other users. The following SQL statement takes away SELECT and INSERT rights on Employee database object from the user user4.

REVOKE SELECT, INSERT ON Employee FROM user4.

10.4.2 DISTRIBUTED AUTHORIZATION CONTROL

Authorization control in distributed DBMSs involves remote user authentication, management of distributed authorization rules, view management and control of user groups. Management of views in distributed database systems was already discussed in previous section. In a distributed database system, users may identify themselves from any sites; therefore, remote user authentication is necessary to prevent unauthorized accessing.

There are two different ways for implementing remote user authentication as described in the following:

- In the **first approach**, the information that is required for authenticating users (i.e., username and password) is replicated and stored at all sites in the system catalog.
- In the **second approach**, each user in the distributed system is identified by its home site. Whenever a user wants to login from a remote site a message is sent to its home site for authentication, and then the user is identified by the home site.

The first approach is costly in terms of catalog management. The second approach is more reasonable, because it restricts each user to identifying him (her) self at the home site. However, site autonomy is not preserved in the second approach.

Authorization rules are used to restrict the actions performed by users on database objects after authentication. In a distributed DBMS, the allocation of authorization rules is a part of system catalog, and enforcement of these rules can be implemented in two different ways.

These are full replication and partial replication as listed in the following:

- In **full replication**, authorization rules are replicated and stored at all sites of the distributed system.

- In **partial replication**, the authorization rules are replicated at the sites where the referenced database objects are distributed.

The full replication approach allows authorization to be checked at the beginning of the compile time, but this approach is costly in terms of data replication. The latter approach is better if localization of reference is high, but it does not allow distributed authorization to be controlled at compile time.

Views can be considered as composite database objects; thus, granting access to a view translates into granting access to the underlying objects. The authorization granted on a view depends on the access rights of the view creator on the underlying objects. If the view definitions and authorization rules are fully replicated, then this translation becomes simpler, and it can be done locally. If the view definitions and their underlying objects are distributed, then the translation is difficult. In this case, the association information can be stored at the site of each underlying object. To simplify the authorization control and to reduce the amount of data stored, individual users are typically divided into different classed known as groups, which are all granted the same privileges. Like centralized DBMS, in a distributed DBMS all users as a group can be referred to as public and all users at a particular site may be referred to as public@sitei. The management of groups in distributed systems is very difficult, because the users belonging to the same group may be distributed at different sites, and the access to a database object can be granted to several groups, where the groups can also be distributed. There are several alternative solutions as listed below.

- One solution is full replication of all authorization rules although maintaining replication is quite expensive in this case.
- Another solution enforces access privileges by performing a remote query to the sites that holds the group definitions.
- Another alternative solution is to replicate a group definition at each site containing a database object that can be accessed by users of that group.

The last two solutions decrease the degree of autonomy. It is obvious that full replication of authorization information simplifies authorization control, as it can be done at compile time. However, the overhead cost for maintaining replicas is significant, if there are many sites in the distributed system.

10.4.3 SITE-TO-SITE PROTECTION

The first security problem which arises in a distributed database is initiating and protecting intersite communication. When two database sites communicate, it is important to make sure that:

1. At the other side of the communicate line is the intended site (and not an intruder).
2. No intruder can either read or manipulate the messages which are exchanged between the sites.

The first requirement can be accomplished by establishing an identification protocol between remote sites. When two remote databases communicate with each other, on the first request they also send each other a password, similar to what happens at the login of users. When two sites decide to share some data, then the two sites are "introduced," by exchanging passwords. This mechanism is used in R*. The second requirement is to protect the content of transmitted messages once the two identified sites start to communicate. Message in a computer network are typically routed along paths which involve several intermediate nodes and transmissions, with intermediate buffering. Requiring that all these intermediate steps be performed after identification and under secure mechanism seems inappropriate and inefficient (because of the large number of nodes involved, which might dynamically change).

The best solution to this problem consists of using cryptography, a standard technique commonly used in distributed information systems, for instance for protecting communications between terminals and processing units. Messages ("plaintext") are initially encoded into cipher messages ("ciphertext") at the sender site, then transmitted in the network, and finally decoded at the receiver site. Encoding involves not only transformations of groups of bits into groups of bits, but also transposition, "confusions," and logical operations (see references [10.8] and [10.9]); these operations need, of course, to e reversible. The rules used for encoding and decoding are called the key of the cryptographic system. Site-to-site cryptography requires the sender and the receiver of the transmission to agree on the key.

10.4.4 USER IDENTIFICATION

When a user connects to the database system, he or she must be identified by the system; the identification is a crucial aspect of preserving security, because if an intruder could pretend to be a valid user, then security would be violated. Assuming a password mechanism, identification requires the password provided by the user to match with the password available to the system. In a distributed database, user could, in principle, identify them at any site of the distributed database.

However, this feature can be implemented in two ways which both show negative aspects.

1. Passwords could be replicated at all the sites of the distributed database. This would allow user identification to be performed locally at

each site, but would also compromise the security of passwords, since it would be easier for an intruder to access them (for example, going to the "less protected" site).

2. Users could each have a "home" site where their identification is performed; in this scenario, a user connecting to a different site would be identified by sending a request to the home site and letting this site perform the identification. The disadvantage of this solution is that site would "trust" the identifications made by other sites. This is not compatible with the preservation of site autonomy.

A reasonable solution is to restrict each user to identifying him (her) self at the home site. This solution is consistent with the idea that users seem to be more "static' than, for instance, data or programs. A "pass-through" facility could be used to allow users at remote sites to connect their terminals to their "home" sites in order identify themselves.

10.4.5 ENFORCING AUTHORIZATION RULES

Once users are properly identified, database systems can use authorization rules to regulate the actions performed upon database objects by them. In a distributed environment, additional problem include the allocation of these rules, which are part of the catalog, and the distribution of the mechanisms used for enforcing them. Two alternative, possible solutions are:

1. **Full replication of authorization rules:** This solution is consistent with having fully replicated catalogs, and requires mechanisms for distributing online updates to them. However, this solution allows authorization to be checked either at the beginning of compilation or at the beginning execution. Thus, the fact that the user does not have the required access rights can be discovered locally and early, increasing the possibility of quickly invalidating compilation or execution.
2. **Allocation of authorization rules at the same sites as the objects to which they refer:** This solution is consistent with local catalogs and does not incur the update overhead as in the first case; however, invalidation of users who have no right to access remote data can be done only by accessing these data at some intermediate stage of compilation or execution. Invalidation in this case requires undoing the already performed actions.

The second solution is consistent with the site autonomy, while the first is consistent with considering a distributed database as a single system; in this case, full replication of authorization rules is appropriate if it is also cost-effective.

Authorizations that can be given to users of a centralized database include the abilities of reading, inserting, creating, and deleting object instances

(tuples) and of creating and deleting objects (relations or fragments). In a distributed database, the additional privilege of "moving" an object from a site to another is added to the previous ones. Having the privilege of moving an object is less than having both insertion and deletion privileges; though moving an object at a different site, no information of the original object is lost, and no new information is created. Therefore, this privilege must be considered as a new one.

10.4.6 CLASSES OF USERS

For simplifying the mechanisms which deal with authorization and the amount of stored information, individual users are typically grouped into classes, which are all granted the same privileges. For instance, all employees of the administration department constitute a class, and all employees of the manufacturing department constitute a different class. Users of the first class can access information about employee salaries, while those of the second class can access information about project management.

In distributed databases, the following considerations apply to classes of users:

1. A "natural" classification of users is the on which is induced by the distribution of the database to different sites; it is likely that "all users at site x" have some common properties from the viewpoint of authorization. An explicit naming mechanism for this class should be provided (R* uses the term Public@Site_X to denote all users of site X;).
2. Several interesting problems arise when groups of users include users from multiple sites; for instance, where should the information about a group's access rights be stored, and which rules should be used for manipulating them? Problems are particularly complex when multiple-site user groups are considered in h context of site autonomy. It appears that any decision concerning the group (revoking privileges or adding and deleting members) cannot really be done on an autonomous basis; thus, mechanisms involve the consensus of the majority or of the totality of involved sites, or a decision made y a higher-level administrator. In conclusion, multiple-site user groups contrast with "pure" site autonomy.

10.5 INTEGRITY

According to Bell and Grisom [BellGris92], preservation of integrity is much more difficult in a heterogeneous distributed database than in a homogeneous one. The degree of central control dictates the level of difficulty with integrity constraints (integrity constraints enforce the rules of the individual organization). The homogeneous distributed database has strong central control and has identical DBMS schema. If the nodes in the distributed network are heterogeneous (the DBMS schema and the associated organizations are dissimilar), several problems can arise that will threaten the integrity of the distributed data.

They list three problem areas:

1. Inconsistencies between local integrity constraints,
2. Difficulties in specifying global integrity constraints,
3. Inconsistencies between local and global constraints [BellGris92].

Bell and Grisom explain that local integrity constraints are bound to differ in a heterogeneous distributed database. The differences stem from differences in the individual organizations. These inconsistencies can cause problems, particularly with complex queries that rely on more than one database. Development of global integrity constraints can eliminate conflicts between individual databases. Yet these are not always easy to implement. Global integrity constraints on the other hand are separated from the individual organizations. It may not always be practical to change the organizational structure in order to make the distributed database consistent. Ultimately, this will lead to inconsistencies between local and global constraints. Conflict resolution depends on the level of central control. If there is strong global control, the global integrity constraints will take precedence. If central control is weak, local integrity constraints will.

10.5.1 INTEGRITY CONSTRAINTS

The integrity constraints in the relational model can be divided into two categories:

1. **Implicit constraints:** Implicit constraints which include domain, relational, and referential constraints enforce the rules of the relational model.
2. **Explicit constraints:** Explicit constraints enforce the rules of the organization served by the DBMS. As such, explicit constraints are one of the two key elements (along with views) of security protection in the relational model [BellGris92].

Accidental or deliberate modification of data can be detected by explicit constraints. Pfleeger [Pflee89] lists several error detection methods, such as parity checks, that can be enforced by explicit constraints. Earlier we discussed local integrity constraints. These constraints are also examples of explicit constraints.

Multilevel classification constraints are another example. A final type of explicit constraint enforces polyinstantiation integrity. Polyinstantiation refers to the replication of a tuple in a multilevel access system. This occurs

when a user at a lower level L2 enters a tuple into the database which has the same key as a tuple which is classified at a higher level L1 (L1 > L2). The DBMS has two options. It can refuse the entry, which implies that a tuple with the same key exists at L1 or it can allow the entry. If it allows the entry, then two tuples with identical keys exist in the database. This condition is called polyinstantiation [Haig91]. Obvious integrity problems can result. The literature contains several algorithms for ensuring polyinstantiation integrity. Typically, explicit constraints are implemented using the SQL ASSERT or TRIGGER commands. ASSERT statements are used to prevent an integrity violation. Therefore, they are applied before an update. The TRIGGER is part of a response activation mechanism. If a problem with the existing database is detected (for example, an error is detected after a parity check), then a predefined action is initiated [BellGris92]. More complicated explicit constraints like multilevel classification constraints require additional programming with a 3GL. So, SQL and, consequently, the relational model alone cannot protect the database from determined inferential attack.

10.5.2 SEMANTIC INTEGRITY CONSTRAINTS

Database consistency is ensured by a set of restrictions or constraints, known as semantic integrity constrains. A database state is said to be consistent if the database satisfies a set of constraints. Maintaining data consistency involves several DBMS modules such as concurrency control, recovery management, protection and authorization control, and semantic integrity control. The responsibility of a semantic integrity control module is to verify whether the updates performed by application programs violate the consistency of database states. If any such violation is detected, the semantic integrity control module rejects the updates or performs some actions to compensate the effects of updates. Semantic integrity constraints are closely connected to integrity constraints in the sense that more semantic information can be captured about applications by using integrity rules or constraints.

Semantic integrity ensures that data entered into a row reflects an allowable value for that row. The value must be within the *domain*, or allowable set of values, for that column. For example, the **quantity** column of the **items** table permits only numbers. If a value outside the domain can be entered into a column, the semantic integrity of the data is violated.

The following constraints enforce semantic integrity:

- **Data type:** The data type defines the types of values that you can store in a column. For example, the data type SMALLINT allows you to enter values from -32,767 to 32,767 into a column.
- **Default value:** The default value is the value inserted into the column when an explicit value is not specified. For example, the **user_id** col-

umn of the **cust_calls** table defaults to the login name of the user if no name is entered.

- **Check constraint:** The check constraint specifies conditions on data inserted into a column. Each row inserted into a table must meet these conditions. For example, the **quantity** column of the **items** table might check for quantities greater than or equal to one.

Those are two different types of semantic integrity constraints:

1. Structural constraints
2. Behavioural constraints

Structural constraints represent basic semantic properties inherent to a model, whereas behavioural constraints control application behaviour. It has been suggested that integrity constraints can be expressed using assertions of predicate calculus. In this approach, one can easily declare and modify complex integrity assertions. The main difficulty in supporting automatic semantic integrity control is the cost of checking assertions. Moreover, enforcing integrity assertions generally requires access to a large amount of data that is not involved in the database updates. Therefore, implementation of automatic semantic integrity control can be prohibitive in distributed database systems. The management of semantic integrity constraints is not discussed in this context as we are mainly concerned about the distributed DBMSs. In a distributed DBMS context, it is very difficult to design a semantic integrity control subsystem. The two major problems are the definition and storage of assertions, and enforcement of these assertions. An assertion is a predicate expressing an integrity constraint that must be satisfied by the database. Domain constraints and referential integrity constraints are special type of assertions. In a distributed system, as assertions can involve data stored at different sites, their storage must be decided to minimize the cost of integrity checking.

Assertions can be classified into three different categories as listed below:

- **Individual assertions:** These assertions involve a single variable and a single relation, and refer only to tuples that can be updated independently. Domain constraints are individual assertions.
- **Set-oriented assertions:** This type of assertions may involve a single relation and multiple variables or multiple relations and multiple variables. Referential integrity constraints are examples of set-oriented assertions.
- **Assertions involving aggregates:** This type of assertions contain aggregate functions and therefore testing of these assertions is too costly.

  The enforcement of assertions in a distributed system depends on the

category of the assertion, the type of update and the nature of the site where the update is issued. The site where the update is issued may or may not store the updated relation or some of the relations involved in the integrity assertions.

- **Enforcement of individual assertions:** There are two methods for the enforcement of individual assertions in a distributed DBMS. If the update is an insert operation, all individual assertions can be enforced at the site where the update is issued. If the update is a delete or a modify operation, it is sent to the sites where the relation resides and update should be performed there. The query processor performs update operation for each fragment. The resulting tuples at each site are combined into one temporary relation in the case of a delete statement, whereas in the case of a modify statement; the resulting tuples are combined into two temporary relations. Each site involved in the distributed update enforces the assertions relevant to that site.
- **Enforcement of set-oriented assertions:** Two cases are considered here. In the case of multiple-variable single-relation set-oriented assertions, the update (may be insert, delete or modify) is sent to the sites where the relation resides, and they return one or two temporary relations after performing the update, as in case of individual assertions. These temporary relations are then sent to all sites storing the specified relation, and each site enforces the assertions locally. Each site storing the specified relation then sends a message to the site where the update is issued indicating whether the assertions are satisfied or not. If any assertion is not satisfied at any site, then it is the responsibility of the semantic integrity control subsystem to reject the entire update program. In the case of multiple-variable multiple-relation set-oriented assertions, the enforcement of assertions is done at the site where the update is issued. Hence, after performing update at all fragments of the involved relations, all results are centralized at the site where the update is issued, called query master site. The query master enforces all assertions on the centralized result, and if any inconsistency is found the update is rejected. On the other hand, if no inconsistencies are found, the resultant tuples are sent to the corresponding sites where the fragments of the relation reside.
- **Enforcement of assertions involving aggregates:** The testing of these assertions is the costliest, because it requires the calculation of aggregate functions. To efficiently enforce these assertions, it is possible to produce compiled assertions that isolate redundant data. There redundant data, known as concrete views, can then be stored at each site where the associated relation resides.

Example 10.2

An individual assertion that involves a single attribute salary and a single relation Employee.

Create assertion salary_constraint check (not exists (select * from Employee where salary <50000)).

The given assertion imposes a restriction that salary should be greater than 50,000 and this condition must hold true in every database state for the assertion to be satisfied.

Example 10.3

A set-oriented assertion that involves two variables salary and deptno and two relations Employee and Department.

Create assertion salary_constraint check (not exists (select * from Employee, Department where salary <50000 and Employee.deptno = Department.deptno)).

The given assertion also represents a referential integrity constraint involving two relations Employee and Department.

10.6 GLOBAL SYSTEM CATALOG

In a distributed database system, the global system catalog stores all the information that are required to access data correctly and efficiently, and to control authorization. The Global Catalog (GC) contains an entry for every object in an enterprise forest but only a few properties for each object. An entire forest shares a GC, with multiple servers holding copies. You can perform an enterprise wide forest search only on the properties in the GC, whereas you can search for any property in a user's domain tree. Only Directory Services (DSs) or domain controllers (DCs) can hold a copy of the GC.

Configuring an excessive number of GCs in a domain wastes network bandwidth during replication. One GC server per domain in each physical location is sufficient. Windows NT sets servers as GCs as necessary, so you don't need to configure additional GCs unless you notice slow query response times.

Because full searches involve querying the whole domain tree rather than the GC, grouping the enterprise into one tree will improve your searches. Thus, you can search for items not in the GC. **The global system catalog is used for the following purposes:**

- **Processing applications:** Catalog information are used in processing application to check whether access plans are valid and the users have the appropriate access privileges.

- **Mapping applications:** Using catalog information data referenced by application programs at different levels of transparency are mapped into physical data.
- **Optimizing applications:** Catalog information are used to produce an access plan for query execution. Typically, the information required for producing access plans include data allocation, statistical information and access methods available at each site.

The updates of data definition (e.g., modification of database schemas, changes in authorization rules) modify the catalog information.

10.6.1 GLOBAL CATALOG IN ACTIVE DIRECTORY

The global catalog is a domain controller that contains attributes for every object in the Active Directory. By default, only the members of the Schema Admins group have rights to change which attributes stored in the global catalog, according to organization's requirements.

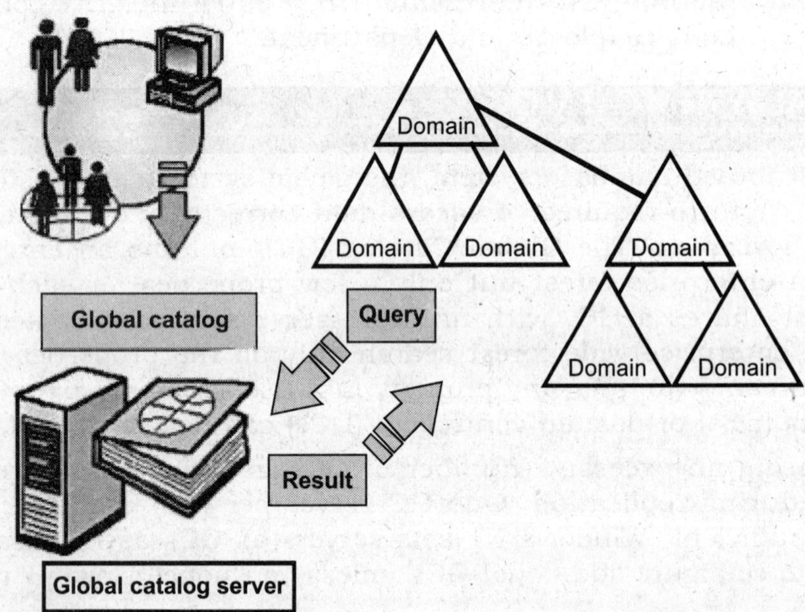

Figure 10.1: Global catalog

The global catalog contains:

- The commonly used attributes need in queries, such as a user's first and last name, and logon name.
- All the information or records which are important to determine the location of any object in the directory.
- A default subset of attributes for each object type.

- All the access related permissions for every object and attribute that is stored in the global catalog. Say, without permission you can't access or view the objects. If you are searching for an object where you do not have the appropriate permissions to view, the object will not appear in the search results. These access permissions ensure that users can find only objects to which they have been assigned access.

A global catalog server is a domain controller that contains full and writable replica of its domain directory, and a partial, read-only replica of all other domain directory partitions in the forest. Let's take an example of a user object; by default user objects have lot of attributes such as first name, last name, address, phone number, and many more. The Global Catalog will store only the main attributes of user objects in search operations like a user's first name and last name, or login name. This partial attributes of that user object which is stored would be enough to allow a search for that object to be able to locate the full replica of the object in active directory. If a search comes to locate objects, then first it goes to local global catalog and reduces network traffic over the WAN.

Domain Controllers always contain the full attribute list for objects belonging to their domain. If the Domain Controller is also a GC, it will also contain a partial replica of objects from all other domains in the forest.

It is always recommended to have a global catalog server for every active directory site in an enterprise network.

10.6.2 CONTENTS OF GLOBAL SYSTEM CATALOG

A global system catalog contains the following information depending on the architecture of the distributed system.

(i) The names of all global relations and their corresponding attributes.

(ii) The details of fragmentation schema, that is, the selection predicates for horizontal fragments, the names of attributes for vertical fragments and both of these for mixed fragments.

(iii) The details of data allocation, that is, the mapping between fragments and physical databases at each site of the distributed system, and the names of local data stored at each site.

(iv) The access method descriptions (e.g., number and types of index, hash function) which are locally available at each site.

(v) The statistical information about the data.

(vi) Consistency information, which include data protection and authorization rules, integrity constraints, security constraints etc.

10.6.3 CATALOG MANAGEMENT IN DISTRIBUTED SYSTEMS

The distributed database catalog entries must specify site(s) at which data is being stored in addition to data in a system catalog in a centralized DBMS. Because of data partitioning and replication, this extra information is needed. There are a number of approaches to implementing a distributed database catalog.

1. **Centralized** – In this approach, the global system catalog is stored at a single site. All other sites in the distributed system access catalog information from this central site. This approach is very simple, but it has several limitations. The system is vulnerable to the failure of the central site. The availability and reliability is very log in this case. The major drawback of this approach is that is decreased site autonomy.
2. **Fully replicated** – In this approach, catalog information are replicated at each site of the distributed system. The availability and reliability are very high in this approach. The site autonomy increases in this case. The disadvantage of this approach is the information update overhead of the global system catalog.

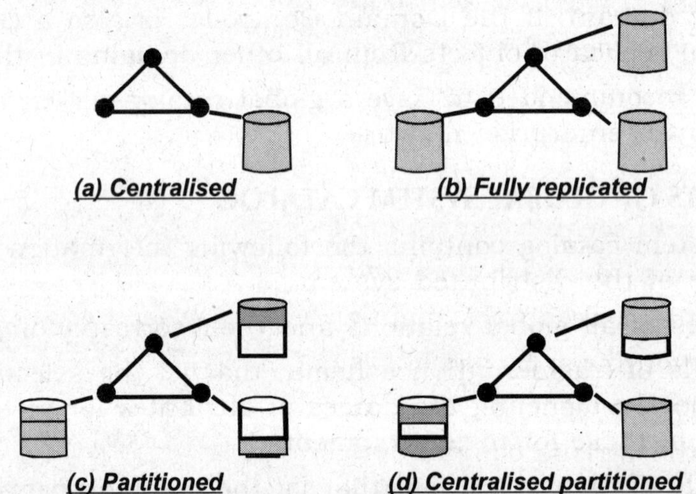

Figure 10.2: Catalog Management in Distributed Systems

3. **Fragmented and distributed:** In this approach, the distributed system R* is used to overcome the drawbacks of the above two approaches. There is a local catalog at each site that contains the metadata related to the data stored at that sit. Thus, the global system catalog is fragmented and distributed at the sites of a distributed system. For database objects created at any site (the birth-site), it is the responsibility of that site's local catalog to store the definition, replication details and allocation details of each fragment or replica of that object. Whenever a

fragment or a replica is moved to a different location, the local catalog at the corresponding site must be updated. The birth-site of each global database object is recorded in each local system catalog. Thus, local references to data can be performed locally. On the other hand, if remote reference is required, the system-wide name reveals the birth-site of the database object, and then the catalog information is accessed from that site.

EXERCISES

1. Explain the distributed database administration?
2. What do you mean by distributed database security?
3. Explain the elements of distributed database management system security?
4. What do you mean by view management?
5. Explain the concept of authorization and protection?
6. Explain the concept of centralized authorization control?
7. Explain the concept of distributed authorization control?
8. What do you mean by site-to-site protection?
9. Explain the concept of user identification?
10. Explain the concept of enforcing authorization rules?
11. Explain the various classes of users?
12. What do you mean by integrity?
13. What do you mean by integrity constraints?
14. Explain the concept of semantic integrity constraints?
15. What do you mean by global system catalog?
16. Explain the concept of global catalog in active directory?
17. Explain the various contents of global system catalog?
18. Explain the concept of catalog management in distributed systems?

GLOSSARY

Aborted transaction: A transaction in progress that terminates abnormally.

Aggregation: The process of transforming data from a detailed to a summary level.

Anomaly: An error or inconsistency that may result when a user attempts to update a table that contains redundant data. The three types of anomalies are insertion, deletion, and modification.

Asynchronous distributed database: A form of distributed database technology in which copies of replicated data are kept at different nodes so that local servers can access data without reaching out across the network.

Authorization rules: Controls incorporated in the data management systems that restrict access to data and also restrict the actions that people may take when they access data.

Access method: The steps involved in storing and retrieving records from a file.

Anomalies: See *Update anomalies.*

Application server: Handles the business logic and data processing layer in a three-tier client–server architecture.

Authentication: A mechanism that determines whether a user is who he or she claims to be.

Authorization: The granting of a right or privilege that enables a subject to have legitimate access to a database system or a database system's object.

Backup facilities: A DBMS COPY utility that produces a backup copy (or save) of the entire database or a subset of the database.

Backward recovery (rollback): The back out, or undo, of unwanted changes to the database. Before-images of the records that have been changed are applied to the database, and the database is returned to an earlier state. Used to reverse the changes made by transactions that have been aborted or terminated abnormally.

Backup: The process of periodically taking a copy of the database and log file (and possibly programs) onto offline storage media.

Bottom-up approach (to database design): A design philosophy that begins by identifying individual design components and then aggregates these components into larger units. In database design, you start at the bottom level by identifying the attributes, and then group the attributes together to form tables that represent entities and relationships.

Cardinality Describes the number of possible relationships for each participating entity.

Centralized approach (to database design): Requirements for each user view are merged into a single set of requirements for the new database application.

Client: A software application that requests services from one or more servers. See also *Two-tier/Three-tier client–server architecture.*

Concurrency control: A DBMS service that coordinates the simultaneous execution of transactions in a multi-user environment while preserving data integrity.

Constraint: A consistency rule that the database is not permitted to violate.

Cardinality constraint: Specifies the number of instances of one entity that can (or must) be associated with each instance of another entity.

Catalog: A set of schemas that, when put together, constitute a description of a database.

Checkpoint facility: A facility by which the DBMS periodically refuses to accept any new transactions. The system is in a quiet state, and the database and transaction logs are synchronized.

Client/server architecture: A LAN–based environment in which database software on a server (called a database server or database engine) performs database commands sent to it from client workstations, and application programs on each client concentrate on user interface functions.

Client/server systems: A networked computing model that distributes processes between clients and servers, which supply the requested services. In a database system, the database generally resides on a server that processes the DBMS. The clients may process the application systems or request services from another server that holds the application programs.

Commit protocol: An algorithm to ensure that a transaction is successfully completed or else it is aborted.

Concurrency control: The process of managing simultaneous operations against a database so that data integrity is maintained and the operations do not interfere with each other in a multiuser environment.

Concurrency transparency: A design goal for a distributed database, with the property that although a distributed system runs many transactions, it appears that a given transaction is the only activity in the system. Thus, when several transactions are processed concurrently, the results must be the same as if each transaction were processed in serial order.

Checkpoint: The recovery manager procedure that performs the checkpointing activity.

Checkpointing: An activity that writes information to stable storage during normal operation in order to reduce the amount of work Restart has to do after a failure.

Checkpoint record: A log record that documents the completion of a checkpoint.

Commit: The transaction operation that a program uses to indicate that it has completed executing the current transaction and that the effects of that transaction should be made permanent.

Commit consistent checkpointing: The checkpointing scheme that stops processing new transactions, waits for all active transactions to commit or abort, flushes all dirty cache slots, and then marks the end of the commit list.

Communication failure: An event that causes two or more sites to be unable to exchange messages.

Conservative TO: A type of TO scheduler that delays operations that could be run without violating the TO Rule, in order to reduce the chance thar it will have to reject other conflicting operations with smaller timestamps later on.

Conservative 2PL: A two phase locking protocol in which each transaction obtains all of the locks it needs before any of its operations are submitted to rhe DM.

Consistent state: A state of the database that satisfies the database's consistency predicates. Intuitively, this means that data item values are internally consistent with each other.

Coordinator: The process that supervises an atomic commitment protocol.

Data: Stored representations of objects and events that have meaning and importance in the user's environment.

Data administration: A high-level function that is responsible for the overall management of data resources in an organization, including maintaining corporate wide definitions and standards.

Database: An organized collection of logically related data.

Database administration: A technical function that is responsible for physical database design and for dealing with technical issues, such as security enforcement, database performance, and backup and recovery.

Database Management System (DBMS): A software system that is used to create, maintain, and provide controlled access to user databases.

Database recovery: Mechanisms for restoring a database quickly and accurately after loss or damage.

Database security: Protection of the data against accidental or intentional loss, dcstruction, or misusc.

Database server: A computer that is responsible for database storage, access, and processing in a client/server environment. Some people also use this term to describe a two-tier client/server environment.

Data control language (DCL): Commands used to control a database, including administering privileges and the committing (saving) of data.

Data definition language (DDL): Those commands used to define a database, including creating, altering, and dropping tables and establishing constraints.

Data dictionary: Repository of information about a database that documents data elements of a database.

Data independence: The separation of data descriptions from the application programs that use the data.

Data manipulation language (DML): those commands used to maintain and query a database, including updating, inserting, modifying, and querying data.

Deadlock: An impasse that results when two or more transactions have locked a common resource, and each waits for the other to unlock that resource.

Deadlock prevention: User programs must lock all records they require at the beginning of a transaction (rather than one at a time).

Deadlock resolution: An approach that allows deadlocks to occur but builds mechanisms into the DBMS for detecting and breaking the deadlocks.

Decentralized database: A database that is stored on computers at multiple locations; these computers are not interconnected bynetwork and database software that make the data appear in one logical database.

Dictionary: An unordered sequence of key-value pairs without any duplicates.

Disjointness constraint: A constraint that addresses the question whether an instance of a supertype may simultaneously be a member of two (or more) subtypes.

Distributed database: A single logical database that is spread physically across computers in multiple locations that are connected by a data communication link.

Dynamic SQL: The process of making an application capable of generating specific SQL code on the fly while the application is processing.

Dynamic view: A virtual table that is created dynamically upon request by a user. A dynamic view is not a temporary table. Rather, its definition is stored in the system catalog, and the contents of the view are materialized as a result of an SQL query that uses the view. It differs from a materialized view, which may be stored on a diskand refreshed at intervals or when used, depending on the RDBMS.

Data administration: The management and control of the company data, including database planning, development and maintenance of standards, policies and procedures, and conceptual and logical database design.

Data dictionary: See *System catalog.*

Data independence: The separation of data descriptions from the applications that use the data. This means that if new data structures are added to the database or existing structures in the database are modified then the application programs that use the database are unaffected, provided they don't directly depend upon what has been modified.

Data model: An integrated collection of concepts for describing data, relationships between data, and constraints on the data used by an organization.

Data redundancy: Same as *redundant data.*

Data security: Covers access and use of database objects (such as tables and views) and the actions that users can have on the objects.

Database: A shared collection of logically related data (and a description of this data), designed to meet the information needs of an organization.

Database administration: The management and control of the physical realization of a database application, including physical database design and implementation, setting security and integrity controls, monitoring system performance, and reorganizing the database as necessary.

(Database) application program: A computer program that interacts with the database by issuing an appropriate request (typically an SQL statement) to the DBMS.

Database design: A stage of the database system development lifecycle that involves creating a design for a database that will support the organization's mission statement and mission objectives for the required database.

Database integrity: Refers to the correctness and consistency of stored data. Integrity is usually expressed in terms of constraints.

Database Management System (DBMS): A software system that enables users to define, create, and maintain the database, and provides controlled access to this database.

Database security: The mechanisms that protect the database against intentional or accidental threats. RDBMSs generally provide two types of security: *data security* and *system security.*

Database server: Same as server (see *Two-tier/Three-tier client–server architecture*).

DBMS engine: Same as server (see *Two-tier client–server architecture*).

DBMS selection: A stage of the database system development lifecycle that involves the selection of an appropriate DBMS to support the database system.

Degree of a relationship: The number of participating entities in a relationship.

Denormalization: Formally, the term refers to a change to the structure of a base table, such that the new table is in a lower normal form than the original table. However, the term is also used more loosely to refer to situations where we combine two tables into one new table, where the new table is in the same normal form but contains more nulls than the original tables.

Design methodology: A structured approach that uses procedures, techniques, tools, and documentation aids to support and facilitate the process of design.

Distributed database: A collection of multiple, logically interrelated, shared data (and a description of this data), physically distributed over a computer network.

Distributed DBMS (DDBMS): The software that transparently manages the distributed database.

Database: A set of data items.

Data manager: The data manager (DM) is a composite module of the database system, consisting of a cache manager (CM) and recovery manager.(RM).

Database operations: Operations on data items that are supported by a database system, typically Read and Write.

Database system: A database system (DBS) is a collection of hardware and software modules that support database operations and transaction operations. In our model, a centralized DBS consists of a cache manager (CM), recovery manager (RM), scheduler, and transaction manager (TM).

Data item: A named memory area that can contain a value.

DBS: Acronym for "database system."

Deadlock: A situation in which each transaction in a set of transactions is blocked waiting for another transaction in the set, and therefore none will become unblocked unless there is external intervention.

Directed acyclic graph: A directed acyclic graph is a digraph that contains no cycles.

DM: Acronym for "data manager."

down The state of a site that has failed (and not yet recovered).

election protocol: A protocol by which a set of processes select a unique coordinator.

Failure transparency: A design goal for a distributed database, which guarantees that either all the actions of each transaction are committed or else none of them is committed.

global waits-for graph: In a distributed database system, it consists of the union of the edges in the waits-for graph at every site.

growing phase: In two phase locking, the phase during which a transaction obtains locks.

Join: A relational operation that causes two tables with a common domain to be combined into a single table or view.

4GL (Fourth-Generation Language): A nonprocedural language, such as SQL, that only requires the user to define *what* must be done; the 4GL translates the *what* into details of *how* this should be executed.

Integrity constraints: Constraints imposed to prevent the database from becoming inconsistent.

Logical database design: The process of constructing a model of the data used in an organization based on a specific data model, but independent of a particular DBMS and other physical considerations.

Local autonomy: A design goal for a distributed database, which says that a site can independently administer and operate its database when connections to other nodes have failed.

Local transaction: In a distributed database, a transaction that requires reference only to data that are stored at the site where the transaction originates.

Location transparency: A design goal for a distributed database, which says that a user (or user program) using data need not know the location of the data.

Locking: Any data that are retrieved by a user for updating must be locked, or denied to other users, until the update is completed or aborted.

Locking level (lock granularity): The extent of the database resource that is included with each lock.

Logical schema: The representation of a database for a particular data management technology.

Multivalued attribute: An attribute that may take on more than one value for a given entity (or relationship) instance.

Multivalued dependency: The type of dependency that exists when there are at least three attributes (e.g., A, B, and C) in a relation, with a well-defined set of B and C values for each A value, but those B and C values are independent of each other. (B)

Normalization: A technique for producing a set of tables with desirable properties that supports the requirements of a user or organization.

Object-oriented DBMS (OODBMS): A manager of an object-oriented database.

Object-relational DBMS (ORDBMS): An extension to the relational DBMS to incorporate some concept of 'object'. There is no single ORDBMS, rather a number of such systems, whose characteristics depend upon the way and the degree to which the extension has been made.

Physical database design: The process of producing a description of the implementation of the database on secondary storage; it describes the base tables, file organizations, and indexes used to achieve efficient access to the data, and any associated integrity constraints and security restrictions.

Recovery control: The process of restoring the database to a correct state in the event of a failure.

Redundant data: Duplicated data that is stored in more than one table.

Referential integrity: If a foreign key exists in a table, either the foreign key value must match a candidate key value of some record in its home table or the foreign key value must be wholly null.

Replication: The process of generating and reproducing multiple copies of data at one or more sites.

Recovery manager: A module of the DBMS that restores the database to a correct condition when a failure occurs and then resumes processing user questions.

Referential integrity: An integrity constraint specifying that the value (or existence) of an attribute in one relation depends on the value (or existence) of a primary key in the same or another relation.

Referential integrity constraint: A rule that states that either each foreign key value must match a primary key value in another relation or the foreign key value must be null.

Relation: A named two-dimensional table of data.

Relational database: A database that represents data as a collection of tables in which all data relationships are represented by common values in related tables.

Relational DBMS (RDBMS): A database management system that manages data as a collection of tables in which all data relationships are represented by common values in related tables.

Relational OLAP (ROLAP) OLAP tools that view the database as a traditional relational database in either a star schema or other normalized or denormalized set of tables.

Replication transparency: A design goal for a distributed database, which says that although a given data item may be replicated at several nodes in a network, a programmer or user may treat the data item as if it were a single item at a single node. Also called fragmentation transparency.

Security: Same as *database security.*

Server: A software application that provides services to requesting clients. See also *Twotier/ Three-tier client–server architecture.*

SQL (Structured Query Language): A nonprocedural database language for RDBMSs. In other words, you specify *what* information you require, rather than *how* to get it. SQL has been standardized by the International Organization for Standardization (ISO), making it both the formal and *de facto* standard language for defining and manipulating RDBMSs.

System catalog: Holds data about the structure of the database, users, applications, and so on.

System definition: A stage of the database system development lifecycle that involves defining the scope and boundary of the database system, including its major user views.

System security: Covers access and use of the database at the system level, such as a username and password.

Schema The structure that contains descriptions of objects created by a user, such as base tables, views, and constraints, as part of a database.

Semijoin: A joining operation used with distributed databases in which only the joining attribute from one site is transmitted to the other site, rather than all the selected attributes from every

qualified row.

Shared lock (S lock or read lock): A technique that allows other transactions to read but not update a record or other resource.

Synchronous distributed database: A form of distributed database technology in which all data across the network are continuously kept up to date so that a user at any site can access data anywhere on the network at any time and get the same answer.

System catalog: A system-created database that describes all database objects, including data dictionary information, and also includes user access information.

Shadow copy: An old version of a data item.

Shadowing: The DM maintains more than one copy of each data item in stable storage, so it may write a data item to stable storage without destroying older (shadow) versions of that data item.

Shadow page algorithm: The no-undo/no-redo algorithm described in Section 6.7.

Shrinking phase: In two phase locking, the phase during which a transaction releases locks.

Start-2PC record: In the two phase commit protocol, the record in the coordinator's distributed transaction log that indicates it has begun the protocol.

Static 2PL: See Conservative 2PL.

Stored serialization graph: The serialization graph maintained by an SGT scheduler.

Strength of locks: Lock type p is stronger than lock type q if for every lock type o, ol,[x] conflicts with ql,[x] implies ol,[x] conflicts with e/Jx],

Strict TO: The TO scheduler behaves like Basic TO, except that it delays each Write WJX] until there is no active transaction that issued a Write on X.

Strict 2PL: A two phase locking protocol where the scheduler releases all of a transaction's locks together, after the transaction commits or aborts.

Subgraph: A graph G' = (N', E') is a subgraph of G = (N, E) if N' E N and E' s E.

System failure: A failure in which the entire contents of volatile storage is lost.

Termination protocol: A protocol invoked by a process when it fails to receive an anticipated message while in its uncertainty period.

Three phase commit: A nonblocking atomic commitment protocol that can tolerate site failures but not communication failures.

Timeout: An alarm that indicates to a process that a predefined time interval has elapsed.

Timeout'action: The action that a process must take if its waiting for an event (typically a message) is interrupted by a timeout.

Timeout failure: A communication failure in which a site believes it cannot communicate with another site because it is using a timeout period that is too short.

Timestamp-based deadlock prevention: A deadlock prevention technique where a transaction T, can wait for another transaction Tj only if T; has higher priority than T.

Timestamp ordering: The scheduling method where each transaction is assigned a unique timestamp and conflicting operations from different transactions are scheduled to execute in timestamp order.

Timestamps: Values drawn from a totally ordered domain. In concurrency control algorithms, timestamps are usually assigned to transactions such that no two transactions have the same timestamp.

TL: Acronym for "tree locking."

TM: Acronym for "transaction manager."

TO: Acronym for "timestamp ordering."

System failures: It models main memory on typical computer systems.

Three-tier architecture: A client/server configuration that includes three layers: a client layer and two server layers. Although the nature of the server layers differs, a common configuration contains an application server.

Time stamp: A time value that is associated with a data value.

Time-stamping: In distributed databases, a concurrency control mechanism that assigns a globally unique time stamp to each transaction. Time-stamping is an alternative to the use of locks in distributed databases.

Top-down planning: A generic information systems planning methodology that attempts to gain a broad understanding of the information system needs of the entire organization.

Transaction: A discrete unit of work that must be completely processed or not processed at all within a computer system. Entering a customer order is an example of a transaction.

Transaction boundaries: The logical beginning and end of transactions.

Transaction log: A record of the essential data for each transaction that is processed against the database.

Transaction manager: In a distributed database, a software module that maintains a log of all transactions and an appropriate concurrency control scheme.

Two-phase commit: An algorithm for coordinating updates in a distributed database.

Two-phase locking protocol: A procedure for acquiring the necessary locks for a transaction where all necessary locks are acquired before any locks are released, resulting in a growing phase, when locks are acquired, and a shrinking phase, when they are released.

Three-tier client–server architecture: Consists of a *client* that handles the user interface, an *application server* that handles the business logic and data processing layer, and a *database server* that runs the DBMS.

Top-down approach (to database design): A design philosophy that begins by defining the main structures of the system and then moves to smaller units within those structures. In database design, you start at the top level by identifying the entities and relationships between the data, then you add more details, such as the information you want to hold about the entities and relationships (called attributes) and any constraints on the entities, relationships, and attributes.

Transaction: An action, or series of actions, carried out by a single user or application program, which accesses or changes the contents of the database.

Transaction Processing Monitor (TPM): A program that controls data transfer between clients and servers in order to provide a consistent environment for OnLine Transaction Processing (OLTP).

Two-tier client–server architecture: Consists of a *client* program that handles the main business and data processing logic and interfaces with the user, and a *server* program that manages and controls access to the database.

Update anomalies: Inconsistencies that may arise when a user attempts to update a table that contains redundant data. There are three types of anomalies: insertion, deletion, and modification.

View: A 'virtual table' that does not actually exist in the database but is generated by the DBMS from the underlying base tables whenever it's accessed.

Wait-Die: A timestamp-based deadlock prevention technique whereby a transaction aborts if it tries to lock a data item currently locked by a higher priority transaction.

Waits-for graph: A graph whose nodes are labelled by transaction names, and that contains an edge T; + Tj whenever Ti is waiting for Tj to release some lock.

Workspace model: Transactions write into a workspace, not the database. When they are ready to commit, the Writes are propagated to the database.

Wound-Wait: A timestamp-based deadlock prevention technique whereby a transaction TI is aborted if a higher priority transaction tries to lock a data item currently locked by r,.

Write(x, vu/): The database operation that changes the value of data item x to vu/.

Write-all: The approach to replicated data where the DBS translates each Read(x) into a Read of some copy of x, and each Write(x) into Writes on all copies of x (not just those copies at operational sites).

Write-all-available: The approach to replicated data where the DBS translates each Read(x) into a Read of some available copy of x, and each Write(x) into Writes on all available copies of x.

Write lock: A reservation to write a data item. Ordinarily (for rw and ww synchronization), if transaction T, owns a write lock on x, denoted wl,[x], then no other transaction can obtain a read lock or write lock on x.

2PC: Acronym for "two phase commit."

2PL: Acronym for "two phase locking."

2PL certifier: A certifier that rejects a transaction's Commit if the transaction issued any operation that conflicts with that of an active transaction.

2PL history: A history produced by a 2PL scheduler.

2V2PL: Acronym for "two version 2PL."

3PC: Acronym for "three phase commit."